Management for Professionals

More information about this series at http://www.springer.com/series/10101

Ferri Abolhassan

Editor

Cyber Security. Simply. Make it Happen.

Leveraging Digitization Through IT Security

 Springer

Editor
Ferri Abolhassan
Telekom Deutschland GmbH
Bonn, North Rhine-Westphalia
Germany

Editing: Gina Duscher, Gerd Halfwassen, Albert Hold, Beatrice Gaczensky, Dominique-Silvia Kemp, Thomas van Zütphen, Martin Farrent
Translation: Dr. Edward M. Bradburn, Daina Jauntirans, Stephen McLuckie, Niamh Ruddy and Jessica Spengler for Malinowski & Partner

ISSN 2192-8096   ISSN 2192-810X   (electronic)
Management for Professionals
ISBN 978-3-319-83536-5   ISBN 978-3-319-46529-6   (eBook)
DOI 10.1007/978-3-319-46529-6

Cover illustration: eStudio Calamar, Berlin/Figueres

Printed on acid-free paper

This Springer imprint is published by Springer Nature
The registered company is Springer International Publishing AG
The registered company address is: Gewerbestrasse 11, 6330 Cham, Switzerland

Foreword

Trust Is the Basis of Digitization

Thomas Kremer

When it comes to the future development of our society and economy, one word dominates the discussion: digitization. The consensus is that people, machines, and devices will become increasingly networked. The debate, however, is whether this is something good or bad. Will digitization unburden people and bring progress, comfort, and freedom? Or will it bring about the collapse of our social and welfare systems, turning us into transparent citizens who have lost control of their own data and whose labor is no longer needed? No single person can answer these questions – and the answers will probably not be black or white but rather somewhere in between. One thing is certain, however: we cannot prevent this development; we can only influence it. Experts predict that by the year 2020, more than 50 billion devices will be connected to one another, from smartphones to cars to industrial machines. This will generate an unimaginable amount of data to be stored and processed. And this data is going to be the most important resource for our digital society, the oil of our economy.

Digitization Offers Great Opportunities

Digitization undoubtedly promises great opportunities: safer road traffic thanks to self-driving cars, for example. Or the prospect of cumbersome tasks being handled by machines that can communicate directly with one another. Or even a longer and healthier life thanks to telemedicine applications and new research results emerging from the analysis of large volumes of data. But for digitization to succeed, it is critical for people to trust in data protection and the security of these new services. Without trust, people will not use the new services. On the contrary: Their knee-jerk reaction will be to try to prevent digital developments.

This is not possible, however. If we undermine the development of digitization in Europe, the new services will be created anyway – mostly on the west coast of the USA. Then, the only option for Europeans would be to send their data there and get modified products in return. Europe would become a kind of digital colony. In the area of services for end customers, this is already largely the case. No one can get around Facebook, Google and Co. The chances are better in the market for business customer solutions. The Internet of Things and Industry 4.0 offer Europeans an opportunity to catch up with digitization.

Data Protection and Digital Business Models Are Not in Opposition

Politics, business, science, and society therefore have a responsibility to establish the right guide rails so that people can trust the new services. The digital sovereignty of the individual must be the priority here. This can be guaranteed by a high degree of transparency, freedom of choice for customers, and the development of solutions amenable to data protection. For this to be possible, data protection experts must be involved right from the start in the development of new products and services that handle personal data. Customers must be able to easily understand how their data will be used so that they can make informed decisions about it. Furthermore, we need effective methods of anonymizing and pseudonymizing data for digital business models so that individuals cannot be identified without their consent.

We have traditionally had a high level of data protection in Germany and Europe. It is good that the EU's General Data Protection Regulation will establish standardized rules throughout Europe which guarantee a high degree of data protection while at the same time enabling new digital business models. The focus cannot be on regulating individual industries or data processing models. Instead, we need clear, standardized guidelines for handling data, which create security and trust for customers and companies alike. People also have to be educated and informed about the use of technologies and their personal data – from an early age.

Security Has to Be Simple

Digitization additionally increases the risk of consumers and companies falling victim to digital attacks. The Center for Strategic and International Studies (CSIS) estimates that the economic damage from cyberattacks amounts to more than 400 billion euros per year worldwide. Up to 400,000 new viruses, worms, and Trojans are found in the network every day. What's more, cybercriminals can now take advantage of vulnerabilities within just a few hours and send deceptively realistic emails in order to sneak in malicious code. These criminals can then use the infected computers to hijack other machines in a corporate network and search for the information they want. It often takes months for the affected companies to notice that there was – or is – an attacker in their network.

Security authorities, companies, and private individuals therefore also have to upgrade in order to protect themselves better. Behavior-based and system-status analyses are the keywords in cyberdefense today. Merely placing firewalls around IT systems is not enough. In many cases, the criminals have used sophisticated social-engineering mechanisms – so they are already in the network. The task then is to find them as quickly as possible. These attackers can be detected by monitoring anomalies in the network. To develop solutions such as this, Deutsche Telekom is currently pooling its expertise in a new organizational unit, "Telekom Security."

There is one principle at the forefront of these new security products: Security has to be simple. Until now, the security of solutions and products has tended to be a supplementary function added to a finished product. But it is increasingly being incorporated right from the start, thus ensuring better integration.

From the user's perspective, too, it is important to remember that four out of five attacks could be prevented using simple security measures. This is why it is so critical for users to always keep their virus protection and operating systems up to date, for example. Incidentally, smartphones are powerful computers that require just as much protection. This personal responsibility is yet another aspect of digital sovereignty.

As you can see, there are many facets to the digitization debate, and security is a critical factor for success. I am delighted that this book is giving cybersecurity the attention it demands, and I hope you enjoy reading it!

Yours,
Dr. Thomas Kremer

Member of the Board of Management for Data Privacy, Legal Affairs and Compliance of Deutsche Telekom

Dr. Thomas Kremer has been Member of the Board of Management for Data Privacy, Legal Affairs and Compliance at Deutsche Telekom since June 2012. He was appointed to the Government Commission on the German Corporate Governance Code in September 2013. He has also been Chairman of "Making Germany Safe on the Net" (DSiN) since November 2015. Before moving to Deutsche Telekom, Kremer worked for ThyssenKrupp AG, joining the company's legal department in 1994. In 2003, as General Counsel, he took over the management of ThyssenKrupp's Holding legal department, which also subsequently went on to develop the company's Compliance program. After taking over the management of the newly formed Corporate Center Legal and Compliance in 2009, Kremer was then appointed Executive Vice President in 2011.

Among other positions held prior to ThyssenKrupp and Telekom, Kremer also was an attorney at law firm Schäfer, Wipprecht, Schickert in Düsseldorf (now CMS Hasche Sigle). After graduating in law, Thomas Kremer worked as a research assistant at the University of Bonn in Germany before receiving his doctorate in law in 1994.

Contents

Security: The Real Challenge for Digitalization

1

Ferri Abolhassan

1.1 Introduction

Predicting train cancellations and thus avoiding what could amount to up to six-figure damages per cancellation. Or telling the purchasing department today which items customers are going to order the day after tomorrow. This is already a reality. Why do CIOs often know more about a company's core business than the CEO or specialist departments – and know it sooner? Because digitalization – with the IoT etc. – gives them access to a huge mass of information about customers, machines and processes. This is what is new. Such information enables CIOs to prepare and make decisions better and, above all, faster – ideally in real time. Now more than ever, the CIO is the most important sparring partner and source of inspiration for the CEO.

But for a CIO to do justice to this role, the technology has to work perfectly. Three things are needed to make sure the CIO is covered in this regard. First, the IT has to be stable. Second, any solutions have to interact reliably. And third, alongside high quality, a maximum level of security must be guaranteed. This is absolutely essential. As digitalization increases, companies are becoming more and more reliant on IT to survive. Quality, reliability **and** security must be ensured in the long term so that CIOs have the freedom they need to innovate. Then they can really pick up the pace with digitalization. The backbone for all this is the cloud. Only the cloud can centrally collect, store and evaluate the mass of structured and, above all, unstructured data and thus draw the maximum benefit from digital technologies – even as the mountain of data continues to grow.

Data and the insights gained from it are becoming increasingly valuable. And they must be protected in every respect: physically, technically and legally. We know this, and yet we do too little about it – because security is complex,

F. Abolhassan (✉)
Telekom Deutschland GmbH, Bonn, North Rhine-Westphalia, Germany
e-mail: ferri.abolhassan@telekom.de

© Springer International Publishing AG 2017
F. Abolhassan (ed.), *Cyber Security. Simply. Make it Happen.*, Management for Professionals, DOI 10.1007/978-3-319-46529-6_1

inconvenient and slow. This has to change. Security has to be simple so that it will be used. This means simple to acquire, to operate and to handle. Security is not an end in itself, after all. It is the prerequisite for digitalization to happen in the first place. Only then can it create real customer value. The only way to do this is with a cloud that offers maximum stability and security. This is the real challenge – and this is what will make security the springboard for digitalization.

1.2   Status Quo: The Cloud Is the Backbone of Digitalization

When analysts such as Gartner say the digitalization hype is already over (see Hagenau 2015), what they mean is this: "Gone are the days when digitalization and cloud computing were repeatedly heralded as the next big thing," as Forrester advisor Dan Bieler puts it. The excitement is giving way to sensible pragmatism. The cloud in particular found its way into companies long ago, and now these companies have to get down to work. The momentum of digital transformation can no longer be stopped, much less reversed. This is true regardless of where an individual company stands – whether it develops services in the cloud, or has to migrate entire legacy systems to the cloud, or wants to explore the Internet of Things.

No matter which current trend a company picks up on today, the basis of it will be the cloud. Something that was a new development just ten years ago is now a prerequisite for nearly every digitalization project. This is because only the cloud offers the capacity, cost-efficiency and agility needed to meet current and future demands of digitalization.

But what does the cloud actually look like? For some it is already a commodity, for others it is still a must-have. And why is it anything but trivial to get a company into the cloud? The answers to these questions are complex – not least because there is no such thing as THE cloud. The cloud has become highly diversified in recent years, so users can now choose from a variety of different options and implement the cloud solutions that best meet their requirements. These options cover everything from on-premise systems to private, public or hybrid clouds. And one question hovers above all of this: How secure will everything be if I connect one thing to the other?

It's a reasonable question. While public clouds are publicly accessible via the Internet, private clouds are designed more individually and offer extra protection by limiting access to a strictly defined user group. The hybrid cloud offers companies the best of both worlds: a combination of a private and public cloud with in-house IT. Customers themselves decide which data they want to host in the private or public cloud.

But the potential target of attack is growing – just look at the Internet of Things. And because up to 50 billion things are expected to be connected by the year 2020, according to IDG, this growth is exponential. As the number of sensors grows, so too will the amount of data they collect and the value of the insights it offers. This means that the need for protection is growing exponentially as well. It is no surprise that the most recent Cloud Monitor study from Bitkom and KPMG reported that while cloud usage is on the rise, the security concerns of potential users are curbing stronger growth (see Bitkom and KPMG 2015). Specifically, 90 percent of the decision-makers in politics and business say that concerns about IT security are currently the most important obstacle to Industry 4.0 (see Hill 2015).

One thing is certain: Both digitalization and the cloud must meet the essential requirements of maximum security, reliability and quality – covering everything from the security of data, processes and networks to the security of data centers, infrastructures, applications and devices. But it is also necessary to protect the interaction between these elements – and to do so without making it arduous for the user. For this reason, security must mirror digitalization, and not just in terms of scalability. It also has to be simple to acquire, implement, operate and use.

1.3   Data Security: Only a Secure Cloud Will Lead to Secure Digitalization

Security – and, in the age of digitalization, data security in particular – is always the prerequisite for business success. The cloud has to be secure if it is going to have a future. Companies need the cloud to explore the potential of the IoT. But if IT security is so fundamentally important, and executives themselves acknowledge this, why do companies struggle to implement it? There are various reasons for this. Security is often perceived as being complex, expensive and difficult to implement – but this can be alleviated by security solutions that are easy and cost-efficient to use. A harder problem to solve in the long term is the lack of technical expertise, especially in small and medium-sized companies. Some security-specific courses of study at universities are already addressing this problem, but the accelerated training of a sufficient number of experts will take some time. Despite all of these obstructions to the implementation of security, urgent action is required. This is because the attacks are getting more professional, and the damage they cause is getting more severe. According to the German data security agency BSI, there are already attackers operating internationally who focus on extorting companies, especially those in the financial services sector. And the attraction of these companies is growing. Studies show that 33 percent of all financial services providers have fallen prey to cybercriminals at least once. The average in every other industry is 17 percent. The attackers specifically look for IT vulnerabilities and systematically exploit them. In the first nine months of 2015, the BSI reported a total of 847 critical vulnerabilities in the eleven most frequently used software products alone (see Sievers 2015).

But how can companies make the leap into a secure future where they are immune to threats of all kinds? And how do secure cloud solutions as the basis of digitalization have to be designed so that companies view them as an opportunity, rather than a risk?

1.3.1   Risk Transformation: It Has to Be Easy to Get into the Cloud

The cloud and digitalization are clearly the future. They promise great technological diversity and immeasurable potential for companies in every industry. But companies have good reasons for hesitating, and these reasons are as diverse as the technology itself. For one thing, these are technologically complex solutions which are almost impossible for corporate IT departments to manage on their own. Then there is the confusing array of providers whose lack of product transparency makes the decision even more difficult. And last but not least, there is investment. Before a company can exhaust the potential of the cloud, it has to make a financial commitment.

Planning risks and financial risks: After choosing a cloud solution, companies are often tied to a provider for a long time. This robs them of the flexibility they need to quickly and easily move to a secure cloud environment. In addition, long contracts scare off potential customers. There are few or no players (i.e., IT service providers) in the market who are seriously trying to absorb some of the business risk for companies. Ideas such as abolishing the vendor lock-in are considered taboo in the industry. The entire history of outsourcing is based on long-term contracts. For customers to leave this contractually protected space, they need to be very confident in the provision and availability of their own services and IT. This is where new concepts come in, such as outsourcing without long contractual commitments and the transformation of legacy applications in the cloud at a fixed price. The option of flexibly cancelling a contract at any time offers real added value and signals that an IT provider is willing to help bear the customer's risk. It also makes investments more calculable and costs more transparent. And faults on the part of the IT provider can be redressed immediately.

Operationalization risks: Complex IT architectures and landscapes that have evolved over years have traditionally been very difficult to transform digitally. They can involve hundreds or even thousands of applications which are often intertwined with one another. If one application is turned off, it is almost impossible to predict how this will impact the others. This is all the more serious because business-critical processes and infrastructures are always affected as well. The implementation of the highest security standards sets the bar even higher. "You don't become a 'cloudifier' – who can handle digital transformation, manage applications in diverse cloud models, and guarantee their security on top of that – overnight." – this comment by Andreas Zilch from PAC hits the nail on the head. Years of experience are needed for smooth cloud transformation and system integration in combination with application-specific cloud orchestration. This problem can be overcome by cooperating with IT integration experts when migrating complex application landscapes to the cloud while modernizing and consolidating systems at the same time. Furthermore, running state-of-the-art cloud and security technologies from high-security, certified data centers helps meet the strictest demands of data security and protection.

1.3.2 Risk of an Incident: Making Sure the Cloud Doesn't Crash

In addition to analyzing business risks and cooperating with IT experts, it is critical for cloud technologies to be secure in and of themselves – which also means they have to offer a high degree of reliability and availability so that users can count on them. Users also have to trust in their inherent security, which must work smoothly. But how are companies protected against failures?

Incident risks: Completely networked value chains and infrastructures in particular harbor a risk of incidents with severe consequences. Networked IT systems are controlling vital machines and processes more and more often today. We need to look no further than intensive care units and operating rooms, high-speed train lines and planes. Perfectly functioning IT is essential here. But it is also clear that incidents are inevitable in IT. The way to counter this is through prevention combined with swift problem detection and reaction – meaning an immediate, structured approach in the event of an incident – embedded in a holistic quality management system.

Comprehensive quality management makes it possible to get very close to 100 percent fail-safety. A three-pillar model has proven effective here. Component one: prevention. Companies identify their business-critical points at platform, process and personnel level – and they take precautions. For example, consistently redundant data center technology can lead to platform availabilities of up to 99.999 percent. This reduces the risk of failures to just a few minutes per year. Furthermore, processes must be classified and emergency plans developed for a variety of scenarios. And finally, quality must be a part of a company culture that is embodied by every employee. This is a process that takes years. Component two: readiness. It literally takes practice to be able to act competently in a crisis. At T-Systems, we hold up to 500 "fire drills" worldwide annually. Regularly simulating emergencies and checking all of the steps necessary for incident management ensures that platforms, processes and personnel are as prepared as possible for component three: action during an actual incident. During any incident, it is also essential that a manager on duty and a representative of top management take responsibility for working on the problem around the clock until it is solved.

Stable, secure cloud services are made possible by coordinated interaction between humans and technology. With this in mind, T-Systems plans to start establishing an ecosystem of partners this year who are all committed to the zero-error principle and comply with common rules for quality management. Cross-industry corporate cooperation will only work in the future if there is a unified industry standard for IT quality. "Made in Germany" is therefore becoming more and more of a seal of approval. T-Systems itself has already reduced its number of system outages by 95 percent to almost zero within just five years through its Zero Outage quality initiative and the certification of around 22,000 employees and 100 system partners. This aspect is gaining importance not only for corporations, but also for small and medium-sized companies and, in principle, for private consumers as well.

Automation of security: This structured and standardized approach is logical – after all, the cloud represents the automation of IT. Consequently, we now need security to be automated on every level. That is the way security can reflect the simplicity of cloud operations – as a managed service, for example. And that is the way products and services can be preinstalled and thoroughly put to the test right from the start. The security-by-design principle must be at the heart of all product development and implementation. This encompasses the security of software throughout a product's lifecycle, as well as all infrastructure and processes. It is also important to ensure intuitive operation so that users are not restricted in their capacity to act. Pioneering solutions already exist that offer companies these kinds of security standards following the quality assurance principle.

1.3.3 Risk of Technical/Physical Attack: A Castle Wall Alone Isn't Enough

Even in the digital age, physical barriers are needed to protect data from attack. Gradually but haphazardly upgrading firewalls and similar solutions is not especially productive on its own. A more promising approach is to continually bring in new fortifications and deploy them in a way that stops attackers in their tracks where previously nothing held them back. This resembles the approach of state-of-the-art, highly secure data centers holding the treasures of digitalization. Take the data center in Biere: This new T-Systems data center near Magdeburg in Germany is separated from adjacent streets by a four-meter-high earth wall. The entire facility is surrounded by a two-meter-high fence topped with barbed wire. Around 300 cameras and motion sensors ensure that attackers cannot penetrate the grounds undetected. For additional security, specially trained security guards patrol the grounds around the clock. Inside the building there are airlock doors, chip-card readers, palm scanners and motion detectors, several hundred sensors and a security center behind mirrored, bullet-proof glass. The heart of the data center can only be reached by crossing an elevated walkway. But physical security does not play the only key role in Biere. To defend against external attackers such as hackers or data thieves, all data flows through encrypted IP VPN tunnels, creating a closed system which is separated from public networks and protected against external access. Intrusion detection and prevention systems supplement the firewall and analyze whether malware has found its way into the data streams. TSL protocols, anti-malware, secure point-to-point connections, and identity and access management solutions ensure that only authorized employees have access to data that may only be used on a need-to-know basis. Unwelcome guests are treated to a veritable labyrinth of intelligent barriers that detect all intrusions, neutralize them and immediately initiate countermeasures. Prevention, detection, reaction – this is what a modern corporate security architecture should look like.

To increase its failure safety, the infrastructure in Biere has been designed redundantly. The data center has an architectural twin in Magdeburg, about 18 kilometers away. Connected by a dual fiber-optic cable and equipped with "twin-core" technology, each data center stores sensitive data redundantly, ensuring its availability even if one of the data centers goes offline. And the effort to ensure high availability goes even further: Connected two times over to a 110-kilovolt power line, the data center's own substation ensures a stable power supply. In the event of an incident, emergency power generators will kick in.

1.3.4   Risk of a Cyberattack: Ensuring Data and Devices Aren't Casualties

Physical attacks in the form of a malicious USB stick – see the Stuxnet virus, for example – are one thing. But the number of cyberattacks has increased even more significantly in recent years. When attackers strike, companies face hefty damages and failures with often far-reaching consequences. In February 2015, hackers acquired the social security numbers, mailing addresses and email addresses of around 80 million customers of Anthem, one of the largest health insurers in the USA. Salary information for customers and employees was stolen as well (see The New York Times 2015). The year before, hackers seized the data of 76 million private and 7 million business customers of the US bank JP Morgan Chase. Attackers apparently also gained access to a list of applications running on JP Morgan's computers. This meant they could examine every program and every web application for known vulnerabilities in order to find an entry point for penetrating the bank's systems again at a later date. Experts say it took the bank months to change its programs and applications (see The New York Times 2014).

Attackers have a variety of motives. They range from a simple "just because they can," through political goals, as is the case with Anonymous, all the way to financial interests, which can be realized through extortion by using crypto-trojans such as Locky (see Eikenberg 2016). Action is urgently required here because these external attacks are becoming increasingly sophisticated, and the attackers are usually well ahead of the companies.

To protect themselves, IT managers have to know where the weaknesses are. But this isn't easy. The opportunities and scenarios for attacks have become very complex. However, technological approaches already exist that can help companies with detection. For example, the defense-in-depth approach divides IT architectures into multiple layers and places security mechanisms on each layer. Once intruders have breached the castle wall – the physical protective barrier – they face the next obstacles: firewalls that prevent unauthorized network access. Then there are honeypots that distract them from their actual goal by simulating the behavior of users, for example. And, to protect the data itself, there are now a variety of encryption solutions available, which make it impossible for attackers to actually use any valuable information they find.

Looking at the security technologies available today, it is clear that their value often depends on how easy they are to implement. Easy-to-install big-data real-time analyses study the behavior of data and detect behavioral and status anomalies – on both stationary servers and mobile devices. It gets even easier for companies when not only the data itself but also its protective mechanisms – including firewalls, intrusion protection systems, and virus or malware protection – are moved to the cloud.

Once security technology has been implemented and its fail-safety is guaranteed, companies must address another, often more serious vulnerability: Human weaknesses must not be underestimated, and they can undermine many of the most sophisticated security mechanisms – and intentionally or not, the consequences are the same. The simplest example is a telephone call from a supposed technician (think "social engineering") who asks for confidential login information. Only training and dissemination of knowledge can help to avoid this kind of error. In general, sharing knowledge and information is an important protection strategy against attackers. Four eyes see more than two – and the same applies to companies who can warn each other before threats spill over and spread. Voluntary organizations such as the Cyber Security Sharing and Analytics (CSSA) association show how this is done. It is equally important to gain an information advantage in your own company. The first cooperative projects have already started here between Deutsche Telekom, the Hochschule für Telekommunikation Leipzig (HfTL) and the Telekom Campus of Ben Gurion University in Israel.

In addition to the technical, human and knowledge-based prerequisites, it is important not to neglect data protection, because as we move toward a digital society, this aspect in particular will be put to the test. However, we must also make a distinction between an American and a European understanding of data protection and data security. Current discussions concerning the EU-US Privacy Shield show where these definitions diverge.

In Germany, companies must comply with especially strict federal data protection legislation. But these strict regulations are what make data-security specifications "Made in Germany" so internationally popular. For instance, the T-Systems cloud data center in Biere is now being used by 50 IT market leaders and has reached a capacity utilization of 70 percent in a very short time. The outstanding technology, architecture and security of our data centers is a good example of how Germany can reclaim value creation for Europe in an IT market dominated primarily by US companies. The traditionally extremely high level of expertise in the area of encryption technologies (encryption/decryption) could be a promising second area of activity in the IT security sector.

1.4 Looking to the Future

This overview of current IT security requirements shows just how complex the issue is. But in which direction will these developments go as they pick up speed – as they undoubtedly will? And where are we headed in the fight against attacks on the security of data, applications and processes? What is certain is that as digitalization progresses, system autonomy will grow as well. The proportion of communication and collaboration not handled by humans will continue to rise in the future. Thanks to smart data and machine learning (ML), machines and systems will become clever enough in the coming years to evolve autonomously. This means that a company's security DNA might also be able to continually optimize itself and adapt to the latest security requirements and threats.

The greatest benefit to users in this context will be the ability of machine learning to identify patterns and further develop this skill by means of independent self-learning. While most of today's security solutions are still rule-based and have to be modified and optimized by people, the security systems of the future will be able to do this themselves – much more efficiently than is currently possible. Just think of intrusion detection systems that can identify out-of-the-ordinary trespassers. Machine learning can detect and reveal such irregularities very quickly.

Or take user authentication and access control: ML systems can differentiate between even the subtlest nuances in how a user hits a keyboard. When a user logs in by typing a sentence, the system knows immediately whether the keystrokes match the user's profile or not. Pattern recognition through machine learning will eventually progress to the point that authentication will be possible using gestures, regardless of the device used. Bank customers might be able to transfer money by writing their name in the air, for example. There are almost no limits to the possible usage scenarios. And even today, we are already using smart, ML-based automation tools in data centers for the cloud.

1.5 Conclusion

The Internet has transformed society. Communication, business models and processes, big data – everything is getting easier, faster and more cost-efficient. The cloud makes it possible. And security has to keep up – taking into account one aspect above all: It must become easy to acquire and easy to use. For security, too, the cloud is the key to success. We must also increasingly turn our attention to protecting data, not just protecting infrastructures. Traditional castle walls that repel attackers are still an important part of security concepts in modern architectures, but a comprehensive security strategy demands additional measures so that companies are prepared if an intruder has already breached the fortifications. Pioneering developments in the field of machine learning already show: As the interface between humans and machines grows simpler, security must adapt to these new processes and user behaviors as well. Otherwise companies run the risk of disrupting their business processes and workflows. And security has to be simple, following the plug-and-play principle. The invention and widespread utilization of the cloud has made this simplicity a reality. Let us use the cloud as our model and create a secure digital future.

References

Bitkom Research GmbH on behalf of KPMG AG Wirtschaftsprüfungsgesellschaft. (2015). *Cloud-Monitor 2015*. Accessed May 30, 2016, from https://www.bitkom.org/Publikationen/2015/Studien/Cloud-Monitor-2015/Cloud-Monitor-2015-KPMG-Bitkom-Research.pdf

Eikenberg, R. (2016). *Krypto-Trojaner Locky wütet in Deutschland: Über 5000 Infektionen pro Stunde*. heise.de. Accessed June 1, 2016, from http://www.heise.de/security/meldung/Krypto-Trojaner-Locky-wuetet-in-Deutschland-Ueber-5000-Infektionen-pro-Stunde-3111774.html

Hagenau, T. (2015). *Cloud computing – der Hype ist vorbei*. computerwoche.de. Accessed May 30, 2016, from http://www.computerwoche.de/a/cloud-computing-der-hype-ist-vorbei,3069749

Hill, J. (2015). *Mit Industrie 4.0 steigt das Angriffsrisiko*. computerwoche.de. Accessed May 30, 2016, from http://www.computerwoche.de/a/mit-industrie-4-0-steigt-das-angriffsrisiko,3219509

Sievers, U. (2015). *Cyber-Angriffe werden immer professioneller*. VDI-nachrichten.de. Accessed June 1, 2016, from http://www.vdi-nachrichten.com/Technik-Gesellschaft/Cyber-Angriffe-professioneller

The New York Times. (2014). *Neglected server provided entry for JPMorgan hackers*. Accessed June 14, 2016, from http://dealbook.nytimes.com/2014/12/22/entry-point-of-jpmorgan-data-breach-is-identified/?_r=0

The New York Times. (2015). *Anthem hacking points to security vulnerability of health care industry*. Accessed June 13, 2016, from http://www.nytimes.com/2015/02/06/business/experts-suspect-lax-security-left-anthem-vulnerable-to-hackers.html?_r=0

Ferri Abolhassan After receiving his doctorate in computer science, Abolhassan began his professional career in R&D at Siemens in Munich, Germany, followed by several years at IBM in San Jose, USA. In 1992, he joined software vendor SAP, where he held a number of senior positions until 2001, including a spell as Senior Vice President of the global Retail Solutions business unit. Following a four-year tenure as Co-CEO and Co-Chairman at IDS Scheer, he returned to SAP in 2005, most recently as Executive Vice President, Large Enterprise for EMEA. In 2008, Abolhassan took over the newly-created position of Head of Systems Integration at T-Systems and at the same time joined the company's Board of Management. His management portfolio was later expanded to include the Production unit. In 2013, Abolhassan was appointed Director of Delivery before becoming Director of the IT division in 2015, overseeing approximately 30,000 employees and 6,000 customers. In December 2015, Abolhassan also took over the task of setting up the Telekom Security business unit, which will bundle all the security departments in the Deutsche Telekom corporation. In October 2016, he moved to Telekom Deutschland, where he heads the newly created business area Service Transformation as its Managing Director.

In 2011, he launched the successful "Zero Outage" program to safeguard T-Systems' quality standards in the face of growing process complexity. Not only is the program now certified by

Germany's technical inspection agency TÜV, but customer satisfaction has also risen to its highest level in the company's history, setting a new benchmark in the industry. T-Systems now plans to work with partners to create a new industry standard based on the Zero Outage principle. Abolhassan also initiated the construction of a new cloud data center in Germany (Magdeburg/ Biere), completed in 2014. The expansion of the facility due to high demand began in 2016. The plan is for storage and computing capacity to have risen by 150 percent on completion in 2018.

To address new IT security challenges, Deutsche Telekom initiated a new organizational unit for security solutions at the end of 2015. In addition to his other tasks, Abolhassan is in charge of launching that unit, which combines and consolidates all of Deutsche Telekom's security activities and will market the company's cyber-security offerings. One primary goal is improved integration of in-house security teams to counter the thousands of daily attacks by cybercriminals. Another objective is to exploit this internal experience to offer customers best-of-breed products and solutions across their entire value chains.

Security Policy: Rules for Cyberspace

2

Wolfgang Ischinger

A computer worm infests Iranian nuclear power plant systems, a cyberattack cripples sections of the Ukrainian electrical grid, intruders penetrate the German Parliament's IT system and steal sensitive data. No longer merely the stuff of science fiction novels cyberspace as a setting for security policy disputes and even a stage for conflicts, has long since become part of our reality.

"I have given Cyber Command ... really its first wartime assignment," declared United States Secretary of Defense Ashton Carter in Washington in early April 2016 (Financial Times 2016) in a statement directed against ISIS and interpreted by many as the first governmental cyberwar declaration. It is no longer possible to address security policy challenges or to lay out strategies today without factoring in the digital realm.

In fact, our current situation is similar to that some 70 years ago, when the invention of the nuclear bomb fundamentally changed the strategic landscape. The technical possibilities offered by the information revolution are less tangible, and their effects are considerably more complex and multi-faceted, but as in the nuclear revolution, they are fundamentally changing the playing field for international security policy. We are already facing massive challenges along with complex ethical, legal and political questions as the result of attacks by hackers on critical infrastructure, the online recruiting of jihadi fighters and the development of autonomous weapons systems. And technological change will march on, bringing new possibilities that open up any number of opportunities, while at the same time further magnifying the potential dangers associated with cyberspace. We must continually assess the opportunities – as well as the risks – of digital progress in terms of security policy and consider the necessary steps for dealing with them appropriately.

W. Ischinger (✉)
Stiftung Münchner Sicherheitskonferenz gemeinnützige GmbH, Prinzregentenstr. 7,
80538 Munich, Germany
e-mail: ischinger@securityconference.de

© Springer International Publishing AG 2017
F. Abolhassan (ed.), *Cyber Security. Simply. Make it Happen.*, Management for
Professionals, DOI 10.1007/978-3-319-46529-6_2

2.1   Taking Stock: Digital Warfare in the 21st Century

The possibilities of cyberwarfare have radically changed the character of modern conflict. In particular, one trend that we have observed increasingly in recent decades continues unabated: Conflicts are often asymmetrical, i.e., they no longer take place between state actors. Compared with the building of nuclear weapons, the barriers to entry for a "cyberwarrior" are, of course, far lower. It is true that major cyberwarfare operations, such as the one that damaged Iranian centrifuges by introducing the Stuxnet virus, are only possible when backed by substantial resources at a level generally only available to state actors. However, a far smaller amount of money combined with the necessary skills is enough to cause significant damage.

Terrorist groups have also discovered the digital world for themselves. ISIS makes use of the opportunities offered by cyberspace extensively and effectively: A significant factor in the organization's expansion is its digital strategy (see Munich Security Report 2016). Whether it is recruiting new members, spreading its propaganda messages, or communicating internally, the group known as the "Islamic State" is constantly expanding – not just physically, but digitally as well. As early as 2014, Robert Hannigan, head of the UK's GCHQ intelligence service, warned that social networks had already become the "command-and-control networks of choice" (Financial Times 2014) for groups such as ISIS. At this year's Munich Security Conference, he underscored this observation and called for more active and more effective measures to be taken in the online fight against jihadi terror (see Munich Security Conference 2016).

This battle is also being fought by private hacker groups like Anonymous, which provides a fitting illustration of today's digital battlefield: "Make no mistake: #Anonymous is at war with #Daesh. We won't stop opposing #IslamicState. We're also better hackers." This tweet was sent out by Anonymous after the Paris attacks in November 2015. In other words, a private hacker group operating in a space that was barely there 25 years ago, has declared digital war on the world's most powerful and dangerous terrorist group, which was non-existent just a few years ago. What would have sounded like an absurd description of a conflict not too long ago, is reality today. And this type of asymmetrical, multi-layered conflict will only become more prevalent in the future.

State actors are becoming increasingly active as well – partly in order to develop offensive capabilities and partly to ready themselves for the countless threats they face in cyberspace – and these activities extend far beyond online jihadism. The dissemination of falsified information for the purpose of intentionally manipulating certain segments of the population has become commonplace and is being given a huge boost by the opportunities offered by the online world. This was demonstrated quite recently in the calculated dissemination of false information in the "Lisa Case" in early 2016 (see Federal Academy for Security Policy 2016). Some states maintain entire "troll armies" that comment on news articles or distribute news and opinions favorable to those governments in social media. The ability of the public in our democracies to form opinions suffers as a result, particularly when this creates alternative public spheres that exist in their own reality, almost entirely walled off from political discourse and the facts.

Another danger stems from attacks on and damage to the institutions of democracy themselves. The large-scale assault on the German Parliament in summer 2015 made this very clear to us here in Germany (see FAZ 2016b). Attacks on critical infrastructure also have the potential to cause untold loss and damage. For instance, more than 700,000 households were temporarily left without electricity as a result of the strike against the Ukrainian power grid in December 2015 (see FAZ 2016a). It is hard to imagine what would happen if such attacks were even more widespread, and mobile communications, transportation and the water supply in densely populated regions were to be crippled in a matter of hours. Speaking on the sidelines of the 2016 Munich Security Conference, the Netherlands' foreign minister Bert Koenders called cyber arms "weapons of mass disruption," in contrast with nuclear, chemical or biological weapons of mass destruction (see Rijksoverheid 2016). Add to that billions in losses for companies as a result of corporate espionage, sabotage and data theft, the cost of which amounts to 51 billion euros each year in Germany alone (see Bitkom 2015), along with other financial losses occurring as "side effects" of digital progress.

Incidentally, such threats are anything but a purely Western problem. The expanding economies of the Global South are particularly vulnerable to the dangers of cyberspace. Often, the digitalization processes in these countries are especially rapid, sometimes occurring without any sort of safeguards whatsoever. A recently published report put economic losses in Kenya due to cybercrime at 146 million US dollars (see Serianu 2015). And South Africa saw approximately 6,000 attacks on its infrastructure, Internet providers and companies in October 2015 alone (see Times Live 2015).

2.2   Challenges for the Political Sphere: Rules, Resources and Expertise

Thus, politicians have to take faster and more effective action against cyberspace threats. One of the most basic problems in this regard is that, in many cases, politicians do not have the necessary expertise in this area. But they must make critical decisions nonetheless. The general public also frequently lacks sufficient understanding and basic knowledge of the topic in view of its complexity and the continual change in cyberspace. This is why we need digital "interpreters" to explain complex processes in simple terms everyone can understand. In the vast majority of cases, today's decision-makers have no affinity for digital issues, let alone professional expertise. And often, there is no common language for dialog between experts and politicians, although this is a basic prerequisite for the implementation of the necessary decisions.

In Germany these days, there is at least awareness of the immense challenges posed by cybersecurity, and initial key steps have been taken. A welcome announcement was made in spring 2016 by the German Federal Ministry of

Defense when it said that the German armed forces (Bundeswehr) would be restructured and a cyberforce added, and that the number of cyberexperts in the Ministry would be massively increased (see Wiegold 2016).

But we still have to ask ourselves whether our efforts are enough. Has society understood how greatly our future security and prosperity will depend on how well-prepared we are digitally? Former US President Barack Obama wanted to earmark line items totaling 19 billion US dollars for cybersecurity in the country's 2017 budget (see Reuters 2016). The British government has announced that it will nearly double its expenditure on cybersecurity over the next five years (see Gov. uk 2015). These are the orders of magnitude in which we must think.

We thus need more expertise, but also more capabilities in terms of resources and structures – well beyond what is called for in the German Ministry of Defense's reform. Universities and other institutions of higher education must be integrated into this effort so that professionals receive training and continuing education at an early stage. Implementation of even the best plans for new cybersecurity structures will fail if we do not succeed in recruiting computer and software specialists, developers and programmers. Thus, one of the key questions will therefore be how to inspire an interest in German military service among younger people who are not necessarily passionately interested in security and defense policy – and how these experts entering the defense ministry can work under Germany's complex public service legislation.

Many significant issues can no longer be resolved by politicians alone: Which technical resources do we have at our disposal for gaining the upper hand over terrorist organizations on the digital battlefield? How can we protect ourselves from attacks by foreign intelligence services that attempt to steal state secrets or sabotage our elected representatives and their independent decision-making process? In order to address these questions together and jointly create the conditions for a free, secure and open Internet, politicians require the support and trust of the private sector and other non-state experts in the field. Last summer, a reporting requirement was introduced in Germany as part of the IT Security Act, which will also be implemented across the EU as part of the Network and Information Security (NIS) Directive. This constitutes another important step toward closer cooperation.

Other questions also remain largely unanswered: What line has to be crossed for cyberattacks to be considered an act of war? How can we respond appropriately to such attacks, and what rules should be followed in carrying out such a response? What happens if there are strong indications as to who is responsible for a massive cyberattack, but no conclusive evidence is available? What implications do these considerations have on Article 5 of the NATO Treaty? NATO has declared that cyberspace will be acknowledged as an independent operational area in the future (see NATO 2016). This could also mean that cyberattacks could trigger the mutual defense clause (see NATO 2015).

Due to the fact that national borders are very fuzzy in cyberspace, transnational forms of cooperation such as NATO play a particularly important role here. Although it is primarily the job of each nation state to guarantee its own security, some responsibilities could be in much better hands at European or NATO level.

In recent years, the practices of some intelligence services have led many Germans to view cooperation with international partners with some skepticism. Particularly their attitude towards the American partner has deteriorated substantially as a result of the NSA affair. According to a survey by the German Marshall Fund, the number of all individuals surveyed in Germany who view the United States positively dropped a full 14 percent points from 2011 to 2014, from 72 to 58 percent (see The German Marshall Fund of the United States 2015). Fortunately, both sides have slowly inched back together in the meanwhile. In May 2015, German confidence in the bilateral alliance had again risen to 62 percent (see Pew Research Center 2015). Some skepticism remains, however, along with fundamental differences in the cyberpolicy of the two countries. This is also reminiscent of the early days of the nuclear age when US allies had to come together before their concerns would be heard by Washington (see Ischinger et al. 2014). For this reason, one of the key objectives must be for Germany and the United States, along with other countries, to build a consensus on the basic pillars of international cyberpolicy. Only based on a clear EU position can we succeed in gradually reaching transcontinental agreement on "reliable rules of the game" (see FAZ 2014) for cyberspace – as called for by Telekom CEO Timotheus Höttges as early as 2014 at the Cyber Security Summit in Bonn, organized by the company and the Munich Security Conference. For several years now, the Munich Security Conference along with Deutsche Telekom has been organizing roundtables and summits on cybersecurity issues, bringing together decision-makers and experts from across the globe, for instance in Silicon Valley in the fall of 2016.

The more sophisticated the possibilities provided by cyberspace become, the more important it is to underpin them with a set of norms and rules. Key here is fundamentally updating international law, which does not yet address or govern cyberwarfare as such. In contrast to nuclear security, for instance, the cyberarena to date has no internationally recognized, multilateral body of regulations that specifically governs the conduct of cyberwar. Nonetheless, some countries, including the two cybergiants – China and the United States – were able to reach initial agreement on the subject of industrial espionage in the fall of 2015. Attempts to arrive at more far-reaching standards for cyberspace have also been underway for some time now. These include the (further) development of the Tallinn Manual, which was initiated in 2009 and elaborated by legal experts from various NATO member states. An initial draft was presented in 2013 (see CCDCOE 2013). However, this standard is not legally binding, and thus international implementation and enforcement of the recommendations have been lacking to date.

Democracies in particular, such as the member states of the European Union, should strive for a free, open and secure Internet as a global public asset. The European Union can still be much more active in this regard and drive the development of international standards. During this process, it will repeatedly run into obstacles. While there already are fundamental differences in cyberpolicy even in transatlantic relations, authoritarian states weigh up security and freedom on the Internet very differently. For this reason, German mistrust of the United States on the issue of data security is largely misguided: We face much greater danger from other directions. According to information by the German Federal Intelligence Service, the attack on the German Bundestag was steered by Russia (see Zeit 2016). And recently, CIA Director James R. Clapper, speaking before the US Senate, emphasized that, "Russia and China continue to have the most sophisticated cyberprograms" (The Diplomat 2016). Many other countries are also working on offensive cybercapabilities. We are, there is no other way to put it, in the middle of a digital arms race. Precisely for this reason, it is all the more important to work out common minimum standards and fundamental rules as quickly as possible.

2.3   Outlook: A Strategy for the Digital Age

As I wrote at the beginning, in some ways we find ourselves in a situation similar to around 70 years ago, when the invention of the nuclear bomb fundamentally changed the strategic landscape. Although the parallels should not be over-emphasized in view of the obvious differences between a nuclear warhead and code, we stand at the beginning of an era of uncertain developments, and that is similar to the post-1945 period. The full effects of new cyber instruments on international security policy and on how wars and conflicts are fought cannot really be foreseen yet. Cyberregulations do not (yet) exist.

But we are experiencing the risks of cyberspace every day. We must seize the opportunity arising from this: the potential for better preparing against these hazards and for developing means of addressing them effectively. For this reason, new approaches are needed. This applies to the national level first of all. The recent restructuring of the German armed forces and the Ministry of Defense is an important step in this regard that must be followed by others. Additional momentum is expected from the new German federal cybersecurity strategy, which will replace the predecessor document written in 2011 (see German Federal Government 2016). At the regional level, what is necessary first and foremost is better coordination within the EU and a drive toward joint initiatives to set comprehensive standards for cyberspace. Ultimately, the greatest challenge appears to be developing and implementing authoritative standards worldwide and agreeing on the basic tenets of international cybersecurity policy.

The process will be long, but it has prospects for success. The attempt in the 1960s to develop rules for the nuclear age was equally complex, but ultimately successful: Steps were taken toward arms control and disarmament, even though the danger was only contained, not eliminated. In this day and age, we must succeed in carrying out a similar international process to develop a common strategy for the significantly more complex digital age. Only then can we ensure together that the potential risks of cyberspace are minimized as much as possible and the numerous opportunities offered by a free, open and secure Internet are realized. It is not yet too late.

References

Bitkom (2015). *Studie zu Wirtschaftsschutz und Cybercrime*. Accessed June 16, 2016, from https://
www.bitkom.org/Presse/Presseinformation/Studie-zu-Wirtschaftsschutz-und-Cybercrime.html

CCDCOE (2013). *Tallinn manual process*. Accessed June 16, 2016, from https://ccdcoe.org/
tallinn-manual.html

Die Bundesregierung (2016). *Kabinettsklausur in Meseberg – Digitalisierung gemeinsam
vorantreiben*. Accessed June 16, 2016, from https://www.bundesregierung.de/Content/DE/
Artikel/2016/05/2016-05-24-digitalisierung-meseberg.html

FAZ (2014). *Cyber security summit – Jeder ist bedroht*. Accessed June 16, 2016, from http://www.
faz.net/aktuell/wirtschaft/netzwirtschaft/telekom-chef-thimotheus-hoettges-jeder-ist-
bedroht-jeder-staat-jedes-unternehmen-jeder-buerger-13243841.html

FAZ (2016a). *Cyber-Sicherheit: Die Hackerdämmerung*. Accessed June 16, 2016, from http://
www.faz.net/aktuell/wissen/physik-mehr/ukrainischer-stromausfall-war-ein-hacker-angriff-
14005472-p2.html?printPagedArticle=true#pageIndex_2

FAZ (2016b). *Netzangriff auf Bundestag – Es begann mit einer E-Mail*. Accessed June 16, 2016,
from http://www.faz.net/aktuell/feuilleton/medien/neue-details-zum-cyberangriff-auf-den-
bundestag-14114851.html

Federal Academy for Security Policy (2016). *The Lisa Case – STRATCOM lessons for European
States (Security Policy Working Paper, No. 11/2016)*. Accessed June 16, 2016, from https://
www.baks.bund.de/sites/baks010/files/working_paper_2016_11.pdf

Financial Times (2014). *The web is a terrorist's command-and-control network of choice*.
Accessed June 16, 2016, from http://www.ft.com/intl/cms/s/2/c89b6c58-6342-11e4-8a63-
00144feabdc0.html#axzz3rjx7E4aL

Financial Times (2016). *US launches online assault against Isis*. Accessed June 16, 2016, from
http://www.ft.com/cms/s/0/4d98edd0-fba5-11e5-b3f6-11d5706b613b.html#axzz4BkAXAl00

Gov.uk (2015). *Chancellor's speech to GCHQ on cyber security*. Accessed June 16, 2016, from
https://www.gov.uk/government/speeches/chancellors-speech-to-gchq-on-cyber-security

Ischinger, W., & Bunde, T. (2014). *Die Zukunft des Westens im digitalen Zeitalter*. FAZ of January
30, 2014.

Munich Security Conference (2016). *Panel discussion "'Daeshing' terror and safeguarding
liberties"*. Accessed June 16, 2016, from https://www.securityconference.de/mediathek/
video/panel-discussion-daeshing-terror-and-safeguarding-liberties/filter/video/?tx_dreipctv
mediacenter_mediacenter[venue]=36&cHash=3c81bfeba609faf81063d1ece9232f09

Munich Security Report (2016). *Munich security report 2016*. Accessed June 16, 2016, from
https://www.securityconference.de/aktivitaeten/munich-security-report/

NATO (2015). *Keynote speech by NATO Secretary General Jens Stoltenberg at the Opening of the
NATO transformation seminar*. Accessed June 16, 2016, from http://www.nato.int/cps/fr/
natohq/opinions_118435.htm?selectedLocale=fr

NATO (2016). *NATO Defence Ministers agree to enhance collective defence and deterrence*.
Accessed June 17, 2016, from http://www.nato.int/cps/en/natohq/news_132356.htm?

Pew Research Center (2015). *Germany and the United States: Reliable allies*. Accessed June 16,
2016, from http://www.pewglobal.org/2015/05/07/germany-and-the-united-states-reliable-
allies/

Reuters (2016). *Concerned by Cyber Threat, Obama seeks big increase in funding*. Accessed June
16, 2016, from http://www.reuters.com/article/us-obama-budget-cyber-idUSKCN0VI0R1

Rjiksoverheid (2016). *Toespraak van minister Koenders bij de Münchner Sicherheitskonferenz*.
Accessed June 16, 2016, from https://www.rijksoverheid.nl/regering/inhoud/bewindspersonen/
bert-koenders/documenten/toespraken/2016/02/12/toespraak-van-minister-koenders-munchner-
sicherheitskonferenz

Serianu (2015). *Kenya cyber security report 2015*. Accessed June 16, 2016, from http://serianu.
com/downloads/KenyaCyberSecurityReport2015.pdf

The Diplomat (2016). *Top US spy chief: China still successful in cyber espionage against US.* Accessed June 16, 2016, from http://thediplomat.com/2016/02/top-us-spy-chief-china-still-successful-in-cyber-espionage-against-us/

The German Marshall Fund of the United States (2015). *Report of the task force on the future of German-American relations.* Accessed June 16, 2016, from http://www.gmfus.org/publications/longstanding-partners-changing-times

Times Live (2015). *It's one hack of a problem.* Accessed June 16, 2016, from http://m.timeslive.co.za/thetimes/?articleId=15801457

Wiegold, T. (2016). *Cyberkrieger, Computernerds und IT-Einkäufer: Bundeswehr stellt sich neu auf.* Accessed June 16, 2016, from http://augengeradeaus.net/2016/04/cyberkrieger-computernerds-und-it-einkaeufer-bundeswehr-stellt-sich-neu-auf/

Zeit online (2016). *Deutscher Bundestag – Hackerangriff wurde aus Russland gesteuert.* Accessed June 16, 2016, from http://www.zeit.de/digital/2016-01/hackerangriff-bundestag-russland-nachrichtendienst-bundesanwaltschaft

Wolfgang Ischinger Ambassador Ischinger is Chairman of the Munich Security Conference and Senior Professor for Security Policy and Diplomatic Practice at the Hertie School of Governance in Berlin.

A graduate in law and international relationships, Ischinger first worked in the cabinet of the UN Secretary-General before moving to the German Federal Foreign Office in 1975.

This included postings to the embassies in Washington, D.C. and Paris, and a period from 1982 to 1990 as a senior assistant to Hans-Dietrich Genscher, the German Minister for Foreign Affairs at the time. From 1993 to 1998, he was Director of the Policy Planning Staff and later Political Director, before serving as State Secretary from 1998 to 2001. He was Ambassador to the USA from 2001 to 2006, and Ambassador to the United Kingdom from 2006 to 2008.

He was appointed Chairman of the Munich Security Conference in 2008. He also held the position of Global Head of Governmental Relations at Allianz SE (Munich) from 2008 to 2015.

Ambassador Ischinger represented the EU in the Troika Kosovo negotiations in 2007 and the OSCE in efforts to establish a national dialog in Ukraine in 2014. In 2015, he was appointed Chairperson of an OSCE-mandated Panel of Eminent Persons to strengthen the European security architecture.

He currently advises companies, governments and international organizations. He is a member of the Supervisory Board of Allianz Deutschland AG and Allianz Private Krankenversicherung (APKV), and a member of the European Advisory Council of Investcorp (London/New York). He also serves on the Steering Committee of the German Council on Foreign Relations (DGAP), the Board of Atlantik-Brücke, the Board of Trustees for SWP (Berlin), SIPRI (Stockholm), AICGS (Washington, DC) and The American Academy in Berlin, the Advisory Board of the Federal Academy for Security Policy (BAKS) and the Center for European Reform (London), and the Board of Directors of the Atlantic Council. He received the Leo Baeck Medal in 2008 and was decorated with the Federal Cross of Merit in 2009.

Data Protection Empowerment

Peter Schaar

The term "data protection" implies that data requires a protective hand. It therefore comes as no surprise that it is often confused or used synonymously with other terms describing similar subject matter, such as IT security. The fact that this misunderstanding seems almost impossible to clear up is due in part to the unfortunate choice of words. Data protection is not about the protection of data per se, but about the protection of personal data in light of the right to informational self-determination and the preservation of the private sphere – which is why another term for it is data privacy.

Data protection laws impose rules on anyone handling personal data. These protection obligations are directed primarily at the state, although government agencies themselves collect huge amounts of personal data, often on the basis of sovereign authority. It is precisely because of these special powers that the data protection laws applicable to government agencies contain especially detailed rules that simultaneously permit and restrict the collection, processing and use of personal information. Data protection is a fundamental right that places limits on the state's thirst for knowledge, as the German Federal Constitutional Court has repeatedly ruled. Data protection regulations for businesses in general, on the other hand, are quite flexible. Companies are allowed to collect, process and use data as long as this is necessary to accomplish a task – such as concluding and executing a contract – or for other justified purposes. Ultimately, personal data may be processed as long as the person affected has consented to this. With the rise of services that are supposedly free but actually financed through the use of personal data, individuals are increasingly being required to give blanket consent to the extensive use of their data in ways they may not even be aware of. Legally defined powers to collect and use personal data stake out the framework within which entities can gather or process data. But even if the goal of this is to secure a space for

P. Schaar (✉)
Spessartstr. 11, 14197 Berlin, Germany
e-mail: peter.schaar@email.de

© Springer International Publishing AG 2017
F. Abolhassan (ed.), *Cyber Security. Simply. Make it Happen.*, Management for Professionals, DOI 10.1007/978-3-319-46529-6_3

individuals in which they can, in principle, control "their" data, this alone does not really guarantee the right to self-determination in a technologized world.

When empowerment is brought up in this context, it is not meant in the sense of prohibition and permission, or even of consent, but rather with respect to designing technology so that control over personal data is returned to the individual.

3.1 Code Is Law

Digital systems whose functionality is determined by hardware and software have at least as much influence as legal regulations when it comes to the options available to the individuals who use these systems or whose data is processed by third parties. "Code is law" – this provocative but nonetheless accurate statement made by Lawrence Lessig (see Lessig 1999) in the last year of the 20th century is more relevant now than ever before. The design and configuration of hardware and software determines what data is collected and how it is handled. The technical decisions made when a system is designed therefore have a decisive influence on what data is gathered and stored, who can access it, and how humans will interact with the machines in question and with other humans. This is not only, or even primarily, about individual pieces of (personal) data, but rather about structural decisions that have an impact far beyond the actual data processing itself. The people in charge of the technology also have the power of decision over how information is used. And they use this "data power" to gain economic or political advantages. As a result, the individuals who use this technology and whose data is processed increasingly become objects.

The mechanisms implemented in hardware and software are moving closer to people and defining more and more aspects of their everyday lives. Smartphones, intelligent kitchen gadgets and digitally controlled heating systems are becoming a norm that only hard-nosed nostalgics try to avoid. Radio-controlled pacemakers and other implants not only measure vital signs, they can also actively influence our health.

An epochal change is currently underway, one driven by increasingly powerful information technology: In the age of Small Data, (personal) data was the material used in processes designed to fulfill a certain task, but the focus of Big Data is to amass as much data as possible (data maximization) and link it beyond the context in which it was originally gathered. The principles of necessity and purpose underlying the classic data protection model are increasingly coming under pressure. Since Edward Snowden's revelations at the latest, no one can deny that the triumphant advance of the Internet, not to mention the Internet of Things, has heralded a golden age for public and private data collectors, leaving individuals relatively helpless in the face of it.

This situation is diametrically opposed to the fundamental right to informational self-determination, which was established by the German Federal Constitutional Court in 1983 in its famous population census decision. "In the context of modern data processing," this fundamental right guarantees.

"... in principle the power of individuals to make their own decisions concerning the disclosure and use of their personal data." (BVerfG 65,1, p.1, headnote 1)

This ruling was based largely on the Court's assessment "that, since personally identifiable information could be collected and processed automatically, individuals must not become mere informational objects." Data processing conditions had to be defined in a way that preserved human dignity and guaranteed the free development of personality. If people had to fear that every aspect of their behavior might be recorded and compiled to create a personality profile, they would not be able to develop or make decisions freely. Instead, they would waive the exercise of certain rights and avoid behaviors that could potentially have negative consequences for them. The Federal Constitutional Court confirmed and expanded upon this view in a number of other rulings. Of particular note here is a decision from 2008 defining a fundamental right to safeguards regarding the confidentiality and integrity of information technology systems (known as the IT Basic Law).

In light of this, data protection cannot and must not be restricted to defining legal limits for processing individual pieces of data. Instead, it must be about designing information technology in compliance with basic rights. The preconditions for this are not all that bad, as the new world of IT offers several points of departure for designs that are compatible with data protection. Unlike the classic mainframe-based data processing systems in the data centers of the 20th century, which operated beyond the reach of the people affected by them, individuals in the 21st-century world of IT are increasingly "users" and thus actors in these information technology systems.

But while it is true that digitalization is leading to growing masses of data – with the corresponding hazards – we must not forget that this same development harbors opportunities for informational self-determination. Unlike the computer dinosaurs in mainframe data centers, modern technical devices are often within our grasp, or at least within our virtual reach. So why not give the affected individuals – us, the users – far more ways of controlling them?

This is why questions about the design, functionality and embedding of information technology have taken on existential significance for the future of society and the personal development of the individual. As "code" influences our life more and more, the question of who determines the code and which rules it follows becomes increasingly important.

3.2 Empowerment

The realization that there is a connection between the legal and technical demands placed on information technology is not new. The basic ideas behind "privacy by design" go back to the 1990s. Under the heading of privacy-enhancing technologies (PET), the Dutch data protection expert John Borking developed a coherent system of information technology measures for avoiding or eliminating personally identifiable data (see IPC 1995). But this concept of data avoidance or data minimization, which has been anchored in the German Federal Data Protection Act since 2001, has barely gained a foothold in practice, especially because economic interests and (at least since the terror attacks of September 11, 2001) public and national security needs have taken precedence.

But as IT systems grow more powerful, it is worth dusting off some of these approaches to privacy-friendly technology design, developing them further and bringing them to life. Now more than ever, technical tools are the only way to rein in the rampant collection, correlation and evaluation of data without foregoing the advantages of using IT. Interactive, multiply networked IT structures and the services provided through them are highly designable. In many cases it is possible to find solutions that allow users or the people concerned to gain or regain control over their data without impacting functionality. Such approaches could center on intelligent devices, such as smartphones, that manage our data protection preferences and enable us to monitor and control where our data is sent.

The P3P (Platform for Privacy Preferences) approach developed more than 15 years ago could be a good starting point for this type of data protection agents. This is an internationally standardized platform (created by the WWW Consortium) for exchanging data protection information for websites. P3P is supposed to give web users a fast, automated overview of which personal data is being processed by website operators or third parties and for what purposes. Users specify their preferences for the protection of their own data in a P3P agent, such as a P3P-enabled browser. The software agent compares these user preferences with the website operator's standardized description of its data processing practices. If there are any discrepancies, the user is alerted. In this case, the website can only be accessed – and the data transferred – if users explicitly release their data.

This model could also be applied to the Internet of Things. However, it would have to be standardized and implemented in the software. For example, a transparent energy management system could be established for digital electricity grids, without energy suppliers or Internet service providers such as Google gaining access to the usage details for devices connected to a smart meter in a household. The decisive factors here, as in other fields of application for smart technologies, are where the data converges, who can access it and who can use it. It is clearly useful for energy users to have more knowledge about their consumption so that they can take action accordingly – with regard to useless standby settings, for example, or replacing power-guzzling electrical appliances. Energy suppliers, on the other hand, do not need to know the details of individual device usage or room thermostat settings in order to plan their network load distribution or to feed energy into the grid. They only need to be aware of the load development in each network segment – not even in each individual household. A privacy-friendly solution could send detailed consumption values to a user's smartphone. If third parties were interested in this data, it would only be sent to them after the user had explicitly consented to this.

Intelligent driver assistance systems can work without centrally collecting data about an individual driver's location and driving habits. Navigation systems can also identify traffic jams without recording personalized driving behavior. We already have powerful systems for measuring traffic loads which use pseudonymized and anonymized data, or even get by without any personal data whatsoever – such as the "smart traffic lights" and traffic routing in the city of Mannheim. As in the case of the electricity network, users should have extensive control over the detailed data they generate in intelligent vehicles. In any event, there must be no chance that this information could be sent to third parties behind the user's back.

In principle, technical systems must be designed to get by without personal data and give individuals the power of decision over their own data. If individualized data has to be stored – for fitness trackers or health apps, for example – there must be a guarantee that the data will be stored under the users' control and only sent to third parties under the conditions stipulated by the users themselves. The widespread practice of automatically storing such data in a cloud controlled exclusively by the provider is highly problematic from the standpoint of data protection laws.

Since individual identity data is generally not needed for data analyses, anonymized data is usually sufficient here. An "intelligent car" equipped with information technology can measure any number of environmental and driving parameters. But much of this data is needed only for a very short period of time, sometimes for just a few seconds. Systems should be designed in a way this information is deleted or at least anonymized once it has served its purpose. If further analyses are to be conducted with the data, the driver or owner must be informed in advance and technical protection measures must be in place, such as anonymization technology. Anonymization and, in some cases – such as long-term medical studies – the use of pseudonyms should become standard practices, with deviations permitted only in special cases and with the full knowledge of the affected individuals. Anonymization and the creation of pseudonyms should be decentralized as much as possible and should not take place on the server side.

Cryptographic methods that protect confidential information from being monitored and recorded are also very important. Efforts to prohibit encrypted communication and install backdoors in information technology for the use of intelligence agencies and other authorities are counterproductive. They interfere with the right to informational self-determination and they weaken IT security – and not just when it comes to exposing criminal activity. With cryptography, too, there must be a stipulation that cryptomaterial – especially the keys that are used – will be generated and managed under the user's control.

Approaches such as P3P and the Do Not Track standard on the web are steps in the right direction, but they must be developed further and, above all, actually implemented. They are essentially limited to the message that Internet services should honor the private sphere. To this day, many websites still ignore the browser preferences set by users. Some "data privacy statements" even say that providers are not prevented from collecting much larger amounts of personal data than the users desire. Future data protection technologies must effectively prevent the disclosure of personal information if this is what the user has requested. The technology used in the latest ad blockers shows that this can work. Additionally, the corresponding measures must be legally enforced – and the opportunities for legal enforcement will rise with the recently adopted European General Data Protection Regulation, which calls for much harsher sanctions against data protection violations than previous data protection laws.

3.3   Information Technology and Social Values

The extent to which we are able to take the achievements and values of civilization into account as our lives are digitalized will determine the character of the information society towards which we are moving at an ever-faster pace.

The success of this also depends on the design of the technology. The "civilization" of IT will only be possible when people – as citizens and consumers alike – can move within a framework of trust in information technology. They must be confident that the technology complies with key rules and regulations, and that the usage conditions are stable. Only then will they be able to rely on the trustworthiness of information technology systems.

All considerations about the future of the information society must center on the individual and his or her right to self-determination and opportunities for personal development. Self-determination is the ability of individuals to control their informational image. Individuals should also have access to technologies that allow them to make their own decisions regarding what they want to reveal about themselves.

References

BVerfG (1983). *Decision from December 15, 1983 (Census decision).* Accessed June 20, 2016, from http://openjur.de/u/268440.html

IPC (1995). *Privacy-enhancing technologies: The path to anonymity* (vol 1). Accessed June 20, 2016, from https://www.ipc.on.ca/english/Resources/Discussion-Papers/Discussion-Papers-Summary/?id=329

Lessig, L. (1999) *Code and other laws of cyberspace* (p. 5). New York: Basic Books.

Peter Schaar is Chairman of the European Academy for Freedom of Information and Data Protection (EAID). He is also President of the Arbitration Body of the Germany Society for Health Insurance Card Telematics Applications (gematik). 2003–2013 he has been a German Federal Commissioner for data protection and freedom of information. Schaar is the author of numerous publications, including "Datenschutz im Internet [Data Protection and the Internet]" (2002), "Das Ende der Privatsphäre [The End of Privacy]" (2007), "Total überwacht – Wie wir in Zukunft unsere Daten schützen [Total Surveillance: Protecting our Data in the Future]" (2014) and "Das digitale Wir – Der Weg in die transparente Gesellschaft [Our Digital Selves: Becoming a Transparent Society]" (2015). His work has received many accolades, including the Political Book Prize from the Friedrich Ebert Foundation and the eco Internet Award in 2008, the GDD's German Data Protection Prize in 2013 and the Louis D. Brandeis Privacy Award in the following year.

Red Teaming and Wargaming: How Can Management and Supervisory Board Members Become More Involved in Cybersecurity?

4

A Traditional Military Approach Applied to Strategy Development in the Field of Cybersecurity

Marco Gercke

4.1 Cybersecurity: A Management Board Issue

When Deutsche Bahn CEO Rüdiger Grube in 2013 was quoted as saying that cybersecurity at his company was a management board issue, not something left to the system administrators (see van Zütphen 2013), this was something out of the ordinary as cybersecurity did not count as a traditional board issue at the time. These days Grube is in the best of company, because the topic of cybersecurity is now on the management board agenda of an increasing number of enterprises. A group of CEOs from 23 German blue chips even discussed it at length at the 2014 Munich Security Conference (see Gercke et al. 2014).

In view of the growing number of attacks on large companies (see Tsukayama 2012) and SMEs (see Securitymagazine 2013) that could jeopardize their future, integrating the management board is a logical move. Even if there is disagreement with regard to the number of attacks, management board members of large companies can ill afford to ignore the threat, in particular because of the liability risk it entails. For stock corporations there is even a legal framework from which the obligation can be inferred. Section 91(2) of the German Stock Corporation Act (AktG) sets out that the management board must establish a suitable risk management system to ensure that developments threatening the survival of the company are detected – as part of the ordinary management of business as defined in Section 93(1) AktG. While the wording of the law does not contain an explicit obligation with regard to cybersecurity, it is widely accepted in literature that cybersecurity is a component of risk management and that a breach of duty under Section 91(2) AktG may lead to the members of the management board being held

M. Gercke (✉)
Cybercrime Research Institute GmbH, Niehler Str. 35, 50733 Cologne, Germany
e-mail: gercke@cybercrime.de

© Springer International Publishing AG 2017
F. Abolhassan (ed.), *Cyber Security. Simply. Make it Happen.*, Management for Professionals, DOI 10.1007/978-3-319-46529-6_4

personally liable (see Bürgers and Israel 2014; Trappehl 2009; von Holleben and Menz 2010).

4.2 Integrating the Management Board into Existing Cybersecurity Strategies

One challenge for companies in general and for their management boards in particular is determining how to integrate management board members into the company's overall strategy. In contrast to the technical aspects of cybersecurity, where standards such as ISO 27001 provide clear structures, there is a lack of appropriate guidance on the involvement of management board and supervisory board members. One of the main issues must be to clarify a company's own cybersecurity strategy to incorporate the decision-makers in a meaningful way, at least when the companies wish to develop a serious strategy – something that is not always the case.

A detailed look at the cybersecurity strategies of countries and private companies reveals that, to this day, the relevant documents are frequently relatively short and focus less on concrete instructions and more on declarations of intent. What is actually needed are strategies that in addition to basic statements contain clear guidelines on responsibility, processes, and technical specifications (see Gercke 2013: 136–142).

When such a complex strategy is being developed, important questions in connection with the inclusion of the management board almost inevitably arise. For example: Which incidents invoke the board's responsibility? While nobody will seriously notify the management board of every single IT incident that occurs at a large company, mundane events may at the same time provide the gateway for complex attacks. Any delegation of responsibilities that has already taken place – for instance from the management board to a crisis unit that becomes active in an emergency – may also be significant in this respect.

4.3 Red Teaming and Wargaming

Since the structures in companies and companies' institutional capacity generally do vary considerably, it is extremely difficult to develop and implement a method for the integration of management board members as a universal blueprint. Customization is what is required here, especially for large companies, which tend to have more complex structures. The question is whether and how the management board can be incorporated in a cybersecurity strategy using military approaches such as red teaming and wargaming.

4.3.1   Red Teaming Defined

Red teaming or alternative analysis is a specific method used to review plans, strategies, and hypotheses (see Fryer-Biggs 2012; Herman et al. 2009; Lauder 2009; Longbine 2008; Sabin 2012). Two teams are formed, a Red Team and a Blue Team (see Wood and Duggan 2002). The Red Team assumes the role of the attacker, while the Blue Team focuses on defense (see CSO 2008). This method has been successfully employed by the military for decades (see Lauder 2009; Longbine 2008) and has also been applied in civil activities for a number of years (see Lauder 2009). It is explicitly not restricted to acting out physical attacks. The methodology can also be used to investigate theoretical issues from different angles and with varying emphases – reaching as far as intangible constructs such as a legislative draft (see Gercke 2014).

Red teaming can be particularly useful when developing cybersecurity strategies, since the attack situation reflects the real threat situation. However, strategies are mostly developed from the defense angle. A change or expansion of perspective enables a company's own strategies to be examined more critically.

4.3.2   Wargaming Defined

Wargaming is the dynamic simulation of genuine threat situations (see Herman et al. 2009; Sabin 2012; Perla 1990; Oriesek and Schwarz 2009). Using simulated situations like this, strategies can be safely tested under realistic conditions. What makes this approach special is its dynamic nature, which is frequently lacking in conventional strategy developments. Another major advantage of simulations is the fact that they create a more realistic environment. In other approaches like the table desk exercise, discussion does take place, but factors such as stress and strain are not taken into account. It is things like this that can generate realistic simulations.

It is therefore not surprising that simulations and wargaming are used not only in a military environment but also in preparing non-military decision-makers (see Herman et al. 2009; Oriesek and Schwarz 2009; von der Gathen 2014). Wargaming offers numerous advantages, particularly in the field of cybersecurity. In cybersecurity incidents, important information about the scope and effects is often unavailable initially. An analysis of attacks also shows that such incidents are becoming increasingly complex. Decision-makers therefore need to come to grips with the situation that decisions must be made rapidly and in some cases on the basis of not very reliable facts.

4.3.3   Differences Compared with Methods Currently in Use

Up to now, companies have often fallen back on theoretical approaches when developing strategies in general and integrating decision-makers in particular, with advisors normally stating where they personally see vulnerabilities and potential for improvement. In many cases, the effects of vulnerabilities are also underpinned by specific examples. However, it is unusual and unnecessary in these formats for the people involved to adopt the perspective of an attacker and consciously attempt to exploit the weaknesses of a strategy for attacks. In traditional approaches, a change in perspective like this is often regarded as counterproductive and not expedient.

The potential of red teaming can be explained using the following example: Is it possible to improve draft legislation through red teaming? At first glance, attacks and legislative procedures appear to be rather incompatible concepts. In a state under the rule of law, however, statutory limits serve as a very important reference point that guide the actions of individuals or organizations and companies. Testing the legal boundaries is often of paramount importance for companies in particular. Loopholes in the law can mean that certain behaviors in exactly this relevant peripheral area might pass unnoticed. Putting oneself in the position of an attacker who is specifically searching for vulnerabilities can make precisely these consequences visible.

This example may sound highly theoretical, but practical experience has been gained with this very concept. Some years ago, red teaming was used as a strategy for the improvement of legislation in the area of cybersecurity in connection with an EU/ITU-funded project for over 50 countries in the Caribbean, the Pacific, and Asia (see Gercke 2013). It was shown that red teaming often brings other vulnerabilities to light than those brought up in round tables with experts. The point was clearly made that possible vulnerabilities in a law can be specifically used for attacks. This was far more impressive and generated a great deal more support in the legislating target group than an academic discussion of dogmatic and legislative problem areas (see Gercke 2014).

Similar experience in connection with cybersecurity has already been gained in the area of wargaming. For example, the dynamic approach of making the practical effects of cyberattacks identifiable was used in 2015 and 2016 at the Munich Security Conference to show participants the threat posed by present-day attacks. While the focus was on members of government and decision-makers from the military and security sector, there are also comparable developments in industry, where management board members use wargaming to prepare for decision-making in the event of an attack (see van Zütphen 2013).

4.4   Use of Red Teaming in Combination with Wargaming at Companies

As noted above, red teaming is designed to improve an organization's planning, operations, and responsiveness. Red teaming reviews the efficiency of existing or chosen strategies by exposing them to a simulated attack. The aim is to find vulnerabilities in existing, ideally field-tested concepts that have been perpetuated and updated over a longer period of time and to anticipate the effects of certain actions. During red teaming, the protagonists explicitly adopt an external perspective. Seeing things from the perspective of an attacker, competitor or adversary allows vulnerabilities to be identified, avoiding cognitive processes that lead to findings being selectively evaluated or disregarded.

In this respect, red teaming builds on a critical point of strategy development: influencing the critical perceptive faculty of the actors involved in the development process. Vulnerabilities are reviewed each time a strategy is developed, but in traditional approaches this takes place from the perspective of those who were involved in the actual design. This carries the risk of selective consideration, which is unconsciously focused on confirmation of the preceding work. Einstein impressively paraphrased the fundamental problem of the approaches that red teaming tries to circumvent when he said, "We cannot solve our problems with the same thinking we used when we created them."

Red teaming offers particular potential in the field of cybersecurity, which generally involves two opposing parties – attacker and target. Yet it must be remembered that red teaming is usually only effectively deployed as part of the development of an overall strategy, not in isolation. This is because the advantage of a realistic review of processes and strategies is partly offset by the disadvantage that time constraints do not allow all attack vectors to be determined and that the respective report also represents a snapshot (see Furtuna et al. 2010).

4.4.1 Classification

Generally speaking, a red teaming approach can be divided into five phases. A combination of red teaming and wargaming results in the following:

1. Definition of a target
2. Composition of the teams
3. Analysis
4. Wargaming
5. Report

The phases may be part of an iterative process and may vary largely depending on their specific implementation.

4.4.2 Definition of a Target

Red teaming begins with the definition of a target (see Furtuna et al. 2010; University of Foreign Military and Cultural Studies 2002). In relation to the integration of the management board, red teaming can specifically address issues such as overlapping responsibilities within a management board or vulnerabilities in reporting processes from middle management. Defining a specific task is of vital importance, especially because of the range of possible deployment. Usually when the task is being defined, the simulated attacks are authorized at the same time (see Furtuna et al. 2010).

4.4.3 Composition of the Teams

Depending on the task defined, the two teams are then put together (see Wood and Duggan 2002), with an attacking team normally pitted against a defending team, as described above (see Herman et al. 2009). Depending on the target defined, it is certainly also possible to use just the attacking team in order to identify vulnerabilities independently of a defense or to review internal resources (see Furtuna et al. 2010). However, the combination of an attacking and a defending team allows defense readiness to be reviewed at the same time.

The success of red teaming depends to a large extent on the team's composition. In addition to professional qualifications, the interpersonal skills of the team members are pivotal in this context (see University of Foreign Military and Cultural Studies 2002). Particularly in the area of cybersecurity, it is important to have subject-area experts in the team (see CSO 2008). Depending on the emphasis, teams may comprise members from a variety of disciplines and professions – such as technical security specialists, management consultants, members of the legal department, strategy advisors, risk managers, psychologists, analysts, experts in simulations and operations research, etc. If the internal resources available in the company are limited or very tied up, an external service provider may take on the role of the attacker.

4.4.4 Analysis: Data Collection and Evaluation

The third phase, which focuses on the collection and evaluation of data (see University of Foreign Military and Cultural Studies 2002), forms the core of the red teaming. By collecting available data on the target of the attack, the attacking team develops its strategy. Task definition can focus on a specific area. The methods used to collect data also vary considerably: Either the necessary information can be supplied to the attacking team or the team has to procure this itself. When it comes to verifying the security of information systems, the measures may range from peer reviews to ethical hacking, where the hacker is hired to actually attack an information system (see Lauder 2009). When integrating management board members into a cybersecurity strategy, developers mainly concentrate on the evaluation of responsibilities, the focal points of delegation and on reporting. In general, making information available to the attacking team prior to the exercise not only saves time, but may be a prerequisite for effective deployment of external experts in particular (see IBM 2005). However, supplying the data radically limits the scope of action for the attacking team.

The decision as to which techniques will be used to collect and evaluate data depends on the task previously set. Typical questions include the following: Have all options and the consequences of a certain approach been considered? Which alternative courses of action exist? Which effects do the actions of others have on a company's own actions? How flexible is the company's own planning? Which of the company's own courses of action has the highest probability of success? Specifically in relation to the integration of management board members, one question could be whether the correct parameters establishing management board responsibility have been chosen.

4.4.5 Wargaming

Red teaming is most effective when it is not solely limited to an analysis of vulnerabilities but is combined with a simulated attack. The method can only be used to its full effect if the Red Team takes the external perspective of an attacker and the typical approaches of an attacker can be applied. In an ideal scenario, the attacking team benefits from its extensive experience in the selection and use of critical, creative methods for the analysis of complex issues and the assessment of different courses of action and is therefore not confined to the mere identification of vulnerabilities.

Developing vulnerabilities into attacks forces attackers not to confine themselves to theoretical concepts but to actually implement attack scenarios based on the identified vulnerabilities. Practical experience shows that nowhere near all vulnerabilities can be automatically transformed into an attack scenario. For example, external attackers may be unable to exploit a vulnerability in an internal system. In this respect, validating that vulnerabilities can actually be used to carry out an attack is a key component of the red teaming process (see Furtuna et al. 2010). Yet in many cases an actual attack is neither possible nor expedient. Using the wargaming methodology, the attack is carried out in a controlled environment in which the actual attack situation is recreated realistically. If the technical side of an attack on information systems is simulated, this may require replication of existing technical structures in a laboratory environment. However, if the decision-maker's basic defense strategies are to be reviewed, the focus is more on the provision of realistic reporting structures rather than on the replication of a technical system.

The simulation approach has proven particularly effective in interaction with members of the management and supervisory boards of large companies. For this approach to work, the decision-making structures in companies need to be depicted realistically. Decision-making processes can then be simulated in both management and supervisory boards. This has the advantage that in just two or three hours the participants can not only be shown the bandwidth of attacks, but the decision-maker's defense readiness can be reviewed and the consequences of decisions can be demonstrated at the same time. Simulations can also provide concrete assistance in process improvement via additional measures, such as language analyses or the recording of data that tracks stress levels.

4.4.6 Report

The last phase involves documenting the entire process. Recommendations for action are often included. The resulting overview of the situation can be used immediately to improve plans and strategies.

4.5 Conclusion

Whereas in the past red teaming and wargaming were primarily used in a military environment and by large companies, the methodology can be easily transferred to the optimization of companies' cybersecurity strategies, particularly the integration of management board members.

References

Bürgers, T., & Israel, A. (2014). *Kommentar zum AktG, 2998, § 91, Rn 12*, in Bürgers, Tobias; Körber, Torsten: Heidelberger Kommentar zum AktG, 2998. C.F. Müller.

CSO (2008). *Red team versus blue team: How to run an effective simulation.* Accessed June 20, 2016, from http://www.csoonline.com/article/2122440/emergency-preparedness/red-team-ver sus-blue-team–how-to-run-an-effective-simulation.html

Fryer-Biggs, Z. (2012). *Building better cyber red teams.* Accessed June 20, 2016, from http://www.thecre.com/fnews/?p=944

Furtuna, A., Patriciu, V.-V., & Bica, I. (2010). *Considerations about red teaming usage in assessing information assurance.* Bucharest.

Gercke, M. (2013). *Cybersecurity strategy, why it is necessary to move from cybersecurity philosophies to true cybersecurity strategies.* CRI 5, 15 ff.; 136–142.

Gercke, M. (2014). *"Red Teaming" Ansätze zur Effektivierung von Gesetzgebungsprozessen? Die Übertragbarkeit einer klassischen, militärischen Methodik auf Gesetzgebungsprozesse im IT-Bereich.* CR 5, 344–348.

Gercke, M., Laschet, C., & Schweinsberg, K. (2014). *Cyber-Risiken als Teil unternehmerischer Leistungsverantwortung.* PHI, 76.

Herman, M., Frost, M., & Kurz, R. (2009). *Wargaming for leaders: Strategic decision making from the battlefield to the boardroom.* New York: McGraw-Hill Education.

IBM (2005). *Red teams: Towards radical innovation.* Accessed June 3, 2016, from http://www-935.ibm.com/services/us/imc/pdf/gt510-6190-red-teams.pdf

Lauder, M. (2009). *Red dawn: The emergence of a red teaming capability in the Canadian forces.* Canadian Army Journal, 12(2), 25–36.

Longbine, D. F. (2008). *Red teaming: Past and present.* Fort Leavenworth: Kansas.

Oriesek, D., & Schwarz, J. O. (2009). *Business Wargaming: Unternehmenswert schaffen und schützen.* Wiesbaden: Gabler Verlag.

Perla, P. P. (1990). *The art of wargaming: A guide for professionals and hobbyists.* Annapolis: US Naval Institute Press.

Sabin, P. (2012). *Simulating war: Studying conflict through simulation games.* New York: Bloomsbury Academic.

Securitymagazine (2013). *$1.5 Million Cyberheist Ruins Escrow Firm.* Accessed June 3, 2016, from http://www.securitymagazine.com/articles/84617-15-million-cyberheist-ruins-escrow-firm

Trappehl, B. (2009). *Arbeitsrechtliche Konsequenzen von IT-Sicherheitsverstößen.* NZA, 18, 986.

Tsukayama, H. (2012). *Report: Chinese hackers breach Nortel networks.* Accessed June 3, 2016, from https://www.washingtonpost.com/business/technology/report-chinese-hackers-breach-nortel-networks/2012/02/14/gIQApXsRDR_story.html

University of Foreign Military and Cultural Studies (2002). *Red team handbook.* Accessed June 6, 2016, from http://www.au.af.mil/au/awc/awcgate/army/ufmcs_red_team_handbook_apr2011.pdf

van Zütphen, T. (2013). *Vorstandsthema Cyber Crime? So sicher wie der nächste Angriff.* Best Practice, 3, 45.

von der Gathen, A. (2014). *Das große Handbuch der Strategie Instrumente.* New York: Campus Verlag.

von Holleben, K. M., & Menz, M. (2010). *IT-Risikomanagement – Pflichten der Geschäftsleitung.* CR, 1, 63–68.

Wood, B., & Duggan, R. (2002). *Red teaming of advanced information assurance concepts.* In DARPA Information Survivability Conference and Exposition, 2002. DISCEX 00 Proceedings (Vol 2, p. 112 ff).

Marco Gercke is one of the world's foremost experts in cybersecurity and cybercrime, having given over 500 papers in more than 80 countries. Gercke is Director of the Cologne-based Cybercrime Research Institute and teaches media criminal law and European criminal law in the Law faculty at the University of Cologne. He is also an external lecturer in the master's program in information law at the University of Oldenburg and visiting professor in international criminal law at the University of Macau (China). His work focuses on advising international organizations – in particular, the United Nations, UNODC, ITU, UNICEF, UNIDIR, UN-CTITF, the European Union, ECOWAS and the European Council – as well as national governments, ministries, experts and large corporations on legal and political issues in connection with cybersecurity. The performance of simulations is a material aspect of this work. Gercke is the author of over 100 publications and has given many expert opinions in comparative law. His most recent monograph was published in six languages.

The Law and Its Contribution to IT Security: Legal Framework, Requirements, Limits

5

Klaus Brisch

Technology is the main way of ensuring that IT security meets perpetrators on a level playing field with weapons of a similar caliber. But technology cannot solve the problem alone. The law can also play a part in IT security, although it is misguiding to assume that legal sanction mechanisms will keep criminal hackers from infiltrating IT infrastructures and harming companies.

In fact, criminal prosecution is quite a blunt instrument, and international legal systems for the prosecution of criminal activities are out of tune with high-tech reality. The level of sophistication possible with technology far exceeds the bounds of our current legal framework. For this reason, legislators concentrate on those who have something to protect and something to lose, i.e., IT users in companies and households. By focusing on users, there is a reasonable expectation of success: They are likely to obey the law and implement the required technical and organizational measures.

From a legal policy perspective, the question then arises as to whether the law and its control mechanisms can possibly address the risks adequately. Can legal responsibility and liability in fact create incentives for IT companies, users, and service providers to effectively combat IT risks?

Are questions of

- duties (who must implement which measures?),
- liability (who is liable when risks materialize, and to what degree?), and
- evidence (who must prove which facts in a dispute?)

asked in a way that aligns with the approach taken by the German Federal Office for Information Security (see BSI 2007)?

K. Brisch (✉)
DWF Germany Rechtsanwaltsgesellschaft mbH, Habsburgerring 2, 50674 Cologne, Germany
e-mail: klaus.brisch@dwf.law

© Springer International Publishing AG 2017
F. Abolhassan (ed.), *Cyber Security. Simply. Make it Happen.*, Management for Professionals, DOI 10.1007/978-3-319-46529-6_5

5.1   Key Features of the Existing Legal Framework

Prior to the entry into force of the German IT Security Act, the only comprehensive IT security regulations in effect for companies of various sizes in various industries stemmed from data protection law or involved the implementation of IT security standards. Since the IT Security Act only applies to companies of certain sizes in certain industries, and merely supplements the general legal framework instead of replacing it, this regulation will be outlined first.

Broadly speaking, the law first and foremost calls for corporate IT suppliers and users alike to set up and maintain data protection systems and to define IT risk management procedures. The focus here is on following IT compliance rules, not least to prevent a company's management board and executives from being held personally liable.

5.1.1   IT Compliance: A Challenge for Management Boards and Executives

According to the definition of "compliance" in the German Corporate Governance Code, "the management board is responsible for ensuring that the applicable statutory provisions and internal company policies are followed, and must work toward adherence by group companies." (Regierungskommission 2015).

Technical standards pertaining to IT are particularly relevant and include the applicable ISO 27001 standard and the IT Baseline Protection Manual (*IT-Grundschutzkataloge*) published by the German Federal Office for Information Security (BSI). These must be complied with although they are not specifically "statutory provisions" or "internal company policies:" Technical standards come into play when the courts need to get to the bottom of statutory standard of care requirements or resolve liability issues. Typical examples are data loss in businesses or a lack of IT availability leading to production or other losses. That is when courts review whether "customary" standards were followed. These standards are considered generally accepted technical guidelines which carry what is known as a "presumption of conformity." According to this concept, a release from liability is justified if such guidelines are adhered to.

5.1.1.1 The Cornerstone of IT Compliance: IT Security

Documenting IT risks is paramount to IT security. A distinction is drawn here between

- organizational,
- infrastructural, and
- application- and process-related risks.

Organizational risks include situations where an IT department is not sufficiently integrated into the corporate structure as an independent entity. Often, the IT organization's responsibilities and requirements are not assigned appropriately in terms of knowledge and skills. Moreover, sensitive data may not be adequately protected to prevent unauthorized access.

Infrastructural risks include the use of heterogeneous or legacy operating systems, data, backup systems, or software packages. This category also includes the technical systems in buildings required to safeguard IT operations, such as suitable protection against water and fire damage, as well as access controls. Finally – and this is pretty much a classic – it is an infrastructural risk when a company has no method of data backup in place or when data backups are only performed sporadically. In practice, users often overlook the fact that backing up data alone is not enough. Rather, it must be possible to seamlessly restore backups to the original IT platform.

Application- and process-related risks can amplify organizational or infrastructure-related risks if a company runs legacy or standalone applications. For example, developers who previously customized off-the-shelf software often leave a company to find other employment. If the customization is not documented, the modified applications can no longer be updated.

5.1.1.2 Liability of the Management Board and Executives

Discussions of IT risk bring up the issue of liability risk for management boards and executives. According to section 93 I of the German Stock Corporation Act (*Aktiengesetz – AktG*) and section 43 of the German Private Limited Companies Act (*GmbHG*), managers of companies are liable for the resulting loss if they breach their duties. To prevent this from happening, they must safeguard the company's interests and protect it from damage while acting within the law and the articles of incorporation, and taking into account the interests of the public. Management must therefore ensure that IT-related legal requirements, particularly data protection regulations, are followed. What's more, if the technical standards relevant to IT security are not adhered to in a corporate setting, the courts consider management personally liable.

5.1.2 Who Is Responsible?

Aside from the question of who is responsible for setting up a fully compliant corporate structure, the division of responsibilities for IT security in the IT value chain is also critical.

5.1.2.1 Requirements for Software Manufacturers

The main laws relevant to software manufacturers are those regarding product liability and product safety. A unique aspect of product liability is that neither a contract between the producer and the user of the product, nor a finding of fault (intent or negligence) is required for producer liability to apply. However, the problem is the unsolved issue of whether software can be classified as a product in the sense of product liability law, in which case intent or negligence would indeed not be conditions of liability. The same problems as with product safety law arise in general tort liability where, in contrast to product liability, the exact crucial point is a finding of fault due to intent or negligence. After all, financial losses are only determined in exceptional cases and a broad interpretation of the concept of property – not yet handed down by the highest courts – would be required to determine damage to data records or databases.

In practice, the company suffering the loss bears the burden of proving that the software is defective, just as it does for proving a link between a defective product and the violation of a legally protected interest as well as the losses in question – an immensely difficult task to accomplish. The complexity of IT systems and infrastructure in companies and the interplay between various products and IT services often do not permit determining one distinct cause of error. In addition, installation or operating errors by the business suffering the loss must be ruled out.

5.1.2.2 Requirements for Network and Platform Operators

Although they enjoy broad liability privileges provided by the German Telemedia Act (*Telemediengesetz – TMG*), network and platform operators must fulfill extensive duties to secure their own IT systems. Section 44a of the Telemedia Act provides those operating their own electronic communication networks to provide telecommunications services with additional liability privileges.

However, these liability privileges do not apply with respect to third parties who suffer losses via the operator's networks. That is because there is no contractual relationship between them, which section 44a of the Telemedia Act requires.

5.1.2.3 Legal Framework for Providers of IT Services

Businesses that provide IT services or manufacture products with the help of IT systems must fulfill numerous duties of protection arising from specific requirements. An example here is online banking, where a comprehensive set of administrative instructions by the German Federal Financial Supervisory Authority (BaFin) stipulates extensive Minimum Requirements for Risk Management (MaRisk) at German banks.

The IT Security Act

Since July 25, 2015, the IT Security Act has been established in Germany. It provides the Federal Republic with a head start regarding a solid legal basis for cyber security. According to the law, operators of critical infrastructure are required to notify the Federal Office for Information Security (Bundesamt für Sicherheit in der Informationstechnik; BSI) of any IT security breach. After evaluation by the BSI, these notifications are processed and made available to all operators.

The IT Security Act focuses on seven branches and about 700 facilities (see Borchers 2016) including but not limited to: information technology and telecommunications, as well as the energy sector, the food industry, the financial and insurance sector, as well as the sectors regarding health and water. These branches are now obligated to orientate themselves to minimal standards for IT security and to notify the BSI of any incidents. The decision as to which attachments fall under the obligation of notification lies with the Federal Government and is based on the "500,000 rule" which claims that as soon as there is a benefit for at least 500,000 people, the corresponding attachment falls under the notification obligation. The actual usage is converted into a threshold value for easy handling.

Most attachments regarding IT security with a notification obligation are found in the energy sector. There are a total of 320 attachments and companies in this sector which reach the following threshold values:

- Electricity generation (or storage): 450 MW per year
- Gas supply: 5,190 GW per year
- Refinery: 620,000 t of fuel oil per year
- Gas station network: 335,000 stations

The **water sector** (including drinking water and sewage drain) comes in second place with 230 attachments. In this sector, sewage treatment plants (that supply about 500,000 people) and water supply companies which are responsible for allocation, processing and distribution of 21.9 million cubic meters of water per year, do have a notification requirement.

Regarding the **food industry** there are currently 70 attachments that are obligated to give notification, namely those that produce, store or distribute 334,000 t of foods a year. Regarding liquids there is a threshold value of 274.5 million beverages.

The **information technology sector**, with its data centers, trust centers and server farms, constitutes the smallest sector that is affected by the notification obligation of the IT Security Act. The 500,000 rule only applies to the trust centers in this sector and refers to the number of registered person-based certificates. In addition to this, every trust center that gives out more than 10,000 TLS certificates becomes obliged to give notification. Regarding the data centers, the notification obligation refers to all installations that have a yearly average of 5 MW. In case of content suppliers, the new rule applies to those that deliver more than 75,000 terabytes a year. Server farms are obligated to notification after an average of 25,000 instances running.

For operators of **telecommunications** that deal with communication and data networks, the notification obligations are already established in the telecommunications law, so that there are only few additions implemented by the IT Security Act. The established threshold value for networks and transmission services lies at 100,000 participants or rather 75,000 terabytes per year. For DNS servers the value lies at 2.5 million IP queries-a-day or accordingly at 250,000 domains, for which the server is responsible. It is currently determined, how many attachments are subject to the reporting requirement.

A threshold value regarding the **health, finance and insurance sectors** is foreseen for the end of 2016. Debates are currently being held.

5.1.3 Regulation on Determining Critical Infrastructure

A legal regulation determines who has to give notification in IT security matters (see Bundesministerium des Inneren 2016). The operators of critical infrastructures can review whether the IT Security Act is applicable with the help of quantifiable and comprehensible criteria for their own company. If that in fact is the case, the operator has to make a contact available for the BSI within six months. Furthermore, the operator has to provide proof that the minimal standards of IT security are being followed within two years. Up to now the regulation refers to the critical infrastructures in the sectors of water, food, energy, information technology and telecommunications. A regulation change foreseen for 2017 includes the sectors of transportation and traffic, as well as health, finance and insurance.

5.1.4 Controversial: Changes Affecting Telemedia Services

An easy-to-overlook requirement of the IT Security Act affecting nearly every business is the amendment to the Telemedia Act implemented in article 4. The key here is section 13 (7) of the Telemedia Act: To the extent technically and economically feasible, service providers must take technical and organizational measures to ensure that no unauthorized access is possible to the technical facilities they use for the telemedia services they offer. In addition, these facilities must be protected against disruptions and unauthorized access to personal information, as well as attacks from outside. The precautions taken, such as data encryption, must be state of the art.

This provision is particularly relevant to companies because in the sense of section 2 of the Telemedia Act a "service provider" is any individual or legal entity offering or providing access to its own or third-party telemedia. In the case of audiovisual media services on demand, a "service provider" is any individual or legal entity effectively controlling the selection and configuration of the content offered. Ultimately, any company that operates its own website for business purposes falls under the security requirements laid down in the IT Security Act. Businesses must therefore immediately begin intense investigations on how to prevent unauthorized access.

5.2 International Issues: The European Union's Directive on Security of Network and Information Systems (NIS Directive)

According to the proposal by the European Parliament and the Council for a Directive on the Security of Network and Information Systems (NIS Directive), operators of network and information systems are expected to do more to ensure network and information security. Because security of information and network systems is of utmost importance for the home markets and is necessary for their smooth proceeding. System malfunctions therefore have to be prevented at all times. In order to achieve this, uniform EU guidelines for the water supply, health, energy, transportation and traffic, internet and finance sector will be enacted. Germany already complies with the planned regulations thanks to the IT Security Act.

The EU member states are required to establish a central base for NIS-notifications so they can inform each other easily and to provide the European Union Agency for network and Information Security (ENISA) with updates for eventual incidents: "The international NIS-notification centers that get the information through these channels are to pass this information on to the companies in their jurisdiction. Reactions to NIS-threats are coordinated by the NIS-authority and the ENISA Europe-wide" (Lepper 2014).

The recommended guideline would provide a minimal security level regarding digital technique, networking and services for all member states alike. These requirements as well as standardized measures in risk management and clear regulations regarding notification will lead to a more stable and trustworthy IT system in the respective sectors.

5.3   Data Protection and Data Security in the United States

There are no comprehensive federal laws governing data protection and data security in the United States. US law governing the collection, use, distribution, and protection of personal information is based on overlapping, and in some cases contradictory, regulations at federal and individual state level. At the federal level, a sector-based approach is taken with data protection guidelines and regulations focusing on industrial sectors such as healthcare and the financial industry. Government agencies such as the Federal Trade Commission (FTC), the Federal Communications Commission (FCC), and the Securities and Exchange Commission (SEC) issue additional rules and regulations that affect the collection, use, and storage of personal information. Finally, US states such as California exercise their right to impose additional requirements – for instance, the obligation to report incidents where the personal data of citizens is threatened.

The amount of questions each individual incident can bring up in the US can be demonstrated by the example of the conflict between the FBI and Apple regarding the data de-codification of a smartphone owned by a potential terrorist (see Martin-Jung 2016). The FBI unlocked the smartphone without the help of Apple, against the court's decision. The reason was simple, that no help was needed from the manufacturer, Apple. Even though the de-codification of the iPhone ended the disagreement between Apple and the FBI, the question remains, if technology companies and other organizations should be obligated to integrate the possibility that in case of investigation, the codified data should be made available to the authorities.

5.4   Data Exchange Between EU and US Companies

The answer to the question of how personal data can be exchanged legally between companies in the EU and the United States is complicated. But one thing is certain: Transferring data without considering the European legal framework unavoidably raises the issue of liability for the company transferring the data as well as the responsible individuals within the company, particularly management.

5.4.1 Safe Harbor

In 2000, the European Commission established a safe harbor arrangement for the purpose of creating legal certainty. It was supposed to facilitate the transfer of personalized data from the EU to the US – and in compliance with the European Data protection regulations.

However, the safe harbor decision was declared invalid by the European Court of Justice on October 6, 2015. Since then, there has been considerable legal uncertainty about whether and on what basis such data can be transferred.

5.4.2 Privacy Shield

The solution for the legal uncertainty is now based on the so-called Privacy Shield, a covenant between the United States and the European Union for the regulation of transatlantic data transfer. Since its announcement on February 2, 2016 the Privacy Shield was fiercely criticized. It was especially complained about the US governments right to collect information on a large scale for purposes of national security. In this form, the agreement would not be upheld by the European Court of Justice (see Beiersmann 2016). According to the European data protection officer, who advises EU institutions, the Privacy Shield must fulfill the requirements of the new EU Data Protection Directive, whose entry into force across the EU is anticipated in May 2018. This directive also applies to the transfer of data to the United States.

Irrespectively of all opposition the EU-Commission established that the new framework protects the fundamental rights of anyone in the EU whose personal data is transferred to the United States as well as bringing legal clarity for businesses relying on transatlantic data transfers (see Europäische Kommission 2016).

Independently of this development numerous cloud providers, such as T-Systems partners Salesforce and SugarCRM, have moved to regional data centers to be on the safe side.

5.5   Conclusion: Many Legal Issues to Consider

IT security is complex in more than just a technical sense. The legal framework underlying it is laced with widely diverse laws, guidelines, rules, and technical standards. Business leaders face a huge challenge if they wish to comply with all of the relevant requirements and limit the risk of personal liability.

The law can shed light on various risk scenarios to which IT providers and users, and network and platform operators are subject. The IT Security Act does not make the general rules on liability obsolete. In fact, they have been enhanced for certain industries.

In the European Union, the harmonization of regulations is proceeding – and the Directive on the Security of Network and Information Systems is pointing in the right direction. Germany is ahead of others in this matter because passing the IT Security Act already implemented large pieces of the directive.

Ensuring security in data exchanges with the United States is a challenge for companies: Legal certainty in the transfer of personal data is currently somewhat questionable due to the rejection of the safe harbor concept despite the implementation of the Privacy Shield. But caution should be exercised because the legal framework in the United States is heterogeneous, and the legal situation in the European Union is fluid. It may be awaited eagerly what judgements the courts will render in the future, especially Court of Justice of the European Union (CJEU).

There is no getting around the fact that companies and their management must clearly see to every aspect of IT security. It cannot simply be seen as a cost factor. In truth, IT security is complex. IT security is expensive, risky and mission critical. IT security must therefore be a top-level management issue. What else could it be?

References

Beiersmann, S. (2016). *Auch EU-Datenschutzbeauftragter lehnt Privacy Shield ab.* Accessed August 16, 2016, from http://www.zdnet.de/88270732/auch-eu-datenschutzbeauftragter-lehnt-privacy-shield-ab/

Borchers, D. (2016). *IT-Sicherheitsgesetz: Wer was wann zu melden hat.* Accessed August 16, 2016, from http://www.heise.de/newsticker/meldung/IT-Sicherheitsgesetz-Wer-was-wann-zu-melden-hat-3096885.html

BSI (2007). *IT-Sicherheit und Recht.* Accessed June 6, 2016, from https://www.bsi.bund.de/DE/Publikationen/Studien/ITSicherheitUndRecht/index_htm.html

Bundesministerium des Inneren (2016). *Kabinett beschließt erste Verordnung zur Umsetzung des IT-Sicherheitsgesetzes.* Accessed August 16, 2016, from http://www.bmi.bund.de/SharedDocs/Pressemitteilungen/DE/2016/04/kabinett-kritis-vo.html

Europäische Kommission (2016). *Europäische Kommission lanciert EU-US-Datenschutzschild: besserer Schutz für den transatlantischen Datenverkehr.* Accessed August 19, 2016, from http://europa.eu/rapid/press-release_IP-16-2461_de.htm

Lepper, K. (2014, August). *Bericht aus Brüssel.* Accessed August 16, 2016, from http://www.bdsv.eu/data/8aae7b7bc3cebbc67ea7aecfbed47bceb9a494cdb9dca0cdc7b798bac7b778d8c3b7b3b88aae957cc2b9d1847dddd093.pdf. In: Newsletter des Bundesverband der Deutschen Sicherheits- und Verteidigungsindustrie e.V. Edition 03.

Martin-Jung, H. (2016). *Datenschutz – Apple trotzt dem FBI.* Accessed August 16, 2016, from http://www.sueddeutsche.de/politik/datenschutz-apple-trotzt-dem-fbi-1.2925671

Regierungskommission (2015). *Deutscher Corporate Governance Kodex.* Item 4.1.3. Accessed June 22, 2016, from http://www.dcgk.de/de/kommission/die-kommission-im-dialog/deteilansicht/kodexaenderungen-2015-beschlossen.html

Klaus Brisch LL.M. (USA), is a partner at DWF Germany Rechtsanwaltsgesellschaft mbH, where he specializes in information technology law. A consultant to national and international companies in the information technology and telecommunications sectors on industry-specific issues relating to commercial law, he also advises end-user companies on the interpretation of IT law. His work focuses in particular on data protection, data security, IT security and cybersecurity in both a national and international context.

Brisch also specializes in providing support for industry-specific acquisitions of companies and shareholdings, as well as the design and management of complex projects in the field of national and international IT and telecommunications, an area that also includes the outsourcing of IT service provision. Other activities include consulting work in the field of IT compliance and e-commerce law.

IT Security: Stronger Together

6

Ralf Schneider

Modern CIOs handle a multitude of roles within their companies, from deciding the strategic orientation of the IT environment to keeping data centers and devices running smoothly. As if this wasn't enough in terms of responsibility, CIOs also bear ultimate responsibility for the security of data, applications and the IT infrastructure. Although ensuring the safety of the company's digital assets has long been one of the core elements of a security strategy, new adversaries such as government-backed hacker groups, cyberespionage teams out for a quick profit and politically motivated activists have resulted in a "red alert" status for digital assets. And yet, while the current threat from these numerous attack vectors should be taken deadly seriously, many companies still believe that antivirus software, a firewall or simply taking a hush-hush approach are adequate precautionary measures. Antivirus software and firewalls are of course essential, even though both systems only form building blocks of an overall security model. But the time has really come to drop the idea of seeing security as a taboo topic not to be discussed in public. "Security by obfuscation" used to be considered a legitimate security strategy: If we don't publish any information on a topic, then we're not giving away any useful data – right? Wrong! Pretty much every proprietary software or hardware has now been hacked, simply because attackers found a loophole that manufacturers had overlooked. Which is why open source software is considered more secure: The multitude of auditors and developers picking through the code maximizes the number of vulnerabilities detected and the speed of their discovery. Going at it alone, hidden away behind closed doors, is not how IT security works. Attackers recognized this a long time ago, of course. Since hacking is a collaborative, team-based effort, why shouldn't the good guys do the same?

R. Schneider (✉)
Allianz SE, Königinstr. 28, 80802 Munich, Germany
e-mail: ralf.schneider@allianz.de

© Springer International Publishing AG 2017   47
F. Abolhassan (ed.), *Cyber Security. Simply. Make it Happen.*, Management for
Professionals, DOI 10.1007/978-3-319-46529-6_6

6.1   The Trinity of IT Security

CIOs must accept the current situation: Observations made by the security company FireEye show that some 95 percent of companies have been victims of cyberattacks for many years without being aware of it. In Germany, the number of attacks against companies and government agencies observed in the second half of 2015 was almost double that of the previous six months. One noticeable trend is the phenomenal rise in attacks made via ransomware across the entire EMEA region (see FireEye 2016a). The threat situation is prodigious. In addition to attacks made at network perimeters, there is the fact that every employee has a couple of tools in daily use capable of routing attacks directly into the heart of the network: the email client and the web browser. If an employee mistakenly clicks on a phishing link, he or she opens Pandora's Box – bypassing firewalls, intrusion detection systems and other perimeter barriers. The same applies to the browser. Drive-by infections by legitimate websites nonetheless polluted with malware dump the poisonous handiwork of clever but criminal hackers directly onto the PC and company LAN. There are no quick remedies to such problems. We live and work in an information society that is becoming increasingly internetworked. Employees without email and with highly-restricted Internet access (or none at all) are unproductive employees. Highly restrictive approaches can really only be deployed in extremely sensitive areas – most office jobs will require a broad range of communication options with the outside world. Nor should one forget that the holy trinitiy of IT security is expressed via the "CIA" principle: Confidentiality, Integrity and Availability should each be given the same level of attention. Plugging every hole also seals off the availability pipeline.

Some protection is of course needed. While it's true that a successful attack doesn't always merit a front-page headline – even if the victims are household names – the consequences of a cyberattack can still be catastrophic. The TalkTalk hack in fall 2015 caused revenue losses of around 60 million pounds and resulted in the UK cellular network provider losing over 115,000 customers (see Wired 2016). And around 61 percent of German consumers would take legal action if their personal data was exposed in a hack (see FireEye 2016b). So it's important to find the right balance between policing and productivity.

But how can one protect a 280,000-node network like the one operated by the Allianz Group? The right hardware and software is of course important, but so is an appropriate model that takes a nuanced approach to threats while conceding that a company has a better chance of mounting a successful defense as part of a team rather than doing it alone. The lion's share of hacks now run as automated processes without a specific target, a simple case of poking around in the dark long enough to find someone who has failed to apply a patch or overlooked a PC backdoor. Once the backdoor is found, there's a good chance that more than one company is affected by it. Often, however, this same vulnerability has already been identified and resolved by another organization. If companies shared this kind of information, everyone would benefit. While this would not offer a remedy against targeted attacks, it would be an effective suppressor of the aggressive "background noise" of digital hackers. Accordingly, the news that cooperative initiatives are now springing up in the traditionally rather close-mouthed sector of IT security is to be welcomed. As just one example, over two dozen companies and organizations have now signed the "Coordinated Vulnerability Disclosure Manifesto." The manifesto declares support for collaboration between companies and the cybersecurity community to find and resolve vulnerabilities in information and communication technology. This kind of cooperation requires a high level of trust between stakeholders. Simply for practicably reasons, only a more exclusive club can be considered for very large firms, whose assets at stake – both in a financial sense and in terms of the company's reputation – are immensely valuable. The role of the partner network for Allianz is played by the German "Cyber Security Sharing and Analytics" (CSSA) association. Within the CSSA, 12 large businesses now work not as partners in crime but partners against cybercrime.

6.2   CSSA – Security Through Collaboration

The founding concept of the CSSA is the peer-based sharing of information about cybersecurity between organizations. Major corporations have other requirements than SMEs, especially in terms of the operating models they use for IT security. The CSSA currently counts 12 heavyweights of German business among its members, including Allianz, BASF, Bosch, Deutsche Bank, Deutsche Börse Group, SAP, Siemens and Deutsche Telekom. United by their strong interest in IT security, they have also recognized that the cooperative approach today is the better option. A non-profit organization, the CSSA develops models that enable the rapid and highly-scalable sharing of information about cyberattacks without compromising the confidentiality of the business transactions involved. The CSSA refers to itself – only half-jokingly – as a kind of "neighborhood watch," warning each other against the digital equivalent of leaving the front door unlocked.

The initiative arose as the logical next move following a meeting of several CIOs. In their meeting, the CIOs not only discovered that they were plagued by similar problems but that each of them also had access to information that could be useful to their counterparts. Companies had previously been prevented from sharing this data due to the lack of a secure and efficient framework. Accordingly, the CSSA was formed in November 2014 as a registered German association with seven founding members, one of whom being Allianz. Membership of the CSSA was and continues to be assessed on the value or information that a new applicant can bring to the group. Participating organizations must contribute both expertise and knowledge and already have a stable security system in place featuring key basic components such as a CERT – and ideally a SIEM, etc. The sharing of information about threats and vulnerabilities would be pointless if a company lacked the tools for implementing protective and counter-measures.

While the CSSA does prioritize the importance of a small, effective group, it is not a static club. New members are welcome if they can meet the acceptance criteria. This includes considering Europe to be the main focus of their business.

6.2.1   Targeted Interaction

"Actions speak louder than words" is the CSSA's unofficial slogan. With it, the CSSA's 12 member companies have mutually agreed their commitment to being active members of the association, i.e., to providing a budget and experts to ensure that the volume of available data can actually be turned into tangible results. All of this is made possible by a manageable number of participating organizations, clearly-defined contacts, and dedicated resources both in the CSSA and member companies.

CSSA members see their most important activity as being the sharing and analysis of actual incidents, threats and vulnerabilities with the aim of improving protection against potential attacks. Weekly conference calls at a technical level plus regular meetings ensure a constant flow of information. By sharing threat intelligence, a joint database is being established. Lessons learned and threat indicators from actual attacks are collected as Indicators of Compromise (IoCs) together with strategic information, while analyses of recently-discovered malware are distributed as Malware Reports. Member companies can import this information into their own systems, thereby enabling them to block potential threats or check infections. At some companies, this process is almost fully automated, while others are still working on integrating the CSSA platform into their security infrastructure.

Since the members are active across a spectrum of industries, the CSSA is generating a large dataset that covers a huge range of threat vectors. This enables information to be isolated from its industry-specific context and to be used to create connections that would be beyond the capabilities of a single company.

Nor does this merely sound good on paper – the reality proves that it's also bearing fruit in the real world. Details from companies about attacks happening on their own turf have been already shared at a strictly technical level with other CSSA members, who were then able to prepare and adapt their defense systems accordingly. A number of those participating had never experienced this level of transparency – some not even within their own company.

The sharing of warnings also plays an important role in the CSSA. A good example of this is last year's wave of "DDoS for Bitcoins" blackmail attacks. One CSSA member was affected early on and warned the other organizations almost a week before the BSI issued a corresponding advisory. So CSSA members were well prepared and able to fend off actual attacks they then experienced.

6.2.2   Network of Trust

Trust is the most important basis for the collaboration within the CSSA: trust that information about individual members is not misused, and that information about a discovered vulnerability or even a wave of attack is passed quickly to the other members. The very founding of the association already involved the definition of policies and processes to ensure the optimum sharing of data among members, with only specific contacts requiring access and nobody else. All individuals involved with the work of the CSSA must sign personal confidentiality statements. The statement includes a version of the Traffic Light Protocol (TLP) adapted for the CSSA. Different levels of confidentiality are shown using the colors green, yellow and red. For publicly-available information, "TLP White" has been introduced. Only green material may be forwarded unencrypted. From the yellow level onwards – which is the default classification within the CSSA – encryption is mandatory. Material at the red level may be shared only within the information's original context. The material is "X eyes only," i.e., only for a specific set of "X" individuals.

Thanks to the small-scale setup of the CSSA, confidentiality breaches are unlikely and have indeed not yet occurred. Furthermore, since the association is based on trust, a breach of this kind would also be treated very seriously. Secure exchange is also naturally essential for the collaboration. In addition to defining a set of general-purpose security rules, the association also deploys specific tools with which information can be distributed securely across multiple media and formats (encrypted email, Secure Data Room, Secure Chat, etc.).

For the future, the CSSA is clearly working towards becoming a competence center and expert panel for its members. Through the network of trust formed between participating organizations and individuals, a database packed with highly relevant and up-to-date information is being established. Here, the trust model is decisive, which is primarily based on personal relationships and designated contacts having direct responsibility. Sharing the database or parts of it with other organizations might be an option for the future, although this is seen only a potential scenario at present. Governmental institutions are currently not granted access as well.

6.3   The Six Elements of an Integrated Defense Strategy

Even when helpful partners are at hand, the primary burden of IT security is borne by a well-configured security system that is correctly dimensioned and monitored on a continuous basis. Past experience has shown that a multi-layered architecture offers the best level of protection and is also the simplest to manage – even for very large networks. In the ideal situation, attacks are intercepted before they even reach the network perimeter. If an attack does slip through, then it is blocked by the subsequent layers. The approach resembles an onion with its several consecutive layers and is capable of handling both a range of attack vectors and heterogeneous corporate structures. At Allianz, a six-level system is deployed that has proven its worth in practice and is undergoing continuous expansion. Virtually every level has been deliberately designed to benefit from information shared between peers and, in turn, to enable the forwarding of information to these partners. Of course, this doesn't automatically work from the outset – this is not an "off-the-shelf" solution. By redesigning its IT processes, however, Allianz was able to streamline many of its processes, adapting them to better suit the needs of its business departments and ultimately its end users.

6.3.1 Prevention Is Better Than the Cure

But how can an attack be blocked before it even happens? Doing so requires neither a crystal ball nor superhuman powers. As the **first layer of protection**, prevention is a crucial strategy, not least because errors that are avoided before hardware or software is even deployed cannot become security holes. Vulnerabilities avoided by prevention can also be beneficial to partners in the information network because the chance that they have also failed to discover the same vulnerabilities is high, given the standard configurations typically applied to devices in company use. From operating systems to applications, no code is error-free. This fact is powerfully illustrated by the monthly "Patch Tuesdays" carried out by Microsoft – although Microsoft is only one prominent example of many, as the problem affects any software development company. In 2015, the US National Vulnerability Database (see National Vulnerability Database 2016) listed 8,822 vulnerabilities – almost 2,000 more than in the previous year. In pole position with 314 entries was Adobe's Flash Player, followed by Microsoft Internet Explorer (231), Firefox (178) and Java Runtime (80).

Another problem is self-inflicted vulnerabilities caused by configuration errors. One recent survey from security company F-Secure (see F-Secure 2016) discovered thousands of cases of incorrectly configured systems and outdated software in use at companies. Indeed, some of the most common vulnerabilities in corporate systems had been caused by misconfiguration issues. In recent months, SSL in particular has proven to be something of a Pandora's Box: Errors made in implementation coupled with careless administration had thrown company gates wide open to attackers, and the confidentiality of SSL-encrypted connections had been compromised. Yet these vulnerabilities were easily avoidable, which would have drastically reduced organizational exposure to attacks.

Surveillance guards against the kind of errors described above. You cannot take the right precautions until you're aware of what needs protecting in your network. Network management/analysis and documentation are key factors that decide whether an IT unit has its network under control or is constantly put on the back foot by a never-ending stream of new problems. And end users are not making life any easier for CIOs and administrators. The words "shadow IT" have now become a feared moniker describing IT systems set up outside official channels. Wi-Fi access points from the local electrical goods store used to be the classic example of shadow IT. Employees frustrated by the speed of the company Wi-Fi network simply took the rough-and-ready approach of installing their own access point in the office – naturally without taking any of the necessary security precautions and without informing the IT department. What was then a minor headache for IT and not without its risks – if an open Wi-Fi network was also accessible outside the building – has now escalated into something else entirely. Cloud services are very popular with employees and even entire departments, and are sometimes used as a DIY solution without official approval.

A survey conducted by the Cloud Security Alliance (CSA) showed that IT management staff receive ten applications for cloud service usage every month on average (see Cloud Security Alliance 2016). The only problem is, they also need about 18 days to process and evaluate an application. This mismatch in time frames can provide dangerously fertile ground for shadow IT, warns cloud security provider Skyhigh Networks. A recent analysis of actual cloud usage in European businesses reveals that a large proportion of the some 1,000 cloud services used on average per company takes place without the knowledge of the IT department (see Skyhigh 2016). If the IT department doesn't know what's being used, it can't protect it – and finding an unauthorized cloud service is more complex than tracking down a rogue access point. This is why proper surveillance of the network and a clear idea of the protocols, services and applications that should run in a specific segment is so important in order to detect changes.

Patching is another aspect of prevention. While it should be self-evident that resolving problems in products with updates, patches and fixes is a good idea, practice tells a very different story. Sometimes, the reasons for this are sound: Not every patch is safe to apply – all too often, updates are well-meant but poorly executed. Even if only one percent of the 280,000 user devices connected to the kind of networks that Allianz runs are taken offline by incompatibilities with other programs, losses in terms of productivity and (indirectly) revenue are nonetheless dramatic. Despite this, patch management is here to stay, and there are now numerous strategies designed to ensure that rollouts proceed smoothly (even in large networks) and side-effects are contained.

6.3.2 Knowledge Is Power

As has already been shown by the very real danger of shadow IT, prevention is only one side of the coin – the status quo must also be reviewed in addition to the desired status. Logically, the **second layer of IT protection** encompasses everything already underway in the company. Surveillance, monitoring, early warning – plenty of security models are available. Above all, however, the collection of data must be automated as far as possible. The 280,000 network nodes at Allianz generate an inordinate amount of data every second. Only an intelligent and largely autonomous filtering system is capable of evaluating the data by relevance and urgency, and correlating it to events. A single failed login to a resource does not by itself indicate the network is under attack. But if the same user also fails to access five other resources in a short space of time, a response is required.

Ideally, a Security Information and Event Management (SIEM) system acts as a high-level information clearinghouse, fed by log files, warnings issued by security software such as IDS/IDP and antivirus systems, as well as the valuable data provided by CSSA members. Normally, a SIEM system merely collects data and prepares it for display. In especially large networks, however, it is also possible to let the SIEM setup or underlying security systems react autonomously. Returning to the above example of the multiple failed logins, the account of the user in question could be locked out or, if a subsequent login succeeded, the user might then be granted only limited rights. While this is technically possible, the consequences at a personal level are rarely thought through in many companies. Should this arrangement also apply to CxO-level accounts? Have staff been properly informed about the people they need to contact to restore login permissions? And is this unit available 24/7 – in the event of an employee being accidentally locked out while working in a different time zone? While a lot can be handled by a SIEM setup and its associated infrastructure, it is often advisable to have a SIEM focus primarily on collection, evaluation and correlation, and leave the job of active system defense to human IT resources.

6.3.3   IT Security Is Not an End in Itself

This brings us to **layer number three** and the employees for whom IT security has been established in the first place. Administrators – and especially those entrusted with security tasks – should not forget that the daily work of the company's employees must be the focus of any security efforts. IT security is not an end in itself but serves to facilitate the productive output of products or services. Accordingly, an IT security strategy must provide answers not only to the issues of securing the working equipment but also to questions about guaranteeing the productivity of members of staff. Although a PC without network access, USB ports or a CD drive is practically impregnable, it's not particularly useful for day-to-day work. While the topic of staff awareness was hyped to breaking-point a few years ago, things have calmed down again since then. Many of the "awareness training" firms that sprang up overnight have vanished again just as quickly. But this doesn't mean that staff are now security-savvy. Quite the opposite, in fact: As network perimeters become increasingly hardened, attackers are becoming increasingly dependent on insider help from within the network. And their chances of success aren't too bad, either. Verizon's Data Breach Investigations Report shows that the number of users opening a phishing email in 2016 has actually risen from 23 percent last year to 30 percent in the current year. A full 12 percent then proceed to click the dangerous link itself – so a certain amount of work still appears to be necessary on the subject of security awareness in the years to come (see Verizon 2016).

Of course, company staff are not solely to blame here. Employees are coming under increasing pressure, as larger workloads are shared among dwindling workforces, and – crucially – proficiency is required in an ever-increasing number of technical and organizational tools. The topic of "password security" alone is met with eye-rolling from users and exasperated groans from administrators. Passwords should be secure, complex and dynamic. And a new password should be set every three months. And a separate password should be used for important services. But it's hardly surprising that employees often sabotage this strategy. The much-loved Post-It under the keyboard, stuck to the monitor or kept handy in a desk drawer bears mute witness to the difference between well intentioned and well implemented. Forcing employees to follow security rules doesn't achieve anything – except less security. Password security problems could have been defused a long time ago by two-factor authentication, for example. As more and more services and operating systems such as Windows 10 support multifactor authentication, this perennial nuisance could perhaps be passé very soon. Interacting with one's staff on awareness and other matters is a highly individual business as every company and department will need to identify and follow their own strategy here. That said, the experience of other partners in similar situations, as gained by CSSA members on a daily basis, can provide help in the form of best practices.

6.3.4 It's Only a Matter of Time: Incident Management

Only a rookie would believe it's possible to stay ahead of the dangers of the digital world. Anyone actually meriting the title of CIO understands that a successful attack will inevitably take place. So the sensible approach is to set up the **fourth layer of the security model** and prepare for this eventuality before it is too late. The time for lengthy discussions is not when the alarms already start to sound. Moreover, the natural response to an attack in progress tends to be panic, nervousness and quite possibly ill-considered responses. Just as it is helpful to regularly rehearse emergency procedures, a detailed code of conduct also helps defuse an ongoing crisis. Knowing the game plan means steps can be taken more quickly. Sometimes it's easier said than done, however. When corporate security is at stake, decisions can have far-reaching consequences. As one example, if a data leak is stopped by effectively cutting network access for more or less the entire organization, this can affect the company's bottom line at the end of the year. If the success of the data hack is unknown, then a sensible precaution might be for everyone to change their passwords. While no one enjoys making such a decision, it needs to be clear that the decision can be made if the risk is serious enough and that the decision-maker also has the backing of company management to do so. Incident Management is also frequently associated with forensic analysis, when the aim is to discover the attack vector and close it against future attacks. Generally, this involves external service providers who then gain access to critical company systems. For a company whose membership in the CSSA means that it is used to confidentiality and the highly selective sharing of information, a fact-finding mission of this kind should only present a low risk of the undesirable disclosure of company internals.

A successful attack on a fellow member is naturally no reason to celebrate for the partners within the CSSA. The organizations can nonetheless benefit from the attack and its attendant circumstances by closing the very same attack vectors within their own networks. Those aware of events in partner companies are better prepared, can take precautions and may even be able to help by providing resources. While it is clear that market forces require two companies to follow their separate objectives, preventing them from simply sharing everything, the clear-cut categorization of the CSSA's Traffic Light Protocol unambiguously clarifies which data can be shared with whom. As a result, the necessary data – and only this data – is provided to take appropriate action.

6.3.5 Fitness Training: Prepare for Emergencies

"Attack is the best form of defense" is a claim made since the Middle Ages. IT security also applies this principle as **another layer of security** – although it does not mean that we attempt to infect hackers with their own malware. At times when there are no acute situations that require an immediate response, the company's own defenses can be put through their paces by simulated attacks. Penetration testing, awareness campaigns using fake phishing mails and social media attacks performed by security service providers are just some of the many strategies with which real-world emergencies can be rehearsed and prepared for. Closer collaboration with the company's ISP can also be a productive strategy against Distributed Denial of Service (DDoS) attacks. Rapid-response defense measures against ongoing attacks require seamless communication, clear-cut competencies and detailed knowledge of the company assets needing protection. Those with the necessary know-how and resources can also try hanging out with the hackers themselves. Many of the underground forums frequented by professional hackers are well-known. Alongside antivirus software makers and other security companies, IT departments of large organizations are often to be found lurking here in the hope of getting tip-offs about forthcoming attacks and the latest malware trends.

6.3.6 Stronger Together

This brings us to the **sixth layer** in our security stronghold. Depending on your viewpoint, this is either the easiest or most difficult level to implement. It involves collaborating with others, implementing insights from one's fellow victims and, naturally, sharing the company's own data. If, like the CSSA members, you have included your partners in the information network for the five security strategies outlined above, then you can draw on a solid, shared repository of data. This helps day-to-day operations with a large volume of data that is fed directly into the SIEM, simplifies trend monitoring thanks to the size of the dataset and spreads the workload across multiple virtual shoulders.

6.4 Conclusion

For a single company, replicating the CSSA's achievements for its members in the months since its formation might be feasible but would certainly be harder. Many companies will (hopefully) rethink their approach in the near future. While discussing IT security was once considered bad form – one might let something slip – the regularity of successful hacks has shown that we all have weaknesses, some of which are already being exploited by attackers. Those who refuse to see IT security as a task that demands integration – as a combination of products, strategies, processes and (above all) partners – are ultimately doomed to fail. But in a world where digital information is used to control trade flows, money transfers, opinion and soon the very cars that drive us, failure is not an option.

References

Cloud Security Alliance (2016). *Website.* Accessed May 24, 2016, from https://cloudsecurityalliance.org

FireEye (2016a). FireEye-Studie: *Doppelt so viele Cyberattacken in Deutschland – starker Anstieg bei Ransomware.* Accessed May 24, 2016, from https://www.fireeye.de/company/press-releases/2016/fireeye-report-finds-almost-twice-as-many-cyberattacks-in-germany.html

FireEye (2016b). *FireEye-Studie zeigt: 61 Prozent der Deutschen würden rechtliche Schritte ergreifen, wenn ihre persönlichen Daten gehackt warden.* Accessed May 24, 2016, from https://www.fireeye.de/company/press-releases/2016/fireeye-consumer-survey.html

F-Secure (2016). *Schwachstellen zu schließen ist eine der wichtigsten Maßnahmen, um Attacken erfolgreich abzuwehren.* Accessed May 24, 2016, from http://www.pressebox.de/inaktiv/f-secure-gmbh/Schwachstellen-zu-schliessen-ist-eine-der-wichtigsten-Massnahmen-um-Attacken-erfolgreich-abzuwehren/boxid/796096

National Vulnerability Database (2016). *CVE and CCE statistics query page.* Accessed May 24, 2016, from https://web.nvd.nist.gov/view/vuln/statistics

Skyhigh (2016). *Cloud adoption and risk in EU Report Q1 2016.* Accessed May 24, 2016, from http://info.skyhighnetworks.com/WPCARRQ12016EU_Download_White.html

Verizon (2016). *Verizon DBIR 2016 shows we haven't learned how to improve security.* Accessed May 24, 2016, from http://searchsecurity.techtarget.com/news/450294161/Verizon-DBIR-2016-shows-we-havent-learned-how-to-improve-security

Wired (2016). *TalkTalk Hack Toll: 100k Customers and £60m.* Accessed May 24, 2016, from http://www.wired.co.uk/news/archive/2016-02/02/talktalk-hack-customers-lost

Ralf Schneider has been Group CIO at Allianz SE since 2010. From 2010 to 2016, he was also responsible for IT as a member of the Management Board at Allianz Managed Operations and Services SE. Schneider was previously CIO at Allianz Deutschland for four years.

In the course of his 21-year career at Allianz, Schneider has worked in several senior IT roles and was always the youngest to hold these positions. His past responsibilities included heading the Information Systems Sales department as well as managing the unit for E-Business and Project Management Accounting Germany. Complementing his successful work at Allianz, Schneider also holds various offices in a number of cybersecurity organizations, such as Cyber Security Sharing and Analytics (CSSA), the German Cybersecurity Organization (DCSO) and the Digital Society Institute of ESMT Berlin.

Schneider studied mathematics and obtained a doctorate in informatics before beginning his professional career at Allianz in 1995.

The German Security Market: Searching for the Complete Peace-of-Mind Service

7

Markus a Campo, Henning Dransfeld, and Frank Heuer

7.1 Challenges for IT Security Managers

Data privacy has a very high priority in Germany. And yet data security is threatened by numerous factors – both internal and external. The typical external trigger for drives towards better security in corporations is an attempt – often successful – by third parties to gain access to IT systems or company data. In recent years, this type of threat has seen fundamental changes, since attacks have become increasingly professional. One reason for this is that advances in security technologies have resulted in a countertrend that has raised attack techniques to at least the same level of sophistication. In addition, state-backed agents and political activists have been joined by organized crime, which has discovered cybercriminality as a lucrative and low-risk source of profit.

Supplementing conventional threats is a new risk that is now spreading rapidly: the "hijacking" of things or machinery controlled by IT systems. Contemporary attacks are about much more than simply hacking IT to steal or disable data or systems. Rather, the term "security" now includes the concept of "safety" – in the sense of security against hazards to life and limb. In the age of the Internet of Things and the steady advance of automation, serious dangers are posed by the unauthorized control of networked industrial robots, control systems – and even cars. The relentless march of progress hugely increases pressure on those responsible for

M. a Campo
Försterstr. 25, 52072 Aachen, Germany
e-mail: markus.acampo@experton-group.com

H. Dransfeld
St. Ursulagasse 19, 61440 Oberursel, Germany
e-mail: henning.dransfeld@experton-group.com

F. Heuer (✉)
Experton Group AG, Königstor 23, 34117 Kassel, Germany
e-mail: frank.heuer@experton-group.com

© Springer International Publishing AG 2017   59
F. Abolhassan (ed.), *Cyber Security. Simply. Make it Happen.*, Management for
Professionals, DOI 10.1007/978-3-319-46529-6_7

security, not least because the theft or manipulation of data in the context of industrial espionage is now practiced on an increasingly larger scale.

A key internal driver for the new requirements faced by corporate IT security professionals is the transformation of the working world, championed by tech-savvy employees at all levels of the hierarchy, who require policy answers from IT units on topics such as Bring Your Own Device (BYOD) and social media. As a result, boundaries between personal and business use and between identities are now increasingly blurred, making the simultaneous fulfillment of existing corporate requirements for business on the one hand and data privacy legislation for employees on the other a growingly complex task for security managers. The intermingling of employees' business and personal lives already began a few years ago, and there are no indications that the trend is set to lose any momentum in the future.

Alongside internal and external threats, corporate IT security managers also see themselves confronted with additional external and internal factors that significantly influence the range of options available to them. These include legislative and regulatory requirements that mandate compliance with applicable security standards (ISO 27001, "IT Baseline Security" from the German Federal Office for Information Security (BSI), etc.) from service providers in sectors such as financial services, energy and telecommunications. Pressure on some segments of German industry is also set to increase still further due to the new IT Security Act (ITSIG). An estimated 2,000 companies will be affected. As operators of critical infrastructure (energy and water supplies, financial services, etc.), they are compelled to comply with a defined minimum standard, and – this is a crucial new requirement – to submit proof of this compliance to the BSI every two years. Once a company has been formally notified that it is now required to comply with ITSIG, it has two years to achieve this compliance.

As can be seen from the range of possible sanctions, this request is not to be taken lightly. In the event of non-fulfillment of the minimum requirements for IT security, the BSI can simply order appropriate measures to be taken. Operators of critical infrastructure are not the only ones affected by ITSIG requirements. The minimum standards specified by the law also apply to relationships with suppliers and service providers. As these are also indirectly affected by ITSIG, the need for security services will increase exponentially in the years to come.

In times where CIOs are increasingly reporting to their CFOs, one extremely significant internal (and limiting) factor is cost pressure within companies. As a consequence, digitization and standardization are now increasingly prevalent, and both business processes and infrastructure are being partially or completely outsourced. CIOs in large companies and corporations in particular are under a lot of pressure to justify their IT expenditure. A report published by the Experton Group discovered no change to the downward trend in dedicated security budgets that has lasted for some years now, finding that outlay for security is either included in the IT budget – itself now an embattled resource – or in the budgets of business departments. As a result, security – viewed as neither productive nor adding value by the business units – is directly competing with current business requirements.

7.2 Choosing the Right Protection in a Fragmented Market

The manifold issues raised by security requirements are matched by a wide choice of solutions and services. In the following sections, we introduce a number of key solutions and note the scenarios in which outsourcing services to a provider can be advantageous. Whether these benefits can actually be realized in practice must of course be assessed on a case-by-case basis.

7.2.1 Data Leakage/Loss Prevention (DLP)

The Experton Group uses the term DLP (Data Leakage Prevention, also Data Loss Prevention) to refer to solutions deployable by the user company for the identification and monitoring of sensitive data. The aim is to ensure that this kind of data is accessible only to authorized users and that no data leaks occur. One technique used here is to identify critical data as it is moving out of the company and to block it if necessary (preventing data loss). Other approaches monitor the infrastructure necessary to gain access to data in order to make the flow of data out of the company more difficult in the first place (preventing data leakage).

In cases where corporate data is stored in the cloud (e.g., Dropbox), there are benefits to be had by outsourcing DLP to a service provider. DLP service providers use specialized interfaces (APIs) to access a wide range of cloud implementations and can therefore offer customers considerable flexibility.

7.2.2 Security Information and Event Management (SIEM)

The Experton Group uses the term Security Information und Event Management (SIEM) to refer to analysis solutions that collect and evaluate security information and events. Some solutions make use of Big Data features to improve their ability to identify hazards for personal and other kinds of confidential data. The particular challenge with SIEM consists of standardizing data from a range of sources and in various formats, and then to analyze this data so that even complex attacks can be identified.

While on-premise solutions in the SIEM field primarily collect and analyze in-house data, SIEM service providers can also use attack patterns identified in data recently harvested from other customers in their analyses.

7.2.3 Email/Web/Collaboration Security

These security solutions offer protection from spam, viruses and malware associated with the use of the Internet and email/collaboration solutions, monitor data traffic. They also protect confidentiality, particularly by means of encryption.

Solutions that guard email against Internet-based attacks are still the "workhorses" of information security. One potential advantage in outsourcing security services in this specific area is the rapid propagation of information about new viruses or spam attacks. Within a provider network, this information is effectively distributed in real time.

7.2.4 Endpoint Security

The protection of user devices against malware is one of the first and oldest themes in IT security architecture. Endpoint Security is one of the key components of a successful defense strategy – both for the safety of the company in general and for cyber security in particular. After all, the first step is crucial for a successful attack on the infrastructure of a company: The attacker must get a foot in the door and set an anchor within the company's systems. Safety experts have, therefore, always been focused on avoiding such initial infections with, for example, Advanced Persistent Threats (APTs).

A key problem with endpoint security occurs in the event of attacks en masse, when the response time for the analysis and distribution of protective measures (e.g., patterns for virus scanners) is very short. Here, outsourced services can offer advantages as providers are able to use the entire customer base to collect data about suspicious files and activities, which can then be analyzed with the aid of Big Data methods to drastically shorten response times. This also applies to sandbox techniques, whereby suspicious files are first executed in a virtual environment (and often within a purpose-built appliance). Here too, centralized data collection by the provider shortens the response time for new attacks.

Another advantage of outsourcing endpoint security to the service provider is flexibility in the integration of new user devices, such as tablets or smartphones. While on-premise solutions often first require the purchase of new software packages that manage and protect these specific devices, service providers typically have most if not all popular user devices in their portfolio.

7.2.5 Identity and Access Management (IAM)

Identity and Access Management (IAM) is the term used by the Experton Group to refer to solutions and services (solution implementation and operation) for the input, logging and management of user identities and their associated access permissions. IAM solutions and services ensure that access permissions are granted in accordance with predefined policies.

The outsourcing of IAM to a service provider is especially advisable in cases where a company operates internationally and therefore needs access to corporate data from a variety of user devices and locations around the world. In this setup, user identification and authentication is handled by the provider, who grants access to the data once users have authenticated themselves successfully.

7.2.6   Mobile Security – Are Employees Really the Biggest Risk?

Employees are now increasingly mobile. Their need for secure access to sensitive data from any location (via tablet or smartphone) demands comprehensive protection for a growingly heterogeneous infrastructure and device landscape. Mobile security is an increasingly important topic. Modern smartphones are now as easy to infect with malware as a traditional PC. In many cases, they are also connected continuously to the Internet ("always-on"), which constitutes an additional security risk. Rapid progress in mobile apps is also generating a broader spectrum of threats. Mobile security is increasingly moving from protection of the user device alone to ensuring end-to-end protection for content, regardless of whether employees are accessing a company application on the go, from a secure office environment or from the much less secure structure of a public Wi-Fi network. In an age where company applications follow the "mobile first" design, integrated models are required to protect user devices, applications and company content from attacks. Here, IT departments are moving to shift company content to a container solution or a virtual application from the cloud. The last option reduces the danger of third-party interference or misuse, as the data is no longer even copied to the user device. The disadvantage of this kind of model is that mobile users have to be online to actually get any work done.

The question often arises as to whether employees themselves are the biggest threat when it comes to the misuse of company data. In the relevant literature, a phrase often heard in this context is that of the "disgruntled employee" – i.e., the members of staff with an ax to grind, who take entire filing cabinets full of corporate secrets home with them on their USB pen drives. How does this kind of mistrust gel with the era of mobility and the promise of "any time, any place, any task, any device" – with the simple freedom of choosing how and where one wants to work, depending on the task at hand? Isn't it the case that these flexible options are actually reducing the numbers of "disgruntled employees" – and thereby lessening the overall risk? Of course companies in the digital age need to protect the data of their business partners and customers in addition to their own. But there is an increasing number of technical measures that can prevent employees with a grudge (identified by the mobility system in use) or staff leaving the company from making off with company secrets. In fact, there are more such measures than ever before. Employers who have implemented a proper process to deal with members of staff leaving the company and their access to mobile user devices or information can eliminate this threat at the touch of a button.

Elsewhere, things are more difficult. Alongside the "disgruntled employee," we also have the "careless employee" – members of staff who take a lackadaisical approach to policy implementation in their company. As the following considerations show, the consequences of such carelessness can be very serious. Attacks from outside are successful only if those attacked are sufficiently vulnerable. Viruses and worms need to discover a vulnerability of this kind in software or hardware in order to deliver their payloads. Security holes need to be identified and patched. Speed is of the essence here to avert the risk of damage. Two factors limit success in this context:

1. **The manufacturer must first identify and respond to the vulnerability**. This isn't always straightforward, as the example of Android and Stagefright has shown. Three months after it became known, a security hole was finally patched – only for a second vulnerability to appear three months later.
2. **Employees need to keep their work devices up-to-date**. Essentially, this only means that they need to have the latest firmware. Everything else can then be centrally deployed to devices with Mobile Device Management. But devices must be enabled and embedded in the system. In the real world, this requirement often implies a good deal of time and effort spent chasing up the last 10 percent of the "careless employees." CSOs and CIOs all agree that one of the most significant security holes is the one created by mobility.

Stopping employees taking information with them when they leave the company is a job that HR and IT must tackle together. Equally, identifying and motivating "careless employees," and encouraging them to upgrade their devices in time, are tasks for the management team. Even the best CIO in the world cannot master this challenge alone.

Due to the wide variety of mobile platforms and the various options for their secure administration, mobile security is a sound business model for a service provider. Everything we have said about endpoint security is especially pertinent in the mobile field. Service providers offer a single, standardized platform to manage and secure a huge variety of devices – a factor that hugely simplifies the work of in-house administrators in the context of Bring Your Own Device (BYOD).

7.2.7 Network Security

Contemporary corporate networks are exposed to a multitude of threats. Alongside unauthorized access to computers by external parties, attacks may also take the form of bringing the target company's servers to their knees (DoS, DDoS) or may simply involve dangers arising from the reckless behavior of the company's own staff. For "lucrative targets," hackers also invest a great deal of effort and an increasing amount of sophistication, penetrating deep into the network infrastructure and using these cyberattacks (Advanced Persistent Threats) to spy on sensitive data undetected for extended periods of time. Effectively countering these threats is a task for network security solutions. In the sense used in this section, "network security" refers to the securing of physical network structures, including wireless LANs.

Protecting against DoS or DDoS in particular is not something achievable by an individual company, since the network bandwidth available is generally insufficient to mount a defense. Accordingly, Internet providers frequently offer the option of providing this type of protection for their customers. Other network security services are also good candidates for outsourcing: For example, firewalls or systems for intrusion detection and prevention can also be configured and supported by a provider. Outsourcing such traditionally internal security services will result in major changes to the nature of the associated admin positions. Staff who have perhaps spent decades running firewalls and configuring their policy files will now need to deal directly with a contractor and monitor the quality of the service provided. When outsourcing conventional network security, a very cautious approach is required if major conflicts are to be avoided.

7.2.8 Conclusion

To protect the company's valuable data, those responsible for IT security can draw on a comprehensive range of on-premise solutions and external services that address a broad spectrum of scenarios. While this situation has the advantage of offering tailor-made solutions for specific needs, the security market seems unnecessarily fragmented for the many security managers who simply need to secure their data and lack the time, know-how and budget to consider specialist solutions. The problem of finding the right package is aggravated by the fact that so many providers and products are essentially offering the same solution.

7.3   Security from a Single Source: Managed Security Services

On the one hand, decision-makers in mid-sized companies in particular are now facing security threats that present multifaceted, highly dynamic challenges. On the other, they have to cope with limited resources in terms of information, time and financing. Security specialists are also in short supply on the labor market. Accordingly, increasing numbers of security managers are now looking for providers who are able to offer a managed security service as a one-stop shop. As with the IT market in general, security is also gravitating towards outsourcing. For the client company, this brings a wide range of benefits, including a lower level of capital outlay coupled with reduced management effort – as a specialized provider (Managed Security Service Provider, MSSP) simply takes over both the operation and the monitoring of security solutions. The customer also benefits from the up-to-dateness of the service provider's expertise, which is hugely advantageous especially in terms of ever-changing cyberthreats. As a service provider that hosts and manages security services, an MSSP operates dedicated IT security infrastructure for one or more customers.

To lower costs, core security functions are often retained within the customer's own company, while day-to-day security business is either partially or fully outsourced as a managed service to an appropriate service provider. This has the advantage of keeping existing expert knowledge about security within the company and enabling more extensive control of security operations. Alongside conventional software licensing and bespoke managed services, standardized "as-a-Service" offers are also becoming increasingly popular. This segment is likely to see disproportionately high growth in the future.

7.3.1 Managed Service or Cloud Solution?

When deciding to outsource security, one question that must always be answered concerns the "distance" permitted between outsourced services and the company's own infrastructure. With a managed service, for example, the equipment running the services usually continues to be based at the client, while the MSSP is responsible for installation, configuration and support. In a cloud solution, on the other hand, network traffic is routed via the provider, who renders the services using in-house systems before ultimately transferring the data back to the customer.

Decisions about the exact variant to choose are made as part of a sourcing strategy, which needs to consider a series of impact factors, including:

- Security and data protection;
- Service flexibility (on the part of the provider);
- Flexibility in handling customer requests;
- Effort required to manage the service (governance);
- Cost;
- Standardization;
- Effort needed to integrate the service into company infrastructure.

Regardless of the sourcing strategy, the two options also come with their respective fundamental advantages and disadvantages:

- Cloud services often offer a broader feature set than managed services. A sandboxing system, for example, which executes and analyzes suspicious files within a self-contained environment, may be offered for any possible operating system variant within the cloud. With a managed service, where the sandbox appliance sits in the client's network and is supported by the MSSP, a decision must generally be made for a single OS environment.
- Cloud services are also easier to integrate into Big Data analyses than managed services, since all of the customer data is already in the cloud and doesn't need to be collected first. This enables new kinds of attacks to be detected more quickly and communicated to the protective systems.
- With cloud services, unencrypted data is first sent to the provider – where it can in principle also be read.
- In addition, encrypted data cannot be analyzed in a cloud solution without first being unencrypted by the cloud provider.
- With a managed service, the risk of unauthorized eavesdropping on data is lower, since the data never leaves the client's own network.

Most of the security features described above are available as a managed service, a cloud solution or a hybrid version of the two. Only protection from DDoS attacks is generally handled exclusively by the cloud, since only a specialized provider can offer the kind of network bandwidth that is necessary when defending against this sort of attack.

7.3.2   Selection Criteria

As the market for MSS now starts to mature, customers are also becoming more demanding. Faced with increasingly sophisticated threats, they are looking for improved service readiness, end-to-end SLAs, on-premise operation where possible – all at affordable prices. Considering these requirements, the Experton Group views the following aggregated criteria as especially relevant for providers of managed security services:

- Breadth of security service portfolio offered, scope of security solutions operated by the provider (see 7.2)
- Range of support strategies intended to secure availability and confidentiality (e.g., failover protection, hotline availability, segregation in multitenancy)
- Security Operations Center (SOC) in Germany or Europe
- Own network (provider offers end-to-end responsibility)

7.3.3   Assessment of Deutsche Telekom/T-Systems as a Managed Security Services Provider

The Experton Group published its second Security Vendor Benchmark in 2015. In this major review of the provider market, the Experton Group also analyzed and rated providers for managed security services based in Germany (see Fig. 7.1). A large number of individual criteria was used to evaluate the providers. These individual criteria were weighted to reflect the respective product category, and used as the basis for assessing the appeal of the security offering ("portfolio attractiveness") and the provider's position in the market ("competitive strength"). These two dimensions form the two axes of the "Experton Market Insight Quadrant." Each of these axes is itself dichotomous, so that the Experton Market Insight Quadrant contains four segments into which providers can be categorized. Providers characterized by a combination of a highly attractive portfolio and high competitive strength are placed in the "Leader" segment. Leader companies can draw on a highly attractive product and service portfolio, plus a strong and well-established competitive presence in the market, and therefore fulfill all of the requirements for successful market development. They are to be viewed as strategic trendsetters and opinion leaders.

In the 2015 Security Vendor Benchmark, Deutsche Telekom (T-Systems and Telekom Deutschland) was placed in the Leader segment for Germany. In the

German market for managed security services, Deutsche Telekom is truly the provider to beat – both in terms of portfolio attractiveness and in competitive strength. Deutsche Telekom's portfolio extends across the entire MSS spectrum, and is supported by an end-to-end service program for securing availability and confidentiality (e.g., failover protection, hotline availability, segregation in multitenancy). One key feature of the portfolio is the inclusion of managed services for network hardening. Internet Protect Pro is just one of Telekom's services in its MSS portfolio, for example. This should be seen in the context of Telekom's view of security as an integral component and basic precondition for its entire product and service portfolio. With T-Systems and the Telekom Deutschland Business Customer Unit, Deutsche Telekom addresses the entire spectrum of industry – from small- and mid-sized enterprises to multinationals. An increasingly powerful argument for Deutsche Telekom – not only in terms of SME customers (cf. the overturning of the Safe Harbor agreement) – is that services are provided from Germany and are governed by the provisions of the German Data Protection Act. As a network operator, Deutsche Telekom can also offer end-to-end responsibility, from the data center/SOC to the customer.

Source: Experton Group AG

Fig. 7.1 Positioning of Managed Security Service Providers in Germany

7.3.4 Specialized Managed Security Services

Managed services is a strong growth market in mobile security, with many companies now utilizing service providers to reduce administrative costs and ensure that the protection of their mobile data is entrusted to experts. Alongside traditional software licenses and bespoke managed services, a firm footing has also been established by Security-as-a Service (SECaaS). For smaller companies in particular, SECaaS offers comprehensive protection from external cloud providers. Advantages include faster antivirus provisioning, continuous and automated virus definition rollouts (saving users from constantly having to update antivirus software themselves) and the outsourcing of tasks such as log management to the external provider. This model is especially attractive for companies with only a limited budget for overall IT security who require an adequate level of security for a large mobile user base. For mobile users, the solution is always a compromise between mobile freedom, the costs for a mobile solution and ensuring optimum protection for corporate data.

Many leading providers now also offer Mobile-Security-as-a-Service, and the Experton Group expects this segment to continue to grow. However, users of this model should always remember that the security of their confidential company data now lies in the hands of an external service provider. Accordingly, steps must be taken to ensure that the SaaS provider is an established company, which has been audited and certified by the German Federal Office for Information Security (BSI).

 **Markus a Campo** works in the Experton Group as a Senior Advisor, specializing in information security with a particular focus on the analysis of IT architecture and IT security models. Other aspects of his work include network security, security audits, incident response, secure smartphone deployment, web application security, payment system security, as well as the ISO 27001 standard and the Baseline Protection Catalogues from the German Federal Office for Information Security (BSI).

As an Advisor, a Campo organizes workshops that address key information security topics of particular interest to customers and works with the customer to develop prospective solutions for meeting these requirements. A Campo studied computer engineering at RWTH Aachen University and received his doctorate in 1991. Following a position in the IT department of a large aluminum company, he has worked since 1997 as a consultant, author and trainer/lecturer in the field of information security. He also is an officially appointed and sworn appraiser for the Aachen Chamber of Industry and Commerce, with his field of expertise being "Information processing systems and applications with a focus on IT security." He is also an ISO 27001-certified Lead Auditor and Lead Implementer.

Henning Dransfeld works for the Experton Group as Manager Advisor and Program Manager Mobile Enterprise, where he specializes in advising ICT users and providers in the field of mobile enterprise on client strategy, mobile productivity, security and staff motivation. Dransfeld is a recognized expert in the analysis of ICT trends, the evaluation of provider strategies and competitive positioning, with over 18 years of experience in the industry. Before moving to the Experton Group, Dransfeld was responsible for Mobile Enterprise in Europe at Forrester Research, where he published a series of analyses on current mobility topics, including "Demystifying BYOD in Europe." Previously, he spent eight years in a number of roles at T-Systems, working as a project manager in the fields of marketing, distribution strategy and corporate strategy. Most recently, he was responsible for Solution Marketing for Mobile Enterprise and Workplace Services. Before moving to T-Systems, Dransfeld spent six years as an analyst at Ovum in London, where he headed the Advisory Service for IP communications services, with responsibility for numerous study reports and forecasts on topics such as IP communications services, and a post as Research Director for ICT Network Strategy.

Dransfeld is an experienced speaker at international conferences such as the European VPN User Association (EVUA) and the European IPQC Mobility Exchange. He is a graduate of the Henley Business School, the University of Wales and Université 1, Institut de Gestion Rennes.

Frank Heuer works at the Experton Group as a Senior Advisor and Lead Advisor for Social Business. He specializes in social business, communications services and solutions, unified communications and cloud computing, with a particular focus on communications-as-a-service. Heuer has worked in ICT market analysis and consulting since 1999. His fields of interest include ICT provider consulting on the topics of strategic and operational marketing, as well as sales. He has overseen go-to-market study reports and analyzes for leading providers on topics as varied as social business, unified communications (as-a-service), cloud computing, IT Security, telecommunications services, convergent solutions and next-generation networks.

Until 2011, Heuer worked at techconsult GmbH as Head of the Competence Center for Communications and Cloud Services. He co-authored the BITKOM Cloud Computing Guide, and is a regular speaker at conferences and webcasts in his fields of expertise. Heuer holds a degree in business administration from the University of Trier.

CSP, not 007: Integrated Cybersecurity Skills Training

8

Rüdiger Peusquens

Whether mid-sized enterprises or corporate giants: In a survey of senior management, 92 percent of respondents stated that IT security has "high" or "very high" priority in the organization (see Telekom 2015). And for good reason: In the Industry 4.0 era, with the growing intelligent networking of humans, machinery and production processes the risk of security attacks also increases simultaneously. Alerts, cyberattacks and other threats must be countered successfully on a daily basis – in a matter of hours, minutes and even seconds. The key challenge here is that IT systems alone cannot win the cat-and-mouse game between the hacker and the target. Well-qualified IT security experts are urgently required; but from where? The market for specialists in this segment is modest – not least because Germany has yet to provide dedicated vocational training and university degrees for defense and security experts. The handful of experts available is much sought-after and therefore very expensive. Long-winded tender procedures also cost time and money – and only provide mid-term solutions to the problem.

8.1 The New Profession of Cybersecurity Specialist: From IT Worker to IT Security Expert

What can be done? Our solution: ensure an adequate skills base within the company, build up expertise and train employees to meet your needs. As a large multinational, Deutsche Telekom employs well over 100,000 people. Among the 9,000 apprentices also working at Telekom are IT experts whose training is of great concern to us; but not necessarily with a focus on security. We need a bridge that leads from vocational training to future employment as a security expert.

R. Peusquens (✉)
Deutsche Telekom AG, Friedrich-Ebert-Allee 140, 53113 Bonn, Germany
e-mail: ruediger.peusquens@telekom.de

© Springer International Publishing AG 2017
F. Abolhassan (ed.), *Cyber Security. Simply. Make it Happen.*, Management for Professionals, DOI 10.1007/978-3-319-46529-6_8

The challenge in the process: A cybersecurity expert effectively requires two occupational training courses, namely a solid standard of education in IT or networks plus dedicated security training. This is where our specialized security advanced training is making a difference: A program that comprehensively, strategically and in a structured manner teaches cybersecurity. The concept emerged in mid-2013 and was formulated thus: We need an entirely new job profile, and a curriculum of advanced training that qualifies IT experts into IT security experts.

In cooperation with the Cologne Chamber of Industry and Commerce (IHK), Telekom developed an advanced training program: The prerequisite is a successfully completed IT-specific vocational training or equivalent dual studies. After two and a half years and successful completion, participants may carry the IHK-certified, nationwide-valid title "Cybersecurity Professional." In addition, the program also partners with the university federation "Open C3S" (Open Competence Center for Cybersecurity) – the largest vocational and further training initiative in the field of cybersecurity in the German-speaking market. The future IT security experts complete appropriate courses there as part of their training.

The IT security positions created especially for graduates of the course attracted over 230 applications. The first development program started in late September 2014.

8.2   Hands-on Experience in All-Round Security

A central element for the advanced training to become a Cybersecurity Professional is hands-on activity in the profession's task area, i.e., practical work in the professional departments. These include all departments that have relevance for IT and network security, and which therefore require employees with sound IT expertise – from the Cyber Defense Center to units working with application security, security-on-access networks and user devices, as well as groups working on fraud detection.

By dealing with the daily requirements from the departments, typically handled in a project format, course trainees develop their expertise step by step. This process is supported in parallel by a modular subject-specific and cross-subject advanced training. Trainees also develop their expertise in a range of formats, from face-to-face seminars to online courses and e-learning. The skills and abilities acquired in these modules can then be immediately applied and further developed directly in workplace projects. In this way, the program integrates practical occupational requirements with the targeted reflection of academic and scientific content, enabling the new IT security experts to apply the latest research in order to resolve challenges in their profession.

To ensure that the course offers both maximum quality and current relevance, the acquisition of specialist professional expertise features strongly in the curriculum. To secure the learning progress, each participant receives support from a subject coach as well as from a course learning process supervisor during the vocational training program. The subject coach is an employee in the department where the trainee also works. This person acts as a mentor to the student and is the first point of contact for day-to-day issues and problems. To avoid hierarchical conflicts from the outset, subject coaches must not be immediate supervisors – e.g., team leaders or managers. The learning process supervisors, however, can be consulted on any general topic concerning the program and also organize communication and networking within the student body. For this purpose, regular face-to-face meetings and workshops are held, in which the budding Cybersecurity Professionals tackle work together on common projects. These events add up to around 40 days of the total time spent in the two-and-a-half-year program. To qualify for the final IHK examination, participants must have an attendance record of 80 percent or more for these classroom-based units.

8.3 Cybersecurity Expertise for Managers, too

At the end of the advanced course, participants must demonstrate their acquired knowledge by autonomously processing and solving a project task. Those who successfully complete this exam receive IHK "Cybersecurity Professional" certification. Once trained, the new specialists can then be deployed to tackle any relevant task areas within the Group. In addition, course participants have the option of taking individual exams for the study units scheduled as part of the program, and thereby acquiring six undergraduate certificates as well as the associated European Credit Transfer and Accumulation System (ECTS) accreditation.

Yet the Cybersecurity Professional course is actually only one of many strategies that Deutsche Telekom is using to combat skills shortages in the field of IT security. In addition, all employees regularly attend security training and are made aware of the issue with a variety of security awareness measures. In addition, modules for managers are also planned, designed to provide management staff with specialist knowledge of selected important IT security topics. These skills will enable prompt and competent decision-making by managers on security-relevant aspects of their day-to-day work.

8.4 Conclusion

Deficiencies in IT security are the Achilles heel of our society, in which humans and machinery are now increasingly networked via the Internet. To achieve greater security in the network, stakeholders need to work together far more closely to create transparency and to establish clear responsibilities and advanced expertise to provide better protection for data and infrastructure. An understanding of the need for IT security must also be established and maintained – both for employees at all levels of the corporate hierarchy as well as for customers. Cybersecurity must stop being seen as an annoying "add-on" for IT: It needs to be presented as a truly critical aspect of day-to-day life until everyone recognizes the hugely important role IT security now plays for us all. In the process, however, security must be simple and easy to obtain and to use – otherwise it will not be implemented.

The great interest of organizations and companies outside the Group in our program confirms the high relevance of the topic in the whole industry. Thus, currently industry associations and the Federal Institute for Vocational Education – the recognized center of excellence for research and development of vocational education and training in Germany – are discussing how specific IT security content itself could be integrated into existing training occupations; and how it could be possible to establish a separate occupational profile such as "IT Security Specialist."

All of this shows just how well the topic resonates with the industry. The major challenge for the future now consists of not resting on one's laurels but instead working to continuously expand the program. As described at the outset, in (cyber) security often a few hours, minutes or even seconds are decisive as to whether an attack is averted or causes damage – and new, entirely novel and unprecedented threats now arise on a daily basis. Looking to the future, one of the primary tasks will therefore be to review the content of this two-and-a-half-year program and adjust the curriculum to the current threat situation – possibly even during ongoing courses.

Reference

Telekom (2015). *Cyber security report 2015*. Accessed July 28, 2016, from https://www.telekom. com/static/-/293656/2/Cyber-Security-Report-2015-si

Rüdiger Peusquens is Vice President Cyber Defense and Situation Management at Deutsche Telekom AG. After receiving his doctorate in nuclear physics, Peusquens began his career as an IT security consultant at debis Systemhaus. During this period, he set up a vulnerability reporting service and completed white hat hacking work for customers in the form of penetration tests.

With the takeover of debis Systemhaus by T-Systems, Peusquens moved to Deutsche Telekom AG, where he used his six years of consultancy experience to contribute his considerable expertise to Group security work. He took on the setup of the internal penetration testing team for quality assurance work in technical security. His most recent work now involves attack detection and defense. His current position brings together the responsive forces of cybersecurity and business security to focus on early detection and rapid countermeasure deployment for security incidents at Deutsche Telekom and its customers.

Human Factors in IT Security

9

Linus Neumann

Imagine you are a hacker suddenly faced with an insurmountable technical challenge: Your target's email server has been well configured, its publicly known vulnerabilities have been eliminated and an as-yet undisclosed vulnerability is either unobtainable or much too expensive. Do you give up? No, you just ask for the password.

One of the most common myths about hacking attacks is that they usually require a high level of technical sophistication. However, you really don't have to possess special technical skills or secrets to be a hacker. In reality, the opposite is often the case: Criminals can successfully gain access with little or no technical knowledge. Most of them make use of "off the shelf" hacking tools which are available either as open source software or from underground online marketplaces. The inconvenient truth is that you – yes, you – are much less secure than your computer. And no attacker wants to do more work than is actually necessary.

9.1 IT Security Is Just Not Very People-Centric

Most people know very little about the inner workings of their computers. Their complexities are indeed quite difficult to fully grasp. It is just as difficult for us to appreciate the principles of computer security. Our understanding is often hampered by something much more basic: IT security does not work the way we intuitively expect it to. It makes assumptions that we often find difficult to fulfill.

L. Neumann (✉)
c/o CCCB, Marienstr. 11, 10117 Berlin, Germany
e-mail: kontakt@linus-neumann.de

© Springer International Publishing AG 2017
F. Abolhassan (ed.), *Cyber Security. Simply. Make it Happen.*, Management for Professionals, DOI 10.1007/978-3-319-46529-6_9

9.1.1 The Thing with Passwords

We have all been there. We need to create a new password for our business account. It should have more than eight characters. It should comprise letters, numbers and special characters. We must not write it down anywhere. And we need to change it after three months. How annoying that we can't just use our standard password: the one we've always used whenever we opened a new account. For our personal email account, for Facebook and for that small online store that had a special offer on some really stylish shoes last year. It's much more convenient to use the same simple password for everything.

We are warned all the time that we have to vary our passwords – but how are we supposed to remember them all? Anyway, how would anyone possibly guess our password? We might have used our partner's name but we were careful to replace the A with a 4. How could anyone figure that one out?

What we tend to forget is that the password is potentially known to every single website on which we use it. How securely it is stored there is anyone's guess.

In fact, reusing the same password for different services is one of the biggest IT risks that we expose ourselves to on a regular basis. A single unauthorized access or a single security hole at one of the many services we use is all it takes to give an attacker control of all of our accounts.

But how are we supposed to remember all these different passwords? Nobody can memorize them all – especially if they have to be totally "random" (i.e., cryptic) and long. And what is all this about anyway? "At least eight characters?" Why not just six?

The exponential relationship is not obvious to us because we cannot imagine how anyone could "crack" a computer password simply by guessing (although sometimes the guessing is far from simple). You start with 'a' and finish with 'ZZZZZZZZ' – if you ever get that far. While you can try all possible combinations of six characters in a few hours, eight characters require months and nine characters years, even with the computing power provided by a modern PC. It is hard for us humans to grasp the two aspects – to imagine, on one hand, how quickly a computer can rattle through all possible combinations; systems optimized for password cracking can easily achieve several million or even billions of attempts per second.[1] And yet on the other hand, it can still take quite some time to guess a few letters, numbers and special characters.

Unfortunately, our desire for ease of use leads us to undermine the very mathematical principles upon which our password protection depends. A "password" is an intrinsically perfect concept: Just a few bytes of information are sufficient to provide us with effective security protection. But our large number of password-protected accounts makes it impossible for us to remember a different password for them all. This is why we resort to simple, popular passwords like "password123," which make it very easy for attackers to penetrate what may have otherwise been a technically secure system.

Our simple, everyday needs make it impossible to reconcile IT security with ease of use, as our first example has demonstrated.

---

[1] The actual speed at which passwords can be cracked depends on whether the cracking takes place locally or remotely, the latter being significantly slower. The technical characteristics of the security system – the hashing algorithm – also make a difference.

9.1.2   The "Security versus Productivity" Dilemma

If you ask the people working for a large company what they see as the biggest brake on their productivity, they are quite likely to say "IT!" They cannot swap files easily and quickly because USB sticks are banned and are not recognized by their computers anyway. Before they can read their emails at a hotel, they first have to set up a complicated VPN connection. And they cannot even configure their company account on their neat new tablet.

There are good reasons for all of these restrictions, but what they have in common is that in reality they hinder users more often than they protect them. This is dangerous in two respects: It decreases satisfaction with and confidence in IT, and it encourages users to find ways to circumvent the restrictions. Instead of carrying out work on their secure corporate laptops, staff use their personal devices – because they will accept USB sticks. Important emails are simply forwarded to a private Hotmail account so that they can be read easily and conveniently on a tablet during a flight.

This causes sleepless nights for the company's IT security professionals because these users are completely outside their control. A common reaction is to impose even stronger restrictions, warnings and prohibitions, thereby antagonizing users even more. The result is an even lower level of security than was the case before the restrictions were introduced.

What those responsible for IT security regularly ignore is that their coworkers really do want to make use of IT in order to carry out their work more efficiently. The last thing they want is constraints on the way they do their work, especially if those constraints don't make any sense to them.

This brings us to IT security's second fundamental problem: A computer either works or it doesn't. It is not able to distinguish between good and bad actions. Users either have permission to open, copy or even overwrite files – or they don't. If users are empowered to do something, that privilege can sooner or later be exploited during an attack. If they are not allowed to do that thing, they will try to circumvent what they consider to be an unnecessary restriction.

9.2   Social Engineering

Attackers know that people are often the weakest link in the security chain. They would have to invest many man-hours to track down and exploit new security vulnerabilities without any guarantee of success. With people, they can be confident of discovering any number of vulnerabilities as long as they employ a little creativity.

In addition, as Fig. 9.1 demonstrates, the organizations and businesses that really need to protect themselves against attacks, often have a wealth of resources at their disposal with which to protect their IT. These massive resources bear no relationship to their investment in "hardening" their staff against hacking attacks.

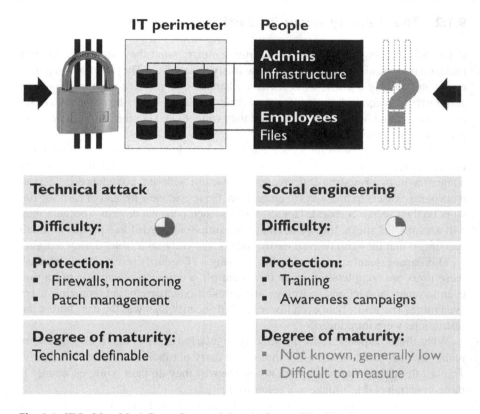

Fig. 9.1 IT Is Often Much Better Protected than the Person Who Uses It

A typical attack can be divided into five phases, which are summarized in Fig. 9.2. Without some sort of vulnerability, an attack is not possible. We also need an "exploit" for the vulnerability, or a way of manipulating the target system so that it does what we want. The actual "manipulating" is done by the "payload," which could, for example, be a trojan horse secretly lurking on an infected computer. Finally, we have the access rights that will allow us to carry out whatever attack we have in mind.

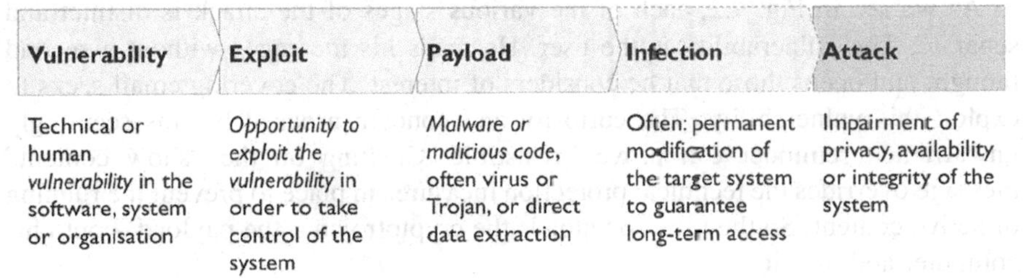

Vulnerability	Exploit	Payload	Infection	Attack
Technical or human *vulnerability* in the software, system or organisation	*Opportunity to exploit the vulnerability* in order to take control of the system	*Malware or malicious code,* often virus or Trojan, or direct data extraction	Often: permanent modification of the target system to guarantee long-term access	Impairment of privacy, availability or integrity of the system

Fig. 9.2 The Phases of a Typical Attack

The human factor is particularly important in the first phase, as attackers are rarely in a position to automatically plant a targeted "drive-by" trojan infection. They have to rely on their victim opening and executing the file. The same is true for passwords: Attackers usually lack the ability to remotely crack a password and depend on their victim's willingness to reveal it to them. But how exactly?

9.3 Human "Weaknesses" Are Often Social Norms or Simple Instincts

Many of these human weaknesses would be strengths in another context. Characteristics such as helpfulness and friendliness are fundamental to our social relationships, just as curiosity is fundamental to our ability to solve problems. Hackers regularly exploit these character traits to get us to infect our own computers or to reveal our passwords.

9.3.1 Would You Mind Installing This Malware on Your Computer?

In early 2016, many people in Germany received one or more email reminders about an unpaid invoice from a company they were not familiar with. The details, it read, were to be found in the attached Word file. "That's just not possible," the recipients thought. "I'd better take a closer look." When they opened the file they saw a blank document, along with a warning from Microsoft Word that the document had "active content" that was currently disabled. The advice – please click on the "Activate content" button to see the active content – might not sound unreasonable to someone staring at a blank page.

Those who accepted this advice would become one of the many victims of the "Locky" cryptotrojan. The "active content" was a macro embedded in the Word file that downloaded the blackmailer's software from the Internet and ran it on the computer. This would be followed by a ransom demand of about 250 euros to restore the files that had been made unusable.

As we see in Fig. 9.2, each of the various stages of the attack is distinct and separate: The vulnerability is the user. He reads his messages without a second thought and opens those that he considers of interest. The covering email seeks to exploit this vulnerability. The curiosity and concern aroused by this seemingly unwarranted reminder can prove irresistible. Clicking on the "show content" message overrides the technical protection measures in place to prevent the running of active content. So the user downloads the cryptotrojan – the payload – onto his computer and runs it.

From a strictly technical standpoint, no technical vulnerability has been exploited here; the attackers are simply exploiting the gullibility of the victim. It did not take long for a considerable number of these infections to occur. Everyone was talking about "Locky" – and not just the specialist IT press. The attackers therefore needed to come up with something new. So they sent out emails with the subject line "Official warning about the Locky computer virus," which asked the recipients to follow the instructions contained in the attachment (see Fig. 9.3). Opening the attachment resulted in a nasty shock.

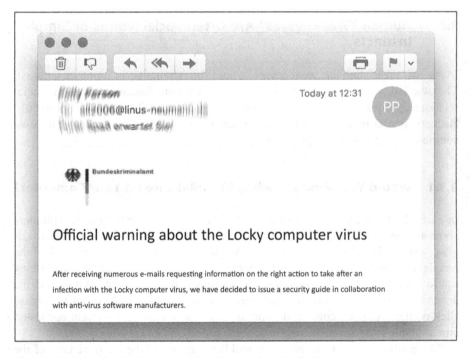

Fig. 9.3 Phishing Email Claiming to Be a Warning from the Police

Another way of getting unsuspecting victims to run malicious software is to deliberately "lose" USB flash drives. These contain a small number of files, named to give the impression that they contain confidential data. Also on the stick is another file, prominently positioned and named "To the honest finder." In reality all the files contain malware configured to attack the systems of curious and honest finders alike.

Some remarkable hacking successes have been achieved at a cost of a few euros for each stick left somewhere on the company's parking lot.

9.3.2   Excuse Me, What Exactly Is Your Password?

Even today, the holy grail of remotely executed espionage and sabotage remains the email password, because this is the gateway to everything else: It enables the intruder to monitor business communications down to the very last detail, to impersonate the victim in communications with third parties, and for good measure, it allows the intruder to reset most other account passwords through email verification. This potentially gives the attacker access to Facebook, Paypal or business bank accounts. But the most dangerous aspect is that the attacker does not even have to use malware, which could be detected by a virus scanner.

Many email servers – particularly those in companies – disconnect after a few failed login attempts and insist on renewed personal authentication. Attackers therefore cannot keep guessing as often as they would need to, but must instead convince victims to reveal their passwords voluntarily.

One popular method is to get a victim to go through the process for changing the password – something users in companies are required to do regularly. The target person receives an email telling them to renew their password. If they fail to do so, access will be disabled within the next few days. The email includes a link to carry out the request immediately. When the target clicks on the link, they see the usual login page, and once logged in, they are presented with an input field in which to change the password.

What likely went unnoticed, is that the linked login page is a near-perfect malicious clone crafted by the attacker. Preparing such a clone does not involve much more than saving the original page and then adding a few additional features to it. The old password is received and stored. The new password will also be stored and automatically changed on the real server. The attacker finally chose a domain name for the malicious website that looks very similar to the real address.

Merely substituting the letter L with the number 1, for example, would change the address https://mail.linus-neumann.de to the deceptively similar https://mail.1inus-neumann.de. Reversing or omitting letters towards the end of the domain name is another popular trick (https://mail.linus-neumnan.de). The human brain doesn't always read words right to the end once it has "recognized" them. It is therefore unlikely that victims would notice the difference.

Following this brief visit by the victim, the attacker is now in possession of both the old and the new login data. He can also see if the victim follows a particular pattern when changing the password – just changing one letter, for example, or incrementing a number. Armed with this knowledge, the attacker does not have to be too concerned if the victim changes his password again. Now, the next thing the attacker does is to download all of the victim's emails and sift through them before deciding how to proceed.

If you are anything like me, you get a couple of dozen emails like this every day. They are often poorly written and are rejected by the spam filter anyway. But all it takes is for you to let your guard down for a second – and an attacker who is skilled at his craft.

Indeed, there is a world of difference between an expert and an amateur, and between mass phishing and a carefully targeted spear fishing attack. With the former, hundreds of thousands of emails are sent indiscriminately to multiple recipients and quickly end up in spam filters, while the latter target specific individuals. These emails refer to their recipients by name and provide faultless instructions in the language they expect to read. A familiar footer with the company logo and callback number also helps to convince the victim of the legitimacy of the request. And spam filters? They are not too worried about a single email; they are trained to detect and block mass mailings. Consequently, most spear-fishing attacks manage to stay completely under the radar.

A recent attack targeted a steelworks in Germany. The 2014 Management Report of the Federal Office for Information Security (see BSI 2014) describes how the attackers tried to use spear fishing emails to get their foot in the door. Over time, they managed to gain access to a number of the plant's control components, causing parts of the plant to fail. They finally caused a furnace to end up in an undefined condition that prevented it from shutting down properly, resulting in massive damage to the plant.

9.4 Would You Please Transfer Me a Few Million?

Most attackers generally have one goal in mind: making money. There are various ways of doing this – making money from an attack they carry out themselves or getting a third party to pay them to carry out an attack. But why make it difficult for yourself – when you can simply request a large transfer of funds?

The boss is out of the office attending an important meeting with business partners. It promises to be a quiet day at the office. But a frantic email causes disquiet. The deal is likely to fall apart because a vital transfer of funds has not taken place. The boss is angry and piles the pressure on his staff: "Please transfer the funds without delay. If the money doesn't arrive tomorrow, all our work has been for nothing. How could this happen?"

The amount? A six- or seven-figure sum payable to an offshore bank account – a run-of-the-mill transaction for a large business. Overwhelmed by a mixture of guilt and indignation, the boss's PA gets to work. Has the boss really not mentioned this payment before, or had it just got stuck in the accounts department? Anyway, something needs to be done about this urgently. The transfer is completed within a few minutes. A short click on "Reply" and the boss sends a friendly thank-you message: "Just in time, thank you."

When the boss returns from his business trip a few days later, his PA thanks him again and asks him if it all went well. "But of course, what could possibly have gone wrong?"

It slowly dawns on the victim. The email claiming to be from the CEO was a well-crafted forgery – and by now the money will have been transferred by a circuitous route from the offshore account to anywhere in the world.

This scam, known as the "Fake President Fraud," relies entirely on the psychological blind spots of the victims. It is usually based on exploiting the universal values professionals live by: authority, speed, trust, and often secrecy. Variants of this method base their approach on the offer of a secret deal that may not yet be public. The employee who receives the message is one of a select few who are being taken into confidence – and is required to keep the matter confidential.

These cases, which are more common than you might think, often end with the employee's dismissal and with a company reluctantly swallowing its losses.

9.5   Defensive Measures

The work of an IT security engineer within an organization is never done. Every day, new vulnerabilities are discovered and have to be dealt with. The IT security engineer has one advantage, however. Once a vulnerability has been eliminated, it is not likely to return soon.

This is not the case when it comes to "human" IT security, where a one-time "immunization" often only has a specific and temporary effect. Even slight variations in attack patterns can increase the chances of finding victims and the odds improve steadily over time.

Many organizations try to warn their staff by sending out regular mass mailings about the risks from such attacks. In practice, however, these warnings have a barely measurable effect that makes them of little practical relevance.

Therefore, hardening an organization against social engineering attacks requires ongoing programs that not only deliver a flow of information about the methods used by the attackers but also include mounting simulated attacks against the users themselves. If they click on the fake phishing messages, they receive an immediate warning and advice.

These simulated attacks should cover the whole gamut of scams employed by hackers. At the same time, the campaigns should be used as an opportunity to strengthen trust between the IT department, IT security and the employees. Allegations and heavy-handed lecturing are unlikely to encourage employees to contact the security specialists if they come across something suspicious.

Since most attacks take place via email and simulated phishing attacks are easily scalable, the principles involved are explained below, based on a typical phishing campaign. By regularly repeating a variety of different attacks, it is possible to evaluate the success of the campaign in terms of the two main learning objectives: Is the number of successful attacks going down? And are attempted attacks being reported more quickly and more often?

9.5.1 Recognizing Social Engineering

Due to their diversity, it is not really possible to devise a technological means of recognizing social engineering attacks. The cover stories are so diverse and the fabricated scenarios are too close to real-world situations. Yet, they often have one thing in common that a trained eye is able to identify: Social engineering attacks usually contain small cues designed to switch us into action-oriented mode without thinking about it much. This can be achieved in two ways: through boredom or excitement.

Familiar, run-of-the-mill situations that we don't think about too much can be exploited. Classic examples are holding open a door for the person in a hurry behind us, getting rid of a familiar warning by clicking on it, or – as described earlier – regularly changing our passwords.

We are just as careless when we are excited: A task must be carried out without delay or else bad things will happen. Classic examples are the software that is supposed to remove what is claimed to be a virus from our computer, the sum of money that must be transferred as a matter of urgency, or the unwarranted payment reminder that we want to refute.

When we are excited or bored, we often do not stop to ask ourselves whether a request is credible or sensible. If we want to immunize organizations against social engineering, we must therefore instill a healthy degree of suspicion. Unfortunately, we have to ensure that this level of suspicion is not so high that it impacts normal working relationships too strongly.

The relevant mechanisms are best demonstrated with some concrete examples. The best time to think about what you have just done is right after you have logged into a phishing site. Users can be alerted to suspicious details that they would normally overlook and can be advised on what they should do in the future. The teaching materials used for this purpose should be memorable and attractive. Specially produced video shorts, no more than two or three minutes long, are particularly effective at getting the point across.

9.5.2 The Learning Objective: Reporting Suspicious Activity

To create a solid defense against attack, an organization must ensure that all targets of a phishing or spear-phishing attack immediately report suspicious messages to the responsible department, usually the IT department or IT security department. Appropriate countermeasures should be taken without delay.

Responses to a phishing email could include the following:

1. Access to the phishing server that is hosting the fake login page is temporarily blocked in the internal network. If the structure of the organization permits, it may also be advisable to temporarily prevent access by external IP addresses to the mail server in question.
2. A warning is sent to all users requesting notification if they have clicked on the link.

3. Affected users receive a detailed debriefing explaining the process and the risks posed by the attack.
4. Working closely with employee representatives, it might be possible to identify the targets of the campaign from the mail server logs. This would make it easier to approach those individuals in order to warn them of the possibility of further attacks, and could also help to explain the motives for the attack.
5. A password reset will be needed for the targets, and in case of doubt, for the entire organization. Steps must be taken to ensure that only reauthenticated users can perform the reset. It is recommended that all affected accounts are frozen until the passwords have been changed. This must be done strictly from within the internal network.

IT should be prepared to take the appropriate measures and to react to the attack quickly but in a calm and collected manner. At the same time, it should expect an increased volume of false alarms as a result of raising employee awareness about the issue. A friendly and encouraging response will help retain the willingness of staff members to report problems. "Rather one report too many than one too few" should be the maxim.

The reporting rate should be evaluated in detail as part of the next simulated attack. How many users fell victim to the attack before it was reported to IT? Experience has also shown that it makes sense to look at whether employees reporting suspicious activity were previously victims themselves and have therefore already seen the teaching materials and the appeal to report anything suspicious. Because attempts to paper over one's own past mistakes can distort the analysis, these reports should not be counted as successes.

9.5.3   Practice Makes Perfect

The first time an organization systematically evaluates its susceptibility to social engineering, the results are often alarming. While the susceptibility of employees to phishing typically lies in the high single-digit percentage range, the success rates achieved with spear phishing normally reach mid to high double digits. It should be assumed that targets who have not proved susceptible have simply ignored or forgotten about the message – because reports of suspicious messages are extremely rare.

But that is not all. These evaluations regularly discover that some employees have not only been unaware that an attack was taking place, but have even gone so far as to establish a cooperative relationship with the attacker. In one particular case, support questions were still being sent by the employees of the targeted organization to the attacker's email address months later. The printer wouldn't print, attachments were too big to send via email, new employees needed to access certain accounts – the problems that the employees communicated to what they believed was the company's IT department were many and varied. Each of these messages gave the hackers another opportunity to compromise the organization all over again.

9.6   Conclusion: IT Must Work for and Not against Users

Social engineering attacks are not just a very effective means of infiltrating an organization; they are another long chapter in the ongoing battle between IT and users. Vulnerability to these attacks can be reduced only by conducting regular campaigns and simulated attacks. These campaigns provide a welcome opportunity to improve relations between users and IT managers.

After all, "normal" users are much more at risk than IT professionals. While the latter are perfectly familiar with concepts such as "email headers" and "spoofing," many users have no idea how easy it is to impersonate an email sender or forge an email.

In an ideal world, the IT department works hand in glove with the rest of the workforce. But often this is no more than wishful thinking. When it comes to defending against social engineering attacks, it is helpful if both sides are able to speak openly. The IT department should therefore think twice before publicly venting their frustration about mistakes users make. The users, for their part, could be more open in discussing their needs with the IT department and more appreciative of the advice they receive – because ultimately, they both share a common goal: making sure that the company and its sensitive information remain secure.

Reference

BSI (2014). *Die Lage der IT-Sicherheit in Deutschland 2014*. Accessed June 6, 2016, from https:// www.bsi.bund.de/SharedDocs/Downloads/DE/BSI/Publikationen/Lageberichte/Lagebericht2014. pdf?__blob=publicationFile

Linus Neumann is a psychologist and hacker. While studying to earn his degree in psychology at Humboldt University in Berlin, he also showed an interest in political science and forensic psychiatry.

He consults German and international organizations on IT security issues and talks about the political and social ramifications of digital transformation in his "Logbuch: Netzpolitik" podcast.

Neumann has appeared as an expert for hacker organization Chaos Computer Club before committees of the German Parliament, contributing his expertise on e-government and the IT Security Act, for example.

Secure and Simple: Plug-and-Play Security 10

Dirk Backofen

These days, companies from all industries and of all sizes – but primarily small and medium-sized enterprises (SMEs) – are required to deal with pressing questions. To remain competitive, they need to introduce and implement new technologies and take account of the demographic trend, globalization, and the continuing shift in the focus of industry to the services sector. This can only be achieved with the aid of digital processes. Digitalization provides a whole range of new possibilities for companies. In particular, the cloud is a cost-effective, simple, and more flexible option for competing successfully.

Yet companies' IT environments are being bombarded – with almost incessant cyberattacks on corporate networks. These, in turn, are ill-protected: Only last year, Germany's National Initiative for Information and Internet Security (NIFIS) said there was a lot of catching up to do in the area of security, especially with regard to securing the Internet of Things. This is especially true for SMEs, says NIFIS (see NIFIS 2015).

Likewise, there is an urgent need to provide greater security for mobile devices such as smartphones and tablets, as techconsult's latest "Security Bilanz Deutschland" shows. In this security poll, 50 percent of German companies stated that they had not found good solutions for identifying viruses and malware. When it came to solutions for mobile devices, this figure increased to as much as 66 percent (see techconsult 2015). Companies are keen to protect themselves better but lack the IT security experts to do so.

For example, a report by the Federal Office for Information Security showed that only one in two companies has the expert capacity to appoint an IT security officer (see BSI 2011). We can see that security is emerging as the final obstacle to digitalization.

D. Backofen (✉)
T-Systems International GmbH, Friedrich-Ebert-Allee 140, 53113 Bonn, Germany
e-mail: dirk.backofen@t-systems.com

© Springer International Publishing AG 2017   87
F. Abolhassan (ed.), *Cyber Security. Simply. Make it Happen.*, Management for
Professionals, DOI 10.1007/978-3-319-46529-6_10

One solution could be an approach that initially sounds paradoxical: In the age of digitalization, the best protection against attacks from the Internet might also come from the Internet. With what are known as managed services, customers receive an easy-to-use all-round protection package from the cloud that secures their industrial networks, data and applications, and gives them early warning of cyberattacks.

10.1 Data Security in the Danger Zone

German companies of all sizes are successful worldwide and often market leaders, yet they worry about security. If the Bundestag (German parliament) and other large organizations are vulnerable to hacking, how, then, are small and medium-sized enterprises in particular supposed to protect business-critical data and applications? Reports of new attacks and infections by computer viruses appear daily. According to Bitkom, Germany's digital association, approximately half (51 percent) of all German companies were victims of digital industrial espionage, sabotage or data theft between 2013 and 2015. The resulting losses to the economy amount to around 51 billion euros per year, with SMEs being hit the hardest (61 percent of the attacks). The sectors that are attacked the most are the automotive industry (68 percent), followed by the chemical and pharmaceutical industry (66 percent), then banking and insurance (60 percent) (see Bitkom 2015b).

What we also know is that cyberattacks are becoming increasingly frequent and more refined. This forces the companies affected to repeatedly invest in new security mechanisms and possibly pay ransoms for stolen data. What is more, such attacks lead to a loss of image and trust, which in turn causes greater customer churn and a drop in revenue. Experts therefore put the global losses resulting from cyberattacks at between 400 billion and 2.2 trillion US dollars (see A.T. Kearney 2015). In most cases, companies are unable to keep pace with criminal IT development. The consulting firm Roland Berger estimates that 250,000 new malware programs are discovered daily (see Roland Berger 2015). The number of programs that actually exist is likely to be significantly higher.

Company managers are well aware of the seriousness of the situation but lack the skills, manpower and easy-to-use solutions to close the lines of defense. How could it come to this, especially as security has always been one of companies' top priorities? A poll conducted last year by Matthias Zacher, senior analyst at IDC, revealed that improving security – especially the security of mobile devices – is one of the three most important initiatives this year for 62 percent of companies. However, techconsult's "Security Bilanz Deutschland" study showed that there are major problems even with relatively simple solutions such as antivirus programs or firewalls for smartphones and tablets. Only one third of the SMEs surveyed professed to be satisfied with the implementation of corresponding solutions at their companies (see techconsult 2015).

This is highly significant because companies feel they are at risk from a whole series of attackers with different objectives ranging from cyberwars, advanced persistent threat (APT) attacks and cybercrime to e-espionage, hacktivism, and e-vandalism. Companies especially do not accord APT due attention, say experts (see IDC 2013). According to a study, one in five companies have not implemented any APT-specific defense mechanisms.

The attacks, aimed at data theft and encryption, have different objectives: extortion, interrupting operations, causing loss of image, and misusing the company's own IT systems for criminal purposes. In a worst-case scenario, the companies involved may end up having to cease operations.

As expected, companies have mainly focused on protecting their data centers and business-critical applications. However, this is not enough. There is now a bewildering number of tablets and smartphones at the periphery of company networks. These are the least secure elements in an enterprise's information technology landscape. This is even more the case when private devices are used for business purposes ("bring your own device").

IT security officers face the task of adequately considering old challenges and new requirements in equal measure (see IDC 2013). This is because cyberattacks are currently only discovered in companies after an average of 230 days, giving the attacker a long time to cause damage unhindered. What companies therefore need are easy-to-use solutions that are able to identify the attacks promptly and initiate defense mechanisms immediately. Malicious code, cyberattacks, and data theft need to be blocked as quickly as possible and, at the same time, suspicious files should be detected through "sandboxing" – by executing them in a protected environment.

A sandbox is a separate area in which processes can run without affecting the software environment. For example, a virus can be safely activated there and its mechanisms can be studied. It is shielded from the rest of the system, just like a child in a sandbox, where it can "play" safely. At the same time, the system time can be accelerated so that system processes can run faster than usual and anomalies such as viruses can be identified within minutes – not after an average of 230 days.

Sandboxes traditionally look like an operating system that builds on a virtual machine or runs in a container. What may sound trivial is actually very tricky, although nowadays even browsers like Google Chrome have built-in sandboxes where they test code on websites to determine whether this is harmful and warn the user if necessary. Solutions for SMEs are naturally far more sophisticated because the attack scenarios are also more complex. In addition, a sandbox must not impact network performance or work.

A sandbox therefore ensures in a simple manner that harmful activities are executed in a closed environment rather than in the company's network. In a closed area, it is possible to study the functioning of a software package that was previously unknown. This was how the cryptolocker "Locky" was detected in March 2016, for example.

Locky and its multitude of variations are what is known as ransomware, to which companies are increasingly exposed. Advanced versions encrypt documents and files on computers and hard drives that are connected on the same network. This enables cybercriminals to paralyze entire organizations and extort money from the victims in bitcoins. One of the companies affected at the beginning of 2016 was a research institution where, in the space of an afternoon, Locky had encrypted the files on a central server and made them unusable (see Heise.de 2016). Many public authorities and companies in smaller communities were also affected during the same period.

Cybercrime has evolved into a separate branch of industry – the underground economy. Trojans like Locky can be purchased on disguised websites, known as the dark web, for a three-figure sum. The suppliers of such harmful code even offer their criminal clients support. And using such ransomware is lucrative: According to calculations by US security specialist Tony Robinson, online criminals can generate over a million dollars per day with it (see T-Online 2016).

In Germany, security experts and the police generally advise companies not to pay ransoms to online extortionists, telling them to focus their efforts on prevention instead. However, in practice many companies and local authorities are obviously unable to cope, because very often the ransomware infects computers through an infected attachment, be it an Office document, a PDF file from the fax machine or even JavaScripts on which the recipient unsuspectingly clicks.

In reality, Trojans and worms are currently the biggest hazard on the Internet, says Bitkom, Germany's digital association, with a reference to a report by the European Network and Information Security Agency (see Bitkom 2015a). Ranking second among the biggest hazards on the Internet are attacks using Web-based software, also known as "drive-by downloads." Visiting an infected website is enough to download harmful code unnoticed. Other hazards are manipulated smartphone apps, remote-controlled computers (called botnets), infected emails, often sent in huge quantities as spam, and attacks on sensitive access data – the dreaded "phishing." All of these hazards continuously keep appearing in new guises.

Here, easy-to-use big data analyses can be of great benefit. They analyze the behavior of data in the system, identify anomalies, and block further exchange where necessary. "Honeypots" have also proven to be very helpful, enticing potentially harmful code with seemingly interesting data and incapacitating it.

In addition, security apps for devices are highly effective: An algorithm capable of independent learning can also identify unknown risks through a real-time analysis of thousands of parameters in the operating system. These include zero-day exploits that target previously unknown gaps in security. Compromised devices can be excluded from the company network as soon as threats arise. They raise the alarm at the system's control center and send forensic data there for a detailed analysis of the attack.

To be able to react in an appropriate manner to all of the attack scenarios outlined, companies have two options: They can either develop and implement their very own security concept or get external help. The first case is anything but trivial – and, as seen, often fails due to the scarcity of experts who can build a powerful defense. In the second case, solutions exist that excel on the basis of their simplicity and come as a bundle from the cloud.

10.2 Digitalization Needs New Security Concepts

All of the problems known to us today relating to the securing of corporate networks can only be understood if we take recent developments in information and telecommunication technology (ICT) into account. Digitalization today is reflected in four major megatrends:

1. **"All is Mobile:"** Knowledge work in the twenty-first century is not possible without electronic aids. Almost every professional now carries a smartphone or a tablet to use for both work and leisure. Although laptops and desktop PCs are still the terminals preferred by 60 percent of users, smartphone use in Germany increased to 29.6 percent at the end of 2015 (see Webtrekk 2016). These days, users are accustomed to being able to access their applications on mobile devices. Needless to say, these applications must be up to date and synchronized at all times. For this, they need to be stored in a central location. This takes us to the second major digitalization trend.
2. **"All is Cloud:"** For centralized storage of applications and data, the PC or server has become obsolete. A centralized, highly secure cloud solution in a data center is what is needed to collect, store, and process the vast quantities of data. Cloud-Monitor 2015 found that 44 percent of companies in Germany deploy such solutions, while a further 24 percent are planning or discussing their use. As many as 74 percent of companies hope that using a private cloud will improve their access to IT resources, while three-quarters of users confirm that this goal has already been achieved (see Bitkom and KPMG 2015).
3. **"All is IP:"** The Internet Protocol (IP) has become the universal language of all communication processes. Instead of the devices of the relevant participants being connected directly as before, communication content is routed in data packages in an IP network. This conserves network resources and makes communication highly efficient. The packages may contain all manner of content – images, texts, videos; in effect, anything that can be digitalized. However, communication no longer solely takes place between people. In the Internet of Things, objects communicate with one another. Here, technology and usage are only in their infancy: Of the some 1.5 trillion objects on Earth that could in principle benefit from an IP address, just one percent are connected to the Internet, according to Roland Berger. It is not only smartphones and computers that use IPs; consumer electronics, communication devices, household devices, clothing, wearables, vehicles and many more objects can also speak this universal language. When the number of devices connected to the Internet reaches the 50 billion mark in 2020, just 17 percent of these devices will be computers or cell phones (see Kückelhaus 2015).
4. **"All is Secure:"** It is a fact that the number of devices connected via an IP is growing on an unimaginable scale. So, too, is the number of possible gateways for data thieves. The fourth aspect of digitalization has thus become the most important: What use is this promising new IP world if it is not secure? This has made the topic of security even more important for company managers.

No business owner can escape this trend. Whether digitalization is in fact worthwhile is no longer the issue – there is simply no way around it now. In this case, it is not the usual situation of large companies swallowing up the small ones; it is about the hare outstripping the tortoise – those who take too long to digitalize will lose out. For user companies the question is therefore not whether they need to digitalize but rather when, where and how securely they will digitalize. These are the decisive issues in the progressive process of connecting all the different devices in companies' distributed networks.

Given these exponentially growing potential gaps in security, how can a user company protect itself from unauthorized access? For providers of security solutions it is vital to understand users' concerns, anticipate them where possible and provide companies with solutions that are genuinely easy to use. What form do the user's digital processes take – a booking process, for instance? Generally speaking, many complex digital processes and mechanisms are used that need to be understood to give attackers no chance.

10.3   Digital Identity Is the New Currency

In the Internet age, the all-important currency is no longer money, but personal data that people divulge online and with which they then "pay" on the Internet, either consciously or unconsciously. But things can even be taken one step further: In the age of the insecure Internet the new currency is one's personal digital identity. Digital identities can take many different forms, and nowadays most people actually have a series of digital identities. People can reveal their identity in the digital world in the same way as in the real world. When users transfer money online, make online purchases, log into forums, social networks or email accounts, they authenticate themselves using a variety of methods. This is where mechanisms that assign individual attributes to a specific person come in. The user name/password combination is a common example (see Bundesdruckerei 2015).

Nowadays, even objects and companies have digital identities. This allows them to be clearly assigned in different process steps and to be traceable, for example in logistics or in Industry 4.0. They must be secured so that they cannot be falsified, manipulated or stolen – by criminals being able to gain access to them, for instance.

As a consequence, the protection of digital identities is closely intertwined with the protection of company data, because access to digital identity is what makes it possible to gain access to the heart of a company. The mechanisms for protection must be equally sophisticated. But how can non-experts know how best to protect themselves? This requires proven experts who ensure the protection of company networks including digital identities and business-critical data.

All-round protection like this is highly complex. However, the experts must not pass this complexity on to users. Their job is to dispel the users' fear of the apparently obscure technological steps in the background. Users should only become aware of the complexity – if at all – when switching a device on or off and as a plug-and-play approach – similar to the electricity that is fed to an appliance unnoticed. SMEs in particular need "plug-and-play security" that is available at all times, quickly and easily. Comprehensive protection for data, networks, applications, and digital identities must ultimately be possible with just a small number of settings. This is the only way data protection can work.

10.4 Does Absolute Protection Exist?

Anyone who has ever had anything to do with security is guided by two ambivalent objectives. On the one hand, they want to get a comprehensive view of a system including all its possible vulnerabilities and weak points, and do everything necessary to achieve this. On the other hand, they have the feeling – in spite of all the analyses and measures – of being absolutely defenseless against a previously unknown threat at the decisive moment. This is the conflict that practically all security experts experience. How can the best possible protection for a company be provided if the company is expanding at the same time and constantly adding new IP connections? After all, it is not only the data and applications that must be made secure, but also the networks on which these run.

There is one thing that all experts can confirm: No security expert in the world can ensure absolute – in other words 100 percent – protection, even with the most sophisticated methods and mechanisms. The reason for this is obvious: Hackers and intruders are constantly competing with the security experts, both sides racing to find solutions or counter-solutions, ideas or opposing ideas. Progressive security experts have therefore proceeded to use intelligent mechanisms not only to identify the patterns that make an attack successful, but also to select the patterns that were atypical or unknown up to now, and to study their harmfulness.

Conventional security technologies, comprising virus scanners, web proxies, and similar mechanisms, perform what are known as deep package inspections, sweeping the network traffic for known threats. If they find such a pattern, the relevant data package, such as an email attachment, is disallowed. These procedures reach their limits as soon as an unknown pattern appears. Using conventional technologies would unleash this potentially harmful pattern on the company. It is important to prevent this in every case, which is why experts have developed processes such as the sandboxing explained earlier. Preventive defense mechanisms must move away from pattern-based analytical procedures that look for known patterns toward mechanisms that hunt for unfamiliar code. In the process, the analysis is expanded to include all elements that are incorporated into the network.

One conceivable approach in this environment is continuous monitoring of mobile devices such as cell phones or tablets – somewhat along the lines of a continuous electrocardiogram for human beings. This would involve compromised devices raising the alarm at the system's control center and sending forensic data there for an analysis of the attack. Other responses to a threat such as notification of the user or other countermeasures via mobile device management solutions can be set up on a case-by-case basis.

Such "continuous ECG monitoring" of a cell phone draws on a great many different vectors and sounds the alarm when, for example, the battery discharges surprisingly rapidly, there is a sudden spike in the CPU load or an excessive amount of storage is used. Whenever something happens that is not in keeping with regular operations, the cell phone is blocked.

Ultimately, the aim is to develop an analytical method that identifies anomalies without initially defining these in more detail. While this still does not provide 100 percent protection, the monitoring of a system increases it to the maximum level possible. And what is possible for smartphones must also be feasible in corporate networks, even though the access scenarios there are considerably more sophisticated and distributed.

10.5   This Is What Attack Scenarios Look Like Today

Denial-of-service attacks show just how elementary an intelligent analysis is. The attack deliberately overloads the computer systems of companies and other organizations. The hacker world generally launches distributed denial-of-service attacks whereby the attack is executed by many different servers previously hijacked by the attacker. These are referred to as zombie hosts. The victim is besieged by large numbers of inquiries, leading to the use of defective IP packages, for instance, and then terminates the service due to overload.

Individual PCs that point the way to a larger, higher-level network are often interesting as a gateway for these attacks. If, for example, the network of a large online mail order company were to malfunction, losses running into millions of euros would be incurred within half an hour. The data stolen from customer bank data could be used to extort a significant amount of money.

Another example is "phishing," the aim of which is to obtain, among other things, online banking login data or other types of passwords. Here, attackers generally use emails that guide the victim to a malicious website or encourage them to open an infected file. Incidentally, according to the Advanced Threat Report by security experts FireEye (see FireEye 2016), malicious code is sent in zip files in over 90 percent of cases. Malicious code like malware has now also started to appear in seemingly harmless email attachments such as ".doc" or ".pdf". This may signal the beginning of an APT attack in which attackers attempt to gain access to corporate networks, identities, and data in several steps, sometimes over a period of several years. DLL files are also increasingly being used instead of the more usual EXE files as they ensure that infections remain undetected for longer.

In the case of malware, attempts are also made to circumvent the sandboxing. For example, incidents are known in which the malware only became active when the mouse was moved – it effectively hid behind the pointer. In addition, there is increased proliferation of malicious code that can identify virtual environments – if the virus believes itself to be in a sandbox, it simply remains inactive.

Attackers and defenders thus continue the hare and tortoise race described at the beginning – like in the case of the aforementioned ransomware "Locky" that caused a furor: This encryption Trojan even captured data from hospitals – both in Germany and in the United States – and tried to extort money from them. It could have been even worse: Not only had results to be communicated by telephone or fax for a while, but patient data could also have been manipulated or deleted – with really serious, i.e., life-threatening, consequences for those affected. Here, too, increased networking of (medical) devices – the Internet of Things – has beneficial goals, but also provides cybercriminals with a growing number of possibilities to access data.

With advanced persistent threat protection, which also prevents more complex access scenarios, the type of malicious code that had been unknown until that point could have been fished out and made harmless. This demonstrates that organizations which considered themselves secure in the past now need to revisit their security situation because the protection they established three, four or five years ago is now obsolete. IT managers and company directors are responsible for keeping the company's safeguards updated at all times and focusing on simplicity of use.

10.6 In Need of Improvement: Security at SMEs

Given the complexity of attacks these days and the defense mechanisms employed to counteract them, only specialists can keep on top of things. And specialists are now in short supply. SMEs and large companies alike are desperate to find suitable staff with the right skills to operate security systems under their own direction. However, these people are very difficult to find.

In many cases, SMEs therefore have little option but to outsource security to a trusted partner. In this respect, it has been found that the best protection against attacks from the Internet likewise comes from the Internet. With what are known as managed services, companies receive the all-round protection package from the cloud – for all targets in the company including the safeguarding of industrial networks and applications as well as the early identification and aversion of attacks. And they acquire all this without specially trained staff having to look after it – again, as quickly and easily as "plug-and-play security."

The mechanisms with which companies of any size protect themselves are nearly always the same. This is because the difference lies not in the attacks themselves, but in the size of the bandwidth of Internet traffic to be inspected. A set of tools comprising virus protection, firewalls, intrusion prevention, load balancer, web proxy, advanced persistent threat protection and some other procedures is generally used for this.

It is not uncommon for managers of SMEs to be overwhelmed by the complexity of the task. They are afraid to take the wrong step at a decisive moment. This often gives rise to security architectures that come in a variety of shapes and forms, are overly complex and heterogeneous and not always very efficient. It would be efficient to use security solutions that constitute "plug-and-play security" or solutions from the cloud. These can be ordered at the push of a button, are delivered as a package, preconfigured and self-installing.

10.7 Expensive Does Not Necessarily Mean Secure: Gaps in Security at Large Companies

Large companies have generally spent significant sums on their protection and therefore frequently consider themselves to be secure. After all, they opted for state-of-the-art technology. But for how long does technology remain state of the art? There is always an even better product out there, and so managers in these corporations spend their time trying to keep up with the latest international security trends. This takes effort and uses up resources.

Another challenge for large companies is that applications have often been written internally and are hosted in their own data center. These applications have always been called up in the company's internal network – because up to now the Internet has only been used for research purposes.

Back at the beginning of this century, security policies focused primarily on safeguarding the transition points from the corporate network to the Internet. Today, this situation is completely different. The Internet has gained immense importance and any number of business applications are available for use in the public cloud. A few of the many examples are the Telekom Cloud, Open Telekom Cloud, MS Office 365, Salesforce, and the Cisco InterCloud. Were companies to host such applications in their own data centers, a variety of measures would be needed – for secure access alone, a corporate security hub would have to be installed between the application and the workforce, for example. The security hub is a security solution that protects mobile devices from attacks and malicious code from the Internet; for this, all data traffic is analyzed in real time. Since large numbers of employees tend to access such applications, the hub must ensure appropriate bandwidth. Encryption of communication also requires a substantial investment and use of resources. Then there is mobile device management, mobile application management, and mobile content management.

Alternatively, companies can simply procure business applications that have been specially developed for their needs as services from the Internet. Users are given direct access to the applications. However, a smart security element from the cloud is installed in between, making the functions of a security hub available for bigger and more diverse user bases and for larger, more complex applications in big firms. This also lays the foundations for more sophisticated security projects.

10.8 The "Made in Germany" Stamp of Quality

It is clear that in the age of the digital transformation the cloud and security are inextricably linked. For a long time, the cloud had an image problem – not necessarily because it would be easy for hackers to break into, but rather because many offerings, particularly from the United States, are not immune to industrial espionage. This was found by the study entitled "IT-Sicherheit und Datenschutz 2016" presented by Germany's National Initiative for Information and Internet Security (NIFIS) (see NIFIS 2016) in the run-up to CeBIT 2016: "The study revealed that 87 percent of companies in Germany attach the greatest importance to their data not being stored on the servers of companies with parents or subsidiaries in the United States, in order to protect against spying. When contracting cloud services, 63 percent prefer to use German or at least European providers only."

Of the companies surveyed for the report entitled "Mobile Content Management in Deutschland 2016" (see IDC 2015), 82 percent stated that the location of the data center of a cloud provider in Germany had become extremely important to them. Both SMEs and large companies rely on providers that operate highly secure cloud data centers in Germany – and only store the data in Germany and in accordance with German legal requirements. It is generally known that Germany is the best place to protect data against unauthorized access due to the country's strict data protection regulations. Encryption of data is also allowed in Germany in contrast to many other countries.

Under data protection law, there are other essential requirements for highly secure data centers. For example, data centers should always have a redundant design so that the data is invariably stored in parallel – even in the event of a failure uninterrupted access to the data is provided on the twin. In addition, the goal should be the highest possible availability of 99.999 percent – the maximum achievable by today's technical means, which corresponds to around five minutes of downtime per year. All data in the data center flows through secured IP VPN tunnels, isolated from the public networks. This creates a closed system, fully guarded against external access. Ultra-modern encryption techniques ensure that data can be viewed by authorized parties only.

10.9   Companies Want the Cloud – But Securely

Cloud offerings furnish solutions to pressing problems of companies wishing to run their applications at minimal cost but also securely. Outsourcing spares them a lot of effort. In-house developments are expensive and lengthy, and they must also be scalable. Large international providers relieve companies of this burden. They give users access to the applications in the cloud and keep these up to date at all times. They also make investments in software and hardware unnecessary. This is a marked difference to the situation in the past, when administrators had to install the latest version of a software package locally on the employees' PCs, often using stacks of CDs.

The cloud makes life so much easier and flexible for IT departments, which is why it can no longer be halted. However, companies must be assured that their data will not spread there. The big challenge is to keep unauthorized parties from seeing this data. This is not just about secure transport routes, but also about access permissions, additional encryption of the data inside the cloud and other mechanisms to make unauthorized access as difficult as possible.

Companies are well advised to investigate a potential cloud provider thoroughly before signing a contract. Under what legislation does the provider operate? Is the potential partner company a German one? Healthcare organizations, for example, are not allowed to store their data outside national borders. Users must therefore take a close look at the provider and ask themselves what is particularly important with regard to the handling of the data (generally this is data protection). Last but not least, customers – especially small and medium-sized enterprises – should make sure that the security can be procured as quickly and easily as if it were plug-and-play security – without interrupting business processes and workflows, yet always unobtrusively in the background. After all, the risks and threats are invariably at the cutting edge of today's technology. Company managers would be wise to keep abreast of the risks at the same speed.

References

A.T. Kearney (2015). *Information security: It's all about trust.* Accessed April 20, 2016, from https://www.atkearney.de/pressemitteilung/-/asset_publisher/00OIL7Jc67KL/content/a-t-kearney-cyberangriffe-werden-in-zukunft-haufiger-und-folgenschwerer?_101_INSTANCE_00OIL7Jc67KL_redirect=%2Fnews-media

Bitkom (2015a). *Die größten Gefahren im Internet.* Accessed April 11, 2016, from https://www.bitkom.org/Presse/Pressegrafik/2015/Maerz/150327-Zehn-groesste-gefahren-Internet/150327-Gefahren-im-Internet.jpg

Bitkom (2015b). *Digitale Angriffe auf jedes zweite Unternehmen.* Accessed April 20, 2016, from https://www.bitkom.org/Presse/Presseinformation/Digitale-Angriffe-auf-jedes-zweite-Unternehmen.html

Bitkom, & KPMG (2015). *Cloud-Monitor 2015.* Accessed March 22, 2016, from https://www.bitkom.org/Publikationen/2015/Studien/Cloud-Monitor-2015/Cloud-Monitor-2015-KPMG-Bitkom-Research.pdf

Bundesamt für Sicherheit in der Informationstechnik (BSI) (2011). *Studie zur IT-Sicherheit in kleinen und mittleren Unternehmen.* Accessed April 11, 2016, from https://www.bsi.bund.de/DE/Publikationen/Studien/KMU/Studie_IT-Sicherheit_KMU.html

Bundesdruckerei (2015). *Was ist eine digitale Identität?* Accessed August 19, 2016, from https://www.bundesdruckerei.de/id-kompass/content/was-ist-eine-digitale-identitaet

Experton Group (2015). *Cloud vendor benchmark.* Accessed March 22, 2016, from http://www.experton-group.de/research/studien/cloud-vendor-benchmark-2015/ergebnisse.html

FireEye (2016). *Annual threat report.* Accessed April 11, 2016, from https://www.fireeye.com/current-threats/annual-threat-report.html

Heise.de (2016). *Krypto-Trojaner Locky wütet in Deutschland: Über 5000 Infektionen pro Stunde.* Accessed April 14, 2016, from http://www.heise.de/security/meldung/Krypto-Trojaner-Locky-wuetet-in-Deutschland-Ueber-5000-Infektionen-pro-Stunde-3111774.html

IDC (2013). *IDC-Studie: Halboffene Scheunentore – Viele Unternehmen in Deutschland zu sorglos bei IT-Security.* Accessed Aug 19, 2016, from http://idc.de/de/ueber-idc/press-center/56521-idc-studie-halboffene-scheunentorse-viele-unternehmen-in-deutschland-zu-sorglos-bei-it-security

IDC (2015). *Mobile content management in Deutschland 2016.* Accessed March 22, 2016, from http://idc.de/de/research/multi-client-projekte/mobile-content-management-in-deutschland-2016/mobile-content-management-in-deutschland-2016-projektergebnisse

Kückelhaus, M. (2015). *Das Unvernetzte vernetzen – das Internet der Dinge in der Logistik.* Accessed August 19, 2016, from https://www.delivering-tomorrow.com/connecting-the-unconnected-the-internet-of-things-in-logistics/

NIFIS (2015). M2M: *Experten warnen vor erheblichen Sicherheitsproblemen im Mittelstand.* Accessed August 19, 2016, from http://www.nifis.de/veroeffentlichungen/news/datum/2015/07/14/m2m-experten-warnen-vor-erheblichen-sicherheitsproblemen-im-mittelstand/

NIFIS (2016). *National initiative for information and internet security.* Accessed April 11, 2016, from http://www.nifis.de/

Roland Berger (2015). *Cyber-security – managing threat scenarios in manufacturing companies.* Accessed April 20, 2016, from http://www.internetworld.de/technik/cybercrime/cyberattacken-verursachen-milliardenschaeden-909741.html

T-Online (2016). Lösegeld-Trojaner – Geiselnehmer haben das Internet entdeckt. Accessed August 04, 2016, from http://www.t-online.de/computer/sicherheit/id_77197720/trojaner-locky-und-co-das-macht-ransomware-so-erfolgreich.html

techconsult (2015). *Security-Bilanz Deutschland.* Accessed April 11, 2016, from http://www.techconsult.de/studien/mobile-security-verursacht-grosse-probleme

Webtrekk (2016). Press release "Webtrekk Quartalsstatistik 2015 Q4: 49 % nutzen Tablets oder Smartphones für Online-Shopping." Accessed March 22, 2016, from https://www.webtrekk.com/fileadmin/PDFs/Press_releases_News/2016/DE/20160115_Webtrekk_DI_Statistik_Q4_2015_DE.pdf

Dirk Backofen has been Program Manager Portfolio Management, Engineering and Operations at Telekom Security since April 2016. In this role, he is responsible for the development of new security products as well as Magenta Security Portfolio Management at T-Systems International GmbH – a position that also involves the provisioning of products and solutions in line with T-Systems' Zero Impact strategy.

Backofen began his career with Deutsche Telekom in engineering in 1991. From 1995 onwards, he held a number of management positions in marketing at Deutsche Telekom. As Senior Vice President Portfolio Management, Presales and Marketing at Telekom Deutschland GmbH, Backofen was most recently involved in portfolio management for fixed-line, cellular and IT/cloud products for business customers. Dirk Backofen holds a degree in information technology, and is an alumni of Chemnitz University of Technology.

Cybersecurity - What's Next?

11

Thomas Tschersich

Companies hoping to successfully use the IT security technologies of the future need to rethink their strategy and shift their focus from a latent arms race aimed at protection against the outside world to detection within the enterprise. After all, every company needs to remember that an attacker will infiltrate its network sooner or later, as many recent examples have shown. The next step is to identify the attack as quickly as possible and remove the threat. In the future, smart data and artificial intelligence will be needed to provide this protection within organizations. Authorized users must be distinguished from attackers rapidly with easy-to-use or automated tools such as behavior-based analysis systems. Zero impact must be the goal. Yet, to understand how to get their company or any company to this point, executives always need to keep in mind how the current situation evolved.

11.1 The Motives of Attackers Are Becoming More Malicious with Each Passing Generation

From private users to companies to governmental organizations or NGOs, the range of potential data thieves is as diverse as the profiles of the participants in global data traffic. Quite a few of today's victims will be the attackers of tomorrow – although unknowingly in many cases. In spite of all the complexity, one thing has always been certain: Nobody enjoys absolute protection against anybody on the other side of the fence. This is something that US security firm HBGary Federal experienced for itself.

Its CEO Aaron Barr had stated very publicly in an interview in the Financial Times that he had infiltrated Anonymous in a month-long campaign and could now

T. Tschersich (✉)
Deutsche Telekom AG, Friedrich-Ebert-Allee 140, 53113 Bonn, Germany
e-mail: thomas.tschersich@telekom.de

© Springer International Publishing AG 2017
F. Abolhassan (ed.), *Cyber Security. Simply. Make it Happen.*, Management for Professionals, DOI 10.1007/978-3-319-46529-6_11

identify all leading members of this group of activists for the FBI (see Menn 2011). Less than 24 hours later, Anonymous retaliated with the theft of 60,000 emails by HBGary's management, disclosing a thorough list of the company's appalling gaps in security. In addition to technical vulnerabilities, these included simple behavioral errors – for example, even the top brass at HBGary such as CEO Aaron Barr and his Chief Operations Officer always used the same, very simple passwords not only for their private email, Twitter, and LinkedIn accounts, but also for the company's key systems (see Schmidt 2011).

Up until about fifteen years ago, when cybercrime or, more precisely, IT security was still in its infancy, hackers were motivated by fame and glory, along the lines of "Look what I can do!" or "Look what I found!" Back then, hacking was not yet about online crime per se, though the foundations for this had been laid. It is only in the last decade or so that we have seen this adaptation of cybercriminal behavioral patterns by, in many cases, organized groups or hacker collectives who are in it for the money on a massive scale. In other words: There has been a commercialization of cybercrime. Phishing emails, DDoS attacks on online shops or the dissemination of SPAM suddenly became the tools of choice in "areas of business" such as fraud, extortion or money laundering.

In the third wave, about five years ago, came the hacktivists, who for politically motivated reasons turned into cyberattackers. DDoS attacks against banks that had blocked the accounts of the whistleblowing platform Wikileaks and attacks paralyzing companies' data traffic in the form of "digital sit-ins" are some of the instruments they use to spread their social, economic or broadly political messages.

Recently, attention has been drawn in particular to state actors, not least as a result of the Snowden leaks. While intelligence agencies have also moved around in cyberspace from year one, in terms of public awareness one can definitely consider the youngest "generation" of cybercriminals to be those who scour the Internet in search of potential targets for acts of sabotage or for the procurement of information under orders from the state or for the purpose of industrial espionage. "Stuxnet" (see New York Times 2016) and "Red October" (see Kaspersky Lab 2013) are just two examples of attacks – allegedly by intelligence agencies or state-controlled organizations – that made headlines around the world.

Admittedly, none of the types of crime and attacks described above are new. But in their order of appearance corresponding peaks have formed. In short, the following assertions can be made:

- The motives and characters of the attackers have changed.
- The attacks are leading to higher and higher financial losses at companies each year. According to security experts, these may currently be as much as 575 billion US dollars and are therefore causing more damage than global drug-related crime (see Bauer 2014).
- The methods and tools used by all groups of perpetrators have remained very similar.
- Yet the resources and the effort in the background differ substantially.

The last point was clearly illustrated by thefts of data such as in the case of Wikileaks or, more recently, the Panama Papers, as compared with attacks like Stuxnet. While in one case it was employees with administrator rights who facilitated the data leak, in other cases attacks use special software that has been developed for this purpose over many years. It is all a question of opportunity, specifically of funding. Using the example of state agencies, there is the telling fact that (according to Wikileaks) the budgets of the five US secret services – CIA, NSA, and Co. – were 45.2 billion US dollars for 2013 alone (see Zeit online 2013). It is a sum that significantly exceeds the annual revenue of quite a few German blue chip companies.

Just how much funding is available to all cyberattackers worldwide does not bear thinking about. The following fact also shows the clear disparities between the concerns of potential attackers and those of their possible victims: A company like Deutsche Telekom must protect over 3,000 proprietary systems directly connected to the Internet in Germany alone, whereas a hacker needs to crack only one of these systems to be successful.

The attacks will become more radical. In the beginning, most attacks were intrusive, with the unwelcome perpetrators simply being satisfied with penetrating the company's line of defense. However, ever since the start of this decade attacks have become increasingly disruptive, compromising the availability of the systems attacked and generally interrupting, blocking or sabotaging their traffic. Digital extortion combined with a ransom demand is the objective of many of these attacks. Attack scenarios in the future, however, will increasingly target the integrity of the data. In other words: While up to now groups of attackers always sought to exploit data in its present form or to impede its availability or communication, the attacks of the future – which scarcely feature today – will be aimed at modifying the data. This will completely transform the risk landscape.

Interference with road traffic is just one example. Remote attacks on cars, their braking performance, sudden failure of wipers or the lighting system – not to mention self-driving cars – could have fatal consequences. The same goes for the manipulation of data in the healthcare system, where, for example, a patient's blood group could be changed in the course of the transfer of the patient's data shortly before an operation. It is very easy to imagine the potential consequences of malpractice during attacks on several hospitals in the German federal state of North Rhine-Westphalia at the beginning of 2016. The worst were only averted because the perpetrators were solely interested in a ransom. As the State Office of Criminal Investigations reported, physicians were unable to continue treating their patients due to data not being available (see Polizei/Landeskriminalamt Nordrhein-Westfalen 2016).

Security homework – or the worst mistakes made by companies. One of the first and most important things that companies need to change is their defense policy, followed by their ecosystem. The next step is to consider everything that needs to be protected in the future. The vast majority of companies protect PCs and servers, and most users also have virus protection, at least for their PCs. The first gaps in security appear when it comes to installing software updates, because this is seen as overly complicated and time-consuming. Although operating systems may actually be updated regularly and promptly, companies often fail to update application software, which may have equally critical security issues. What is more, the update cycles at companies are frequently far too slow. This enables attackers to exploit new gaps on a massive scale just hours after they become known, as companies frequently only implement manufacturers' updates weeks or months after their release. Not to mention that there is also a whole series of other IT systems such as cell phones, system controls, etc., most of which are still left out of the equation entirely. Such carelessness, once discovered by cybercriminals, is almost an invitation for attackers and makes one thing clear: Security and laissez-faire are two irreconcilable worlds.

The fact that this understanding has still not become entrenched in people's minds is one of the main reasons why – in 84 percent of the cases investigated in a study last year by the US telecommunications group Verizon – it took attackers only a few hours to prepare an attack and subsequently reach the actual target system. By contrast, in 62 percent of the cases the attacks were not identified by the companies themselves until months later (see Verizon 2016).

Significantly larger gaps in corporate security will be caused in the future due to the fact that we still regard the smartphone as a telephone rather than a computer. In this connection, people still completely underestimate how quickly smartphones can be turned into remote-controlled cyberweapons to be misused as a listening device, to access photos and videos or to serve as a Bluetooth interface to the user's peripheral application systems.

Cell phones are an even more attractive target for hackers who harness these devices for botnets, for instance, in order to launch automated attacks against third parties from a network of externally controlled devices or computers. Botnets are used for distributed denial of service (DDoS) attacks against websites or other services, for example. Ultimately, hackers can thus paralyze any e-commerce platform with just ten captured smartphones. One of the methods used for this is the NTP reflection attack (see Akamai Technologies 2015), in which the Network Time Protocol standard used to synchronize the time of computer systems is abused to prompt one server to attack other servers in the Internet with NTP packages (see NTP 2016).

What do attackers need to carry out such attacks? – High bandwidth and a low level of protection. Very few smartphones these days have security software, but they have far superior bandwidth to most PCs. What also plays into the hands of criminals is open architectures such as in Google's Android operating system. Owing to the Americans' business model of monetarizing user behavior and user data in advertising, for which a lot of content is generated from any number of sources, Android, the smartphone operating system with a market share of over 80 percent, is becoming an open invitation to any criminal. It took around 14 years for 450,000 malware versions to be identified in the Windows operating system, but not even 10 months for this to happen in Android.

Companies that give their employees iPhones for work purposes should not feel any safer. Even though Apple's operating system is more homogeneous and its architecture affords better protection because the business model works differently from Google's, it is not perfect either. One of the reasons for this is the ever-popular practice of jail breaking, which involves removing the restrictions imposed by a cell phone manufacturer – in this case Apple – in order to download software to an iOS phone from alternative marketplaces instead of using the Apple Store.

Tests we performed showed that a jailbroken iPhone connected to the Internet suffered around 300,000 automated attacks in one year. About 330 of these attacks were so successful that the attackers were able to move around freely in the system of the phone we had designed as a honeypot. But especially in the areas of jailbreaking and rooting, not everything is black or white: By obtaining elevated privileges to their device, experienced users can also raise their level of security – if they know what they are doing. In addition, there is a lively CustomRom scene that also develops operating systems with the latest security updates for many of the popular models.

Yet even iPhones that have not been jailbroken are not immune to being hacked. In an analysis of Operation Pawn Storm, which has been running worldwide for four years now (see Trend Micro 2014), Security company Trend Micro (see Trend Micro 2015) discovered a tool that was specially designed for iOS phones (see iPhone Ticker 2015). This extensive malware campaign is directed at companies as well as at the political organizations and the military in different countries. The target persons are never attacked directly. Instead, the hackers attempt to initially infect the communication devices of other people from their target's personal or business environments, obviously based on the idea that a subsequent attack or the transmission of malicious software via news or emails from trusted sources has significantly greater chances of success. That is why this approach is called "pawn storm" after the chess strategy.

Cheap smartphones, put on the market by the manufacturer at a particularly reasonable price but not receiving any further security updates, constitute a fundamental problem, not just for companies. Here, what is needed is a policy that requires all manufacturers to ensure security updates throughout a phone's life, which generally lasts at least two years.

In the future, gaps in our defense will also show that we underestimate the growing risk of increased networking. Be it air-conditioning systems and elevators in companies or household appliances such as fridges, televisions etc., many of the devices that can be networked today were not originally designed for this purpose at all. In most cases, the software is installed in these devices during production; interaction with the user – e.g., for update installation – is not envisaged or not possible. Consequently, protection for these devices must come from the network. Going forward, security solutions that are incorporated into network infrastructures will therefore have even greater significance than today.

The traditional perimeter approach adopted by companies of building their castle walls increasingly higher, wider and thicker led to companies continuously investing in security. Ultimately, though, they were only ever able to maintain the status quo and therefore hardly able to achieve their goal of increasing the level of protection. Instead of being forced to spend money on repairing damage, they should free up resources whose investment actually improves their own security. But how does this square with the growing need for security from the network? As easy as it may sound, the first step is finally to do our old, but perennial homework and to continue to do this without fail.

11.2 Cybersecurity – The Sleeping Giant in the Company

A successful defense against cybercrime is based on three pillars: prevention, detection, reaction. I would go so far as to say that at least 95 percent of the millions upon millions of cyberattacks that are carried out around the world each day would come to nothing if companies took the basic rules of prevention to heart. The fact that end users and unfortunately also companies (because they dread the effort involved in testing) do not implement software updates as quickly as possible and, after putting them off several times, eventually end up letting things slide is by far the greatest vulnerability.

In addition, most of the attacks that exploit the gap created by missing software updates follow a set pattern: The fundamental principle of the protection concepts in the company is based on the fact that there is an internal (trusted) infrastructure and an (untrusted) outside world. Broadly speaking, these worlds are separated using firewalls. The principle governing these firewalls is simple: Everything coming from outside is "bad" by definition and is blocked, whereas everything that comes from within the company is good and is allowed to happen. This is where attackers begin. Using social engineering, the environment of potential addressees is spied out using enticing emails which successfully function as bait – if not on the first or second attempt, then on the third or fourth attempt – essentially by awakening the recipient's interest so that they read the email and open the attachment that is generally enclosed. This may be a PDF that looks completely normal but immediately executes malicious software in the background, downloading a Trojan from the network and installing it automatically.

Unfortunately, neither of these steps raises any suspicions for conventional firewalls. This is because emails per se are treated as a communication channel that is always kept open to the outside world. Moreover, a Trojan is downloaded by means of an action that is initiated by the computer from the inside and is therefore classified as "okay" by the firewall, as would be expected from it. Having penetrated the castle walls in this way, every attacker has free access to the system. Getting from the attacked computer to the file server, where data is spied out, exfiltrated, and the attacker's tracks are obliterated, is a process that in some cases takes no more than a few minutes. With one fatal consequence: While the firewall as the "castle wall" continues to defend the perimeter, the attacker is now in the house and can move around freely.

APT detection solutions provide help here. APT stands for Advanced Persistent Threat, effectively a permanent individual vulnerability. Solutions like Fire Eye, which review the behavior of all incoming emails and any attachments enclosed, provide protection. If the behavior of the emails being examined is inconspicuous, these are effectively waved through after being checked in a virtual machine. However, if the file being examined suddenly starts to develop unexpected activities such as wanting to install software updates or change the operating system or the configuration, Fire Eye assumes that this file has been manipulated by malicious functionality and blocks it. The entire check is performed in milliseconds without causing a perceptible delay in email traffic for the owner of the mailbox. In terms of functionality, the safeguards that will be needed in the networks in the future are vastly different from the long-established "castle walls." Future security models will be based on the behavior of software rather than on the principle of admission control at the wall.

A second new way of protecting company networks is by using sensor technology like in alarm systems. All PCs could also be fitted with sensors, just like every smartphone today – for example to receive GPS signals or capture data on health or environmental data. These sensors can continuously review incoming and outgoing data traffic and attachments, files, etc. for conspicuous behavior, identify anomalies immediately, and report them to a central instance. In many company networks, for example, there is no direct client-to-client communication. If a PC starts contacting another PC directly without going via the email server or group shares, this can only mean one of two things for a security officer who has been alerted by an alarm triggered through corresponding sensors: Either an employee introduced a service and forgot to tell anyone about it, or an attacker is moving sideways in the network from one PC to the next.

Although such sensory solutions for detection purposes are unable to reverse the attack, which may have taken place long before, they can minimize its effects. This is no mere small comfort, because these days no company should assume that it can permanently protect itself against attacks. Today, every security officer's goal must be zero impact, in other words, reducing the repercussions of attacks to zero. To this end, a logical step, which at the same time entails a radical change in IT security overall, is to move away in the future from a purely preventive approach and to equally divide capital expenditure on security between detection and reaction.

Before this happens, however, it can be assumed that the preferred (and simple) method among attackers of exploiting the fact that software updates have not been installed will remain successful for quite some time – simply because users lack the necessary awareness, be it at work or in their own personal environment. This, in my opinion, may be the main reason why cybercriminals always seem to use Formula 1 cars, while the security experts – usually unnecessarily – trail after them in Bobby cars.

In the past, it normally took months to find out which vulnerability was closed by an update and then to develop an exploit (attack tool) for this. Through reverse engineering, which makes the original program code and therefore also the measure implemented for its improvement easier to extract, this now takes the underground economy not even half a day. On average, only a few hours elapse between the supply of a patch for the vulnerability and the large-scale, fully automated use of tools that can exploit an identified vulnerability. For companies and the providers that protect them, this means that the time frame for an appropriate reaction is relatively minute. Speed is of the essence here. Relying on the virus protection installed on each company PC does not provide adequate assurance, as this only recognizes threats that are already known to it. However, when criminals use an exploit for the first time – or possibly once only – the chances of this being detected are virtually zero. This is because virus protection works along the same lines as a police fingerprint file. If a method, a line of attack or a perpetrator has already appeared, the virus protection will be able to identify it. Otherwise, there is not a chance. This means that malicious software of which the antivirus industry is not yet aware may "work" for months before being exposed. When the update is installed at some stage and sounds the alarm – "malicious software on this computer" – it is often far too late.

This makes it very important for companies to be able to keep track of how long malicious software was actually active. It may require a great deal of time and effort to eliminate all of the damage because attackers naturally know that their "break-in" through the front door – via email access – will be discovered sooner or later and be blocked by the software update. This is why they generally use the time to set up their own back entrances and exits. Identifying these is extremely time-consuming and nearly impossible in some cases. In the attack on the German Bundestag, in which hackers gained access to 14 parliament servers in May 2015 (see Zeit online 2016), the computer system had to be set up again from scratch (see Holland 2015). In cases of doubt, this is actually the last remaining useful measure to at least bring the traditional hare-and-tortoise game between attackers and victims back to the starting line.

Unfortunately, in the reality of business every update is considered a brake, true to the motto "never touch a running system." The real message should be that people who do not install software updates promptly only have themselves to blame. To put it plainly: it is a worthwhile investment. This is because simple updates are the key to foiling virtually all attacks with the exception of zero-day exploits.

11.3   What Will Protect Us?

The first step is to create a much better awareness of threats. In many companies these days, investment decisions about IT security are made by managers who throughout their career – apart from using their PC – have had nothing whatsoever to do with IT, never mind IT security. IT security is normally studied as part of a computer science degree – but is actually an interdisciplinary topic spanning all sectors, i.e., all courses of study. A mechanical engineering contractor who installs remote maintenance modules in his equipment is taking a quantum leap in terms of servicing. This is called predictive maintenance. The only thing he is generally unable to guess is how the module will function and what scope for attack his equipment will provide at any given time.

However, as IT security is an issue that affects everybody, from the janitor up to the CEO, and as everyone will be a link in the security system of their future employer, this subject should already be firmly anchored in school curricula. It not only hones people's security awareness, but also trains them to keep in mind at all times that every hacked PC is a potential cyberweapon against third parties. Continuously sharpening this awareness, also in employees' personal spheres, will need to become an important part of companies' defense strategy. The effects will be twofold: Companies will reduce the possible scope for attack against themselves and will increase the motivation of employees to address this issue – even more so when those employees see there is something to be gained in their private IT lives, too.

When it comes to concrete solutions, a whole series of solutions can be identified. Encryption will be the technology of choice in the future for protecting the integrity of data. It effectively provides secure transportation for the data. It would never occur to the central bank to transport pallets with gold bars or the latest generation of freshly printed 20 euro bills on flatbed trucks on the public highway. However, this is precisely what we do in the digital world. What applies to virtually all security applications also applies here. When their use is to be mandatory – keyword "user acceptance" – defense and protection solutions such as encryption must fulfill three requirements: easy to procure, easy to implement and easy to use – ideally even running automatically.

In order to provide optimum protection for the email gateway, as mentioned before, behavioral analyses in the network or in virtual machines are particularly suitable for advanced persistent threats (APTs) that use malware, possibly individually tailored for just one person. Whether in large corporations, SMEs or start-ups – cutting-edge technologies as potential prey make it worthwhile for criminals to invest a great deal of time and effort in developing tools, even though these might only be used once for one specific purpose.

In the future, sensor technology in the network will also be essential for detecting and remedying conspicuous client-to-client communication, for instance, as quickly as possible through behavioral analyses. Cybersecurity sensors like honeypots will take on greater importance, not only at strategic points in the company network but in all devices (smartphones), computers, and equipment. This is because nobody is capable of analyzing over 400,000 new variants of malware every day, as now registered worldwide by the antivirus industry. For this reason, behavior-based detection will play a key role in the future for initiating fully-automated defense mechanisms. If sensors are to be extensively employed, however, the hardware industry has a particular responsibility to make the first move. "One sensor for each PC" must be the standard in the future.

Rethinking a company's own security practice must also involve systematically keeping critical and uncritical applications apart and fitting each component with sensors and safeguards. The exchange of data between systems should always be authenticated in every case.

A future trend will be that security is set to become a component of the data itself rather than of the infrastructure that transports and processes the data. Digital rights management (DRM) technologies are one example, ensuring that data cannot be viewed or modified during transfer and could thus also be given a kind of digital best-before date. Data or documents themselves will then contain information as to who is authorized to access and modify them. This will progressively reduce the importance of the infrastructure in guaranteeing security. At least in terms of approach, the photo service Snapchat provides an example of an alternative, deleting a photo once it has been viewed by the recipient. This is a useful feature – and not only for potentially embarrassing selfies.

In addition to all of the new technical possibilities, it is also important to keep the castle walls high, at least to ward off intruders, but to no longer exclusively rely on them for protection.

Otherwise, I believe that two ideas are especially important. Firstly, keeping silent about having fallen victim to a cyberattack should be a thing of the past for companies. Let's rather view it as joining the club. The list of companies already in the club is effectively a Who's Who of international industry. And who believes that any company is unassailable?

This idea leads on to the next one: Why shouldn't potential victims of cybercrime not join forces just like the attackers do? After all, I believe that security is for sharing. Sharing at many different levels, from the Cyber Security Sharing and Analytics (CSSA) platform, on which the largest German blue chips already share their experience and information about new methods and types of attack with one another (see CSSA 2016), to the operations of the cyberdefence centers of major providers. Once these have initially identified the attack and the underlying tool at just one of their customers, the security solution implemented for defense purposes is automatically transferred to all of the other customers. This form of digital neighborhood watch will allow us to implement better defense strategies more easily overall.

One aspect that in my experience tends to be neglected by companies in nearly all security discussions at C-level is the nonetheless obvious consideration of where administrators stand in the company hierarchy and salary structure. This is because the objective of all attacks is to gain administrative rights – giving any attacker "carte blanche." Companies may be making a strategic mistake in keeping the employees with the highest authorization level ("they are allowed to do more than any CEO") and who know every IT secret – in other words, the "Access Almighty" – at the lowest level of the hierarchy in some cases. Here, I would urgently advise checking to what extent it is recommendable for such employees to be promoted in line with their level of responsibility and the value they add for the company. This might keep the scope for attack that vital bit lower.

Urgent need for action – Yet even the supposed all-inclusive package still has gaps when it comes to providing security for the future. Security officers claim to have rightly complained: "If everything were encrypted, it would be impossible to identify malware in the network." Unfortunately, though this is true, who says it will always be the case? Developing technologies that overcome this obstacle should be a future research assignment for IT chairs the world over.

11.4   Conclusion

From my point of view, companies are well advised to stay with what has been proven to work (and also implement it properly), but to implement many new measures and solutions at the same time. In companies' protection concepts, internal sensor technology – the installation of sensors in practically all hardware used – is only in its infancy. However, this technology is necessary to ensure that future security models work and new job norms such as "bring your own device" do not turn into "bring your own disaster."

Where appropriate, small and medium-sized enterprises (SMEs) and other companies should replace their own in-house security operations center with external cyberdefense centers that work with broader analytical capabilities, forensics, hunter teams and anomaly recognition on the basis of sensors and logic; with the objective of deriving preventive solutions and defense mechanisms from these and initiating them immediately.

Companies should seriously consider the benefit of the swarm intelligence amassed by a service provider who protects many systems, has the specialists for this, and averts threats that arise at a given point for everyone in an automated manner. Companies that are not there yet should at least use the knowledge available in their own community – that of the potential victims. This is because, despite all competitive thinking, companies will always remain a community. And, last but not least – patch, patch, patch.

References

Akamai Technologies (2015). *Reflection-Techniken für DDoS-Angriffe*. Accessed May 18, 2016, from http://www.itseccity.de/virenwarnung/statistiken/akamai110215.html
Bauer, H.-P. (2014). Mehr Schaden durch Cyberkriminalität als durch Drogenhandel. Interview in Manager Magazin. Accessed May 18, 2016, from http://www.manager-magazin.de/unternehmen/it/enormes-wachstum-cyberkriminalitaet-ueberholt-drogenhandel-a-976184.html
CSSA (2016). Website. Accessed May 18, 2016, from http://www.cssa.de/
Holland, M. (2015). *Nach Bundestag-Hack: Parlament bekommt neue IT-Sicherheitsstruktur*. Accessed May 18, 2016, from http://www.heise.de/newsticker/meldung/Nach-Bundestags-Hack-Parlament-bekommt-neue-IT-Sicherheitsstruktur-2810587.html
iPhone Ticker (2015). *Operation Pawn Storm: Malware zielt auf iOS-Geräte ohne Jailbreak*. Accessed May 18, 2016, from http://www.iphone-ticker.de/operation-pawn-storm-malware-zielt-auf-ios-geraete-ohne-jailbreak-77204/
Kaspersky Lab (2013). Kaspersky Lab Identifies Operation "Red October," an Advanced Cyber-Espionage campaign targeting diplomatic and government institutions worldwide. Accessed May 18, 2016, from http://www.kaspersky.com/about/news/virus/2013/Kaspersky_Lab_Identifies_Operation_Red_October_an_Advanced_Cyber_Espionage_Campaign_Targeting_Diplomatic_and_Government_Institutions_Worldwide
Menn, J. (2011). *Cyberactivists warned of arrest*. Accessed May 18, 2016, from http://www.ft.com/intl/cms/s/0/87dc140e-3099-11e0-9de3-00144feabdc0.html#axzz490kpLOzQ
New York Times (2016). *Cyberattacks on Iran – Stuxnet and Flame*. Accessed May 18, 2016, from http://www.nytimes.com/topic/subject/cyberattacks-on-iran-stuxnet-and-flame

NTP (2016). *Website des Network Time Protocol Projekts.* Accessed May 18, 2016, from http://www.ntp.org/

Polizei/Landeskriminalamt Nordrhein-Westfalen (2016). *Cybercrime-Angriffe auf Infrastrukturen von Krankenhäusern, Behörden, Unternehmen.* Accessed May 18, 2016, from https://www.polizei.nrw.de/lka/artikel__13193.html

Schmidt, J. (2011). *Ausgelacht.* Anonymous kompromittiert US-Sicherheitsfirma. Accessed May 18, 2016, from http://www.heise.de/ct/artikel/Ausgelacht-1195082.html

Trend Micro (2014). Pawn Storm Espionage Attacks Use Decoys, Deliver SEDNIT. Accessed May 18, 2016, from http://www.trendmicro.com/vinfo/us/security/news/cyber-attacks/pawn-storm-espionage-attacks-use-decoys-deliver-sednit

Trend Micro (2015). *Pawn Storm Update: iOS Espionage App Found.* Accessed May 18, 2016, from http://blog.trendmicro.com/trendlabs-security-intelligence/pawn-storm-update-ios-espionage-app-found/

Verizon (2016). *Cybersecurity's most comprehensive investigations report.* Accessed May 18, 2016 from http://www.verizonenterprise.com/verizon-insights-lab/dbir/

Zeit online (2013). *Geheimes Budget von US-Nachrichtendiensten veröffentlicht.* Accessed May 18, 2016, from http://www.zeit.de/digital/datenschutz/2013-08/geheimdienste-haushalt-snowden-nsa-cia

Zeit online (2016). *Hackerangriff wurde aus Russland gesteuert.* Accessed May 18, 2016, from http://www.zeit.de/digital/2016-01/hackerangriff-bundestag-russland-nachrichtendienst-bundesanwaltschaft

Thomas Tschersich As Senior Vice President Group Security Service at Deutsche Telekom AG, Thomas Tschersich is responsible both for cybersecurity and all other operational security topics in the Group. Since April 2016, he has also led the Internal Security and Cyber Defense team for the future Telekom Security unit. In this position, he directs high-level services for the new unit and is responsible for strengthening internal hazard control and managing the external launch of the Telekom's cyberdefense portfolio. With Telekom Security, Deutsche Telekom is bringing together security teams from across the group.

Since joining Deutsche Telekom, Tschersich has established a Group-wide security team and held a number of roles, including Senior IT Security and Information Security Officer at Group HQ, as well as managing the Security Strategy and Policy unit in the core Group Security division and the Technical Security Services unit within Group Business Security. In February 2009, Tschersich was appointed Senior Vice President Group IT Security – the cybersecurity unit within Deutsche Telekom. In this role, he has Group-wide responsibility for the security of production and IT infrastructure. Alongside his work at Deutsche Telekom, Tschersich also sits on numerous committees as an advisor to the German Federal Government and the European Parliament.

Conclusion

12

Ferri Abolhassan

12.1 The Internet Has Become Ubiquitous

Within a few short years, the Internet has fundamentally changed the way we live, work and perceive our surroundings. According to the German digital association Bitkom, using the Internet is now more or less a daily routine for most Europeans: "Three out of four EU citizens between the ages of 16 and 74 (76 percent) go online at least once a week" (Bitkom 2016). In Germany, the average is actually 84 percent. The Internet has thus become part of our everyday lives. We surf, chat and play there. We book trips, buy insurance and transfer money. Digitalization has taken hold wherever apps have made services faster, easier and cheaper than conventional offerings.

The advantages of digitalization are even more tangible and extensive in the business world. The Internet of Things alone is revolutionizing entire business models and processes. "Faster, more efficient and more flexible," is the motto when it comes to accessing real-time maintenance data from machines, for example, or logistics data from transported goods. Or when big, traditional, global banks work together with alternative payment providers such as PayPal or new financial services companies – the dynamic "fintechs" – in order to jointly develop offers for bank customers. One thing is certain: Digitalization has led to exponential growth in the volume of data, and thus in the lures of abusing this data – either by hackers and their ilk, or by intelligence services who disregard the right to informational self-determination and preservation of the private sphere.

F. Abolhassan (✉)
Telekom Deutschland GmbH, Bonn, North Rhine-Westphalia, Germany
e-mail: ferri.abolhassan@telekom.de

© Springer International Publishing AG 2017
F. Abolhassan (ed.), *Cyber Security. Simply. Make it Happen.*, Management for Professionals, DOI 10.1007/978-3-319-46529-6_12

12.2   Good Internet, Bad Internet

John Doe and even corporate employees and executives might like to close their eyes to the hazards of the Internet and ignore the risks inherent in handling digital information every day, but one user group has long been aware of the Internet's value potential: cybercriminals. They have a decisive advantage here. As opposed to crimes in "real life," online crimes are much less dangerous for them. If a theft is discovered at all, it is usually only after some time has passed. And there is no need to fear being apprehended with a loaded gun and thus facing risk to life and limb. As a consequence, the biggest bank robberies these days are digital. For example, the Carbanak gang was able to steal up to one billion US dollars worldwide from around 100 financial institutions in the space of about two years. They committed the biggest online bank heist of all time. And according to the latest information, the criminals have not yet been stopped (see Computerwelt 2016).

After seeing attacks such as these covered by the media, every last user and IT officer must now be aware of one thing: Data is exposed to very high risks online. For this reason, extensive protective measures must be taken to ensure its safety. And yet, most users still do little or nothing. Why is that? For the majority, especially private consumers, security measures seem too expensive and complicated. "Things have been fine so far," they think. So why bother with the latest encryption solution, firewall or a new password? What's even more concerning is that the situation is not much better in industry. Many companies are not sufficiently protected against attacks by cybercriminals. And in companies, too, people are often the weak points. What good is the best firewall if a user reveals personal login data over the phone to someone claiming to be from IT support? Or when someone finds a USB stick at a trade fair and tests it on their office computer, just out of curiosity? In the case of social engineering attacks such as these, the only thing that usually helps is a short, sharp shock – that is, confronting users with their mistakes through simulated attacks, combined with subsequent risk training. But very few companies – not to mention private users – have reached this point yet. Urgent action is needed here.

12.3   Cyberhare vs. Cybertortoise

The high speed and dynamics of digitalization suit the schemes of cybercriminals. Digital transformation moves more quickly than people or the society we live in, and it moves much more quickly than legislation. The law appears very antiquated indeed in the face of the quantum leaps made by digitalization in recent years. And legislators have realized that data protection regulations no longer meet current requirements. Thanks to the IT security law that came into force in July 2015, Germany is a pioneer in cybersecurity legislation, with extensive reporting requirements for the operators of critical infrastructures. However, the EU-wide harmonization of regulations demands even more work from everyone involved. Another set of rules will come into play with the new EU data protection directive, which is due to take effect in 2018. Here, too, IT officers must keep their fingers on the pulse of development in order to stay abreast of what is required and what is prohibited.

But private Internet users and companies are not the only ones affected. Cyberthreats have long had global political dimensions. We need look no further than the hacker attacks on globally important critical infrastructures, the online recruitment of jihadi fighters, and autonomous weapons systems. Here, too, the barriers to entry for cyberwarriors are much lower than they would be in a traditional battlefield situation. Not just anyone can build an atomic bomb, but anyone can develop a virus or gain access to an insecure password. These possibilities have fundamentally changed the nature of modern conflict. The attack scenarios call for worldwide security alliances, and they are forcing even global organizations to take action. NATO, for instance, recently declared the Internet to be an independent theater of operations, and attacks via data networks are treated in the same way as those by land, sea or air forces. If such virtual attacks were to take place, they could even trigger NATO's collective defense article. The threshold for this has not yet been defined. But there is no doubt that these threats are being taken very seriously.

The German armed forces are also employing more cyberspecialists to protect themselves as well as possible from the continuously growing threat. However, it is not clear where this large number of required cyberexperts will come from because – as if there were not already enough to do in the field of IT security – such experts are in short supply. This affects every industry as well as organizations and companies of every size. But the problems are particularly acute among small and medium-sized enterprises. Though the first security-specific courses at universities are already available, it will take a good deal of time to train a sufficient number of experts in the long run. Additionally, this training is more demanding than other subjects, where the same syllabus can be used for years. Since the threats from cybercriminals evolve so rapidly, security experts must be trained in an equally dynamic way so that they are always up to date.

Security experts and legal regulations are not the only things in short supply. A valid, resilient strategy for dealing with emergencies is also lacking. Very few CEOs or CIOs know how to respond properly to a cyberattack. They would do well to deal with this problem, however, because depending on the legal structure of a company, its management may be held personally responsible if the company's risk management system fails. This in itself gives management the opportunity to hone its responsiveness and cybersecurity strategy. By applying military methods such as red teaming or wargaming to the business world, dangerous real-world situations can be simulated dynamically, so that the interaction of internal teams can be tested without risk. A comprehensive risk management strategy is also critical for large international companies whose global activities mean they must take numerous regulatory and legal IT security requirements into account. The situation is even more difficult if they serve different B2B and B2C customer groups and work with diverse partners and suppliers. The resulting complexity of their IT landscape raises the potential threat to almost unimaginable levels. Risk management goes a long way toward helping companies maintain an overview in the face of this.

Cooperation with other large corporations is another opportunity available to CEOs and CIOs. Associations such as Cyber Security Sharing and Analytics (CSSA) work closely together so that their members can mutually warn each other of potential attacks ahead of time. And they are extremely successful at it: During the "DDoS for Bitcoins" wave of extortion in 2015, for example, potential damages in the millions were prevented when a company that had been attacked warned its CSSA partners – a week before any notice was published by the BSI, the German Federal Office for Information Security. A week is worth a fortune in the digital age, so the CSSA members were able to protect themselves and ward off subsequent attacks. These and other approaches are models for companies looking for appropriate ways of managing IT security in the future.

12.4 Simple and Secure Is the Motto

The expert essays in this book from the fields of business, politics and society make it clear that there is still much to do, but also that we already have some outstanding strategic approaches and IT solutions that can help users protect themselves against cybercriminals. Users can easily get lost in the multitude of technological options available – from data leakage prevention, through security information and event management, to mobile security and identity and access management. Managed security services delivered in all-inclusive packages such as security-as-a-service or mobile-security-as-a-service can prevent this from happening. This is a central component of IT security strategy. Another component is teamwork, and not only because four eyes see more than two. From in-house security operations centers to expanded, external cyberdefense centers – security will soon come down to extensive analytical expertise combined with forensics, hunter teams and anomaly recognition with the help of sensors and logic, enabling preventative solutions and defensive actions to be triggered.

But we also need much more. For example, the exchange of personal data must be contained so that as little user information as possible is exposed to these risks in the first place. We already have models for this, such as the P3P (Platform for Privacy Preferences) approach, an international standardized platform developed by the WWW Consortium for the exchange of data protection information for websites. The goal of P3P is to return a substantial amount of data sovereignty to Internet users by automatically informing them when third parties want to access their personal data so that they can prevent this. This approach is feasible in other areas as well, such as the Internet of Things. Service providers do not always need all of an individual's personal data; they could often get by with pseudonymized or anonymized information. When dealing with personal data, even apparently minor measures such as these can help ensure that essential information does not fall into the hands of criminals who could abuse it. These tools also show that security does not always have to be complex; it can actually adapt itself to work and usage processes.

After all, in order to stay safe from future threats as well, it is important to bear one thing in mind: If IT security is going to be broadly used and useful, it has to be even easier to handle, operate and acquire – following the plug-and-play principle of security from a socket. The cloud is the most important foundation for this, because only the cloud offers the necessary resources and flexibility – along with a secure basis for digital transformation via hosting in German data centers, which are comprehensively protected in accordance with national IT security law. The cloud also enables the pioneering of automated solutions in the areas of smart data and machine learning (ML), which will soon make it possible for the security DNA of a company to optimize itself, recognize patterns in real time and evolve through autonomous self-learning.

This long-term strategy for success also depends on factors such as the comprehensive and seamless implementation of security solutions in companies and organizations, proper training of security experts, and measures to make employees aware of the importance of the issue. Finally, users can also benefit from the best practices of other economic sectors, such as the sharing economy, and they can share their own knowledge of how to fight cyberthreats. Together we are stronger. This is particularly true when it comes to IT security – because the attackers are working together, too, and they are often several steps ahead of us. We can not allow this to continue. We have made a start.

References

Bitkom. (2016). *Internet*. Accessed July 5, 2016, from https://www.bitkom.org/Marktdaten/ Konsum-Nutzungsverhalten/Factszu-Internet.html

Computerwelt. (2016). *Carbanak: Der Online-Bankraub geht weiter*. Accessed July 4, 2016, from http://www.computerwelt.at/news/technologie-strategie/security/detail/artikel/ 115084-carbanak-der-online-bankraubgeht-weiter/

Appendix

Eleven Rules for a Secure Internet of Things (IoT)

1. **Think about security from the start**: Retrofitting is always hard
2. **Know what's connected**: If you are aware of the individual connections between things, you can protect and monitor them better
3. **Don't connect everything just because you can**: Follow the minimization principle – only make connections that are sensible and necessary!
4. **Only allow essential communication**: Networked things will communicate with each other only in predefined cases
5. **Separate critical and non-critical systems**: For example, do not connect industrial controllers directly with office communication networks
6. **Create logical zones**: Make sure to break the whole into parts so that damage is contained in the event of an attack
7. **Conduct pen tests**: When you know where your vulnerabilities are, you can protect yourself in advance
8. **Keep your software up to date**: 95 percent of attacks could be prevented if every system worldwide was patched promptly
9. **Encrypt the connections between things**: Encrypted communication ensures that no information can be picked off along the transmission route
10. **Use certificates to securely identify each thing**: Only authorized individuals can control the devices that are supposed to be controlled
11. **Rely on strong partners**: When in doubt, seek professional help and have a comprehensive protection concept drawn up, like that offered by companies such as Deutsche Telekom

© Springer International Publishing AG 2017   119
F. Abolhassan (ed.), *Cyber Security. Simply. Make it Happen.*, Management for
Professionals, DOI 10.1007/978-3-319-46529-6

The Magenta Security Portfolio

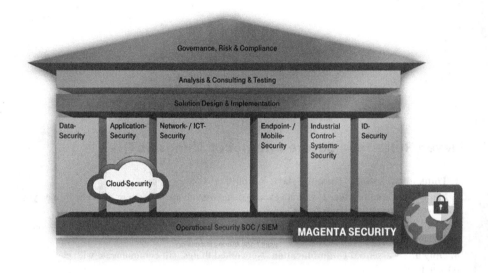

Technical Literature

Abolhassan, Ferri (Ed.): Security Einfach Machen. IT-Sicherheit als Sprungbrett
    für die Digitalisierung. Springer Gabler (2016), ISBN 978-3-658-14944-4

Abolhassan, Ferri/Kellermann, Jörn (Eds.): Effizienz durch Automatisierung – Das
    Zero-Touch-Prinzip im IT-Betrieb, Springer Gabler (2016), ISBN 978-3-658-
    10643-0, eBook ISBN 978-3-658-10644-7

Abolhassan, Ferri (Ed.): The Drivers of Digital Transformation – Why There's No
    Way Around the Cloud, Springer Gabler (2016), eBook ISBN 978-3-319-
    31824-0

Abolhassan, Ferri (Ed.): Was treibt die Digitalisierung? – Warum an der Cloud kein
    Weg vorbeiführt, Springer Gabler (2015), ISBN 978-3-658-10639-3, eBook
    ISBN 978-3-658-10640-9

Abolhassan, Ferri (Ed.): Kundenzufriedenheit im IT-Outsourcing – Das Optimum
    realisieren, Springer Gabler (2014), ISBN 978-3-658-04748-1, eBook ISBN
    978-3-658-04749-8

Abolhassan, Ferri (Ed.): The Road to a Modern IT Factory: Industrialization –
    Automation – Optimization, Springer Gabler (2014), ISBN 978-3-642-40218-0,
    eBook ISBN 978-3-642-40219-7

Abolhassan, Ferri (Ed.): Der Weg zur modernen IT-Fabrik: Industrialisierung –
    Automatisierung – Optimierung, Springer Gabler (2013), ISBN 978-3-658-
    01482-7, eBook ISBN 9783658014834

Abolhassan, Ferri/Scheer, August-Wilhelm/Jost, Wolfram/Kruppke, Helmut (Eds.): Innovation durch Geschäftsprozessmanagement: Jahrbuch Business Process Excellence 2004/2005, Springer (2004), ISBN 978-3540220374; eBook ISBN 9783642171383

Abolhassan, Ferri/Scheer, August-Wilhelm Scheer/Jost, Wolfram/Kirchmer, Mathias (Eds.): Change Management im Unternehmen: Prozessveränderungen erfolgreich managen, Springer (2003), ISBN 978-3-540-03437-7, eBook ISBN 978-3-642-19020-9

Abolhassan, Ferri/Scheer, August-Wilhelm/Bosch, Wolfgang (Eds.): Real-Time Enterprise – Mit beschleunigten Managementprozessen Zeit und Kosten sparen, Springer (2003), ISBN 978-3540023562, eBook ISBN 978-3-642-55458-2

Abolhassan, Ferri/Scheer, August-Wilhelm/Jost, Wolfram/Kirchmer, Mathias (Eds.): Business Process Change Management: ARIS in Practice (english), Springer (2003), ISBN 978-3-540-00243-7

Abolhassan, Ferri/Arend-Fuchs, Christine/Georgi, Hans-Peter/Müller, Peter/Zentes, Joachim: Der Handel im Internet-Zeitalter – Perspektiven für Handel und Konsumgüterindustrie mit mySAP.com, Galileo Press (2001), ISBN 3898421147

Practical Report from the Graduates

Sarah Schuchardt and Alexander Schmitz

> In each beginning dwells a magic, protecting us and helping us to live...
>
> *(Hermann Hesse)*

It was with these words that our fascinating top-up qualification as Cybersecurity Professionals began in September 2014 after a work-study course (Sarah Schuchardt) and training as an IT specialist for systems integration (Alexander Schmitz). At an interesting kick-off event attended by Deutsche Telekom board members and external cybersecurity experts, we gained many insights into the subject that will occupy us well into the future: cybersecurity.

Practical Projects as the Focus of Instruction

The Cyber Security Professional program focuses on practical work. We were therefore given interesting projects right from the start. In the Cyber Defense Center, Sarah worked on the development of a prototype for visualizing firewall log data for small and medium-sized companies (the Cyber Threat Detector), which was subsequently presented at CeBIT 2015. The Cyber Threat Detector is an entry-level solution that works according to the principle of a cyberdefense center – though on a smaller scale and in a more standardized way. The solution collects, aggregates and visualizes all log data generated by a connected firewall. The detector then compares this data with information about current and past cyberattacks and their control structures. If the solution identifies such communication patterns, it sounds the alarm so that action can be taken quickly. The detector also clearly displays traffic streams into and out of the company in real time and visualizes them according to their destination countries, internal network segments and the protocols used. This makes it possible to see in real time whether data is leaving network segments from which no data is usually allowed to flow. The new tool offers various filtering options right in the user interface to easily display relevant data for analysis purposes. Companies using the Threat Detector benefit from the broad networks and analyses of Deutsche Telekom. The solution compares attack indicators from the German Federal Office for Information Security, known attack patterns, data from general attack analyses, as well as data from 180 traps set by the company to provoke and analyze cyberattacks.

From the start, Alexander worked in the Network Services and Data Centers units on projects for protecting cloud storage devices. We were each immediately assigned an employee from our new team as a professional coach. In the early days in particular, these colleagues supported us with suitable projects and points of contact that were important to our day-to-day work.

Virtual Detective Work as Final Module Assignment

The last two successful years of continuing education have included a variety of university modules. Topics such as network and application security, programming in an IT security environment and forensics were all covered. The latter was an especially noteworthy highlight. In the module on digital forensic methods, an Internet crime was presented for our final assignment. The case involved a web server that was compromised through a local file inclusion vulnerability. This made it possible for the attacker to read the system's password file. We were given two operating system descriptions for the potential criminal. Using our newly acquired forensic skills, we had to identify the perpetrator – a virtual manhunt, so to speak.

Along with the university modules, we received additional soft-skills training. Sessions such as "Compact IT Security Knowledge" at the start of the program, and workshops such as "Rhetoric" and "Intercultural Communication" were special highlights. We used a "cyberlogbook" to record our progress and the knowledge that was conveyed in the modules and training sessions. This served as evidence of what we had learned and as an exam prerequisite for the Chamber of Commerce and Industry, and it was discussed in personal meetings every two months with our learning process advisors and professional coaches. Reflection workshops were held every six months to foster communication among the CSP participants. In the course of these we discussed the current university modules, contemporary security issues and general suggestions for the program.

There was a lot of interest in our further education program right from the start. Because we were the first candidates for this entirely new job profile, there were internal and external (press) inquiries about our training. We also represented the new program at the Chamber of Commerce and Industry Education Awards 2016 and were on hand to witness the presentation of the third-place prize.

Cyber Security Professional Training for Jobs of the Future

At the end of the program, we have to complete an exciting final project. The only requirement in terms of content is that it has to be practically relevant to our everyday work, so the focus must be on the current issues handled by each security team. At the end of the two and half years there is an oral exam, during which we'll be asked about the final project and what we have learned. After graduating, we will be certified "Cyber Security Professionals" who are highly motivated to start these jobs made for the future. But we know: "...it won't always be easy to feel the magic... never put an end to the beginnings!"

Alexander Schmitz is a Cybersecurity Professional at Deutsche Telekom AG, where he works in the Group Security Services, primarily in the field of cloud security. A specialist in IT system integration by trade, Schmitz focused in particular on using software component integration to model and implement complex IT technology systems during his training as a Cybersecurity Professional. He was also involved in networked IT system installation, configuration and administration, and the presentation of system solutions.

Sarah Schuchardt is a trainee in Deutsche Telekom's Cybersecurity Professional program and works in Group Security Services, the Cyber Defense Center and the CERT. Schuchardt studied Applied Informatics at Baden-Wuerttemberg Cooperative State University and worked for T-Systems International GmbH, with projects including development of the application lifecycle management and version control for complex projects. She also used Metasploit exploits for vulnerability grading work.

Glossary

Advanced Persistent Threat (APT) A targeted attack and stealthy attempt to spy on confidential data and IT infrastructure.

Big Data The rapidly growing volume and complexity of corporate data, which needs to be stored and structured efficiently, and made available for analytical purposes within a very short timeframe – to perform risk appraisals in financial or energy-sector applications, for example.

Bring Your Own Device (BYOD) The trend for employees to use their personal mobile devices such as smartphones and tablets in a corporate environment. BYOD requires a comprehensive concept for the integration of such hardware.

Cloud Computing IT infrastructure and applications (such as software or storage capacity) sourced from a network generally operated by a service provider. Data is no longer hosted on the company's own storage servers, but in the provider's data center. (See also Private Cloud and Public Cloud.)

Cryptolocker An encrypted Trojan that is smuggled into a system where the cryptolocker encrypts files and then demands payment of a fee to decrypt them. (See also Ransomware and Trojan.)

Cyberwarfare The conduct of warfare with information technology as the battleground. Involves attacks targeting computers, data, information and systems.

Distributed Denial of Service (DDoS) A multi-pronged attack against computers, networks or servers. Typically, the attack target will be overloaded by the sheer volume of connection requests, leading to it becoming unavailable and its service therefore "denied."

Firewall A security system placed between local and public IT infrastructures to prevent outside intrusion into local systems.

Hacktivism Exploiting IT infrastructure for ideological, grassroots and/or politically motivated activism.

Honeypot A program or system offering an attractive target to distract intruders from their original objective and render them harmless.

Internet of Things The networking of everyday objects with the Internet, enabling them to communicate independently and carry out various tasks. (See also Wearables.)

Internet Protocol (IP) A network protocol that transports data packets from a sender to a receiver via multiple intermediate networks.

Intrusion Prevention Monitoring of data traffic within the network with the aim of detecting and blocking attacks by analyzing network usage patterns.

Load Balancing Distribution of loads within server environments or data centers to increase the speed of the overall system.

Machine Learning (ML) Generic term for the artificial generation of knowledge from experience. An artificial system learns from examples and can generalize this experience once the learning phase is over. The system therefore not only memorizes the examples but also identifies laws and patterns in the data.

Major Incident (MI) A severe fault – such as the failure of an entire IT system – that results in a serious interruption of business activities and must be resolved with great urgency in order to avoid significant loss or damage (such as damage to the company's reputation or financial losses).

Malware Undesirable and damaging pieces of software. (See also Trojan, Virus and Worm.)

Managed Services Provisioning of information and communications services by a specialized provider in accordance with a framework contract.

Mobile Application Management (MAM) Software and solutions that provision internally developed and publicly available mobile applications for use in a business environment. Alongside apps on work devices, this also covers apps on personal devices within the framework of a BYOD policy. (See also Bring Your Own Device.)

Mobile Content Management (MCM) Provisioning, administration and backup of company-internal documents and content on mobile devices.

Mobile Device Management (MDM) Software-based and centralized administration of mobile devices in terms of inventory, software, data distribution and security.

Network Time Protocol (NTP) Standard for clock synchronization between computer systems.

Outsourcing Moving of services or units to external providers.

Patch Piece of code correcting software vulnerabilities in software or systems.

Phishing Luring users to enter personal data with fake websites or messages for the purposes of identity theft. If successful, bank accounts or email accounts from affected users can be viewed and used without restriction.

Predictive Maintenance (PdM) Monitoring a system to forecast potential defects or failures with the aid of data collected on a continuous or cyclical basis.

Private Cloud A non-public implementation of cloud computing. The cloud infrastructure here is operated for a single company or a specific group of people – either by the company itself or by a provider. (See also Cloud Computing and Public Cloud.)

Public Cloud A public implementation of cloud computing. The cloud is made available to a broad group of users and is freely accessible over the Internet. (See also Cloud Computing and Private Cloud.)

Ransomware Malware that not only seeks to restrict or prevent data usage or access but which actively demands payment of a fee to decrypt or release this data. (See also Cryptolocker.)

Red Teaming Testing method for plans, strategies and hypotheses in a simulation scenario. While the term originated in a military context, the method is now also deployed by companies. (See also Wargaming.)

Reverse Engineering Creation of a blueprint or source code from a finished system for the purposes of reconstructing its design and/or further developing the system.

Sandbox An isolated software environment that can be used to test program code. Deployed in a security context to safely activate malware and study its mechanisms.

Smart Data Generating added value from Big Data by the intelligent use of very large volumes of data. (See also Big Data.)

Social Engineering Manipulation of interpersonal relationships to cause people to perform a certain action (e.g., to disclose personal data, purchase specific products or services, pay sums of money, etc.).

Trojan A piece of computer malware that disguises itself as a useful application but executes other actions in the background. (See also Malware.)

Underground Economy Economic activities that proceed in parallel to and undetected by the Government taxation system.

Vendor Lock-In Dependency on a specific manufacturer.

Virus A piece of computer malware that self-propagates by infecting other programs. (See also Malware.)

Wargaming Simulation of dangerous real-world situations to test strategies without risk under realistic conditions. While the method originated in a military context, it is now also used by companies as a means of testing their security strategies. (See also Red Teaming.)

Wearables Computer technology that is worn by the user. Generally used to help the user in the collection, processing and sharing of information and data. (See also Internet of Things.)

Web Proxy Communications interface within a network which accepts queries and establishes a connection to the recipient using its own address.

Worm A piece of computer malware that self-propagates without infecting other files or boot sectors. (See also Malware.)

Zero-Day Exploit Possibility of exploiting a vulnerability in a system or program before a patch is available as a countermeasure. (See also Patch.)

Printed in the United States
By Bookmasters

No Other Gods

Other Books by the Same Author

The Trial of the Assassin Guiteau: Psychiatry and Law in the Gilded Age
The Cholera Years: The United States in 1832, 1849, and 1866

No Other Gods

On Science and American
Social Thought

Charles E. Rosenberg

The Johns Hopkins University Press

Baltimore and London

The Johns Hopkins University Press, Baltimore, Maryland 21218
The Johns Hopkins Press Ltd., London

Originally published, 1976

Johns Hopkins paperback edition, 1978

Library of Congress Catalog Card Number 75–36942
ISBN 0–8018–1711–0 (hardcover)
ISBN 0–8018–2097–9 (paperback)

Library of Congress Cataloging in Publication data
will be found on the last printed page of this book.

For my parents,
Bernard and Marian Rosenberg

Contents

Preface

Science and society, science and values, science and social thought —all familiar phrases, almost embarrassingly familiar. Yet the very ease with which we invoke them underlines the shallowness of our understanding.

Historians must bear a good share of the responsibility for perpetuating such casual superficiality. The relationship among science, society, and social thought has been a marginal topic for historical inquiry, its devotees respectable, but rarely major figures among the interpreters of American history. There are some recent exceptions. Daniel Boorstin's ambitious multivolume American history employs data drawn from the realms of science, technology, and the learned professions. Science and technology were to have played a major role in Perry Miller's projected study of the nineteenth-century American mind. Perhaps more significantly, the past decade has seen the publication of a small but steadily growing number of monographic studies relating developments in American science and technology to specific social contexts.

But these are beginnings only, especially as measured against a growing social concern. First the atomic bomb, more recently our emerging awareness of environmental deterioration, our parallel consciousness of the technological as well as political myths which helped structure and legitimate our war in Southeast Asia, the growing debate over medical care, even the civil rights and women's movements have sharpened our awareness of the relationship between social thought, social policy, and the prestige and data of science.

This book is intended as a preliminary exploration of such questions. It is necessarily tentative; given the current state of the art, no historical analysis of science and American society could pretend toward definitiveness. The organizational structure conforms neither to a framework based on a conventional time-periodization (science in Jacksonian America, the idea of science in Progressive America, and so forth) nor to an equally conventional scheme of intellectual periodization (the era of evolutionary naturalism, let us say, or the influence of the Newtonian world-view in the eighteenth century). It is structured, instead, around an attempt to define certain fundamental ways in which science, social thought and values, and the institutional structures of science itself have interacted. In the following pages science will be assumed to mean a number of different things: an accumulating body of knowledge and the techniques for acquiring it, a community with peculiar ideas and values, and, in addition, the images and emotions which scientific knowledge and the figure of the scientist have conjured up in American minds.

(This American mind, encountered with such baleful frequency, is, of course, a conventional fiction. Most of the descriptive generalizations which follow refer, if unqualified, to the educated, moderately articulate, and modestly—if insecurely—prosperous, churchgoing folk whom we associate with the middle-class consensus. And even within this group, values and attitudes existed in particular configurations of emotional need and formal expectation—expectations dependent on regional, religious, and ethnic variables.)

The formal structure of the book is simple enough. A long introductory section attempts to categorize and briefly illustrate certain basic relationships between science and social thought, while succeeding chapters seek to elaborate these relationships in terms of particular ideas, individuals, and institutions. The problem of relating science and social though is complex and our understanding so rudimentary that a chronological or narrative structure seemed inappropriate either for exposition or analysis; thus the structural logic of the book, its assumption that a series of more-or-less detailed case studies would most adequately illustrate fundamental relationships.

Part One explores ways in which scientific images and ideas have performed the ideological function of rationalizing and communicating a conventional understanding of fundamental social realities; in one chapter the problem of male sexual identity, in another woman and her role serve to illustrate such prescriptions. Another chapter, dealing with nineteenth-century ideas of heredity, demonstrates how disease incidence and human difference could be explained in similarly rationalistic terms. A later chapter, more narrowly defined, traces the social uses of hereditarian explanation into the twentieth century in sketching the career of Charles B. Davenport, an influential eugenicist. Because Davenport was a holder of the doctorate, a reputable biologist, and a scientific administrator, this chapter reflects as well the interaction between social needs and values, and the prerogatives of a newly self-conscious world of academic science. The chapter on George M. Beard and his concept of neurasthenia deals with the latent social function of a seemingly novel clinical entity: the neurasthenia construct expressed a more general disquietude in regard to post-bellum America's increasingly urban and alarmingly labile society. At the same time it served both to legitimate the neurologist's newly proclaimed and still precarious specialized status *and* to explain the clinical reality of those marginal psychiatric conditions which loomed so large in his practice.

The final two chapters in this part deal more directly with the increasing emotional relevance of science as a source of authority in nineteenth-century American social thought. One chapter illustrates the pietistic motivations of pioneers in the seemingly secular and pragmatic mid-nineteenth-century movement for reform in public health; social activism in mid-nineteenth-century America was marked by a characteristic emotional continuity between evangelical and secular modes in social reform. The last chapter in this first part elaborates the theme of science as an emotionally compelling source of authority and continues that theme into the twentieth century as it explores the "spiritual"—transcendent—function of science in the moral structure of Sinclair Lewis's *Arrowsmith*, a book at first thought brashly secular.

Part Two is composed of studies focusing not on appeals to science as a source of emotional assurance and understanding, but on the development of the American scientific community. These chapters center on the scientist himself, his perception of his role, his relation to his discipline, his attempts to work within society so as to create a secure and intellectually appropriate institutional base. More specifically, four of the five chapters deal with the growth of the agricultural experiment station in the late nineteenth and early twentieth century. The stations constituted an extremely important precedent in the willingness of American government to support scientific research. These chapters emphasize the role of individual scientists, their self-perceptions and discipline-specific aspirations in creating these novel institutions. By examining an applied-science context—and especially one in which scientists were extremely effective in securing research support—we can begin to understand how complex and ambiguous was the relationship between certain scientists' needs and preconceptions and those of their lay constituency.

The first chapter in this section is an informal collective biography of the pioneer generation of institution builders—Americans who made the atypical career decision to study chemistry in Germany in the mid-1850s. (Since religion played so prominent a role in motivating these young men, this study elaborates the theme of the two chapters immediately preceeding; for all deal with a gradual shift in emotional relevance from religious to scientific imperatives.) The next two chapters deal specifically with the creation of the agricultural experiment station as a milieu suitable—at least in some states—both for scientific achievement and for the shaping of economic realities. The scientist's conception of appropriate work and appropriate conditions in which to perform that work became an indispensable dynamic element in shaping America's agricultural experiment stations specifically and the state universities more generally. Their commitment to science structured and legitimated ambition, while their commitment to a particular discipline provided a specific blueprint for social action.

It must be understood that the discipline or subdiscipline is the scientist's primary orientation, the context which defines success or failure, which specifies appropriate problems and the technique for solving them. Each discipline serves, then, as a kind of self-defined subculture, explicitly prescribing the behavior and aspirations of its adherents. In the final chapter, a case study in the development of genetics as a discipline, I have sought to suggest how social priorities and institutional realities and rigidities interacted to create the specific structure of a developing field. The penultimate chapter examines two innovations—hybrid corn and vitamin A—in an attempt to illustrate their origins in perceived social needs and particular institutional realities.

These chapters have been written over the period of a dozen years. But, with the exception of the introductory essay, they have been rewritten only in places where their relation to certain themes seemed not entirely explicit. At first I was troubled by the seeming diversity of case studies; but an analytical unity grew persuasively out of this seeming diversity. Again and again the same kinds of relationships, the same patterns of interdependence asserted themselves; their recurrence in different contexts asserts—I think convincingly—the centrality and character of the relationships which constitute the book's analytical center.

The bare statement that such relationships exist is no longer a meaningful one; it is the task of historians to explore specific instances and define the texture of specific relationships. There is an aesthetic of complexity in history; in history, at least, less is not more, but less. Any way in which the historian can bring together seemingly disparate elements, any way in which he can juxtapose unfamiliar materials so as to shed light on the interdependence of human life and thought is inherently laudable. Certainly the interaction between science and social thought is one such relationship.

Acknowledgments

I should like particularly to thank Carroll Smith-Rosenberg, who is coauthor of Chapter 2, "The Female Animal: Medical and Biological Views of Women," and Chapter 6, "Piety and Social Action: Some Origins of the American Public Health Movement." Even more importantly, she has criticized and encouraged me for more than a decade in the writing of this book.

I should also like to thank the following publishers and journals for permission to reprint material: The Dorsey Press for permission to reprint portions of the Introduction, which originally appeared in *Science and American Society*, ed. David Van Tassel and Michael Hall (Homewood, Ill., 1966), pp. 135–62; *The Journal of the History of Medicine* for permission to reprint Chapter 6, which appeared in Vol. 23 (1968), pp. 16–35, and Chapter 12, which appeared in Vol. 22 (1967), pp. 27–46; the *American Quarterly* for permission to reprint Chapter 3 (May 1973), pp. 131–53, and Chapter 7, which appeared in Vol. 15 (1963), pp. 447–58; *Agricultural History* for permission to reprint Chapter 9, which appeared in Vol. 44 (January 1971), pp. 1–20, and Chapter 10, Vol. 38 (1964), pp. 3–21; *Perspectives in American History* for permission to reprint Chapter 1, which appeared in Vol. 8 (1974), pp. 189–235; *Science and Values* for permission to reprint Chapter 8 (New York, 1974), pp. 21–42; and *Journal of American History* for permission to reprint Chapter 2, which appeared in Vol. 60 (September 1973), pp. 332–56.

Chapters 4 and 5 are reprinted from the *Bulletin of the History of Medicine*, Vol. 35 (May–June 1961), pp. 266–76, and Vol. 36 (May–June 1962), pp. 245–59.

All of the essays have been revised, and Chapter 11 appears for the first time in this form.

Introduction: Science, Society, and Social Thought

One can distinguish at least four kinds of relationship between science and American social thought. Perhaps the most important has been the increasing emotional relevance of science, its expanding role as an absolute, able to justify and even motivate the behavior of particular individuals. But the role of science in social thought has been expository as well as emotional. Science has lent American social thought a vocabulary and a supply of images; it has served as a source of metaphor and, like figures borrowed from other areas, the similes of science have variously suggested, explained, justified, even helped dictate social categories and values. Both of these relationships are pervasive, somewhat limited by class and region but otherwise widespread. Both are flexible as well, dependent for their particular configuration upon social needs and the consequent manipulation of available ideological forms.

A third relationship between science and American society is much less familiar, but perhaps easier to describe in that it is more sharply defined both by content and by relevance to particular individuals in particular institutional settings. I refer primarily to the role in society of the professional scientist's values and attitudes.[1] The scientist shares certain values and preconceptions with his disciplinary peers. These are different from those of society at large, indeed sufficiently different and sufficiently compelling to have served as a necessary input in the development of modern industrial society. The scientist's aspirations and behavior have certain rather general aspects, characteristics which apply to all those who see themselves as scientists or would-be scientists; at the same time each field of learning has a peculiar identity (structured by a generation-specific body of knowledge and technique

1

which at once defines, legitimates, and constitutes the discipline's intellectual texture). However, the scientist's role exists outside its embodiment in the shared lives of particular disciplines; it exists in quite another realm—in the popular mind, as an intellectual construct having only a problematic relationship with the scientist's actual behavior, but much to do with the recruitment of scientists and the willingness of society to support the activities of a scientific community.

Such a point of view implies a fourth relationship between science and American social thought. This is the obverse of the third—that is, not the effect of the scientific community's values in bringing an element of change and diversity to society, but that of society's attitudes and demands upon the scientist's work and thought. For on many levels—not only that of institutional support—society constantly helps shape the scientific enterprise; even the internal texture of scientific ideas is not entirely insulated from such pressures.

II

In the nineteenth century, science for the first time assumed a significant place in the hierarchy of American values. As it did so, the realm of science played a necessarily increasing role in the communication of social norms; for every culture needs to create and communicate an appropriate social ideology and in doing so must draw upon those sources of authority clothed with the greatest emotional relevance. As the nineteenth century progressed, the world of science increasingly played such a legitimating role.

Faith in science did not originate in nineteenth-century America; nor is it true that science was until relatively recent times a somewhat distrusted competitor of religion. As modern studies of seventeenth- and eighteenth-century American intellectual life have shown, science occupied a real and in some ways prominent place in the intellectual life of America's colonial elite. Science and medicine, as much as Greek verbs and systematic theology, were accepted parts of a learned man's intellectual equipment. Certainly the study of God's works never implied skepticism toward their Author. Quite the contrary. "Nature" was, in the stylized categories of nineteenth-century formal rhetoric, "one volume of God's Bible; and the more *thorough* your acquaintance with God's book of nature, written in character, the more clear and consonant will appear its harmonious correspondence with God's book of revelation, written in letter."[2] Without undue oversimplification, it can be argued that this was the position of most educated

Americans from the seventeenth century until the beginning of the twentieth.[3]

The advance of secularism in the nineteenth century should be seen, not as a struggle between conflicting ideologies, but as a constantly shifting equilibrium between secular and religious imperatives. The similarity between scientific and religious values made it natural for most Americans to move fluidly from one intellectual and emotional realm to another. Science, like religion, offered an ideal of selflessness, of truth, of the possibility of spiritual dedication—emotions which in their elevating purity could inspire and motivate, could legitimate the needs of particular individuals to achieve and control—but in a context seemingly far-removed from the sordid compromise implied by most other careers. Moral and scientific progress did not seem contradictory but, to the ordinary American, inevitably parallel and complementary. "The three great civilizing influences of the age," Josiah Strong, spokesman of militant Protestantism, was able casually to state, "are Christianity, the press, and steam, which respectively bring together men's hearts, minds, and bodies into more intimate and multiplied relationships."[4]

Bitter hostility did on occasion mark the relationship between science and religion in American history. Yet such conflict has been much exaggerated, originally by some of the protagonists, later by a Whiggish and conflict-oriented historical canon. There never was a pervasive and genuinely divisive discontinuity between scientific and religious imperatives in the minds of most educated Americans; the remarkable thing about Darwinism, for example, is not the conflict it inspired, but—considering its implications—the lack of conflict. The comparatively rapid acceptance of Darwinism by the scientific community meant its acceptance, within a relatively short time, by most articulate Americans. The majority of educated, servant-employing, churchgoing Americans could not help ultimately accepting knowledge endorsed by men of science, its epistemological implications notwithstanding. How could it be otherwise? The structure of accepted and acceptable knowledge is very much a part of social structure, and thus of social order. To reject an idea endorsed by men of learning was to reject, at least partially, order and stability in society. Even the most zealous in their piety, even those educated Americans most hostile to particular aspects or manifestations of a seeming materialism, ordinarily made it clear that they had no intention of attacking science as such. "Whatever is scientifically defended and maintained," admonished Noah Porter, orthodox president of Yale in 1872, "must be scientifically refuted and overthrown." The most profound scientific inquiry would, he never doubted, serve inevitably to "strengthen and brighten the evidence for Christian faith."[5] Insofar as social discord has revolved about Darwinism in America, it has been largely a class and regional conflict. Students of American social and intellectual history will find it more profitable not to assume a necessary conflict between religion and science, but to describe and understand the intricate yet ever-changing symbiosis which they maintained.

III

Most aspects of social thought in any culture deal with universal human problems, problems which must be answered by each generation in its own way—the need, for example, to explain why some persons are wealthy, others poor, some healthy and vigorous, others sickly and weak, why children of the same parents differ widely. Every aspect of the life cycle, from birth and puberty to sickness and death, demands meaningful explanation; these universal realities are never seen as random, but inevitably find explanations consistent with a culture's particular world-view. In Europe and North America these explanations have, since the seventeenth century, assumed increasingly scientific forms. Indeed, almost every American social problem in the nineteenth century attracted scientific discussion: the role of women, ethnic difference, appropriate sexual behavior, the logic of class, the effects of urban life, for example.

Throughout the nineteenth century science provided ever-greater understanding of natural phenomena, and thus materials for more plausible because increasingly prestigious mechanisms with which to underwrite traditional modes of understanding and ordering human behavior. Late-nineteenth-century science, for example, had provided publicists and scholars with the tools of the Darwinian synthesis; we are well aware that these ideas were then used to explain almost every aspect of social structure and social function.[6] But this was only one example of a far more pervasive phenomenon.

At the same time, to cite an example, metaphors originating in physics and electro-physiology were made to explain variation in human capacities. Neither folk wisdom nor the physician's clinical acumen doubted that human beings differed greatly in intelligence. They differed as well in their resistance to disease and in keenness of perception. Some were able to respond—even thrive—in a stressful environment, while others succumbed to a variety of physical and emotional ills. Some recovered easily from an illness which might leave others permanently disabled. For centuries physicians had spoken of "vital force" and of "irritability" in an effort to explain such innate differences.

By mid-nineteenth century scientists had come to accept the electrical nature of the nervous impulse. In 1852 Hermann von Helmholtz, the German physiologist and physicist, successfully measured the rate of nervous conductivity. His achievement suggested that nervous force might well be the same as vital force and that this vital force, if not electricity itself, must be some form of energy closely allied to it. "It matters not," as one mid-century physician explained it, "whether, with Cullen, we call the power or agency residing in the nervous system, the Energy of the Brain; or, with Darwin, the Sensorial Fluid; or, with more recent physiologists, we regard it as a Vital Electro-Magnetic power—the fact of its existence cannot be questioned."[7] In addition, popular understanding of the second law of thermodynamics seemed to emphasize man's necessarily limited quantity of vital energy and the innumerable possibilities for energy loss from within the closed system that was the human organism.[8] Yet the body and its environment were traditionally seen as intricately and inextricably related; as in the millennia-old humoral theory, an emphasis on the role of vital energy implied labile relationships of challenge and response. An adequate physiological response meant equilibrium and health, an inadequate one instability and thus disease.

The nervous system as visualized before the acceptance of the neuron theory was a closed and continuous channel. A fixed quantity of nervous force, a hereditary endowment assumed to be electrical in nature, filled and coursed through this channel. It was generally assumed that the capacity to generate such nervous force was determined by "cellular nutrition" and thus by a variety of environmental and physiological realities. (Popularizers grew fond of comparing the human brain and nervous system to the headquarters and wires of a great telegraph system. "The brain is the central office, and in it there are nine hundred million cells generating nerve fluid. . . .")[9] Using this schematic model, physicians and social thinkers could explain the most varied aspects of human behavior. Thus, for example, it was thought that the artistically gifted maniac was the result of a particularly abnormal imbalance of nervous energies.[10] The origin of both mental and physical ills could be explained in these terms, as could the undoubted stress of such periods as puberty, pregnancy, and menopause.[11] Each "critical period" demanded a necessary—because developmental—adjustment of forces and thus implied particular stress until a new equilibrium was reached. Energy relationships provided as well a natural metaphor with which to explore conflict and dominance-submissiveness within interpersonal relationships, particularly marriage—thus the commonly accepted idea that union between individuals of unequal vital endowment could mean either weakening the stronger or, possibly, the gradual debilitation and death of the weaker.[12] This speculative argument was sometimes employed by writers suspicious of sexuality as a rationale for condemning the sharing of a single bed by married couples; it was clearly an occasion of physiological sin. We may smile at the arbitrary and simplistic quality of these explanations; but it must be recalled that late-nineteenth-century thinkers as diverse as Sigmund Freud and Henry Adams were captivated by explanatory models in which energy relationships were made to explain individual and collective behavior in a fashion not very different in form from these ingenuous schemes.

The electrical nature of the nervous impulse and the conservation of energy served thus as sources of didactic metaphor, figures clothed in the authority of science yet dramatizing fundamental social concerns. And metaphors based on energy relationships were only one among a number of such pervasive and culturally reassuring formulas. Not surprisingly, as the nineteenth century grew increasingly secular, such arguments became more frequently scientific in form, increasingly dependent upon the rising status of science in the hierarchy of American values. Though the formal content of such arguments changed as the century progressed, their social functions often did not. Old wine can easily find its way into new bottles.

Let me try to make these generalizations somewhat more explicit, while exploring another pervasive example. Moderation was, in the pantheon of nineteenth-century American social values, almost synonymous with morality. Excess was considered not only immoral but physiologically foolhardy as well. This emphasis was, of course, age-old, a characteristic of suggested medical regimens since the time of Hippocrates; but in the nineteenth century new mechanisms had to be found with which to underwrite these traditional beliefs, and thus to fulfil the social functions they always had. And here again arguments based on vital force could be made to play a significant role. Man's limited complement of nervous energy, if considered in light of the normal human need to indulge in a great variety of activities, meant that one should not indulge immoderately in any particular activity. Those which stimulated the emotions were thought to be especially dangerous, for it seemed clear that the expression of strong emotion implied the copious expenditure of nervous energy. The effects of excessive devotion to business might be the same as those of an obsessive love affair. All sensual pleasure was—in excess, of course—perilous. As Alexander Bain put it, "Every throb of pleasure costs something to the physical system; and two throbs cost twice as much as one."[13] Yet nervous energies must be discharged, for without physical or emotional release, these energies would accumulate and ultimately create pathological conditions. Thus, for example, the frequency of hysteria in the more delicate and protected of middle-class maidens. Morality denied to young ladies the opportunity to discharge accumulating sexual energies, while fashion dictated their refraining from the active work or outdoor play which might also have reduced to a safe level the body's normal production of nervous energy.

In addition to refurbishing and reinforcing conventional admonitions, analogies and arguments drawn from science became, as the nineteenth century progressed, an increasingly plausible idiom in which to formulate—and in that sense to control emotionally—almost every aspect of an inexorably modernizing world. Perhaps most central was the need to deal with an achieving society. More than a few Americans have felt misgivings in contemplating the dangerous and unsettling freedom of American life, and throughout the nineteenth century physicians warned that a good many aspects of American life made massive and unnatural demands on the nervous system. Constant choice and opportunity in business and religion, a lack of standards in personal and social life, all created tension and excitement. Competition began in the schools. The smallest of children were forced to specialize and to overwork in the quest for narrow academic distinction, their physical well-being all but forgotten. Even if the average American survived his education with a minimum of psychic or physical damage, he had then to face an adulthood filled with insecurity. American customs seemed often pathogenic when compared with Europe's more settled institutions. On the Continent religion seemed to many Americans a source of security and passive reassurance; in the United States, on the other hand, Protestantism's uncompromising demands for individual piety implied challenge and stress. Similarly, in politics and business any American, regardless of social origin, might be subject to the stress created by his own unbounded aspirations —and consequent alterations of hope, elation, and despair. "The result of this extreme activity is exhaustion and weakness. Physical bankruptcy is the result of drawing incessantly upon the reserve capital of nervous force."[14] Those characteristics, moreover, which helped make the self-made man were not necessarily consistent with those endorsed by traditional morality. Disease sanctions were one obvious way of expressing such cultural inconsistencies—and in that sense dealing with them. With a peculiar appropriateness science provided a vocabulary and a source of imagery in which these contradictions could be expressed with some subtlety—indeed, with an unselfconscious sensitivity which might well have been unattainable in more formal modes of speculation (and the formal recognition of which might well have been uncomfortably threatening). Physicians and social thinkers since the day of Thomas Jefferson and Benjamin Rush have criticized the peculiar tensions of American life. The speculative pathologies which explain precisely how these tensions injured the mind and body have changed in form since the days of Rush, but the ambivalent attitudes which they express toward American life have not.

Yet neither Benjamin Rush nor his successors later in the century —Weir Mitchell, Isaac Ray, and G. M. Beard, among others—were willing, warn as they might of the psychic perils of American life, to exchange its liberties for the placid tyranny of the Russian or Turkish empires (or, most Americans felt, their Protestantism for the formalistic reassurances of Catholicism). Throughout the nineteenth century American warnings of the dangers of modern life to mental stability were not a negative but, in sum, a positive, even nationalistic, doctrine. Progress and liberty were unquestionably desirable, and the ailments which they induced in American minds were in a sense additional bits of evidence for the superiority of American ways of life. Technological change might be the cause of mental unease, but almost all Americans were relatively sanguine in their attitude toward the future of such material change. Many Americans believed, indeed, that the very processes of technological change that appeared to threaten mental health would ultimately provide remedies. Such ills as might develop in the interval were those of a transitional period in history and a small price paid for social progress. "We must not go backward, but forward," Irving Fisher wrote in 1908. "The cure for eye strain is not in ignoring the invention of reading, but in introducing the invention of glasses. The cure for tuberculosis is not in the destruction of houses, but in devices for ventilation."[15]

A function central to the social thought of any time or place—and another form in which to express both cultural values and anxieties—is the creation and communication of ideal social types. And here too, scientific idiom and authority have played a significant role. Throughout the nineteenth and into the twentieth century, for instance, a major theme in formal American rhetoric was the responsible, middling, yeoman farmer. The virtues attributed to this thinking agriculturist were physical as well as moral; a rural upbringing seemed to guarantee a far healthier life than that of a youth spent in the city's debilitating air. It seemed equally clear (at least in the categories of didactic prose) that a "middling" life was more wholesome physically—as well as far more likely to be wholesome morally—than that of either the very poor or the very rich. The lower classes, poorly fed, addicted to drink and vice, kenneled in filthy and ill-ventilated apartments, had little chance to live out a natural life span. The rich, whether they had inherited wealth or risen to it, were similarly prey to physical and nervous ills. Luxury implied excess in food and drink and, especially for women, health-sapping idleness. The scion of wealthy parents was exposed to the mental atrophy of inactivity, if not to the effects of dissipation as well; the self-made man was necessarily debilitated by the tensions and stress which accompanied his financial ambition. The ideal citizen was rural, moderately prosperous, of good though not brilliant mental endowment. Genius, authorities agreed, was frequently accompanied by insanity, moral obtuseness, or ill-health; it could hardly be viewed as an ideal. Therefore, in the words of a prominent eugenicist expressing a long-felt American conviction, "it would seem wise not to breed for geniuses, but for a solid middle class."[16]

And, he might have added, to raise them in contact with nature. Even the least credulous of eighteenth- and nineteenth-century physicians found it difficult to question the presumed immunity of primitive peoples from most of the diseases which plagued civilized man. Mental illness, heart disease, even liver ailments seemed rarely to be found in non-Western peoples. Travelers reported that childbirth among American Indians was a relatively casual if not absolutely painless function. Pain in labor and post-partum disability were consequences of civilized women having ignored the laws of health. Even pauperism, it seemed natural to assume, "does not exist in the natural state of man. Under the sweet influence of the skies, he is in the woods as quick and nimble as the bird or deer he pursues. Only in the atmosphere, thick with moral and physical poison of crowded cities, he degenerates into a pauper, robbed of all that elasticity and high potency by which man masters every resistance. . . ."[17] Yet those Americans who eulogized the health and virtue of primitive peoples would hardly have favored a return to their unsophisticated ways. Though it may have had its questionable aspects, late-nineteenth-century Western civilization offered advantages far superior to the health guaranteed by the savage's rude life. The crudeness of nervous organization which protected these simple folk from nervous ills prevented them as well from creating a complex society. The highest of human activities—morality, religion, art, and literature—were all consequences of Western man's more finely developed "nervous organization." Darwinism only provided—and, in providing, endorsed—a mechanism with which to explain these attainments. "There can be no question," physicians assumed, "as to whether the nervous systems of highly cultivated and refined individuals among civilized peoples are more complex and refined in structure and delicate in susceptibility and action, at least in their higher parts, than the nervous system of savages."[18] The sensitivity and complexity of this superior nervous organization, its greater "area" for the reception of sensation, its greater capacity for imagination, all helped explain the susceptibility of civilized man to a growing variety of nervous ailments.

There is a logic here, arbitrary and makeshift as these "scientific" analogies may seem. It is to be found not in their particular scientific content, but in their function. We must look not at the internal logic of the scientific ideas appropriated, but at their external logic—their social function. The ultimate coherence of these ideas lies, indeed, in their very inconsistency, in the willingness of Americans to tolerate contradiction, indeed demand it. For the ambivalence of American cultural attitudes implied the use of images and analogies flexible enough to express the structure of this ambivalence.

The social use of scientific ideas is hardly arbitrary, however. The more tenuous an area of scientific knowledge, the smaller its verifiable content, the more easily its data may be bent to social purposes. Thus, as we shall argue in some detail in the next chapter, rejection of the assumption that acquired characteristics could be inherited inevitably forged a connection between consistent hereditarianism and socially conservative views. Gradual acceptance of the new genetics after 1900—with its fundamental assumption of a categorical distinction between the hereditary and the acquired—created a situation in which hereditarianism became increasingly and almost exclusively endorsed by social conservatives; the reformist in temperament tended, as their emotional position dictated, to disassociate behavioral characteristics entirely from a possible genetic basis. They had no choice, for they too felt hereditary characteristics to be immutable. Yet their motivation was primarily humanitarian, and this humanitarianism demanded the performance of melioristic acts which social conservatives derided as useless in the face of implacable heredity.

Nowhere did the ideological and emotional symbiosis just suggested have a longer history than in medicine, and nowhere does it have a more direct applicability to human affairs. Anthropologists have long been aware of the centrality of medical theory and practice in the understanding of a particular culture's beliefs. Indeed, it is probably fair to say that the use of disease as a sanction in enforcing behavioral norms is almost universal and that the speculative etiologies which justify such social usage are always consistent with a culture's most fundamental patterns of belief.

Just as naturalists and physical scientists assumed that their research illuminated the glory of God in his works, so did most nineteenth-century American physicians assume that there could be no conflict between their findings and the truths of morality. The human organism was a thing both material and divine, and offenses both physical and moral were necessarily punished with disease. Drinking, overeating, sexual excess, all carried with them inevitable retribution, not because the Lord deigned to intercede directly in human affairs, but because He had created man's body so that infringing on God's moral law meant disobeying the laws of physiology. Moralism thus drew upon the prestige of science, while medicine was pleased that its findings supported the dictates of morality. "True education, all genuine civilization, and pure Christianity, in order to have a permanent basis and progress," one mid-century physician explained, "must have their foundation and support in the laws of the physical system. . . . And who," he concluded, "are to be the interpreters, the expounders of these laws, unless the members of the medical profession?"[19] It was an admirable and internally consistent network of relationships. Disease explanation served not only to sanction and communicate behavioral norms, but helped individuals deal with the emotional reality of disease itself, both directly and indirectly, inasmuch as popular faith in his speculative pathologies supported the physician's prestige (a prestige necessary to the emotional structuring of disease by the sick and their families).

Nowhere were such arguments more pervasive than in nineteenth-century pleas for temperance reform. As early as the 1820s and 1830s temperance advocates used medical and statistical data to support their cause. Benjamin Rush had, a generation earlier, phrased a plea for temperance in scientific terms, but his was an appeal to the traditional humanitarianism of the educated eighteenth-century gentleman. In the 1820s, however, the nation's growing evangelicalism broadened and democratized the temperance cause. Yet these pious reformers saw no inconsistency in employing temporal arguments in their efforts to hasten the millennium. Addiction to alcohol was a consequence of both moral and physiological factors. Alcohol was a material substance with particular physiological properties; the decision to drink, however, was a moral failing, a failure of will. Once habituated, nevertheless, it was almost impossible for the drunkard to return to morality and sobriety without the supernatural strength imparted by conversion and God's saving grace. The ravages of alcohol, the argument continued, deadened man's higher moral centers, making it impossible for him to respond to conscience—even, some implied, to accept the grace of God. (The most zealous refused even to accept alcohol as part of God's natural order. It never occurred in nature, they argued, but was a product of man's depraved ingenuity—not a natural substance, but one formed through degradation and decay. The appetite for spirits, it followed, was not part of man's normal physical make-up but itself a symptom of disease, an unnatural craving induced by the effects of the alcohol already consumed.)[20]

Though such appeals by religious reformers to the prestige and data of science were common well before the Civil War, the habit of mind they foreshadowed did not become pervasive until well after mid-century. In the decades after Appomattox, science tended to play an increasingly important role in the minds of generations still inspired by the zeal of an earlier, more specifically religious earnestness, but unable any longer to accept solutions formulated in traditional religious terms. The absolute of science became increasingly autonomous.

As early as the 1840s and 1850s, for example, sanitation and hygiene had come to be accepted as a necessary auxiliary to reform, either temporal or eternal. The soul, religious reformers assumed, could not be saved while the body it inhabited remained in filth.[21] By the 1870s and 1880s, however, the ultimate goal of religious conversion had been relegated to a subordinate place in the efforts of American reformers. Sanitation and tenement reform were becoming goals sufficient in themselves. Filth was no longer in essence an external symptom of spiritual decay; it had become a sin in itself, irredeemable without cleanliness. Yet the zeal which inspired certain reformers to improve tenement conditions and abolish sweatshops clearly reflected the emotional heritage of an earlier generation. Though perhaps phrased in the measured terms of empirical analysis, proposals for reform in late nineteenth-century America were often suffused by a vision of transcendent moral benefit. Eugenical sterilization, for example, in the mind of one enthusiast was not simply a means of reducing criminality and mental retardation. It would rid man of all "the ills which flesh is heir to." They would "vanish with the mists of its night of suffering and sorrow, dissatisfaction and jealous rage, before the glorious dawn of its millennial day of comfort, hope, peace, and promise." "Social Science," an undergraduate orator announced in the mid-1880s, "is the Healer, the life-thrilled Messianic Healer of the human race. It is the herald on the misty mountaintop, proclaiming, through all this burdened earth, that THE KINGDOM OF MAN IS AT HAND." And it will be recalled that this is the generation of college students which provided so much of the leadership in that political movement which we have come to call progressive.[22]

The faith of many progressives in science was a real one. But it was more than an allegiance to a program of specific measures scientifically determined. Expertise, efficiency, disinterested inquiry were the means by which social injustice might be approached, not as an indictment of American society as a whole, but as a series of specific solvable problems. Thus conceived, reform could proceed by limited, manageable steps. Reform measures which could be presented as the product of disinterested inquiry benefited not only from the uncritical faith of most Americans in the procedures of science but as well from their belief that such proposals were untinged with narrow and sordid partisanship, untainted by the treacherous ideology of the political extremist.

These are optimistic, even exhilarating attitudes. Yet it must be emphasized that the appeal of science as an absolute was limited largely to the educated, to the elite and articulate. Science did not appeal with the same cogency to the urban lower class or, with some exceptions, to the less educated or provincial generally. Scientific absolutes, with their self-consciously moralistic quality, appealed as little to an Irish longshoreman in 1910 as the pietistic dogmas which justified reform in antebellum America would have appealed to his grandfather.

Which suggests another caveat. The relevance of scientific ideas and authority is shaped by a number of interrelated variables. One, of course, is class; another, ethnicity; another, religious orientation; another, education. Social location determines social experience and thus the *likelihood*—but hardly the necessity—of individuals embracing particular aspects of their generation's conventional wisdom. Society provides intellectual options; it does not dictate the choice individuals make among them in a more-than-statistical sense. Individual personality must choose among available vocational and ideological choices. For example, one of the chapters in this book describes the career of Charles B. Davenport, an ardent advocate of eugenics, an activist social conservative (if this seeming anomaly be excused), and a descendant of Connecticut's prominent Davenport family. His career of academic respectability but economic marginality, his hostility to a new society and its increasingly alien inhabitants, make him an almost-too-precise exemplar of a displaced, hostile, and anxious old order. Yet, while I was investigating Davenport's personal papers some years ago, I was amused to discover that his brother was an advocate of environmental reform—a city missionary among Italian immigrants whose occasional antisocial behavior he sought to explain as resulting from a hostile environment rather than ineluctable heredity. Both social and vocational orientations, with their differing yet presumably functional psychic equities of emotional commitment and reassurance, existed as alternatives to men of their time and class. These options had been structured by society; the brothers' personalities chose between them.

Obviously the relationships between social location, individual personality, and vocational choice are hardly random. And once vocational choices have been made, institutional factors can play a role of their own in shaping receptivity toward particular ideas. We have, in the interest of analysis, been seeking to isolate variables which in terms of individual lives could hardly have been separable. Let me cite an example to illustrate this interdependence: Charles D. Meigs and Hugh Hodge, Philadelphia's leading teachers of obstetrics in the 1840s and 1850s were vociferous in rejecting the suggestion that puerperal fever might be contagious, indeed often spread by the obstetrician himself.[23] The intensity of their response suggests that something more than mere intellectual difference was involved; one of the roots of their hostility to a contagionist point of view lay in the threat it implied for the physician's status, especially in relation to female patients. Medicine—and particularly gynecology—may thus have constituted for men such as Meigs and Hodge a sort of adjustment, possibly even a mode of securely structuring their relationships with women.[24] A theory which placed responsibility for the spread of a fatal disease upon the physician thus jeopardized their status both as males and as professionals, and necessarily evoked an emotional response.

IV

The use of science as an idiom of social thought and its place as a transcendent motivating value are both pervasive. This is not true of our third relationship between science and American society—that between social values generally and those values peculiar to the scientific community. This subrealm of society at large, created by a shared vocation, is in some ways a distinct subculture, marked by a configuration of values and attitudes which distinguish its members from those of other social groups.[25]

One can, I think, mark the beginning of modern academic science in the United States at the moment investigators began to care more for the approval and esteem of their disciplinary colleagues than they did for the general standards of success in the society which surrounded them. All students of American intellectual history are aware that the decades between 1850 and 1880 saw Americans in a number of the sciences beginning to accept these values. All students realize as well that this process was connected with the experiences of scores of Americans at European universities (and in the case of other less affluent or less fortunate Americans, with the images, at least, of these universities). It was not simply scientific data and laboratory techniques which were transferred, but those values and attitudes which make the life of science seem important and define the way it should be lived. Once he had accepted the values of the world of academic science, the American scholar could measure achievement only in these terms. And success in this world meant acceptance as a creative scholar by one's disciplinary peers. Concretely, such success demanded the publication of books and articles and the research support which could alone make publication possible. And the formulation of aspirations in terms of research, in terms of adding to the fund of human knowledge, did not seem sordid but selfless, indeed spiritual. The scientist's role implied rejection of the seemingly materialistic standards by which success was ordinarily judged in American society. As an absolute good, the cause of abstract research justified, even encouraged, any steps which could be seen as furthering scientific investigation—a cause transcending mere personal ambition. Such attitudes legitimatized the personal ambitions of at least some men who have sought achievement within American society—but who were repelled by the moral compromise seemingly implicit in most paths to success.

A subsequent chapter illustrates this dynamic in terms of the collective experience of a group of young American chemists who found in academic science—or in the variant role of scientific entrepreneur—an emotionally appropriate vocation. In traveling to Europe in the 1840s and 1850s to prepare themselves for a scientific career, these young Americans made a strikingly atypical career choice.[26] Their German teachers, as one put it, gave them "a contempt for that superficial smattering of everything without even an idea of what thoroughness is in anything which is too characteristic of our American system of education." A scholar's true calling was not to disseminate knowledge but to add to it. Once exposed to these values, and to the scientific knowledge and technique which at once legitimated and constituted their new disciplinary consciousness, these young men could no longer accept as laudable the vague gropings of American science. Popular or democratic science was a contradiction in terms: "When it becomes so popular as to be understood by a promiscuous audience, who had never been trained in the classroom by the study of its abstractions, it loses that scientific *essence* from which it derives its value, and is therefore no longer science, but simply . . . so much worthless '*claptrap.*' "[27] The letters of these young chemists and their friends written after returning to the United States were filled with wistful nostalgia for their *alte Heimat* in Göttingen and Leipzig and Würzburg, sprinkled with amusingly gratuitous German phrases and puns and a pervading frustration at the limitations placed by American conditions upon their desire for achievement as scientists. They wanted time for research and funds to support it; they needed students to help in their work (and to fulfill that part of the academic ethos which placed a high value on the training of successors); they sought leisure in which to write the books and articles which alone could win the respect of their disciplinary peers. It is hardly surprising to learn that as soon as they returned home the more entrepreneurially minded among these young Americans began to write memorials, to cultivate politicians, and to seize every possible opportunity in which to spread the gospel of science. Nor is it surprising that they began to instill in their students a reverence for original investigation and a contempt for the American scientific environment. To accept these conditions was to deny the values which ruled the world of international science. "I can never adjust myself to my surroundings here," an unhappy Göttingen graduate wrote from rural Kentucky, where he taught in a small college; "to do so would be to proclaim my stay in Europe a failure."[28]

Such desires acted as a catalyst not only in the creation of laboratories, but in the reshaping of American higher education generally. Innovations in higher education must not be thought of simply in terms of farsighted reformers struggling to introduce electives and graduate programs; it must be seen as well in terms of young scholars attempting to create an environment in which they could find achievement within their own disciplines. These working scientists provided the motivation and specific scientific knowledge necessary to crystallize in institutional form the amorphous enthusiasm of Americans for science and the progress it seemed to imply. College administrators soon found that they could hire and keep such young men only if they accepted at least some of the young men's goals. No academic position could attract the most eligible candidates if research facilities were not available and a typically heavy teaching schedule was imposed. In 1889, President James K. Patterson of the University of Kentucky wrote to T. H. Morgan, a young Kentuckian studying at the Johns Hopkins University, offering him a position as professor of natural history. Though refusal would involve financial hardship, Morgan could not accept the position. "Today," he wrote in explanation, "a man is known in his own field by his original work—& this takes both time & energy—& now to give up one's strength to the classroom would leave little or no opportunity for original work."[29]

That Morgan was to become a Nobel laureate merely dramatizes the personal decision made by many Americans of his generation. As these scholars achieved status within their chosen field, and as it became difficult to ignore such criteria in employment, these young men became candidates for the leading chairs in American universities. Once appointed, they utilized their strategic positions to help create an academic environment suitable for professional achievement. This environment included, of course, graduate training programs, freedom of research and teaching, all those idealized standards which have played so central a role in the creation of modern higher education.

And in the creation of modern society as well; for the establishment of academic science in this country was a necessary step in the economic and technological development of modern America. American enterprise and the North American continent's natural resources had, by mid-nineteenth century, created a complex and in some ways technologically sophisticated economy. But, as the history of the electrical industry was to show, progress beyond this steam and iron technology could occur only with the help of academic science. This was a lesson which German technological success had taught not only to scientists but to many educated and articulate Americans. The only way, however, in which the scientific disciplines could establish themselves in this country was through the antecedent creation of a group of would-be scholars and academic entrepreneurs, enthusiastic in their motivation, secure in their righteousness, and confident in their special knowledge. The perception, adoption, and acting out of these new roles played a necessary part in the process of modernization, constituted an input into American institutional and economic growth available from no other source.

The relationship between society and the scientific community it supports is, however, no unilateral one. Just as the creation of each new scientific discipline meant the creation of a novel substrain in American social thought, so American thought and values have and still do affect the scientist in his intellectual and institutional life. The needs and attitudes of society at large have had a significant influence upon the development of scientific institutions in America, first preparing a social and economic climate in which science could ultimately flourish, then dictating the patterns of research and support, and—at times—even influencing the scientist in his attempts to evaluate and explain research findings.

Though abstract science and the institutions in which it can be pursued did not flourish in antebellum America, a social climate favorable to its ultimate growth did. It is axiomatic that the basic values of a culture must be sufficiently congruent with those of the scientific community to allow this vocation to seem a plausible choice for at least some individuals and to insure a minimum level of support. And, as we have contended, science was on the whole unchallenged by religion, encouraged by a vigorous faith in the social efficacy of rational means, and reinforced by a romantic interest in the things of nature. Americans could view science as an admirable, even socially prestigious, avocation—if not as a practical vocation. Science clubs and botanical and mineralogical trips sponsored by academies and secondary schools all helped to provide a good many young men—and even young ladies—with a sedate interest in science and left in the minds of a few inspiration sufficient to encourage the devotion of later years to its pursuit.

Despite such indications of a congenial climate for the development of scientific institutions, it must be emphasized that much of this enthusiasm was rhetorical—until relatively recent generations the academic practitioners of science have not enjoyed enthusiastic or widespread public support. Though overemphasized, there is certainly some truth in the conventional historical view of a materialistic, success-driven America, willing to tolerate a roseate view of science in the abstract or a zealous enthusiasm for science when it appeared in the guise of a promising technology, but hostile to anything which seemed mere idle speculation, which did not promise an immediate return. Only occasionally and then in circumscribed areas did Americans before 1914 demonstrate a willingness to support systematic investigation. One thinks, for example, of the Coast and Geodetic Survey supported by the federal government; similarly, state geological surveys were created throughout the Union, and in some cases, maintained with comparative generosity a generation before the Civil War. (As might have been expected, there were sometimes bitter misunderstandings between the legislators who paid—as they understood it—for practical results and the scientists in whose charge the surveys had necessarily to be placed. The goals of geologists and paleontologists were not precisely those of the state representatives whose votes assured their salaries.)

The simple desire for gain in an optimistic and expanding economy was not the only factor influencing the pattern of research support in nineteenth-century America. Other social values and attitudes played a role as well, modifying and interacting with more strictly economic assumptions. Why, for example, did agricultural science receive such early and comparatively generous government support? One reason, of course, was the vulnerable position of agriculture in an increasingly competitive world market, coupled with the political power of rural areas. Perhaps equally significant, however, was the farmer's ideological status. Like science itself, agriculture assumed a neutral and benevolent cast in the nation's store of ideal social types. It was thought peculiarly virtuous and deserving of support; legislation in support of the yeoman's needs was not class legislation, for his interests were indistinguishable from those of the nation. At least some congressmen could assuage their constitutional qualms in voting support for scientific agriculture with the conviction—in some cases possibly even sincere—that the infusion of science and systematized knowledge into the farmer's workaday routine would not only benefit his economic condition but also improve his lowly status (in reality, if not in the categories of social mythology, where his status remained lofty). Agriculture might, it seemed, become a learned profession.

It was such oddly assorted ideas which some among America's first generation of European-trained and applied-science-oriented academic entrepreneurs were able to exploit in their campaign for government support of scientific research. (This was a goal which they achieved gradually, first through state governments, then through the national Bureau of Agriculture, finally in 1887 and 1906 by direct federal subvention.) Thus major precedents in the development of federal support for scientific research in the universities and states were created almost through inadvertence, not because of a reasoned commitment to the need for supporting the scientific enterprise, but because of the political power and peculiar ideological status of agriculture in American life.

We have been illustrating only one *kind* of relationship between the scientific enterprise and society—and an indirect relationship, inasmuch as it derived essentially from those social needs and perceptions which have made nonscientists willing to support scientific activity. Society can have, as well, a direct effect upon the particular texture of scientific thought; just as scientific vocabulary and metaphors can serve as ideological building blocks in the creation of a usable worldview, scientists have—especially in medicine and certain areas of biological research—incorporated social perceptions into the formal texture of their work.

Such values not only have helped dictate the problems to which scientists have directed their efforts, but also, in some cases, have shaped their answers to those ostensibly scientific questions. The more closely related to felt social problems, the more likely is a scientist's work to be influenced by society's importunate demands. (And those sciences, the behavioral and biological, which still seem difficult of reduction to physical and mathematical terms and controlled experimental situations, are those closest to social concerns.) Human genetics, for example, was slow in developing, not simply because of difficulty in working with the human organism, but because of society's imperative demands for immediate answers to social problems. The gauche solutions so readily provided by certain geneticists early in this century discredited the field among most academic biologists and may well have retarded less spectacular work in this area.

But this is not true of genetics alone. At about the same time that some of the earlier and more enthusiastic of the Mendelians were establishing the new science of eugenics, eminent nutritionists had come to argue that energy requirements were the key factor in determining a correct human diet. Prior to the 1890s it had been generally believed that a ration sufficient for man or experimental animals could be calculated in terms of a balance among fats, carbohydrates, and proteins (plus appropriate inorganic salts). At the end of the nineteenth century, however, scientists began to add a new and centrally important factor to the traditional equation—energy as measured by the calorie.

The vogue of the calorie resulted from a number of different factors: one of them, a concern for the poor and their physical well-being; another, the seeming impasse reached by more conventional means of scientifically analyzing the value of foods and the prestige accorded techniques which promised hard, quantitative results. Metabolic studies seemed to show that the worker should spend his food allowance on starches and carbohydrates, the cheapest source of calories. Meat and fresh vegetables were—calorie for calorie, scientists believed—far more expensive, and their place in the diet might well be curtailed. Thus the diet of the poor could be improved without burdening their already low income. (Studies in the first decade of the century seemed, moreover, to show that protein requirements were greatly overestimated; a low-protein diet seemed, indeed, to be far healthier than one rich in protein.) Here was a concept equally attractive to legislators, to philanthropists, to newspapermen, and to ambitious yet public-spirited scientists. This research seemed rigidly scientific and yet eminently practical and humanitarian. It is hardly surprising that metabolic studies, with their immediate human implications and enticingly precise results, found comparatively generous support in a generation still sparing in its support of most physiological research; nor is it surprising that scientists were perhaps overenthusiastic in their acceptance of the calorimeter and its results. That many of the leaders in calorimeter research were slow to accept newer problems and methods was equally predictable. At the turn of the century it could hardly have been anticipated that understanding of nutrition would soon take a novel turn, that research would turn from a concern with energy balance to the significance of trace nutrients and ultimately their implications for the study of intracellular processes. None of the disciplines potentially relevant to an understanding of nutrition in the opening years of the century incorporated in their customary training the appropriate mixture of biochemical sophistication, animal experimentation, and experimental pathology which might easily have led to the vitamin concept. As shall be illustrated in a later chapter on the discovery of vitamin A, social need, institutional context, and the intellectual texture of the relevant scientific disciplines all played necessary roles in shaping this innovation.

Each scientist's particular reality can be conceived of as the consequence of a particular adjustment between discipline and context, between the generation-specific intellectual demands of his discipline and the needs and attitudes of society as expressed through the context in which that discipline is pursued. Each area of knowledge provides a different kind of sensitivity to its social environment. Pure mathematics or theoretical physics are not immune to the need for support, but are obviously less sensitive to perceived social priorities than, let us say, plant pathology or even genetics. Yet insofar as particular social realities influence the internal life of particular social contexts—university, government laboratory, or private industry—they influence the disciplines conducted within them. To define the interaction between the internal and external, intellectual and institutional, development of science, historians must address themselves to the fine structure of these interactions.[30]

PART ONE

Science, Authority, and the Logic of Social Explanation

1

The Bitter Fruit:
Heredity, Disease, and Social Thought

Since at least classical antiquity men have sought to explain individual differences and to understand how parents' physical and emotional characteristics were transmitted to their children. Heredity has always played some role in both medical and social thought. It was not until the second half of the nineteenth century, however, that it became a prominent component not only in accepted schemata of medical explanation, but of social analysis and rationalization as well.

Historians tend to think of late-nineteenth-century hereditarianism in terms of positivism, of a self-indulgent *fin-de-siècle* determinism, of an unfortunate ethnocentrism; we think of it as well as an intellectual movement beginning formally with Darwin and Galton, finding institutional fulfillment in the eugenics crusade, and reaching a peak of popular acceptance in the years immediately following the First World War. This is an oversimplification at best. For the deterministic ideas which we associate with the world-view of the Progressive generation are the somewhat atypical descendants of an intellectual lineage far more rich and ambiguous. The vogue of social hereditarianism was already well under way by the mid-nineteenth century, while the optimism and confident manipulativeness which characterized these ideas in the middle third of the century was far different from the self-conscious pessimism which had come to inform them by the early years of the twentieth.

This shift in tone and social relevance is particularly apparent since the body of scientific knowledge which legitimated and served as a vehicle for the communication of social hereditarianism changed hardly at all in the course of the century. Between 1800 and 1900 the vast majority of physicians, publicists, and biologists who sought to understand human heredity shared the same working assumptions. But while the formal content of scientific knowledge remained essentially unchanged, its social applications shifted markedly in scope and emphasis. It is an intellectual evolution which illustrates with remarkable clarity the way in which ideas putatively scientific can be shaped by the need of society to rationalize, to understand, to find plausible sanctions for social action.

The following pages are in this sense a venture closer to the domain of what might be called the history of ideology than to that of the history of scientific ideas (assuming that this is a useful if ultimately treacherous dichotomy).[1] The discussion will not be limited to a high culture of elite physicians and articulate biologists and publicists, but will rather emphasize that broad middle ground of social discourse occupied by articulate and educated Americans—most prominently by medical men whose professional ideas concerning heredity were, for the greater part of the century, separated only tenuously from those of laymen. In regard to conceptions of human heredity, moreover, only comparatively minor differences distinguished the elite within the profession from their less educated and articulate colleagues. We are dealing, that is, with ideas which enjoyed a relatively broad social currency, though sanctioned by formal biological and especially medical doctrine.[2]

A final word in regard to tactics: This chapter will, first, outline those views of human heredity generally accepted in the first half of the century, then suggest areas of mid-century concern in which hereditarian explanatory schema were beginning to be applied in social contexts. I should like then, more tentatively, to suggest a framework of explanation in which this particular configuration of ideological form and social function might possibly be placed.

As the nineteenth century opened, heredity was hardly a subject for controversy. It was understood—or at least it seemed to be. "Like," after all, did "beget like." This is an assumption so primitive that it demands an effort of imagination to understand that it was, indeed, an assumption, and how fundamental a role it played in the explanation of health, disease, and behavior.

Though unquestioned, this assumption required elaboration if it were effectively to rationalize observable human differences and misfortunes. One can identify at least four building blocks of presumption and exposition which fleshed out this basic generalization, all as unquestioned as the fundamental truth itself. First, both physicians and laymen assumed that acquired characteristics were inherited. Second, they assumed that heredity was a dynamic process beginning with conception and extending through weaning (an assumption not unrelated to the first). Third, they assumed that the inheritance of character, disease, and temperament was a protean affair of tendency and predisposition, not of discrete and unitary qualities. Fourth, contemporaries agreed that the sexes played a necessarily different role in heredity.

Perhaps most significant was the assumption that acquired characteristics, even patterns of behavior, could be inherited. At the moment of conception the particular biological identities of both parents were resultants of the cumulative interaction of all those habits, accidents, illnesses—and original constitutional endowments—which had intersected since their own conception. Some authorities, for example, believed it important to determine whether an insane mother had become so before or after the birth of her children; if afterward, the "hereditary entailment" need not be quite so ingrained. Thus, for example, the persistent belief that the ordinarily greater resemblance between twins than between other siblings was a result of the time which elapsed between the birth of siblings—time during which the parents' physical attributes had necessarily changed.[3] Any unwise habitual aspect of an individual's regimen, from lack of exercise to overwork, could lead to a physical deterioration inevitably passed on to children.

Such influences did not end with conception. The fetus and then nursling remained labile and malleable until weaning, its development a dynamic response to its environment. Certain moments were considered particularly critical. Most sensitive was the moment of conception itself; if the parents, for example, were inebriated, the child might well—the improving argument followed—prove idiotic, alcoholic, or insane. These assumptions were remarkably tenacious. As late as 1885 a professor at the School of Medicine of the University of Pennsylvania could warn "that the indulgence of a man's grandfather at his [the grandfather's] wedding feast [may] be written upon his body in the unmistakable characters of a debilitated and dyspeptic stomach."[4] Thus both popular and scientific treatises warned throughout the century of the need to conceive children only when both parents were relaxed, well-rested, and affectionate. Tension, hostility, even exhaustion during intercourse could result in weak and unhealthy offspring.

During gestation, either significant trauma or such chronic states as depression and malnutrition could leave their imprint upon the fetus. Many cautious physicians doubted that particular psychic or physical traumas could produce specific blemishes—such as lesions in the shape of the snake or dog which had frightened the mother—but none doubted that protracted anxiety, overwork, or malnutrition in the mother could and would cause constitutional ills in the child she bore.[5] Physicians had little difficulty in providing hypothetical mechanisms with which to explain this phenomenon; the mother's blood supply unquestionably sustained the growing child, and as late as the 1880s and 1890s some eminent physicians held that physical and emotional states could interfere with the pregnant woman's ability to assimilate food and thus with the child's fetal development.[6]

The nervous system provided another mechanism to help explain the assumed ongoing interaction between mother and fetus. Even after anatomists had shown that no direct connection existed between mother and embryo, the "reflex" ability of the human nervous system to modify other aspects of the body's physiological equilibrium seemed to explain adequately how maternal stress could "mark" the developing fetus. The pregnant woman was urged to be calm and reassuring, unaggressive and pious. "Cheerfulness, contentment, gratitude, hope, joy, and love," one mid-century author catalogued as desirable maternal qualities, while another warned against exciting the pregnant woman's "combativeness, destructiveness or revengeful feelings," for all could be communicated to her child and create lasting moral damage.[7] It seems almost too apparent that heredity thus served as a sanction in the communication and enforcing of accepted gender roles; those women who failed to live as women should were threatened with punishment through moral and physical debility in their children.

The child retained its passively malleable quality during nursing. "The new being," as one popular writer explained, "is dependent upon the state of the mother's blood from the moment of conception till weaned from the breast." Physicians accordingly warned nursing mothers of the danger of allowing themselves to succumb to inappropriate emotional states, such as anger, sexual desire, or envy; all could potentially injure the nursling by contaminating its milk. So sensitive was this presumed relationship that even momentary emotional states, such as anger, fear, or jealousy, could transform the mother's milk into a dangerous substance, one capable of producing anything from colic to congenital criminality in the suckling.[8] No one doubted that chronic illness or flawed temperament could be similarly transmitted to children. So assumed was this relationship that an accepted remedy for a weak or suspect hereditary endowment was the employment of a wet nurse whose health might counteract the biological mother's constitutional weakness. Thus incipient tuberculosis could be averted in the child of a nervous and run-down middle-class mother by procuring a vigorous farm woman as wet nurse. More common, however, was the opposite anxiety: a wet nurse, of lower-class origin, might impart in her milk the seeds of sensuality, alcoholism, and criminality.[9] At the very end of the century an earnest medical student carefully recorded his professor's warning that "cancer and insanity . . . marked tuberculosis, scrofula or syphilis . . . violent temper, or, at times, nervous temperament," all disqualified a biological mother from nursing her infant; the seeds of all these ills might be transmitted to the child in its milk.[10]

A third major aspect of early-nineteenth-century hereditarian views lay in their protean quality. One inherited, to employ nineteenth-century terminology, a diathesis or constitutional bent. Most authorities saw such predispositions as manifesting themselves in several inclusive patterns or configurations, the scrofulous and nervous being the most common. A diathesis was, in the words of a well-known clinician in 1884, "little other than an exceedingly chronic disease. It is a disease or taint which may be active at times, and which may be handed on to another generation."[11] Until the mid-nineteenth century, the idea that disease was in general a discrete entity—or even a well-defined physiological process with a peculiar natural history—was not generally accepted. This was still a period when both learned physicians and the common man saw disease as the sum of one's transactions with the environment—the resultant of a total physiological process. Hereditary constitutional endowment was one given, the peculiar pattern of life through which that original endowment passed, another. Many physicians and laymen assumed, moreover, that these patterns of diathetic weakness could exhibit an underlying unity. "Thus," as one physician explained it, "the insane, as a class, are unsound alike in mind and body. They inherit the multiform varieties of scrofula, and among them abound the Protean forms of nervous disease, hysteria, chorea, neuralgia and epilepsy."[12]

Such diathetic weakness did not imply the necessary emergence of a particular ill, but rather the potential for such disease, a potential which constituted the occasion for early and thoughtful prophylaxis. Tuberculosis, cancer, and mental illness seemed to fit naturally into this pattern. These "diathetic" conditions were not assumed to be *necessarily* hereditary; they might develop in any individual. But if they were "hereditarily entailed," they tended to appear, it was believed, earlier in life and to be far less amenable to cure. Chronic illnesses with little tendency to lasting remission obviously demanded an explanation consistent both with this pattern of development and with the physician's acknowledged helplessness.

Psychological aspects of individuality were assumed to be related intimately to his underlying constitution. An individual's emotional set and intellectual attributes had been assumed since classical antiquity to be determined by his fundamental constitutional pattern; and this humoral tradition was still very much alive through the middle of the nineteenth century. An army surgeon could, for example, warn medical examiners in 1840 that "a flabby phlegmatic habit, and a dull, stupid mind are often found together." These assumptions were well-nigh universal in pre-bellum medicine; case reports, for example, frequently began with a routine notation of the patient's constitutional type—whether phlegmatic or sanguine, plethoric or asthenic—along with age and sex.[13] The late-nineteenth-century emphasis on the hereditary origin of behavioral traits grew naturally out of such ancient habits of thought.

It was generally assumed, finally, that father and mother, male and female, played different roles in shaping the physical attributes of their child. The mother, for example, was generally seen as contributing temperament, the father intellect, the mother internal viscera, stamina and vitality, the father external musculature. This traditional conviction was, seemingly, documented by "sex-limited" ills such as color blindness and hemophilia, which suggested patterns of heredity dependent upon the particular sex of parents. Because color blindness and hemophilia, in particular, seemed connected with patterns of sexual transmission, they served to reinforce the popular, and psychologically resonant, assumption that the mother was directly responsible for the transmission of many constitutional ailments and that the closest influences often existed between mother and son, father and daughter.[14]

Most importantly, woman's responsibility continued throughout gestation and nursing, while the father's role ended at the moment of conception. This emphasis upon the role of the mother in shaping her child's ultimate psychic and physical health grew markedly in the second quarter of the century; while many authors before this period placed little emphasis upon the role of the mother during gestation—she was simply the nurturant incubator in which the father's seed matured—mid-nineteenth-century authorities on heredity tended to define the mother's responsibility as well-nigh inclusive, the father's as relatively minor and limited to the moment of conception.[15]

This configuration of ideas was well established by the beginning of the nineteenth century and went largely unchallenged through the century. The situation was stable; the empirical data—observations by both clinicians and laymen in regard to disease and human difference—did not and could not well change, while understanding of these phenomena changed almost as little as the phenomena themselves.[16]

Hereditarian assumptions had necessarily to be consistent with two categories of observation. First was the resemblance between parent

and child—a resemblance hardly invariable, however, and often contradicted by differences between siblings. Such impressionistic views of
individual differences and familial resemblance were, however, difficult to shape into explanatory forms; these observations could not be
doubted, but neither could they be precisely defined.

A second kind of data—one seeming to illustrate a connection
between disease and heredity—played a disproportionately prominent
role in the discussion of human heredity. Diseases seemed to fall into
three general categories. Acute infectious diseases were not considered
to be hereditary. Such ills as smallpox, influenza, cholera, and acute
fevers fell into this category.[17] At the other end of the spectrum,
physicians recognized a few seemingly discrete and absolutely hereditary conditions such as polydactylism and color blindness; but these
commanded little attention.[18] Since no one *doubted* that disease and
deformity could be hereditary, these were seen as atypically clear
examples of a general and unquestioned truth, too rare and too
intractable to serve as appropriate challenges to the physician's intellectual and clinical abilities.

Nineteenth-century attitudes toward heredity thus reflected peculiarly the existence of a third class of ailment, the chronic and constitutional—cancer, gout, mental illness, tuberculosis, and heart disease.
And these ills served sharply to underwrite the general views of heredity
we have tried to outline: they seemed to be inherited in patterns of
general, though not inevitable, constitutional weakness. They appeared to be progressive, largely idiopathic, and related to individual
idiosyncrasies of temperament and resistance. By the end of the
eighteenth century such constitutional ills were seen as largely hereditary in origin.

The conventional wisdom was clear and unequivocal. Physicians
and moralists warned from the late eighteenth century on against
marriage for money alone in defiance of considerations of health and
temperament. Erasmus Darwin expressed this consensus with characteristic exuberance at the very end of the century:

> Parental taints the nascent babe imbibes;
> Eternal war the Gout and Mania wage
> With fierce uncheck'd hereditary rage;
> Sad Beauty's form foul Scrofula surrounds
> With bones distorted, and putrescent wounds;
> And, fell Consumption! thy unerring dart
> Wets its broad wing in Youth's reluctant heart.[19]

Constitutional disease could be entailed as irrevocably as lands and
rents. "Family constitutions," William Buchan warned in his *Domes-*

tic Medicine, the most widely read popular health manual of the period between 1775 and 1830, "are as capable of improvement as family estates; and the libertine, who impairs the one, does greater injury to his posterity, than the prodigal, who squanders away the other."[20]

In the absence of verifiable knowledge, it is only to be expected that the interaction of social need and casual observation would create just such a flexible body of assumption. Social context, not empirical research or internal logic, determined the contours of nineteenth-century hereditarian thought. Some of these contextual factors were of a general sort, applying to all articulate members of society; others were peculiar to the needs and perceptions of the medical profession.

The physician's perspective is in many ways easiest to understand. Most important was his need to find explanations for the disease phenomena which made up his everyday routine, formulas at once flexible yet consistent with lay assumptions. Laymen, for example, recognized that most constitutional ills were generally unaffected by medical art; the physician's situation thus demanded an explanation which minimized the possible relevance of medical intervention.[21] Heredity provided just such a framework—indeed, one which the laity accepted with alacrity. Even the educated were convinced that most chronic and constitutional ills were rooted irrevocably in "the blood." Physicians felt called upon to denounce the "vulgar notion" that gout and tuberculosis, for example, were inherited as simply and absolutely as blue eyes, that they depended "upon some peculiar taint in the system."[22]

One inherited a weakness or predisposition toward a particular family of ailments, physicians explained; and if a well-developed case of hereditarily-entailed illness could not be cured, judicious prophylactic counsel might still make the difference between being a merely potential and an actual victim. The children of consumptive parents were certainly born with a predisposition to the disease itself, but, as one authority put it, there was "no reason to suppose that in the majority of instances, prophylactic treatment would not be attended with success."[23] Gout was almost universally assumed to be hereditary in origin and yet physicians urged that even children of the gout-ridden were not unavoidably doomed to its agonies. An individual with a strong hereditary predisposition might escape entirely if he avoided wine, meats, and a sedentary or dissipated life; conversely, an individual with normal metabolism or even a minor tendency toward gout who spent his life in idle and luxurious living could fall victim (and thus entail upon his children a much-increased likelihood of their becoming gouty). Similarly, with regard to insanity, the child of "nervous" and dyspeptic parents might well succumb to business or family stress which would only strengthen the character of an individual endowed with normal emotional resilience. In both instances a physician's timely counsel might make the difference between sickness and health.

These ideas are no arbitrary arrangement of unstructured speculation and traditional lore. They were informed by an unavoidable social logic: the age-old need of the medical profession to find an intellectual framework with which to help rationalize its basic function, the treatment of disease, and its subsidiary role, the explanation of human differences. For the physician to have thrown up his hands, to have confessed ignorance and impotence would have been a very real failure of commitment. Heredity thus became one of the necessary elements in the endlessly flexible etiological model that served to underwrite the social effectiveness of the late-eighteenth- and early-nineteenth-century physician. Natural endowment, environmental stress, inadequate or improper diet, climate—all interacted to produce health or disease. In a period before the germ theory, before Weismann, before immunology, no single element in this etiological equation could be defined and evaluated. The physician was thus rarely at a loss to explain and reassure.

These explanatory models also played a more diffuse social role, serving as disease sanction within the culture generally. Doctors were, on the whole, little different from others of their class and time; and hereditary predispositions helped dramatize the need for temperance, for moderation in diet and sexual relations.[24] The sins of the fathers could thus act literally as a plague debilitating and stigmatizing their children. Such homiletic uses were to become increasingly prominent in hereditarian formulations as the nineteenth century progressed.

Until the 1840s these concepts were accepted components of conventional medical wisdom—but neither particularly prominent nor controversial. Perhaps most striking—at least in retrospect—they were employed comparatively little in the rationalization of social problems. Criminality, pauperism, and prostitution were not ordinarily seen as peculiarly hereditary in origin. Even in regard to mental illness and mental deficiency, where a substantial degree of hereditary causation was assumed, there were no calls for eugenic marriage laws, for sterilization of the criminal and the retarded. (Physicians and clergymen warned routinely, as we have seen, against marriages for wealth alone or to the nervous and scrofulous, but only in the form of

individual admonition.) The determinism which characterized hereditarian thought in the last decades of the nineteenth century was
conspicuously absent.

Beginning in the 1840s emphases changed markedly. Hereditarian
explanations of both individual disease and antisocial behavior became
with each succeeding decade increasingly pervasive and emotion-filled.
Yet the body of knowledge and observation which legitimated such
ideological usage remained stable. No new insights or discoveries
altered the configuration of assumption already outlined. The vast
majority of the publicists, social thinkers, and physicians who popularized hereditarian ideas never questioned their truth or adequacy;
they simply used them more frequently, more deterministically, and in
increasingly social contexts. "Like begets like," as a prominent advocate of social hereditarianism explained in 1869, "is for the existing
state of science an ultimate fact."[25]

A few relevant details were added to the body of scientific knowledge. A growing number of clinical entities were identified and shown
to be hereditary—Huntington's chorea, for example, and Friedrich's
ataxia. But no one ever doubted that such absolutely hereditary
conditions existed, while their comparative rarity militated against
their having any major impact. A growing body of would-be empirical
studies of institutional populations also bolstered the assumption that
insanity, mental deficiency, deafness, and blindness were frequently
hereditary in origin, often, indeed, the result of consanguineous
marriage. (By far the most widely quoted was S. G. Howe's study of
idiocy in Massachusetts.)[26] But such data only reaffirmed in appropriately positivistic terms the traditional beliefs already described.

An objection would now seem to be in order. Surely Darwin and
evolutionary thought must have focused attention on the importance
of heredity in human affairs? The answer is problematical. A growing
interest in hereditarian modes of social explanation was firmly established in the 1840s. Forces independent of the formal debate on
species and evolution—and antedating it—must therefore have played
an autonomous role. Moreover, Darwin's own formulations—though
they clearly had the effect of increasing the prevalence, legitimacy, and
emotional relevance of hereditarian explanatory models—had little, if
any, effect in reshaping generally accepted attitudes toward human
heredity. Darwin's doctrine of pangenesis was consistent with—indeed,
essentially a formalization of—mechanisms used traditionally to explain heredity in general and the inheritance of environmental effects
in particular.[27]

That other great bench mark in the history of biology, the germ
theory, also played an ambiguous role in the shaping of nineteenth-

century hereditarian thought. One might suppose that it would have served, both immediately and by implication, to reduce dependence on hereditarian models. Yet the reality was far more complex; for the period of most enthusiastic hereditarianism—let us say the years between 1885 and 1920—coincided with the most enthusiastic and uncritical acceptance of the germ theory.

The explanation is apparent. The germ theory certainly did seem to explain acute infectious ailments; but these had, as I have suggested, never been explained in constitutional and hereditarian terms. The paradigmatic constitutional ills—cancer, gout, mental illness, diabetes, epilepsy, heart disease—were not clarified by early bacteriological findings and continued routinely to be seen as constitutional and frequently hereditary in origin. (And, with the exception of syphilis, behavioral characteristics would not have been plausibly explained in terms of the germ theory's new insights.)

Most revealing is the case of tuberculosis, the greatest single cause of death in this period. Though the causative organism was discovered in 1882 (a discovery widely and instantly publicized in both lay and medical circles), tuberculosis continued for some time to be seen as an essentially constitutional ailment. It was all very well, as contemporaries argued, to identify the organism connected with the characteristic lesions of tuberculosis. But was it useful? The germ was distributed everywhere, and almost all were exposed; the problem lay in understanding why some succumbed and others did not. Hereditary predisposition and unfortunate environmental circumstances still seemed the most plausible explanation.[28] Hereditary transmission would have to be banished from the public mind, the antituberculosis agitator Lawrence Flick wrote in 1888, if the public campaign against the disease was to be successful. "So long has it held sway," he explained, "and so thoroughly has it been woven into our literature, into our ways of thinking, and even of acting, that it has actually become a remote cause of the disease." As late as 1912 a prominent English physician complained that it was still difficult to "disentangle men's thoughts from this erroneous teaching."[29] What hereditarian thought and the germ theory had in common was their ability to provide material and increasingly reductionist answers to problems of human individuality and pathology.

As with the germ theory, one might assume a priori that the public health movement with its origins in the 1830s and 1840s and its strongly environmental emphasis would have been in implicit conflict with hereditarian explanations of social phenomena. Again the truth is different. The assumption that acquired weakness and disability would be transmitted to children only added a new dimension of urgency to environmental appeals. Thus public health advocates could argue that pauperism not only lowered the health and vitality of urban and industrial populations, but passed on to slum children a burden of constitutional inadequacy which ill-suited them to cope with urban life. Both hereditarian arguments and environmental criticism were products of the same critical attitude toward certain aspects of social organization and the same desire to find a framework scientific in form with which to confront this intractable reality.

Though assumptions about the actual process of human heredity remained generally stable throughout the nineteenth century, hereditarian modes of explanation were utilized quite differently in the latter half of the century. The most dramatic trend was the increasingly aggressive employment of hereditarian arguments in the analysis of human behavior, especially antisocial behavior. But even within this growing commitment to social hereditarianism, there were major shifts in emphasis and nuance over time. The period between the 1840s and 1870s was marked by a tone sharply different from that which characterized the century's last two decades.[30]

The mood which characterized the growing use of hereditarian ideas in the middle third of the century was one of confidence that man's most fundamental attributes could and should be manipulated. "Who," as one publicist asked at the end of the period, "does not see that the terrific seriousness of the laws of hereditary descent, instead of being an injustice, is a proclamation to every man to institute a reform?" Such confident activism was characteristic of those who sought in this period to understand and articulate their generation's accepted wisdom about the relationships among health, heredity, and morality. Though such would-be reformers conceded that the human race inherited at least some seeds of disease, all was not hopeless. "There is a bright side to this view," William Alcott explained in his widely read *Laws of Health*: "Few persons are so much affected by inheritance as to render their condition necessarily one of misery." One need only "obey the whole physical and moral code," Alcott promised, and life "in nine cases out of ten, if not in ninety-nine out of a hundred, would, on the whole, be a blessing." Man's free will had brought him sickness and inherited constitutional weakness; free will could reverse this process. Thomas L. Nichols expressed this conviction in characteristically enthusiastic terms: "With all things in nature working together for good, we must not despair, but try to improve by culture and education. With good conditions, and surrounded by good influences, the faults and diseases of birth are gradually eradicated and cured, until scarcely a sign of them remains; and children born ugly, diseased, and with unfortunate mental and moral tendencies, may come to be more

beautiful, healthy and good than seemed possible in their infancy."
Hereditary taint implied striving, not despair.[31]

These bravely confident attitudes may seem paradoxical, for we have
become accustomed to equating hereditarian thought with determinism. Yet even a schematic examination of the mid-century roots of
hereditarian thought should indicate how appropriate, even predictable, was this tone of optimism and activism. Let me simply list—and
then elaborate—those areas of social concern and debate that fostered
the use of social hereditarianism. One such area was the contemporary
health reform movement—and thus indirectly the activist heritage of
religious enthusiasm which helped motivate overtly secular reformers
of health and diet.[32] Hereditarian modes of explanation were used increasingly as well in explaining America's newly created, rapidly
growing, and dismayingly intractable institutional populations. The
mechanisms of hereditary influence were also invoked in discussions
of marriage, sex roles, and the nurture of children. Finally, there were
the more limited and in a sense adventitious influences of phrenology
and temperance, in both of which hereditarian arguments figured
prominently.

Though it may seem at first thought inconsistent, the enthusiastic
religion which played so characteristic and prominent a role in
Jacksonian America helped to create an intellectual and emotional
atmosphere receptive to hereditarian explanations of behavior. The
Second Great Awakening had left a goodly number of pious activists in
search of a rationale for their activism; in an increasingly secular
society a failed millennialism might well have been expected to reassert
itself in reformist and material terms.[33] The zeal of health reformers
such as William Alcott, Sylvester Graham, and Thomas Nichols,
though expressed in attacks on tea and coffee, alcohol and sexual
excess, had a manifestly transcendent end which informed even their
most ingenuously materialistic appeals.[34]

It was only natural that these health reformers should have emphasized heredity; for heredity seemed to provide a mechanism which need
only be manipulated by the well-intentioned and well-informed to
bring about improvement in man and his society. The mother's ability
to shape the child she bore provided—with careful attention paid to the
avoidance of mating with the infirm and immoral—a means of
achieving social perfection.

... in its plastic state, during ante-natal life, life, like clay in the hand of the
potter, *it can be molded into absolutely any form of body and soul the
parents may knowingly desire.*

With human intelligence, conscience and moral aspiration, what might not
be accomplished in a few generations? It makes one dizzy to think of it. I
have known several couples of average capacity to set themselves seriously
at the task of producing a beautiful, bright and vigorous child. Not one of
them missed.

"The reformation of the world," as another enthusiast revealingly
contended, "can never be accomplished—the millennium of purity,
chastity, and intense happiness can never reach this earth except
through cheerful obedience to ante-natal laws. Whose heart does not
beat high at the bare possibility of becoming the progenitor of a world,
as it were, of pure, holy, healthy, and greatly elevated beings—a race
worthy of emerging from the fall—and of estamping on it a species of
immortality?" The possibility of such transcendent achievement implied a didactic truth; responsibility lay heavily upon those who would
beget children.[35]

Though extreme versions of this biological perfectionism were
intoned only by an "ultraist" minority, less literal, more meliorist
versions pervaded the health and moral reform literature so abundant
in mid-nineteenth-century America. It is hardly surprising that didactic authors should, in their transition from the spiritual to the secular,
have begun to employ hereditarian arguments routinely in their
homiletic arsenal. The traditional medical conception of ominous
taint averted through the exertion of will (as manifested in a wholesome regimen) provided an emotionally viable framework in which to
express a familiar American cultural stance, characteristic both in its
burden of anxiety and its promised relief through moral activism.
Heredity not only provided a sanction useful in enforcing traditional
standards of behavior but also served to express in this more secular
generation a sense of the sin and moral inability borne by all men—a
sin immanent yet not *quite* inevitable.

Health reformers managed, not surprisingly, to nurture a still
vigorous Biblical literalism. God could not well have created disease;
physical as well as moral deformity and inability were therefore a
consequence of man's fallen nature. "Who ever imagined Adam
suffering from dyspepsia," Elizabeth Blackwell asked, "or Eve in a fit
of hysterics? The thought shocks us—our Eden becomes a hospital."
The disease and constitutional weakness which, to some degree at least,
blighted the health and happiness of all men resulted from the effects
of millennia of sin—a cumulative sediment of impaired capacity.
There had been neither physicians nor disease in the Garden of Eden.
"Every human being is the product of a principle which has been
taking careful note of the lives and habits, the neglects, the excesses,

and the abuses of every crime against the body through all the generations from Adam down to the individual man in question."[36] In the post-Darwinian years especially, a surprising variety of articulate Americans found in heredity a plausible mechanism with which to restate in appropriately secular form a lingering commitment to "original sin." As Edward Bellamy's Julian West comments, in *Looking Backward*, on being informed that criminals were treated as atavisms, "I was brought up a Calvinist, and ought'nt to be startled to hear crime spoken of as an ancestral trait."

A related interest in heredity, one which developed in parallel fashion and often among the same publicists and health reformers, was a growing need to rationalize—and, in the case of particular individuals, to redefine—the role of women and of sexual relationships generally. Hereditarian arguments were used both by those who sought to expand the area of female autonomy and by those who sought to limit and define woman's role exclusively in terms of childbearing.

Traditional rhetorical formulas magnified and dignified woman's home-centered role; wives were warned routinely that failure to devote themselves to maternity, a willingness to practice birth control or abortion, might have baleful consequences for their children (as might a mother's failure to nurse). Emphasis on the centrality of the mother's relationship to her child during gestation and nursing probably reflected the emotional reality of many mid-nineteenth-century American families. Certainly it was consistent with the romantic justifications of domesticity conspicuous in the didactic literature of this period—and particularly with a certain revealingly strained emphasis on the need for emotional closeness. Physical and moral weakness in children served as a natural sanction in regard to such relationships, threatening punishment for lack of maternal commitment, for the father's failure to defer to the mother's emotional needs. "The rule, then, for the production of good children is exceedingly simple," as one widely read publicist explained: "Keep the mother happy and comfortable. The rule extends through the entire period of gestation and lactation."[37]

This nexus of image, admonition, and sanction was equally well suited to the ideological needs of feminist and crypto-feminist authors who sought to increase woman's autonomy within marriage. Some were quite explicit in their feminist use of social hereditarian arguments. Bad marriages, warned Harriot Hunt, make bad children: "Stultify, cramp, fetter, and blind woman, and you will see perpetuated what is now in our midst—dwarfish, puny physiques with ever active, nervous temperaments." Or, as another feminist explained in referring to the personal and sexual tyranny of a pious and oppressive husband:

"But can any one, who has any knowledge of the laws that govern our being—of heredity and pre-natal influences—be astonished that our jails and prisons are filled with criminals, and our hospitals with sickly specimens of humanity? As long as the mothers of our race are subject to such unhappy conditions, it can never be materially improved." Woman must first improve their own lot if their children were to enjoy moral, healthful, and successful lives.[38]

There is a strong correlation between the social convictions of such women and belief in phrenology on the one hand and a mechanistic and secularized vision of sin and salvation on the other. Harriot Hunt, for example, recorded her reaction to George Combe's phrenological lectures in the following terms: "They brought to light hidden affinities, they revealed indirect influences; and thus robbed metaphysical subtleties of their mysticism, effecting a reconciliation in the mind between sin and its consequences."[39]

Most of those mid- and late-nineteenth-century physicians and publicists who emphasized the centrality of the gestating mother's control of her child's eventual attributes were far less explicit; they seemed to accept the institution of marriage in general, but hoped to alter the texture of relationships within it. Much of such discussion revolved about the related questions of sex, power, and childbearing.[40] Woman's sexual autonomy, one such argument ran, would have to be ensured if a family were to remain free of the moral deterioration consequent upon sexual excess. (Such excess was attributed to the husband's often unbridled desires.) Heredity was the sanction most frequently employed in the proscribing of exploitative sexual relationships. Children conceived by a sexually exhausted father and sexually abused mother would, according to such formulas, suffer from one of those diathetical conditions that guaranteed a brief and miserable life. Publicists who employed such arguments tended consistently to emphasize the positive aspects of the mother's potential influence on her gestating child—her ability to shape thoughts, behavior, and hygienic regimen so as to produce "better babies," healthy, happy, moral, even talented in preselected directions. Alice Stockham, for example, a popular advocate of "marital hygiene" and birth control, suggested as a plausible course that a woman might study natural history or botany while pregnant, so that her child might be "a Humboldt, an Agassiz, or an Audubon."[41] Such tirelessly repeated admonitions are suggestively consistent with the emotional needs of a society in which birth rates were decreasing and career options for children increasingly diverse and problematical.

The temperance movement, influenced itself by both evangelicalism and covert feminism, served also to disseminate hereditarian explanations of behavior. Temperance advocates turned early in the nineteenth century to statistical arguments to prove that inebriety tended to become hereditary, that it led to ever more dramatic neurological and psychiatric problems in children. "In fact," as one such polemicist put it blandly, "a drunken parent can never be the father or mother of sound and healthy children." Few doubted that the habitual use of alcohol and other drugs could lead to deterioration of germ cells; even an isolated drinking bout might warp children conceived while their parents were under the influence. Institutional reports had, since the 1820s and 1830s, sought routinely to identify the proportion of such ills caused by parental alcoholism. As late as 1882 a prominent American psychiatrist could warn his colleagues: "That the brain and nervous system are conditioned by the intemperate habits of the parents, or by occasional indulgence in the use of intoxicants, is proved beyond all dispute by the facts of idiocy and imbecility of children conceived when one or both parents were under the influence of liquor."[42] Well into the twentieth century, indeed, the damage which alcohol could inflict on germ plasm remained not only a truism for publicists and reformers, but even a research theme for academic laboratory investigation.

Phrenology played a role similar to that of temperance in popularizing hereditarian ideas and reinforcing their importance in the explanation of human behavior. (In the vulgarized form in which most Americans encountered it, phrenology was the doctrine that certain areas of the brain controlled and embodied discrete cognitive, sensory, and emotional faculties—and that these were evident in the external configuration of the skull.)[43] Phrenology was the "new psychology" of the second quarter of the nineteenth century; and the connection between the assumption that there existed a specific material locus for particular emotions and psychological functions and an emphasis upon constitutional—and, by implication, hereditary—endowment is clear. Not surprisingly, the exhortatory literature of phrenological improvement became in the 1840s increasingly involved with explicit discussions of heredity and the means it provided for ensuring a desirable assortment of qualities in one's children. An appropriate maternal regimen could guarantee the development of particular phrenological traits. "Lay it up in your memories," Lorenzo Fowler urged, "that *we* give to our *children* their bad heads and bodies." If mothers understood and obeyed the principles of heredity, Fowler argued, "they would do far more towards perfecting the human race, and ridding the world of vice and immorality, than all the benevolent and moral reform societies united." Through such attention to proper mating, new generations would people the earth, he proclaimed in another tract, with "generations of *men* and *women*, having all that is great, and noble, and good in man, all that is pure, and virtuous, and beautiful, and angelic in woman. . . . Then shall God be honored, and man be perfectly holy and inconceivably happy, and earth be paradise."[44]

A consistent theme in the *American Journal of Phrenology*—indeed, in the writings of almost every important publicist of phrenology, whether English or American—was the need to contract eugenic marriage, and then to take every precaution during gestation and early childhood to ensure the development of healthy, moral, and intelligent children.[45] George Combe's *Constitution of Man*, the most widely read and influential exposition of phrenology, relied heavily on hereditarian assumptions, and these were quoted repeatedly by would-be reformers of health and heredity.[46] Mid-century advocates of health reform tended to endorse phrenology, while publicists of phrenology urged the need for hereditary improvement.

Temperance and phrenology were widely accepted and diffused in ante-bellum American society. It is hard to associate either concern with any specific social location—or at least with one more specific than that of the would-be middle class as a whole. Another and increasingly important nineteenth-century source of hereditarian thought was connected, however, with a very explicit social location—the use of hereditarian etiologies by those connected with institutions for the insane, prisons, and schools for the "idiotic." With the growth of such institutional populations and the parallel expansion of groups defined by an increasingly secular and urban society as deviant, heredity became useful in explaining the nature and intractability of the incarcerated and the stigmatized—and thus the specific policy commitments of proto-social scientists and administrators. Historians during the past decade have already begun to concern themselves with aspects of this development, so let me simply suggest that the relationship between the development of institutional populations and the gradual professionalization of their custodians implied the increasing attractiveness of hereditarian etiologies.[47] The use of such arguments was already commonplace by mid-century; that such formulations had already been well established in Europe only underlined their plausibility.

Through many aspects of mid-century America encouraged the use of hereditarian arguments, the exploitation of these ideas was by no means confined to America, though particular emphases may well have been characteristically American.[48] It was in France, indeed, rather than in the United States, that the application of broad hereditarian schemata to the explanation of social realities first became important in academic circles. These ideas were soon assimilated not only in the English-speaking world but in Germany and Italy as well.

In its most influential and crystallizing formulation, the emphasis on heredity was a product of mid-century French psychiatry and appeared in the guise of what later came to be called the "degeneration thesis." In the most significant exposition of this doctrine—by Benedict Morel in 1857—there are revealing parallels with contemporary American reform hereditarianism. Most important is the ultimate optimism which marked both. Morel, a pious French psychiatrist, also assumed that degeneration meant, literally, a deterioration from the state of physical perfection granted man before the fall. Drugs, alcohol, environments inimical to human health and development—such as mines and urban slums—progressively impaired the ability of men to pass on to their children even that tenuous state of health which they had themselves inherited. In a formulation that was to become increasingly influential in succeeding decades, Morel suggested the inheritance not of specific ills but of a neuropathic constitution which tended to deteriorate in a specific and progressive pattern from generation to generation; alcohol and neurosis in one generation might be followed by hysteria in the next, insanity in the third, then idiocy and sterility. Though much of this argument was simply a plausibly stated and plausibly timed fusion of elements already present in medical views of heredity, especially the protean diathesis concept, it did contain several new emphases.[49]

One was the focus on antisocial behavior, another the suggested pattern of cumulative degeneracy. Morel's degeneration concept was to become an explanatory cliché, first in the writings of psychiatrists, then among proto-social scientists, and even—in the hands of Zola and like-minded naturalists—among novelists. Frank Norris's *McTeague* (1899) provides a good example of the use of such hereditarian ideas by an American would-be naturalist.[50] It must be re-emphasized that Morel's original views (and those of his more immediate successors) were neither socially conservative nor oppressively deterministic. Since acquired characteristics could be inherited, environmental reform was all the more important; Morel, for example, vigorously opposed the use of alcohol and narcotics. His degeneration model was, moreover, self-liquidating in that its final stage was sterility.

The specter of neuropathic constitution, a basic inherited weakness which might manifest itself in any number of psychological ills, became a commonplace in the last third of the nineteenth century and survived well into the twentieth. Perhaps most significantly, it helped to establish the scientific legitimacy of all those marginal conditions —migraine headache, hysteria, obsessional states, anxiety and depression, homosexuality—which were gradually becoming part of the newly specialized neurologist's clinical world.[51] If such "nervous" conditions were to be accepted as true disease states and not mere impostures or wickedness, they would have to be seen as resting at some ultimate level upon a physical, and thus often by implication heredi- tary, reality. Neurosis was thus a kind of undifferentiated precursor state out of which insanity or other more specific conditions might develop. "To put it briefly," as one contemporary argued, "it is not only the insane diathesis which we dread, but it is also the nervous diathesis, which under favoring conditions may become the possibly insane diathesis." A prominent Boston psychiatrist was able to argue that neurosis could be far more significant—as indicating hereditary predisposition—than actual episodes of insanity in evaluating the prospects of those seeking to marry.[52] Not all such ideas were derived specifically from Morel and his intellectual successors, but they repre- sented a generally consistent expansion and generalization of his viewpoint (and of the tradition of diathetic heredity he subsumed).

Even in the writings of men who sought to disassociate themselves from absolute hereditarian formulations, the idea of neuropathic constitution maintained a tenacious hold throughout the nineteenth century. Let me cite two contrasting statements by James Jackson Putnam—soon-to-be-defender of Freudianism. "We bear no ticket-of- leave which stamps us as drunkards or maniacs on probation. . . . There is no original sin, and not even as it seems to me, original propensity, but only original capacity and original limitation, and even limitation is only another name for latent capacity." Yet in the same 1899 lecture, when he was speaking of those persistent neuroses which he treated so frequently, Putnam explained that "these disorders arise more readily, strike their roots wider and deeper, and keep a more tenacious hold if there is a native defect in the mechanism of the nervous system such as we see in the great class of cases which for convenience's sake may be grouped as *constitutional neurasthenias*."[53]

The degeneration concept was soon popularized outside the psychi- atric community, most conspicuously in the study of criminal behav- ior. The assumption that most crime should be interpreted as the normal behavior of a hereditary criminal type—one marked by pecu- liar physical "stigmata" of degeneration and thus determinable—be- came an intellectual foundation stone in the development of criminol- ogy as proto-social science. Crime and the criminal could now become the subject of concerted and orderly study. These deterministic theories of criminality were associated with the name and prestige of the Italian "criminal anthropologist" Cesare Lombroso. In Lombroso's formula- tion the criminal is seen not as a degenerate, but as an anomalous example of nonevolution, a type of atavism more akin to primitive man than to nineteenth-century man's more highly evolved and thus moral state. The links with evolutionary thought and hereditarian explanations of behavior are obvious.[54]

In the decades between 1875 and 1895 students of psychiatry generally and of abnormal and antisocial behavior particularly frequently
turned to somatic and mechanistic etiological models. This was only
one aspect of an international shift in the world-view of nineteenth-
century medicine. The development of pathological anatomy in the
first half of the century had created a need to see all diseases as consequences of—and necessarily legitimated by—discrete and determinable lesions.

Physicians naturally began to find hereditarian explanations for the
constitutional and degenerative diseases that played so important a role
in their social and intellectual world—explanations phrased in terms
of a somatic pathology. Cancer, heart disease, renal or circulatory ills
might be based on inherited structural differences, perhaps too small to
be observed by available techniques but capable over an individual's
life of causing impaired function and ultimately chronic and then fatal
illness. "The pathological variations of internal structure," as a
Philadelphia pathologist argued in 1871,

> which are conditional causes of disease, may now be handed down from
> parent to child, just as the peculiarities of feature, form of the skull, etc. of
> the Aryan and semitic races have been transmitted from generation to
> generation. . . . *Inheritance of microscopic peculiarities* of formation
> would do much towards further explaining many obscurities concerning
> the way in which hereditary idiosyncrasies of disease occur. Thus, for
> example, a congenital smallness of the arteries supplying the feet may be the
> direct cause of senile gangrene coming on when the powers of life become
> feeble in old age. . . .[55]

In medicine generally, as elsewhere in nineteenth-century thought,
emphasis upon heredity increased, although knowledge of the process
itself remained—perhaps necessarily—imprecise.

American popularizers of hereditarian ideas in the 1870s reflected all
these themes and influences: the ideas of the French degeneration
theorists, a need to elaborate mechanisms appropriately and reassur-
ingly scientific, an emphasis on environmental reform, a characteristically American social activism, and a diffuse evangelicalism.

Richard Dugdale was almost certainly the most influential of such
immediately post-bellum publicists. Though well known to his contemporaries as an omnipresent social reformer, Dugdale was to become
better known to posterity as delineator of the infamous Jukes family,
eponymous representatives of the role played by hereditary taint in
shaping a class of congenital criminals, prostitutes, and paupers.
While working as secretary of the New York Prison Association, one of
the numerous benevolent associations in which he played an active
role, Dugdale studied the hereditary criminal and pauper proclivities

of a particular family in upstate New York. After accumulating an impressive array of history, hearsay, local tradition, and rumor, Dugdale was able to conclude that the descendants of a particular revolutionary officer's misalliance had already cost the state of New York some million-and-a-third dollars. But his remedy was not what it would have been half a century later; Dugdale pleaded not for sterilization but for environmental reform and control. Missions and schools could alter even the most ominous predisposition in young people. As Dugdale himself explained, "environment tends to produce habits which may become hereditary, especially so in pauperism and licentiousness, if it should be sufficiently constant to produce modification of cerebral tissue. . . . From the above considerations the logical induction seems to be, that environment is the ultimate controlling factor in determining careers, placing heredity itself as an organized result of invariable environment." Thus, he reasoned, the control of pauperism and crime would become a possibility if the necessary training could be made to extend over two or three generations.[56]

The policy implications of Dugdale's work seemed clear enough to reformers of his generation. As Elisha Harris, pioneer public health advocate and author of an even earlier survey of heredity in a prison population, commented in 1877, "I have seen the 'Juke' family that Mr. Dugdale has described, and I have not seen one of them that could not have been saved as a child, except those that were born without the use of their faculties."[57] Only the idiotic and imbecile were beyond help. Similarly, Charles Loring Brace, founder of New York's Children's Aid Society, argued in an ingenuously optimistic blend of Darwinism and Morelian degeneration that the "struggle for existence" in the American environment removed the most vicious and ungoverned among the poor. "Probably no vicious organization," he contended, "with very extreme and abnormal tendencies is transmitted beyond the fourth generation; it ends in insanity or cretinism or the wildest crime."[58]

Perhaps the most remarkable aspect of Dugdale's work is the systematic misuse of his conclusions by succeeding generations. Beginning in the late 1870s and early 1880s and continuing in a rising crescendo of positivistic hand wringing, Americans explained phenomena as varied as class identity, criminality, and "pauperism" in terms increasingly hereditarian and deterministic.[59] The environmentalism and optimism which had characterized mid-century discussions of heredity were gradually replaced in the 1880s by a growing biological reductionism and emphasis on authoritarian solutions. Thus one medical enthusiast could argue casually in 1891 that fifteen minutes with the surgeon's scalpel would have prevented all the crime and pauperism of the Jukes heritage and steered a good deal of money into more constructive channels.[60]

Since the 1830s and 1840s would-be reformers of health and morals had chastised those who would contract dysgenic marriages, but almost none had called for legislative intervention.[61] Both in England and the United States such critics conceded that the national character forbade a mandatory interference with individual liberties; education and persuasion, not statutes, were the appropriate tools of social reform. This changed in the mid-1880s and early 1890s. Now demands were beginning to be made for the absolute interdiction of reproduction among the defective and delinquent. This "final solution" to the social problem manifested itself in a more moderate form in the demand for stringent and well-enforced marriage laws. The habitual recourse to environmental solutions could hardly survive unaltered in this climate; it was already in short supply in the 1880s in minds beginning to reflect and articulate a growing race consciousness and demanding sterilization of the idiotic and criminal, restriction of immigration, and passage of eugenic marriage laws. The change in tone and emphasis from the reform hereditarianism of mid-century is sharp and unmistakable. By the end of the 1880s the eugenics movement had come into being in all but name.

Yet the scientific substrate upon which these ideas rested had not changed substantially. Most significantly, the assumption that acquired characteristics could become hereditary remained essentially unchallenged until the twentieth century; the dualism of Weismann, so plausible in retrospect, was still controversial among the advanced thinkers who debated it in the 1890s.[62] The physicians, publicists, and social thinkers who concerned themselves with human heredity did not in general grasp the full social implications of Weismannism until well into the twentieth century. Physicians still assumed, as they had for generations, that the inheritance of mental illness, "pauperism," and other constitutional ills was a protean affair of diathesis, habit, and predisposition. They had simply become more rigid and despairing in their formulations.[63] Absolute distinction between the innate and the acquired was a concept so novel, so contrary to traditional common sense, that it was not generally assimilated until the second decade of the twentieth century.

Equally significant in the last decades of the nineteenth century was the fact that eugenic goals and the programs with which to achieve them were still legitimated in traditional and ultimately transcendent terms. As one anonymous early advocate of eugenic sterilization argued,

In vain will we continue to plead the ordinary Religious and Moral Reforms of the day, for the salvation of the individual, or for the race. In vain will we apply the Moral plasters and blisters of cure.

Every effort thus made is so much waste of vitality in the wrong
direction. . . .

If human beings were made right—with perfect mental, moral and
physical organizations, there would be no necessity for the Doctors of Law,
Divinity or Medicine—prisons, dram-shops, poor-houses, gallows all other
necessary evils would cease to exist. . . .

This would be the coming of the Messiah—the dawning of the Millennium—the establishment of divine law on earth—the religion of the future! . . .

It is to the destiny of the unborn millions, that the Scientist, the Moralist,
and friend of the race should direct their efforts for the regeneration and
purity of mankind.[64]

The possibility of attaining such ultimate social good could justify the
harshest of eugenic measures.

We have thus far studiously avoided the two intellectual themes
which have received particular attention from historians concerned
with explaining the use of biological metaphors in late-nineteenth-
century American society—scientific racism and Social Darwinism. Yet
both were related logically and emotionally to hereditarian ideas.

In the closing years of the nineteenth century and opening years of
the twentieth, when nativism and racially tinged eugenics were accepted with widespread and generally uncritical enthusiasm, the
hereditarian assumptions necessary to these positions were, as has been
suggested, long-familiar clichés to social activists and would-be reformers and analysts of society. Most fundamental was the assumption
that behavioral characteristics had a biological and thus presumably
racial basis. Moreover, all the qualities associated with a hypothetically
malevolent hereditary diathesis were attributed to one or more of the
new immigrant groups. Even in the writings of committed urban
reformers, "racial realities," as they were sometimes called, helped to
explain the seemingly disproportionate incidence of insanity, tuberculosis, criminality, and alcoholism among particular ethnic groups.
Though distinct in their origins, racial and hereditarian modes of
social explanation were ultimately consistent, synergistic—and responsive to many of the same social needs.[65]

Yet there were illuminating differences as well. Most conspicuously,
hereditarian thought was not necessarily bound up with xenophobia.[66]
Hereditarian thinkers entertained as well a positive vision of social
good embodied in the concept of racial identity and communality.
Such assumptions are explicit in the writings of many late-nineteenth-
century reformers and social commentators, as in this example: "as
all members [of the body] constitute but one whole, and each is linked
to the other by a chain of sympathy, if by no stronger tie, so the full
development of all must be essential to the perfection and full play of

each. Besides, it is not the mere continuation of the race that should be sought, but its improvement and perfection." Racial health was thus a sum of individual energies, as an individual's health reflected a particular balance of vital energies accumulated or expended; "each man represents an unit in the energy that is expended today to influence the future."[67] Such tribalism in a period of social change and individualism served to order and reassure; to some Americans at least, the rewards of individual achievement had to be placed in a communal and in that sense selfless, transcendent, and morally acceptable context. Commitment to physical and moral health was far more than an individual concern. "Beyond the welfare of the individual," as one physician expressed it, "it means health and happiness to descendants and that earthly immortality of the race which must precede that of heaven."[68]

Certainly evolutionary ideas played a role in underlining the relevance as well as in articulating particular aspects of late-nineteenth-century hereditarian thought. Yet it is almost impossible to be precise in explicating chronological, logical, and social relationships between the two; their interpenetration was too complex and too labile—especially since in lay hands both evolutionary and hereditarian thought drew upon a common heritage of tenaciously assumed, yet loosely formulated, intellectual reflexes. Lomboso's criminal anthropology was, for example, a mélange of Morel, of physical anthropology, and of derivative evolutionism. All such discussions of the characteristics of particular races or the biological basis of particular behavior tended to confirm hereditarian and constitutional explanations of disease and personality.

By the last years of the century social hereditarianism had already undergone a complex evolution since its mid-century origins; the stage had been set for its tenaciously aggressive, nativistic, and formally eugenic metamorphosis. The vogue of Mendelism in the first decade of the twentieth century only crystallized and added impetus to well-established intellectual and emotional concerns. In the last quarter of the nineteenth century publicists, physicians, proto-social scientists, and social workers had already applied hereditarian explanations to the analysis of almost every visible social problem. Hereditarian explanations of human behavior had the virtue of seeming to embody the concepts and prestige of science, while at the same time being devoid of verifiable content—a remarkably functional combination that made hereditarianism usable in a wide variety of social contexts.

As the complexity and indeterminacy of human heredity became increasingly apparent in the second, third, and fourth decades of the twentieth century and as German National Socialism provided an ultimate comment on racial politics, the great majority of laboratory scientists and even social thinkers disassociated themselves from interventionist eugenics.[69] The vogue of deterministic and socially oriented hereditarianism was thus limited to a period between the late 1880s and the realization by the 1930s that human heredity and its social implications had no simple solutions. These had been peculiar years, years in which hopes and possibilities had grown out of a fortuitous combination of social need and imprecise scientific knowledge.

Why were hereditarian doctrines so pervasive in the nineteenth century? Why did their emphases shift in the last half of the century? Clearly no single explanation will do; the vogue of hereditarianism was too broad, its emotional relevance too visceral. Moreover, although certain trends imparted a characteristically American cast to hereditarian arguments, it was a much broader trend, characterizing late-nineteenth-century social thought in England and on the Continent as well as in the United States.

There are a number of obviously relevant explanatory factors. Most all-encompassing is the relationship between these ideas and structural change in nineteenth-century America—the growth of industry and of cities, a decreasing birth rate, the bureaucratization of work roles. In this sense, the vogue of social hereditarianism can be viewed as one response to the emotional needs created by modernization. But generalization on this level is hardly illuminating; one must look at specific textures and relationships.[70]

There is an obvious parallel between the vogue of hereditarianism and the growth of secular modes of thought—the shift from formally religious to formally scientific schemes of reference as a source of value legitimation and as specific structuring elements in the world view of the educated and articulate. As the social problems connected with structural change became more pressing, it was perhaps inevitable that a good many Americans would seek solutions framed and justified in scientific terms. Heredity seemed to provide not only a meaningful explanation for individual and even collective behaviors but a mechanism as well (even if we would not regard it as such). Emphasis on the "laws" of heredity, "as definite and fixed as those of chemistry," on "like producing like," on the "determination of criminality" provided a kind of spurious yet functional order. Heredity, as one cynical female physician remarked in 1881, had become "the fashion of the hour for those who affect science."[71]

These doctrines brought comfort to a generation needful of imposing order upon ominously changing social phenomena. The rhetorical content of such arguments was far more important than the formal; to find and intone an explanation was to reassure, even if the logical content of the intonation pointed to deterministic, even despairing conclusions. The seemingly deterministic trend of late-nineteenth-century hereditarian ideas did not in fact breed a pessimistic quietism. Precisely at its most pessimistic moments one finds in social hereditarianism a kind of rhetorical euphoria, a self-conscious satisfaction in understanding; for understanding implied not only control and emotional reassurance but also a necessary rationale for the manipulative activism that many Americans still admired.

For some Americans the logic of a particular institution informed their receptivity to hereditarian explanations. Such ideas were useful in helping justify the social position of practicing physicians in general, and especially of those individuals who dealt with institutional populations; the criminal or lunatic who could be defined and classified within the same complex of ideas that explained why he could not ordinarily be cured was a less threatening and more manageable reality.[72]

Another institutionally structured aspect of hereditarian thought in this period was its use by the emerging social and policy sciencies The role of Lombroso's criminal anthropology in the development of criminology and penology is only exemplary. Hereditarian ideas also pervaded the superstructure of formal knowledge which helped legitimate other new disciplines such as sociology and social work. To those who sought to understand and cope with the increasingly visible and alarming increase of pauperism and dependency, heredity became an important tool.[73] Moreover, heredity could explain criminality and dependency in ultimately individual terms and thus obviate the more ambiguous task of evaluating the role of society in human failure. As one student of prisoners and paupers explained: "There is never found in the pauper or criminal class, except by accident, a normal, well developed, healthy adult. At least not in America, where the will of the majority is recognized as rational law by all rational beings, and the opportunities of self-support are ample for the healthy and strong."[74]

Late-nineteenth-century hereditarian ideas served another, more diffuse though perhaps even more fundamental purpose. The formulas of social hereditarianism helped to ensure a continuity in general social norms and provided an emotionally persuasive source of sanctions to guard against their infringement; indeed, it might well be argued that only through such shifts in formal content and sources of authority could traditionally prescribed norms find adequate ideological support in this period of rapid social change.

Hereditarian ideas helped to maintain social value continuity in a number of different and not necessarily consistent ways. Perhaps most importantly, heredity seemed a largely individual problem; biological realities were individual realities and social problems the sum of such individual realities and actions. Demands for governmental intervention in enforcing eugenic measures—as in analogous trends with respect to temperance and prostitution—reflected frustrated moral suasion as much as a reasoned commitment to the need for expanded power for the state. One finds echoes of a traditional religious commitment in even the most overtly secular visions of eugenicists and social reformers who sought to restore national vitality and racial purity. Social hereditarianism served as one avenue through which pre-bellum activist and reformist, even millennial, trends could find emotional and social policy continuity.

Nineteenth-century social hereditarianism provided a framework within which behavior was explicable in terms of will and consequent action. One could change, one could *will* to have happy, healthy, intelligent children—-children able to control their own will and thus destiny, able to grapple successfully with the ominous and often unmanageable tendencies toward moral entropy and lack of control that seemed to lurk within almost all individuals. If, as some social historians have argued, structural change was creating more and more emotional demands upon the family, demands increasingly harsh upon the individual's capacity for self-control, if careers were becoming more and more problematical in an increasingly urban, economically unstable society, then assurances of hereditary ability would have been functional indeed.[75]

Many middle-class or would-be middle-class parents needed the assurance that their children would have the will and ability to compete and could ill tolerate the thought that they might be the cause of their children's failure. "All men naturally feel anxious about themselves," one mid-century physician explained; "each one asks, am I the tainted? Will my offspring suffer from me?" A child met with sufficient obstacles without having to struggle against "a lessened power of self-control and resistance." Chance, as another reformer put it, is unknown to nature; if children "were formed for the practice of virtue, they could not follow vicious habits so easily."[76] By the 1880s the child's right "to be well born" had become a cliché in the appeals of health reformers.

The theme is unmistakable, and not limited to programmatic statements but deeply internalized by many Americans. Here are two passages from personal letters, the first written in 1837, the other in 1903. The former is contained in a letter from W. H. Channing to Dr. James Jackson and describes his reaction at seeing an infant in its cradle. Where else, he suggested, could one see

might justice & mercy of providence more clearly than in the relation of the
character of children to their parents. Here before you in miniature are your
own characters—your own virtues and faults. There all sleeping peacefully
are the results of the . . . passions and efforts of generations. You are to reap
in your intercourse with that as yet insignificant *thing*, so soon to be a most
[expressive] *person*, what you & your father have [sowed] in your turns of
careless nursing, of [unbent?] relation, of strenuous toil, of faithful principle. Here is justice.[77]

Or again, in the altered yet reminiscent words of Charles B. Davenport,
a trained zoologist and soon-to-be advocate of eugenics, in a 1903 letter
to John Shaw Billings: "For what greater encouragement can there be
for the teacher, the philanthropist or the man himself than to be
assured that the improvement of the individual means an improvement
of the race through a permanent bettering of the germ-plasm: that our
children will, on the average, reap an advantage and be born on a
higher plane because of all our strivings."[78] This was the irreducible
core of the hereditarian commitment—the desire for assurance that
one's children would somehow be endowed with the virtues required to
make their lives successful—and thus allay the guilt, the anxious
striving, the ambivalence of their parents.

Men do not easily tolerate indeterminacy and, with the decreasing
emotional relevance of a predominantly religious world view, medical
and scientific ideas, metaphors, and vocabulary would have to perform
social functions previously fulfilled by a more traditionally spiritual
configuration of ideas and authority. Thus the racism, the xenophobia,
the movements for sterilization and "positive eugenics" can be seen as
adaptational tactics, helping to create a cognitive world picture
through which particular individuals could impose a consoling order
upon a continually shifting reality. Such ideas reaffirmed in terms
comfortingly scientific the importance of the individual and his moral
choices; their emotional appeal was strong indeed. The concern of
social hereditarianism with the explanation of deviance and the
predictability of children's behavior was consistent with this pattern of
belief.

Yet all such conclusions must be tentative. What can be demonstrated with some certainty, however, is a specific configuration of
ideas, the structure of which at least suggests particular relationships
between form and function, and thus a relevance to particular social
needs. Most insistently, these ideas illustrate the strength and continuity of nineteenth-century social thought, its ability to find appropriate
forms in which to fulfill the traditional need to prescribe and proscribe.

2

The Female Animal: Medical and Biological Views of Women

Since at least the time of Hippocrates and Aristotle, the roles assigned to women have attracted an elaborate body of medical and biological justification. This was especially true in the nineteenth century as the intellectual and emotional centrality of science increased steadily. This chapter is an attempt to outline some of the shapes assumed by the nineteenth-century debate over the ultimate bases for woman's domestic and childbearing role.[1] In form it resembles an exercise in the history of ideas; in intent it represents an attempt to use the form of conventional ideas to gain insight into their social and psychological function.

This approach was selected for a variety of reasons. Role definitions exist on a level of prescription beyond their embodiment in the individuality and behavior of particular historical persons. They exist, rather, as a formally agreed upon set of characteristics understood by and acceptable to a significant proportion of the population. As formally agreed upon social values they are, moreover, retrievable from historical materials. Such social role definitions, however, have a more than platonic reality, for they exist as parameters with which and against which individuals must either conform or define their deviance. When inappropriate to social, psychological, or biological reality, such definitions can themselves engender anxiety, conflict, and demands for change.

During the nineteenth century, economic and social forces at work within Western Europe and the United States began to compromise traditional social roles. Some women at least began to question—and

This chapter was written with Carroll Smith-Rosenberg as coauthor.

a few to challenge overtly—their constricted place in society. Naturally enough, men hopeful of preserving existing social relationships, and in some cases threatened themselves both as individuals and as members of particular social groups, employed medical and biological arguments to rationalize traditional sex roles as rooted inevitably and irreversibly in anatomy and physiology. This chapter examines the ideological attack mounted by traditionally minded men against two of the ways in which women could express their dissatisfaction and desire for change: women's demand for improved educational opportunities and their decision to resort to birth control and abortion.

Much of this often emotionally charged debate was oblique and couched in would-be scientific and medical language. The Victorian woman's ideal social characteristics—nurturance, intuitive morality, domesticity, passivity, and affection—were all assumed to have a deeply rooted biological basis. These medical and scientific arguments formed an ideological system rigid in its support of tradition, yet infinitely flexible in the particular mechanisms which could be made to explain and legitimate woman's role.

Woman, nineteenth-century medical orthodoxy insisted, was starkly different from the male of the species. Physically, she was frailer, her skull was smaller, her muscles were more delicate. Even more striking was the difference in the nervous system of the two sexes. The female nervous system was finer, "more irritable," prone to overstimulation and resulting exhaustion. "The female sex," one physician explained in 1827, "is far more sensitive and susceptible than the male, and extremely liable to those distressing affections which, for want of some better term, have been denominated nervous, and which consist chiefly in painful affections of the head, heart, side, and indeed, of almost every part of the system."[2] "The nerves themselves," another physician concurred a generation later, "are smaller, and of a more delicate structure. They are endowed with greater sensibility, and, of course, are liable to more frequent and stronger impressions from external agents or mental influences."[3] Few if any questioned the assumption that in males the intellectual propensities of the brain dominated, while the female's nervous system and emotions prevailed over her conscious and rational faculties. Thus it was only natural, indeed inevitable, that women should be expected and permitted to display more affect than men; it was inherent in their very being.

Physicians saw woman as the product and prisoner of her reproductive system. It was the ineluctable basis of her social role and behavioral characteristics, the cause of her most common ailments;

woman's uterus and ovaries controlled her body and behavior from puberty through menopause. The male reproductive system, male physicians assured, exerted no parallel degree of control over man's body. Charles D. Meigs, a prominent Philadelphia gynecologist, stated with assurance in 1847 that a woman is "a moral, a sexual, a germiferous, gestative and parturient creature."[4] It was, another physician explained in 1870, "as if the Almighty, in creating the female sex, had taken the uterus and built up a woman around it."[5] A wise deity had designed woman as keeper of the hearth, as breeder and rearer of children.

Medical wisdom easily supplied hypothetical mechanisms to explain the interconnection between the female's organs of generation and the functioning of her other organs. The uterus, it was assumed, was connected to the central nervous system; shocks to the nervous system might alter the reproductive cycle—might even mark the gestating fetus, while changes in the reproductive cycle shaped emotional states. This intimate and hypothetical link between ovaries, uterus, and nervous system was the logical basis for the "reflex irritation" model of disease causation so popular in middle- and late-nineteenth-century medical texts and monographs on psychiatry and gynecology. Any imbalance, exhaustion, infection, or other disorder of the reproductive organs could cause pathological reactions in parts of the body seemingly remote.[6] Doctors connected not only the paralyses and headaches of the hysteric to uterine disease but also ailments in virtually every part of the body. "This disease," one physician explained, "will be found, on due investigation, to be in reality no disease at all, but merely the sympathetic reaction or the symptoms of one disease, namely a disease of the womb."[7]

Yet despite the commonsensical view that many such ailments resulted from childbearing, physicians often contended that far greater difficulties could be expected in childless women. Motherhood was woman's normal destiny, and those females who thwarted the promise immanent in their body's design must expect to suffer. The maiden lady, many physicians argued, was fated to a greater incidence of both physical and emotional disease than her married sisters and to a shorter life span.[8] Her nervous system was placed under constant pressure, and her unfulfilled reproductive organs, especially at menopause, were prone to cancer and other degenerative ills.

Woman was peculiarly the creature of her internal organs, of tidal forces she could not consciously control. Ovulation, the physical and emotional changes of pregnancy, even sexual desire itself were determined by internal physiological processes beyond the control or even the awareness of her conscious volition.[9] All women were prisoners of the cyclical aspects of their bodies, of the great reproductive cycle bounded by puberty and menopause, and by the shorter but recurrent cycles of childbearing and menstruation. All shaped a woman's personality, her social role, her intellectual abilities and limitations; all presented as well possibly "critical" moments in her development, possible turning points in the establishment—or deterioration—of future physical and mental health. As the president of the American Gynecological Society stated in 1900: "Many a young life is battered and forever crippled in the breakers of puberty; if it crosses these unharmed and is not dashed to pieces on the rock of childbirth, it may still ground on the ever-recurring shallow of menstruation, and lastly, upon the final bar of the menopause ere protection is found in the unruffled waters of the harbor beyond the reach of sexual storms."[10]

Woman's physiology and anatomy, physicians habitually argued, oriented her toward an "inner" view of herself and her worldly sphere. (Logically enough, nineteenth-century views of heredity often assumed that the father was responsible for a child's external musculature and skeletal development, the mother for the internal viscera, the father for analytical abilities, the mother for emotions and piety.)[11] Their secret internal organs, women were told, determined their behavior; their concerns lay inevitably within the home.[12] In a passage strikingly reminiscent of some mid-twentieth-century writings, a physician in 1869 depicted an idealized female world, rooted in the female reproductive system, sharply limited socially and intellectually, yet offering women covert and manipulative modes of exercising power:

> Mentally, socially, spiritually, she is more interior than man. She herself is an interior part of man, and her love and life are always something interior and incomprehensible to him. . . . Woman is to deal with domestic affections and uses, not with philosophies and science. . . . She is priest, not king. The house, the chamber, the closet, are the centres of her social life and power, as surely as the sun is the centre of the solar system. . . . Another proof of the interiority of woman, is the wonderful secretiveness and power of dissimulation which she possesses. . . . Woman's secrecy is not cunning; her dissimulation is not fraud. They are intuitions or spiritual perceptions, full of tact and wisdom, leading her to conceal or reveal, to speak or be silent, to do or not to do, exactly at the right time and in the right place.[13]

The image granted women in these hypothetical designs was remarkably consistent with the social role traditionally allotted to them. The instincts connected with ovulation made her by nature gentle, affectionate, and nurturant. Weaker in body, confined by menstruation and pregnancy, she was both physically and economically dependent upon the stronger, more forceful male, to whom she necessarily looked up with admiration and devotion.

Such stylized formulas embody, however, a characteristic yet entirely functional ambiguity. The Victorian woman was more spiritual than man, yet less intellectual, closer to the divine, yet prisoner of her most animal characteristics, more moral than man, yet less in control of her very morality. While the sentimental poets placed woman among the angels and doctors praised the transcendent calling of her reproductive system, social taboos made woman ashamed of menstruation, embarrassed and withdrawn during pregnancy, self-conscious and purposeless during and after menopause. Her body, which so inexorably defined her personality and limited her role, appeared to woman often degrading and confining.[14] The very romantic rhetoric which tended to suffocate nineteenth-century discussions of femininity only underlined with irony the distance between emotional reality and the forms of conventional ideology.

The nature of this formalistic scheme implied as well a relationship between the fulfilling of woman's true calling and ultimate social health. A woman who lived "unphysiologically"—and she could do so by reading or studying in excess, by wearing improper clothing, by long hours of factory work, or by a sedentary, luxurious life—could produce only weak and degenerate offspring. Until the twentieth century—as we have seen—it was almost universally assumed that acquired characteristics in the form of damage from disease and improper life styles in parents would be transmitted through heredity; a nervous and debilitated mother could have only nervous, dyspeptic, and undersized children.[15] Thus, appropriate female behavior was sanctioned not only by traditional injunctions against the avoidance of individual sin in the form of unnatural modes of life but also by the higher duty of protecting the transcendent good of social health, which could be maintained only through the continued production of healthy children. Such arguments were to be invoked with increasing frequency as the nineteenth century progressed.

In mid-nineteenth-century America it was apparent that women—or at least some of them—were growing dissatisfied with traditional roles. American society in mid-nineteenth century was committed—at least formally—to egalitarian democracy and evangelical piety. It was thus a society which presumably valued individualism, social and economic mobility, and free will. At the same time it was a society experiencing rapid economic growth, one in which an increasing number of families could think of themselves as middle class and seek a life style appropriate to that station. At least some middle-class women, freed economically from the day-to-day struggle for subsistence, found in these values a motivation and rationale for expanding their roles into areas outside the home. In the Jacksonian crusades for piety, for temperance, for abolition, and in pioneering efforts to aid the urban poor, women played a prominent role, a role clearly outside the confines of the home. Women began as well to demand improved educational opportunities—a few even admission to colleges and medical schools. A far greater number began, though more covertly, to see family limitation as a necessity if they would preserve health, status, economic security, and individual autonomy.

Only a handful of nineteenth-century American women made a commitment to overt feminism and to the insecurity and hostility such a commitment implied. But humanitarian reform, education, and birth control were all issues which presented themselves as real alternatives to every respectable churchgoing American woman.[16] Contemporary medical and biological arguments reflected and sought to eliminate two of these threats to traditional role definitions: demands by women for higher education and family limitation.

Since the beginning of the nineteenth century American physicians and social commentators generally had feared that American women were physically inferior to their English and Continental sisters. Young women of the urban middle and upper classes seemed in particular less vigorous, more nervous than either their own grandmothers or European contemporaries. Concern among physicians, educators, and publicists over the physical deterioration of American womanhood grew steadily during the nineteenth century and reached a high point in its last third.

Many physicians were convinced that education was a major factor in bringing about this deterioration, especially education during puberty and adolescence. It was during these years that the female reproductive system matured, and it was this process of maturation that determined the quality of the children which American women would ultimately bear. During puberty, orthodox medical doctrine insisted, a girl's vital energies must be devoted to development of the reproductive organs. Physicians saw the body as a closed system possessing only a limited amount of vital force; energy expended in one area was necessarily removed from another. The girl who curtailed brain work during puberty could devote her body's full energy to the optimum development of its reproductive capacities. A young woman, however, who consumed her vital force in intellectual activities was necessarily diverting these energies from the achievement of true womanhood. She would become weak and nervous, perhaps sterile, or more commonly—and in a sense more dangerously for society—capable of bearing only sickly and neurotic children, children able to produce only feebler and more degenerate versions of themselves.[17] The brain and ovary could not develop at the same time. Society, mid-century physicians warned, must protect the higher good of racial health by avoiding situations in which adolescent girls taxed their intellectual faculties in academic competition. "Why," as one physician pointedly asked, "spoil a good mother by making an ordinary grammarian?"[18]

Yet where did America's daughters spend these years of puberty and adolescence, doctors asked, especially the daughters of the nation's most virtuous and successful middle-class families? They spent these years in schools; they sat for long hours each day bending over desks, reading thick books, competing with boys for honors. Their health and that of their future children would inevitably be marked by the consequences of such unnatural modes of life.[19] If such evils resulted from secondary education, even more dramatically unwholesome was the influence of higher education upon the health of those few women intrepid enough to undertake it. Yet their numbers increased steadily, especially after a few women's colleges were established in the East and state universities in the Midwest and Pacific Coast began cautiously to accept coeducation. Women could now, critics agonized, spend the entire period between the beginning of menstruation and the maturation of their ovarian systems in nerve-draining study. Their adolescence, as one doctor pointed out, contrasted sadly with those experienced by healthier, more fruitful forebears: "Our great-grandmothers got their schooling during the winter months and let their brains lie fallow for the rest of the year. They knew less about Euclid and the classics than they did about housekeeping and housework. But they made good wives and mothers, and bore and nursed sturdy sons and buxom daughters and plenty of them at that."[20]

Constant competition among themselves and with the physically stronger males disarranged the coed's nervous system and left her anxious, prey to hysteria and neurasthenia. One gynecologist complained as late as 1901:

> The nervous force, so necessary at puberty for the establishment of the menstrual function, is wasted on what may be compared as trifles to perfect health, for what use are they without health? The poor sufferer only adds another to the great army of neurasthenia and sexual incompetents, which furnish neurologists and gynecologists with so much of their material. . . . Bright eyes have been dulled by the brain-fag and sweet temper transformed into irritability, crossness and hysteria, while the womanhood of the land is deteriorating physically.

She may be highly cultured and accomplished and shine in society, but her future husband will discover too late that he has married a large outfit of headaches, backaches and spine aches, instead of a woman fitted to take up the duties of life.[21]

Such speculations exerted a strong influence upon educators, even those connected with institutions which admitted women. The state universities, for example, often prescribed a lighter course load for females or refused to permit women admission to regular degree programs. "Every physiologist is well aware," the Regents of the University of Wisconsin explained in 1877, "that at stated times, nature makes a great demand upon the energies of early womanhood and that at these times great caution must be exercised lest injury be done. . . . Education is greatly to be desired," the Regents concluded: "but it is better that the future matrons of the state should be without a University training than that it should be produced at the fearful expense of ruined health; better that the future mothers of the state should be robust, hearty, healthy women, than that, by over study, they entail upon their descendants the germs of disease."[22] This fear for succeeding generations born of educated women was widespread. "We want to have body as well as mind," one commentator noted, "otherwise the degeneration of the race is inevitable."[23] Such transcendent responsibilities made the individual woman's personal ambitions seem trivial indeed.

One of the remedies suggested by both educators and physicians lay in tempering the intensely intellectualistic quality of American education with a restorative emphasis on physical education. Significantly, health reformers' demands for women's physical education were ordinarily justified not in terms of freeing the middle-class woman from traditional restrictions on bodily movement, but rather as upgrading her ultimate maternal capacities. Several would-be physiological reformers called, indeed, for active participation in housecleaning as an ideal mode of physical culture for the servant-coddled American girl. Bedmaking, clothes-scrubbing, sweeping, and scouring provided a varied and highly appropriate regimen.[24]

Late-nineteenth-century women physicians, as might have been expected, failed ordinarily to share the alarm of their male colleagues when contemplating the dangers of coeducation. No one, a female physician commented sardonically, worked harder or in unhealthier conditions than the washerwoman; yet would-be saviors of American womanhood did not inveigh against this abuse—washing, after all, was appropriate work for women. Women doctors often did agree with the general observation that their sisters were too frequently weak and unhealthy; however, they blamed not education or social activism but artificialities of dress and slavery to fashion, aspects of the middle-class woman's life style which they found particularly demeaning. "The fact is that girls and women can bear study," Alice Stockham explained, "but they cannot bear compressed viscera, tortured stomachs and displaced uterus," the results of fashionable clothing and an equally fashionable sedentary life. Another woman physician, Sarah Stevenson, wrote in a similar vein: " 'How do I look?' is the everlasting story from the beginning to the end of woman's life. Looks, not books, are the murderers of American women."[25]

Even more significant than this controversy over woman's education was a parallel debate focusing on the questions of birth control and abortion. These issues affected not simply a small percentage of middle- and upper-middle-class women, but all men and women. It is one of the great and still largely unstudied realities of nineteenth-century social history. Every married woman was immediately affected by the realities of childbearing and child rearing. Though birth control and abortion had been practiced, discussed—and reprobated—for centuries, the mid-nineteenth century saw a dramatic increase in concern among spokesmen for the ministry and medical profession.[26]

Particularly alarming was the casualness, doctors charged, with which seemingly respectable wives and mothers contemplated and undertook abortions, and how routinely they practiced birth control. One prominent New York gynecologist complained in 1874 that well-dressed women walked into his consultation room and asked for abortions as casually as they would for a cut of beefsteak at their butcher's.[27] In 1857 the American Medical Association nominated a special committee to report on the problem; then appointed another in the 1870s. Between these dates and especially in the late 1860s medical societies throughout the country passed resolutions attacking the prevalence of abortion and birth control and condemning physicians who performed and condoned such illicit practices. Nevertheless, abortions could be obtained in the 1870s in Boston and New York for as little as ten dollars, while abortifacients could be purchased more cheaply or through the mail. Even the smallest villages and rural areas provided a market for the abortionist's services; women often aborted any pregnancy which occurred in the first few years of marriage. The Michigan Board of Health estimated in 1898 that one third of all the state's pregnancies ended in abortion. From seventy to eighty percent of these were secured, the board contended, by prosperous and otherwise respectable married women who could not offer even the unmarried mother's "excuse of shame."[28] By the 1880s English medical moralists could refer to birth control as the "American sin" and warn against England's women following in the path of America's faithless wives.[29]

So general a phenomenon demands explanation. The only serious attempts to explain the prevalence of birth control in this period have emphasized the economic motivations of those practicing it—the need in an increasingly urban, industrial, and bureaucratized society to limit numbers of children so as to provide security, education, and inheritance for those already brought into the world. As the nineteenth century progressed, it has been argued, definitions of appropriate middle-class life styles dictated a more and more expansive pattern of consumption, a pattern—especially in an era of recurring economic instability—particularly threatening to those large numbers of Americans only precariously members of the secure economic classes. The need to limit offspring was a necessity if family status was to be maintained.[30]

Other aspects of nineteenth-century birth control have received much less historical attention. One of these needs only to be mentioned, for it poses no interpretative complexities; this was the frequency with which childbirth meant pain and often lingering incapacity. Death from childbirth, torn cervixes, fistulas, prolapsed uteri were widespread "female complaints" in a period when gynecological practice was still relatively primitive and pregnancy every few years common indeed. John Humphrey Noyes, perhaps the best-known advocate of family planning in nineteenth-century America, explained poignantly why he and his wife had decided to practice birth control in the 1840s: "The [decision] was occasioned and even forced upon me by very sorrowful experiences. In the course of six years my wife went through the agonies of five births. Four of them were premature. Only one child lived. . . . After our last disappointment, I pledged my word to my wife that I would never again expose her to such fruitless suffering. . . ."[31] The Noyeses' experience was duplicated in many homes. Young women were simply terrified of having children.[32]

Such fears, of course, were not peculiar to nineteenth-century America. The dangers of disability and death consequent upon childbirth extended back to the beginning of time, as did the anxiety and depression so frequently associated with pregnancy. What might be suggested, however, was that economic and technological changes in society added new dimensions to the age-old experience. Family limitation for economic and social reasons now appeared more desirable to a growing number of husbands; it was, perhaps, also more technically feasible. Consequently, married women could begin to consider, probably for the first time, alternative life styles to that of multiple pregnancies extending over a third of their lives. Women could begin to view the pain and bodily injury which resulted from such pregnancies not simply as a condition to be borne with fatalism and passivity, but as a situation that could be avoided. It is quite probable, therefore, that in this new social context, increased anxiety and depression would result once a woman, in part at least voluntarily, became pregnant. Certainly, it could be argued, such fears must have altered women's attitudes toward sexual relations generally. Indeed, the decision to practice birth control must necessarily have held more than economic and status implications for the family; it must have become an element in the fabric of every marriage's particular psychosexual reality.[33]

A third and even more ambiguous aspect of the birth control controversy in nineteenth-century America relates to the way in which attitudes toward contraception and abortion reflected role conflict within the family. Again and again, from the 1840s on, defenders of family planning—including individuals as varied and idealistic as Noyes and Stockham, on the one hand, and assorted quack doctors and peddlers of abortifacients, on the other—justified their activities not in economic terms, but under the rubric of providing women with liberty and autonomy. Woman, they argued with remarkable unanimity, must control her own body; without this she was a slave not only to the sexual impulses of her husband but also to endless childbearing and rearing. "Woman's equality in all the relations of life," a New York physician wrote in 1866, "implies her absolute supremacy in the sexual relation. . . . It is her absolute and indefensible right to determine when she will not be exposed to pregnancy." "God and Nature," another physician urged, "have given to the female the complete control of her own person, so far as sexual congress and reproduction are concerned."[34] The assumption of all these writers was clear and unqualified: women, if free to do so, would choose to have sexual relations less frequently and to have far fewer pregnancies.

Implied in these arguments as well were differences as to the nature and function of sexual intercourse. Was its principal and sole legitimate function, as conservative physicians and clergymen argued, the procreation of children, or could it be justified as an act of love, of tenderness between individuals? Noyes argued that the sexual organs had a social, amative function separable from their reproductive function. Sex was justifiable as an essential and irreplaceable form of human affection; no man could demand this act unless it was freely given.[35] Nor could it be freely given in many cases unless effective modes of birth control were available to assuage the woman's anxieties.

A man's wife was not his chattel, her individuality to be violated at will, and forced—ultimately—to bear unwanted and thus almost certainly unhealthy children.

Significantly, defenders of women's right to limit childbearing employed many of the same arguments used by conservatives to attack women's activities outside the home; all those baleful hereditary consequences threatened by overeducation were seen by birth control advocates as resulting from the bearing of children by women unwilling and unfit for the task, their vital energies depleted by excessive childbearing. A child, they argued, carried to term by a woman who desired only its death could not develop normally. Were women relieved from such accustomed pressures, they could produce fewer but better offspring.[36]

Many concerned mid-nineteenth-century physicians, clergymen, and journalists failed to accept such arguments. They emphasized, instead, the unnatural and thus necessarily deleterious character of any and all methods of birth control and abortion. Even coitus interruptus, obviously the most common mode of birth control in this period, was attacked routinely as a source of mental illness, nervous tension, and even cancer. This was easily demonstrated. Sex, like all aspects of human bodily activity, involved an exchange of nervous energy; without the discharge of such accumulated energies in the male orgasm and the soothing presence of the male semen "bathing the female reproductive organs," the female partner could never, the reassuring logic ran, find true fulfillment. The nervous force accumulated and concentrated in sexual excitement would build up dangerous levels of undischarged energy, leading ultimately to a progressive decay in the unfortunate woman's physical and mental health. Physicians warned repeatedly that condoms and diaphragms—when the latter became available after mid-century—could cause an even more alarmingly varied assortment of ills. In addition to the mechanical irritation they promoted, artificial methods of birth control increased the lustful impulse in both partners, leading inevitably to sexual excess. The resultant nervous exhaustion induced gynecological lesions, and then through "reflex irritation" caused such ills as loss of memory, insanity, heart disease, and even "the most repulsive nymphomania."[37]

Conservative physicians similarly denounced the widespread practice of inserting sponges impregnated with supposedly spermicidal chemicals into the vagina immediately before or after intercourse. Such practices, they warned, guaranteed pelvic injury, perhaps sterility. Even if the woman seemed in good health despite a history of practicing birth control, a Delaware physician explained in 1873 that "as soon as this vigor commences to decline . . . about the fortieth year, the

disease [cancer] grows as the energies fail—the cancerous fangs penetrating deeper and deeper until, after excruciating suffering, the
writhing victim is yielded up to its terrible embrace."[38] Most importantly, this argument followed, habitual attempts at contraception
meant, even if successful, a mother permanently injured and unable to
bear healthy children. If unsuccessful, the children resulting from such
unnatural matings would inevitably be weakened. And if such grave
ills resulted from the practice of birth control, the physical consequences of abortion were even more dramatic and immediate.[39]

Physicians often felt little hesitation in expressing what seems to the
historian a suspiciously disproportionate resentment toward such
unnatural females. Unnatural was, of course, the operational word; for
woman's presumed maternal instinct made her primarily responsible
for decisions in regard to childbearing.[40] So frequent was this habitual
accusation that some medical authors had to caution against placing
the entire weight of blame for birth control and abortion upon the
woman; men, they reminded, played an important role in most such
decisions.[41] In 1871, for example, the American Medical Association
Committee on Criminal Abortion described women who patronized
abortionists in terms which conjured up fantasies of violence and
punishment:

> She becomes unmindful of the course marked out for her by Providence,
> she overlooks the duties imposed on her by the marriage contract. She
> yields to the pleasures—but shrinks from the pains and responsibilities
> of maternity; and, destitute of all delicacy and refinement, resigns herself,
> body and soul, into the hands of unscrupulous and wicked men. Let not the
> husband of such a wife flatter himself that he possesses her affection. Nor
> can she in turn ever merit even the respect of a virtuous husband. She sinks
> into old age like a withered tree, stripped of its foliage; with the stain of
> blood upon her soul, she dies without the hand of affection to smooth her
> pillow.[42]

The frequency with which attacks on family limitation in mid-nine-
teeth-century America were accompanied by polemics against expanded roles for the middle-class woman indicates with unmistakable
clarity something of one of the motives structuring such jeremiads.
Family limitation necessarily added a significant variable within conjugal relationships generally; its successful practice implied potential
access for women to new roles and a new autonomy.

Nowhere is this hostility toward women and the desire to inculcate
guilt over women's desire to avoid pregnancy more strikingly illustrated than in the warnings of "race suicide" so increasingly fashionable in the late-nineteenth century. A woman's willingness and
capacity to bear children was a duty she owed not only to God and

husband but to her "race" as well.[43] In the second half of the nineteenth century articulate Americans forced to evaluate and come to emotional terms with social change became, like many of their European contemporaries, attracted to a world-view which saw racial identity and conflict as fundamental. And within these categories, birth rates became all-important indices to national vigor and thus social health.

In 1860 and again in 1870 Massachusetts census returns began to indicate that the foreign-born had a considerably higher birth rate than that of native Americans. Indeed, the more affluent and educated a family, the fewer children it seemed to produce. Native Americans in the Bay State were not even reproducing themselves, and the social consequences seemed ominous indeed.

The Irish, though barely one quarter of the Massachusetts population, produced more than half of the state's children. "It is perfectly clear," a Boston clergyman contended in 1884, "that without a radical change in the religious ideas, education, habits, and customs of the natives, the present population and their descendants will not rule that state a single generation."[44] A few years earlier a well-known New England physician, pointing to America's still largely unsettled western territories, had asked: "Shall they be filled by our own children or by those of aliens? This is a question that our own women must answer; upon their loins depends the future destiny of the nation." Native-born American women had failed as individuals and as mothers of the Anglo-Saxon race. If matters continued for another half century in the same manner, "the wives who are to be mothers in our republic must be drawn from trans-Atlantic homes. The Sons of the New World will have to re-act, on a magnificent scale, the old story of unwived Rome and the Sabines."[45]

Such arguments have received a goodly amount of historical attention, especially as they figured in the late-nineteenth and early-twentieth centuries as part of the contemporary rationale of immigration restriction.[46] Historians have interpreted the race suicide argument in several fashions. As an incident in a general Western acceptance of racism, it has been seen as product of a growing alienation of the older middle and upper classes in the face of industrialization, urbanization, and bureaucratization of society. More specifically, some American historians have seen these race suicide arguments as rooted in the fears and insecurities of a traditionally dominant middle class as it perceived new and threatening social realities.

Whether or not historians care to accept some version of this interpretation—and certainly such motivational elements seem to be suggested in the rhetorical formulas employed by many of those bemoaning the failure of American Protestants to reproduce in adequate numbers—it ignores another element crucial to the logical and emotional fabric of these arguments. This is the explicit charge of female sexual failure. To a significant extent contemporaries saw the problem as in large measure woman's responsibility; it was America's potential mothers, not its fathers, who were primarily responsible for the impending social cataclysm. Race suicide seemed a problem in social gynecology.

Though fathers played a necessary role in procreation, medical opinion emphasized that it was the mother's constitution and reproductive capacity which most directly shaped her offspring's physical, mental, and emotional attributes. And any unhealthy mode of life—anything, in short, which seemed undesirable to contemporary medical moralists, including both education and birth control—might result in a woman becoming sterile or capable of bearing only stunted offspring. Men, it was conceded, were subject to vices even more debilitating, but the effects of male sin and imprudence were, physicians felt, "to a greater extent confined to adult life; and consequently do not, to the same extent, impair the vitality of our race or threaten its physical destruction." Women's violation of physiological laws implied disaster to "the unborn of both sexes."[47]

Although such social critics tended to agree that woman was at fault, they expressed some difference of opinion as to the nature of her guilt. A few felt that lower birth rates could be attributed simply to the conscious and culpable decision of American women to curtail family size. Other physicians and social commentators, while admitting that many women felt little desire for children, saw the roots of the problem in somewhat different—and perhaps even more apocalyptic—terms. It was not, they feared, simply the conscious practice of family limitation which resulted in small families; rather, the increasingly unnatural life style of the "modern American woman" had undermined her reproductive capacities so that even when she would, she could not bear adequate numbers of healthy children. Only if American women returned to the simpler life styles of the eighteenth and early-nineteenth centuries could the race hope to regain its former vitality; from childhood women must see their role as that of robust and self-sacrificing mothers. If not, their own degeneration and that of the race was inevitable.

Why the persistence and intensity of this masculine hostility, its recurring echoes of conflict, rancor, and moral outrage? There are at least several possible, though by no means exclusive, explanations. One centers on the hostility implied and engendered by the sexual deprivation—especially for the male—implicit in many of the modes of birth control employed at this time. One might, for example, speculate—as Oscar Handlin did some years ago—that such repressed middle-class sexual energies were channeled into a xenophobic hostility toward the immigrant and the black and projected into fantasies incorporating the enviable and fully expressed sexuality of these alien groups.[48] A similar model could be applied to men's attitudes toward women as well; social, economic, and sexual tensions which beset late-nineteenth-century American men might well have caused them to express their anxieties and frustrations in terms of hostility toward the middle-class female.[49]

Such interpretations are, however, as treacherous as they are inviting. Obviously, the would-be scientific formulations outlined here mirror something of post-bellum social and psychic reality. Certainly some middle-class men in the late-nineteenth century had personality needs—sexual inadequacies or problems of status identification—which made traditional definitions of gender roles functional to them. The hostility evident in the violent imagery expressed toward women who chose to limit the number of children they bore indicates a significant personal and emotional involvement on the part of the male author. Some women, moreover, obviously used the mechanisms of birth control, and not infrequently sexual rejection, as role-sanctioned building blocks in the fashioning of their particular adjustment. Their real and psychic gains were numerous: surcease from fear and pain, greater leisure, a socially acceptable way of expressing hostility, and a means of maintaining some autonomy and privacy in a life which society demanded be devoted wholeheartedly to the care and nurture of husband and children. Beyond such statements, however, matters become quite conjectural. At this moment in the development of both historical methodology and psychological theory great caution must be exercised in the development of such hypotheses, especially since the historians of gender and sexual behavior have at their disposal data which from a psychodynamic point of view is at best fragmentary and suggestive.[50]

What the nineteenth-century social historian can hope to study with a greater degree of certainty, however, is the way in which tensions surrounding formal definitions of gender roles may have reflected social change. Obviously, individuals as individuals at all times and in all cultures have experienced varying degrees of difficulty in assimilating the prescriptions of expected role behavior. When such discontinuities begin to affect comparatively large numbers and become sufficiently overt as to evoke a marked ideological response, one can then speak with assurance of having located fundamental cultural tension.[51]

Students of nineteenth-century American and Western European society have long been aware of the desire of a growing number of women for a choice among roles different from the traditional one of mother and housekeeper. It was a theme of Henry James, Henrik Ibsen, and a host of other, perhaps more representative if less talented, writers. Women's demands ranged from that of equal pay for equal work and equal education for equal intelligence to more covert demands for abortion, birth control information, and sexual autonomy within the marriage relationship. Their demands paralleled and were in large part dependent upon fundamental social and economic developments. Technological innovation and economic growth, changed patterns of income distribution, population concentrations, demographic changes in terms of life expectancy and fertility all affected woman's behavior and needs. Fewer women married; many were numbered among the urban poor. Such women had to become self-supporting and at the same time deal with the changed self-image that self-support necessitated. Those women who married often did so later, had fewer children, and lived far beyond the birth of their youngest child. At the same time ideological developments began to encourage both men and women to aspire to increased independence and self-fulfillment. All these factors interacted to create new ambitions and new options for American women. In a universe of varying personalities and changing economic realities, it was inevitable that some women, at least, would—overtly or covertly—be attracted by such options. For such women the normative role of homebound nurturant and passive woman was no longer appropriate or functional, but rather a source of conflict and anxiety.

It was inevitable as well that many men, similarly faced with a rapidly changing society, would seek in domestic peace and constancy a sense of the continuity and security so difficult to find elsewhere in their society. They would, at the very least, expect their wives, their daughters, and their family relationships generally to remain unaltered. When their female dependents seemed ill-disposed to do so, such men responded with a rigidity sanctioned increasingly by the new gods of science.

3

Sexuality, Class, and Role

Any historical consideration of sexuality necessarily involves a problem in method. Most would-be students are concerned with behavior, but must satisfy themselves with the materials of myth and ideology: such scholars must somehow extrapolate a relationship between the content of this ideology and the behavior it presumably reflected and legitimated.

This difficulty manifests itself in a particularly intractable form to those attempting to understand the nineteenth century.[1] Historians and social scientists still tend to see mid and late-nineteenth-century sexuality as peculiar; Victorian is still a synonym for repressive. The few social historians concerned with sexuality have written in emotional and intellectual consistency with immediately post-Victorian reformers of sexual behavior who perpetuated the vision of a "neurotic" or, perhaps more accurately, pathogenic nineteenth century (at least for the middle class), a period in which the sexual impulse was systematically repressed and deformed.

Such diagnoses are necessarily suspect. One cannot solve problems of historical interpretation by describing a whole society, or a major class grouping within it, as though it were some poorly adjusted individual. We may find many mid- and late nineteenth-century attitudes toward human sexuality both alien and alienating, but it is quite another matter to characterize these ideas as simply and inevitably dysfunctional.[2]

Perhaps this is not quite accurate: for on one level, that of the total society, some historians have begun to assume that this repressive ideology was indeed functional. They have, that is, argued that sexual repression (and impulse deferral in general) served the needs of an increasingly bureaucratized society by helping to create a social discipline appropriate to a middle class of managers, professionals, and small entrepreneurs. But such views simply reinforce a traditional irony; for on the individual level we still tend to see these ideological justifications for repression as dysfunctional, indeed pathogenic, in their stifling of basic human needs.[3]

Should one simply assume this irony and elaborate a chastening discontinuity between the needs of society and those of the individuals who make it up? I think not, if only because it is too simple: one must distrust any approach which fails to recognize that human beings, in any culture, come in assorted psychological shapes and sizes. No analytical strategy which assumes that the behavior of groups can be explained by considering them as undifferentiated individuals writ large can prove intellectually adequate (especially when our understanding of individual psychodynamics is far from definitive and our understanding of the relationship between individual and group processes more tenuous still).

The discussion of sexuality which follows is based on the assumption that all individuals have peculiar needs and "choose" particular configurations of roles appropriate to these needs (though social location defines the structure of available choice). Although all individuals must play a number of such roles simultaneously, all are necessarily interrelated—with each other and with each individual's pattern of sexual behavior. This chapter begins with an evaluation of one element relatively discernible in historical materials: formal prescription of sex and gender roles. A second and more tentative portion of the argument suggests some of the ways in which these roles may have related to the actual expression of sexuality.

To delineate role prescriptions is, of course, not to describe behavior: no particular individual need have lived his or her life in accordance with these projected values. On the other hand, one never escapes them entirely: every member of a particular generation has somehow to find an individual accommodation with respect to these ideal prescriptions. Even those who reject a life entirely consistent with such ideals cannot elude them completely, for they constitute a parameter which helps define the nature and content of their deviance. In the series of choices which can be said to describe growth, options rejected as well as those accepted form a part of one's self-image, become an element in the configuration of emotional resonance which ultimately defines individuality.[4]

A recent critic has suggested that the fundamental literary reflections of Victorian sexuality were "pornography and expurgation."[5] This may indeed be true of belles-lettres. There does exist, however, a class of materials that attempts to explain, rationalize, somehow come to terms with the sexual impulse. Most are medical and the argument which follows is based upon such writings.

The medical and biological literature relating to sexuality in nine-teenth-century America is a mixed and surprisingly abundant lot, ranging from earnest marriage manuals to the insinuating treatises of quacks advertising their ability to treat venereal disease or procure abortion. It includes careful academic monographs and cheaply printed paperback guides to midwifery and domestic medicine. It is a genre complex, disparate, and ambiguous.[6] And as such it reflects the needs and attitudes of almost all elements among those who could, or hoped to, consider themselves middle class, that is, from the educated and economically secure to the shopkeepers, skilled workers, and clerks who sought this secure identity.

Yet one can, I think, identify a number of characteristic aspects. The first is a tone of repressiveness which marks much of the material written in the two generations after the 1830s; by the 1870s this emphasis had moved from the level of individual exhortation to that of organized efforts to enforce chastity upon the unwilling.[7] Closely related to this theme of repressiveness is a virtual obsession with masturbation; the tract on "secret vice" became a well-defined genre in this period.[8] Not surprisingly, sexual activity in youth and adolescence was explicitly and emphatically discountenanced. Almost every one of these themes was expressed before the 1830s, but they were intoned with increasing intensity and frequency in succeeding generations.

A second general trait is that of ambivalence and inconsistency; not only within the genre as a whole but within the same article or treatise—even within a single paragraph—facts casually assumed are directly contradicted. A third theme, one not unrelated to the second, is the persistence of an older, male-oriented antirepressive behavioral ethos. Though the evidence is less explicit, the existence of this variant norm is undeniable. A final quality of these arguments is their employment of a common vocabulary and store of images, a kind of lingua franca of scientific authority and metaphor doing service as scientific fact.

The trend toward repressiveness, not surprisingly, correlates in time with the pious activism of the generation following the Second Great Awakening, that is, the decades following the 1830s. Authorities of the eighteenth and early-nineteenth centuries routinely indicted "sexual excess"; yet their injunctions have a calm, even bland tone. These writers accepted sexual activity after puberty as both normal and necessary; though all assumed that an intrinsically limited quantity of vital force might be depleted through excess, all assumed as well that physiological functions unfulfilled could be pathogenic. Thus the not infrequent advice that marriage might cure hysteria, that masturbation could be cured only through sexual intercourse, that maidenhood and celibate bachelorhood were unnatural and potentially disease-producing states.

Beginning with the 1830s, however, the ritualized prudence of these traditional admonitions sharpened and was applied far more frequently, while for some authors any expression of sexuality assumed a problematical cast.[9] Thus, for example, "excessive" sexual intercourse *within* marriage became, for the first time, a subject of widespread censure. Such warnings applied, moreover, to both sexes: only the need for propagating the species, more extreme authors contended, could justify so dangerous an indulgence. Even if the female did not suffer the physical "drain" that ejaculation constituted for the male, she suffered an inevitable loss of nervous energy. "With the male, excessive indulgence frequently causes general debility, weakness, and lameness of the back, dyspepsia, impotency, and a predisposition to almost innumerable diseases, by rendering the system susceptible to the action of other causes of disease. In the female, such excesses frequently cause uterine inflammation, and ulceration, leucorrhoea, deranged menstruation, miscarriage, barrenness as well as debility, hysteria, and an endless train of nervous and other diseases."[10] A generally wary attitude toward the dangers of sexual activity can also be seen in advice suggesting the proper frequency of intercourse. A month's interval was probably the most common injunction, though some more flexible writers conceded that even weekly "indulgence" might not be harmful to a "healthy laboring-man." Almost all such authorities strongly opposed sexual intercourse during gestation and lactation—periods, it was argued, when nervous excitement would divert vital energies needed for the fullest development of the fetus or nursling.[11]

Logically related to the increasing prevalence of such repressive attitudes was a growing concern with masturbation. It was, according to scores of writers both lay and medical, the "master vice" of the period, the source of a variety of ills ranging from tuberculosis to myopia. Many of the tracts dedicated to combating this evil were, of course, cynical appeals to fear and guilt by business-seeking quacks.[12] Yet the concern demonstrated by would-be health reformers and phrenologists, as well as the more specifically evangelical, indicates a depth of anxiety transcending the individual and the cynically exploitive. Such widespread concern can only be interpreted as reflecting a more general emotional consensus; even the calculating arguments of quack physicians can be presumed to reflect a not unsophisticated evaluation of where emotional appeals might most profitably be made. Perhaps most alarming to contemporaries was the universality of the practice. "This polluting stream flows through all grades of society . . . and even the shepherd and shepherdess, who have been surrounded by every thing that could inspire the heart with sentiments of virtue and purity, have desecrated the scene, where Heaven has displayed in rich profusion, the evidences of its love and power, by indulgence in a vice, in view of which angels, if possible, weep, and creation sighs."[13] Not even the youngest child could be presumed immune; one physician noted that even infants of eighteen months had been taught the "horrid practice."[14] Such undoubted instances of "furious masturbation" which could be observed in mere infants demonstrated the power of this instinct; but the very strength of this animal attribute only underlined the need for controlling it.

Control was the basic building block of personality. To allow the passions—among which sexuality was only one—to act themselves out was to destroy any hope of creating a truly Christian personality. "Self-respect" was impossible if mind could not control emotion. Sexual health lay fundamentally in the ability to "restore the calm equilibrium of mind and senses; put down the terrible mastery of passion." One could not relax even momentarily, for such emotions intruded themselves "upon the attention of all alike, with more or less power of impertinent distraction."[15] This was, of course, in many ways a traditional view; the ability to deal with such "impertinent distractions" lay at the emotional center of a time-hallowed male ideal of Christian stoicism. But as the nineteenth century progressed, this emphasis on self-control was expressed with an intensity alien to the tradition of gentlemanly virtue through prudent moderation. It was, moreover, oriented increasingly toward sexuality as such; earlier guides to the good life had always discussed the insidious effects of the "passions," but in such tracts the dangers of gluttony, anger, or envy figured as prominently as those posed by sexuality.

Consistent with the need for self-control was a parallel emphasis upon the need to repress childhood and adolescent sexuality. Physicians warned with increasing sharpness as the century progressed that marriage contracted before the attainment of full maturity resulted inevitably in the stunting of both husband and wife; any children they might conceive would embody this constitutional weakness. Elizabeth Blackwell, for example, argued that both sexes—and especially males—should remain continent until the age of twenty-five. Puberty was assumed to be crucially important in both psychic and physical development; and thus sexual activity during this formative period was particularly dangerous. It was never too early, health reformers warned, to train children in respect for the Seventh Commandment. "In the unformed immature condition of the physical system, at the date of the first evolution of the reproductive instinct, an unbridled indulgence could not fail to prove destructive to the perfection of the bodily powers, as well as highly detrimental to the moral and mental development."[16] This view was almost unquestioned. A physician undertaking a gynecological survey of the Oneida Community, for example, where sexual activity in youth was accepted, could only express surprise that the women of the Community seemed no different from other American females: "However repugnant it may be to our sense of manhood, we cannot resist the conclusion that sexual intercourse at this tender age does not arrest the steady tendency to a fine and robust womanhood."[17] Consistently enough, traditional admonitions that women marry early so as to avoid sexual frustration and its consequent psychic dangers began to disappear by the generation of the Civil War. Newer hygienic ideals urged mental discipline and physical exercise as appropriate modes for the discharge of nervous energy.[18] An increasingly urban and bureaucratized middle class might obviously be expected to create sanctions justifying postponement of the normal age for marriage. Not surprisingly, this ideological trend coincides both with statistical evidence that urban family size was decreasing and with a growing and acrimonious debate over birth control and abortion.

Another general characteristic of this medical and biological literature is its remarkable inconsistency. Sex was natural, yet unnatural. Children were innocent, yet always at risk because of their ever recurring sexual appetite. Most strikingly, female sexuality was surrounded by an ambivalence so massive as to constitute one of the central analytical dilemmas in the understanding of nineteenth-century social history. H. Newell Martin, first professor of biology at the Johns Hopkins University, was able in a widely used text on the human body to cite on one page the opinion that few women of the more luxurious classes regarded sexual congress as anything more than a nuisance after the age of twenty-two or twenty-three, and on the next page quote an even more authoritative opinion noting that orgasm is necessary for health of both sexes, but especially for women.[19] A popular writer, to cite another example, warned paradoxically that women were "not affected so much by over indulgence as by Masturbation. Delicacy not allowing an ardent woman to tell her husband of her needs, she is apt to relieve herself by this unnatural practice. There are, however, but few women who crave sexual intercourse. The excess is generally on the part of the man." Laymen believed that woman could not conceive unless she felt sexual pleasure; and some wives, indeed, sought to suppress sexual excitement—consciously, at least—as a mode of birth control.[20] Women, on the one hand, were warned that excessive sexuality might cause illness—and, at the same time, that sickness, physical unattractiveness, and lack of sexual responsiveness might well lead to the loss of their husbands' affection to "other women." Most men seem to have desired sexually responsive wives, yet some feared that "excessive" sexuality might lead either to infidelity or, less consciously, to dangerous and demanding impositions upon their abilities to perform adequately. As the century progressed, the term "nymphomania" was applied to degrees of sexual expression which would be considered quite normal today. H. R. Storer, for example, a prominent Boston physician, could refer casually to the case of a "virgin nymphomaniac."[21]

As if in response to the mixed emotional cues implicit in these inconsistent ideals of sexual behavior, middle-class Americans began to elaborate a synthetic role—that of the Christian Gentleman. The Christian Gentleman was an athlete of continence, not coitus, continuously testing his manliness in the fire of self-denial. This paradigmatic figure eschewed excess in all things, and, most important, allowed his wife to dictate the nature of their sexual interaction. A pious father should instruct his son "as to a gentleman's duty of self-control and respect toward a lady, and as to the proper occasions for exercising such self-control in the marital relation."[22] Too frequent intercourse was physically draining and led to a striving after ever greater sensation, to a "constitutional irritability" which required ever more frequent and diverse stimulation; this "sick irritability" had clearly to be distinguished, publicists argued, from the healthy and sparing strength of true manliness. Continence implied strength, not weakness.[23] "Reserve is the grand secret of power everywhere." "Be noble, generous, just, self-sacrificing, continent, manly in all things —and no woman worthy of you can help loving you, in the best sense of the word." Yet the majority of men, most mid-century evangelically oriented authors had to confess, were still slaves of the "love of domination, ungoverned passion, grossness," and "filthiness of habit."[24] Continence and manliness were still far from synonymous.

Which suggests our third major theme: the implacable persistence of an older male-oriented behavioral ethos, one which placed a premium on aggressive masculinity. "I regret," a self-consciously horrified physician recorded in the early 1880s, "to say that I have known some fathers to tickle the genital organs of their infant boys until a complete erection of the little penis ensued, which effect pleases the father as an evidence of a robust boy."[25] Obviously, of course, premarital chastity and marital fidelity hardly serve as an inclusive description of mid-nineteenth-century behavior. The prostitution, the venereal disease rate, the double standard itself all document the gap between admonition and reality. Equally striking evidence is to be found in male fears of weakness, impotence, and premature ejaculation—widespread anxieties to which the century's abundance of quack specialists in "secret diseases" appealed. Insofar, moreover, as particular males internalized the transcendent behavioral prescriptions embodied in the idea of the Christian Gentleman and thus avoided premarital sexual activity, they would necessarily experience increased anxieties as to their ultimate sexual capacity. Thus the often brutal and impulsive behavior of husbands on honeymoons (a universal complaint of would-be defenders of woman's marital rights) is in some cases plausibly explained by the husband's fear of inadequacy (in addition to possible ambivalence toward the act itself). The marriage night was an institutionalized trauma for the pure of both sexes.[26]

The masculine ethos, like its evangelical counterpart, could justify itself in physiological terms; most prominent among these justifications was the assumption that sexual energies had somehow to be discharged if health was to be maintained after puberty. As late as 1891, a regretful physician complained that such beliefs were still frequently used to justify the double standard: "There are those among the males of our generation, who attribute to men an inherent natural need to gratify passions, claiming that the weaker sex understand it to be necessary to man's nature, and willingly tolerate lustful ante-nuptial and post-nuptial practices."[27] Evangelicals still accused physicians of backslapping recommendations of fornication as cure for masturbation and other ills; to more "realistic" and worldly physicians—perhaps individually more committed to the masculine ethos—masturbation was a normal, if not indeed whimsical, sympton of adolescence, to be cured by the application of copulation in required doses. Fathers still proudly sent their sons off to bawdyhouses to establish their masculinity. Perhaps most pervasive were warnings that men be assertive and avoid the slightest hint of femininity; as one physician explained, "a woman admires in man true *manliness*, and is repelled by weakness and effeminacy. A womanish man awakens either the pity or the contempt of the fair sex."[28]

A final characteristic of nineteenth-century American and English writings on sexuality is of a general kind, and relates not so much to content as to formal structure. All these books, pamphlets, and articles, no matter what their particular orientation, spoke in the same vocabulary, used the same images, made the same appeal to such standard expository modes as that of argument from design. Even more generally, all these authors used disease sanctions as their basic framework for exposition and admonition; their hypothetical etiologies served, of course, to shape and sanction particular life styles. Almost all these accepted modes of argument were, moreover, so open-ended that appeals of the most varying kind could employ the same figures and analogies. Both sides, for example, employed arguments drawn from design; liberals emphasized that the function implicit in the secretion of semen implied expulsion and use; the more repressive argued that woman's menstrual cycle implied the maximum frequency for sexual intercourse. The more evangelically oriented similarly emphasized that copulation in lower animals took place infrequently, only at the initiative of the female, and only for the purpose of reproduction. These practices were thus "natural"—that is, more primitive—and man's comparatively frenetic sexuality a sign of civilized degeneracy. Lack of control, on the other hand, was always seen as animal, as characteristic of a brutal, less highly organized being. Like any alphabet, these traditionally accepted modules of image and assumption could be manipulated into vastly different configurations.[29]

At this point a word of caution is indicated. We have, thus far, emphasized the repressive. Yet most physicians who discussed such questions endorsed a rather more moderate position. They assumed that the sexual powers had necessarily to be exercised, but that morality and social policy demanded that they be limited until marriage. "Although function is the natural destiny of organs," as the editor of the *British Medical Journal* noted blandly in 1882, "considerations, both of morality and expedience, and even of health, concur in the advice that it is better to hold over the formation of a certain habit until the bodily frame is thoroughly consolidated and the practice can be indulged in a legitimate manner."[30] Such stolidly nontranscendent prudence was as close as the majority of physicians ever came to endorsing wholeheartedly the evangelical attitude toward sexuality. Few, however, were willing to publicly challenge the more intensely repressive formulations routinely offered the public by their more evangelically inclined colleagues. Significantly, however, even the handful of physicians explicitly hostile to the evangelical view of sexuality were convinced that "intellect" must always dominate, that no passion must ever escape conscious control.[31]

These were the most obvious characteristics of medical and biological views of sexuality in nineteenth-century America. Now let us consider some of the ways in which c'ass and gender roles helped shape and are, in turn, reflected in this literature.

But first a minor caveat. For the purposes of this discussion we must very largely limit our remarks to those Americans who considered themselves part of the "respectable" middle class, for it is they who produced the sources upon which we must depend, and whose needs and anxieties these sources mirror. Yet, it might be objected, class status is an extraordinarily difficult commodity for the sociologist, let alone the historian, to measure objectively. Vocation, income, religion, birth, all play a role, but in particular configurations not always amenable to orderly historical reconstitution. At the same time, however, consciousness of class identity is a primary emotional reality, especially when such identity is marginal or ill-defined. And status definitions in nineteenth-century America were, contemporaries and historians have agreed, particularly labile and would thus have tended to make class identification stressful and problematic. A good many Americans must, it follows, have been all the more anxious in their internalization of those aspects of life style which seemed to embody and assure class status. And contemporaries clearly regarded overt sexuality, especially in women, as indicative of a way of life demeaning to middle-class status. Virtue and self-denial, on the other hand, like evangelical religion itself, could be embraced by any man who so willed—and thus serve as transcendent and therefore emotionally reassuring tools in the forging of a life style appropriate to assuaging both the expected scorn of established wealth and breeding and the economic anxieties symbolized by the ominous existence of the poor.

In the social categories employed by nineteenth-century writers on sexuality, the "immoral" rich and the debauched poor equally embodied "depravity" and license. It was assumed, for example, that domestic servants were a source of moral contagion, that they took particular pleasure in teaching masturbation and salaciousness generally to the innocents placed in their charge. "It seems," one physician complained, "as if this class took special delight in poisoning the minds of the young and innocent and initiating them into habits of vice." For every case, another physician charged, in which precocious sexuality was aroused through idiopathic causes, "three to five" were incited by servants. Such views continued almost unchanged into the opening years of the present century; in 1910, for example, a well-meaning female physician warned against servants playing a role in the sexual education of children, for their "point of view can hardly fail to be coarse and may be really vicious."[32]

Servants, it must be recalled, were a part of every household with any pretension to respectability; as such they represented an intrusive emotional reality. The widespread hostility toward domestics to which we refer might well have mirrored middle-class repression of the sexuality which the lower orders were presumed to enjoy. However, it may have reflected as well some measure of reality. Servants may, in "seducing" their youthful charges, have been simply acting out an older sexual ethos, one still normal in the lower and rural classes.[33] The social and psychological meaning of such behavior, whether real or fantasied, is not at all clear.

Public health advocates assumed that sexual license was characteristic of slum life and, like drink, one of those traits which kept the poor poor. The rich too were, consolingly, seen in these mythic categories as victims of sensuality. In the United States, perhaps even more than in England, the ideal type of the Christian Gentleman served as one mode of legitimating the lives which so many Americans had necessarily to lead: lives of economic virtue, sexual prudence, of a chronic need to evaluate and reassert appropriate life styles.[34]

I have, thus far, emphasized the repressive—and in their intensity and pervasiveness, novel—aspects of nineteenth-century attitudes toward sexuality. Yet a great deal of evidence points to nineteenth century patterns of sexuality not so much absolutely repressive as sharply variant. No critical observer has failed to note the inconsistency between a growing ideological discountenance of sexuality, an increasing and reciprocal emphasis upon the ideal of domesticity, and a behavioral reality which included widespread prostitution, illegitimacy, birth control, and abortion.

The key, I feel, to this apparent paradox lies in the nature of existing gender roles. For a primary reality to men and women was precisely their ability to act out their socially prescribed roles as men and women; and nineteenth-century gender roles embodied and implied conflict, conflict not only with those characteristics assigned the opposite sex, but with other components of contemporary social values (including prescriptions of class-appropriate behavior). To be more specific: despite a superfluity of evangelical exhortation, the primary role model with which men had to come to terms was that which articulated the archaic male ethos—one in which physical vigor and particularly aggressive sexual behavior was a central component. There is an abundance of evidence supporting the emotional relevance of this masculine ethos, as well as of its prescribing and informing behavior.

Consistently enough, the most hated target of mid-nineteenth-century feminist advocates of moral reform was the double standard which recognized and, in a sense, legitimated the male ethos. And gradually male and female writers extended the area of conflict and control to include sexuality within marriage; until woman controlled access to her own body, she could not enjoy true freedom—or physical and mental health. For the husband came to marriage, as one woman physician put it, "imbued with the belief—an ironclad tradition of the ages—that marriage gives him a special license, and under this license often and often he puts to shame the prostitution of the brothel."[35] Moral reformers not only demanded that men conform to the same standards of sexual morality as women, but taught that the best means of achieving this goal was through woman's control of the male child's moral education and the ending of sexual segregation in childhood. Such reformers warned again and again that the polarization of male and female traits perpetuated in this segregation guaranteed that true sexual morality would never be established.[36]

The depth and significance of the conflict which characterized this polarization of gender role traits is particularly well illustrated in the nineteenth century's masturbation literature—not only in its very existence, but even more clearly in its internal themes. That of the need for control is self-evident; but an equally prominent theme is the fear of sexual failure. Was masturbation, after all, not an ultimate confession of male sexual inadequacy? Such tracts warned melodramatically of its demeaning and emasculating consequences. The confirmed onanist's genitals might, for example, "shrink and become withered, and cases have been known, in which, faded and entirely decayed, the little remains of them have disappeared into the abdomen." Finally he would become impotent, unable to "penetrate the finest woman in the world." These threatened consequences indicate, moreover, the emotional centrality of a particular individual's consciousness of male-female orientation. Thus warnings against the consequences of prolonged masturbation tended to incorporate personality traits associated with the female role stereotype. "All the intellectual faculties are weakened. The man becomes a coward; sighs and weeps like a hysterical woman. He loses all decision and dignity of character."[37] The intonation of such symptom catalogs assumes a ritual character—and to some individuals presumably an expiatory one. The ideological emphasis on secret vice and its consequences served, that is, to ritually express and thus perhaps allay a subconscious ambivalence in regard to masculine identification. Only the transcendent categories of Christian commitment could serve as an adequate counter to the behavioral demands implied by the masculine ethos. Thus the need to impart the intensity of millennial zeal to that ritual of self-denial which underwrote the social logic of the Christian Gentleman.

Significantly, the masturbator's alleged characteristics also served to project the vision of a figure emotionally and socially isolated: "They drivel away their existence on the outskirts of society; they are at once a dead weight, a sluggish, inert mass in the paths of this busy, blustering life, having neither the will nor the capacity to take a part in the general matters of life." The demand for economic achievement, in other words, served in synergistic parallel with that for sexual achievement; and just as many men were not prepared to live in terms of the ideals demanded by the masculine ethos, so many were uncomfortable with those characteristics which tended in reality to make the self-made man.[38]

Admonitions proscribing female masturbation are, not surprisingly, quite different in content. Perhaps most obviously, disease sanctions varied in emphasis; failure or inadequacy in childbearing played an extraordinarily prominent role, though cancer, insanity, and tuberculosis were also frequently cited consequences of female addiction to "solitary abuse."[39] Even more significantly, male authors express a pervasive disquiet in the presence of female sexuality. A central issue, of course, is still control, but in this context it is not self-control, but control of women's sexuality.[40] Masturbation is, as a few of our twentieth-century contemporaries have argued, the ultimate in female autonomy; to mid-nineteenth-century physicians, perhaps not coincidentally, it threatened to result either in frigidity or nymphomania —both means through which the husband might be humiliated.[41] Evidence indicating male anxieties in regard to female sexuality are as old as history itself and have attracted an elaborate, if dissonant, body of discussion; whatever metapsychological interpretation one places upon this phenomenon, its existence seems undeniable.

And it is, as a matter of fact, no difficult matter to locate a group of mid- and late-nineteenth-century male authorities on sexuality whose moral admonitions would document a defensive and monolithic antisexuality.[42] It was, such zealots charged, the individual physician's moral responsibility to denounce casual and "excessive" marital sex. "All excess in that direction he will discountenance. . . . Unmastered importunity and too submissive an affection must be met by separate beds, by uncommunicating rooms, and if need be, by strong expostulation."[43] Significantly, all emphasized the need for limiting, and ideally for absolutely eschewing, all sexual activity during pregnancy and lactation. William Alcott, for example, warned that intercourse during gestation was particularly dangerous, especially if the mother should experience orgasm. "The nervous orgasm," he explained, "is too much for the young germ."[44] Procreation was the purpose of sexual intercourse; once the child had been conceived, every energy should be bent toward nurturing the young life.

The specific emphases and emotional tone of these authors fall into a pattern so consistent that one is tempted to suggest a common psychic function for their ideological commitment. All, for example, tended to deny the intensity of female sexual needs; all tended to see sexual relationships as normally exploitive; all tended to identify woman with a higher moral calling. This strong identification with woman—assuming that she exhibited the appropriate passive, asexual, and nurturant qualities—suggests not only the possible roots of the author's own needs, but the ways in which the several dimensions of behavior had come to be seen as rigidly male or female. They suggest a family milieu in which power and autonomy, emotional loyalty, and identification were consistently defined in terms of either/or—father or mother, male or female. (These novel emotional realities may possibly be seen as reflecting an increasingly urban family pattern, one in which the removal of economic functions from the home had created sexually polarized patterns of emotional identification.) These writers consistently associated woman's sexual innocence with her maternal function: Dio Lewis, a popular advocate of temperance and health reform, "liked," for example, "to think that the strong passion of my mother was the maternal." Men, Lewis continued, "can hardly understand the childlike innocence in which the pure woman considers this whole class of subjects."[45]

Beginning with the second third of the nineteenth century, moreover, a new sanction became increasingly—and, I feel, revealingly —plausible: that of the primacy of the mother in determining heredity and the need, therefore, to grant her dominion in the structuring of sexual relations. "DESTINY IS DETERMINED BY ORGANIZATION," as abolitionist Henry C. Wright put it. "ORGANIZATION IS DETERMINED BY MATERNAL CONDITIONS."[46]

We have become accustomed to thinking of such formulas as in some sense ultimately dysfunctional; we assume as well that such attitudes may have encouraged aggression or other inappropriate—deflected—modes of response. Yet this is at best a partialistic way of approaching a most complex problem; for such generalizations are based not only on a transparently monolithic view of actual behavior patterns, but upon an equally schematic view of human psychodynamics. In the first place, many Americans simply paid no attention to these pious injunctions.[47] Some men ignored them at no particular psychic cost, others only at great cost. But to others, it may be argued, these seemingly unreal and—it would seem—dysfunctional views were functional indeed. For some men at least, the glorification of denial, with its transcendent justification in the categories of evangelical Christianity, could well have served as an ideological defense against the ever-present demands of the masculine ethos, demands which some men at least could not meet (demands, moreover, in conflict with other social norms and values).

In Victorian England and America, moreover, the repression of sexuality could mean security, the ability to predict economic and social reality, in short, autonomy and social respectability. In a period when the urban lower and lower-middle classes had few enough areas for the establishment of ego function, the very process of deferring pleasure—with its ideological sanction in the evangelical world view and social sanction in its organic relationship to status definition —provided one mode through which individuals of marginal social status might begin to find security and dignity.[48] Others, as I have suggested, incapable for individual reasons of living an assertive sexual life, could find in this ideology of denial a sanction for their particular disability. Hardly ideal perhaps, but any option is better than none, and in terms of social reality the uncontrolled expression of sexuality was—and presumably is—hardly a real option for most individuals. In terms of individual psychodynamics (since members of a particular generation fall into varied categories of potential behavior) it is not clear that all, or even most, Americans would have found the freedom to act out some fundamental sexual need a healing ordinance. Even in the self-consciously liberated 1970s, when the expression of sexuality is sometimes seen as a moral imperative, we seem not to have produced a generation of psychically fulfilled and sexually adequate citizens.

American society in the past century offered, in other words, a variety of behavioral options in the area of sexuality. And if some individuals suffered as a result of the conflict implied by the emotional inconsistencies embodied in these options, other Americans presumably benefited from the availability of varied behavioral options. Let me be a bit more specific. For some individuals, the expression of aggressive sexuality would have an important relationship to ego function generally; those males, that is, able to live out the imperatives of the masculine ethos would find in this virility a source of strength generalizable to other areas of activity. (Some women, similarly, could find achievement within the traditional role of nurturant wife and mother; others would find only tension and ambiguity.) To certain other American men, internalization of the pieties implicit in the Christian Gentleman ideal (combined with a measure of worldly success) provided a viable framework for personality adjustment, despite a stressful ambivalence in regard to the imperatives of the masculine ethos. For still other men, of course, neither of these options provided usable solutions; indeed, the particular neurotic needs of some could well have found an ideal focus in the very structure of ambiguity which so characterized available gender roles. One might argue that it was not so much repression as such which characterized Victorian sexuality, but rather a peculiar and in some ways irreconcilable conflict between the imperatives of the Masculine Achiever and the Christian Gentleman. Few males were completely immune from the emotional reality of both.

Woman had also to create an appropriate emotional balance between two conflicting roles; she could retreat to passivity and purity (often in the form of maternity) and reject the male's proffered sexuality, but only at the expense of failing within the even more traditional role of female as giving and nurturant; for true nurturing implied sexual warmth and availability.

These gender roles must be understood, moreover, as a basic variable in the emotional structuring of particular marriages. The need of the male to achieve sexually, to act out his frustrations and insecurities in the form of aggressive sexuality in conjunction with the female's socially legitimate "spirituality" provided the wife with a natural emotional leverage. The power to reject was the power to control—and one of the few avenues to such power and autonomy available to women within the Victorian family. It was, as well, a power now sanctioned in the newly forged categories of the female-oriented evangelical view of sexuality. Women's characteristically ambivalent sexual role must, that is, have helped structure—if not indeed occasion—intramarital conflict. Both husband and wife were in this sense prisoners of the same ritual pattern.

Sexual adjustment within the urban middle-class family would, moreover, naturally reflect any stress peculiar to the changing social environment of mid-nineteenth-century America. Shifting patterns of work and residence associated with urbanization and industrialization must certainly have implied parallel shifts in available emotional options within the family. Economic or career tensions affecting the husband, role anxieties in the wife would all have had to find some expression if not resolution in the marriage bed, that potential context of reassurance or rejection. Such realities can be illustrated concretely by the conflict surrounding birth control, a fact for many nineteenth-century urban families. One dimension of family decisions to practice birth control (or abortion) was economic. But this was only one aspect of an inevitably complex and ambiguous situation. Many husbands, for example, must have experienced deep ambivalence, desiring, on the one hand, a small family to ease economic burdens, yet regretting the loss of male status symbolized by abundant fatherhood—not to mention the control of his wife implied by the existence of numerous children. Whether decisions to limit family size actually affected sexual intercourse per se depended, of course, on the means employed, the confidence of the woman in such means, and the personality needs of husband and wife.

Another aspect of nineteenth-century sexual prescriptions thus far not discussed systematically is the ideological function of these formulas, their relationship to the maintenance of a particular social order. In examining the ideological content of the scientific intonations and disease sanctions we have been describing, there are some obvious points of structural reference. Most apparent is the emotional centrality of a fundamental expository metaphor, one which might best be called "mercantilist." The body is visualized in this metaphor as a closed energy system, one which could be either weakened through the discharge of energy or strengthened through its prudent husbanding.

These omnipresent images of control and physiological penury lend credibility to interpretations which emphasize the parallelism between those modes of behavior implied by the needs of a developing capitalism and the rationalization and ordering of sexual energies to this purpose. "The gospel of continence," in the words of Peter Cominos, a forthright recent advocate of this position, "reveals its meaning when it is related to the dynamic quality inherent in the structure and functioning of the Respectable Economic System, the compulsion to accumulate and reinvest capital."[49] This ideology of sexual penury would thus be as functional to the Western European bourgeoisie as its equivalents in those non-Western cultures where ecological realities demand that reproduction be curtailed; one would normally expect in such a culture to find a well-articulated ideology of taboo, ritual, mythic constructs, and disease sanctions enforcing and legitimating the logic of sexual frugality.

All well, and possibly even good. But the interpretive problem is a good deal more complex. We are dealing with a world of ideology and behavior more fragmented, more obviously inconsistent than that characteristic of most traditional cultures. The attempt, moreover, to associate repression of sexuality with the creation of an ethos appropriate to capitalism presents grave chronological problems. Why, for example, should the mid-nineteenth century see the efflorescence of this doctrine? Efforts by the new bourgeoisie to forge an appropriate life style had been in process since at least the sixteenth century; one must, that is, in attempting to employ this line of argument, relate this peculiarly repressive ideology not simply to "capitalism," but to a particular stage in its development—the crystallization of industrialism and its structural implications in the shape of urbanization, bureaucratization, a declining birth rate, and the like. Even so, the connection between these themes and images and the supposed needs of this society cannot simply be assumed. Thus, for example, similar ideas concerning the drain of sexual expenditure upon bodily health—especially in the case of semen—have a long and astonishingly mixed cultural history; Taoism, for example, in which such ideas figured prominently, would seem at first glance—and perhaps the second as well—to have little in common with the social and intellectual world of nineteenth-century England and America.

The preceding pages have attempted to suggest *one* possible perspective through which to view sexuality as it was perceived and acted out by nineteenth-century Americans: the effect of two basic social roles, class and gender, in shaping sexual behavior. Using expressions of ideology as indices to more fundamental change, I have sought primarily to describe and then to suggest possible forms of interaction, and thus areas for further investigation. What, for example, was the relationship between evangelicalism and the peculiarly structured role characteristics we have described? What were the effects of an urban bureaucratized life upon the emotional structure of the family? There are no simple answers to such profound questions, and only recently have historians become aware that these were, indeed, questions. In point of fact, we do not now possess a generally agreed-upon model appropriate to explain the precise relationships between structural change—economic, demographic, and technological—and the microsystem of the family and the individual.

There is, on the other hand, a plausible framework in which to place the intellectual and emotional phenomena we have sought to describe. The pervasive emphasis upon control, the temporal correlation between these repressive formulas and a parallel commitment to the transcending reassurance of evangelical religion can be seen as acculturation phenomena—mechanisms facilitating adjustment to a new social discipline.

Yet even were this interpretation "correct," in the limited sense that so general a formulation can be termed correct, it must remain schematic, useful only in a heuristic sense. Almost every element in this complex, and largely implicit, model remains still to be made explicit.[50] The present discussion has sought, in a thus necessarily tentative way, to contribute to this discussion, to examine some of the ways in which available role prescriptions may have functioned in the particular configuration of emotional and structural reality which faced Americans in the latter half of the nineteenth century.

I have sought, moreover, to avoid the use of certain now-traditional psychodynamic categories, especially the tendency to interpret sexual behavior in terms of a value-laden and one-dimensional polarity of expression versus repression. I have assumed, on the contrary, that individuals vary, that most manage somehow to grow and differentiate, and that the social and sexual values of the mid- and late-nineteenth century were probably no more inimical to human potential than those of any other period—or that, if they were, it remains still to be demonstrated. Granting that certain Victorian attitudes toward sexuality and the types of ideal behavior these ideas legitimated may have imposed costs—to particular individuals perhaps tragic and irreparable costs —does not compromise the essential logic of this position.

4

Charles Benedict Davenport and the Irony of American Eugenics

Though men have always speculated as to the nature of heredity, it was not until the second half of the nineteenth century that the principles which govern it became the object of concerted scientific investigation. The statistical methods of Galton and Pearson had for the first time, it seemed, provided a means of determining the elusive laws of human heredity. Yet within a few years of its creation, the new discipline of biometrics had, in the minds of many biologists, become obsolete.

In 1900 the rediscovery of Gregor Mendel's neglected conclusions seemed to provide an explanation for those phenomena which previously dominant statistical methods were capable only of describing. It was inevitable that the laws which the Austrian monk had found to govern inheritance in garden peas would soon be applied to human heredity. It was equally inevitable that this work should prove inconclusive. Man is not an ideal experimental animal, and the tools and concepts of biology at the turn of the century were not equal to unraveling the complexities of human genetics. Equally important, the very attitudes which inspired scientists to apply Mendelianism immediately to the inheritance of human traits made an objective study of these traits impossible. To many of the early workers in the field, human genetics was indistinguishable from eugenics; their findings were blueprints for social action. Charles Benedict Davenport was the most active and prominent of such early American geneticists.

Charles Benedict Davenport was born in 1866. Though raised in Brooklyn, this descendant of Puritan divines always prided himself on his New England ancestry. "I have been an American for three-quarters of a century," he wrote in 1942. "No, longer than that—for over three hundred years. For this 'I' is composed of elements that were brought to this country during the seventeenth century."[1]

Despite an absorbing childhood interest in natural history, young Charles was destined by his authoritarian father for a career in the financially more reliable profession of engineering. It was only after he had graduated from the Brooklyn Polytechnic Institute, earned a bit of money with his engineering skills, and, still more important, attained his majority, that the prospective scientist was capable of defying his father's wishes.

Davenport finally entered Harvard College in 1887, at the age of twenty-one, and within two years received his bachelor's degree. Another three years in Cambridge brought him a doctorate in zoology. Davenport then served Harvard for seven years as an instructor, until delivered from this Egyptian bondage by the newly established University of Chicago's offer of an assistant professorship. In 1901 he was promoted to associate professor, only to resign three years later. He had been offered something which he had always wanted and which he could not well refuse—the directorship of his own research institute.

Largely at Davenport's initiative, the Carnegie Institution had established a Station for Experimental Evolution at Cold Spring Harbor, Long Island, and appointed the ambitious young zoologist as director.[2] Davenport was to occupy this position for thirty years, from his appointment in 1904 until his retirement in 1934. During these three decades he devoted his research almost entirely to human genetics.

While at Harvard and Chicago, Davenport had already established himself as a leader in the use of biostatistics. The years spent in engineering school had not been entirely wasted. Davenport brought to his zoological studies a mathematical preparation far greater than was customary among biologists of his day. Until his acceptance of Mendelianism, Davenport had been convinced that the future of biology lay in these new quantitative methods. The application of such procedures, he wrote enthusiastically in 1900, had already borne fruit. "The role of natural selection, the method of evolution, and the laws of inheritance are being discovered. Already we are able to predict greater results from the quantitative methods in biology, especially where combined with experimentation, than any which have yet appeared."[3] These central problems of biology all seemed within reach of solution—even the vexing question of heredity; for heredity was, as Davenport put it, "only a special case of correlated variation; a correlation between parents and offspring or between any two blood relatives."[4]

With scientific opinion of heredity in so murky and ill-defined a state, the generalizations of Mendel appeared with almost the power of revelation. For the first time heredity could be understood and even predicted.

Charles Davenport had always been interested in heredity and evolution, and he lost no time in acquainting himself with these new ideas. He was, in fact, the author of one of the earliest, if not the very first, American discussions of the papers by Correns and De Vries, who along with Tschermak—whose work was not known to Davenport— had independently rediscovered the Mendelian principles. (The article appeared in June of 1901 in the *Biological Bulletin* of the Woods Hole Marine Biological Laboratory, though Davenport's diary records his having written it in November of the previous year.)[5] Though he did not immediately discontinue his biometric studies of variation and selection, Davenport had, by 1904, become a thorough convert to the ideas of Mendel and De Vries.[6]

Mendel's work had an almost euphoric effect on the biology of the early 1900s, an effect which can, with some justice, be likened to that which the germ theory had had upon the medical profession in an earlier generation. Both theories opened new areas of research, and in both cases much of this research was premature and uncritical. And Charles Davenport was not only uncritical; he was almost painfully ambitious and emotionally committed to the results of his studies. There could be no more important social goal, he believed, than the enactment of genetic truths into law.

Even before 1900 Davenport had been deeply interested in the eugenics movement. His original enthusiasm for Galton's biometrics was at least partially a reflection of this interest. True progress, he believed, could come only through improvements in man's germ plasm. Heredity, as Davenport warned in 1910, "stands as the one great hope of the human race; its savior from imbecility, poverty, disease, immorality." Davenport was never to be shaken in this conviction. Social problems, he admonished a group of medical students in 1940, three decades later, were coming more and more to be recognized as biological problems.[7]

Unfortunately, human beings are not so easily studied as garden peas or drosophila. Nor are most human traits adequately explained by the simplistic doctrine which Mendelianism seemed to most biologists to be in the century's first decade. Indeed, as late as 1912 Davenport wrote confidently that "modern studies in heredity have made that science relatively simple."[8] The same year Davenport wrote to economist Irving Fisher, stating that there wasn't "very much more mathematics to Mendel's law than that 1/2 of 1/2 is 1/4." When he began research in genetics, Davenport assumed that human traits were discrete, unit characters determined by pairs of distinct immutable factors, one of which might often mask or dominate the other. Davenport tended to assume as well that dominance meant the presence of something, and recessiveness, its absence. It was not yet customary to think in terms of alternatives. Working after 1900 almost exclusively with human material, he was, moreover, forced to rely for data upon pedigree studies.

Yet, despite these conceptual and methodological limitations, Davenport made real contributions to the study of human genetics. He was, for example, one of the first investigators to apply the concept of polygenic inheritance to a human trait. In 1910, in a paper published with his wife Gertrude, Davenport concluded that the gradations of human skin color might well be determined by the combined action of two independent pairs of factors.[9] Indeed, as early as 1908 Davenport had suggested that so-called blending inheritance was probably due to "a Mendelian inheritance of minute units."[10] He was also one of the first to explain the determination of a human trait (eye color) in terms of multiple alternative genes. Where the pedigree method was of value, as in a number of hereditary or supposedly hereditary defects such as albinism, Huntington's chorea, and otosclerosis, Davenport was able to contribute valuable data.

To Charles Davenport, however, those traits which most demanded study were those determining human behavior. Yet it was in the field of behavior genetics that the pedigree method was most inadequate and in which Davenport's social commitments were in sharpest conflict with his scientific objectivity. It was also, ironically enough, the area in which the discarded correlations and standard deviations of the biometric approach would have been most useful. Not only mental disease and mental deficiency, but such characteristics as "shiftlessness," "licentiousness," and "criminality" were all attributed to the presence or absence of one or more Mendelian determiners.

But how could such aspects of human behavior be studied? Let us look at one of Davenport's personality studies and see how he attempted to approach such problems. In 1917, with war imminent, he undertook to isolate those criteria which might be useful in predicting the success of future naval officers. Davenport began by choosing sixty-eight historically prominent naval commanders and, making use of biographies, memoirs, and biographical dictionaries, compiled a list of those characteristics which they had displayed as children and which, Davenport asserted, could be used to predict the likelihood of their success as officers. Foremost among such desirable traits, he concluded, was an inborn love of the sea, or thalassophilia. This lust for the sea, Davenport contended, was almost certainly due to a sex-linked recessive factor. (That it was sex-linked seemed apparent, because men, not women, ran away to sea.)[11]

Other social traits could, similarly, be shown to depend upon genetic determinants. Prostitution, for example, was a consequence neither of economic nor psychological factors, but of hereditary predisposition. In a study of 350 "wayward" girls, only one, Davenport reported, had entered the ancient trade for economic reasons. Innate eroticism was the causative factor, and this was produced by "an additional germinal determiner that less licentious persons do not have." Unfortunately, eroticism was, he argued, a Mendelian dominant.[12]

Charles Davenport was to adhere consistently to such interpretations of human behavior until his death in 1944. His convictions were too deeply rooted in his opposition to social change and too much a product of the scientific concerns and presuppositions of the generation in which he grew to maturity.

Like many of his scientific contemporaries, Davenport was a rigid biological mechanist. Every aspect of human behavior had its origins in definite physiological and anatomical mechanisms. Behavior, he wrote in 1917, "is reaction to stimulus, and the nature of the reaction is determined in part by the nature of the reacting nervous machinery."[13] Thus variations in behavior implied underlying structural and functional differences. If Negroes and whites differed in their performance on psychological tests, it was because they differed in neurological attributes just as they did in skin color or hair texture. "The brains," Davenport asserted in 1926, "of great speakers are of one type; those of philosophers of another type; those of the menial another type; those of morons, imbeciles, Mongolian idiots of still other types. The mental output is what it is, to a great degree, because of the nature of the machinery that controls the output."[14]

Nor did it seem arbitrary to Davenport that he should regard such traits as industry, sympathy, or loyalty as though they were well-defined unit characters. Influenced by concepts of cerebral localization which had begun with the neuroanatomical theories of Gall, many nineteenth-century neurologists and psychiatrists found it increasingly natural to think of intellectual and emotional traits as discrete entities, localized in particular areas of the brain. The only way to conquer an individual failing such as criminality, Davenport argued, was to use another trait, such as fear, to counteract it. "Cutting out physical pain from punishment is the invention of the sentimentalist," he wrote in 1928; "not of the student of physiology and of Nature's laws."[15] If there was a speech center, then why not a center for eroticism as well? And, assuming as Davenport did that such traits were anatomically grounded and functionally independent, it was equally natural to assume that they should have a genetic basis. For Davenport it was unquestionable.

All organic phenomena were seen by Davenport's generation of biologists in relation to their place in the process of evolution. Davenport, unlike many of his colleagues, however, regarded not only physical, but cultural and social traits as being products of this same evolutionary process. It was second nature to Davenport—and many of his contemporaries—to think in phylogenetic terms. In his 1901 article on Mendel, for example, Davenport noted in passing that "in some cases the dominating form is the systematically higher; in others, it is the older or ancestral form." In his later years after increasing criticism of his genetic work drove him toward physical anthropology, Davenport's anthropomorphic researches frequently consisted of gathering data to prove that ontogeny really did recapitulate phylogeny.[16]

Criminals, prostitutes, and tramps—the feebly inhibited in Davenport's terminology—were simply those unfortunates lacking the gene, or genes, whose appearance through mutation in man's distant past had allowed him to control his more primitive asocial instincts and thus develop civilization. Ontogeny, as Davenport believed, recapitulated phylogeny in the child's socialization as well as in his physical growth. The child, like prehistoric man, was selfish, violent, and erotic. Normal children, however, were able as they grew older to control, to shunt off, as Davenport put it, these primeval impulses. The criminal was a criminal, the prostitute a prostitute, because their genetic make-up had not provided them with the neurological or physiological means of circumventing these brute urges.[17] Feeble-mindedness too resulted from the persistence of more primitive genes. It was, as Davenport declared, "an uninterrupted transmission from our animal ancestry. It is not reversion; it is direct inheritance."[18]

Davenport's debt to Lombroso and criminal anthropology is apparent, as is his debt to the earlier theory of degeneration. In addition to his acceptance of the idea of "atavism," Davenport believed, for example, in the connection between insanity and genius, in the possibility of physical stigmata marking the insane and feeble-minded, as well as in the existence of a basic "neuropathic weakness," which might manifest itself in insanity, pauperism, mental retardation, or criminality.

Social and physical evolution were one. Attempts to improve man by changing his environment were, Davenport believed, doomed to futility. The efforts of social workers, even of medicine and public health, were ultimately contrary to the direction of evolution. In the years before 1900, liberal intellectuals had formulated a detailed indictment of Social Darwinism, an indictment based on the assumption that a qualitative distinction existed between physical and social evolution.[19] In Davenport's hands this dichotomy disappeared; cultural change merely reflected underlying physical developments. The ideas of Mendel and De Vries had been used to adapt those of Herbert Spencer to the demands of a new century. "Barring a few highly exceptional conditions," Davenport wrote in 1911, "poverty means relative inefficiency and this in turn usually means mental inferiority." Wages and salaries, profits and honors were the rewards given by society to its "effective" and moral members. The principle of equality was a biological absurdity.

Yet these truths seemed to him increasingly ignored in twentieth-century America. The values which Davenport had assumed as a child were, he felt, being replaced by those of paternalism. "A demand for more social workers," he warned in 1912, "and larger institutions for defectives will be the first alarm of the approaching end of the old regime." And, as the century progressed, his fears seemed to have justified themselves. Welfare agencies, he wrote to Frederick Osborn in the terrible December of 1932, were a "force crushing out civilization."[20]

A preoccupation with the idea of race was characteristic of European and American minds in the half-century between 1880 and 1930. Charles Davenport was no exception: two of his major research interests were the effects of race-crossing and the comparative social traits of different races. Davenport never doubted that racial traits were as immutable as the genes which produced them.

America, as Davenport interpreted the nation's history, was the product of Anglo-Saxon genes, and it seemed to him questionable whether this democracy could long survive the dilution of the blood which had created it. The only hope of the republic, he believed, lay in the success of the immigration restriction movement, a cause to which he gave his wholehearted support and to which he lent without reservation the prestige of his scientific position. As a consequence of the tremendous influx of immigrants from Southeastern Europe, Davenport wrote in 1911, the American population would "rapidly become darker in pigmentation, smaller in stature, more mercurial, more attached to music and art, more given to crimes of larceny, kidnapping, assault, murder, rape and sex immorality."[21] Davenport's views changed little in succeeding decades, though his optimism sometimes flagged. The racial situation seemed to be deteriorating steadily, he confided to a friend in 1925. "Our ancestors drove Baptists from Massachusetts Bay in to Rhode Island but we have no place to drive the Jews to. Also they burned the witches but it seems to be against the mores to burn any considerable part of our population."

By the late twenties and early thirties such pronouncements were being received by American scientists with increasing uneasiness. After the National Socialist party had implemented these ideas in Germany, such concepts began to seem not merely gauche but dangerous. The intellectual break which most geneticists had made with the eugenics movement in the twenties had become a public one by the late thirties. "It seems to me," Harvard geneticist W. E. Castle explained in 1924, "that we are scarcely as yet in a position to do more than make ourselves ridiculous in this matter. We are no more in a position to control eugenics than the tides of the ocean." This was in a personal letter. The more outspoken Raymond Pearl published a slashing would-be eulogy over the eugenics crusade in 1928. "For their public teaching," he charged, "their legislative enactments, and their moral fervor are plainly based chiefly upon a pre-Mendelian genetics, as outworn and useless as the rind of yesterday's melon." The literature of eugenics, Pearl explained, "has largely become a mingled mess of ill-grounded and uncritical sociology, economics, anthropology and politics, full of emotional appeals to class and race prejudice, solemnly put forth as *science.*" It was, Pearl continued, the geneticists' responsibility to disown such sentiments, for "the public is told that the eugenic *pabulum* it is fed is the latest and considered word from the science of genetics."[22] Both a faith in democracy and a prudent sensitivity toward the integrity of their discipline had made eugenics no longer a plausible enthusiasm for the great majority of professional geneticists.

In 1940 the Carnegie Institution withdrew the last of its support from the eugenics program at Cold Spring Harbor. Davenport was now seventy-four, six years in retirement, a prophet without followers. Yet, though the crusade which had filled his life had ended in failure, he did not despair, but continued to work actively until almost the day of his death in 1944. In his ten years of retirement Davenport published forty-seven papers, wrote one book, and revised another.[23]

Human genetics has been recreated in the past three decades. Eugenics is more the concern of the historian than that of the scientist.[24] What, then, were the contributions of Charles Benedict Davenport to the nation and the science he wished to serve?

If only because of his acceptance and championing of both biostatistics and Mendelianism, Davenport would have been of real importance in the development of human genetics. Though never a major contributor in either field, he had the imagination to realize at once the significance of these new ideas.[25] Perhaps more important, Davenport was an early example of that much-neglected figure in the history of science and medicine, the statesman administrator, the ambassador to the laity from the world of science. Davenport not only created a wide interest in genetics with his writings and addresses, but was able as well to attract what were, for his time, enormous research funds. The Harriman, Huntington, and Rockefeller families, as well as the Carnegie Institution, contributed to his research programs. Such blessings were not so common in the first quarter of the century as they have become today; there were few American geneticists of note in the first three decades of the century who did not spend at least a summer at Cold Spring Harbor.

To the historian of American society generally, Davenport's career is—most obviously—an illustration of the ways in which personal and social needs can appropriate the prestige and data of science to their own purposes. Davenport's career spanned a particularly ambiguous moment in the establishment of the biological sciences in America. Over-confident in their ability to apply new scientific insights to problems of social policy, sharing the concerns and anxieties of most other articulate, middle-class Americans, Davenport and not a few other scientists sought to use their knowledge and status to help solve the problems of their society and at the same time establish their own discipline and within it a meaningful personal career.

5

George M. Beard and American Nervousness

George M. Beard occupies a small, but apparently secure, place in the accepted canon of medical history. His discovery of neurasthenia—or nervous weakness—and his contention that it was a legitimate disease won him an international reputation in the late nineteenth century and has gained him the attention of historians of psychiatry in the twentieth. To these historians, Beard was a pioneer in the study of the neuroses, a forerunner of Freud and modern theories of dynamic psychiatry.

Yet Beard was neither a profound nor a critical thinker. His medical writings are a mosaic of the intellectual commonplaces of his time; it was the familiarity rather than the novelty of Beard's theories which made them so easily and rapidly accepted. His role in the development of modern psychiatry, though a real one, was no greater than that played by a score of his contemporaries. The opinions of George M. Beard are, nevertheless, of more than antiquarian interest, for his pages record with ingenuous fidelity the intellectual temper of post-bellum America. Most significantly, they illustrate the utility of scientific metaphor and authority in helping rationalize a rapidly changing and stress-filled world. Neurasthenia served too as a central component in the framework of clinical assumption within which the neurologist, a new species of urban specialized physician, could at at once justify his novel pretensions and in doing so explain the very real sufferings of patients seemingly unable to function within this labile enviroment.

George Miller Beard was born in 1839, in Montville, Connecticut. After two years of teaching school, Beard entered Yale in 1858; he graduated in 1862, spent one year in medical school in New Haven, then served for two years as assistant surgeon in President Lincoln's navy.[1] He completed his interrupted medical education at New York's College of Physicians, from which he graduated in 1866. Upon receiving his medical degree, Beard turned almost immediately to specialization in electrotherapy and diseases of the nervous system. To have specialized in such fields would have been well-nigh inconceivable for a regularly educated young physician a generation or two earlier. Beard was, naturally enough, a vigorous and self-conscious defender of specialization.[2]

Only two years after beginning practice, in 1868, Beard began to lecture on nervous diseases at New York University. Beard felt no distaste for hard work: in the seventeen years between his graduation in 1866 and his premature death in 1883, he managed to write and revise a standard treatise on "medical electricity," edit a popular medical encyclopedia, write widely on health for the layman, experiment with hypnotism, defend the rights of the insane, and suggest possible means for preventing mental illness—as well as carry on a busy practice. Yet these efforts were all subordinated to what he considered a more important contribution to medicine—his discovery of neurasthenia.

Those American physicians who, like Beard, began their careers at the close of the Civil War entered a new and rapidly changing medical world. It was to Germany, not France or England, that George M. Beard and his classmates came to look for inspiration. "The Anglo-Saxon peoples," Beard noted acidly in 1882, "have in modern days a genius for nonexpertness in science. . . . Were we not constantly nursed at the breast of Germany, both England and America would long since have starved to death scientifically."[3] German science and German method had seemingly reduced the mysteries of life to the physical and mathematical terms so congenial to many of Beard's contemporaries. One recent contribution of the "Anglo-Saxon mind," however, had already become a central assumption of scientific thought by the 1870s. This was the theory of evolution—"the highest generalization," as the enthusiastic young neurologist put it, "that the human mind has yet reached."[4] And though raised in a pious home and educated at Yale, George M. Beard felt that there could be no truths higher than those verifiable by the human mind.

And there was no challenge to science greater than the study of this mind, Beard contended. Psychology was to be "the one science of the future." Not supernaturalism and metaphysics, but chemistry, mathematics, and physics would be the tools of this new discipline. "Law reigns in the throb of passion as in the rush of a planet, and the atoms of the cell within the brain, like the hairs without it, are all numbered."[5] Insanity was a physical ailment, as much so as smallpox or a broken leg. This held true, Beard soon decided, not only for insanity, but for the numberless and amorphous ills which physicians traditionally described as "nervous."

The nervous patient, easily fatigued, anxious, complaining of vague physical ailments, was hardly a novelty to the medical profession in Beard's day. Such symptoms had even received literary recognition—and perhaps encouragement—in the well-cultivated sensitivity of the romantic hero and in that of his domesticated epigone, the delicate Victorian lady. The medical profession had always tended, however, to regard such tenuous ailments with skepticism. The patients displayed no physical symptoms and were not really ill; it was "all in their minds." Hysteria was merely an extreme form of such complaints, more imposition than illness. The hysteric, most medical and popular opinion agreed, could always run well enough in event of fire.[6]

Unlike the asylum physician, however, the neurologist in private practice had necessarily to spend much of his time with neurotic patients; and Beard, like other neurologists of his day, soon discovered that a good many of his patients complained not of clearly defined ailments, but of vague and unclassifiable symptoms, of morbid anxiety, unaccountable fatigue, irrational fears, of erratic sexual behavior. The youthful specialist was soon convinced that such symptoms could not be dismissed by labeling them hysteria or hypochondria. Fevers might kill, Beard argued in 1880, "but to many death is by no means the most disagreeable of the many symptoms of disease."[7] Most important, Beard was convinced that an underlying kinship existed among the bewildering variety of ailments tormenting his patients. All were manifestations of a single disease or condition; all stemmed from the same original cause. And by 1869, when Beard first described neurasthenia, it seemed unquestionable to most physicians that the basis of any real disease must be somatic.

The great clinicians of Paris, Vienna, and Dublin had taught their lessons well. Disease, to Beard's generation, was a well-differentiated clinical entity with distinct cause and pathology. If neurasthenia was to become a matter of scientific concern and not remain an occasion for moral condemnation, it too must be shown to fulfill these criteria; the behavior of both physician and patient must, that is, find appropriate scientific legitimation. It was to this task that Beard immediately applied himself.

The seemingly endless symptoms of the disease had first to be described. Beard did not hesitate at their diversity or apparent lack of organic connection, but methodically catalogued dozens of "characteristic" symptoms. These ranged from dyspepsia to an aversion of the eyes, from tenderness of the teeth and gums to chronic indecision. After filling two pages with a list of some three dozen symptoms, Beard modestly concluded that the list was "not supposed to be complete, but only representative and typical."[8] Though these symptoms could be described minutely, it was a seemingly impossible task to prove their common origin (as clinical-pathological correlations had, for example, done with the varied lesions of tuberculosis). For lack of such proof, Beard was forced to define neurasthenia as a "functional" disease. This was not meant to imply that nervous exhaustion was any less a material phenomenon than typhoid or cholera: it was simply, Beard argued, that science had not as yet progressed to the point where it was capable of studying disease processes which did not involve gross structural change. "I feel assured," he wrote in 1869, "that it [neurasthenia] will in time be substantially confirmed by microscopical and chemical examinations of those patients who died in a neurasthenic condition."[9]

Though unable to provide such empirical proof, Beard had at his disposal the intellectual tools with which to fashion a plausible, if speculative, etiology for his new disease. He called with casual impartiality upon physics, neurophysiology, and technology, upon Herbert Spencer, Thomas Edison, and Herman von Helmholtz for the building blocks with which to construct a mechanistic model explaining the pathology of nervous exhaustion. DuBois-Raymond supplied proof of the electrical nature of the nervous impulse, Helmholtz and Meyer their work in thermodynamics, Marshall Hall and others the reflex concept, and Brown-Sèquard "proof" of the heritability of acquired characteristics. With such new and prestigious insights at his disposal, Beard found it no difficult task to explain how a disease might be functional and yet the product of tangible material change. "Nervousness," he reiterated, "is a physical not a mental state, and its phenomena do not come from emotional excess or excitability."[10] Though paradoxical to mid-twentieth-century minds, precisely such formulations were demanded if the disease was to be seen as the appropriate object of a physican's concern.

Though characterized by dozens of apparently unrelated symptoms, neurasthenia, as Beard defined it, was simply what the word meant—a weakness of the nervous system. No two persons would be born with precisely the same amount of nervous force; no two persons would be subjected to the same external pressures. Only those individuals whose endowment of nervous force was inadequate to the demands of daily life succumbed to neurasthenia.

The nervous system, as Beard visualized it, was a closed and continuous channel. A fixed quantity of nervous force, assumed to be electrical in nature, coursed through this channel. It was this nervous force which carried messages from one part of the body to another, from the brain to the several organs, and, in addition, served as the "raw material" of consciousness. This mechanistic design provoked little criticism in Beard's self-consciously materialistic generation; electricity was not metaphysics and nervous energy seemed far removed from vital force. By calling upon three central ideas—the reflex theory, the electrical nature of the nervous impulse, and the conservation of energy—Beard was able to fashion a schematic explanation for every aspect of human behavior.[11]

The energies of the nervous system, for example, were limited, and their expenditure in one area resulted in their being unable to meet demands in others. Through this invocation of physical laws, Beard was able to explain the notoriously inconsistent development of human abilities (far better, he argued, than the traditional faculty psychology). Thus the idiot savant or the artistically gifted lunatic was the result of a particularly abnormal imbalance of these nervous energies. "The force which is turned away from some channel that is blocked up by disease rushes through the channels of sanity that remain unobstructed with heightened velocity." Hypnotism or trance was the consequence of nervous force being concentrated in "one direction." Physiology, Beard explained at the end of his life, "is the physics of living things . . . [and] pathology is the physics of disease."[12]

The effect of environmental tensions in causing nervous illness was easily explainable within the same system of ideas. A dynamo, Beard pointed out, capable of supplying power for a thousand lamps would fail if another five hundred were added to the circuit. The human body, like the dynamo, could produce only a limited amount of nervous force, while the stress of nineteenth-century life acted upon the human nervous system as so many added lamps would upon an electrical circuit. In those inadequately endowed with nervous force there would be a "dimming," possibly even a failure of normal nervous function. Business anxieties, excessive use of mental at the expense of physical powers, even extremes of temperature might all cause such an "overload."[13]

But what was the origin of such differences in nervous force? These variations, Beard felt, were essentially hereditary. Few of his medical contemporaries doubted the importance of a "nervous diathesis" in the etiology of mental illness. "Inheritance," as Beard put it, "is more than important; it is almost everything. To be born is, in the life of any man, the chief fact, all else being but a trifle."[14] Of course, not every case of neurasthenia involved a hereditary weakness; impotence or even sexual perversion might, for example, be traceable to youthful excesses—though even such sexual debility, Beard believed, might become "organized in families."[15] Hereditary explanations of mental illness were in the air. The pervasive degeneration theory provided an intellectual context in which neurasthenia found a natural and immediate place; it was the primary and generalized state of a nervous weakness which might in later life or in succeeding generations manifest itself as something more serious—as mania, or general paralysis, or epilepsy.

Beard found no difficulty, moreover, in explaining what might seem the most vexing problem in the pathology of nervous exhaustion—the means by which a primary weakness manifested itself in the endlessly varied symptoms which characterized the disease. The explanation lay in the "reflex function" of the nervous system. Man, Beard warned, was a "bundle of reflex actions, with a very small margin of volitional life."[16] Any lesion or irritation might, through "reflex action," cause disturbances almost anywhere else in the body. (In the 1870s and 1880s reflex irritation was a ubiquitous mechanism—or perhaps, more accurately, metaphor—helping to explain ailments undeniable as clinical phenomena but in which no discernible anatomical change could be demonstrated.)

There were, Beard emphasized, "three great centres of reflex action—the *brain*, the *stomach* and *digestive apparatus*, and the *reproductive system*." When "any one of these three reflex centres is irritated by over-use or direct abuse, the injury is likely to radiate or reverberate in any or in all directions; we cannot tell just where lightning will strike."[17] Thus masturbation might cause insanity, or a lacerated cervix hysteria. In this form the doctrine of reflex irritation was a commonplace to Beard's contemporaries. He, however, carried the doctrine one step further, asserting that mental strain or a generalized weakness of the nervous system might cause apparently physical ills. Lacerations of the uterus and perineum during childbirth, he suggested, occurred "because they have previously been reduced to the tearing point by general nervous exhaustion."[18]

With so earnestly somatic a pathology, Beard's therapy placed little reliance on "moral"—that is, psychological—treatment. Though few neurologists emphasized more clearly than Beard the influence which the mind was capable of exerting upon the body, he felt that the only way in which the physician could utilize this relationship was to assure the patient that his ailments were quite real, that they bore no stigma of malingering and were amenable to traditional therapy. As Charles L. Dana recalled: "Dr. Beard was intensely therapeutical and believed in drugs and instruments, and in anything that would help to cure. He had a long list of special and often ingenious and unusual formulas, which were put up for him in certain drug stores. . . . He had all kinds of devices for his neurasthenics: He used deep injections into the urethra, cold sounds and local electricalization. . . . While intensely interested in hypnotism, he did not use it therapeutically."[19] Though the mind might act upon the body to produce physical lesions, once produced these lesions were very real. To rely upon a therapy which would merely "wish them away" would be to call the legitimacy of the disease concept itself into question. Disease was a material phenomenon and could not be cured with words and kindly treatment.

There is no hint in Beard's writings of a psychological etiology for the grab bag of complaints he gathered under the rubric "neurasthenia." It is undeniable that George M. Beard was one of the first to advocate the systematic study of what is today ordinarily diagnosed as neurosis. That he suggested, moreover, a common etiology underlying such varied symptoms is, in the light of twentieth-century ideas, a credit to his discernment; that he helped remove the social disapproval attached to such ailments and helped make their diagnosis a medical and not a moral one is, in itself, a historically significant—if culturally ambiguous—accomplishment. That he is in any more specific way related to the theoretical development of modern psychiatry is doubtful.

Most twentieth-century historians of psychiatry have tended to project the values of a genetic psychology into the past and thus have failed to evaluate with sympathy the ideas of Beard and his contemporaries. They are either "bad" insofar as they were somaticists, or "good" insofar as their writings foreshadowed those of Freud.[20] Thus Beard's preoccupation with the environmental causes of mental illness has been seen exclusively in terms of the later ideas which it seems to prefigure, and not as part of a long and varied tradition of such thought. Because Beard studied behavior to which we tend to attribute a psychogenic etiology does not necessarily imply that he too was a self-conscious pioneer in such etiological thought.

The provision of a serviceable pathology for neurasthenia was only a part, and perhaps the least part, of Beard's work —though a necessary one if his ideas were to be accorded serious consideration. Another aspect of his thought seems most relevant today. This is his attempt to shed light upon the role played by society in the production of mental illness. Nervous exhaustion was, to Beard, the immediate consequence of a particular kind of social organization; it was as peculiar a product of the nineteenth century as the telegraph.

This was a natural-enough belief. Even the least credulous of nineteenth-century psychiatrists found it difficult to question the assumed connection between the tensions and artificialities of civilization and the existence of nervous disease. It was absurd, Beard held, even to suggest that a Congo Negro should suffer from neurasthenia or a South Sea Islander from epilepsy. Such primitivistic assumptions were, moreover, reinforced by the experience of acute clinicians who could not help observing cases in which stress had seemingly affected the course of a patient's illness.[21]

Beard contended, however, that it was not civilization as such, but rather the nineteenth-century variety of it, which caused neurasthenia. There had been no nervous exhaustion, he argued, in classical Greece or Rome. These ancient civilizations, Beard contended, lacked five characteristics peculiar to nineteenth-century civilization: steam power, the telegraph, the periodical press, the sciences, and the mental activity of women.[22] In each of these aspects of modernity, Beard casually noted, America was a quarter century more advanced than any European country. Thus it was only to be expected that nervous exhaustion should be most prevalent in the United States. And it was, in fact—Beard contended—so much more prevalent that it might almost be considered a peculiarly American disease.

Such conclusions were in keeping with a long and familiar tradition. Since at least the time of Benjamin Rush, American physicians had, almost as a matter of course, conceded that the unique pace of American life, its competitiveness, its lack of stability in religion and government, was somehow related to an incidence of mental illness higher than that of other Western countries.[23] After the Civil War, moreover, a new prop had been added to this traditional belief in the relationship between civilization and nervous ailments.

This was the idea of evolution. The almost instinctive belief in the immunity of barbarous peoples from mental afflictions now boasted a scientific explanation. Insanity, feeble-mindedness, crime, and immorality were all instances of what Herbert Spencer christened "dissolution," of a reversion to that which had been man's state in more primitive times. "Insanity," as Beard phrased it, "makes us children, makes us savages, makes us animals."[24] Such ideas, as they appeared in the pages of Spencer, Tuke, Lombroso, and Hughlings Jackson, were accepted with unqualified enthusiasm by Beard and the majority of his medical contemporaries.

Though Beard explicitly disowned a faculty psychology, it found a place in his thinking and in that of his contemporaries. The traditionally "higher" faculties, the aesthetic and moral, were as a matter of course identified with those highest in the scale of evolution. These were Spencer's "most altruistic" or John Hughlings Jackson's "most voluntary" attributes. Criminality and the mental illness or epilepsy which seemed so frequently to accompany it was simply a failure—due to either disease or heredity—of the higher and more complex centers. Such complex mechanisms were naturally more liable to malfunction than simpler ones; civilized man had, to use twentieth-century shorthand, too many moving parts.

The evolution of the nervous system had brought with its increasing complexity the ability to create a complex and moral civilization. Unfortunately, however, this highly evolved nervous system was, by virtue of its very "fineness of organization," vulnerable to the tensions characteristic of the civilization its evolution had made possible. It was the duty of the psychologist, Beard argued, to study the effects of such social stress upon the human nervous system. Until these relationships were understood, the etiology of nervous ailments would remain a mystery. Medicine was incomplete without an understanding of sociology (while the sociologist, Beard felt, could learn much from the observations of the physician).[25]

Why, for example, did neurasthenia seem to be limited almost exclusively to the wealthy and refined? The reason was clear enough to Beard. The educated and affluent enjoyed their places in the social order by virtue of their more sensitive "nervous organization." And it was this sensitivity which made them susceptible to neurasthenia. Indeed, the higher incidence of nervous exhaustion among the more successful classes of society seemed to provide clinical proof of the biological basis for their favored social position. Neurasthenia was to be found in the pulpit and counting room, not in the fields or factory, among the sensitive and cultivated and not among those "who have made the least advance beyond the savagery of our ancestors."[26] Beard's speculative etiology fitted unobtrusively into the assumptions of Social Darwinism.

The etiology of American nervousness was as much social comment as medical theory. It not only implied a justification of social relationships as they were, but—and with seeming inconsistency—constituted an indictment of many of this society's failings, of premature industrialization, of materialism, and of the futile anxieties which this materialism fostered. It provided as well an opportunity for expressing the unformulated misgivings which Beard, like many other Americans, felt in regard to the dangerous and unsettling freedom of American political and religious life. Russian peasants chose neither their rulers nor their religion and suffered from none of the symptoms of nervous exhaustion. Of course, there was no hint in Beard's writings that free Americans could find anything to envy in the lot of such peasants. Religious and political liberty might create insecurity, constant choice, and inevitable nervous strain, but it was unthinkable that Americans should exchange their unique liberties for the placid tyranny of the Russian or the Turkish empire.

Beard's doctrine of nervous exhaustion was, in sum, an optimistic, even nationalistic, concept. Each case of neurasthenia in the United States was an additional bit of evidence for the superiority of American institutions. American government was incomparably better than that of any other nation, its ordinary citizens more prosperous and better educated, its women more attractive and vivacious than those of other lands. Beard's was an ambivalence characteristically American. Like many men of his day, Beard's thinking was marked by unresolved and ordinarily unstated contradictions, between an ingenuously arrogant nationalism and a chronic national insecurity, between optimism and pessimism, between primitivism and progress. His ultimate position, however, was never in doubt. Beard questioned the desirability and inevitability of progress as little as he doubted that science and technology were the only sources of such progress.

The inventions of one man, Thomas Edison, Beard contended, had made and were making enormous demands upon the nervous force of Americans. Each new invention brought with it change, speed, and complexity—additional drafts upon the limited resources of nervous force allotted by heredity. Yet, as he concluded, "any school or college in which his labors were not recognized and the results of his labors were not taught would be patronized only for those who prefer the eighteenth century to the twentieth."[27]

Like Freud, George Beard saw the demands made by society upon the individual as an essential factor in the etiology of nervous illness. But the similarity between their views extends no further. Beard, unlike Freud, saw in the continued advance of material progress a solution for the evils of what Beard regarded as the essentially transitional period in which he lived. The conquest of neurasthenia need involve no change in man himself. The technology which had produced the telegraph, the railroad, and the factory had already begun to provide innovations which helped to reduce the tensions of nineteenth-century life. (Beard cited as specific examples the elevator, the sewing machine, and the palace car.)[28] The gradual dissemination of wealth would, moreover, help ultimately to provide immunity from mental illness as it had already provided some Americans with protection against infectious disease. By the beginning of the twentieth century, Beard believed, the incidence of nervous ailments would have reached its peak and have begun to decrease. Neurasthenia was merely one of the growing pains of a new and better society.

Beard was an American, an optimist, something of an evangelist. Many of his European contemporaries shared his conviction that there existed a relationship between the nature of nineteenth-century society and the causation of mental illness; few, if any, shared his unquestioning faith in the necessary triumph of progress. An equally small number could have shared in the sense of mission which accompanied this faith. Especially in the realm of human psychology, Beard felt, every discovery meant a victory for science and truth and defeat for the forces of ignorance and superstition. It was the duty, he wrote, of the physician not only to heal, but to enlighten, to make of himself "a power in society."[29]

Not all of Beard's fellow Americans accepted his ideas with enthusiasm. To a number of them, indeed, he was little more than a charlatan. He published the same articles again and again in different journals, then wove them together into books. And in these books Beard seemed more concerned with establishing his own reputation than with providing evidence for the existence of neurasthenia. Edward C. Spitzka, a painstaking neuroanatomist and one of the founders of the New York Neurological Society, characterized Beard as a kind of Barnum of American medicine. (The content of Beard's *American Nervousness*, Spitzka added in another review, was "not worth the ink with which it is printed, much less the paper on which this was done.")[30] Many medical men—hostile in any case to avowed specialists —continued to dismiss neurasthenia as a fashionable self-indulgence afforded themselves by the wealthy and idle.

Yet these were minority opinions. Within a decade of Beard's death in 1883, the diagnosis of nervous exhaustion had become part of the office furniture of most physicians. Few textbooks and systems of medicine failed to discuss it, and in 1893 neurasthenia received its ultimate legitimization—the publication of a German *Handbuch der Neurasthenia*.[31]

Nevertheless, Beard was careless, visionary, uncritical, and ambitious to a degree which compromised his ability as a scientist. Yet such criticisms seem today essentially irrelevant to the central issues raised by his work—the role of social organization in creating stress and possible mental illness. More original and more critical thinkers in the generations which followed Beard's—Freud, Durkheim, Adler, Horney, Sullivan, and many others—have sought to illuminate these relationships.[32] And though none of their solutions seems final, at least part of their stature lies in the very magnitude of these questions they sought to answer, questions which challenged the imaginative mind of George M. Beard almost a century ago. We can hardly be said to have banished those cultural anxieties which so forcefully expressed themselves in Beard's exposition of ostensibly clinical problems.

Piety and Social Action: Some Origins of the American Public Health Movement

In 1842 Robert M. Hartley, a pious and charitable New Yorker, helped found the New York Association for Improving the Condition of the Poor. That same year John H. Griscom, M.D., City Inspector, submitted to New York's Common Council an elaborately critical report on the city's sanitary condition. These two events initiated the first more-than-episodic public health movement in any American city.

During the decades before the Civil War, New York seemed the filthiest and least healthy of American cities. In the 1840s and early 1850s the two New Yorkers most concerned with the need for reforming such baleful conditions were John H. Griscom and Robert Hartley. These men were in some ways dissimilar: one was a physician, the other a businessman turned innovator in social welfare; one a Quaker, the other an orthodox Presbyterian. In other ways they had much in common. For the social historian, their most pertinent similarity lies in both having become involved in public health reform as a result, essentially, of their commitment to a pietism widespread in their generation.

That evangelical religion had a broad impact in antebellum America has become a historical commonplace.[1] Such spiritual dedication played an important role in helping to create a concern for health conditions in the nation's cities, as well as for more familiar reforms such as abolitionism and temperance. The vast majority of respectable urban Americans, including physicians, found no great difficulty in ignoring the medieval filth and misery which surrounded them.

This chapter was written with Carroll Smith-Rosenberg as co-author.

English and French crusaders for public health reform found only a handful of North American disciples before the late 1850s. The motivations which inspired America's pioneer sanitarians cannot therefore be explained alone in terms of European influences or as an inevitable, almost instinctive, rejection of intolerable conditions. The following pages attempt no comprehensive study of either Hartley or Griscom, but hope only to suggest the place of religious motives in shaping their dedication to social reform—as such pietistic convictions did in inspiring the work of virtually every urban philanthropist in this period. In an even more general sense their concerns and motives illustrate the creative interpenetration of religious and scientific values in the shaping of a characteristic mid-century commitment to social activism.

To historians of American public health and American urban development, John H. Griscom is known primarily as the author of an eloquent pamphlet entitled *Sanitary Condition of the Laboring Population of New York* (1845).[2] Yet this is only a small part of his efforts in the cause of public health. Beginning with his tenure as New York's City Inspector—the community's principal health officer—in 1842 and culminating with his presidency of the Third National Quarantine and Sanitary Convention in 1859, Griscom labored constantly to alert his fellow New Yorkers to the need for sanitary reform. Griscom was for a number of years almost alone among New York physicians in his crusade.[3] This reformist impulse was indeed so atypical in the medical world of the 1840s that it seems logical to explain Griscom's involvement in public health matters not in terms of his role as a physician, but in terms of his being his father's son.

The senior John Griscom was a Quaker educator and philanthropist who exemplified in his long career of benevolence a characteristically American respect for science and learning coupled with an intense pietism. Griscom was born in 1774 into an established Quaker family in New Jersey. He studied briefly in Philadelphia, then turned to secondary school teaching in Burlington, New Jersey. Griscom was remarkably successful, and at the invitation of a number of wealthy New Yorkers he moved in 1807 to the emerging metropolis and began to conduct a private school. This was the beginning of more than half a century of ceaseless benevolence.[4] In addition to his teaching, Griscom was, for example, instrumental in founding the House of Refuge for destitute and vagrant children and a Society for the Prevention of Pauperism, as well as half a dozen similar philanthropies. He was very much a part of New York's interdenominational evangelical establishment; though a Quaker, he worked closely with Methodists, Episcopalians, and Presbyterians to found and manage some of the city's most ambitious charities.[5]

In one area, however, Griscom's activities were quite individualistic. He was fascinated by science generally and chemistry specifically. The Quaker schoolmaster was one of the first Americans successfully to attempt the popularization of chemistry; he spoke at schools and lyceums and to mechanics' groups, and gave other public lectures.[6] Such scientific proselytizing implied no concession to materialism. Quite the contrary, Griscom's world was of a piece and the study of nature could, he assumed, only illuminate God's greatness. Griscom assumed, indeed, that any and all learning must inevitably have a spiritual effect. "It seems to me almost an axiomatic truth," he explained, "that sound learning and science do, by a natural law, gravitate towards virtue."[7] And as a man of piety he never shirked his duty of serving as an evangelist of science, helping to make his fellow Americans at once more learned and moral.

Griscom soon became one of the handful of respectable New Yorkers alarmed by the misery of so many among the city's poor. In his work with school-age children, and especially as a result of his years with the House of Refuge and the Society for the Prevention of Pauperism, Griscom accumulated detailed knowledge of the conditions in which his less fortunate fellow New Yorkers lived. With such broadly social concerns, and in a society in which scientific knowledge was uncommon, Griscom was gradually drawn into areas which seem to the twentieth-century reader specifically medical. In 1822, for example, he became embroiled—as a reigning expert on chemistry and thus on disinfection—in debate over the best means of preventing the spread of yellow fever. In similar fashion Griscom was called upon to act as an adviser on ventilation.[8] Yellow fever, ventilation, science education, and, most importantly, the condition of the poor—these were to be central concerns in the life of his physician son.[9]

John H. Griscom was born in 1809 and attended his father's New York school. Not surprisingly, with the elder Griscom so well connected in New York's scientific and philanthropic circles, the younger traveled the path of accepted success in New York medicine. He attended several full sessions of the Rutgers Medical College, where his father served as professor of chemistry and natural philsophy, and studied successively under two eminent preceptors, John D. Godman and Valentine Mott. After the final collapse of the Rutgers school in 1830, Griscom attended the University of Pennsylvania School of Medicine and was graduated in 1832. Returning to New York from Philadelphia, he was awarded an appointment at the New York Dispensary. In 1842 Griscom was also made attending physician at the Eastern Dispensary and a year later received a coveted appointment as attending physician at New York Hospital. Griscom was a founding member of both the New York Medical and Surgical Society and the New York Academy of Medicine. When the Academy was organized in 1847, Griscom served on five of its committees the first year, an unmistakable indication—as both common sense and political scientists tell us—of establishment membership.[10]

In addition to his responsibilities as a practitioner, Griscom found time to express a passion for intellectual improvement similar to that which had marked his father's career. The younger Griscom began in the late 1830s to devote a good deal of time to popular education in physiology and hygiene. He wrote several school texts, and soon began to offer public lectures. Fundamental improvement in the health of Americans would depend ultimately, he always held, upon disseminating the truths of hyigene at all levels throughout the community; there was no subject so important and so unfortunately neglected in the curriculum. "The general introduction of this subject," he wrote in 1844, "as a branch of school learning, would, I hesitate not to say, have a greater meliorating influence upon the human condition, than any other." Griscom believed that hygiene and physiology had a spiritual as well as material content. What subject, for example, could more effectively demonstrate to children their total dependence upon the Lord and the need for obeying His admirably contrived laws? "Indulgence in a vicious or immoral course of life," Griscom assured his young readers, "is sure to prove destructive to health."[11] An understanding of anatomy and physiology would, in addition to preserving health and morality, draw the mind upward toward the Contriver of this marvelous "animal mechanism."

Griscom drew habitually upon arguments from design. New York's mortality rates, for example, could not be a normal part of God's world; could He have planned so inefficient a system? A goodly portion of the sickness which afflicted men, Griscom argued, resulted not from some mysterious and ineluctable dispensation of Providence, but from man's own ignorance. (And in the moral calculus of the Griscoms, sin and ignorance unimproved were hardly distinguishable.) Were men only to utilize properly the fresh air, the pure water, the intelligence granted them by the Lord, they would escape unnecessary sickness and premature death. Yet air, water, and food—the necessities of life—became all too often the channels through which disease attacked. "Left to the care of nature herself," Griscom lectured, "these would be far less frequently, to man, the sources of disease; but by his own wilfullness and intermeddling, and sad to say, by his own ignorance, he creates the poison which he presents to his own lips."[12]

Like many of his contemporaries, Griscom emphasized the unnatural quality of city life, the essentially more healthful—because more natural—life of the savage. One need only compare the rude health of the American Indian with Griscom's wan and narrow-chested fellow New Yorkers.[13] The contrast was easily explained: the savage lived a simple life, in unthinking harmony with the bounties supplied abundantly by the Lord. The ignorance and cupidity of civilized man, on the other hand, everywhere polluted the sources for a healthful life.

This emphasis was consistent with Griscom's essentially optimistic and melioristic tone; civilized life was not inevitably or necessarily unhealthy. To remedy its evils, one need only apply knowledge already available; ventilation was a case in point. The true fault lay not in the existence of cities as such, but in man's obstinate failure to use his intelligence in making city life as healthy as it might be. In this sense, Griscom was certain, such neglects were culpable, an affront to God. "Cleanliness," he noted in 1850, "is said to be 'next to godliness,' and if, after admitting this, we reflect that cleanliness cannot exist without ventilation, we must then look upon the latter as not only a *moral* but *religious* duty." What was needed, Griscom urged, was a "*sanatory* regeneration of society."[14]

But, it may be objected, all these arguments were quite commonplace, formulas so traditionalistic that it would be unsafe to assume from them any overwhelming degree of pietism in their user. This may, to some extent, be conceded; but Griscom's lasting significance does not rest upon the formal content of his writings. His historical reputation is based on the Quaker physician's tenacious commitment to bettering the living conditions of deprived New Yorkers. For this was a period when such concerns were atypical in the medical profession, when the filling of public health posts was often a badge of professional inadequacy or second-rate careerism. It does not seem likely that the well-connected Griscom was simply an opportunist seeking notoriety and the sinecure of a political appointment.[15] And if this is not the case, the only apparent motivation for his untiring concern was religious—for a truly secular humanitarianism was still essentially alien to Griscom's time and social class. Even in his explicitly detailed appeals for public health reorganization, Griscom displayed a persistent tone of moral concern, a guiding dependence upon moral imperatives in shaping his understanding of individual behavior and the place which such reform might play in the upgrading of civic virtue.

Most famous of these appeals is his *Sanitary Condition of the Laboring Population of New York*, delivered in December of 1844 as a public lecture and published soon after. (This pamphlet was in its turn

an expansion and elaboration of remarks Griscom had appended to his
1842 report as City Inspector.)[16] The Quaker physician emphasized the
contrast between the city's essentially healthful physical setting and its
disgracefully high mortality rate. There was an unmistakable connection between New York's excessive premature deaths and the miserable
condition of the city's tenements. Most deplorable was the plight of
thousands who inhabited underground apartments, prey to cellar
dampness—even flooding—and poor ventilation. As he describes such
conditions, Griscom's decorous prose suggests the emotional impact of
the squalor he—unlike most "respectable" New Yorkers—had seen. "It
is almost impossible," he explained, "when contemplating the circumstances and conditions of the poor beings who inhabit these holes, to
maintain the proper degree of calmness requisite for thorough inspection, and the exercise of a sound judgment, respecting them."[17] The only
solution lay in the use of the state's regulatory powers; New York City
needed a board of health endowed with broad powers and staffed by
properly trained medical men.[18] Griscom reiterated such arguments for
two decades—at legislative hearings, in journal articles, at meetings of
the New York Academy of Medicine and the American Medical Association.

Public health reform would result not only in healthier New Yorkers,
but in more moral and law-abiding ones. John H. Griscom's world, like
his father's, was an organic one. Physical health and living conditions,
morality and religion, were a tightly knit series of causes and effects. The
cellar resident, no matter how pious or industrious at first, could not
long remain a productive, churchgoing member of society. Damp ill-
ventilated apartments soon brought disease, depressed vital energies,
and, inevitably, lowered the "moral tone" as well. Unemployment,
neglect of person and God soon followed. Such debilitated slum
dwellers turned then to alcohol for the physiological stimulation
lacking in their inhospitable environment; the picture of the filthy,
drunken, immoral pauper was complete. "From a low state of general
health," Griscom explained, "whether in an individual or in numbers,
proceed diminished energy of body and of mind, and a vitiated moral
perception, the frequent precursor of habits and deeds, which give
employment to the officers of police, and the ministers of justice.
. . . The coincidence, or parallelism, of moral degradation and
physical disease, is plainly apparent to an experienced observer."[19]
How, for example, could man's innate love of modesty and decorum
manifest itself in New York's reeking tenements? Was it surprising that
incest, prostitution, and venereal disease should thrive in districts where
families had to perform all their biological functions in one small and
crowded room? Just as man had an innate feeling for morality, he had an

instinctive feeling for order and cleanliness; but, Griscom asked, how could these homely virtues be encouraged in such circumstances? Rents were so high and accommodations so shoddy that even with a steady job and the best of will, working men found it almost impossible to find decent quarters for their families.[20] Man's natural capacity for virtue, like his natural state of health, was everywhere corrupted—by individual sin and ignorance and by the inequities of social organization.

And the atmosphere, the most universal of God's blessings, was in American cities everywhere polluted. Not only did a vitiated atmosphere deplete the slum dweller's vital powers, it served as a medium for the spread of disease. Epidemic and "miasmatic" diseases —cholera, yellow fever, malaria—were, of course, presumed to be spread through the atmosphere. Griscom believed, however, that even those diseases normally assumed to be contagious might in confined circumstances also be airborne. "The contagious viri of small-pox, measles, scarlet fever, and all others of that class," Griscom explained,"are also admitted to be communicated through the intermedium of the atmosphere. . . ."[21] The more contaminated the atmosphere, the more concentrated the infectious principle—and the more likely one was to contract it. In crowded tenements all these circumstances coincided; diseases normally noncontagious might often become so, while the slum dwellers, with vital energies chronically reduced by breathing such vitiated air, succumbed readily whenever they were unfortunate enough to come in contact with "contagious viri." It was only to be expected that Griscom should have emphasized the evils of a vitiated atmosphere and the need for improved systems of ventilation in his calls for reform. Not only was ventilation a fashionable cause but also it provided a scientifically reassuring vehicle for Griscom's need to instruct and improve.

It is tempting to interpret Griscom's rejection of early ideas of the specific etiology of epidemic disease within the same humanitarian framework. Like many other public health leaders of his first generation—Edwin Snow of Providence and H. G. Clark of Boston, for example—Griscom found it difficult to modify his earlier emphasis upon the importance of local conditions in creating the necessary environment for epidemic disease. For an emphasis upon local causes implied a system in which man's own actions were the ultimate cause of the pestilence which afflicted him; to place the blame for an epidemic upon some impersonal and specific contagion—as the English sanitarian John Snow seemed to do in the case of cholera—was to create an etiological scheme in which Griscom's habitual demands for environmental reform would be deprived of their immediacy. In 1866, for example, Griscom argued that the presence of cholera on a ship in quarantine was due not to some specific and unavoidable contagion, but to the ship's filthy conditions. If the ship had been equally filthy and there had been no cholera influence present, ship fever would have resulted; if the ship had been clean, there would have been neither cholera nor typhus.[22]

Griscom could at first muster scant support in his attempts to gather data on slum conditions and in demanding their reform. Both in his 1842 report as City Inspector and in his *Sanitary Condition of the Laboring Population* Griscom relied heavily upon the testimony of missionaries of the New York City Tract Society. For they, with the city's dispensary physicians, were the only emissaries of respectable society to the tenement districts in which the poor lived and died.[23] Griscom's dependence upon the help of city missionaries indicates not only something of his personal ties, but something of the origins of a growing awareness of slum conditions among proper and articulate New Yorkers. It is no accident that public health reformers in this generation spoke so often and so casually of the need for health missionaries and the distribution of health tracts. The reviewer of Griscom's *Sanitary Condition* in the *New York Journal of Medicine* actually suggested, by way of conclusion, that it be reprinted and distributed by the City Tract Society.[24] In ideas, in actions, and in his personal associations, Griscom consistently displayed the pietistic origin of his concern for public health.

In subsequent years, as increasing numbers of physicians became interested in public health problems, this motivating pattern of religiously oriented humanitarianism persisted. Stephen Smith and his wife, for example, were both active in the affairs of the American Female Guardian Society, an organization occupying a "left-wing" position in the evangelical united front. John Ordronaux, another prominent writer on public health matters, urged in his 1866 anniversary discourse to the New York Academy that the American Tract Society print and distribute health tracts among the poor: "Let the poor be taught that there is religion in cleanliness, in ventilation, and in good food; let them but once be induced to put these lessons into practice, and we may rest assured their spiritual culture and moral elevation will be rendered all the more easy and certain." "Disease, like sin," he explained, "is permitted to exist; but conscience and revelation on the one hand, and reason and science on the other, are the kindred means with which God has armed us against them."[25]

More influential than Griscom in illuminating the misery and sickness which existed in New York of the 1840s was his contemporary Robert M. Hartley. Hartley was a man of great vigor and tenacity, and, as a principal organizer and long-time director of the New York Association for Improving the Condition of the Poor, is ordinarily considered the shaper of America's first proto-social welfare agency. One of the most significant of Hartley's accomplishments was his leadership of the Association's pioneer involvement in tenement and public health reform, an involvement which in point of time exactly paralleled Griscom's.

Despite Hartley's self-consciously pragmatic attempts to professionalize charity, the history of the A.I.C.P. and Hartley's own life illustrate how directly the origins of his social activism were rooted in the evangelical enthusiasm of his youth. Robert Milham Hartley was born in England in 1796 and came to the United States as a three-year-old with his merchant father. The family settled in western New York State, in an area known to historians and contemporaries as the Burned-Over district, for the intensity of the religious revivals which swept through it. Like his father, young Hartley went into business, making a mercantile career in New York City. But, as in the case of many of his contemporaries, the competitive urgings of commerce did not fill his life. As a boy, Hartley experienced a conversion to evangelical Protestantism and even before arriving in New York City, while still a clerk in upstate New York, he organized prayer meetings and crusaded for proper Sabbath observance. Soon after moving to New York City, Hartley became active in the affairs of his Presbyterian church, serving as an elder and assuming leadership in the church's program of house-to-house missionary visiting. Hartley also began to play an active role in the work of the New York City Temperance Society and in 1833 became its corresponding secretary and agent. Hartley was instrumental in formulating the latter Society's policy of total abstinence—a novelty at a time when temperance still meant temperance.[26]

The perfectionism implied in Hartley's advocacy of total abstinence was a characteristic of the late 1820s and early 1830s, a period of increasingly millennial enthusiasm. Hartley's spiritual life was informed by this intense pietism throughout his career, even when dedicated as an older man to ostensibly secular goals (as the rational distribution of charity and the construction of model tenements). Fortunately for the historian, Hartley kept a diary which demonstrates clearly the continuity of his spiritual commitment. The entry of October 15, 1845, for example, reads: "Revised a plan for the press, long under consideration, to remodel all the city dispensaries so as to distribute the physicians and the medical depots generally over the city. And now, O my soul, how hast thou this day withstood the assaults of an evil world? Answer ere thou sinkest to the insensibility of sleep, as under the searching eye of him with whom thou has to do." And that for March 19,

1856: "I am, on a review, much dissatisfied with my labors today. I have done but little of that I designed to do. Truly I am an unprofitable servant; yet God mercifully forbears to punish. O for a higher wisdom than my own to direct the labors of my calling! At evening attended a sanitary lecture at the Cooper Institute. Today my mind has been pervaded with a deep seriousness, and a desire to dwell on spiritual things." Such sentiments were habitual with the one-time merchant who could, by 1856, write that sanitary reform was "the basis of most other reform in this city." There was not, nor could there be, any conflict between Hartley's vigorous pragmatism and intense pietism; the spiritual energies of his youth had been gradually rechanneled so as to shape and motivate his career of overtly secular benevolence. His pious activism had always to be maximized; it could alone placate his consciousness of sin and spiritual imperfection. "My failures," Hartley wrote when he was past 70, "I believe, were less owing to insuperable difficulties, than to my lack of earnestness and energy."[27] The contemplative life had few appeals for the pious in Jacksonian America.

These spiritual compulsions and the slum contacts they engendered had made Hartley and a number of like-minded evangelicals aware of their city's unsavory health conditions well before the formation of the A.I.C.P. in 1842. By the mid-1830s, for example, the New York City Tract Society, of which Hartley had been a member since 1827, began with New York's other city missions to take notice of the sickness and poverty encountered by their missionaries and volunteer tract distributors. Conditions already bad were harshly exacerbated by the panic of 1837 and the lengthy depression which followed; with growing frequency, the annual reports of these evangelical societies lamented in detail the misery of the city's slums. It had begun to seem increasingly unlikely that the souls of the poor could be saved while their bodies remained in such wretchedness.[28] Hartley's temperance work too, though it may seem today a moral, if not moralistic, concern, drew him increasingly into an understanding of the brutal facts of slum life.

It was, indeed, through temperance that Hartley first became involved with a specific public health problem. New York's infant mortality rate was remarkably high, and by the mid-1830s Hartley had become aware of what he considered a central role played by contaminated milk in swelling these dismaying statistics. He was particularly indignant when investigations showed that a good portion of the city's milk supply came from animals closely confined in filthy and unventilated stalls, and—worst of all—fed exclusively on distillery swill. In the winter of 1836–37 Hartley wrote a series of articles exposing these evils, and in 1842 a full-length treatise on the subject.[29]

Hartley's discussion of the milk problem displays a characteristic nineteenth-century mixture of pragmatic scientism, religious metaphor doing duty as medical logic, and unmistakable piety. Arguments from Liebig nestle comfortably against those drawn from moral imperative and providential design. Hartley appealed, as did Griscom, to the ultimate value of the natural—read "godly"—in condemning the unhealthfulness of the milk produced in such grossly unnatural conditions. Cows kept without exercise in filthy and unventilated stables, without room even to turn about, fed on hot and reeking swill—such animals could be expected to live but a short time and to produce milk as foul as their own conditions and diet. Could men of good will fold their arms and blame the death of so many innocents upon some inscrutable and unavoidable dispensation? "Can such be the purpose of the benevolent Creator?" Hartley, like Griscom, asked fellow New Yorkers. "Is so large a number of His rational offspring born with such feeble powers of vitality that life necessarily becomes extinct on the threshold of existence? Such conclusions, being inconsistent with the teachings of His Word and Providence, must be rejected as impious and absurd." And to an activist like Hartley, the conclusion was unmistakable: no truly pious New Yorker should purchase milk from this tainted source. "Can you continue so, and feel that you have discharged your duty to God, to your families, and to the community? Are you not bound by the most powerful obligations to wash your hands from all participation in so great an evil?"[30]

Hartley's argument from design was, of course, a commonplace in this generation, among physicians as well as laymen and the clergy. This was vigorously illustrated by Dr. A. K. Gardner, a prominent specialist in diseases of women and children, when he was testifying at an 1858 hearing in which he recalled the condition of swill-fed cows he had seen: "And I drew the conclusion that they were not in a state of nature; and the next conclusion that I drew was, that cows not in a natural condition, could not give milk of a natural character. . . . I then considered that if God made the milk in a certain way, that it could not be improved upon; and if any milk was totally opposite from the natural milk, God's milk, that it must be totally wrong."[31]

It takes no great sophistication to discern the moralism, the temperance zeal, in Hartley's overtly pragmatic concern for pure milk. And one could, indeed, make a great deal of the function played by images of pollution, of unnatural alcohol defiling that most natural of foods, God's pure milk (as one could with Griscom's discussion of the manner in which men violated the air they breathed).[32] Their habitual dependence upon such emotion-laden metaphors do not prove Hartley or Griscom to have been pious obscurantists; they were simply utilizing a traditional idiom in rationalizing and dramatizing a deeply held philanthropic commitment. (This was in a period, it must be recalled, when existing etiological knowledge seemed only to underscore the unity between moral and medical truths expressed by such time-honored images and admonitions.) The distinction between that which we regard as pragmatic environmentalism and that which we dismiss as mere moralism is, in regard to the public health movement of the 1840s and 1850s, far more confusing than enlightening. Both styles of thought supplemented each other, interacting with the energies of pietism to motivate and broaden the concern of a man like Hartley with the human problems of his city.

Hartley's interest in public health only began with his crusade for pure milk. As corresponding secretary and agent of the A.I.C.P. Hartley soon involved himself and the Association he guided in a varied group of measures aimed at improving the health of New Yorkers. For Hartley, like Griscom, assumed that man could be neither provident nor moral without health. As one surveys American cities in the 1840s and early 1850s, it soon becomes apparent that the A.I.C.P. had, indeed, the most coherent and far-seeing public health program of any benevolent group, while medical societies still concerned themselves only marginally with such matters.

The Association's managers were certain of the means by which the city's health conditions could be improved; the provision of decent housing was an indispensable first step. As early as 1846, only a few years after the organization had begun independent life, its directors voted to form a committee to investigate New York's slums. The committee issued its report the following year; the city's tenements, they concluded, were utterly inadequate to the preservation of either human health or Christian morality. Echoing Griscom's arguments of 1842, the Association's committee contended that New York's crowded, filthy, and ill-ventilated tenements eroded not only good health and moral standards, but also self-respect and religious sentiment. Man, a weakened creature at best, needed a decent environment in order to preserve his industriousness, cleanliness, and morality. This environment, the committee reported to their fellow New Yorkers, could not be found in the city's ever-widening slums. The committee concluded by warning the Association firmly that if they hoped to reduce the amount of poverty in New York and improve the morale of the poor, they must first reform tenement conditions. "Great value should be attached to this much-desired reform, seeing it lies at the basis of other reforms; and as the health and morals of thousands are injured or destroyed by the influence of circumstances around them, an improvement of the circumstances, in connection with other appropriate means, afford the only rational hope of effectively elevating their character and condition, and of relieving the city from numerous evils which now exist."[33]

Following European precedents, Hartley and the Association turned first to private investment. Model tenements could be constructed—buildings which would provide light and air and still bring a six percent return to the Christian capitalists who, it was hoped, would finance their construction. Despite years of effort, however, and the launching of one substantial experiment, these plans never came to fruition.[34] By the mid-1850s the Association, still dedicated to the amelioration of tenement housing, had turned largely to legislative solutions; only the power of the state could end the worst of such abuses, and thus allow the possibility of physical and moral regeneration.[35]

Most notably, the A.I.C.P. sponsored an ambitious study of New York's housing conditions, a study far more detailed than Griscom's earlier report. The committee presented a detailed, ward-by-ward description of New York's slums. A model of lucidity for its time, this document remained until the mid-sixties a source of data for American housing reformers and public health workers.[36] Throughout the 1850s, in legislative investigations, in medical articles and reports, in the activities of the New York Sanitary Association and the National Quarantine and Sanitary Conventions, the findings of the A.I.C.P. played a significant role in demonstrating the need for improved housing in safeguarding the health of the city's working population.[37]

In their broad concern for New York's "dependent classes," the A.I.C.P. did not limit its health program to demands for housing reform. It endorsed an eclectic range of public health measures, including the provision of medical care for the indigent. No sooner, indeed, had the A.I.C.P. been founded than it began to investigate the health of the poor and the adequacy of medical care available. In 1845, even before the appearance of its first annual report, the Association published Hartley's *A Plan for the Better Distribution of Medical Attendance*, a proposal for the increased provision of outpatient care. Within six years the A.I.C.P. established two new medical dispensaries. Association visitors worked closely with dispensary physicians, bringing them to the sick poor, even distributing medicines from central depositories. Throughout the 1850s and 1860s the A.I.C.P. continued to concern itself with such practical health needs. In 1852 it opened a Bath and Wash House, where for a minimal charge (imposed to prevent pauperization of the users) the poor could bathe and wash their clothing. This was New York's first public bath. In 1862, as well, the Association's legislative efforts at last won a state law regulating the production and sale of milk. During these same years the A.I.C.P. also supported such general public health measures as the improvement of the city's sewers, the regulation of slaughterhouses and bone-boiling establishments, and the prevention of tenement dwellers from keeping pigs, goats, and cows in their apartments. It fought among a growing number of allies and with final success—in 1866—to secure an effective, professionally staffed metropolitan Board of Health.[38]

The preceding pages have not sought to contend that all Americans who called in the 1840s and 1850s for public health reform were "secularized" evangelists, but rather to argue that a certain number, especially among this pioneer generation, found a central motivation for their activism in a pervading spirit of millennial piety. English example and influence were certainly strong, indeed crucial; the writings of Hartley and Griscom reflected again and again their familiarity with contemporary English public health appeals. Yet the question remains: why were these men—unlike the great majority of their medical contemporaries—so receptive to the ideas of the pioneer English sanitarians? The only plausible explanation lies, as we have suggested, in their religiously based commitment to saving and helping the unfortunate, in their assumption that an intimate relationship existed between environment, health, and morals.

Perhaps "pietistic" or "evangelical" is not quite precise enough a word to describe the motivations of men so different as the orthodox Hartley and the Quaker Griscom. And it must be confessed that they differed markedly in their attitude toward the poor and the poverty both sought to alleviate. (Griscom, for example, was at heart an environmental determinist, concerned far more with the implacably forbidding conditions of the slum than with the sins of those who inhabited them. Hartley, on the other hand, never escaped the conviction that original sin was the ultimate cause of all human misery, despite his understanding of the environmental factors which seemed often to cause and always to exacerbate the demoralization of poverty.)[39] Yet these individual differences suggest all the more unmistakably the overarching commonality of feeling which bound Griscom and Hartley together—an urgent need to help and in helping to convert, whether one understands the term "conversion" in the narrowly orthodox sense of predestined salvation, or in the humanistic sense which characterized the Griscom family's millennial faith in education, in science, and in moral improvement. It meant, in operational terms, a need to reach out to the disadvantaged, an inability to tolerate wrongs which through one's efforts might be ameliorated.

7

Martin Arrowsmith:
The Scientist as Hero

With the manuscript of *Babbitt* almost complete in the fall of 1921, Sinclair Lewis had already planned his next novel. Perhaps, he wrote Alfred Harcourt, his friend and publisher, it would not be satiric at all, "rebellious as ever . . . but the central character *heroic.*"[1] His next novel was *Arrowsmith*. Its heroic protagonist is a research scientist, the first of consequence in American fiction. To Sinclair Lewis he was far more than that.

Martin Arrowsmith is a new kind of hero, one appropriate to twentieth-century America. Journalists and historians inform us that the 1920s were years of intense and aggressive materialism. Yet Arrowsmith is obviously a hero not of deeds, but of the spirit. His scientific calling is not a concession to material values, but a means of overcoming them. In the austere world of pure science and in the example of Max Gottlieb, Arrowsmith finds a system of values which guide and sanction his stumbling quest for personal integrity. It is this quest which provides the novel's moral structure. Martin Arrowsmith's professional career is the record of his deepening understanding and acceptance of these scientific values and of their role in assuring Arrowsmith's ultimate triumph in his struggles with a succession of increasingly plausible material temptations.

Other centuries have accepted patterns into which such moral achievement could be projected—the martyr, the pilgrim, the evangelist, and, in more recent generations, the creative artist. None of these seemed particularly relevant to Sinclair Lewis in 1922. He had emphatically rejected the forms of traditional religion, despite the appeal which they had held for him as a lonely adolescent. Religion had become just another marketable commodity; its purveyors could not easily be pictured as heroic.[2] Nor was the sensitive artist a potential hero; Lewis knew too many and knew them too well. Yet Sinclair Lewis was very much a novelist of society, very much bound to the particular. His hero had to have a vocation. The problem was to find one in which dignity and integrity could be maintained in a world of small compromise and petty accommodation.

Yet America did have a heritage of dignity and individualism, Lewis believed. It lay in the pioneering spirit of the men and women who had settled the nation's West. Their heroic qualities had created America, yet theirs were the very characteristics which seemed to be disappearing most rapidly in a twentieth-century America, settled and implacably confining. *Arrowsmith* begins with an almost crudely pointed vignette: Martin Arrowsmith's great-grandmother, aged fourteen, is seated at the reins of a wagon. Her father, lying racked with fever in the wagon's bed, begs her to turn aside and ask shelter at her uncle's. But she will be obligated to no one and turns west. "They's a whole lot of new things I aim to be seeing," she exlaims. On the opening page of *Main Street*, Lewis describes another restless young girl. Carol Milford, like Arrowsmith, is the descendant of pioneers. Though the days of their exploits are "deader than Camelot," the spirit of her daring ancestors survives to animate this rebellious girl.[3] In the future Mrs. Kennecott, however, the divine discontent which helped people a continent becomes an unfocused and almost pathetic dissatisfaction with the commonplace world of Gopher Prairie. Arrowsmith is gifted with the same vigor and curiosity, but is able to attain through it the heroic stature denied Carol. In the life of the pure scientist he discovers a vocation in which his spiritual endowments find meaningful expression.

During the early part of 1922 the *Century Magazine* published a series of anonymous articles attacking the pretensions of American medicine. The articles were entitled "Our Medicine Men" and were written by Paul de Kruif, a junior staff member at the Rockefeller Insitute. By the end of 1922 he was unemployed.[4]

In the summer of 1922 Sinclair Lewis still sought a suitable protagonist for his heroic novel. He had begun his customarily detailed research for a novel of the American labor movement, its hero to be a Christlike leader modeled after Eugene Debs. But the novel did not seem to coalesce. On a hot August day in Chicago, Morris Fishbein, associate editor of the *Journal of the American Medical Association*, introduced Lewis to the young bacteriologist from the Rockefeller Institute.[5] *Arrowsmith* was the result of this meeting. No one but Sinclair Lewis could have written quite such a novel; yet insofar as *Arrowsmith* is a comment on the world of American medicine and biological research, insofar as it makes use of scientific values and preoccupations, it reflects clearly the attitudes of Paul de Kruif.

De Kruif provided Lewis with the vitae for his principal characters, with the details of laboratory procedure, and with a plausible scientific setting for Arrowsmith's exploits. Even more important, Lewis believed, was his contribution of the scientist's "philosophy."[6] De Kruif entertained few doubts concerning the nature of the scientific endeavor or of the intellectual and personal integrity it demanded. He was equally certain that most American research was slipshod and careless, simply cluttering the journals and indices. De Kruif's influence can be documented not only in Sinclair Lewis's own words, but in the youthful bacteriologist's published writings. Before the appearance of *Arrowsmith* in March of 1925, he had written, in addition to the articles in the *Century*, an essay on Jacques Loeb which appeared in *Harper's* and the section on medicine, also anonymous, in Harold Stearns's *Civilization in the United States*.[7] His discussion of Loeb, both in *Harper's* and in Stearn's *Civilization*, is particularly significant, for it is Jacques Loeb's values which are those professed by Max Gottlieb. De Kruif's "philosophy" is not a philosophy at all, but the recent convert's overenthusiastic reflection of a philosophy—of Loeb's biological mechanism.

Loeb's methodological scruples, even his style of life, had, moreover, a particular significance for American medicine in the early 1920s. He lived and expressed the gospel of pure science. In at least a limited sense, *Arrowsmith* is an incident in the birth of a new scientific medicine.[8] De Kruif's hostility toward the medical profession is an extreme, though not unrepresentative, instance of the laboratory scientist's hostility toward the clinician. Such attitudes, formed in the uneasy coexistence between laboratory and clinical medicine, shaped many of the particular incidents and emphases in *Arrowsmith*.

Martin Arrowsmith's professional biography is a record not only of the progress of a confused and easily misled young man toward emotional and intellectual fulfillment; it is the recapitulation in one man's life of the development of medicine in the United States. Each stage of Arrowsmith's career corresponds to a particular stage in the evolution of American medicine. Doc Vickerson's practice—and Martin's own practice in Wheatsylvania—dramatizes, for example, the trials and rewards of what De Kruif called "the splendid old type of general practitioner."[9] Both he and Lewis were sympathetic to this aspect of American medicine. It seemed informal, individual, at moments even heroic; at least it was free of that mixture of ersatz science and sordid commercialism which De Kruif regarded as having corrupted contemporary medical practice.

At Winnemac University both teachers and classmates of young Arrowsmith exemplify particular types and trends in medicine's coming of age. Dean Silva, for example, the pious disciple of Osler and Laennec, represents the understanding and craftsmanship to be found in clinical medicine. Professor Robertshaw, the self-exiled Brahmin physiologist, who always spoke—with elaborate casualness—of his student days in Leipzig with Carl Ludwig, illustrates the transference of German laboratory medicine to the United States—and with his "fuzzy little . . . maiden-aunt experiments" proves that the progress of science demands the spirit and not simply the techniques of German science.[10] Roscoe Geake, the professor of otolaryngology and future minion of the New Idea Instrument and Furniture Company, is a representative of the most sordid and ignoble aspects of clinical medicine, his specialism simply a device for the multiplication of fees.

Unlike most of his fellow medical students, Arrowsmith is the graduate of a four-year liberal arts curriculum. He is confident in his abilities as he enters medical school and looks forward to increasing his scientific knowledge. But, except for the inspiring example of Max Gottlieb, he is to be sadly disappointed. Arrowsmith's disillusionment is identical with that experienced by a hypothetical college graduate whose medical career was depicted by Paul de Kruif in the *Century*. He "enters his first medical course with confidence, aware of his superiority over the majority of his fellows. It is easy, then, to imagine his dismay when he discovers that he knows far more of physics and chemistry than many of his medical instructors, and finds himself surrounded by glib-memoried, poorly-prepared ignoramuses who shine by reason of their parrot-like ability to reel off an enormous number of facts crammed out of text-books."[11] After a short residency at a metropolitan hospital, an experience which at first stimulates then bores him, Arrowsmith begins practice in Wheatsylvania, North Dakota. But a newly inspired enthusiasm for public-health work earns him only the scorn of the small farming community. Fortunately, he is able to leave. Through the agency of Max Gottlieb and Gustav Sondelius, he obtains a position with the health department of a small Iowa city. In Nautilus, Arrowsmith's zeal quickly fades before the boosterism of his chief, the improbable Almus Pickerbaugh. Public-health programs, Martin discovers, are to be conducted in newspaper columns and on the lecture platform, not in the laboratory. De Kruif had, before meeting Lewis, recorded his intense dislike for such "shouters for public health," for these "dubious Messiahs who combine the zealous fanaticism of the missionary with the Jesuitical cynicism of the politician."[12] Boards of health, he argued, should be administered by engineers, statisticians, and bacteriologists —not by half-educated physicians.

Driven finally from his post in Nautilus, Arrowsmith is forced to accept a position with that "most competent, most clean and brisk and visionless medical factory, the Rouncefield Clinic."[13] In the early years of the 1920s the clinic seemed to all observers the most advanced form of medical practice. And De Kruif, like many other laboratory men, had already demonstrated his distaste for these gilded repair shops. Research, Arrowsmith soon learns, is regarded simply as a means of securing free advertising for the clinic. After a year of bondage at the Rouncefield Clinic, Arrowsmith's first paper is published in the *Journal of Infectious Diseases* and he is offered a research position at the McGurk Institute (of course, Lewis's conception of the Rockefeller Institute). At first Arrowsmith feels that he has reached a kind of scientific Elysium. He has a well-equipped laboratory, competent assistants, the company of his revered Max Gottlieb. Yet this too proves less than idyllic. Its demands for social graces, for premature publication, in short, its cultivation of success leads Arrowsmith toward his final and most important decision. He resigns from the Institute and joins his friend, the irreverent chemist Terry Wickett, who had already fled the compromising security of McGurk, at a wooded Vermont lake. Here, with a few like-minded investigators, they plan to conduct years of uninterrupted research. Thus the novel ends; Arrowsmith has conquered the final and most plausible obstacle in his quest for personal integrity—he has renounced success itself[14]—or at least success by the ordinary standards of American life. Like Max Gottlieb, Martin Arrowsmith is destined for fame, but in a world whose judgments are eternal, international, and ultimately untouched by material considerations.

One of the tentative titles for *Arrowsmith* was *The Shadow of Max Gottlieb*—an unfortunate title perhaps, but in a way justified. For Gottlieb *is* the scientific vocation. He had, inevitably, to be German. It was not simply that Paul de Kruif was immensely impressed by Jacques Loeb. To the young men of Lewis's and De Kruif's generation, science was German science, its embodiment the German professor. Gottlieb is a symbol not only of the transfer of European knowledge and techniques to the New World, but an expression of the peculiar mystique of German academic life. His worship of research qua research and his reverent attitude toward this pursuit of knowledge are very much the product of the German university. Such beliefs never established themselves with quite such intensity in France, in England, or in the United States. Yet the almost religious texture of this attitude toward the scientist's task is essential to the moral structure of the novel. It clothes Arrowsmith's long hours in his laboratory with a spiritual, an inherently transcendent quality.

As in the legends of the saints, every sordid aspect of Max Gottlieb's life is only evidence of his grace and a comment upon the tawdry standards of those who mock him. He lives in a "small brown weedy" house, rides to his laboratory on an ancient and squeaky bicycle, and wears the shabby topcoat of a poor professor. Most Americans could only regard him as something of a crank. His was "no work for the tall man at a time when heroes were building bridges, experimenting with Horseless Carriages, writing the first of the poetic Compelling Ads, and selling miles of calico and cigars." Yet on the crowded desk of Gottlieb's little bungalow, letters from the "great ones" of Europe awaited his reply—and mocked the collective wisdom of Mohalis and Wheatsylvania and Sauk Centre.[15] But Arrowsmith is vouchsafed the grace to understand and find inspiration in Max Gottlieb's life and ideas. Arrowsmith too shares something of his curiosity, something of his indignation at the shoddy and imprecise.

Sinclair Lewis created Max Gottlieb, but with raw materials provided by Paul de Kruif. Gottlieb, De Kruif later recalled, was an amalgam of Frederick G. Novy and Jacques Loeb. Novy was the austere and scientifically elegant professor of bacteriology at the University of Michigan who introduced De Kruif to biological research. Loeb was his idol at the Rockefeller Institute.[16] Though Gottlieb is a bacteriologist and immunologist like Novy, not a general physiologist like Loeb, his personality and mannerisms obviously represent the novelist's rendering of the articulate and sardonic German—or at least the picture of him which De Kruif had presented to Lewis. In his memoir Paul de Kruif describes Gottlieb as a "muddy mélange" of Novy and Loeb. There is little evidence, however, of his having been dissatisfied with this sentimentally didactic figure when, in 1924, he first read the manuscript of *Arrowsmith*.[17]

The genuine scientists in *Arrowsmith*—Gottlieb, Terry Wickett, and Arrowsmith himself—all share the same conception of truth. It is knowledge obtained in rigidly controlled experiments, knowledge analyzed and expressed in quantitative terms. There is only one assurance in life, Gottlieb warns the youthful Arrowsmith: "In this vale of tears there is nothing certain but the quantitative method."[18] Though many biologists today would approve such methodological sentiments, they would hardly express them with such passionate conviction. Our contemporaries are almost a century removed from the philosophical preoccupations which meant so much in Jacques Loeb's youth. The emotional intensity with which he, and his fictional counterpart Max Gottlieb, express such quantitative goals is clearly the reflection of an ancient conflict within the scientific community. This is the struggle between vitalism and mechanism.

Physical chemistry and mathematics were more than a method to Jacques Loeb; they were his reason for becoming a biologist. As a very young man, he recalled, he had read Schopenhauer and Eduard von Hartmann.[19] And while he was a student of philosophy at Berlin, the problem of free will seemed to him the most central of intellectual concerns. Loeb soon found himself unable to accept the existence of such individual freedom. Nor could he accept the techniques of philosophical analysis traditionally employed in the discussion of such problems. Loeb turned to physiological research in an attempt to prove that animal behavior was simply the sum of inorganic phenomena no different in kind from those studied by the physical scientist. Human behavior too, he believed, was no more nor less than the product of such physical and chemical forces. The "mystical" aspects of life were to be dissolved in the acid of mathematics and physical chemistry.

Naturphilosophie had been thoroughly vanquished by the late 1840s; yet the struggle against it had left a lasting impression on German biological thought.[20] The men most articulate in opposing formal idealism were imbued with an instinctive sensitivity to philosophical implications and many embraced mechanistic materialism with an absolutist zeal inevitably paralleling the idealistic convictions of an earlier generation. It was this period of conflicting ideologies which shaped Loeb's intense and consistently generalizing mind.

Jacques Loeb was, for example, an assistant of Adolf Fick. Fick was one of the greatest of Carl Ludwig's students and perhaps the one most inclined toward the study of physiological processes in physical and mathematical terms. And Ludwig—with his great colleagues Helmholtz, du Bois-Reymond, and Brücke—had been a leader in the struggle against a romantic or purely descriptive biology.[21] Loeb himself always regarded the significance of his classic experiments on artificial parthenogenesis "to be the fact that they transfer the problem of fertilization from the realm of morphology into the realm of physical chemistry." His earlier investigations of animal tropisms were, he explained, crucial because they proved that animal movements were regulated "by the law of mass action."[22] (Max Gottlieb remarks to Arrowsmith, when the young man arrives at McGurk, that he hopes "to bring immunity reactions under the mass action law.")[23] When Gottlieb feels that Arrowsmith has learned the elementary principles of his trade, he warns that true scientific competence requires a knowledge of higher mathematics and physical chemistry. "All living things are physicochemical," he points out to his disciple; "how can you expect to make progress if you do not know physical chemistry, and how can you know physical chemistry without much mathematics?" Arrowsmith's maturity as a scientist comes only in the last few pages of the book. His papers are praised in Paris and Brussels and Cambridge. But the socially impeccable Dr. Holabird is simply bewildered. What, he asks, did Arrowsmith "think he was anyway—a bacteriologist or a biophysicist?"

In a very real sense the values which sanction and direct Arrowsmith's quest for truth reflect those of Jacques Loeb and of a generations-old debate within the academic confines of German biology. As I have suggested, moreover, Max Gottlieb's values record accurately the laboratory scientist's impatience with the impressionistic and empirical aspects of clinical medicine. The essence of medicine is the functional relationship which the individual physician bears to his patient. It is his task to heal—or at least to console. It is the scientist's task to understand.[24] At best, De Kruif argued in 1922, the physician is a skilled technician of applied science. The attempt to train each practitioner as a scientist was simply delusive; a return to the preceptorial system of medical education would be preferable.[25] Lewis too found it natural to accept the pure scientist's vocation as a higher one. The very social necessity which created the medical profession tied it to the exigencies of everyday life, to compromise and commercialism, to the collection of bills and the lancing of boils. As able, self-sacrificing, and understanding as the best physician might be, he could never transcend the social relationships which formed the fabric of his professional existence. And to Lewis the essence of heroism, the measure of a man's stature, lay in the extent to which he was able to disengage himself from the confining pressures of American society. His heroic protagonist had to be a scientist; he could not be a physician. And certainly not an American physician.

Both De Kruif and Lewis agreed that American society had debased even the pursuit of science. For both men the essential factor in scientific progress was the initiative and creativity of the individual investigator. There seemed increasingly little provision for such individualism in twentieth-century America. To De Kruif no development within American science was more dangerous than its growing "barrack spirit."[26] Centralization and bureaucratization of scientific research were not simply the inevitable concomitants of an increasing complexity within society and within the body of scientific knowledge—they were developments inimical to the impulse of spontaneous creativity. Hence Lewis's acid portraits of Rippleton Holabird, of A. De Witt Tubbs and of his League of Cultural Agencies. ("If men like Koch and Pasteur only had such a system," Tubbs bubbles to Martin, "how much more *scope* their work might have had! Efficient universal *cooperation*—that's the thing in science today—the time of this silly, jealous, fumbling individual research has gone by.")[27] The young scientist, in an unfortunate image of De Kruif's, was to be denied the "privilege of wandering forth equipped only with the rifle of his intelligence, and thus to remain for long periods of lawless and impudent penetration of the forests and jungles of ignorance."[28] No great man had ever drawn his inspiration from the memo pad of a research coordinator. Their hypotheses, De Kruif argued, were drawn directly from the observation of natural phenomena. The investigator who sought his inspiration in a library could hardly be considered a scientist at all.

Jacques Loeb was fond of aphorisms. He was especially fond of one coined by his friend and teacher, the great botanist Julius von Sachs. "All originality," Sachs observed, "comes from reading."[29] Loeb was acutely conscious of history and of the communal nature of the scientific endeavor. He might mock the institutions of science and the mediocrities who so often found shelter within such institutional bulwarks, but he realized the futility of rejecting the scientific community as such. He died full of honors on the staff of the Rockefeller Institute. J. H. Northrop, model for Terry Wickett, even though a lover of the outdoors, always maintained his academic connections. Neither Loeb nor Northrop was a failure; neither renounced the corruptions of academic science and both learned to live with success. Even the criticisms and preoccupations of the restless Paul de Kruif were, as I hope to have shown, themselves characteristic products of the intellectual and institutional history of the biological and medical sciences. The conclusion of *Arrowsmith* is not only an indictment of the handicaps placed in the scientist's path by American society; it is a rejection at the same time of the scientific community whose values justify this indictment.

The novels of Sinclair Lewis are peopled with the wistful figures of Americans whose spiritual potentialities are unfulfilled. Arrowsmith is a conspicuous exception. Paul Riesling in *Babbitt* and Frank Shallard in *Elmer Gantry*, for example, were gifted with something of the sensitivity granted Arrowsmith. But, unlike him, neither was able to enter a vocation in which his spiritual endowments could find expression. Their inability to conform brought only their own destruction. The tragedy of George Babbitt lies in the pathetic and overwhelming defeat administered his vague idealisms by the forces of organized Zenith. In the scientist's life, however, such chronic questionings find a recognized social function. Even Arrowsmith's social inadequacies, his lack of humor, his callousness toward the old and the lonely and the workingman are simply evidence of his spiritual stature. It is the small people who make good administrators, who are attuned enough to the petty circumstances of life to function successfully within them.

It is this pervading air of compromise which finally drives Arrowsmith from his wife, from his child, and from his laboratory in New York.[30] His ultimate rejection of society and its demands has been criticized as callow romanticism—and perhaps it is. But it is the logical result of Lewis's desire to depict greatness and his inability to conceive of its being allowed to exist within American society.

PART TWO

Institutional Forms and
Social Values

Science and Social Values in Nineteenth-Century America: A Case Study in the Growth of Scientific Institutions

In any culture some values favor and others retard or positively oppose the development of science. Even within Western Europe, national and religious differences have been seen as peculiarly immanent in shaping variant patterns of scientific and technological growth. Hesitant mid-twentieth-century experience with social engineering in the so-called developing nations has simply dramatized the intricate relationship between social values, institutional forms, and the growth of a scientific community. Like the transplant of any tissue, the organic structures of science may well be rejected by inappropriate hosts.

The following pages represent a case study in the role of social values in the creation of a particular scientific and technological institution—the agricultural experiment station—in a particular developing society, the United States in mid-nineteenth century. The beginnings of agitation for the creation of experiment stations in the United States can be traced to the 1850s, and in particular to the ideas and efforts of a group of young chemists who studied together in Germany in the mid-1850s.[1] The most articulate and tenaciously entrepreneurial of these German laboratory companions were Evan Pugh of Pennsylvania and Samuel William Johnson of New York State. Upon his return to the United States, Pugh guided the development of Pennsylvania's agricultural college into an early model for other such institutions before his premature death in 1864. Johnson returned to New

Haven, an eventual professorship in Yale's Sheffield Scientific School, and leadership in the establishment of America's first agricultural experiment stations. Because of their importance as institution builders, I have singled out Pugh and Johnson for somewhat more detailed discussion. There existed, nevertheless, a revealing similarity in the shared values and experiences which shaped the motivational structure of all the Americans who studied chemistry in Europe during the 1850s—and a particular unity of commitment among some half dozen who were to make a career in agricultural chemistry.[2]

None of these young men came from particularly wealthy backgrounds—one at least, Evan Pugh, from relatively humble origins.[3] All had to overcome formidable obstacles in acquiring an education and in establishing a scholarly career. Though chemistry had, in the 1840s, come to replace geology as the generation's "glamor" science, it offered at best a problematical career in a society still unwilling to recognize and support the professional research scientist. When these young men boarded ship for study in Europe, it constituted a very real act of faith.

In mid-nineteenth century most practicing American scientists served as college teachers; such positions entailed enormous teaching burdens and assorted pastoral duties. Research was never assumed to be a condition of employment. Most American professors, as a student chemist writing from Berlin expressed it, "are worked to death and many [never] in the course of their lives publish one single original paper or contribute one single new fact to science." Desks in the government's patent office, even though politically compromised, were an extremely desirable place for a young chemist; such posts paid better than almost any professorship and work ended at three, allowing "time enough for study or research."[4]

Not surprisingly, there were no provisions for formal graduate training. Until the late 1840s advanced training in chemistry was to be found only in a handful of private analytical laboratories, ad hoc, expensive, and often inadequate by contemporary European standards. Even Yale's Analytical Laboratory—opened in 1847 and a prototype for true graduate training—was in form not much different from competing private analytical laboratories; fees for analysis and the tuition of private students provided its only income.[5] And, despite America's theoretical acceptance of the self-made man, scientists complained again and again that material success alone seemed to determine such social acceptance. A European student, one American explained by way of contrast, "may dress in the coarsest & cheapest garb & . . . be admitted to that society for wh. his intellectual powers fit him." American attitudes provided a dismaying contrast. Despite such consistent discouragement, however, a growing number of American would-be chemists were, by the early 1850s, in residence in European laboratories. What, one cynic among them wondered in 1853, would become of them when they returned to the United States? Even the ordinarily sanguine Samuel W. Johnson could joke that a rich wife was a young chemist's only hope for success.[6]

Why, then, did these Americans make the difficult decision to study abroad? Even more specifically in terms of our case study, how did those among them concerned with the growth of agricultural chemistry justify their commitment? There were, it seems to me, four principal sources of motivation and legitimization.

First, many sought an avenue for the fulfillment of individual aspirations in a role seemingly untainted by the demeaning compromises and materialistic standards of the business world. A second and related factor was the stimulus provided by the energies of evangelical pietism. The decades between the 1820s and the 1850s had been marked by a mood of intense, even millennial enthusiasm. Men accepting this strenuous faith had necessarily to pursue their chosen vocation with an intense seriousness of purpose—and for a few Americans the career of scientist seemed a higher vocation than that normally undertaken by ambitious young men of their generation. Thirdly, all shared an unquestioning faith in the unambiguous virtue of progress—and, as we shall emphasize, distinctions between the material and spiritual aspects of economic, technological, and scientific progress were almost never made. A shared nationalism also legitimated what might have been seen as elitist and personal ambitions. Within the assumptions of this nationalism, moreover, agriculture played a particularly significant role; providing technological and thus economic aid to American farmers was a goal of more than temporal dimensions, for the individual landowning farmer had come to assume a pivotal role in the accepted structure of America's virtue-embodying social order. What I am suggesting, then, is a configuration of logically distinguishable, yet emotionally consistent—indeed, synergistic—assumptions and sources of emotional reassurance. Such a world-view served to legitimate personal ambition and thus the desire for both institutional innovation and intellectual achievement.

In examining the careers of America's pioneer agricultural chemists, perhaps the most striking similarity is their religiosity. Even though they came from widely varied backgrounds (Johnson, for example, was a Congregationalist, Pugh a Welsh Quaker), they all adhered to a peculiarly evangelical and intensely pietistic faith, their lives necessarily consecrated to a worthy stewardship. Samuel Johnson, for example, worried frequently about the vitality and strength of his commitment

to science. "My studies have been profitably and steadily pursued," he
wrote home from Yale in 1850, "and the way seems open for further
prosecution. Yet I have sorrow that some hours have not been well
spent,—that the motive of my industry and zeal in study has not been a
higher one, such as my Heavenly Father could approve. But I have a
greater joy. It is that I am determined through Christ who strength-
eneth me to walk in all the ordinances of the Lord, blameless." On
another occasion Johnson wrote to his father, "Since I left home 2
months have elapsed, 6 times 2 months is a year, 20 or 30 is all I can
hope to live—Have I time to do more than my duty to God? Have I
time to jest and trifle when so short a time only separates me from the
presence of my God?" Precious hours could not be wasted; the
discipline of the laboratory was a necessary improvement of whatever
skills God had granted. It was only natural that Johnson's brother-in-
law should have encouraged him in this scientific vocation with the
injunction that "agricultural science is your missionary field and you
are responsible to the amount of some talents for its cultivation."[7]

Johnson was not atypical. Pugh was even more ascetic in his
personal habits; he detested all artificial stimulants—tea and coffee as
well as alcohol and tobacco. His meticulously kept European journal
provides a good many expressions of muscular indignation at German
beer drinking and casual hygienic attitudes; such habits implied no enviable state of spiritual health.[8] Similarly, John P. Norton, cofounder
of Yale's Analytical Laboratory and Johnson's teacher, also worried about the strength of his vocational commitment. "God
has been good to me," he confided to his journal in 1846 as he contemplated a second European study trip, "though I have done little
to deserve it. May he keep me from all evil ways during this second
absence, and may I be led to improve my time so that I shall be fitted
to do much on my return." When, on another occasion, his child
lay seriously ill, Norton reflected in his journal: "This uncertainty of
life ought to prove to me also a solemn warning and to remind me how
imperfectly I am performing any one particular of my duties, and how
many things I leave undone."[9] Obviously there is much of the conventional in such rhetoric; yet in its pervasiveness and intensity one senses
genuine emotional conviction. It implied that scholarship would be
undertaken with an unswerving seriousness of purpose; and it goes far
to explain why men such as Norton, Johnson, and Pugh would have
embarked upon that very act of faith with which they mounted the
gangplank for their European apprenticeship.

This pietistic commitment to science as vocation was not, of course,
limited in mid-nineteenth-century America to would-be agricultural
chemists. It marked the careers of many other scientists as well. Edward

Hitchcock, for example, professor, geologist, and probably the most widely read expositor of natural theology in his generation, could conclude in examining the state of his spiritual health that scientific pursuits were indeed "a means of personal sanctification."[10] It was, in many ways, the similarity rather than the difference between scientific and religious values which made it natural for many Americans to move fluidly from one intellectual realm to another.

The scientific vocation provided many of the spiritual compensations demanded by men of this generation. It represented no conflict in life style with that of the traditional religious leader, but served, rather, as an alternative, offering many of the values embodied in the ideal type of the spiritual teacher. It was a role in which success could be achieved not in terms of demeaning material standards, but as a result of contributing to human knowledge—and thus, they never doubted, to human welfare and morality. Pugh, for example, explained in his journal that he knew "no higher standard of greatness (other conditions such as morality, etc., being equal) than that of being a great scientific man." More poignant are the words of a contemporary unable for personal reasons to enter upon the life of science: "But after all it is something to be conscious of such a life. It is right to feel oneself allied to a higher order of beings by holding in common with them faculties which the base votaries of Mammon all around us do not possess, and for possessing which they despise us. They will brand me a *visionary* and cast me from the pale of their fellowship—nay this is daily done and I am made to feel the biting pangs of their sarcasms. . . ." "The pursuit of knowledge," Samuel W. Johnson explained, "furnishes its own exceeding great reward, independent of the voice of human flattery. Yet reputation is not to be slighted, for where well-founded it enlarges the field of usefulness and enables its possessor to wield a mighty influence upon the minds and hearts of his fellow men." The inspiring lives of great scientists, Johnson explained, encouraged him "to tread cheerfully the path of science, though alone and exposed to the sneers of the vulgar and ignorant."[11] Images of isolation and moral heroism appear with illuminating frequency in the writings of would-be American scientists in this generation.

The self-contained and protectively removed quality of the scientific confraternity must also have seemed attractive for at least a few lonely and introspective young men; the life of science promised a secure and legitimate identity. It was an identity, moreover, in which one's hopes for achievement could be defined in terms outside those of the local community. One senses in America's sprawling, scattered, and relentlessly masculine society a group of young men who sought contacts outside the frustrating, perhaps even threatening routine of daily existence. Let me simply quote a few wistful phrases from a letter exchanged between two young midwestern botanical correspondents: "I enclose my photograph," one wrote; "do you think we will do to be intimate friends?"[12]

Religion and the peculiar qualities of the scientific role were not alone in shaping the configuration of values and assumptions which motivated our protagonists. They also shared a similar attitude toward progress, an attitude central in their commitment to applied science. As workers active in a field potentially relevant to human needs, these young Americans assumed that their work would have a moral and social significance—and not simply prove a source of personal intellectual satisfaction.

The vast majority of nineteenth-century Americans never doubted that human beings had progressed and that this progress—inevitably —subsumed dimensions both moral and material. It was inconceivable to them that the steam engine and morality were not somehow interconnected. It was unthinkable that the failure of, let us say, the Burmese to produce such artifacts was not somehow related to their lack of evangelical Christianity. Progress and technology were not only integral but justifying elements in the widely accepted vision of America's higher moral order.

Improvements in man's material comfort created precisely those conditions in which his moral and spiritual health might improve—or so it seemed. Even so careful and pious a thinker as Evan Pugh entertained no reservations. Scientific progress, he explained to a farm audience, is certainly not of a "higher character than moral and religious advancement. It only stands," he elaborated, "in such relation to these as does the engine upon the railroad to the human freight which it hurls along the iron track."[13] Derailments did not enter into this design and the destination was never in doubt. Let me refer to the sentiments of Samuel W. Johnson's father, a pious and prudent New York State farmer. "It is right and proper," he urged his son,

> that every one should be well employed in doing and being useful, in bettering the condition of our fellow-beings in the concerns of the present life, in making improvements. The steamboat was a wonderful achievement in 1807. . . . But who thought of five hundred or more persons in ten or twenty coaches flying on iron rails at the rate of 30 or 40 miles an hour without horse or mule, but more than twenty years ago was that event consummated. Then the electric telegraph soon followed. . . . It would seem that the Lord is lavishing temporal blessings in great abundance upon Christendom, and particularly upon that part now Protestant. "Has God so dealt with any other people?"[14]

That men who lived in increasing material comfort would also live more piously was an assumption so visceral that the vast majority of mid-nineteenth-century Americans never realized it was an assumption—let alone questioned it.

So ingrained was this faith in the ability of science and technology to improve man's spiritual condition that it remained ineluctably alive while the explicitly spiritual energies which inspired the generation of the 1850s began to recede. Thus Johnson's most successful student, W. O. Atwater, a leading nutritionist and prominent Methodist layman, could in 1893 justify his devotion to nutrition investigations by declaring that "the time has come when we must get at the physical basis of human living if we are going to make the best provision for intellectual and moral progress." From such a position it demanded no great leap of intellectual evolution to arrive at the characteristic—if vulgar—sentiment of an agricultural college dean who explained in 1912 that "efficiency and morality may not be synonymous, but they are mighty good chums."[15]

The worship of productivity as the essence of and index to progress and the infusion of this assumption with an aura of nationalism and morality has persisted into the present with a dismaying weight of moral inertia. The generation of the 1850s played an unavoidable role in forging the habit of seeing all social and economic problems as solvable through the deus ex machina of increasing productivity—a position which has conveniently obviated the need to examine social alternatives.

In this complex of attitudes toward science and human progress, a vigorous nationalism assumed a natural place. To the earnest young advocates of agricultural science in the 1850s, America's peculiar virtues were unquestionable, despite the powerful counterattraction of European culture and learning. Their ambivalence toward Europe was particularly marked in relation to Germany. Its government seemed despotic, its common people ignorant, impious, and tradition-bound. Though American students might concede that German pure science led the world, their own American countrymen seemed far more skillful and ingenious in the application of science and technology to the improving of man's lot.[16] Even more important to many Americans was the vast difference between German and American moral expectations. A Göttingen friend of Johnson and Pugh observed of German students that their "only pleasure seems to be in drinking beer, smoking pipes, and fighting duels." A generation later—in the 1870s—Americans continued to express a similar ambivalence toward things German. Henry Rowland, Johns Hopkins physicist, confessed, for example: "It is only since coming to Europe that I have been able to understand my own countrymen and appreciate their good qualities. . . . I believe that I can say with pride that there is not a more moral people on earth than our own, and this will account for some of our social habits which I often see criticized." Religion seemed dead in Germany, mere ritual and social convention. Perhaps this secularism, another agricultural chemistry student at Göttingen wrote in 1870, explains "an intellectual development in the upper classes that stands in marvelous contrast with the bestiality of all classes."[17]

Yet many Americans did develop a warm feeling for some at least of their German hosts, their drinking and good fellowship, their hospitality, their relaxed attention to eating, to music and literature. And, of course, German cultivation of the sciences found no parallel in America. The German professor, moreover, in his dedication to research and apparent disdain for material goals provided an appropriately ascetic model for idealistic young men. Students recalled their shared hardships, their scrimping to buy books, their vacation-time sightseeing and hiking, their crude efforts at cooking. Not surprisingly, almost every American who studied chemistry in Germany in the 1850s strained his—or his family's—financial resources to the utmost in an effort to extend his stay.

But none, so far as the available evidence indicates, even contemplated the possibility of leaving their native soil for Germany or any other country. Would-be agricultural chemists—whose particular ambitions I should not like to lose sight of in delineating the more pervasive attitudes in which they shared—felt not the slightest temptation to deny their social responsibility. Evan Pugh, for example, though engaged in important research at England's Rothamsted experimental farm, explained to Johnson that "they have offered me $500 to stay next summer but I feel that I must get home. There is a field there upon which the harvest is great and the laborers are few." Johnson, too, though anxious to extend his European stay, felt that he ought "to go home and put a shoulder to the wheels of progress in my young native land with all her youthful stains vastly more glorious than the monarchies of Europe."[18]

But before following these student travelers to their North American homeland, let me reemphasize that their European years in sum intensified original motivations and imparted a new unity of vision to disparate views. The shared experience of feeling alien in a civilization to which one maintained a consistently ambivalent position, combined with the peculiar ideological regalia of the German academic world, only strengthened commitments both to science and to the role of purveyors of science in service to society. (A reciprocal ambivalence toward things American would only have provoked guilt and thus a renewed activism.) Perhaps most important, the German experience gave to American students a particular body of techniques and concepts, knowledge which at once justified and, in a sense, constituted the peculiar status of the man of learning. One cannot well disentangle the consciousness of adherence to a discipline from the specific techniques and ideas which constitute the intellectual content of that discipline at any moment in time.

Once he had accepted the values of the world of academic science, the American scholar could measure achievement primarily in terms of acceptance as a creative scholar by his disciplinary peers. Such acceptance was, of course, based on research and publication. Thus American chemists necessarily returned to their native land not only with the reformer's zeal, but with a blueprint to guide them. The need for adequate laboratory facilities and research time dictated a specific program for institution building. Conditions appropriate for research and publication were thus always an organic part of the demand for agricultural education and experimentation formulated by this handful of German-trained chemists. In agriculture, moreover, the legitimacy of such demands was generally underscored by their unquestioned conviction that only first-rate research would prove ultimately most beneficial to the agricultural producer; there could be no conflict between science pure and applied.

Pugh and Johnson as well as a number of their friends had been particularly impressed during their student years by Germany's infant network of agricultural experiment stations. To these young men, committed to help in bettering man's lot, the need for improving American agriculture was especially pressing, not only because of the farmer's place in the pantheon of national values, but because of a shared faith that chemistry could and would be readily applicable to farm problems. Thus the establishment of agricultural experiment stations on the German model promised not only the opportunity to contribute personally to a growing research area, but to do good in a more general and fundamental way. For some Americans at least, the entrepreneurial impulse could manifest itself only in limited and morally suitable contexts.

As early, indeed, as 1854 Pugh and Johnson already planned a campaign of educational and scientific reform. In discussing the possibility of establishing an agricultural school in Pennsylvania, Pugh warned Johnson, "It still may be best to '*compromise*' matters; and after the thing is once going, and its operations acquire the confidence of the public and those interested in its maintenance, &c., it may be made what (and all what) we could want it to be." A year later

Pugh wrote again, urging Johnson to cultivate the "really scientific agriculturists" as a necessary first step in creating a base of support for their reforms. "I don't doubt but that if one got into a place where the arrangements were not the best in the world for the promotion of Ag. science he might bend matters gradually into a proper course. One must first gain the confidence of interested persons, and then *influence* over them follows."[19] Allies in editorial circles and in state and local agricultural societies were necessary paths to such influence—and both Pugh and Johnson wrote and spoke widely, assiduously cultivating personal contacts. Their themes were predictable enough.

Agriculture, they reiterated, must be made rational and scientific. Only trained scientists could ultimately guarantee true progress; the farmer's fear of the "mere theorist" was sadly misplaced. Standards in agricultural education and research would have to be raised and only through agricultural colleges and related experiment stations could these goals be achieved. As early as the mid-1850s both Pugh and Johnson saw experiment stations as a necessary component in a proposed agricultural college system. By the late 1850s and early 1860s Pugh in particular began to emphasize the need for federal support if experiment stations—and the research opportunities they implied —were to become a reality. Pugh had become frustrated after years of lobbying with his state's unsympathetic legislature. "I have spent the whole vacation," he wrote in 1861, "dogging at our legislature for money. I have been put off, trifled with, cheated, deceived and humbugged in a great variety of ways till now the session is nearly to a close and yet not one dollar voted. . . . I am a little blue about it. Blue because all my vacation was wasted with those legislator blockheads— blue because honesty has not availed us in a righteous cause." Proper agricultural research, Pugh reassured Johnson during the Civil War, could never be undertaken until government paid "back a tythe of what it already owes science in order to carry them out. But my dear fellow get at it, starve along as best you can and I will point at you starving when the proper time comes to lay the question of a *station* before Uncle Sam. I am satisfied the old man will help you just as soon as he arranges matters on his cotton estates."[20]

In *all* education, Pugh and Johnson urged farmers and legislators, especially in agriculture and industry, science would have to constitute the essential substance. To establish an agricultural college and not place it under the guidance of a man with the most advanced scientific training would be to create a watch, as Pugh put it, without a mainspring. There was no doubt in his mind that he and other German-trained scientists should and would perform this function. Not surprisingly, when Pugh was called in 1857 to assume presidency of

Pennsylvania's infant agricultural college—christened at first the Farmer's High School—he began almost immediately to offer advanced and specialized analytic training in chemistry. Both in public and private, though in somewhat different terms, Pugh defended his atypical commitment to excellence and specialization. The great German universities, he explained in 1864 to the state legislature, base their superiority not upon facilities, "but it consists in the large number of their professors and the profoundness which necessarily results from this large number and from their unceasing devotion to the subjects they teach, so that the student lives, moves, and breathes in an intellectual atmosphere. . . . Our Industrial Colleges must be experimental institutions, because they are devoted to subjects which need much more investigation before they can be taught with entire satisfaction. . . ."[21] There was no possible conflict, these would-be reformers argued, between the needs of scientists and those of the American economy. Fundamental scientific progress—and thus, all assumed, economic growth as well—would not come about through the popularizing of science to a virtuous yeomanry, but through cultivating "a few students to a high standard." "What a good influence," Pugh congratulated himself,[22] "the European system has in giving us a contempt for that superficial smattering of everything without even an *idea* of what thoroughness in anything is which is too characteristic of our American system of education and our American notions of what education should be." Mid-nineteenth-century American scientists had often to be entrepreneurs and publicists as well as investigators; Johnson and Pugh were clearly well suited to this promotional role. They accepted as necessary and inevitable the long hours spent in cultivating men of influence, in speaking at fairs and farmers' clubs, in writing popular articles for farm weeklies. The sordid arts of the lobbyist had been harnessed and tamed by the transcending logic of piety and patriotism.

Despite these vigorous efforts, however, it was not until the 1870s that American experiment stations actually came into being. And even then, as we will emphasize, the founding generation's particular ability to compromise laid the groundwork for an endemic ambiguity in the history of this institution—an ambiguity characteristic of a good many other relationships between the American scientific community and the society which has supported it. Yet it would, I think, be a mistake to emphasize only the negative implications of the mutually ingenuo quid pro quo which underlay this ambiguity. Though the structu political alliance and ideological assumption forged by the gene of the 1850s became increasingly habitual and confining perhaps a necessity in an open society seeking to maximiz

growth yet generally tolerant of science only in the form of rhetoric—
or when it promised tangible returns.

It was a grimly inhospitable reality which confronted German-
trained chemists in mid-nineteenth-century America as they disem-
barked after sailing homeward. A few returned to an expected business
career. Here laboratory skills and the motivation implied by a willingness to study in Europe made success plausible; J. F. Magee, for
example, founded a firm specializing in photographic chemicals; R. H.
Lamborn became a prosperous mining engineer and entrepreneur;
both had been good friends of Pugh and Johnson in Germany.[23] But
for those who sought academic careers, prospects were still bleak
indeed. Pugh, as we have noted, was made president of an embryonic
and physically isolated agricultural college—by European standards a
secondary school. J. P. Kimball, another of the Göttingen American
colony, could at first find work only as an assistant in the geological
survey, then a brief position with an abortive agricultural college in
New York State, an experiment destroyed by the Civil War and, as
Kimball put it, "apathy and neglect." Even men who were to make
eminent careers in later decades found readjustment to American soil
painful indeed. George C. Caldwell, later a professor at Cornell, spent
almost a decade in grimly depressing teaching positions before arriving at Cornell's comparative luxury. Caldwell's diary records a
typical day during this trying period:

> My own work presses me hard. . . .I am up at six, work over notes of
> lectures till 7:30—then breakfast. . . . Then up to the college and get
> experiments ready for classes. Lecture at 10, recitation . . . at eleven. From
> about 11:45 to 12:45 I rest and behold my wife and enjoy her blessed
> company and my dinner. From 1 to 3 is the distracting Doctor here and
> Doctor there of my sixteen or eighteen laboratory students. . . . By the time
> 4 o'clock comes I am pretty well used up and ready for recreation, but must
> find my recreation in continuation of Laboratory work on my own account.
>
> I must be doing something, even though it be but little to save my
> reputation or myself from being forgotten by the circle of my scientific
> friends. . . . The evening is my only time to study—but with boys to keep in
> their rooms in study hours, I sometimes don't get much time to study.[24]

The laboratory bench still seemed a dubious place for gentlemen.
les F. Chandler, another Göttingen friend of Pugh and Johnson,
professor at Columbia University, was forced in 1862 to
at misapprehension on the part of some persons in regard
ht in the laboratory. They have an idea that the
spend their time in mechanical operations, in
of the technical part of various branches of
by the lower classes of society."[25] Johnson,

the real father of America's first agricultural experiment stations, if any one individual can be presumed to deserve that title, received an assistantship at Yale's Sheffield Scientific School soon after returning to the United States. And though this was probably the most desirable academic position received by any of the Göttingen American colony, Johnson too had to spend countless hours in writing for popular audiences, in lecturing, in serving more than metaphorically as missionary of agricultural chemistry to the "spiritually dead" among Connecticut farmers.

Obviously, advocates of scientific research in agriculture had to deal with the assumptions—and power—of a laity at once skeptical and credulous. Though scornful of "mere theory," interested laymen still entertained a number of ingenuously optimistic scientific hopes. Most important was an uncritically positive attitude toward chemistry and its potential efficacy in solving economic problems. In regard to agriculture specifically, the popular impact of Liebig's work had made the rationalization of farming through chemistry an enormously and insidiously popular hope. (A student of Pugh's wrote, for example, from his father's farm that "the barbarians expect me to raise corn without a cob I should think by the way some of them talk.") "Every farm should be considered a chemical laboratory," a representative popularizer explained, "and every farmer a practical chemist and philosopher: farming would then be honorable and lucrative." Were rhetoric alone a useful index to social priorities, the chemist would have been a favored citizen indeed.[26]

Unfortunately, the ordinarily vague expectations of laymen sometimes assumed embarrassingly concrete forms. Perhaps the most awkward of the popular assumptions which faced young agricultural chemists in the 1850s and 1860s was the illusion that simple testing procedures could ensure soil fertility; once missing constituents were identified in the test tube, they need only apply the prescribed fertilizer —and a marginal farm would become a source of profit. Worse yet, a number of chemical entrepreneurs—our European-trained chemists referred to them as quacks—deliberately ministered to such hopes by "promising to satisfy that vulgar notion."[27] Another pervasive misapprehension, even among those "intelligent farmers" most willing to support science, was that an experimental farm should show a profit. "Would it not be profitable," one supporter wistfully asked Pugh, "would the students and faculty commit wilful injury?"[28] Laymen in general demanded immediate and tangible rewards in return for their willingness to support science. In the words of another supporter of agricultural science, "the peculiar genius of our people must have something *practical*, something from which *dollars and cents* may be realized." Naturally enough, American scientist-entrepreneurs quickly learned to cast their appeals for support in the form of an enticing quid pro quo. An entomological contemporary of Pugh and Johnson, for example, was soon convinced that farmers would support entomology only if assured that it would increase their profits. "Much as I despise this sordid test of the utility of a science," he concluded, "I am forced to own its necessity when the public is to be enlisted."[29]

Yet men such as Pugh and Johnson could not turn their backs on fields ripe for harvesting. For both practical and ideological reasons they persisted in their attempts to wring support from American society. "No worthy enterprise," Pugh wrote encouragingly to Johnson,[30] ". . . can be accomplished without effort. If effort at first appear unavailing—if continued labor fail to produce the desired effect—if those for whom we labor close their eyes and stop their ears, and open their mouths to let *quacks* and *knaves* feed them still let not despair raise its scowling curtains before us." But such missionary work was slow indeed, and the gathering of souls a difficult and discouraging task. Even after twenty years of devoted "political education," most enlightened and sympathetic laymen still failed to accept or comprehend the Göttingen world-view.[31] But the help of such influential laymen could still be solicited upon the convenient basis of mutual misunderstanding.

It was not until 1875 that Johnson's policies brought results. Under the immediate leadership of his politically acute student W. O. Atwater and influential farm publisher Orange Judd, the state of Connecticut established an agricultural experiment station. This was the formal initiation in the United States of an institution which has, as much as any other single factor, been responsible for the remarkable growth of productivity in twentieth-century American agriculture. In the dozen years after 1875, a number of states followed Connecticut's example and in 1887 the national government provided $15,000 a year to each state for the support of an agricultural experiment station—thus establishing the first significant instance of federal support for scientific research and development in states and universities.[32] In mid-twentieth century the importance of such precedents can hardly be overestimated.

By the 1880s conditions for research-oriented American chemists had begun only marginally to improve. The fledgling experiment stations promised relatively desirable positions. Yet the compromises demanded by an applied-science context were making such positions less and less attractive to the best-trained among a new scientific generation. A measure of improvement in other areas—symbolized by the opening of the Johns Hopkins University and other pioneer graduate

programs, as well as expanding possibilities in industrial chemistry
—paralleled the growth of an increasingly indigenous scientific esprit,
one mirroring and utilizing the absolute self-justifications of the
German professoriate in a fashion quite different from that of the
young men of Pugh and Johnson's generation. In 1887, for example,
the year that the Hatch Act establishing a national system of experiment stations was passed, the graduate-oriented Johns Hopkins University had already been in existence a dozen years and it was only
natural for a Hopkins student to observe: "As far as I can see the
chance for advanced research work in this country is very poor—the
country is not old enough—such things will come only after the present
race of money muckers has been turned to some agricultural use, I fear.
Nothing *pays* here unless advertised and acceptable to the public and
nothing is thought sane unless it is expected to pay."[33] This kind of
alienated posturing would have been impossible for men like Pugh
and Johnson, though they might well have agreed with the substantive
burden of this criticism. Their peculiar commitment to their countrymen, to the necessity of improvement through pious activism, would
have made such a position distasteful indeed.

Even in the mid-nineteenth century, of course, some American scientists with different backgrounds and assumptions had tried to maintain a distance from the immediate demands of any particular client
constituency. For example, two Harvard scientists—W. G. Farlow, a mycologist, and F. H. Storer, an agricultural chemist—though both active
in training experiment station scientists, always maintained substantial reservations in regard to the possibilities of conducting ultimately
meaningful research in so pragmatically oriented a context. As early as
1880 Storer had warned S. W. Johnson, a close friend since their
European student days, that "for successful research something more
than good intentions is necessary; viz. technical training, modesty of
thought, and an open mind." Farlow was even more openly scornful of
the scholarly pretensions of station and state mycologists. An Iowa
farm boy commented after observing Farlow's reactions to a visit from
an experiment station botanist: "They do like to kick things & people
here and set on them."[34]

It is probably fair to concede that most experiment stations never
achieved that successful synthesis of the pure and applied which had
been so central to their founders' vision. The irony was complete. By
1900 the experiment stations still provided desirable and in some ways
practically advantageous positions for young organic chemists. Yet the
better-trained among these had become increasingly unhappy with the
casual standards for original investigation maintained by many of the

experiment station administrators and the unceasing pressure of these same administrators and an aggressive farm constituency for immediate results; farm leaders had already been courted assiduously for two generations with euphoric visions of prosperity to follow hard upon increased research appropriations. To this newer generation of scientists, Samuel W. Johnson's well-worn policies of farm-oriented research were narrow and constricting. He had become part of an old guard, an old guard whose peculiar contribution of energy, of idealism, and of advanced scientific training had long been forgotten.

The dilemma was probably insoluble. Working in an experiment station context before the First World War, the scientist had either to adjust to a lack of autonomy, to shaping research hours in response to the demands of a client constituency—or leave. "When I got through in Germany," one chemist trained in Germany in the 1870s put it in 1906, "I was für die Wissenschaft, but since I have been connected with the expt. Sta. my thought has unquestionably [been] influenced by being constantly in close touch with practical men who make [their] livelihood fr. cultivating the soil. The question with them was always *how* can I do this or that to grow better crops for less money."[35] Experiment station research had to be shaped in response to the equally categorical, yet only partially consistent, demands of the scientific discipline on the one hand and, on the other hand, those of an imperious lay constituency. This implied sharing (if not surrender) of institutional autonomy bequeathed an ambiguous heritage to even the best agricultural research laboratories, as in the twentieth century they sought to become contexts for high-level research in the biological sciences.

But such difficulties were in some ways explicit in the attitudes and contextual realities of the founding generation of the 1850s. "We must," one of these German-trained scientists wrote in 1852, "go out into the unscientific portions of our country and there raise up science; by so doing, we shall render a much more acceptable service to science than if we were propounders of some abstruse theories or the discoverers of new elements, planets or comets."[36] These men could not overcome the influence of this moral gradient; their European training served only to add immediacy and personal legitimacy (in the form of their recently acquired specific knowledge). To this small group of scientists and scientist-entrepreneurs, the discipline-oriented and self-conscious elitism of some of their contemporaries and many of their successors would have seemed egocentric indeed.

And in a sense they were correct. To accept the ultimate worth of applied research in mid-nineteenth-century America was necessarily to accept the constraints of working with and through an economically oriented client constituency. And in accepting these terms such gifted institution builders as Pugh and Johnson played an important role in the economic growth of American agriculture (and thus indirectly in that of the state universities and "basic" sciences as well). For it is hard to imagine how the historical circumstances which gave birth to the American experiment station movement would have allowed any alternative method of subsidizing agricultural research. Nor would these resources have been diverted to other means of underwriting pure or applied research. Neither individual units of production—the farmers—nor agriculture-related business would have considered such allocations of funds in the late-nineteenth century.

The agricultural colleges and experiment stations have played an important role in the twentieth-century growth of American agricultural productivity, with its economic, social, and demographic consequences. Equally important, many of the precedents for government-designed and supported research—and the ramifications of this dependence for the scientific community—were forged most prominently in the agricultural colleges and experiment stations. In this particular sequence of historical development, the ideas and assumptions of the far-seeing and energetic founders of the 1850s played an important role, helping transmit ideas and institutional forms from the European metropolis to a similar yet distinct and physically distant culture. Their willingness to commit their energies to applied science provided an important element in ensuring in America an ultimately symmetrical development of the sciences, of technology, and of a technologically oriented economy. Their energy and commitment were, as we have seen, as peculiar a product of this society as their assumptions about the nature of society and the scientist's social role—so meaningful to them, yet so wistfully distant today.

Let me conclude with several more general observations in the form of a defense of some assumptions implicit in the organization of this case study. It might be objected that only a handful of Americans embraced a scientific vocation in the mid-nineteenth century and that, as our own discussion has made clear, if some values pervasive in the culture were congenial to such a vocational choice, others were just as clearly antithetical. True enough. But it must be understood that we are dealing with a universe of individual personalities and coexisting if not always consistent cultural values. As they reached adulthood, Americans with individual personality needs chose among those careers made available to them by their culture, and, if successful, found embodied in this choice a configuration of values appropriate to their emotional needs. In terms of our case study, I refer of course to those implications of antimaterialism, selflessness, service, and a potentially benevolent activism promised by the research scientist's role. Of course, the scientific calling was a highly atypical one in mid-nineteenth-century America; indeed, it seems fairly obvious that those very elements which made it atypical—even scorned by some—served only to enhance its attractiveness for those idealistic young men whose careers we have tried to explain.

In implying that individuals chose the life of science as a form of adjustment, I do not mean to imply that all who made this decision were necessarily similar in personality. A commitment to the scientific vocation might be equally functional to the personality stabilization of individuals with quite different needs. Evan Pugh seems—if I may be excused such instant psychobiography—on the basis of personal documents to have been extremely achievement-oriented, dominant in personal relations, as physically vigorous as he was ambitious; yet many of his culture's normal paths to achievement—politics and the law, for example—seemed to him tainted by materialism and sordid compromise. The role of scientific entrepreneur, on the other hand, promised accomplishment and a spiritually irreproachable strategy for ego aggrandizement. Science was, moreover, an interest traditionally sanctioned by the Pennsylvania Quaker community in which Pugh had grown to maturity. The youthful Samuel W. Johnson seems, on the other hand, to have been equally ambitious, yet quiet and intro-spective. He too had been raised in an area in which enthusiastic religion had coexisted peacefully with a surprisingly strong interest in natural philosophy.[37] In both cases a commitment to science provided an appropriate means for attaining status and individual achievement, as well as the expression of dominance and authority. What I would suggest, then, is that their choice of the scientist's life was equally functional in the adjustment of both these young men to maturity—not that the function was precisely the same. Many other mid-nineteenth-century American scientists seem to have had other needs—ones for which the otherworldly and self-consciously elitist aspects of the scien-tific career seemed particularly congenial. To such investigators a de-votion to applied science and its inevitable institutional compromises would have been intolerable, a denial of the emotional distance with which their vocation helped them to structure their relationship to society generally.[38]

Science, Technology, and Economic Growth: The Case of the Agricultural Experiment Station Scientist, 1875–1914

Clichés of historical explanation are not always wrong, but they are never very useful. A familiar example of the species urges the importance of the relationship between science, technology, and economic development in the historical evolution of Western society. Can one object? The problem, of course, lies not in an unwillingness to concede this general point, but, given the present state of the art, in understanding this relationship in particular contexts and at particular times. Yet, despite its obvious importance, students of American society have devoted little attention to the historical interaction between science, technology, and social context; aside from a handful of case studies, the historical literature is spotty and unsystematic.

This chapter constitutes such a case study. Its central theme is the behavior of scientists and scientist-administrators within an institutional context defined by social and economic factors. More specifically, this is a study of the scientists employed by American agricultural experiment stations between the 1870s and 1914. In the hope of imposing some order upon a complex story, I will first briefly outline the nature of lay expectations—a primary dimension of the scientist's contextual reality—then characterize the response of scientists to what was originally a far from satisfactory work situation; the pressure of an aggressive lay constituency seemed particularly intolerable in a period during which ambitious young scientists were increasingly influenced by the German research ideal.

In 1875 the state of Connecticut established an agricultural experiment station. A dozen years later the federal government made the experiment station a national institution by providing in the Hatch Act $15,000 a year to each state for the support of a station.[1] The motivations of the state and national legislators who approved these measures seem transparent enough. These subventions for research were concessions to farm power in the form of a pork-barrel issue easily clothed in the neutrality of science and justified in terms of the traditional virtues granted the yeoman cultivators of the nation's farms. The stations would help the farmers adjust to an increasingly competitive world market, would rationalize and systematize his operations—would provide, that is, a conservative alternative to more radical schemes for adjusting to changed economic and demographic realities.

Although the desire of politicians and farm spokesmen for scientific aid was real enough, their conception of the scientst's role was dismayingly imprecise. Professional scientists had since the 1850s been leaders in a campaign of "education" and agitation in favor of the experiment station idea, but they had found it both difficult and impolitic to be quite candid in their predictions of what an experiment station might be and do.

To many interested farmers and journalists, on the other hand, the role of the experiment station seemed all too clear; it was to perform the experiments which the individual farmer, lacking time and opportunity, could not; common sense, order, and precision allied with the American's native ingenuity were qualities adequate to the task. This was stated explicitly even in the writings of farm journalists and legislators enthusiastic in support of the experiment station movement.[2] "The average farmer," as the *Rural New Yorker* editorialized in 1886, "cannot afford to experiment in a careful systematic way for himself. Hence the value of Experiment Stations, if only they be conducted by intelligent, earnest, practical men." A goodly proportion of the stations' lay advocates as well as their self-appointed critics expected, even into the twentieth century, that the experiment station would be operated as a model farm, indeed a model farm which would show a profit on its operations. (How, after all, could it be presumed a model if it lost money?) Up through the First World War experiment station workers had to answer the criticism of visitors who could not understand why a stand of wheat might be dwarfed or why scores of horticultural varieties were not to be seen in vigorous profusion.[3] Such conceptions had a long and tenacious history. J. B. Turner, for example, one of the putative fathers of the land-grant college, argued in his 1848 plan for an industrial university that the professor of agriculture should be judged by his ability to plan experiments in which no money would be lost. "I would put no public funds into the professor's hands (certainly none beyond the original outfit) to squander in any day dreaming or absurd speculations. I would have every new experiment bear directly on his own private purse."[4]

Only with respect to chemistry did the "intelligent farmer" assume that special training might be a prerequisite for the experiment station staff member. Indeed, to many Americans agricultural science *was* chemistry; the name and doctrines of Liebig were by the late 1840s familiar in comparatively remote farm communities. But, even with respect to chemistry, the experiment station scientist found that assumptions underlying the expectations of his farm constituency implied career problems. One difficulty was the popular illusion that simple testing procedures could ensure soil fertility; once missing constituents were identified in the test tube, the farmer need only apply the prescribed fertilizer—and a marginal farm would become a source of profit. Throughout the last decades of the nineteenth and even into the twentieth century, farmers confidently sent in samples of soil for analysis and requested individually tailored advice in purchasing fertilizers.

The marketing of chemical fertilizers provided the occasion for another ambiguity which faced the first generation of station scientists. Perhaps the most telling single argument for the creation of experiment stations in the late 1870s and 1880s lay in their potential for regulating the composition of chemical fertilizers. Station supporters in older farming areas, conscious of competition from newer and more fertile states and indignant at the sometimes casual ethics of fertilizer manufacturers and dealers, assumed that experiment stations would act as "fertilizer control" agencies. (The North Carolina and Maine stations actually bore this designation as part of their formal title.) Experiment station advocates were willing enough to cater to these desires, as they were a source of leverage in gaining the support of influential farm and business leaders. Yet once the stations were established, the young chemists who staffed their laboratories often found themselves prisoners of a deadening routine of fertilizer analysis.[5] The functions of research and development were never clearly distinguished in the public mind from those of regulation and inspection.

In addition to the sharp consciousness of economic need and the vagueness of lay expectations in regard to science, other more general ideological factors played a role in shaping the experiment station scientist's environment. Perhaps the most important factor in setting intellectual guidelines was the generally assumed and morally absolute

vision of an intelligent and prosperous yeomanry as a necessary basis
for an enduring democracy. Clearly the personal aspirations of station
scientists were secondary to the well-being of this virtue-embodying
class. Experiment station scientists in the years before the First World
War had thus to deal with a constituency aggressive in its rectitude and
casual in its assumption of the right to enforce demands upon the
performance of station scientists. Were these chemists and botanists not
public servants?[6] Government in the nineteenth century was not
something of which to stand in awe, but something to despoil. Thus, for
example, the plaintive complaint of experiment station directors that
visitors thought it their right to pick anything growing on the "state
farm."

The station scientists not only faced arbitrary and inconsistent lay
demands, but they were outside the established structure of administrative authority as well. As scientists or scientist-administrators they
were newcomers at the mercy of a not always sympathetic hierarchy of
college presidents and faculties. (The Hatch Act, which endowed the
stations in 1887, required that they be part of the land-grant college,
except in those states where an independent station already existed.)
Imposed from above by federal fiat, yet at first unprotected by federal
regulation and control, the station and its budget were at the mercy of
existing—and almost always undercapitalized—academic administrators. To secure a responsive and appropriate context for scientific
research, or even for the adoption and dissemination of empirical
findings, power would have to be gained by the stations within each
state's hierarchy of economic and political power and this power then
utilized in the academic sphere as well.

Some of the problems faced by experiment station scientists were not
peculiar to the stations, but were characteristic of the late-nineteenth-
century American academic world generally. The pressure of an
aggressive nonprofessional constituency seemed particularly intolerable in a period during which ambitious young scientists were increasingly influenced by the German research ideal. The intellectual and
behavioral demands of the several scientific disciplines made it difficult
for the scientist who defined his aspirations in disciplinary terms to
accept the constraints of American academic institutions. Most station scientists had college-teaching assignments as well as station
duties and, in this capacity, were expected to teach a multitude of
courses for long hours at small wages. A combination of German,
chemistry, and botany—with certain disciplinary duties as well—was
not atypical.[7] Particularly frustrating, especially to that increasing
number of American scientists exposed to the values of the European
academic disciplines, was the universal assumption that research was

not a part of the college professor's expected duties. Standards other than competence in one's field were still routinely applied; even chemists, for example, found religious criteria important in securing a college position.

Southern institutions demanded not only piety but also Democratic orthodoxy—and at salaries even lower than those offered in the North. As late as 1889, for example, Texas hoped to hire a "competent analytical chemist" for $800 to $900. An applicant for a position as professor of natural history assured the president of the University of Kentucky, "Your last three requirements are perhaps the easiest met. I am a *Southerner*, intensely so, both by birth and education; a *democrat*, because I could be nothing else, since I was born of democratic parents, and in a democratic state, and nourished on democratic pabulum." The gentleman concluded wanly that he was a "passive" Methodist. It was well known that Southern institutions hesitated to hire Northerners, while Northerners felt great hesitancy in accepting Southern positions.[8]

An experiment station position implied, moreover, a number of peculiar problems in addition to those normally faced by American would-be scholars. Personality, for example, was an important consideration in hiring and firing, for station workers were expected to be effective in contacts with farmers.[9] Thus, for example, Cornell felt some doubt in considering the promising young Alabamian Benjamin Duggar for an experiment station position because of some possible "southern peculiarity" which might interfere with his success in working with New York farmers. Another problem lay in the demand for regular publication; bulletins and annual reports had to make their appearance even if there was little or nothing in the way of original findings to fill them. Experiment station bulletins, an editorialist complained in *Agricultural Science* in March of 1887, were published "ostensibly to report progress, [but] practically to propitiate a constituency who unreasonably expect the most important problems settled as though by sleight of hand." And research plans reflected economic needs, not the training and aspirations of staff members. If, let us say, no entomologist were available, a chemist or botanist would simply have to make do—answering farmers' questions, preparing bulletins, perhaps giving spraying demonstrations. Vacations had often to be sacrificed to rural lecture tours. In some states, moreover, days were filled with the endless detail of regulatory work, not only fertilizer testing, but the evaluation of seeds, horticultural varieties, and the like.

No problem was more exasperating to station scientists than the assumption that they should be responsible for answering any and all questions which might be addressed to them. Indeed, a number of directors were proud to list among their accomplishments the fact that their stations had become "general bureaus of information." This achievement seemed far less positive to staff members increasingly occupied in answering a bewilderingly varied correspondence. As one station scientist complained in 1881: "This is the *very busiest* time of the year for us. Farmers are busy making their plans for the coming year & they write to me on all sorts of subjects. And the trouble is every one has an equal right to an answer. I am a public man, and belong to the people & the people are relentless and exacting in their demands."[10]

With the exception of those few stations created by states before the Hatch Act, the majority of stations were departments of the several land-grant colleges. And in this relationship still another ambiguity confronted the would-be scientist. Proximity to a university, though in some ways an intellectual stimulus, had drawbacks as well.[11] The most important, as we have implied, was the tendency of college and university administrators to exploit experiment station budgets. The most common form of such exploitation lay in charging the salaries of men whose duties were essentially teaching college science courses to the experiment station fund. Some administrators, however, displayed even more imagination, charging insurance, a portion of the president's salary, students' laboratory supplies—in one case, even a carpet—to the Hatch fund. Professors of agriculture at land-grant colleges were in many cases appointed director of the new agricultural experiment station—at no increase in salary or reduction in teaching responsibilities. And, though administrators might demand a profit from farm operations, they ordinarily applied this income to general college purposes.[12] "The average agricultural college trustee," one scientist commented after three years' experience under the Hatch Act, "believes that the government appropriation for experiment stations is a sort of windfall to the colleges, and is to be used to help these institutions."[13] Not surprisingly, station scientists often opposed these practices which denied them time and resources for investigation.

The able and articulate among experiment station scientists and administrators had to respond by seeking to restructure an environment which seemed on every hand to compromise their autonomy. Idealism as well as self-interest at once prompted and legitimated such policies. Few experiment station scientists could accept the possibility that an irreconcilable conflict might indeed exist between the scientist's needs and those of his agricultural constituency; for none doubted that the conditions most appropriate for "high-grade" research were the optimum conditions for economic growth. A career in station work almost demanded such a point of view; the scientist's need to create a vis-à-vis between the demands of his own discipline and the requests of farm spokesmen made this formulation a logical and emotional necessity.

Some experiment station scientists did refuse to accept any version of this justifying doctrine, convinced that the incessant demands of the station's agricultural constituency made any true scientific vocation impossible. As an example let me mention only the experiences of several students of Harvard mycologist W. G. Farlow, who, unable to secure "appropriate" university positions, became botanists and plant pathologists in experiment stations. The scorn of a man like Roland Thaxter for the Connecticut farmers who besieged him with demands for practical help was acid and unbending. "Bordeaux mixture is the vilest compound imaginable," Thaxter complained to his teacher, Farlow, "but it would give me intense satisfaction to spray a select committee of Connecticut farmers with it till they couldn't see out of their eyes and the moss started from their backs. . . ."[14] Other station scientists, oriented toward a more mundane careerism, used misleading rhetoric and political skills to advance themselves. Most occupied positions somewhere between the genteel scorn of a Thaxter and the unalloyed boosterism of certain other station men.

In discussing the professionalization of experiment station science in the following pages, I will be describing two principal social roles. One is that of the working scientist. Another and more specialized role is that of the research-entrepreneur—a role increasingly important in the twentieth century, but still novel in the formative years of the American experiment stations. These leaders—usually station directors—were forced to mediate between the world of science on the one hand and, on the other, the social and economic realities of a particular state constituency. The best of these research-entrepreneurs (who might or might not be productive scientists themselves) were able to forge political alliances of mutual convenience with farm leaders and businessmen. At the same time, however, they had to maintain some commitment to and understanding of the world of the scientific disciplines. The successful research-entrepreneur had not only to tailor a research policy to the needs of his lay constituency, but still remain aware of professional values and realities, for institutional success was dependent not only upon the research-entrepreneur's political skills but upon his ability to recognize and hire men of talent and provide them with an at least minimally adequate environment.

Inevitably, so complex and demanding a role was pioneered successfully by only a handful of men. Inevitably as well, client-oriented policies which had brought success in the last decades of the nineteenth century became increasingly ambiguous as the twentieth century progressed. But the forging of this entrepreneurial role was still a necessary step in the development of the agricultural experiment station (as it was in the development of twentieth-century scientific institutions generally). I should like to suggest briefly how three such research-entrepreneurs—William A. Henry of Wisconsin, Eugene Davenport of Illinois, and Eugene W. Hilgard of California—sought and achieved institutional security. The parallels are obvious and instructive.

At the University of Wisconsin the first formal provision for agricultural "experimentation" had been made two decades before the passage of the Hatch Act in 1887. An "experimental farm" had existed on the Madison campus since 1866, but it was not until the arrival of William A. Henry in 1880 that Wisconsin's agricultural program began to make progress.[15] Though a graduate of Cornell's four-year course in agriculture, Henry had had no further advanced training. Appointed as professor of agriculture, he realized immediately that it would be impossible to build institutional strength upon the college's teaching program; students simply failed to attend. "The other line of work left open to us is experimentation," he explained to the Board of Regents. "By advancing agricultural science and getting our farmers interested in our work, we can justly hope, I hope, for more prosperous days in the future."[16]

Henry's attitude toward the success of the station and college of agriculture was based on three policy assumptions. The first was a recognition of the necessity for improving relations with the state's influential farmers, and the conviction that this could be accomplished only through tailoring research to their needs and then convincing this skeptical farm constituency of the station's potential usefulness. Second, the realization that the ability to solve such problems could come only through the work of scientists with the best possible training. Third, the assumption that the success of both college and station would depend upon the ultimate success of Wisconsin's agricultural community in shifting from a dependence upon grain to more specialized and diversified crops.

Not surprisingly, Henry's most strenuous efforts were directed toward the conversion of the state's wealthier and more influential farmers. He insisted that all his staff scientists, no matter what their personal inclinations, play an active role in popularizing the station and college of agriculture. "I have a man I have been training for seven years," Henry explained, "and though he groans when he sees a visitor coming and feels like running, he knows he has got to stay and take it." Henry and his staff explained again and again to visitors that an experiment station demanded an excellent chemical laboratory, that it

was not a model farm and could not be expected to make a profit.
Henry reminisced: "The first thing we are met with every day is this
statement: 'Well, professor, this farm will be satisfactory when you
make it pay.' . . . I knock that man right down and drag him off the
farm. Some one says: 'Professor, what does it cost you to make a pound
of butter?' expecting me to say 15 or 18 cents, but I say, 'Gentlemen,
most of our butter this winter is costing us $5 a pound, I think.' I knock
them right down at once and then explain. . . ."[17] In addition to such
face-to-face contacts, Henry wrote widely for farm papers and lectured
at Grange meetings and farmers' institutes throughout the state. He
sought, in addition, to find ways of bringing farmers to Madison. In
attaining this latter goal, Henry proved a vigorous educational innovator, pioneering the use of practical winter short courses as a means of
spreading the gospel of scientific agriculture and at the same time
building support for the university.

Although interested in several areas of agricultural production,
Henry chose to endorse dairying with particular vigor. By the middle
of the 1880s he had begun urging Wisconsin farmers to adopt dairying
as a remunerative and stable response to a changing market.[18] When he
hired S. M. Babcock as station chemist in 1887, it was because of the
Göttingen-trained New Yorker's demonstrated success in milk chemistry. With Henry's talent for choosing first-rate investigators and his
understanding of how such intellectual resources might best be
applied in economic contexts, the Wisconsin station had by 1905
contributed a number of innovations instrumental in the reshaping of
traditional dairy practice—the proper use of silage, cold curing of
cheese, and the Babcock butter-fat test, for example.

As a successful research-entrepreneur, Henry was blessed with not
only an understanding of the economic needs of his state's agricultural
community, but a measure of sympathy for the professional needs and
attitudes of scientists. When hiring Babcock and dairy bacteriologist H.
L. Russell—the latter a coworker of Babcock and Henry's successor as
college dean and station director—Henry was careful to emphasize the
light teaching duties and opportunities for research which their
positions implied.[19] And, though Wisconsin's presidents were generally friendly to his work, Henry discouraged even small encroachments
upon research funds for general university purposes. By judicious
cultivation of agricultural politicians and editors, and through an
ability to produce tangible results, Henry and his successor H. L.
Russell had by 1914 raised state appropriations for agricultural research to the then handsome figure of $75,000.[20]

This accumulation of institutional strength had certain negative
concomitants. Perhaps most important was Henry's commitment to

the need for "practicality" in research, a commitment justifiable in the 1880s but decreasingly fruitful in the first decade of the twentieth century. ("As between the so-called theorist and the practical man," he wrote just after leaving his administrative duties in 1908, "I would take the practical man every time.")[21] Henry could be a harsh taskmaster for those scientists unwilling or unable to commit themselves to agricultural improvement at the cost of sacrificing an opportunity for achievement within their particular discipline.[22] The heritage, moreover, of justification in terms of popular approval could handicap even the most creative laboratory men. Biochemist E. V. McCollum, for example, codiscoverer of Vitamin A, found it at first impossible to get financial support for the rat colony which he hoped to establish for nutrition studies; the Wisconsin legislature could hardly be expected to look with favor on tax monies being used to provide board and room for the farmer's bitter enemy.[23] Similarly, geneticists at Wisconsin and other stations anticipated opposition to plans for using small mammals—rats, mice, guinea pigs—in breeding experiments; why, critics asked, should state and national funds pay for information on the breeding of pests? Ultimately even more compromising was the heritage of extension work created by Henry's policy of attracting farm support through service. These politically strategic contacts with farmers had by the turn of the century produced an exhausting load of correspondence and lecturing.

The central irony lay, as we have seen, in Henry's very ability to gather statewide support. For the mechanisms which brought this success necessarily compromised the working scientist's autonomy. Yet, as contemporaries argued, no other approach would have been appropriate to the social and political realities of the 1880s and 1890s. Henry's tactics were, indeed, so successful that administrators in a number of other states found in them a model for their own policies.

No research-entrepreneur was more assiduous in such efforts than Eugene Davenport, Henry's counterpart at the University of Illinois. Though perhaps less successful than Henry in promoting real contributions to agricultural productivity—possibly because he was less skillful in his choice of staff—Eugene Davenport was even more successful in garnering support for his research program.

Agricultural education and research had borne comparatively little fruit at Illinois before Davenport was hired in 1895 as dean of the College of Agriculture.[24] With feeble backing from a president uninterested in the college and station, Davenport was forced to turn for support to the state's agricultural producers and agriculture-related industries. A man of acute political sensitivity, he was quick to cultivate leaders in the state's specialized producers' associations, gaining legislative strength by having these representatives of the state's commercial agriculture lobby for categorical appropriations —for research in soils, in crops, in livestock, even in floriculture. "There is no question," Davenport explained again and again, "but that money devoted to investigation pays, and pays immediately." "In the final roundup before the legislature," he confined to an aspiring Iowa administrator, "nothing counts so much as a delegation of actual farmers representing organizations. Their influence does not depend upon their numbers; while anything like a popular movement, when organized, requires a good deal of work to arouse it in the first place, and is liable at any moment to subside." Ultimately, of course, Davenport realized, he would have to seek research funds without hemming them in with specific requirements.[25]

Ironically, however, his very success in building support for the college and station was to make the desired autonomy difficult to achieve. Even more than Henry, Davenport became the prisoner of his own political acumen. In administering the station, Davenport worked closely with advisory committees of prominent agriculturists to oversee the several lines of investigation the state had opted to support. (The Illinois Grain Dealers' Association and Corn Growers' Association, for example, jointly appointed the committee on crops, the Illinois State Horticultural Society, the committee on orchards, the Dairyman's Association, the committee on dairying, and so forth.) Enmeshed in so intimate a relationship, Davenport found it difficult consistently to maintain the initiative in formulating station research policy. Farm leaders directly influenced hiring and firing, while large appropriations brought pressure for immediate results.[26] Such close relations between experiment station staff and their clients also maximized the likelihood of nonprofessional conduct; incidents of premature disclosure of work in progress—accompanied by grandiose claims—as well as staff members' involvement in indiscreet business enterprises all troubled Davenport's directorship.

Yet he could, by the First World War, point to a record of outstanding growth for the Illinois College of Agriculture and Experiment Station. In terms of staff, research support, and number of students, the college and station had become firmly established. This is demonstrated vividly in Davenport's ability to bypass university presidents James and Draper (neither of whom were enthusiastic advocates of agricultural education and research) in gaining access to the legislature.[27] Davenport was ultimately able to mobilize a network of statewide influence in gaining support for general university needs; by 1910 the university's orphan child had become at once a leading advocate of and argument for legislative largesse.

Of our three examples, that of Eugene W. Hilgard of California is perhaps the most complex. For Hilgard was both scientist and re-search-entrepreneur, a geologist of international reputation and at the same time a gifted publicist and molder of public opinion.

When he arrived in Berkeley as professor of agriculture in 1875, Hilgard found a campus beset with problems; the Grange was actively hostile to an institution in which agriculture was clearly held in small regard.[28] Berkeley had failed as a college of agriculture, and Hilgard, like Henry and Davenport, turned to research as justification for continued legislative support. Hilgard immediately set out to placate the Grange through personal contacts and by undertaking work relevant to the needs of California agriculture, especially in viticulture —most notably his campaign against phylloxera—and, closer to his original interest and training, the study of California's varied soils. Central to these plans was an experiment station. (Even before arriving in Berkeley, Hilgard had sought to popularize the need for American agricultural experiment stations on the German model.) Within a few years of his arrival, Hilgard could boast of having created such a station, in function if not in name.[29] By the mid-1880s Hilgard had built a respectable base of support for his work.

The logic of Hilgard's position implied the necessity of an almost exclusive emphasis upon immediate economic goals; by the 1890s he was forced to defend his service-oriented policy against frequent criticisms from the USDA's Office of Experiment Stations and other would-be upgraders of station research. In an environment as novel as that presented by California, Hilgard argued, such policies were the only appropriate response. These were the arguments Hilgard em-ployed, for example, in justifying to the Office of Experiment Stations his policy of encouraging branch stations throughout the state, a policy vigorously opposed by the OES. Hilgard was, moreover, forced to embrace an at-least-rhetorical unity with the working farmer and rancher. Despite his academic credentials, Hilgard assured farm au-diences, he had had personal experience as a farm owner and under-stood their problems. He was not one of those professors who "fight shy" but one "who has been there and knows how it is himself." As a result of this responsiveness, however, Hilgard soon found the de-mands upon his time oppressive. "There is no rest here for anyone, wicked or otherwise," Hilgard complained to F. A. P. Barnard in 1886, "least of all for a man who, like myself, is in a position which author-izes everyone from the shock-haired and hayseed-bestrewn granger to the justices of the supreme court to ply me with questions on their pri-vate business." His routine correspondence alone, he complained, would "do credit to a wholesale business house."[30] But, as in Wisconsin and Illinois, such contacts were unavoidable if Hilgard's work was to find adequate support.

Like Davenport at Illinois, moreover, Hilgard had to contend with a president—and in California elements of the Board of Regents as well—unsympathetic to agriculture. As dean of the college of agriculture he had thus to wage a bitter biennial campaign for appropriations. Though generally successful in his lobbying efforts, Hilgard looked forward in the early 1880s with keen anticipation to the availability of permanent federal support for his state's experiment station; not surprisingly, he worked vigorously for passage of the Hatch Act. "I am getting heartily tired," he explained to a friend, "of my biennial fight for existence."[31] But even after passage of the Hatch Act he continued to lobby in Sacramento for the categorical appropriations which helped to ensure the continued growth of his college and station. And Hilgard was justifiably proud of his achievements: "I have built up the whole," he explained to President George Atherton of Pennsylvania State University, "by an aggressive policy in the face of many discouragements, even the regents tolerating it at first only as a sop thrown to the Cerberus of the Grange. But the work has acquired an impetus that renders it unsafe for legislators or regents to ignore it."[32]

Differences in personality and local economic conditions implied minor tactical differences, but in all three cases the research-entrepreneur's strategy was the same—the creation of institutional strength through alliance with members of the business, agricultural, and political communities. In terms of the scientist's immediate work environment, these relationships could, as we have suggested, become a mixed blessing. Even those laymen most sympathetic to the stations and most euphoric in their hopes for scientific agriculture often entertained quite narrow views of the tasks appropriate to the experiment station scientist.

Scientists reacted in several ways to such constraints. A principal response, as we have illustrated in the case of three states, was to work for power and thus autonomy through cooperation with existing sources of economic and political influence. Another was to appeal to competing sources of power and reassurance—one the United States Department of Agriculture's Office of Experiment Stations; another, of a more general kind, the shared values of the several scientific disciplines. (These recourses were particularly important for scientists in states where deans and directors were more attentive to the demands of local clients than to the desires of their own staff members.) A third was the creation of new applied-science disciplines with norms more appropriate to the demands of the experiment station context than those of older pure-science fields. And, finally, agricultural scientists in almost every discipline reassured themselves and their clients by endorsing a rhetorical stance which emphasized the need for pure research if applied science was to prove ultimately fruitful.

The Office of Experiment Stations played a particularly strategic role in attempts by station scientists to shape their own professional lives. Under the control of men sympathetic to the scientist's point of view, the OES administration was consistently alert to the dangers of local obstructionism. In the 1890s the OES gained increased powers of audit and inspection, powers which it used to discourage the exploitation of Hatch funds.[33] (And such exploitation meant, it must be recalled, in day-to-day terms either the scientist's assignment to wearying teaching and extension work, or the diversion of funds which might have benefited research.) Functioning, moreover, as a semiformal employment agency for workers in the agricultural and biological sciences, the OES was able to make tactful suggestions to the well-meaning, find jobs for innocent victims of local power conflicts and better places for the competent. In the early years of the twentieth century, the elite among experiment station leaders united with the OES to lobby for passage of the Adams Act (1906), which doubled the funds available for the several state stations, but with the important and innovative proviso that the money be spent for "original investigation."[34]

Scientists also appealed to disciplinary peers for moral support and endorsement, and to such values as academic freedom and professional competence against local political or administrative pressures. Significantly, however, scientifically oriented station men also charged that certain administrators, in catering blindly to laymen, were performing a disservice to American agriculture as well as to freedom of inquiry. Such assumptions had become habitual by the turn of the century. For most American agricultural scientists had, as we have argued, adopted a rhetorical stance which justified science pure as a necessity if science applied was to function properly; only upon a base of high-quality research could ultimate economic gains be predicated. This assumption was a necessity for the great majority of station scientists, who could neither consider themselves mere implements of their agricultural constituency nor reject the structure of compromise exacted by this lay clientele.

Indeed, this argument—with its corollary that *all* insights gained into the laws of nature would, through some serendipitous process, be transformed into immediate practical benefits—was so frequently reiterated that it became a source of unmet hopes and unreal expectations. Let me refer, by way of example, to the area of animal and plant breeding in the first dozen years of this century. The insights of Mendel and DeVries not only implied the creation of a new and promising discipline, but seemed to guarantee immediate practical results. (One station writer noted wryly at the time that "members of the legislature who have the dispensing of funds will certainly find more comfort in the theory of DeVries than in that of Darwin.")[35] Such ingenuous hopes were soon blighted; Mendel added little or nothing to the technical armamentarium of the skilled empirical breeder. As geneticist Raymond Pearl noted sharply before the First World War, all that the new genetics had really done thus far was to help the breeder interpret his accustomed techniques. He explained, "This may seem too mild a statement of the potential value of genetic science to the animal breeder. It undeniably does lack the grandeur of the vision sometimes opened out by the extension lecturer in his zeal to inspire farmers to do better things, and at the same time pave the way for increased appropriations for his institution."[36]

The rhetorical emphasis upon the necessary and mutually beneficial relationship between science pure and applied did, however, begin to change at the end of the nineteenth century. This accustomed emphasis became a subject of debate in a growing conflict between an older generation of scientist-administrators strongly committed to the legitimacy of the demands made by their agricultural clients, and younger—often European- or graduate-school-trained—laboratory men. These younger scientists tended to assume much higher ground in discrediting policies which allowed the perceived needs of a lay constituency to define research programs. As state support for stations increased in the early years of the century, and as the Adams fund became available after 1906, American experiment stations turned increasingly to the nation's doctoral programs for staff members. Agricultural colleges produced few doctorates and station directors had—in some cases unwillingly but with the consistent encouragement of the OES—to turn to basic science departments for well-trained men.[37] As their numbers increased, criticism of the older generation of politically sensitive research-entrepreneurs grew sharper and more frequent.

Reformers were willing to concede that accommodation was necessary in the pioneer years of the experiment station movement; it was appropriate both to political realities and to the stations' limited technical capacities. But by 1900, articulate critics submitted, American agricultural research was ready to outgrow such immature relationships; it was no longer necessary to dramatize the immediate relevance of station science to the farmer's economic needs. American scientists must now emulate their German counterparts and educate laymen and administrators to the need for higher standards of research if substantial increases in productivity were to be attained.[38]

It would be easy enough to emphasize ways in which the experiment station context and traditions played a negative role in the development of the sciences in America. A tradition of client-centered research led to much trivial and redundant work. The need to achieve institutional and individual autonomy did result in a habit of compromise—a habit easily justified by a democratically tinged rhetoric of service as ultimate goal.

Yet, despite such constraints, the agricultural experiment station played in sum a positive role in the development of the scientific disciplines in the United States. Though the relationship between agricultural scientists and the economic substrate which supported them was ambiguous, it served as a formative stage in the gradual shaping of a research context increasingly hospitable to more fundamental work.[39]

In specifying some components of this complex relationship, one can begin with a positive generalization. The stations played a substantial role in the careers of individual scientists and in the formative periods of a number of the biological sciences in America—most prominently bacteriology, biochemistry, and genetics. The reasons are obvious enough. First, in years of austere academic budgets almost any position was a good one. A job, moreover, in which research and publication were formal aspects of one's duties seemed particularly attractive; though often disappointed, would-be scientists were again and again attracted to experiment station work. The better state stations and colleges of agriculture offered greater freedom than the United States Department of Agriculture, [40] while research positions in industry were still scarce indeed.

The most important direct relationship between the experiment stations and the development of the scientific disciplines in America lay, I feel, in the stations' role in strengthening the state universities. The strategies for accumulating political influence adopted by college and station interests had helped bring about a more secure level of support for many state universities; the relationship between college and station was essentially constructive—though as ambivalent and ambiguous as marriages generally. Examples of successful technological innovation had helped make investment in the production and dissemination of such innovation a plausible course of action, while at the same time creating a group of potential lobbyists in farmers and businessmen who had themselves benefited from station work. (And, of course, whatever role the stations played in increasing agricultural productivity ultimately increased the resources potentially available for expenditure on public purposes.)

Indeed, even though it may be argued that the relatively crude level of pre-First World War agricultural technology served to limit the stations' capacity for actually increasing productivity, the role of the experiment station in strengthening the state university—as at Wisconsin, where such extremely strong departments as bacteriology, biochemistry, and genetics all grew up within the college of agriculture and experiment station—became increasingly important as the twentieth century progressed and a more intricate and fruitful relationship between basic and applied science became both necessary and possible.[41] The experiment station with its professionally oriented staff of disseminators, adaptors, and innovators existed to provide a nexus in which such relationships could be created, exploited, and its products disseminated.[42]

At least as important, perhaps, as the direct role played by the stations in the development of American science was the effect they exerted upon economic growth and thus, inevitably, upon science as well. Obviously this distinction—that between the role of the stations in promoting economic growth and in the development of the scientific disciplines—is arbitrary at best. Yet granted the difficulty of evaluating specific inputs and relationships in a system so complex and interdependent, let me try to suggest in general terms some of the ways in which the existence of the stations and the consequent movements toward professionalization among station scientists served as a component of economic growth.

First, the gradual professionalization of the experiment station scientist constituted a specific input into the expansion of agricultural productivity. Put another way, the agricultural scientist's perception of an appropriate role and his efforts to narrow the gap between this ideal and his originally unsatisfactory circumstances altered his behavior and thus served as an agent of economic change. This influence was exerted in two general ways: in terms of innovation and adoption, and in the provision of mechanisms for the dissemination of knowledge.

Whether the experiment station scientist defined his role in terms of applied science or some more traditional discipline, conformity to a professional role implied publication; it meant mastery of a literature inexorably growing in both quantity and complexity, and, more fundamentally still, commitment to an acceptance by his fellow scientists as an ultimate measure of achievement. And such acceptance was defined with increasing circumstantiality in terms of knowledge and publication. Even the creation of new applied science disciplines—economic entomology, horticulture, or poultry husbandry, for example—was shaped by such general criteria as well as others more discipline-specific. In addition to the general values which we have discussed, agricultural scientists of all disciplines tended to accept service as an absolute value. In an era before the Smith-Lever Extension Act of 1914, this ethic of service helped (with the institutions' own need for ensuring public support) create an extension program in function if not in name, bringing and adapting agricultural innovation to an industry often resistant to change.

The political needs of the station scientists guaranteed that the educated, adequately capitalized farmer would be their natural ally in the achievement of power. Indeed, the larger the scale of an enterprise, the more likely it was, in general, to find experiment station scientists relevant. Innovation and adoption implied both capital and appropriate values. (And these values—education particularly—implied in their turn a degree of prosperity.) "I am sorry," W. A. Henry wrote in 1898, "to say that we have not accomplished much with the lower stratum of Wisconsin farmers, but the more intelligent ones who are leaders of their community and who help others by example are for the most part strongly with us."[43] In inspection work or efforts at control, it was the less-educated general farmer who was often inhospitable to "book-farming" and to agricultural colleges which seemed remote from his needs and those of his children. Similarly, it was the small nurseryman or fertilizer manufacturer who frequently objected to station regulation, the larger producers who often welcomed it.[44] The experiment stations served with some efficacy to strengthen and rationalize—exacerbate, if one likes—trends already apparent within American agriculture and society generally.

Logically enough, the stations tended to be most successful in states developing a specialized urban-market-oriented agriculture, and at the same time states in which respect for science and education as instrumentalities for economic progress and moral improvement was most apparent. With such a constituency eager to rationalize their methods, and capable of being convinced by station arguments and demonstrations, conditions for the interaction of the needs of station scientists and the parallel development of agricultural productivity were maximized. The effectiveness of station efforts, even by the First World War, in increasing productivity in particular states and particular industries seems clear enough, though dairying was perhaps the most striking example.

Not only in Wisconsin, but in New York, Connecticut, Minnesota, Illinois, Iowa, Vermont, and New Hampshire, dairying was actively promoted by station directors, beginning in many cases in the 1880s. Working at first with a handful of large farmers, farm editors, and farm business leaders, some directors were able by the 1890s to create a vigorous interest in this stable, year-round enterprise. A number of the more alert directors were sensitive to the economic contours of the budding dairy industry and thus aware of production and marketing problems potentially solvable by technological means. Thus at least five stations were at work in the late 1880s on a practical butter-fat test for commercial creameries. (Without such a test, there could be no satisfactory mechanism for payment to individual producers.) And, as we have already noted, S. M. Babcock, who proved successful in this search, had been hired by Wisconsin because of his proven skills in milk chemistry. Once the test was described in 1890, other stations acted quickly to popularize it among their constituencies, not only publishing special bulletins, but also organizing winter short courses in dairying with instruction in the Babcock test as a key inducement.

The economic consequences of the Babcock test extended beyond the provision of a rational method for paying producers. It served as well as a criterion for culling nonproductive animals from dairy herds and thus led to a general upgrading of dairy stock (including the more general adoption of the Holstein-Friesian).[45] Finally, of course, the test provided a public relations argument for greater support of agricultural research and the state universities generally. (Dean Davenport could, for example, inform the chairman of his state's committee on appropriations that the Babcock test alone had been worth more to the state of Wisconsin than the cost of running the entire university throughout its history.)[46] And the Babcock test was only one among a series of technological innovations which helped reshape the American dairy industry between 1890 and 1914.[47]

It is, of course, impossible to make any quantitative evaluation of the efficacy and wisdom of the investment of intellectual and capital resources by state and national governments in the stations before 1914. This is hardly a meaningful question. The problem was not, and could not, have been formulated in these terms; it is hard to imagine how the historical circumstances which gave birth to the American experiment station movement would have allowed any alternative method of subsidizing agricultural research. Nor would these resources have been diverted to other means of subsidizing pure or applied science. Neither individual units of production—the farmers—nor agriculture-related business would have considered such allocation of funds in the late-nineteenth century. Only the political power and ideological primacy of both agriculture and science, in their different fashions, allowed the stations to be created.

Interest-group politics created the American experiment stations; once created, the men who staffed these new institutions, motivated by their own values and institutional needs, became an interest group of their own, forging pragmatic alliances and a research policy based on a shared interest in the growth of productivity through the rational application of technology. The fragmented quality of American institutional life meant that the values of professionalization would —shaped into concrete institutional forms—establish themselves within this shifting intellectual and institutional landscape. The station scientist's increasing commitment to professional norms was power too, power to determine a pattern of behavior which stimulated economic development and the growth of both pure science and agricultural technology.

10

The Adams Act:
Politics and the Cause of
Scientific Research

On March 2, 1887, President Grover Cleveland signed the Hatch Act, a novel measure which granted $15,000 annually to each state for the maintenance of an agricultural experiment station.[1] In 1906 Theodore Roosevelt, with much greater willingness, signed another act, sponsored by Representative Henry C. Adams of Wisconsin, which gradually increased each state's appropriation to $30,000. The text of Adams's bill was very similar to that of the Hatch Act. In one crucial phrase, however, they differed; while the Hatch Act had provided funds for conducting scientific investigations and for dissemination of the results, the funds appropriated nineteen years later were to be used only for "original" scientific research[2]—a triumph, one might assume, for the idea of abstract research over the narrow-mindedness and prejudice of legislators. And in a sense it was; but only in a carefully qualified sense.

More specifically, the Adams Act can be seen as the consequence of a generation's experience with agricultural research under the Hatch Act. Even more meaningfully, the Adams Act can be understood as the product of three different though interrelated contexts of power. First were the sometimes conflicting and sometimes complementary needs and identities of four different agencies—the experiment stations, the agricultural colleges, and United States Department of Agriculture, and the agricultural department's Office of Experiment Stations. A second sort of power was that exerted by the agricultural colleges and experiment stations within their own states and upon their representatives in Washington. The third sphere of power is one somewhat different in form, but no less real or important. This was the influence of the institutional values of the scientific disciplines which sanctioned and shaped the ambitions of the American scientists and administrators involved in promoting the Adams Act. If the first two factors suggested —institutional growth and rivalry and local political relationships— explain the enactment of Congressman Adams's bill, the third explains the particular form which it assumed, and a good portion of the impetus for its passage.

The passage of the Hatch Act posed a number of administrative problems, but none was more urgent than that of establishing a pattern of formal relationships between the several state stations and the USDA. In an effort to solve this dilemma, Congress sanctioned the creation in 1888 of a division within the Department of Agriculture to coordinate experiment station work. This was the Office of Experiment Stations, and the solution it provided to the problem of state-federal relations was a surprisingly successful one.

This success was the result of the work of three men who shared a remarkable practicality and an equally remarkable clarity of purpose —Wilbur O. Atwater, Alfred C. True, and Edward W. Allen. Atwater, a chemist of national reputation at Wesleyan, was the first director of the Office and although he served for only two years, he succeeded in formulating a coherent statement of research aims for the infant stations. Atwater brought with him to Washington a young colleague from Wesleyan's Classics Department, Alfred C. True, who was to serve as director of the Office from 1893 until its reorganization in 1915. It was he, more than any other man, who made Atwater's theoretical goals the basis for administrative reality.[3] Though True was a classicist by training, he had absorbed from Atwater and from Allen, his long-time administrative associate—both German-trained chemists—a precise conception of the goals proper for America's experiment stations. Truly abstract investigations, neither Atwater nor Allen ever doubted, were a necessity, not only for the advancement of scientific knowledge, but for the solution of the economic problems facing American agriculture. The history of the Office of Experiment Stations between 1893 and the passage of the Adams Act in 1906 is very largely the record of a consistent and stubborn war of attrition against the shoddy and opportunistic elements in experiment station science.

In its first years of existence, the Office limited itself to the making of policy statements and to the compilation and indexing of station publications. But this quickly changed. In 1893 A. C. True began his directorship, and a year later the Office acquired the power to audit and pass upon station expenditures.[4] With each succeeding year True narrowed his interpretation of permissible expenditures under the Hatch Act. At first he found an abundance of obvious infringements of the act's intent; agricultural colleges used the Hatch endowment for everything from paying fire insurance premiums to the purchase of fish and cats for dissection in student laboratories.[5] True struggled constantly against the use of Hatch funds for the support of work that was essentially regulatory or preventive. Station veterinarians and chemists, True stated again and again, were being paid to do research, not to perform routine fertilizer analyses or to administer preventive inoculations. Most important, the Office of Experiment Stations had to fight a continuous and dispiriting war against the pilfering of station funds and the misuse of station personnel by college deans and presidents. These administrators saw in the Hatch Act a windfall for undernourished instructional budgets, and Allen and True were forced to write scores of letters each year, demanding that men who taught fulltime no longer be paid with Hatch funds.[6]

By the late 1890s the Office of Experiment Stations had begun to exert its influence in a more positive fashion. True, for example, consistently encouraged stations wishing to study feeding to discard the routine analysis of the economic value of feeding stuffs. They would, instead, do well, he suggested, to hire chemists and physiologists and attempt to discover something of the physiological nature of digestion or of the biochemical make-up of foodstuffs.[7] In the dozen years between 1894 and 1906, the Office of Experiment Stations had evolved a persistent and well-articulated policy aimed at converting the Hatch appropriation into a research fund exclusively. But it could never become quite that. The wording of the original act, calling as it did for the dissemination of research findings and permitting the "verification" of experiments, would have defeated so narrow an interpretation. The Hatch Act was ultimately unsatisfactory, either as an administrative tool to control station research policies or, on the other hand, as a source of funds sufficient to subsidize the kinds of research which, by 1906, needed so badly to be undertaken.

The Adams Act not only increased the financial resources of the stations, but in its specification of "original investigations" provided the administrative leverage with which to control the expenditure of these funds. It is hardly surprisingly to learn that A. C. True wrote the original draft of the Adams Act or that he and his Office of Experiment Stations consistently supported the measure—despite the unspoken hostility of a number of bureau chiefs in True's own Department of Agriculture.[8]

In the dozen years before 1906 the Department's scientific bureaus had expanded enormously. As they did so, and as their work extended into individual states, the bureaus came into inevitable conflict with state colleges and experiment stations. Two agencies in particular, Milton Whitney's Bureau of Soils and Beverly T. Galloway's Bureau of Plant Industry, seemed inordinately imperialistic to experiment station leaders.[9] Plant pathologists or soil mappers were simply unwelcome interlopers to many experiment station spokesmen—highly subsidized bureaucrats competing with colleges and stations for public favor within their own states. It was difficult, however, to attack these bureaus directly—that is, through Congress—for their support in the House was surprisingly strong; few congressmen could easily resist assenting to an appropriation which promised to manifest itself conspicuously in their own districts. Though the stations had hoped that the Secretary of Agriculture, "Tama Jim" Wilson, originally an experiment station man, might be a bulwark of state interests in Washington, he had been a disappointment. Wilson seemed to many station leaders insufficiently aggressive and dangerously dependent upon his bureau chiefs.[10] Realizing that they had little chance of decreasing Congressional appropriations to the Department's scientific bureaus, station leaders soon decided that their only hope of keeping pace with the Department lay in increasing their own financial support. It would be accurate to describe the Adams Act as a strategic victory for the stations in a continuing conflict with the Department of Agriculture.

This was a conflict based on far more than personal pique or offended prerogative. Station leaders were convinced that they could not tolerate the competition of a powerful and prestigious rival within their own states; each successful research program of the national department threatened some segment of local support for college and station. And, as we have seen, it was upon the continuance of such local support that the security of college and station interests depended.

Agricultural opinion is not made by some undifferentiated group of hard-working farm operators. It is made by the articulate, the prosperous, and the influential both within and without the community of agricultural producers. Educated and more highly capitalized farmers, editors of farm and rural papers, country bankers, insurance agents, merchants, and implement dealers make up the visible agricultural consensus. These were the men active in most farmers' organizations and specialized producers' associations—those who had come to accept scientific knowledge as necessary for successful economic competition. Their letters filled the correspondence files of experiment station directors and agricultural college deans. Naturally, these men of consequence met station workers, deans, and directors at meetings, at farmers' institutes, and at social gatherings. Editors came habitually to call upon station directors for columns of free copy, while politicians turned to the same men for sympathetic and knowledgeable speeches on agricultural questions. It was inevitable that experiment station workers should play increasingly important roles in the affairs of farm organizations; it was equally inevitable that these farm associations and the rural lawyers and editors connected with them should become the backbone of college and station support in state legislatures.[11]

Each of the more successful stations based its research policy at least partially on the needs of farm associations. State Granges and boards of agriculture, associations of dairymen and fruit growers, florists, poultry raisers, and cranberry growers—even apiarists might be the source of much-needed political support.[12] The research of station scientists was, on the other hand, often of real help to such groups—thus strengthening these producers and ultimately the station which had contributed to their prosperity. It was not by chance that the Babcock butter-fat test was discovered in Wisconsin; nor was it an accident that E. M. East was allowed to work on hybrid corn investigations in Connecticut. Dean William A. Henry of Wisconsin's College of Agriculture had brought Stephen M. Babcock to Madison with the specific intention of having this New York authority on the chemistry of milk develop a commercially practicable butter-fat test for Wisconsin dairymen. Director Edward Jenkins of Connecticut's New Haven Experiment Station had similarly decided that dairying would be an appropriate field of specialization for Connecticut farmers. Jenkins realized as well, however, that in order to compete with newer soils Connecticut farmers would need more efficient feeds for their dairy herds—hence his interest in the possibilities of improved corn varieties.[13] Both Henry and Jenkins had spent many years in preaching the importance of specialization in agricultural production. The future, they believed, lay not simply in exporting staples to a world market, but in applying science and efficiency to production for a changed domestic market.

Not only did the political influence of college and station increase as farm associations and rural businessmen prospered, but it grew as the number of graduates of agricultural courses increased. In Wisconsin, in New York, and in Ohio, for example, associations of agricultural alumni organized ostensibly to sustain interest in scientific agriculture, served as interested and articulate wedges of support for station and college policies. More important, in states predominantly or largely agricultural, was the fact that at least some editors, lawyers, legislators, even bankers and businessmen were likely to have attended or at least to have had some contact with their state university. By 1900 the more successful and dexterous station directors were, as we have seen in the case of Henry, Davenport, and Hilgard, able to call a well-organized network of influence to the aid of favored measures in local statehouses or in Washington. If, for example, A. C. True needed support for a pet item in an agricultural appropriation bill, he could and did call upon this nationwide web of power.[14] When the Adams Act appeared on the floor of Congress, it passed with a voice vote; no Congressman would needlessly record himself against progress, against science, and against the articulate sentiment of his state's organized farm groups.

Representing scientific progress in agriculture was not simply discreet; it might even be a means of creating or strengthening a political career. This was certainly apparent in the case of Henry C. Adams, Wisconsin Representative from 1903 until his premature death in 1906. No contemporary political career could, indeed, have more clearly demonstrated the existence of that nexus of political, social, and economic relationships in which worldly college and station leaders had forged so strategic a position. Adams had attended the University of Wisconsin for several years and, though never in robust health, had found time to serve as a farmer's institute worker, as president of the State Dairymen's Association, as secretary of the State Horticultural Society, and as State Food and Dairy Commissioner. Moreover, at the university he had come under the influence of Dean W. A. Henry and Henry's relentless faith in progress through science. A sincere convert to this faith, Adams found, moreover, that his gradually acquired skills and his conspicuous promotion of scientific agriculture were a secure bit of bedrock in the shifting sands of Wisconsin politics. It is hardly surprising that he introduced a bill increasing experiment station appropriations, and that his advocacy of the Adams Act was a central appeal in a hard-fought struggle to maintain his congressional seat in 1906.[15]

The deans, the station directors, A. C. True, and Congressman Adams all had immediate stakes in the passage of the Adams Act. However, above this maelstrom of conflicting needs lay a system of values which gave force, direction, and justification to the strivings of the deans and scientists involved in promoting the Adams Act.

That the bill called for "original investigation" only was far more than a reflection of A. C. True's desire to increase his bureaucratic powers—or of the state stations to compete with the United States Department of Agriculture. It was a recognition by the better-trained station scientists and administrators of their adherence to the value system of the scientific disciplines, and of their attempts to make its tenets a program and a rationale for American agricultural science. Political manipulation was sanctioned because it was in a good cause. Opposition to the Bureau of Soils was not simply sordid competition

for public funds, but a defense of academic freedom.[16] Petty bureaucratic restrictions were a necessity because they pointed, if ever so
slightly, toward the path of an absolute good—the cause of abstract
research. Sensitive as they were to popular desires and rural attitudes,
leading experiment station figures never doubted that ultimate progress, expressed either in terms of farm practice or absolute knowledge,
could come only through a willing adherence to the standards accepted
by the academic scientists of France and Germany.

To many scientists, however, the Adams Act meant something far
more concrete than a recognition of principles and far more important
than an increase in research funds. It promised a new era for the
experiment station scientist. Agricultural science was still not quite
respectable academically; the agricultural scientist still had to bear the
gibes of his liberal arts colleagues and the inattentiveness of his
European contemporaries. He was, moreover, saddled to teaching,
often to routine regulatory and analytical work, and to endless speaking engagments. The Adams fund promised freedom from such tasks
and the consequent opportunity to perform the research and write the
books and articles which alone could gain for the agricultural scientist
the recognition of his disciplinary peers. And this recognition was, for
many, the only sort of success that ultimately mattered.[17]

The Hatch Act had been little more than a beginning; the pressures
against research had been too great, the number of scientists trained
to perform it pathetically few.[18] The Adams Act was the product of a
younger generation, better trained, more numerous, and with a far
clearer idea of the essential quality of the scientific endeavor. To
such scientists, the Adams Act was a necessary first step in the direction of a final emancipation from the duties of teacher and analytical
drudge; the Smith-Lever Act supporting extension work eight years
later marked a second step, helping free agricultural scientists from
the routine of lecture platform and institute meeting.

The elevating pursuit of pure science had made enemies as well as
friends. For every administrator like Cornell's Liberty Hyde Bailey or
A. C. True, there were other college presidents and members of station
boards of control who fought stubbornly to continue using Hatch
funds for teaching and extension work. For each able and ambitious
station scientist, there were others untrained and unequal to the
demands of original investigation. To such men, the incessant demands of experiment station spokesmen for abstract research were
simply officious threats.[19]

In the American Association of Agricultural Colleges and Experiment Stations the more scientifically oriented deans and directors

possessed a device with which to put formal pressure on weaker and less reputable stations and, of course, a device for the presenting of unified demands to Congress.[20]

The passage of the Adams Act was a very real personal triumph for Dean W. A. Henry and his protégé, Congressman Henry C. Adams. Adams received scores of letters congratulating him for his intelligent and persistent championing of the measure; a knowing minority, however, sent their letters of congratulations to Henry. For, as Adams himself was happy to acknowledge, the bill which bore his name was far more the result of Henry's initiative than his own.[21]

Henry was, of course, not alone in his desire for an increase in the experiment station endowment. Farm leaders and experiment station spokesmen had, almost from the passage of the Hatch Act, suggested the necessity of such action. By 1902 research needs had expanded to the point where this was at least an ultimate necessity—and the competition of the Department of Agriculture's scientific bureaus served to make this ultimate need an immediate one. Late in 1902 the agricultural college association resolved to authorize its executive committee to propose to Congress "at the earliest practicable date" that Hatch funds be augmented.[22]

While in Washington late in 1903, Dean Henry called on his long-time friend, the newly elected Representative Adams. The dean spent much of his visit in outlining experiment station needs and in emphasizing the danger of competition from the Department of Agriculture; he concluded by urging Adams to introduce in Congress a measure increasing experiment station appropriations. Adams was naturally sympathetic and immediately promised to do what he could. His first step was to visit Secretary Wilson and A. C. True; Wilson was noncommittal, but True, of course, was enthusiastic, indeed so enthusiastic that he set about drafting a bill which Adams introduced that winter in the House.[23] Despite a generally friendly reaction, however, the measure was not to reach the floor until early in 1906.

Two principal obstacles stood in its way: first, the skepticism of several members of the House agricultural committee; and second —and more difficult to overcome—the opposition of Speaker Cannon, hostile toward almost any new continuing appropriation and doubly hostile toward the ivory-tower "book-farming" which the experiment stations seemed to represent.[24]

Fortunately, there was little opposition from the Department of Agriculture's politically influential bureau chiefs. Neither Whitney nor Galloway, involved as they were in public squabbling with the experiment stations—and in private disputes with each other—could afford to oppose the bill openly. Harvey Wiley, on the other hand, at odds with both Whitney and Galloway, who were, he believed, poaching in the research preserves of Wiley's Bureau of Chemistry, promised to use his influence in favor of the measure. Thus growth and differentiation within the Department of Agriculture had created a countervailing need within experiment station circles to press for increased financial support, while the Department's growth had, ironically, at the same time created an internal situation in which opposition to the station measure was impossible.[25]

The first opposition to Adams's proposal came from within the House Committee on Agriculture. Both James Wadsworth of New York, the committee's chairman, and Gilbert Haugen of Iowa were opposed to the bill and suspicious in general of the experiment stations. The stations, Wadsworth was convinced, simply duplicated the same experiments over and over again. Haugen doubted the wisdom of the entire program; a practical farmer could teach more in ten minutes than a scientist in an hour and a half, he assured his committee members; while the Adams bill, he concluded, was designed "to furnish stalls for a lot of public grafters to get their noses into the crib of the public treasury."[26] Adams, a junior member of the committee, found that his arguments and statistics had little effect on these unsympathetic committee members. But he could call upon a force more powerful than words in his fight to obtain a favorable committee report. This was the local political influence which Dean Henry and the agricultural college association's exective committee put at Adams's disposal. Dean Charles Curtiss of Iowa's College of Agriculture, for example, was requested by Henry to have Iowa farm groups put pressure on Haugen; and Liberty Hyde Bailey was asked to use his influence to change Wadsworth's adamant position. Dean Henry, at the same time, promised Adams that he would turn the editorial columns of the *Rural New-Yorker* and the *Breeder's Gazette* against Wadsworth. The refractory committee members were finally brought into line; and on March 24, 1904, the agricultural committee reported the bill favorably.[27]

But now the measure met the stubborn opposition of "Uncle Joe" Cannon. There was nothing personal in this opposition, the Speaker assured Adams: it was simply that he could not at the moment approve of any new appropriations. Despite Cannon's opposition, however, Adams felt that the bill did have a chance to be passed, but only because of the effective organization which he had created to support it. Without such local support, he admitted, "it would not stand a ghost of a show."[28] Dean Henry and his fellow station directors had made certain that congressional support would not lag. Early in 1904 Adams set about the organization of what he called a chain-letter system; employing the statewide connections of deans, directors, editors, and farm leaders, Adams was able to create a deluge of letters and petitions to congressmen calling for the passage of the proposed experiment station bill. In Pennsylvania, for example, station director Henry P. Armsby was at the center of a carefully planned letter-writing campaign, a campaign which benefited from the support of the state Grange and Pennsylvania's united farmers' organizations. Armsby's preparations were extremely successful; Representative Thomas S. Butler of Pennsylvania complained that he was being driven simply insane by letters from what seemed to be every farmer and farm organization in his state.[29] But throughout 1904 and 1905 the unyielding Speaker refused to smile upon the Adams proposal; and it was not until February of 1906 that Cannon permitted the bill to reach the floor, where it passed without opposition.[30] Now only the approval of the Senate was needed and Adams's network of local influence was again put to work. As soon as the measure was approved in the House, Adams dispatched telegrams to farm leaders and college administrators, urging them to write to their senators in support of his bill.[31] There was no Speaker Cannon in the Senate and the experiment station measure passed unopposed in the upper house, to be signed by President Roosevelt a week later.

American scientists realized that most of the Adams fund would at first be wasted, since there were hardly enough trained scientists to spend it effectively. But the very existence of the endowment played a significant role in the development of the sciences in America. It provided much-needed support for new and centrally important disciplines, for genetics, for biochemistry, and for bacteriology.[32] It permanently strengthened the scientific departments of the land-grant colleges. The Adams Act provided the opportunity for willing men to enter upon the path of abstract research. More than this, however, it demanded a precise definition of agricultural research and—by implication—of the experiment station's proper task. Few leaders had ever had occasion to define agricultural "research" in more than homiletic terms; now, however, "original investigation" would have to become not merely a theoretical rallying point, but a concrete standard for the evaluation of particular research proposals.

Secretary Wilson announced immediately after the passage of the Adams Act that its administration would be entrusted to the Office of Experiment Stations and its director, A. C. True.[33] This was no easy task for True and his lieutenant, E. W. Allen, but they were neither without experience nor without preconceptions. An investigation could be considered original, Allen and True agreed, only if it was clearly limited to the solution of a specific problem and only if its solution would shed light on the natural laws which underlay agricultural production. "Lots of people," Allen remarked, "think they are doing investigational work if they are conducting some variety tests or testing South Carolina rock against ground bone for potatoes.[34] Such fertilizer or variety tests might be useful, but they were hardly original. Crop rotations were a perfectly proper field of research, but not if limited to the comparative trials conducted by so many of the stations. An appropriate rotation experiment might, for example, seek to investigate the effects of a particular plan's growth on the nitrogen or phosphorus content or bacterial population of the soil. Nutrition research was a particular favorite with True, and he often suggested it to stations as a proper field for Adams's work. Such research, however, could not be conducted as it had so often been in the past—simple experiments to determine the most economical feeding mixtures for a particular animal or locality. Again and again, the Office of Experiment Stations pointed as an inspiring example to the precise research of Thomas B. Osborne at Connecticut's New Haven station. Osborne's decades-long search for the composition of plant proteins was work which every experiment station scientist could admire.[35] Though it roused the sarcasm of Connecticut Valley farmers, Osborne's research won only praise in Leipzig and Berlin.

True and his coworkers knew, of course, that good examples and encouraging letters were not enough to bring immediate compliance with their interpretation of the Adams Act. The Office of Experiment Stations established, therefore, an essentially new administrative tool for the enforcing of these views. This was, in mid-twentieth-century usage, the project system. After being entrusted by Secretary Wilson with the enforcement of the Adams Act, True announced that all plans for the conducting of research with Adams fund had to be submitted for approval before the work itself should be undertaken. This arrangement provided an excellent means of coercive persuasion; if proposals seemed vague or ill-considered, they need not be refused outright. Suggestions might be given; particular problems and approaches—even changes in personnel—might be urged on the misguided station.[36] At the same time the Office of Experiment Stations assumed an increasingly rigid attitude toward expenditures under the Hatch Act. True hoped, insofar as this was possible, to make the Hatch fund into a research endowment similar to that created by the Adams Act. The passage of the Adams Act, True wrote to station directors and college deans, was no cause for ending pressure on state legislatures. On the contrary, it provided an occasion to demand greater financial support, especially for that extension work so popular with farmers, so demanding to the laboratory scientist, yet so necessary if the research sponsored by the Hatch and Adams funds were to become part of the farmer's world.[37]

It was not by chance that the Adams fund was available to provide research support for American genetics and biochemistry at formative stages in their development. These new sciences and the Adams Act itself were equally characteristic products of Western society's generally symmetrical and increasingly complex development. America had produced markets and transportation for dairymen and fruit growers and political representation for their economic interests in capitol and statehouse. The increasing size and complexity of this new society demanded corresponding increases in the complexity of institutional forms; and inevitably these institutions had different and conflicting interests. An industrial society, the America which produced the Adams Act, was deeply dependent upon scientific knowledge and was beginning to provide a secure context for the development of the scientific professions. By 1906 these had become well-organized disciplines with peculiar systems of values and attitudes. And by 1906 as well, these ideas had become generally enough accepted and clearly enough articulated to provide a specific and appropriate form for the Adams Act.

11

Science Pure and Science Applied: Two Studies in the Social Origin of Scientific Research

In the three previous chapters I have tried to describe the role several generations of scientists played in the creation and evolution of the agricultural experiment station. Historians have paid little attention to the work done in these novel institutions. Yet, as in all applied science contexts, interaction between the demands of the several scientific disciplines and those of a lay constituency created a sometimes-strained research climate. Each discipline, pure or applied, offered a unique relevance to economic realities; every state represented a somewhat different social context. In states bereft of an appropriate system of social support—a respect for education, well-differentiated local leadership, available capital, and the beginnings of a stable commercial agriculture—federal support produced little useful research or effective cooperation between agriculture and state-supported scientific institutions.

In some states, on the other hand, a peculiar configuration of scientific possibilities and social need created a context which fostered innovation. This chapter examines two instances of such productive experiment station research: the discovery of vitamin A and the development of hybrid corn. In both cases, the problem of innovation as an intellectual task cannot be understood apart from its specific institutional and social contexts. To understand the solution of any core of scientific problems, the historian must not look simply at the work of the few men associated with particular discoveries, but at the manner in which the discipline as a whole shaped the particular research area in which they labored and the specific institutional contexts in which practitioners of that discipline were able to practice their craft. In each instance, a particular interaction of discipline and context created unique institutional conditions—and, to the scientists concerned, a unique reality.

This is apparent when one traces the development of American nutrition research in the years before the First World War. Previous to 1900 a goodly proportion of the laboratory hours of American chemists was spent in what could be characterized as nutrition studies. But those pursuing this work were neither physiological chemists nor physicians. They were agricultural chemists, and their analysis of feeding stuffs and agricultural products was not motivated by a concern for some ultimate physiological truth but was dictated and supported by the economic needs and political power of agriculture. Equally important, their work was shaped by the dominant assumptions, and limited by the standard techniques, of German organic chemistry. For in the United States, as in Germany itself, agricultural chemistry was simply a specialized branch of organic chemistry. And no doctrine of German agricultural science was more sacrosanct than the assumption, held generally between the 1870s and 1900, that a diet balanced with a proper mixture of proteins, fats, carbohydrates, and inorganic salts would, irrespective of the source of protein, provide an adequate diet for men or animals.[1] This convenient belief was reinforced by a need to provide advice for agricultural constituencies; farmers did find that the feeding mixtures recommended by agricultural chemists increased milk yield and rate of growth. There was little incentive for the fraternity of agricultural chemists to investigate more precisely the constituents of foods which seemed completely adequate as sources of all the nutrients necessary for growth and maintenance. (Some nutrition workers did entertain a healthy skepticism toward these conventional ratios. C. S. Plumb, for example, remarked in 1890 that he had found a higher complement of nutrients—calculated according to accepted doctrine—in the feces of experimental animals than in food they had consumed.)[2]

Even had they wished to, even had they been generally skeptical of the traditional means of expressing food values, agricultural chemists before 1900 lacked the requisite tools for deepening their research. Analytical techniques were obviously inadequate. The analysis of proteins, for example, was exceedingly crude: quantities of protein in foodstuffs were estimated by multiplying the factor 6.25 times the amount of nitrogen obtained from a sample—though much of the nitrogen might have come from compounds unrelated to proteins.

Even the most sophisticated of American analysts had, moreover, been trained as organic chemists, and German organic chemistry had few connections with experimental physiology or pathology. Chemists performed few experiments with animals, while medical men and physiologists seldom received highly specialized chemical training. Certainly biologists and medical men had not accepted the assumption—natural to the chemist—that research should, if possible, be conducted with substances of known chemical composition and structure. Chemists, on the other hand, were relatively unfamiliar with the technique of using experimental animals to test the physiological activity of known chemical substances or to differentiate closely related compounds. As a group, chemists were comparatively unacquainted with the literature of clinical medicine. By the early years of this century, moreover, clinicians had become aware that a number of pathological conditions were related to dietary factors. Rickets, scurvy, and beriberi were definitely connected with diet. It was known, moreover, that comparatively small quantities of iodine and iron had significant effects in goiter and certain types of anemia.[3]

Nevertheless, the origins of the work which led Americans to the discovery of vitamin A came not through an interest in the deficiency diseases, as one might naturally suppose, but through an interest, on the one hand, in cattle feeding and, on the other, in the nutritional role of particular proteins and amino acids. The pioneer American vitamin work was performed not by medical men, but by organic chemists working at agricultural experiment stations.

Essential to the establishment of this line of research was an increasing sophistication in analytical chemistry and especially in our knowledge of the proteins. By 1906 a handful of dedicated protein chemists, Ritthausen, Fischer, Kossel in Germany, and Thomas B. Osborne in this country had shown that proteins of different origin differed widely, that their amino acid composition was far from uniform, and, finally, that these amino acids played specific roles in influencing human nutrition. The availability of purified proteins, such as those prepared by Osborne, constituted in itself something of a quantum jump in the study of nutrition, for their existence made possible, indeed implied, new types of experimental situations. In 1908, for example, a prominent Yale physiological chemist emphasized the "divergent chemical structure of individual proteins," and concluded that it was "obvious that a new standard of comparison is at hand, the suggestions it may offer to be tested by appropriate feeding experiments on man and animals."[4] It is out of this tradition of protein chemistry that F. G. Hopkins had in 1906 explicitly formulated the idea that certain—as yet unknown—accessory substances might be necessary for normal growth and maintenance. Though Hopkins was English, Americans too played a conspicuous role in this early work.[5]

Half a dozen years after Hopkins's theoretical conjecture, E. V. McCollum at the University of Wisconsin and L. B. Mendel and Thomas B. Osborne at the Connecticut Agricultural Experiment Station discovered almost simultaneously that a fat-soluble substance was necessary for the carrying on of normal life processes. The project at Wisconsin had begun before McCollum arrived, having had its origin in the skepticism of Stephen M. Babcock, one agricultural chemist who had never placed much confidence in the nutritive ratios so faithfully observed by a generation of farmers and chemists alike.[6] Babcock suggested that cows be fed a ration supposedly equal—at least in terms of the generally accepted balance of fat, carbohydrates, and protein—but derived from different plants. One group of cows was to be fed on wheat alone, a second only on corn, and a third on oats. It soon became clear that the animals reacted very differently to their diets: the cows fed on wheat did not thrive and were unable to bear live calves, while the corn-fed cows appeared to be perfectly normal.

How was this to be explained? An explanation had to be found, for the experiment's implications were of great significance to Wisconsin's dairy industry. Federal research funds were, as we have seen, doubled in 1906, and with new financial resources the Wisconsin Experiment Station sought to employ a chemist capable of isolating the substances in the grains responsible for their differing feeding characteristics. They were equally fortunate in finding a most promising young man, Elmer V. McCollum, an organic chemist trained at Yale's Sheffield Scientific School. Unlike most organic chemists, however, McCollum had taken a year's work in physiological chemistry—a fortuitous year, it should be noted, spent not because of a consuming interest in this comparatively new field of specialization but, on the contrary, because McCollum was unable after receiving his doctorate to find a suitable teaching position in organic chemistry. McCollum had, in addition, spent several months working as an assistant in Thomas Osborne's laboratory at the Connecticut Agricultural Experiment Station. Osborne was one of the world's leading authorities on protein chemistry and had for almost two decades been at work on the purification and analysis of plant proteins.[7]

Though somewhat unwilling to accept an appointment at a midwestern experiment station, in 1907 McCollum accepted the position offered by Wisconsin; unlike several other teaching offers, this professorship promised ample time for research.[8] Though unfamiliar with the literature of agricultural chemistry, McCollum soon realized that the traditional experiment station practice of studying metabolism in farm animals exclusively—a seeming necessity because of the need to ensure farm support in state legislatures—was simply impossible if one assumed the need to work with chemically known dietaries; small mammals would be far more suitable. After a thorough training in organic chemistry and a tour in Osborne's laboratory, McCollum had come to assume the necessity of working with substances of known chemical content, and these could hardly be made available in suffi- cient quantity to provide an adequate diet for a group of cows or pigs. Choosing the white rat as his experimental animal and taking advan- tage of Osborne's techniques for the preparation of proteins, he was able to begin work. McCollum had to keep the rats in his office and pay for materials and cages personally; the dean had qualms about farm supporters learning that their state's College of Agriculture was providing "board and room" for rats.

Osborne and Mendel were almost at the same time beginning feeding experiments with white rats, work supported by the Carnegie Institution of Washington and Connecticut Agricultural Experiment Station funds. Both laboratories sought to raise experimental animals on diets of known chemical make-up—not, of course, in the form of naturally occurring foods. Both laboratories failed and both concluded eventually that some previously unknown substance present in butter fat was necessary to growth. Both groups, however, found their research a difficult and lengthy procedure, partially because of the limitations of their training. McCollum, for example, recalled being so unfamiliar with medical literature that he did not become aware until 1913 that beriberi was connected with diet.[9] In a similar vein, Osborne wrote one summer to his vacationing coworker Mendel, bewailing the outbreak of an eye infection among one group of his experimental rats, asking his colleague's advice, and noting that he was treating the local infection with Argyrol![10] (Clinicians were, on the other hand, well aware of a connection between lesions of the eye and inadequate diet.) Yet physicians, often aware of a possible relation between diet and disease, were ill-prepared to undertake the chemical work necessary if a specific dietary factor was to be isolated. Nor were they as a group ready to think in such terms. Inhibited by the attractions of more fashionable etiological models, they found it difficult to believe that disease might be caused by the absence of some nutrient substance necessary in minute quantities.

It is impossible to understand the development of this work, as I hope to have suggested, without some knowledge of the status of American chemistry at the beginning of the twentieth century. A tra- dition of applied research had to be sharpened and deepened by an increase in the sophistication of technical means. The tradition of practical nutrition work, on the other hand, both at the Wisconsin and Connecticut Experiment Stations, had provided funds to make research facilities available and a context in which the traditional split between organic chemists and biologists tended to be counteracted.[11] Though this was a period of bold programmatic statements calling for the application of chemical and physical techniques to the traditional concerns of biology and medicine, this new synthesis was slow to develop because of the limitations imposed by the specialized training and values of the men involved. Certainly an appropriate context for such work did not yet exist within the medical schools and was not easily created. Yet agricultural research, despite its background of compromise and ambiguity, was at times able to provide just such an intellectually appropriate context.[12]

The story of hybrid corn has been told a number of times and the following pages are by no means intended to serve as a history of this innovation.[13] So far as I am aware, however, none of the available accounts adequately place the beginnings of hybrid corn investigation in the complete institutional and economic context which gave it birth. And this is unfortunate, for the origin of this research demonstrates rather clearly some interactions and parallels between structural economic change, technological innovation, and the institutional needs and disciplinary assumptions of the scientists and administrators involved.

As the University of Illinois is pleased to recall, scientists at Urbana originated the inbreeding work which was to lead four decades later to the first commercially successful hybrid corn. Why did the university's College of Agriculture and its dean, Eugene Davenport, undertake this work? The reasons, I think, lay in the nature of the state's maturing agricultural economy and in Davenport's relationship to that economy. In the 1890s the Illinois College of Agriculture was far from secure financially.[14] Hearings on appropriation bills were chronic academic crises and not surprisingly the dean's was a familiar face in Springfield. Thus research programs necessarily assumed a twofold aspect. The college employed scientific methods in the solution of specific economic problems and, in doing so, sought to strengthen and ensure the support of individual farmers and agricultural producers' associations throughout the state. It was only natural that the dean should count upon the sympathy of those who had benefited tangibly from the technological abilities of college scientists.

Since the early 1890s the university's College of Agriculture had sponsored attempts to improve corn varieties. Every farmer was familiar with the upgrading of domestic animals which had been brought about through careful breeding. Selection and crossing had brought about even more remarkable improvements in plants. European investigators, for example, had more than doubled the sugar content of sugar beets through the application of "careful scientific selection." Experiment station advocates pointed again and again to such enticing results. "There are no crops," a Minnesota scientist, for example, enthused, "but that can be gradually and materially improved as to yield and quality." Nothing beyond "careful selection" would, of course, be necessary.[15] Corn, however, was the key crop in Illinois and detailed and well-publicized chemical analyses performed at the Connecticut Agricultural Experiment Station had demonstrated that existing and well-established strains of American maize varied enormously in composition. Different varieties grown in different locations varied, for example, from eight to seventeen percent protein; similar variability was found in fat and carbohydrate composition.[16] It seemed clear enough to Dean Davenport and to his long-time friend and college agronomist P. G. Holden that prosperity for corn growers in an increasingly competitive market might well depend upon the availability of specialized strains of corn. "We can," as one Urbana agronomist promised in 1900, "have a high oil corn, high starch corn, and a high protein corn, just as we have developed the beef and dairy types of cattle and the light and draft types of horses, or as we have developed the per cent of sugar in the sugar beet."[17]

A specific impetus to this work came from the desire of the College of Agriculture to win the support of the state's largest farmers—men influential in agricultural producers' associations and in the state legislature as well. Large farmers like F. A. Warner of Sibley or E. D. Funk of Bloomington saw a profitable field for expansion in the sale of guaranteed strains of seed corn to farmers increasingly conscious of the need to increase the efficiency of their farm practice. At the same time that the Illinois inbreeding work was being undertaken on the college's experimental plots, agronomists P. G. Holden and later A. D. Shamel were helping to organize a seed-corn growers' association, publicizing its products, guaranteeing their reliability, even steering prospective customers in the direction of prominent seed-corn raisers and friends of the university like Warner and Funk. (The College of Agriculture was, indeed, so prominent in the organization of the seed-corn association that Dean Davenport feared these policies might lead to criticism.)[18] In exchange, the influential men who were turning their lands to the production of seed corn provided needed political support. And the production of seed corn would, of course, always be the province of the large producer, the man with hundreds, if not thousands, of acres in cultivation. Through personal friendships and shared attitudes, moreover, the larger producers were the natural friends and supporters of the university. Small farmers were, on the whole, less educated and had neither the capital nor the attitudes necessary for their immediate acceptance of an innovation such as the cultivation of specialized commercial seed corn.[19]

Corn-breeding work at Illinois was thus closely related to the growing scale and complexity of the state's agricultural economy. And growing complexity and specialization, of course, implied a growing dependence upon the College of Agriculture's technological capabilities. The relationship of the college to the would-be seed-corn growers was similar to that which it sought to maintain with other specialized groups—with dairymen, horticulturists, implement dealers, bankers, agricultural processors. In 1900, for example, College of Agriculture authorities arranged for a joint meeting of the Illinois Corn Growers, Grain Dealers, and Seed Corn Breeders; a key point in their local arrangements was a plan to have toasts offered at the banquet by the presidents of the Chicago and St. Louis boards of trade and the head of the "glucose trust."[20] Each of these groups could benefit from a quid pro quo with the College of Agriculture; each was a potential source of support for research and development.

It might be objected at this point that the inbreeding work done at Illinois was simply a crude beginning, one which led to the development of hybrid corn only by the most circuitous of paths. One might indeed argue that this beginning was a peculiarly misguided one at that. The aim of men like Holden and chemist C. G. Hopkins, was not hybridization, a procedure considered risky and unreliable, but the creation of merchantable specialized pure lines of corn. ("Crossing," Holden wrote in 1900, "nine times out of ten . . . results in securing a type of poorer quality. It is a risky business and generally proves unsatisfactory.")[21] They hoped to develop reliable guaranteed strains —like the Holstein-Fresian or other registered breeds of domestic cattle. This goal was to be attained through careful selection, selection guided by the analyses of Hopkins's chemical laboratory.[22] Hence the cul-de-sac which the Illinois workers soon reached: selection and inbreeding for a character such as high protein content meant the inevitable appearance of unproductive strains. The lack of vigor and lower yields of these lines seemed to mean failure; the college's specialized strains would never, apparently, become commercially feasible.

The actual creation and commercial introduction of hybrid seed corn did not take place in Illinois. The men associated with the crystallization of the work begun at Urbana were George Shull of the Carnegie Institution's Station for Experimental Evolution at Cold Spring

Harbor, New York, and Edward East and his student Donald Jones at the Connecticut Agricultural Experiment Station. It was Shull's work particularly and his Mendelian explanation of the well-established fact of hybrid vigor which rationalized the procedure and inspired the culminating work of East and Jones.[23] (And even then, of course, there was a lag of twenty years before hybrid corn was at all widely accepted by American farmers.) Perhaps, it might be argued, the economic context in which the Illinois College of Agriculture functioned merely posed a technological problem which, because of this economy's own importunities, could not be solved at Champaign. Perhaps a somewhat different context was needed—one in which the techniques and attitudes of world science rather than the needs of the corn grower shaped research designs. Perhaps such problem-bound research tends to be sterile, dependent ultimately upon the tools and insights made available by academic science.

Undoubtedly, there is a good deal of truth to this widely held opinion. But without elaboration it is a somewhat simplistic truth. The line between science pure and science applied is a tenuous one. Applied, empirical experimentation had, for example, demonstrated quite clearly the phenomenon of hybrid vigor by 1900 and as well the frustrating loss of vigor which seemed inevitably to accompany selection for particular characteristics. The economic needs which helped shape research policies at Urbana were, moreover, hardly unique, but similar to those encouraging technological innovation in a number of other states. Thus still another strand in the development of hybrid corn can be traced to economically oriented research, to New Haven and the Connecticut Agricultural Experiment Station. It will be recalled that the analyses of corn which influenced Dean Davenport and the Illinois College of Agriculture in their search for spcialized strains of maize were performed at New Haven. Even more directly, Director E. H. Jenkins of the Connecticut Station had hired Edward East from the University of Illinois in 1905 because of East's participation in their well-known inbreeding work and with the assumption that he would continue this research in Connecticut, Jenkins had stated repeatedly since the 1889s, both in private correspondence and in published arguments, the need for Connecticut agriculture to specialize in such fields as dairying and horticulture, integrating itself more intimately with nearby urban areas. If the eastern farmer was successfully to compete with the rich lands of the West, he must produce the largest possible quantity of feed per acre. Hence his interest in improved strains of corn—and hence the hiring of East. By the growing season of 1909, only a year after Shull and East had clarified their theoretical views of hybridization, Jenkins had already set a large number of cooperating Connecticut farmers to work in planting single-hybrid crosses.[24] (And Connecticut was only one among a number of state agricultural colleges and experiment stations working in the immediately post-Mendelian years between 1900 and 1908 with inbreeding and crossbreeding of corn.

George Shull, it must be confessed, however, whose insights were central to the development of commercial hybrid corn, came to the problem from an essentially academic background, though he had been employed for several years by the Department of Agriculture's Bureau of Plant Industry. Yet it might be noted in conclusion that Shull's salary was paid by the Carnegie Institution of Washington. It would not be unreasonable to suggest some connection between this particular benevolence of the Scottish iron maker and the rapidly maturing economy dramatized in Carnegie's own career (though this sort of relationship is, of course, of a more general kind and does not exhibit quite the same organic parallelism and interaction between patterns of economic development and the evocation of technological innovation as does the situation in Illinois or Connecticut).

The relation of experiment station and agricultural college to the surrounding society, though a complex and in some ways fertile one, did have a number of disadvantages. Most obvious, of course, was the need to produce results, to think not only in terms of the internal dimensions of a scientific problem, but of the effect its solution might have upon the agricultural community. Thus the dead end reached in the Illinois corn-breeding work; poor yields in inbred lines meant failure, for their goal was defined not in terms of understanding the nature of heredity, but of producing a reliable, merchantable product. This desire of the experiment stations to produce such merchantable results, often the product of a real commitment to the needs of the agricultural population, sometimes led to premature and unwarranted announcements of research findings and to the waste of both time and money in the attempt to find answers to inappropriate questions.[25] Perhaps most unfortunately, it led in some cases to the sacrifice of time and energy by men of talent in projects either trivial or misguided. Ultimately, however, and despite such compromising circumstances, the state universities did much to help elaborate and rationalize the economic structure of American agriculture and in doing so strengthened not only the nation's economy but in proportion their own ability to function as secure contexts for research and teaching of an inevitably more and more advanced character. Perhaps it is in this relationship that we can see most clearly the ultimate interdependence of pure and applied science in the case of hybrid corn.

Once created, the agricultural colleges and experiment stations were guided by institutional needs. Staff members needed support for research and salaries and relief from physically exhausting teaching and extension duties. Given the economic and political structure of most American states the only way in which these goals could be achieved was through integrating the work of the institution with the economic needs of the community. This was a situation which from the scientist's point of view was not always ideal, but one which could, in some states, result in a productive context for the application of science and technology to the problems of agriculture—and, beyond this, contribute to the definition and solution of more fundamental scientific problems. As we saw in the case of vitamin A, contextual pressures helped overcome the intellectual rigidities of particular disciplines and thus create new research options.

12

The Social Environment of Scientific Innovation: Factors in the Development of Genetics in the United States

Americans played an extraordinarily important role in the formative period of modern genetics—the years immediately following 1900. By the First World War this new subdiscipline was being pursued at least as successfully in the United States as in any other country. And this is not simply a nationalistically tinged impression. It was a circumstance agreed upon by contemporary biologists and is confirmed by a study of the references in any monograph on heredity written in the first two decades of this century. T. H. Morgan's *The Mechanism of Mendelian Heredity*, for example, published in 1915, lists a bibliography of 330 items, of which 201 are verifiably American in authorship.[1] Morgan, it must be conceded, was an American, and the most prominent champion of what was then still a somewhat idiosyncratic cytological approach. Other works, however, tend to confirm the impression garnered from Morgan's bibliography. A check, for example, of the bibliography in William Bateson's 1913 edition of *Mendel's Principles of Heredity* shows that 108 of the 323 publications listed were of American authorship—and this despite the author's English nationality and well-known skepticism toward the interpretations of Morgan and his "Drosophilites."[2]

Why did American biologists do so well in this new field? Or, perhaps more precisely, how could they have done so well? Throughout the nineteenth century the United States occupied a provincial place in world science. Even in the early part of the twentieth century it

196

is difficult to find parallels in other disciplines or subdisciplines, other fields in which Americans produced not merely one or two men of real importance, but a host of thorough, well-trained, and representative workers.

National bias is one of the chronic ills associated with the writing of the history of science. It encourages provincialism and partiality, leads to inaccuracy, to bitter and undignified squabbles. The baleful influence of nationalism is only exacerbated by the scientist's concern for priority, a concern mirrored in the writing of many historians of science. There are, however, certain compensations in studying science in a particular nation. Occasionally, for example, such studies underline disproportionate and seemingly anomalous instances of extraordinary scientific productivity. Social values, patterns of economic development, individual genius, educational innovation, have all been used to explain the scientific prominence of particular countries at particular times. Like many other atypical phenomena, these efflorescences of creativity can be made to provide insight into the normal social functions which necessarily underlie scientific as all other human endeavors. Hence the natural interest of any student of the social underpinnings of science in a case study such as that represented by the formative years of genetics in this country.

The intellectual interest of the problem inherent in explaining American achievement in genetics is sharpened, moreover, by the manner in which modern genetics can—with more accuracy than is usual in such cases—be said to have begun at a specific date. This date is 1900, the year of the rediscovery of Mendel's laws. Certainly roots of interest and research accomplishment extend much further back in time; the dramatic and illuminating quality of the Mendelian insights had the effect, however, of catalyzing interest in heredity in very broad segments of the scientific community.[3] The nature of these reactions was necessarily determined by the intellectual and institutional configuration of this scientific community's various components. Thus a study of the varying reactions to the same ideas at the same time should indicate something of the character of America's scientific establishment at the beginning of the present century.

There were, I think, three potential contexts in which genetic research might have been expected to develop. These were medicine, plant and animal breeding, and—finally—university departments of biology. In each there had been a good deal of interest in problems of heredity before 1900; in each there was widespread interest in the implications of the Mendelian principles. Yet each provided quite different conditions for the pursuit of research based on these new insights.

In some ways the tradition of support for work in heredity was strongest in the area of animal and plant breeding. The connection between the necessities of an agriculture increasingly aware of the need to rationalize production and the political power of this constituency had, as we have seen, resulted by the late 1870s and 1880s in state and in 1887 in federal subventions to the states for research in agriculture.[4] By the 1890s every state had at least one agricultural experiment station and in many of these breeding work was being actively pursued. In addition, countless amateurs, gentlemen farmers, businessmen, physicians—even clergymen—pursued more or less coherent breeding experiments.

Careful breeders had since the eighteenth century been perfecting animal and plant types. And in such hands economically profitable introductions were regularly perfected—through an empirical system of intuitive selection and judicious inbreeding and outbreeding. The work of the Vilmorins, for example, in increasing the sugar content of the sugar beet had helped create an important agricultural industry in France and Germany. Such tangible results did much to encourage experimental breeding in the United States. At the same time, however, they helped to create an unfortunate sense of confidence, one which seemed to underwrite the ultimate adequacy of the empirical methods which led to these accomplishments. As a pioneer agricultural scientist put it in 1879, there was little opportunity for originality in writing a treatise on breeding, "an art that is almost exclusively based upon the experience of practical men."[5] The sum total of knowledge in this field, aside from the understanding of particular strains and qualities, could probably be expressed in the two phrases "breed from the best" and "like begets like." As an Alabamian wrote in 1884: "With this principle [that is, that like begets like] . . . as a guide, the stock-breeder need only exercise a sound judgment, guided by a close and careful observation to effect the most marked improvement in the character and type of his stock, and perpetuate his improvement when once made."[6] This was a doctrine appealing to farmers, to legislators and administrators, and, indeed, to the scientists themselves.

Oriented, moreover, toward the needs and problems of their agricultural constituency, breeders at agricultural colleges and experiment stations attempted to elucidate research problems formulated by the farmer's needs and often in terms of the farmer's beliefs. How, for example, could one determine a bull's potency from his external appearance? What was the influence of previous impregnations upon subsequent matings? Would dehorning of bulls affect their potency? George Morrow at the University of Illinois, for example, spent a good deal of time in the 1880s testing the validity of traditional rural beliefs.

By semicastrating a male pig, in one characteristic experiment, he attempted to test the ancient theory that semen from the right testicle produced male offspring and that from the left, female.[7] The bulk of the work undertaken was, of course, selection—that is, "breeding from the best." Undoubtedly such work was performed more carefully—by the 1890s often with the help of chemical analysis in plant-breeding—at agricultural colleges and experiment stations, but in no essential differently from that of the experienced seedsman or stock raiser. As late as 1902, after two decades of such experimentation, A. C. True, director of the Department of Agriculture's Office of Experiment Stations, could write that "almost all the work thus far by the experiment stations has been empirical in character. There is at present no satisfactory manual on the breeding of animals written from a scientific standpoint, and I am informed that the data for such a treatise are not available."[8] When, in 1906, the federal government granted $15,000 a year to each state for original scientific investigations relating to the problems of agriculture, almost none of the agricultural colleges and experiment stations was prepared to undertake work of this kind in breeding. Even those institutions active in such research had always conceived of it as simply that—efforts to produce better-tasting, hardier, or more rapidly maturing varieties of plants and animals. By 1900, then, the needs of American agriculture had created an institutionally secure—if, in a sense, intellectually compromising—context for the pursuit of studies in heredity.

Physicians too were affected by the demands which society made upon their profession. The primary role of the American doctor, as both he and his society saw it, lay in caring for the sick. Yet a part of his task was to provide explanations, to reduce uncertainty and the fear of sickness and death to an understandable and, in that sense, comforting system. Few physicians were able to confess their inability to explain the causes of disease or to guarantee its cure. Accepting ignorance and articulating it was in the nineteenth century the intellectual indulgence of some academics and a constitutionally cynical minority among clinicians. And ideas of heredity were particularly murky, peculiarly difficult to test—and tenaciously held.

As late as the beginning of the present century the physician's knowledge concerning heredity was essentially speculative, his data limited largely to random clinical observations and to a comparative handful of pedigree studies. Like the agricultural scientist, moreover, the physician interested in heredity was handicapped by a false sense of knowledge. As one medical writer put it in 1869, the homely phrase "like begets like" is "for the existing state of science an ultimate fact."[9] Medical theory traditionally assumed that much disease was hereditary in origin and in the nineteenth century asylum statistics, studies in consanguineous marriages, clinical observations of families with marked hereditary anomalies—all, as we have seen, seemed to prove with scientific impersonality that sickness did beget sickness, deformity did breed deformity.[10]

In any case, hereditarian thought in medical circles was closely tied to a nexus of social needs and interests, while the profession itself had yet to provide any institutionalized support or encouragement for the investigation of such questions. In only a handful of the very best medical schools and then only in traditionally defined areas—anatomy, for example—was there either provision for or expectation of investigation by faculty members.[11] In only a small proportion of cases was medical school appointment or promotion based primarily on research and publication.

The university provided a radically different context. By 1900 higher education in the biological sciences had made a firm beginning in the United States. American universities were benefiting for the first time from the nation's economic growth; men of means were beginning to help endow and support higher education, and state legislatures with more income at their disposal were becoming increasingly liberal in their provision for state universities. But in only a handful of institutions had true graduate education become a reality. At Johns Hopkins, at Columbia, at Chicago, Harvard, and Pennsylvania, for example, the would-be biologist could acquire a truly professional graduate education (although in many fields a European sojourn was still considered advisable). And these pioneer graduate programs were staffed and inspired by men who considered themselves part of the world of international science, men whose values and hence aspirations were determined largely by those of their disciplinary peers both in Europe and the United States. The work of these investigators would inevitably be shaped, not by the needs of an economic interest group, not by the social necessities of the physician's role, but by the forms and values of the several biological disciplines. Their task was not to answer questions but to publish papers. If these papers were to be acceptable—and this, of course, was ultimately the only road to recognition by one's scientific peers—they must contribute to an area already defined by a substantial body of verified knowledge and accepted technique. Neither the observations and gratuitous explanations of the clinician nor the empirical findings of the agricultural breeder were ordinarily relevant.

Academic biology had, moreover, been vitally concerned with a number of areas which would, after 1900, become a source of ideas, techniques—and men—central to the development of modern genetics.

Cytology and experimental embryology had, by the 1890s, pointed with some clarity toward the nature of the mechanisms which might explain heredity. Both fields had grown through half a century of sustained and increasingly refined work; new contributions would have to be evaluated in terms of methods and data already accumulated. It was not that the canon of accepted research designs necessarily snuffed out speculation—Weismann, for example, infuriated many of his methodical contemporaries with what seemed to be gratuitous philosophizing[12]—but that generally accepted criteria of knowledge and the means for its validation and reproduction had come into being. Thus, within the context of academic biology, Darwinism had been substantially transmuted from a philosophical problem into a stimulus toward statistical, cytological, and embryological studies. (E. B. Wilson, for example, in the introduction to the first edition of his magisterial *Cell in Development and Inheritance,* describes the origin of his synthesis in an attempt "to trace the steps by which the problems of evolution have been reduced to the problems of the cell.")[13] As was not the case with the physician attempting to explore disease causation, or the breeder concerned with maturation in hogs, the academic biologist assumed that heredity would eventually have to be reduced to microscopic material mechanisms. And these would necessarily reside in the cell. By 1900 the work of two generations of biologists had provided a relatively clear understanding of the mechanics of reduction division. It is hardly surprising that soon after 1900 the connection should be made between these intracellular phenomena and the Mendelian laws.[14]

The Mendelian revolution of 1900 affected all three potential research areas. Each the product of a particular configuration of ideas and institutions reacted, of course, quite differently and at different rates of speed.

The medical profession responded, on the whole, comparatively slowly and then in a traditional fashion. It sought to utilize these new, prestigious, and only partially understood ideas to explain the age-old problems to which society demanded solutions; Mendelian factors now explained how like begat like. But the concerns and responsibilities of the profession had not changed. Not surprisingly, mental retardation and genius, insanity and criminality, tuberculosis, cancer, and alcoholism, as well as scores of other conditions were soon explained by the presence or absence of a single Mendelian factor. Such excesses might well have been expected, for they were solutions—and satisfyingly scientific ones at that—to social problems so pressing that they could not be avoided. And these ideas were inherently appealing. Perhaps with this new knowledge it might be possible to change man himself, to ordain a new and superior race. Certainly Mendelianism might explain the seemingly ineradicable inferiority of racial groups unfamiliar to Americans and seemingly inimical to American ways of life.[15] In the minds of many social thinkers, the teachings of Mendel and Weismann justified and exacerbated already pessimistic attitudes toward the role of race and heredity in the etiology of social problems.

Paradoxically, however, the rather melodramatic pessimism so characteristic of hereditarian social thinkers at the turn of the century often contained an optimistic, even utopian quality. Though the prospects for the race might at the moment appear bleak, the reasons for its decline were understood; that science which explained the logic of racial degeneracy might ultimately guide the medical and governmental reforms necessary to reverse this trend. During the first decades of this century, it must be recalled, an understanding of Mendel's principle of segregation was credential sufficient for certification as an expert on heredity.

Not only within the medical profession but also in the minds of most students of human genetics, social and even utopian aspects were foremost. Hence the vogue of eugenics, begun as a movement before 1900, but increasing enormously in influence during the first two decades of this century.[16] Faith in the new knowledge of heredity as a tool for social engineering was not limited to the incompletely educated or the obsessive. Even Karl Pearson, for example, in spite of his mathematical sophistication, felt able to say as late as 1912 that a few trained field workers could easily solve the problem of mental retardation. William Bateson, to cite another example, like Galton, believed that the ultimate possibilities of racial betterment were very real. And in the general climate of unquestioning confidence so characteristic of hereditarian thought in the early years of this century, the comparatively cautious hopes of such scientists were soon outstripped by their less knowledgeable fellow eugenicists. It was such misplaced enthusiasm, coupled, of course, with the inherent difficulties of using man as a research animal, which made human genetics an object of increasing suspicion in academic circles. "We are," as Harvard geneticist William Castle put it in 1924, "scarcely as yet in a position to do more than make ourselves ridiculous in this matter. We are no more in a position to control eugenics than the tides of the ocean." Such suspicions were deepened and confirmed by the increasingly ominous manner in which eugenics became connected in the 1920s with conservative social thought and in the 1930s with the racist doctrines and practices of Hitler's Germany.[17]

Certainly many academic biologists had become deeply involved with the eugenics movement.[18] As was not the case, however, with many of the physician-eugenicists, university biologists had necessarily to maintain an awareness of the limitations in their knowledge. The excesses of what might be called premature Mendelism in the years before the First World War seemed not only to indicate the inherent difficulty of studying human genetics, but at the same time left a collective skepticism, a kind of intellectual bad taste, in the profession, especially among younger, research-oriented men. Thus human genetics, the natural field of research for the physician, never quite recovered from the excesses of eugenics and the racism which so frequently accompanied it; not until the past two decades have American medical schools become generally enthusiastic about true research programs in genetics.[19]

The new insights into heredity which we associate with the names of Mendel and Weismann affected medical thought, however, in broad and lasting and not always very apparent ways. Despite the rather simplistic explanations of the first years of the century, i.e., the attribution of tuberculosis or alcoholism to a single Mendelian character, medical men became accustomed to connecting disease and constitutional factors with specific, concrete heredity carriers. For better or worse, the concept of diathesis, the medical profession's expression of its traditional emphasis on flexible constitutional factors, suffered a growing eclipse in formal medical thought; etiological designs tended to become increasingly "hard" and reductionist.[20] Similarly, the age-old assumption of the heritability of acquired characteristics succumbed to Mendelism; it was not until the dramatic impact of the Mendelian laws that the medical profession began at all generally to accept the idea that acquired characteristics might not be transmitted to future generations. This was, of course, a gradual and selective process. "Weismannism" could not be said to have penetrated to the medical profession as a whole until the time of the First World War. It seemed almost perverse to deny that diseased and damaged tissues could somehow exert a malevolent influence in the reproductive process. In socially sensitive conditions, moreover, physicians were particularly slow in rejecting the idea that one generation's sins could be visited upon its progeny. Thus, for example, well into the 1920s, elaborate speculative pathologies explained how a mother's alcoholism might affect the fetus or ovum.[21]

The reaction to the Mendelian insights among plant and animal breeders illuminates a situation far more complex. The existence of jobs and research support in agricultural colleges and experiment stations meant that each of these institutions was a potential nexus for the reception of the new genetics, for its dissemination, and—in some cases, at least—for research based on these new concepts. The better

state universities, for example, would by the time of the First World
War hire only men with doctorates to guide experimental breeding
programs. Thus, almost inevitably, they appointed scholars oriented
toward academic values and with specialized laboratory training, men
who in many cases had small knowledge and in some cases little
sympathy for the problems of their agricultural constituency. At the
University of Wisconsin, for example, a chair in "experimental breeding"—forerunner of the university's present Department of Genetics
(which, it might be noted, is still in the College of Agriculture)—was
not established until 1910. When filled, however, it was with a Har-
vard-trained scientist, L. J. Cole. Cole, who had worked for a time at
the Rhode Island Agricultural Experiment Station, was never to be
more than a representative geneticist.[22] Yet almost from the day he
reached Madison, Cole began teaching not only Mendelism, but the
other more recent insights which were already becoming a part of the
new discipline of genetics. As early as 1911 he wrote to T. H. Morgan
asking for a culture of his mutant flies to use in students' laboratory
exercises. Even more significant was the manner in which a man like
Cole served as a cultural intermediary, offering advice and suggestions
to biologists at other colleges and universities within Wisconsin's
sphere of influence. After breeding several generations of mutant
drosophila, Cole dispatched cultures to colleagues at Beloit, Illinois,
Iowa State, and North Dakota.[23] A tracing of the path followed by
Morgan's fruit flies serves, indeed, as a kind of schematic diagram
illustrating the pattern in which new knowledge and techniques were
diffused—from the East Coast, that is, to regional centers, thence to
smaller institutions tributary to these larger regional centers. And in
this network of ideas and knowledge the state universities and experiment stations played an important role.

These institutions, on the other hand, and of course their genetics
programs, were often handicapped by the demands of the very farm
constituency which provided their original support. Agricultural
scientists could rarely avoid working with domestic animals—while it
seemed clear enough to the well-trained men among them that such
animals with their long reproductive cycles were simply not suited to
many kinds of genetic research. Cytology and biochemistry had little
place in the world of agricultural research, except in traditionally
accepted areas such as plant pathology and nutrition. The introduction of such work in new contexts always had to be done in fear of rural
criticism for being excessively abstract and impractical.

It was clear, however, especially after the passage of the Adams Act
in 1906, that there were more positions for "breeders" than there could
possibly be well-trained scientists to fill them. At the same time,

moreover, teaching positions in the major universities and better liberal arts colleges were few, for beginners poorly paid and filled with lengthy hours of teaching. Nevertheless, when such conditions drove well-trained scientists into accepting positions in agricultural colleges and experiment stations, they often found the environment unsympathetic. They had to lecture to farm groups, to design their research programs in response to the needs of these same farmers, and in their classroom hours to spend precious time dispelling ancient notions of heredity and putting in their place the simplest of biological truths.[24] A. F. Blakeslee's early career represents a case in point. One of W. G. Farlow and Roland Thaxter's most promising students in mycology at Harvard, Blakeslee found it almost impossible to locate an appropriate position in a liberal arts college or university, upon returning from a Carnegie-endowed postdoctoral sojourn in Europe. He finally accepted a post at the Connecticut Agricultural College at Storrs, then a remote farm school at which doctorates were as scarce as freethinkers. For the next half-dozen years, Blakeslee taught long hours and as a research area worked on modes of selection for egg production in chickens and milk production in cows. "Agricultural colleges," as a friend of Blakeslee's put it, "as a rule would shy at a man of your attainments. No money in it. Your zygospores are no good to eat."[25]

Even the most devoted lay supporters of scientific research in agriculture had an ingrained suspicion of abstract research and what they often conceived to be its egocentric and, in a sense, antisocial practitioners. James Wilson, Secretary of Agriculture under Presidents McKinley, Roosevelt, and Taft and renowned as a leader in the development of the Department's scientific bureaus, constantly reassured agricultural correspondents that the Department pursued no abstract work; its scientists were devoted unanimously to the interests of the man who worked with his coat off in the fields. Similarly, W. D. Hoard of Wisconsin, one of the state university's firmest political supporters and publisher of an influential farm weekly, *Hoard's Dairyman*, was severely critical of anything smacking of the abstract and impractical. He wrote indignantly to Cole, for example, when the professor proposed to collect data on the pedigree of freemartins. This was a useless and arbitrary whim, Hoard complained; it was the professor's duty to study more practical problems, as, for example, the external evidences of potency in bulls.[26] Inevitably, the economic context within which the experiment station breeder worked turned him into a lobbyist and publicist. Money for research had often to be torn from the grasp of a reluctant legislature, and scientists wishing to continue their work had no choice but to convince men of influence that new ideas could, with a modicum of support, be turned to practical account. Thus the work of Mendel and DeVries—as the work of Luther Burbank or the Vilmorins in the nineteenth century—was immediately fashioned into arguments for the support of science and scientific research. Inevitably these arguments were oversold. The claims of Mendelism fell somewhat flat when it became apparent that "scientific breeders" produced in practice results no more impressive than those which practical men had reached without the benefit of intellectual apparatus other than a sharp eye and a willingness to work.[27]

Yet despite such embarrassments, the more enterprising among research-oriented college and station leaders were able to utilize their locus of institutional security to support research programs of constantly increasing quality. As early as 1906, for example, Liberty Hyde Bailey at Cornell wrote in search of a man skilled in cytology and physiology to head a program in breeding. Officials in the Office of Experiment Stations in Washington similarly used their administrative influence to raise research standards at state agricultural colleges and experiment stations. Within a few years of T. H. Morgan's first drosophila publications, for example, Office of Experiment Station administrators were urging state directors and deans to turn to the Morgan group at Columbia in their search for men to conduct breeding programs.[28] Later in the century, not surprisingly, in the stronger state universities, distinguished genetics departments could develop upon the institutional base established by these economically oriented and at times short-sighted agricultural breeding programs.

There were other ways, as well, in which agricultural research worked to foster American genetics. State and federal research programs provided comparatively well-paid postgraduate and graduate research training at a time when financial support for such training was almost nonexistent. Men later to make their reputations in more abstract work often began their research careers in this somewhat compromising context of economic need and legislative subvention.

It would seem clear enough, however, that in the first decades of this century there was no counterpart in agricultural research, certainly not in American medical institutions, to the significance of the work accomplished by Morgan and his "Columbia group." Their cytological approach to the explanation of breeding experiments suggested the mechanism and ultimately explained the anomalies which seemed to mar the uniformity (and in some minds to impair the plausibility) of the Mendelian laws. "Cytology," as T. H. Morgan phrased it in an early paper, "furnishes the mechanism that the experimental evidence demands."[29] Even more important—or so it would seem with the benefit of mid-twentieth-century hindsight—was the role of the cytologists in unifying the diverse strands of breeding experiment and cytology, thus creating in the cell a new nexus for the investigation of heredity—and implicitly a new discipline. It constituted no great shift in interest, if indeed a shift at all, for men working in experimental embryology or the mechanisms of cell division and sex determination to turn to the insights of Mendel and apply them in a revealing new context.

The leadership of academic zoologists, embryologists, and cytologists in the new-model genetics was inevitable. It was, similarly, no accident that Columbia University assumed the lead in this fledgling discipline. For at the beginning of the twentieth century, Columbia was easily the strongest of American universities in cytology. With E. B. Wilson and T. H. Morgan as senior men, Columbia offered rigorous training in a traditionally Germanic and exacting field.

In 1902 two Columbia graduate students, Walter Sutton in zoology and W. A. Cannon in botany, both suggested that the behavior of the chromosomes during reduction division might provide a mechanism explaining the segregation of the putative Mendelian factors. Their individual perspicacity, of course, led these particular young men to this conclusion. But their working at Columbia might only have been expected. Sutton, for example, was a Kansas farm boy deeply influenced by C. E. McClung, who at that time taught at the University of Kansas; it was only natural that McClung should have advised Sutton to attend Columbia when the young man decided to continue his cytological training.[30]

Our original problem, of course, still remains unsolved. Why did so many Americans do so well in genetics? Why was there a Columbia group at all, with its hard-working, imaginative, and well-trained young men? Let me, in this connection, return for a moment to our analysis of the bibliography in Morgan's *Mechanism of Mendelian Heredity*—to the statistics with which we began this discussion—and pursue them a bit farther.

Fifty-two separate first authors contributed to the 201 items of American authorship. All but five of these men had earned the doctorate; one possessed a medical degree. Significantly, however, only one of these investigators held a European doctorate and only a few had studied extensively in Europe. Seven of the 51 were women, all but one of whom held a doctor's degree. Of the 46 earned American doctorates, 15 had been granted by Columbia, 9 by Harvard, 8 by Chicago, 3 each by Bryn Mawr and Johns Hopkins, and 2 by Pennsylvania. Clark, Missouri, Nebraska, Kansas, Michigan, and Illinois had each granted one.[31]

The lesson implicit in these simple figures is, I think, obvious. America had, by 1914, been able to train and employ a generation of academic biologists. In 1876, when The Johns Hopkins University opened its doors, the United States offered for all practical purposes no graduate training in the biological sciences. By 1915, when Morgan's synthesis appeared, he was able to cite the writings of some four dozen American scientists, all trained essentially in the United States. (Many of their teachers, of course, had European training.)[32] This is certainly a remarkable development—the creation of a self-reproducing group of academicians within one generation. The pattern of distribution of the earned doctorates illustrates as well the manner in which the development of graduate education was becoming a truly national phenomenon. Though a few Eastern institutions had awarded the lion's share of the doctorates, the inclusion of Kansas, Nebraska, Missouri, Illinois, and Michigan indicates the increasingly general diffusion of new modes in education. The University of Chicago, third on our list of degree-granting institutions with eight, had, indeed, not even come into existence when Johns Hopkins was founded. Even more striking, as indicating the national character of this upgrading of American higher education, is the manner in which the holders of doctorates on our list were scattered through out the country, colonizing a far greater number of institutions than those which had originally granted their degrees.[33] The relatively high proportion of women among the Americans cited by Morgan, as well as the three doctorates awarded by Bryn Mawr, symbolizes the manner in which American society was making higher education available to increasingly large numbers.

It would indeed seem likely that a fundamental reason for Americans having done so well in genetics was the very number of Americans exposed to the opportunity of performing such work. But why genetics particularly? Perhaps this was a function of the prominence of these new developments (and their antecedents in botany, cytology, and experimental embryology) at the very period during which Americans could for the first time in relatively large numbers take advantage of opportunities for higher education. It was a field as well which drew for its acolytes upon those Americans still fascinated by an endemic romantic interest in nature—an interest invigorated and in some ways intensified by the impact of Darwinism.

All these developments must, of course, be understood as having parallels in the maturation of the nation's economy. Graduate education had to be underwritten; it could not be managed on the sketchy financing which sufficed for most collegiate programs throughout the nineteenth century. The number of students able to afford the years of financially unrewarding graduate training (small though it was in proportion to the total population) was, of course, related directly as well to the increasing complexity and productivity of the economy generally. Perhaps the prominence of Americans in genetics was an incident similar to their country's participation in the First World War, both symbolizing the emergence of the United States as a modern technological society.

We have not, it must be confessed in conclusion, answered finally the question which began this discussion: why did Americans play so prominent a role in the new discipline of genetics? Perhaps one can never provide definitive answers to such questions; chance and individual abilities play too great a role in determining precise patterns of innovation. I have sought, instead, to outline some of the reasons why it was *possible* for Americans to have accomplished so much in this new field, not why particular men accomplished particular things.

More generally still, I have sought to emphasize the need for studying the total circumstances surrounding the scientific investigator as a necessary preliminary to a full understanding of his work. The scientist is not only an individual but a member of society generally and of a specific learned discipline. Each of the potential research contexts we have discussed—agricultural institutions, medicine, the universities—provided a quite different scientific environment. Each presented a characteristic texture, a mosaic of the social, economic, and institutional factors which ordered the roles and expectations of the men functioning within them. At the same time, however, the scientist's conception of his task was shaped by the techniques, the ideas, the values and aspirations which education in a particular discipline had instilled in him. The sum of scientific achievement in any one field is clearly shaped by the interaction of external circumstances (the manner in which society supports work in this field) and the scientists's personal, internal aspirations (especially the role of his discipline in shaping a particular research orientation). This is no more than a truism, but a truism too often ignored by historians of science (while general historians tend to ignore science and its cultural implications). If we are to uncover patterns of historical interaction between scientific ideas and institutions and the society in which they existed, we must resign ourselves to a quest for the complex and the ambiguous. Yet this is hardly a cause for despair; for only such difficult quests are worth the undertaking.

Notes

Introduction

1. Physicians constitute a distinct—and, in terms of numbers, far more numerous —group whose institutional position dictates a special relationship to the ideas and prestige of science. Theories of disease causation and treatment have always served to legitimate the physician in the performance of his necessary healing tasks.

2. An excellent place for the prospective inquirer to begin the study of the history of the relationship between science and religion in America is James Ward Smith and A. Leland Jamison, eds., *Religion in American Life*, Princeton Studies in American Civilization, no. 5, vol. 4, *A Critical Bibliography of Religion in America*, by Nelson R. Burr et al. (Princeton, N.J., 1961). See the section "Theology and Modern Sciences," pp. 1043–1109. (This book is bound in two separate volumes, with continuous pagination to 1219 pages and separate index.)

3. Although science, or the idea of science, unquestionably played a liberating role in the social philosophy of America's revolutionary generation, and throughout the nineteenth century for at least some Americans, it was only gradually in the course of the century that science as an emotionally meaningful value came to be accepted outside of a relatively small intellectual elite. Even in the age of Jefferson, and among the more educated classes, it seems questionable how genuinely "popular" science may have been. John C. Greene, "Science and the Public in the Age of Jefferson," *Isis* 39 (1958): 13–25. For a study of the place of science in the world of Jefferson and his immediate circle, see Daniel J. Boorstin, *The Lost World of Thomas Jefferson* (Boston, 1960).

4. Josiah Strong, *Our Country. Its Possible Future in Its Present Crisis*, rev. ed. (New York, [ca. 1891]), p. 121. See also, in this connection, Arthur A. Ekirch, Jr., *The Idea of Progress in America, 1815–60* (New York, 1951), chap. 4, "The Advancing Faith in Science."

5. Introduction, *Half-Hours with Modern Scientists. Lectures and Essays by Prof. Huxley, Barker, Sterling, Cope, and Tyndall*. First Series (New Haven, 1872), pp. x–xi. It would seem apparent that one of the reasons for the time-lag between the publication of the *Origin* and *Descent* and the most egregious aspects of the evolution controversy lay in the decades necessary for these new ideas to become better-known outside of opinion-forming urban centers. Though many educated Americans did have their reservations, it is clear that by the late 1870s and early 1880s, they—and their children, certainly—felt little active hostility toward Darwin and his doctrines. This statement is based primarily but not exclusively on my reading of the obituaries and editorials written at Darwin's death in some forty religious publications (1882). See also Norman Furniss, *The Fundamentalist Controversy, 1918–1931* (New Haven, 1954).

6. The standard general survey of Social Darwinism in this country is still that by Richard Hofstadter, *Social Darwinism in American Thought* (Boston, 1955). See also

211

Stow Persons, ed., *Evolutionary Thought in America* (New Haven, 1950). There is some question as to how pervasive Social Darwinism as a well-articulated doctrine actually was. See Irvin G. Wyllie, "Social Darwinism and the Businessman," *Proceedings of the American Philosophical Society* 103 (1959): 629–35. It is clear that many of the ideas associated with Social Darwinism had a pedigree long antedating the *Origin of Species*.

7. John P. Spooner, *The Different Modes of Treating Disease; or, The Different Action of Medicines on the System in an Abnormal State* (Boston, 1862), p. 13. The Darwin referred to is Erasmus, not Charles.

8. The second law of thermodynamics states that in a free and continuous heat exchange, heat is always transferred from the hotter to the colder body.

9. W. J. Hunter, *Manhood Wrecked and Rescued: How Strength, or Vigor is Lost, and How it May be Restored Through Self-Treatment* (Passaic, N.J., [ca. 1900]), p. 129. It was assumed in most of these analogies that man's endowment of nervous energy was not an absolute quantity provided at birth but, rather, the body's potential for the production of this nervous energy during life.

10. These formulations, it should be noted, preserved the traditional assumption that both heredity and environmental stress played a role in the etiology of nervous disease. There is, so far as I am aware, no study available of the metaphorical use of energy relationships in American social thought. For Freud, see S. Bernfeld, "Freud's Earliest Theories and the School of Helmholtz," *Psychoanalytic Quarterly* 13 (1944): 341–62; for Henry Adams, see William Jordy, *Henry Adams, Scientific Historian* (New Haven, 1952). For an account of research relating to the discovery of the electrical nature of the nervous impulse, see E. G. T. Liddell, *The Discovery of Reflexes* (Oxford, 1960), chap. 2, "Animal Electricity," pp. 31–47.

11. A traditional medical unwillingness to entertain a distinction between the realms of the material and psychological meant that interpretations of such events in the life cycle always incorporated biological, social, environmental, and psychological dimensions.

12. Such views were well-nigh universal in nineteenth-century America. A prominent scientist could, for example, write the following to a relative in the mid-1890s: "It is with all experienced physicians and hygienists a settled maxim that two persons in weak health should never sleep together, as experience shows that they are almost certain to hurt each other. How, goodness knows—nervous influence or something, but there is no doubt about the fact. A healthy person having nervous force to spare may benefit immensely another by lending him some of it; but in the long run few are strong enough to resist entirely such depleting influence. Young children sleeping with their grandparents become wretched while the ancestors thrive, and there is a standing maxim against permitting it. Some women as you know will kill half a dozen husbands, and vice versa some husbands half a dozen wives, unintentionally, by the same influence." E. W. Hilgard to Alice Hilgard (from letterpress book covering the period February 1894–October 1896), E. W. Hilgard Papers, Bancroft Library, Berkeley, California. Compare the exchange between a correspondent and the editor of *Lancet*, April 7, 1883, p. 621.

13. "The Correlation of Nervous and Mental Forces," in Balfour Stewart, *The Conservation of Energy* (New York, 1875), p. 228. Bain, a professor at Aberdeen, was widely read in this country.

14. R. V. Pierce, *The People's Common Sense Medical Adviser in Plain English: or, Medicine Simplified* (Buffalo, N.Y., 1895), p. 619. For a clear exposition of the assumption that American life held dangers to mental health, see the many references in Norman Dain, *Concepts of Insanity in the United States, 1789–1865* (New Brunswick, N.J., 1964). See also George Rosen, "Social Stress and Mental Disease from the Eighteenth Century to the Present: Some Origins of Social Psychiatry," *Milbank Memorial Fund Quarterly* 37 (1959): 5–32, and Mark D. Altschule, *Roots of Modern Psychiatry* (New York, 1957), pp. 119–39.

15. Irving Fisher, *Bulletin 30 of the Committee of One Hundred on National Health, Being a Report on National Vitality, Its Wastes and Conservation* (Washington, D.C., 1909), p. 96. J. Leonard Corning, *Brain Exhaustion, with Some Preliminary Considera-*

tions on Cerebral Dynamics (New York, 1884), p. 135. For influential statements in regard to the influence of American life on mental health, see Isaac Ray, *Mental Hygiene* (Boston, 1863), esp. pp. 219-23, and Benjamin Rush, *Medical Inquiries and Observations upon the Diseases of the Mind* (Philadelphia, 1812), pp. 65-69 and passim. See also chap. 5, below.

16. Charles B. Davenport to D. Starr Jordan, January 27, 1922. Davenport Papers, American Philosophical Society. The literature relating to the connection between genius and other forms of mental abnormality is immense. An excellent guide is Wilhelm Lange-Eichbaum, *Genie, Irrsinn und Ruhm* (Munich, 1961).

17. Samuel Royce, *Deterioration and the Elevation of Man through Race Education* (Boston, 1880), 1: 49.

18. J. S. Jewell, "Influence of Our Present Civilization in the Production of Nervous and Mental Diseases," *Journal of Nervous and Mental Disease* 8 (1881): 4. With the acceptance of Darwinism these hypothetical mental attributes of civilized man were provided with evolutionary credentials. The traditionally higher faculties—the aesthetic and moral—were as a matter of course identified with those highest in the scale of evolution. Being the "highest," they were naturally man's last acquisition in his upward path.

19. Nathan Allen, *The Physiological Laws of Human Increase*. Extracted from the Transactions of the American Medical Association (Philadelphia, 1870), p. 26. "It is an admitted fact," as one mid-nineteenth-century physician explained, "that nearly all the chronic diseases to which the system is liable, are the consequence of some violated laws that Infinite Wisdom has imposed upon the animal economy." S. S. Purple, *New York Journal of Medicine* 3 (1849): 207-8.

20. Marcus Cross, *The Mirror of Intemperance, and History of the Temperance Reform* (Philadelphia, 1850), p. 18; American Temperance Society, *Permanent Temperance Documents* (Boston, 1835), p. 1. The latter publication provides a convenient compendium of temperance arguments. For references to twentieth-century materials, see Bartlett C. Jones, "Prohibition and Eugenics, 1920-1933" and "A Prohibition Problem: Liquor as Medicine, 1920-1933," *Journal of the History of Medicine* 18 (1963): 158-72, 353-69.

21. For a more elaborate discussion of this development, see chap. 1, below.

22. The first quotation is from Henry M. Boies, *Prisoners and Paupers: A Study of the Abnormal Increase of Criminals, and the Burden of Pauperism in the United States* (New York, 1893), p. 291; the second is from Florence T. Griswold, "The Social Problem," *The Badger* (Madison, Wis.) 4 (June 13, 1885): 201-3. The generalization in regard to student opinion is based on a study of student publications of the 1880s at Wisconsin, Lehigh, and the University of Pennsylvania. Student newspapers and magazines provide important and little-used sources for social and intellectual history.

23. For the most important statements by participants in the puerperal-fever debate, see Charles D. Meigs, *On the Nature, Signs, and Treatment of Childbed Fevers; In a Series of Letters Addressed to the Students of his Class* (Philadelphia, 1854); O. W. Holmes, *Puerperal Fever as a Private Pestilence* (Boston, 1855); Hugh L. Hodge, *On the Non-Contagious Character of Puerperal Fever. Delivered Monday, October 11, 1852* (Philadelphia, 1852). "What rewards," Hodge rhetorically questioned his medical-student audience, "can possibly compensate the obstetrician, who has reason to believe that he has actually poisoned even one of those valued and lovely beings who rested confidently and implicitly on him for deliverance?" (p. 10).

24. Geographical location, it must be confessed, may also have been a factor in their hostility to these ideas, associated as they were with Oliver Wendell Holmes and Boston. A contagionist emphasis was also associated with British etiological thought, an anticontagionist bias with the more fashionable French clinical school which had so influenced Meigs and Hodge.

25. This is not to imply that any of the constituent attitudes and norms are in themselves in conflict with those of society generally. Indeed, in some important ways many of the norms and aspirations of the scientific community are entirely consistent with those of the larger society. See chap. 8 for a more detailed case study.

26. But deviant only in the sense of atypical, for their peculiar commitment was justified in terms of values accepted as legitimate by their society generally. See chap. 1, below.

27. The first quotation is from Evan Pugh to S. W. Johnson, November 18, 1861, Pugh Papers, Pennsylvania State University; the second is from Pugh, *Address to the Cumberland County Agricultural Society* (Carlisle, Pa., 1860), p. 24. Representative letters of the Göttingen circle have also been published in Elizabeth A. Osborne, *From the Letter-Files of S. W. Johnson* (New Haven, 1913), and C. A. Browne, "European Laboratory Experiences of an Early American Agricultural Chemist—Dr. Evan Pugh (1828-1864)," *Journal of Chemical Education* 7 (1930): 499–517.

28. W. B. Smith to Stephen M. Babcock, November 23, 1879, Babcock Papers, State Historical Society of Wisconsin.

29. Morgan to James K. Patterson, June 13, 1889, Patterson Papers, University of Kentucky Educational Archives. It is hardly surprising that many American scholars were beginning to argue that professional standing, rather than moral or other personal criteria, should be the deciding factor in the hiring of faculty; see F. W. Clarke, "The Appointment of College Officers," *Popular Science Monthly* 21 (1882): 173–74.

30. Social values also affect the scientific enterprise through the person of the scientist himself, insofar as he shares the social assumptions of his peers and insofar as his choice of a scientific vocation is in itself a response to a particular image projected by the life of science and the values incorporated in that image.

Chapter 1

1. Although historians have paid a good deal of attention to scientific racism and Social Darwinism, we still have no systematic study of nineteenth-century attitudes toward human heredity.

2. At least one explicit social location—that of the practicing physician—can, however, be correlated with this complex of ideas. One other minor caveat: this discussion is limited somewhat arbitrarily to human heredity and ignores the interpretation of animal breeding, although examples from this realm were often utilized by writers concerned with human heredity.

3. Cf. J. F. Nisbet, *Marriage and Heredity. A View of Psychological Evolution*, 2d ed., rev. (London, 1890), pp. 126–27. See also A. S. Couch, "Heredity and the Higher Duties of the Profession," *Transactions of the Homeopathic Medical Society of New York* 16 (1880–81): 122–34.

4. J. G. Richardson, "Address in Hygiene," *Transactions of the Medical Society of Pennsylvania* 17 (1885): 94–95. Cf. F. E. H. Steger, "Hereditary Transmission of Diseases," *Nashville Journal of Medicine and Surgery* 8 (1855): 182; [Hester Pendleton], *Husband and Wife; or, the Science of Human Development through Inherited Tendencies* (New York, 1863), p. 46; J. B. Newman, *The Philosophy of Generation* (New York, 1849), p. 46. There is, of course, an ancient lore describing putative relationships between particular aspects of or attitudes toward sexual intercourse and their effect on the child which might result.

5. The problem of "maternal impressions" and their ability to "mark" a child has, of course, an equally ancient pedigree. For examples of the tentative acceptance of this doctrine by mid-century authorities, see W. B. Carpenter, *Principles of Human Physiology*, 4th Amer. ed. (Philadelphia, 1850), pp. 720–21; C. Rokitansky, *A Manual of Pathological Anatomy*, 4 vols. (London, 1854), 1: 11–12. For attacks of gradually increasing absoluteness, see Alexander Hamilton, *The Family Female Physician* (Worcester, Mass., 1793), p. 131; Michael Underwood, *A Treatise on the Diseases of Children*, 3 vols. in one (Philadelphia, 1818), 2: 83; T. Gaillard Thomas, *Abortion and Its Treatment* (New York, 1890), p. 43.

6. A respectable Philadelphia physician could repeat such warnings as late as 1911: Myer Solis-Cohen, *Girl, Wife, and Mother* (Philadelphia, 1911), p. 110.

7. Stephen Tracy, *The Mother and Her Offspring* (New York, 1860), p. 244; John Bovee Dods, *The Philosophy of Electrical Psychology* (New York, 1851), esp. pp. 242–43. Dods urged the systematic cultivation of the mother's impressions during gestation as a means of perfecting her offspring. Like many such tracts of this period, Dods's argument betrays strong if covert feminist overtones.

8. Rebecca Crumpler, *A Book of Medical Discourses* (Boston, 1883); Samuel Busey, "Maternal Impressions . . . ," *Gynecological Transactions* 11 (1886): 18; Sydney B. Elliot, *Aedology: A Treatise on Generative Life* (New York, 1892), pp. 44–46; E. Seguin, *Idiocy* (New York, 1866), p. 300; William A. Hammond, "On the Influence of the Maternal Mind over the Offspring during Pregnancy and Lactation," *Quarterly Journal of Psychological Medicine* 2 (1868): 1–28.

9. A. Portal, "Considerations on the Nature and Treatment of Some Hereditary or Family Diseases," *Medical and Physical Journal* 21 (1809); 293–94; Henry Belinaye, *The Sources of Health and Disease in Communities; Or, Elementary Views of "Hygiene"* (Boston, 1833), p. 35; Tullio S. Verdi, *Maternity: A Popular Treatise for Young Wives and Mothers* (New York, 1870), pp. 186–89; Joseph E. Winters, "The Relative Influences of Maternal and Wet-nursing on Mother and Child," *Medical Record* 30 (November 6, 1886); 504–14, and discussion, p. 525. Treatises on domestic medicine written for middle-class families always emphasized the need, first, for the mother to nurse her own children, but, failing this, to be extremely careful in her choice of wet-nurse. Such warnings might only have been expected in a period when children who were not nursed stood little chance of survival.

10. George W. Colby, [Notebook on baby and child care, with notes taken at Long Island College Hospital, 1895], Rare Book Room, New York Academy of Medicine, p. 3.

11. Jonathan Hutchinson, *The Pedigree of Disease; Being Six Lectures on Temperament, Idiosyncrasy, and Diathesis* (London, 1884), p. 71. See also the extremely enlightening remarks by Archibald E. Garrod, *The Inborn Factors in Disease* (Oxford, 1931), pp. 9–12.

12. D. T. Brown, *Report of the State of the New York Hospital and Bloomingdale Asylum, for the Year 1854* (New York, 1855), p. 35.

13. Thomas Henderson, *Hints on the Medical Examination of Recruits for the Army* (Philadelphia, 1840), p. 14. It was assumed, of course, that such basic constitutional patterns were related to heredity.

14. On the differing contribution of male and female parents to their children, see Nathan Allen, "Physical Degeneracy," Reprinted from the *Journal of Psychological Medicine . . . 1870* (New York, 1870), p. 25; Tandy L. Dix, *The Healthy Infant: A Treatise on the Healthy Procreation of the Human Race* (Cincinnati, 1880), p. 16; J. B. Thomson, "On the Comparative Influence of the Male and Female Parent upon the Progeny," *Edinburgh Medical Journal* 4 (1858): 502; 4 (1859): 696–99; William Sedgwick, "On Sexual Limitation in Hereditary Disease," *British and Foreign Medical and Chirurgical Review* 27 (1861): 447–89, 198–214.

15. This growing emphasis upon the mother's role in shaping her child's heredity endowment during gestation and nursing was, indeed, the most conspicuous exception to the generally unchanging quality of nineteenth-century hereditarian views. I have found only one prominent mid-nineteenth-century American physician who consciously attacked this doctrine, Hugh Hodge, who argued that the contribution of both parents was established at the moment of conception. Interestingly, however, Hodge was also an early and outspoken critic of abortion. *On Criminal Abortion; A Lecture Introductory to the Course on Obstetrics . . . University of Pennsylvania* (Philadelphia, 1854), p. 9.

16. Since clinicians never believed in the invariability of hereditary transmission of constitutional disease, negative data could hardly accumulate, while seemingly positive examples were encountered by every busy practitioner in the course of his daily rounds. Tuberculosis, cancer, mental illness, all seemed to both lay and professional eyes constitutional and thus generally hereditary.

17. Some authorities went so far as to argue that "habit" could indirectly predispose even to acute epidemic ills. See Julius H. Steinau, *A Pathological and Philosophical Essay on Hereditary Diseases* (London, 1843), p. 26.

18. By mid-century conditions considered undoubtedly hereditary included harelip, lack of fingers, polydactylism, deafness with age, near-sightedness, cataract, color blindness, and amaurosis. For a representative list, see B. Lincoln Ray, *Hereditary Transmission* (Providence, R.I., 1861), p. 10; James Whitehead, *On the Transmission, from Parent to Offspring, of Some Forms of Disease* (London, 1851). The undoubtedly hereditary conditions, despite the comparative lack of interest which they evinced, did reinforce particular aspects of the conventional wisdom in regard to human heredity; one was the recognition of what contemporaries called "atavism"—the ability of a disease or condition to remain dormant through one or more generations and then reassert itself in succeeding ones.

19. Darwin, *The Temple of Nature; or, The Origin of Society: A Poem* (New York, 1804), p. 50.

20. Buchan, *Domestic Medicine; or, A Treatise on the Prevention and Cure of Diseases . . .* Adapted to the Climate and Diseases of America by Isaac Cathrall (Philadelphia, 1797), p. 28. Consistently enough, insurance companies were in this period generally hesitant to insure the lives of individuals whose parents had died of constitutional ailments, most conspicuously tuberculosis. For examples of attacks on parents for entailing disease upon their children, see Elizabeth Blackwell, *The Laws of Life* (New York, 1852), p. 145; Richard Carmichael, *An Essay on the Origin and Nature of Tuberculous and Cancerous Diseases* (Dublin, 1836).

21. It is significant that mid-nineteenth-century academic medicine began to entertain increasingly critical attitudes toward existing therapeutic means.

22. *Hints to a Fashionable Lady. By a Physician* (New York, 1831), p. 13; [William A. Alcott], "Hereditary Disease," *Library of Health* 2 (1838): 55. One of the first monographs in English devoted specifically to hereditary disease—and sometimes referred to as significant in establishing the legitimacy of this concept—was dedicated in part to allaying popular fears. Published in London in 1814 and written by Joseph Adams, it was entitled *A Treatise on the Supposed Hereditary Properties of Diseases, Containing Remarks on the Unfounded Terrors and Ill-judged Cautions Consequent on such Erroneous Opinions.* Similarly, a speaker at the 1857 meeting of the American asylum superintendents' association suggested that it might be much better if the public knew less of the hereditary transmission of insanity, for the knowledge often induced anxiety which might cause the feared result. *American Journal of Insanity* 14 (1857): 85.

23. Translator's note in P. C. A. Louis, *Pathological Researches on Phthisis,* trans. Charles Cowan (Boston, 1836), p. 446n. See also Adams, *Hereditary Properties of Diseases,* p. 84; John Ellis, *Marriage and Its Violations* (New York, 1860), p. 16; William Mavor, *The Catechism of Health* (New York and Baltimore, 1819), p. 11.

24. For an example of the similar use of disease as sanction in the case of an acute disease in this period, see Charles E. Rosenberg, *The Cholera Years: The United States in 1832, 1849, and 1866* (Chicago, 1962).

25. Nathan Allen, *The Intermarriage of Relations* [from the *Quarterly Journal of Psychological Medicine,* April 1869] (New York, 1869), p. 25. "Heredity is," as another medical publicist put it, "one of the exact sciences, although we know so little of it that it seems to most persons to be almost anything but exact, and even those who have given it the most attention are often puzzled to account for its seeming vagaries." H. S. Pomeroy, *The Ethics of Marriage* (New York, 1888), p. 107.

26. [S. G. Howe], *On the Causes of Idiocy; Being the Supplement to a Report by Dr. S. G. Howe and the other Commissioners Appointed by the Governor of Massachusetts to Inquire into the Condition of the Idiots of the Commonwealth, Dated February 26, 1848* (Edinburgh and London, 1848). For a useful summary of knowledge and conviction in regard to consanguineous marriage, see Robert Newman, "Report of the Committee on the Result of Consanguineous Marriages," *Transactions of the Medical Society of the State of New York,* 1869, pp. 109–30. Cf. Alfred H. Huth, *The Marriage of Near Kin,* 2d ed. (London, 1887).

27. A similar argument may with some justice be applied to Francis Galton. His studies, impressively empirical though they appeared to contemporaries, simply reasserted and reaffirmed long-familiar doctrines; Galton's vogue documents and encou-

raged the trend toward hereditarian explanations of social phenomena. Yet it is not clear whether his work is best seen as progenitor or product of this tendency; clearly his case is analogous to that of Darwin himself, his influence similarly complex and ambiguous (though Galton certainly played a central role in the eugenics movement qua movement, in contemporary debates on the nature of individual class differences and as well—ultimately—in the development of biostatistics.) On Galton, see Ruth Schwartz Cowan, "Sir Francis Galton and the Study of Heredity in the Nineteenth Century" (Ph.D. diss., John Hopkins University, 1969).

The widely quoted experimental results of physiologist Brown-Séquard, which seemed to prove that neurological trauma could have hereditary implications, served similarly to document what was—to most contemporaries—self-evident. For a discussion of Brown-Séquard's work, see J. M. D. Olmsted, *Charles-Edouard Brown-Séquard, a Nineteenth-Century Neurologist and Endocrinologist* (Baltimore, 1946).

28. These generalizations are based on a survey of the diffusion of Koch's discovery in the year following its announcement.

29. Flick, "The Hygiene of Phthisis," *Transactions of the Philadelphia County Medical Society*, January 11, 1888, pp. 4–5; R. Clement Lucas, *The Bradshaw Lecture on Some Points in Heredity* (London, 1912), pp. 7–8.

30. And by a revealing shift in genre as well: from the late 1830s through mid-century it had been the abundant literature of health reform, phrenology, and social perfectionism which utilized hereditarian arguments most frequently in the explanation of social phenomena. By the end of the century they were expressed as well in the new literature of the social sciences.

31. Joseph Cook, *Heredity, with Preludes on Current Events* (Boston, 1879), p. 240; William Alcott, *The Laws of Health* (Boston, 1857), p. 12; Thomas L. Nichols, *Esoteric Anthropology* (London, n.d.), p. 150. A parallel source of scientific reassurance lay in the traditional emphasis upon the tendency of variations to return to type. Cf. Isaac Ray, *Mental Hygiene* (Boston, 1863), p. 27; L. W. Pendleton, "Transmitted Tendencies," *Transactions of the Maine Medical Society* (1877–79), p. 447.

32. For a parallel interpretation of the pietistic origins of the public health movement, see chapter 6. The influence of pietism in other areas of social reform—such as abolitionism, temperance, communal perfectionism—are comparatively well known to American historians.

33. The popularity of hereditarianism among left-wing or "ultra" reformers was obvious to contemporaries; one regular physician complained in 1861, for example, that for the past thirty years the subject of heredity had been well-nigh monopolized by the "absurdities" of "phrenologists, spiritualists, ultraists of every hue." Most of these enthusiasts were, of course, doctrinally unorthodox. The phrases are from Ray, *Hereditary Transmission*, p. 35.

34. In reformist circles, indeed, it became acceptable to assume a material basis, not only for cognition but for emotion and morality as well. Traditional medical assumption of an intimate connection between body and mind provided one source of legitimation for such views, just as medicine provided the basic framework of formal assumption used in nineteenth-century hereditarian ideas generally. It should also be noted that the vogue of Swedenborgianism played a significant role in helping to popularize these attitudes which so casually confounded mind and body; both an emphasis on heredity and a spiritualization of matters seen traditionally as temporal can be seen in New Church—and New Church–influenced—writers of this period. See, for example, Henry C. Wright, *The Empire of the Mother over the Character and Destiny of the Race* (Boston, 1866); Henry C. Wright, *Marriage and Parentage; or, The Reproductive Element in Man as a Means to his Elevation and Happiness* (Boston, 1854); Woodbury M. Fernald, *A View at the Foundations; or, First Causes of Character, as Operative before Birth, from Hereditary and Spiritual Sources* (Boston, 1865); Andrew J. Davis, *The Genesis and Ethics of Conjugal Love* (New York, 1874).

35. John Cowan, *The Science of a New Life* (New York, [ca. 1869]), p. 137; Dio Lewis, *Chastity* (New York, 1894 [orig. copyright 1874]), p. 144; [William Alcott], *The Physiology of Marriage* (Salem, 1856), p. 96; [Dr. Porter], *Book of Men, Women, and*

Babies. The Laws of God applied to Obtaining, Rearing, and Developing the Natural, Healthful, and Beautiful in Humanity (New York, 1855), p. 175; *Esoteric Anthropology,* p. 103; Wright, *Marriage and Parentage,* p. 17, noted forthrightly that "functional derangements of souls, as well as bodies, are transmitted. It is true of the soul, as well as of the body, that parents reproduce in their likeness" (p. 53).

36. Elizabeth Blackwell, *Laws of Life,* pp. 16–17; J. H. Kellogg, *Chastity and Health* (Battle Creek, Mich., 1895), p. 4. For an assortment of statements of this position, see Daniel Haynes, "Reflections on the Origin, Progress, and Treatment of Hereditary Diseases," *Transactions of the New York State Medical Society,* (1841), pp. 196–204; [Hester Pendleton], *Husband and Wife* (New York, 1836), pp. 64–65; Calvin Knerr, *A Memorial of Constantine Hering* (Philadelphia, 1880), p. 153.

37. R. T. Trall, *Sexual Physiology* (New York, 1866), p. 258.

38. Harriot Hunt, *Glances and Glimpses; Or Fifty Years Social, Including Twenty Years Professional Life* (Boston, 1856), pp. 259–60; "Reminiscences: Emily Collins," in *History of Woman Suffrage,* ed. Elizabeth C. Stanton, Susan B. Anthony, and Matilda J. Gage (New York, 1881), 1: 9. One female advocate of hereditary improvement argued, in terms amusingly contemporary: "The common, ideal woman is a weak, disingenuous, cowardly creature. She has no earnest convictions, no purposes, no sincerities within her." Georgianna Kirby, *Transmission; Or, Variation of Character through the Mother* (New York, 1879), p. 52.

39. Harriot Hunt, *Glances and Glimpses,* p. 143.

40. Only a handful of liberals dared openly to espouse birth control through mechanical means in the mid-nineteenth century; a far greater number, however, did demand the limitation of offspring through abstinence and—even when the autonomy of women was consciously seen as one end of such abstinence—clothed these appeals in the transcendent categories of evangelical piety.

41. *Tokology: A Book for Every Woman* (Chicago, 1887), p. 346. For other examples of such biologically justified feminism, see Elizabeth E. Evans, *The Abuse of Maternity* (Philadelphia, 1875), p. 100; Mary E. Walker, *HIT* (New York, ca. 1871), p. 61; E. H. Heywood, *Cupid's Yokes; or, The Binding Forces of Conjugal Life* (Princeton, Mass., 1877), p. 17; James C. Jackson, *American Womanhood: Its Peculiarities and Necessities,* 2d ed. (Dansville, N.Y., 1870), pp. 83–84. In many such writers there is a revealing coincidence of arguments for family limitation, woman's control of the sexual relationship, and the legitimation of these goals through invocation of woman's control over the physical and moral qualities of the child she bore. This particular discussion cannot hope to evaluate the psychological variables which made these ideas emotionally relevant to particular men and women.

42. J. Curwen, *Alienist and Neurologist* 3 (1882): 198. For a note on the persistence of arguments emphasizing the connection between alcohol and heredity, see Bartlett C. Jones, "Prohibition and Eugenics, 1920–1933," *Journal of the History of Medicine* 18 (1963): 158–72.

43. John D. Davies, *Phrenology, Fad and Science: A Nineteenth-Century American Crusade* (New Haven, 1955), is still the only survey of the impact of phrenology on American society. On the European background see Owsei Temkin, "Gall and the Phrenological Movement," *Bulletin of the History of Medicine* 21 (1947): 275–321; Erwin H. Ackerknecht and Henri V. Vallois, *Franz Joseph Gall: Inventor of Phrenology and His Collection,* trans. Claire St. Léon (Madison, Wis., 1956); Robert M. Young, *Mind, Brain, and Adaption in the Nineteenth Century: Cerebral Localization and Its Biological Context from Gall to Ferrier* (Oxford, 1970), pp. 1–53.

44. Lorenzo Fowler, *The Principles of Phrenology and Physiology Applied to Man's Social Relations; Together with an Analysis of the Domestic Feelings* (New York, 1842), p. 89; idem, *Hereditary Descent: Its Laws and Facts Applied to Human Improvement* (New York, 1847), p. 281. Hester Pendleton, author of the first widely read American book on hereditary improvement, was a zealous advocate of phrenology. *Facts and Arguments on the Transmission of Intellectual and Moral Qualities, from Parents to Offspring* (New York, 1843).

45. This generalization is based in part on a reading of the first ten volumes of the *American Journal of Phrenology.* Publication began in October 1838.

46. Combe's *Essay on the Constitution of Man and Its Relations to External Objects* first appeared in Edinburgh in 1827 and was reprinted many times in pre-bellum America; in terms of its impact on popular social thought in ante-bellum America, Combe can—with only minor exaggeration—be compared to Darwin in the decades after the Civil War. Alexander Walker's explicitly titled *Intermarriage; or, The Mode in which, and the Causes why, Beauty, Health and Intellect, Result from Certain Unions, and Deformity, Disease and Insanity from Others*, 1st Amer. ed. (New York, 1839), was also read and quoted widely.

47. See, for example, Norman Dain, *Concepts of Insanity in the United States, 1789–1865* (New Brunswick, N.J., 1964); Gerald N. Grob, *The State and the Mentally Ill: A History of Worcester State Hospital in Massachusetts, 1830-1920* (Chapel Hill, N.C., *1966)*; Edward Jarvis, *Insanity and Idiocy in Massachusetts: Report of the Commission on Lunacy, 1855*, with a critical introduction by Gerald N. Grob (Cambridge, Mass., 1971).

48. This raises some interesting questions in relation to the movement and diffusions of ideas across time and class. Despite the widespread acceptance of hereditarian assumptions by both the medical profession and articulate laymen before the Civil War, the explicit borrowing of European forms and authority may still have been the central event in the acceptance of such formal models by a post-bellum elite oriented increasingly toward the ideas and authority of their European disciplinary peers. Though the precise configuration of events and relationships may be unclear, it is certain that these European precedents and authorities were a critical element in the shaping of late-nineteenth-century American social hereditarianism.

49. Morel's most significant work is not available in English. *Traité des dégénérescences physiques, intellectuelles et morales de l'espèce humaine et des causes qui produisent ces variétés maladives* (Paris, 1857). Two recent Zurich dissertations are useful: Peter Burgener, *Die Einflüsse des zeitgenössischen Denkens in Morels Begriff der 'dégénérescence'* (Zurich, 1964); Helmut Semadeni, *Die Erbkrankheiten um 1850* (Zurich, 1960). The most detailed study of the influence of the degeneration idea is still that by G. P. H. Genil-Perrin, *L'Idée de dégénérescence en médecine mentale* (Paris, 1913). See also Annemarie Wettley, "Zur Problemgeschichte der 'dégénérescence,'" *Sudhoff's Archiv* 43 (1959): 193–212; Annemarie Wettley, *Von der "Psychopathia sexualis" zur Sexualwissenschaft* (Stuttgart, 1959); Erwin H. Ackerknecht, *A Short History of Psychiatry* (New York, 1968).

50. On the influence of degeneration in fiction, see A. E. Carter, *The Idea of Decadence in French Literature 1830-1900* (Toronto, 1958), esp. chap. 3, "Nerve-Storms and Bad Heredity." Mario Praz's *Romantic Agony* (New York, 1951) also contains material on hereditarian motives and imagery.

51. For the use of somatic models in the legitimization of marginal psychological states see chap. 5. See also Nathan Hale, Jr., *Freud and the Americans: The Beginnings of Psychoanalysis in the United States, 1876-1917* (New York, 1971), esp. pp. 47–97. Charles E. Rosenberg, *The Trial of the Assassin Guiteau: Psychiatry and Law in the Gilded Age* (Chicago, 1968), discusses the place of hereditarian factors in the causation of mental illness and notes their implications for legal medicine. Not surprisingly, a number of leading authorities were concerned with attempts to define an anatomical basis for the *predisposition* to insanity; most still felt uneasy with formulations which defined insanity as absolutely and unavoidably hereditary. Cf. Theodor Meynert, *Psychiatry; A Clinical Treatiese on Diseases of the Fore-Brain Based upon a Study of Its Structure, Functions, and Nutrition* (New York, 1885), p. viii.

52. George D. Stahley, *The Relation of Education to Insanity. Read before the Lehigh Valley Medical Association . . . January 31, 1889* (Philadelphia, 1889), p. 3; comment by Dr. Charles Folsom at a meeting for the Boston Society for Medical Observation, *Boston Medical & Surgical Journal* 108 (May 31, 1883): 514.

53. James Jackson Putnam, *Not the Disease Only, but also the Man. The Shattuck Lecture, Delivered at the Annual Meeting of the Massachusetts Medical Society. June 13, 1899* (Boston, 1899).

54. There is a vast literature on "criminal anthropology." The best summary of such arguments is still that in Arthur E. Fink, *Causes of Crime: Biological Theories in the*

United States, 1800–1915 (Philadelphia, 1938). For a brief evaluation of Lombroso by a contemporary criminologist, see Marvin Wolfgang, "Cesare Lombroso," in *Pioneers in Criminology*, ed. Hermann Mannheim (Chicago, 1960), pp. 168–227. An invaluable source of bibliography is Arthur MacDonald, *Abnormal Man, Being Essays on Education and Crime and Related Subjects, with Digests of Literature and a Bibliography* (Bureau of Education, Circular of Information no. 4, 1893 [Washington, D.C., 1893]).

55. Joseph G. Richardson, *Introductory Lecture to the Course on Pathological Anatomy at the University of Pennsylvania . . .* (Philadelphia, 1871), p. 12. Cf. James Paget, *Clinical Lectures and Essays* (London, 1875), p. 380; Henry Holland, *Medical Notes and Reflections* (Philadelphia, 1857), pp. 38, 47.

56. Richard Dugdale, *The Jukes: A Study in Crime, Pauperism, Disease, and Heredity*, 4th ed., with an introduction by Franklin H. Giddings (New York, 1910), p. 66. The first separate edition of Dugdale's *Jukes* was published by Putnam's in 1887. Like many of his contemporary reformers of man's biological nature, Dugdale was clearly aware of the formulations of Morel and his school. "Hereditary pauperism," Dugdale explained, "rests chiefly upon disease in some form, tends to terminate in extinction, and may be called the sociological aspect of physical degeneration" (p. 38). Dugdale is not an isolated example; compare his position with that expressed in Samuel Royce, *Deterioration and Race Education* (Boston, 1878), which reflects the same predilection for social manipulation and activism and an even more detailed knowledge of contemporary European writings on heredity.

57. From remarks by Elisha Harris in a discussion of a paper by Dugdale, *Proceedings of the National Conference of Charities* (1877): 90–97.

58. Charles Loring Brace, *The Dangerous Classes of New York, and Twenty Years' Work among Them* (New York, 1872), pp. 44–45. Despite the logically quietist implication of these ideas, Brace was, of course, an indefatigable social reformer.

59. Particularly enlightening is the contrast between Dugdale's *Jukes* and H. H. Goddard's *The Kallikak Family: A Study in the Heredity of Feeble-Mindedness* (New York, 1912), with its simplistic and would-be Mendelian conclusions. But this reductionist trend had manifested itself well before the turn-of-the-century rediscovery of Mendel's work. See, for example, Oscar C. McCulloch's study, "The Tribe of Ishmael: A Study in Social Degradation," which appeared in the *Proceedings of the National Conference of Charities and Corrections for 1888*.

60. Such surgical procedures were, of course, technically more feasible than at mid-century and thus provided a new policy option. The phrase is from Gonsalvo Smythe, *Influence of Heredity Introducing Disease and Degeneracy: The Remedy . . .* (Indianapolis, Ind., 1891), p. 7. By the turn of the century a popular writer on heredity could casually report that Dugdale had "plainly demonstrated the merely palliative character of our whole system for the treatment of vagrancy, drunkenness, prostitution and crime." W. Duncan McKim, *Heredity and Human Progress* (New York, 1900), p. 11. The best-balanced account of the eugenics movement in America is still that by Mark H. Haller, *Eugenics: Hereditarian Attitudes in American Thought* (New Brunswick, N.J., 1963); but see also Kenneth M. Ludmerer, *Genetics and American Society: A Historical Appraisal* (Baltimore, 1972), and Donald K. Pickens, *Eugenics and the Progressives* (Nashville, Ind., 1968). The best account of the English eugenics movement is Lyndsay A. Farrall, "The Origins and Growth of the English Eugenics Movement, 1865–1925" (Ph.D. diss., Indiana University, 1969).

61. There were, of course, exceptions to this generalization. E. B. Foote, for example, a widely read author of popular medical texts, argued in the 1864 edition of his *Medical Common-Sense* (New York, 1864), p. 297, that Americans should do away with the "present rotten system of legalizing marriages." He would have substituted a Board of Phrenologists and Physiologists in every county seat with power to approve physiologically desirable pairings and grant divorces to those unhappily married.

62. Even among convinced social hereditarians at the end of the century it was still generally assumed that behavior was ultimately defined by the interaction of heredity and environment. "Organization limits the influence exerted by environment, while environment limits and modifies the development of the capacities of the organization." William G. Stevenson, *Genius and Mental Disease: An Address Delivered before the*

Vassar Brothers Institute (Poughkeepsie, N.Y., 1886), p. 7. For representative examples of authors concerned with the dangers of hereditary ills but still sensitive to the environmental variable, see Amos G. Warner, *American Charities: A Study in Philan-thropy and Economics* (New York, 1894); Eugene S. Talbot, *Degeneracy: Its Causes, Signs, and Results* (London, 1899); William Osler, "On the Brains of Criminals," *Canadian Medical Journal* 10 (1882): 385. Physicians, of course, still continued to emphasize the need for an appropriate regimen in averting a potential hereditary taint. Cf. J. R. Black, *The Ten Laws of Health* (Philadelphia, 1885), p. 322; M. L. Holbrook, *Parturition without Pain* (New York, 1882), p. 20; Samuel Peters, "Family Taints," *Medical and Surgical Reporter* 41 (1879): 184-88. One of the themes of public health advocates in this period was the need for physicians to assume responsibility for teaching this necessary attention to those endangered by hereditary weakness.

63. Patrick Geddes and J. A. Thomson, for example, in their influential *The Evolution of Sex* (London, 1898), refer to the "speculative views of Professor Weismann" as having been very recently introduced to English readers (p. vi). As late as 1908 Yale economist Irving Fisher could still urge that "there is strong reason to believe that inheritance depends largely upon the physical condition of both parents at the time of conception." *Bulletin 30 of the Committee of One Hundred on National Health. Being a Report on National Vitality, Its Wastes and Conservation* (Washington, D.C., 1909). Even physicians who avowed themselves converts to the teachings of Weismann could casually—and traditionally—warn that the condition of the parents during intercourse, alcoholism, or inadequate diet might weaken the parents' germ plasm. In addition to the need of the medical profession to find plausible social explanations and to use heredity as a disease sanction, many publicists and physicians found it difficult wholeheartedly to embrace a doctrine which seemed to allow no easy road to social progress. As one such reformer put it, "Unless characteristics acquired by an individual, that is, the modifica-tion of the organism due to his own life experiences, are capable of being handed down to his offspring, it is difficult to see how any progress could be made in the development of the race." M. L. Holbrook, *Homo-Culture* (Ann Arbor, Mich., 1897), pp. 72-73. Cf. H. Whitfield, "The Hereditary Transmission of Mental and Physical Impressions, How and When Produced." *British Medical Journal* 1 (1862): 602.

64. *Homocultology* (New York, [1875?]), pp. 16, 19.

65. While scientific racism was becoming widely accepted in European intellectual circles, it seemed at least as relevant and familiar in the United States, for these ideas created a particular resonance in terms of the American experience. An ethnically diverse immigration—and one plausibly connected with the egregious evils of the city and factory—coupled with a view of black inferiority traditionally legitimated in scientific terms created a ready social and intellectual climate. There is an interesting and instructive divergence, however, in European and American hereditarian emphases. The European emphasis upon attempting to explain the logic of class membership in biological terms was replaced in the United States by a comparative—though not exclusive—emphasis on race and ethnicity. It is significant that a good many American social hereditarians urged that a solid and stable middle class should be the goal of eugenic efforts. "Give me neither riches nor poverty seems to be the golden mean which can secure the attainment of race superiority," *Independent* 33 (September 22, 1881): 10; cf. H. S. Pomeroy, *Ethics of Marriage* (New York, 1888), p. 120.

66. Historians have tended to emphasize the interrelationship between nativism and deterministic hereditarianism in this period. See, for example, John Higham, *Strangers in the Land: Patterns of American Nativism, 1860-1925* (New Brunswick, N.J., 1955); Barbara Miller Solomon, *Ancestors and Immigrants: A Changing New England Tradi-tion* (Cambridge, Mass., 1956); Oscar Handlin, *Race and Nationality in American Life* (Garden City, N.Y., 1957), esp. chap. 6, "The Horror," pp. 111-32.

67. Nathan Allen, "The Normal Standard of Woman for Propagation," *American Journal of Obstetrics* 9 (1876): 4; Max B. Gomberg, *Neuroses. Read at a Meeting of the James Tyson Medical Society, April, 1895* (Philadelphia, 1895), p. 24.

68. Yet despite such emotional continuities, there were changes of tone as well as of formal content in American use of race concepts. The value of "race health" had a more specifically tribal and defensive quality—a posture never altogether absent, but consist-

ently muted in the more universalistically oriented perfectionism of the Jacksonian evangelicals. The citation is from Charles Chaddock, *Moral Health. Valedictory Address . . . Marion-Sims College of Medicine* (St. Louis, 1894), p. 28.

69. In this connection see Bernhard J. Stern, "Human Heredity and Environment," *Historical Sociology: The Selected Papers of Bernhard J. Stern* (New York, 1959), pp. 316-27; L. C. Dunn, "Crosscurrents in the History of Human Genetics," *American Journal of Human Genetics* 14 (1962): 1-13.

70. Obviously differences between individuals, differences based on social location and individual personality, meant that these same ideas would have a different relevance for individual Americans (although, as we have previously argued, the practicing physician's social location implied a particular function and thus relevance for these hereditarian ideas). In the analysis that follows, the more general suggestions refer to Americans who would have considered themselves—or would have liked to consider themselves—middle-class. It would be naïve to try to define this group with great precision—or to deny the emotional reality of such categories to individuals who had necessarily to define their particular social identity.

71. Sarah Stevenson, *The Physiology of Woman* (Chicago, 1881), p. 44.

72. The mid-century commitment by a number of states to the need for public mental hospitals—a seeming victory for rationalism and humanitarianism—soon turned ironically into a far more ambiguous situation as these new hospitals became overcrowded and increasingly custodial (and as the patient population both in its scale and often in its social make-up became decreasingly amenable to available modes of "moral"—that is, environmental and nonmedical—therapy). Similarly, in pioneer institutions for the mentally retarded, the optimism which informed their mid-century founders' hopes that these institutions could be regarded as schools from which their charges would emerge to function in the community was dissipated in a generation of negative experience—experience which seemed to indicate that a permanent custodial status seemed necessary in a discouragingly large number of cases. This emphasis on hereditarian etiologies was also consistent with the intellectual presuppositions of this generation of prestigious European psychiatrists and pathologists—men whose leadership the elite in American medicine and social thought normally followed with little hesitation. See the references in note 47, above, for the historical consensus in regard to the evolution of the state hospital in nineteenth-century America. In regard to institutions for the retarded, see the recent thesis by Peter L. Tyor, "Segregation or Surgery: The Mentally Retarded in America, 1850-1920" (Ph.D. diss., Northwestern University, 1972).

73. In a very general sense hereditarian explanations of human behavior were a consequence of and stimulus to the more general intellectual movement which saw man becoming a part of the natural world, his behavior and moral attributes an appropriate subject for disciplined inquiry. In this context both environmental and hereditarian explanations played the same role.

74. Henry Boies, *Prisoners and Paupers* (New York, 1893), p. 266.

75. Obviously not all Americans were part of an urban, economically changing world, but a large number of the articulate were; and whether particular careers were more unstable or not, contemporaries certainly regarded them as being so.

76. The phrases cited are drawn from M. A. Pallen, "Heritage, or Hereditary Transmission," *St. Louis Medical and Surgical Journal* 14 (1856): 501; Maria King, *Social Evils: Their Cause and Cure* (New York, 1870), p. 19; Henry Reynolds, "The Effect of Intemperance on the Offspring," *Zion's Herald* 59 (January 18, 1882): 18. See also [Pendleton], *Facts and Arguments*, pp. 13-15. This commitment to the establishment of desirable qualities in children—and the race—in the hands of some authors could assume a consciously religious quality. For example, Abbott Kinney, *Conquest of Death* (Boston, 1893), pp. ix, 58, argued, "There is, however, ground to expect that the grand motive of immortality of the body instilled into children may become a natural and practical religion . . . not subject to the periodic overthrow of systems based on the undemonstrable dogmas of religion. . . . The grand aim and object is self-improvement continued in children to perfection. . . . The necessity is such by reason of individual death, and is the only means to overcome this." Compare the parallel sentiments of

Jonathan Hutchinson, a leading English clinician and late-nineteenth-century authority on heredity in disease: Herbert Hutchinson, *Jonathan Hutchinson: Life and Letters* (London, 1946), pp. 217-18.

77. Channing to Jackson, September 27, 1837, James Jackson Papers, Countway Library of Medicine, Boston. Compare the exhortatory words of a contemporary New York physician: "If therefore, we wish to have the blessing of a healthy child; it there be any delight to us in contemplating the child of our own loins, in associating its resemblance to ourselves, or to those fond relatives long laid in the dust—if there be any pleasure in watching its lively movements and growth and secretly devoting ourselves incessantly to toil for its future welfare—in short, do we desire to see this child live, and live a life of happiness, our lives must be lives of temperance, and our habits the habits of the good." G. Ackerly, *On the Management of Children, in Sickness and in Health*, 2d ed. (New York, 1836), p. 44.

78. Davenport to Billings, carbon, May 3, 1903, C. B. Davenport Papers, American Philosophical Society. In the late nineteenth and early twentieth centuries a flourishing subliterature, much of it published by obscure publishers and clearly aimed at a lower-middle-class audience, still emphasized the possibility of a mothers's shaping her gestating child's ultimate attributes through appropriate intellectual activities and physical regimen.

Chapter 2

1. For historical studies of women's role and ideological responses to it in nineteenth-century America, see William L. O'Neil, *Everyone Was Brave: A History of Feminism in America* (Chicago, 1969); William Wasserstrom, *Heiress of All the Ages: Sex and Sentiment in the Victorian Tradition* (Minneapolis, 1959); Eleanor Flexner, *Century of Struggle: The Woman's Rights Movement in the United States* (New York, 1968); Aileen S. Kraditor, *The Ideas of the Woman Suffrage Movement, 1890-1920* (New York, 1965). For studies emphasizing the interaction between social change and sex role conflict, see Carroll Smith-Rosenberg, "Beauty, the Beast and the Militant Woman: A Case Study in Sex Roles and Social Stress in Jacksonian America," *American Quarterly* 23 (October 1971): 562-84; Carroll Smith-Rosenberg, "The Hysterical Woman: Sex Roles and Role Conflict in Nineteenth–Century America," *Social Research* 39 (Winter 1972): 652-78.

2. Marshall Hall, *Commentaries on Some of the More Important of the Diseases of Females*, in 3 parts (London, 1827), p. 2. Although this discussion centers on the nineteenth century, it must be understood that these formulations had a far longer pedigree.

3. Stephen Tracy, *The Mother and Her Offspring* (New York, 1860), p. xv; William Goodell, *Lessons in Gynecology* (Philadelphia, 1879), p. 332; William B. Carpenter, *Principles of Human Physiology: With Their Chief Applications to Pathology, Hygiene, and Forensic Medicine*, 4th ed. (Philadelphia, 1850), p. 727. In the mid-nineteenth century many of these traditional views of woman's peculiar physiological characteristics were restated in terms of the currently fashionable phrenology.

4. Charles D. Meigs, *Lecture on Some of the Distinctive Characteristics of the Female. Delivered before the Class of the Jefferson Medical College, January 5, 1847* (Philadelphia, 1847), p. 5.

5. M. L. Holbrook, *Parturition without Pain: A Code of Directions for Escaping from the Primal Curse* (New York, 1882), pp. 14-15. See also Edward H. Dixon, *Woman, and her Diseases, from the Cradle to the Grave: Adapted Exclusively to her Instruction in the Physiology of her System, and all the Diseases of her Critical Periods* (New York, 1846), p. 17; M. K. Hard, *Woman's Medical Guide: Being a Complete Review of the Peculiarities of the Female Constitution and the Derangements to which it is Subject. With a Description of Simple yet Certain Means for their Cure* (Mt. Vernon, Ohio, 1848), p. 11.

6. In the hypothetical pathologies of these generations, the blood was often thought to serve the same function as that of the nerves; it could cause general ills to have local manifestations and effect systemic changes based on local lesions. By mid-century, moreover, physicians had come to understand that only the blood supply connected the gestating mother to her child.

7. M. E. Dirix, *Woman's Complete Guide to Health* (New York, 1869), p. 24. So fashionable were such models in the late-nineteenth century that America's leading gynecologist in the opening years of the present century despaired of trying to dispel these exaggerated notions from his patients' minds. "It is difficult," he explained, "even for a healthy girl to rid her mind of constant impending evil from the uterus and ovaries, so prevalent is the idea that woman's ills are mainly 'reflexes' from the pelvic organs." Gynecological therapy was the treatment of choice for a myriad of symptoms. Howard A. Kelly, *Medical Gynecology* (New York, 1908), p. 73.

8. [Dr. Porter,] *Book of Men, Women, and Babies, The Laws of God applied to Obtaining, Rearing, and Developing the Natural, Healthful, and Beautiful in Humanity* (New York, 1855), p. 56; Tracy, *Mother and Offspring*, p. xxiii; H. S. Pomeroy, *The Ethics of Marriage* (New York, 1888), p. 78.

9. On the involuntary quality of female sexuality, see Alexander J. C. Skene, *Education and Culture as Related to the Health and Diseases of Women* (Detroit, 1889), p. 22.

10. George Engelmann, *The American Girl of To-Day: Modern Education and Functional Health* (Washington, D.C., 1900), pp. 9-10.

11. Alexander Harvey, "On the Relative Influence of the Male and Female Parents in the Reproduction of the Animal Species," *Monthly Journal of Medical Science* 19 (August 1854): 108-18; M. A. Pallen, "Heritage, or Hereditary Transmission," *St. Louis Medical and Surgical Journal* 14 (November 1856): 495; William Warren Potter, *How Should Girls be Educated? A Public Health Problem for Mothers, Educators, and Physicians* (Philadelphia, 1891), p. 9.

12. As one clerical analyst explained, "All the spare force of nature is concerned in this interior nutritive system, unfitting and disinclining the woman for strenuous muscular and mental enterprise, while providing for the shelter and nourishment of offspring throughout protracted periods of embryo and infancy." William C. Conant, "Sex in Nature and Society," *Baptist Quarterly* 4 (April 1870): 183.

13. William H. Holcombe, *The Sexes here and hereafter* (Philadelphia, 1869), pp. 201-2. William Holcombe was a Swedenborgian, and these contrasting views of the masculine and feminine also reflect New Church doctrines.

14. In regard to pregnancy many middle class women "sought to hide their imagined shame as long as possible" by tightening corsets and then remaining indoors, shunning even the best of friends—certainly never discussing the impending event. Henry B. Hemenway, *Healthful Womanhood and Childhood: Plain Talks to Non-Professional Readers* (Evanston, Ill., 1894); Elizabeth Evans, *The Abuse of Maternity* (Philadelphia, 1875), pp. 28-29.

15. For a brief summary of late-nineteenth-century assumptions in regard to human heredity, see the preceding chapter.

16. Since both male and female were ordinarily involved in decisions to practice birth control, the cases are not strictly analogous. Both, however, illustrate areas of social conflict organized about stress on traditional role characteristics. This discussion emphasizes only those aspects of the birth control debate which placed responsibility on the woman. Commentators did indeed differ in such emphases; in regard to abortion, however, writers of every religious and ideological persuasion agreed in seeing the matter as woman's responsibility.

17. "The results," as Edward H. Clarke put it in his widely discussed polemic on the subject, "are monstrous brains and puny bodies; abnormally active cerebration, and abnormally weak digestion; flowing thought and constipated bowels; lofty aspirations and neuralgic sensations. . . ." Edward H. Clarke, *Sex in Education; or, A Fair Chance for Girls* (Boston, 1873), p. 41. Thomas A. Emmett, in his textbook of gynecology,

warned in 1879 that girls of the better classes should spend the year before and two years after puberty at rest. "Each menstrual period should be passed in the recumbent position until her system becomes accustomed to the new order of life." Thomas Addis Emmett, *The Principles and Practice of Gynecology* (Philadelphia, 1879), p. 21. For a more detailed discussion of this subject, see Carroll Smith-Rosenberg, "Puberty to Menopause: The Cycle of Femininity in Nineteenth-Century America," *Feminist Studies* 2 (1974).

18. T. S. Clouston, *Female Education from a Medical Point of View* (Edinburgh, 1882), p. 20; Potter, *How Should Girls be Educated?*, p. 9.

19. The baleful hereditary effects of woman's secondary education served as a frequent sanction against this unnatural activity. Lawrence Irwell, "The Competition of the Sexes and Its Results," *American Medico-Surgical Bulletin* 10 (September 19, 1896): 319-20. All the doyens of American gynecology in the late-nineteenth century—Emmett, J. Marion Sims, T. Gaillard Thomas, Charles D. Meigs, William Goodell, and Mitchell—shared the conviction that higher education and excessive development of the nervous system might interfere with woman's proper performance of her maternal functions.

20. William Goodell, *Lessons in Gynecology* (Philadelphia, 1879), p. 353.

21. William Edgar Darnall, "The Pubescent Schoolgirl," *American Gynecological and Obstetrical Journal* 18 (June 1901): 490.

22. Board of Regents, *University of Wisconsin, Annual Report, for the Year Ending, September 30, 1877* (Madison, 1877), p. 45.

23. Clouston, *Female Education*, p. 19.

24. James E. Reeves, *The Physical and Moral Causes of Bad Health in American Women* (Wheeling, W. Va., 1875), p. 28; John Ellis, *Deterioration of the Puritan Stock and Its Causes* (New York, 1884), 7; George Everett, *Health Fragments or, Steps toward a True Life: Embracing Health, Digestion, Disease, and the Science of the Reproductive Organs* (New York, 1874), p. 37; Nathan Allen, "The Law of Human Increase; or, Population based on Physiology and Psychology," *Quarterly Journal of Psychological Medicine* 2 (April 1868): 231; idem, "The New England Family," *New Englander*, March 1882, pp. 9-10.

25. Sarah H. Stevenson, *The Physiology of Woman, Embracing Girlhood, Maternity, and Mature Age*, 2d ed. (Chicago, 1881), pp. 68, 77; Alice Stockham, *Tokology: A Book for Every Woman*, rev. ed. (Chicago, 1887), p. 257. Sarah H. Stevenson noted acidly that "the unerring instincts of woman have been an eloquent theme for those who do not know what they are talking about." Stevenson, *Physiology of Woman*, p. 79. The dress reform movement held far more significant implications than one would gather from the usually whimsical attitude with which it is normally approached; clothes were very much a part of woman's role. Health reformers, often critical as well of the medical establishment whose arguments we have, essentially, been describing, were often sympathetic to women's claims that not too much, but too little, mental stimulation was the cause of their ills, especially psychological ones. M. L. Holbrook, *Hygiene of the Brain and Nerves and the Cure of Nervousness* (New York, 1878), pp. 63-64, 122-23; James C. Jackson, *American Womanhood: Its Peculiarities and Necessities* (Dansville, N.Y., 1870), pp. 127-31.

26. For documentation of the progressive drop in the white American birth rate during the nineteenth century, and some possible reasons for this phenomenon, see Yasukichi Yasuba, *Birth Rates of the White Population in the United States, 1800-1860: An Economic Study* (Baltimore, 1962); J. Potter, "American Population in the Early National Period," Paul Deprez, ed., *Proceedings of Section V of the Fourth Congress of the International Economic History Association* (Winnipeg, Canada, 1970), pp. 55-69.

27. A. K. Gardner, *Conjugal Sins against the Laws of Life and Health* (New York, 1874), p. 131. H. R. Storer of Boston was probably the most prominent and widely read critic of such "conjugal sins." Abortion had in particular been discussed and attacked since early in the century, though it was not until the post-bellum years that it became a widespread concern of moral reformers. Alexander Draper, *Observations on Abortion. With an Account of the Means both Medicinal and Mechanical, Employed to Pro-*

duce that Effect . . . (Philadelphia, 1839); Hugh L. Hodge, *On Criminal Abortion; A Lecture* (Philadelphia, 1854). Advocates of birth control routinely used the dangers and prevalence of abortion as one argument justifying their cause.

28. *Report of the Suffolk District Medical Society on Criminal Abortion and Ordered Printed . . . May 9*, [1857] (Boston, 1857), p. 2. The report was almost certainly written by Storer. The Michigan report is summarized in William D. Haggard, *Abortion: Accidental, Essential, Criminal. Address before the Nashville Academy of Medicine, August 4, 1898* (Nashville, Tenn., 1898), p. 10. Much of the medical discussion centered about the need to convince women of the falsity and immorality of the traditional view that abortion was no crime if performed before quickening and the need to pass and enforce criminal laws and medical society proscriptions against abortionists.

29. Compare the warning of Pomeroy, *Ethics of Marriage*, pp. v, 56, with the editorial, "A Conviction for Criminal Abortion," *Boston Medical and Surgical Journal* 106 (January 5, 1882): 18-19. It is significant that discussions of birth control in the United States always emphasized the role and motivations of middle-class women and men; in England, following the canon of the traditional Malthusian debate, the working class and its needs played a far more prominent role. Not until late in the century did American birth control advocates tend to concern themselves with the needs and welfare of the working population. It is significant as well that English birth control advocates often used the prevalence of infanticide as an argument for birth control; in America this was rarely discussed. And one doubts if the actual incidence of infanticide was substantially greater in London than New York.

30. For a guide to literature on birth control in nineteenth-century America, see Norman Himes, *Medical History of Contraception* (Baltimore, 1936). See also J. A. Banks, *Prosperity and Parenthood: A Study of Family Planning among the Victorian Middle Classes* (London, 1954), and J. A. Banks and Olive Banks, *Feminism and Family Planning in Victorian England* (Liverpool, 1964); Margaret Hewitt, *Wives and Mothers in Victorian Industry* (London, ca. 1958). For the twentieth century, see David M. Kennedy, *Birth Control in America*.

31. John Humphrey Noyes, *Male Continence* (Oneida, N.Y., 1872), pp. 10-11.

32. It is not surprising that the design for a proto-diaphragm patented as early as 1846 should have been called "The Wife's Protector." J. B. Beers, "Instrument to Prevent Conception, Patented August 28th, 1846," design and drawings (Historical Collections, Library of the College of Physicians of Philadelphia).

33. In certain marriages, for example, even if the male had consciously chosen, indeed urged, the practice of birth control, he was effectively deprived of a dimension of sexual pleasure and of the numerous children which served as tangible and traditional symbols of masculinity—as well as the control over his wife which the existence of such children implied. In some marriages, however, birth control might well have brought greater sexual fulfillment because it reduced the anxiety of the female partner. Throughout the nineteenth century withdrawal was almost certainly the most common form of birth control. One author described it as "a practice so universal that it may well be termed a national vice, so common that it is unblushingly acknowledged by its perpetrators, for the commission of which the husband is even eulogized by his wife." [Cook,] *Satan in Society*, p. 152. One English advocate of birth control was candid enough to argue that "the real objection underlying the opposition, though it is not openly expressed, is the idea of the deprivation of pleasure supposed to be involved." Austin Holyoake, *Large or Small Families* (London, 1892), p. 11.

34. R. T. Trall, *Sexual Physiology: A Scientific and Popular Exposition of the Fundamental Problems in Sociology* (New York, 1866), pp. xi, 202. As women awoke to a realization of their own "individuality," as a birth control advocate explained it in the 1880s, they would rebel against such "enforced maternity." To radical feminist Tennie C. Claflin, man's right to impose his sexual desires upon woman was the issue underlying all opposition to woman suffrage and the expansion of woman's role. Tennie C. Claflin, *Constitutional Equality: A Right of Woman; or A Consideration of the Various Relations Which She Sustains as a Necessary Part of the Body of Society and*

Humanity; With Her Duties to Herself—together with a Review of the Constitution of the United States, Showing that the Right to Vote is Guaranteed to All Citizens. Also a Review of the Rights of Children (New York, 1871), p. 63. Particularly striking are the letters from women desiring birth control information. Margaret Sanger, *Motherhood in Bondage* (New York, 1928); E. B. Foote, Jr., *Radical Remedy*, pp. 114–20; Henry C. Wright, *The Unwelcome Child; or, The Crime of an Undesigned and Undesired Maternity* (Boston, 1858). This distinction between economic, "physical", and role considerations is, obviously, justifiable only for the sake of analysis; these considerations must have coexisted within each family in particular configurations.

35. Noyes, *Male Continence*, p. 16; Frederick Hollick, *The Marriage Guide; or, Natural History of Generation; A Private Instructor for Married Persons and Those About to Marry, Both Male and Female* (New York, ca. 1860), p. 348; Trall, *Sexual Physiology*, pp. 205–6.

36. Indeed, in these post-Darwinian years it was possible for at least one health reformer to argue that smaller families were a sign of that higher nervous evolution which accompanied civilization. [M. L. Holbrook,] *Marriage and Parentage* (New York, 1882). For the eugenic virtues of fewer but better children, see E. R. Shepherd, *For Girls: A Special Physiology: Being a Supplement to the Study of General Physiology*, 20th ed. (Chicago, 1887), p. 213; M. L. Griffith, *Ante-Natal Infanticide* (n.p., [1889]), p. 8.

37. See Louis François Etienne Bergeret, *The Prevention Obstacle; or, Conjugal Onanism*, trans. P. de Marmon, (New York, 1870); C. H. F. Routh, *Moral and Physical Evils Likely to Follow If Practices Intended to Act as Checks to Population Be not Strongly Discouraged and Condemned*, 2d ed. (London, 1879), p. 13; Goodell, *Lessons in Gynecology*, pp. 371, 374; Thomas Hersey, *The Midwife's Practical Directory; or, Woman's Confidential Friend: Comprising, Extensive Remarks on the Various Casualties and Forms of Diseases Preceding, Attending and Following the Period of Gestation, with Appendix*, 2d ed. (Baltimore, 1836), p. 80; William H. Walling, *Sexology* (Philadelphia, 1902), p. 79.

38. J. R. Black, *The Ten Laws of Health; or, How Disease Is Produced and Can Be Prevented* (Philadelphia, 1873), p. 251. See also C. A. Greene, *Build Well. The Basis of Individual, Home, and National Elevation. Plain Truths Relating to the Obligations of Marriage and Parentage* (Boston, ca. 1885), p. 99; E. P. LeProhon, *Voluntary Abortion, or Fashionable Prostitution, with Some Remarks upon the Operation of Craniotomy* (Portland, Me., 1867), p. 15; Myer Solis-Cohen, *Girl, Wife, and Mother* (Philadelphia, 1911), p. 213.

39. There is an instructive analogy between these ponderously mechanistic sanctions against birth control and abortion and the psychodynamic arguments against abortion used so frequently in the twentieth century; both served precisely the same social function. In both cases the assumption of woman's childbearing destiny provided the logical basis against which a denial of this calling produced sickness—in the nineteenth century through physiological and, ultimately, pathological processes; in the twentieth century through guilt and psychological but again, ultimately, pathological processes.

40. A. K. Gardner, for example, confessed sympathy for the seduced and abandoned patron of the abortionist, "but for the married shirk, who disregards her divinely-ordained duty, we have nothing but contempt. . . ." Gardner, *Conjugal Sins*, p. 112. See also E. Frank Howe, *Sermon on Ante-Natal Infanticide delivered at the Congregational Church in Terre Haute, on Sunday Morning, March 28, 1869* (Terre Haute, Ind., 1869); J. H. Tilden, *Cursed before Birth* (Denver, ca. 1895); J. M. Toner, *Maternal Instinct, or Love* (Baltimore, 1864), p. 91.

41. It must be emphasized that this is but one theme in a complex debate surrounding the issue of birth control and sexuality. A group of more evangelically oriented health reformers tended to emphasize, instead, the responsibility of the "overgrown, abnormally developed and wrongly directed amativeness of the man" and to see the woman as victim. John Cowan, Henry C. Wright, and Dio Lewis were widely read exemplars of this point of view. This group shared a number of assumptions and presumably psychological

needs, and represents a somewhat distinct interpretive task. John Cowan, *The Science of a New Life* (New York, 1874), p. 275.

42. W. L. Atlee and D. A. O'Donnell, "Report of the Committee on Criminal Abortion," *Transactions of the American Medical Association* 22 (1871): 241.

43. The most tireless advocate of these views was Nathan Allen, a Lowell, Massachusetts, physician and health reformer. Nathan Allen, "The Law of Human Increase; or, Population based on Physiology and Psychology," *Quarterly Journal of Psychological Medicine* 2 (April 1868): 209-66; idem, *Changes in New England Population. Read at the Meeting of the American Social Science Association, Saratoga, September 6, 1877* (Lowell, Mass., 1877); idem, "The Physiological Laws of Human Increase," *Transactions of the American Medical Association* 21 (1870): 381-407; idem, "Physical Degeneracy," *Journal of Psychological Medicine* 4 (October 1870): 725-64; idem, "The Normal Standard of Woman for Propagation," *American Journal of Obstetrics* 9 (April 1876): 1-39.

44. Ellis, *Deterioration of Puritan Stock*, p. 3; H. R. Storer, *Why Not?* (Boston, 1868), p. 85.

45. Clarke, *Sex in Education*, p. 63. For similar warnings see Henry Gibbons, *On Feticide* (San Francisco, 1878), p. 4; Charles Buckingham, *The Proper Treatment of Children, Medical or Medicinal* (Boston, 1873), p. 15; Edward Jenks, "The Education of Girls from a Medical Stand-Point," *Transactions of the Michigan State Medical Society* 13 (1889): 52-62; Paul Paquin, *The Supreme Passions of Man* (Battle Creek, Mich., 1891), p. 76.

46. These arguments, first formulated in the 1860s, had become clichés in medical and reformist circles by the 1880s. See Barbara Miller Solomon, *Ancestors and Immigrants: A Changing New England Tradition* (Cambridge, Mass., 1956); John Higham, *Strangers in the Land: Patterns of American Nativism, 1860-1925* (New Brunswick, N.J., 1955). Such arguments exhibited a growing consciousness of class as well as ethnic sensitivity; it was the better-educated and more sensitive members of society, anti-Malthusians began to argue, who would curtail their progeny, while the uneducated and coarse would hardly change their habits. H. S. Pomeroy, *Is Man Too Prolific? The So-Called Malthusian Idea* (London, 1891), pp. 57-58.

47. Ellis, *Deterioration of Puritan Stock*, p. 10.

48. Oscar Handlin, *Race and Nationality in American Life*, 5th ed. (Boston, 1957), pp. 139-66.

49. One might postulate a more traditionally psychodynamic explanatory model, one which would see the arguments described as a male defense against their own consciousness of sexual inadequacy or ambivalence or of their own unconscious fears of female sexual powers. These emphases are quite distinct. The first, though it also assumes the reality of individual psychic mechanisms such as repression and projection, is tied very much to the circumstances of a particular generation, to social location, and to social perception. The second kind of explanation is more general, time-free, and based on a presumably ever-recurring male fear of female sexuality and its challenge to the capacity of particular individuals to act and live an appropriately male role. For the literature on this problem see Wolfgang Lederer, *The Fear of Women* (New York, 1968).

50. At this time, moreover, most psychiatric clinicians and theoreticians would agree that no model exists to extend the insights gained from individual psychodynamics to the behavior of larger social groups such as national populations or social classes.

51. Most societies provide alternative roles to accommodate the needs of personality variants, as, for example, the shaman role in certain Siberian tribes or the accepted man-woman homosexual of certain American Indian tribes. In the nineteenth-century English-speaking world such roles as that of the religious enthusiast and the chronic female invalid or hysteric may well have provided such modalities. But a period of peculiarly rapid or widespread social change can make even such role alternatives inadequate mechanisms of adjustment for many individuals. Others in the same society may respond to the same pressures of change by demanding an undeviating acceptance of traditional role prescriptions and refusing to accept the legitimacy of such cultural variants. The role of the hysterical woman in late-nineteenth-century America suggests many of the problems inherent in creating such alternative social roles. While offering both an escape

from the everyday duties of wife and mother, and an opportunity for the display of covert hostility and aggression, this role inflicted great bodily (though nonorganic) pain, provided no really new role or interest, and perpetuated—even increased—the patient's dependence on traditional role characteristics, especially that of passivity. See Carroll Smith-Rosenberg, "The Hysterical Woman," pp. 652–78. For useful discussions of hysteria and neurasthenia, see Ilza Veith, *Hysteria: The History of a Disease* (Chicago, 1965); Henri F. Ellenberger, *The Discovery of the Unconscious: The History and Evolution of Dynamic Psychiatry* (New York, 1970). Esther Fisher-Homberger has recently argued that these diagnostic categories masked an endemic male-female conflict: "Hysterie und Mysogynie—ein Aspekt der Hysteriegeschichte," *Gesnerus* 26 (1969): 117–27.

Chapter 3

1. Among the more important, and characteristically diverse, recent attempts to deal with this general problem are Peter T. Cominos, "Late-Victorian Sexual Respectability and the Social System," *International Review of Social History* 8 (1963):18–48, 216–50; Steven Marcus, *The Other Victorians: A Study of Sexuality and Pornography in Mid-Nineteenth-Century England* (New York, 1966); Stephen Nissenbaum, "Careful Love: Sylvester Graham and the Emergence of Victorian Sexual Theory in America, 1830–1840" (Ph.D. diss., University of Wisconsin, 1968); Graham Barker-Benfield, "The Horrors of the Half-Known Life: Aspects of the Exploitation of Women by Men" (Ph.D. diss., University of California, Los Angeles, 1968); Nathan G. Hale, Jr., "American Civilized Morality, 1870–1912," in *Freud and the Americans. The Beginnings of Psychoanalysis in the United States, 1876–1917* (New York, 1971), pp. 24–46; David M. Kennedy, "The Nineteenth-Century Heritage: The Family, Feminism, and Sex," chap. 2 in *Birth Control in America. The Career of Margaret Sanger* (New Haven, 1970), pp. 36–71.

2. We have come to think in such terms as a result of our tendency to impose individual psychodynamic models upon a total culture, thus allowing the convenient "diagnoses" of its modal personality—and ills. For an early criticism of this position, see Erwin H. Ackerknecht, "Psychopathology. Primitive Medicine and Primitive Culture," *Bulletin of the History of Medicine* 14 (1943): 30–67, reprinted in Ackerknecht, *Medicine and Ethnology. Selected Essays* (Baltimore, 1971).

3. An important question, both for historical method on the one hand and psychiatric theory on the other, relates to whether such discontinuities between the content of a particular ideological set and certain irreducible human needs can be explicitly and absolutely pathogenic, or whether it is simply the immediate occasion for conflict in individuals otherwise predisposed.

4. The strategy of examining role options in terms of their emotional meanings to the individuals who choose to embrace them is, of course, not limited to sex and gender roles. It is even more easily applied to certain adult roles: for a study of the choice by a number of mid-nineteenth-century Americans of the highly atypical role of research scientist, see chap. 8, below.

5. The phrase is from a review by Robert Ackerman in *Victorian Studies* 14 (1970): 108.

6. Many of these materials are rare. I have used the excellent collections at the National Library of Medicine, Bethesda, Maryland; College of Physicians of Philadelphia; and the Countway Library of Medicine, Boston, and would like to thank John B. Blake, L. M. Holloway, and Richard Wolfe of these institutions for their aid and courtesy. There is no adequate bibliographical guide to such writings, with the exception of the appropriate subject categories in the *Index-Catalogue of the Library of the Surgeon-General's Office* Washington, D.C.:1879–). The bibliographies in Nissenbaum, "Careful Love," and Norman Himes, *Medical History of Contraception* (Baltimore, 1936), provide valuable supplementary materials.

7. As personified in the career of Anthony Comstock most conspicuously and in the social purity movement generally. For an important description of this moral reform, see David J. Pivar, *Purity Crusade. Sexual Morality and Social Control, 1868–1900* (Westport, Conn, 1973); see also R. C. Johnson, "Anthony Comstock: Reform, Vice, and the American Way," (Ph.D. diss. University of Wisconsin, 1973).

8. A recent student has emphasized the eighteenth-century origin of this subgenre, but the mid-nineteenth-century saw a proliferation of such tracts and pamphlets so distinct as to constitute a more than quantitative change. Robert H. MacDonald, "The Frightful Consequences of Onanism: Notes on the History of a Delusion," *Journal of the History of Ideas* 29 (1967): 423–31. S. A. Tissot's (1728–97) widely read and influential tract on onanism was, significantly, not reprinted in the United States until 1832, almost half a century after its original publication. The anonymous English pamphlet "Onania" was, so far as is known, reprinted only once (1724) before 1820 and apparently in a relatively small edition, since a single copy only is known to survive. See entry 1435, Robert B. Austin, *Early American Medical Imprints. . . 1668–1820* (Washington, D.C., 1961), p. 152. English books dealing with masturbation, however, almost certainly did circulate in the early national period. Probably the most widely read was Samuel Solomon's *A Guide to Health; or, Advice to Both Sexes, in Nervous and Consumptive Complaints. . .* (n.p., n.d.). The imprints on this famous quackish tract are all deliberately vague, but one copy at the Countway Library is inscribed with the date 1804 in a contemporary hand.

9. In parallel fashion the rationalistic and pragmatic temperance reform of the late-eighteenth-century had been metamorphosed in the same period into an uncompromising crusade for teetotalism. The connection of both instances of activist—even punitive—moralism with the pietistic energies of the Second Great Awakening which immediately preceded it seems clear enough, but difficult to specify in terms of precise relationships. The tendency toward such repressiveness was nowhere so clearly marked as during the years of the Second Great Awakening itself. One possible explanation for the tone of intrusive moralism which marked the generations after the 1830s centers on the possibility that childhood socialization was altered during the years of the Awakening so as to create a peculiar collective experience for many of those brought up in these years, later to become prominent in social and moral reform movements. Certainly the attitude toward childhood sexuality might, for example, be seen in this context; such an explanation would also help to explain the sudden concern with masturbation in mid-century and succeeding decades. But such suggestions are, of course, speculative. That the cooling ardors of pietism were succeeded by a more rigid and formal moralism is, however, unquestionable.

10. John Ellis, *Marriage and its Violations. Licentiousness and Vice* (New York, 1860), p. 21. Cf. Nissenbaum, "Careful Love," p. 4.

11. Three years might thus intervene between conception and weaning, a period during which no sexual intercourse was to be tolerated. This taboo is relatively common in non-Western cultures and its latent function is generally presumed to be that of population control. Impressionistic evidence indicates that few mid-nineteenth-century Americans obeyed this injunction; in those who urged it most strongly, its function must be sought ultimately in the area of individual psychodynamics.

12. Their tone of conscious manipulativeness indicates that at least some individuals in the culture did not share these phobic attitudes.

13. John Fondey, *A Brief and Intelligible View of the Nature, Origin, and Cure of Tubercular or Scrofulous Disease* (Philadelphia, 1860), p. 45.

14. Parents were warned again and again that it was their responsibility to "repress the premature development of the passions," "natural instincts" though they may have been. W. S. Chipley, *A Warning to Fathers, Teachers, and Young Men, in Relation to a Fruitful Cause of Insanity. . .* (Louisville, Ky., 1861), pp. 169, 174.

15. These phrases, typical of many scores of others, are from Walter Preston, *The Sufferer's Manual. A Book of Advice and Instruction for Young Men. . .* (Chicago, 1879), p. 37; William Capp, *The Daughter: Her Health, Education, and Wedlock. Homely Suggestions for Mothers and Daughters* (Philadelphia, 1891), p. 72.

16. *An Hour's Conference with Fathers and Sons, in Relation to a Common and Fatal Indulgence of Youth* (Boston, 1840), p. 26; Elizabeth Blackwell, *Counsel to Parents on the Moral Education of Their Children* (New York, 1880), pp. 94–95. Cf. L. N. Fowler, *The Principles of Phrenology and Physiology Applied to Man's Social Relations* (Boston, 1842), p. 18.

17. Ely Van De Warker, "A Gynecological Study of the Oneida Community," reprinted from *American Journal of Obstetrics* 17 (1884): 11.

18. As hereditarian ideas became increasingly plausible in the second half of the century, they were naturally made to underwrite this argument; the sanction of individual sin was reinforced by that of potential race degeneration.

19. James Ashton, *The Book of Nature; Containing Information for Young People Who Think of Getting Married* (New York, 1861), p. 45; H. Newell Martin, *The Human Body*, 2d ed., rev. (New York, 1881), appendix, pp. 20–21.

20. Though physicians tried to scout the idea throughout the century, it seems, significantly, to have had a tenacious hold on the popular mind. Cf. Alice Stockham, *Tokology. A Book for Every Woman* (Chicago, 1887), p. 326; Frederick Hollick, *The Marriage Guide, or Natural History of Generation...* (New York, 1860), p. 339; T. S. Verdi, *Maternity. A Popular Treatise for Young Wives and Mothers* (New York, 1870), p. 25; M. K. Hard, *Woman's Medical Guide* (Mt. Vernon, Ohio, 1848), p. 51.

21. *Causation, Course, and Treatment of Reflex Insanity in Woman* (Boston, 1871), pp. 211–12; Robert T. Wakely, *Woman and Her Secret Passions* (New York, c.1846), p. 92; M. Larmont, *Medical Adviser and Marriage Guide...* (New York, 1861), pp. 320–22.

22. M.L. Holbrook, *Parturition without Pain: A Code of Directions for Escaping from the Primal Curse* (New York, 1882), p. 36.

23. William Alcott, probably the most widely read of such authors, was, for example, never able to escape the ambiguity inherent in these contradictory orientations. Sex itself he always praised as a gift of God, a necessity for preserving the species, and sexual vigor he admired as a sign of health. Thus the emotional logic inherent in his plaintive distinction between sexual "power," which he could only characterize as healthy and admirable, and "excitability," which he saw as "pathological," as tainted by loss of control. Cf. introduction by Charles E. Rosenberg in Alcott, *Physiology of Marriage* (1866; reprinted, New York, 1972).

24. A. E. Newton, *The Better Way: An Appeal to Men in Behalf of Human Culture through Wiser Parentage* (New York, 1890), p. 29.

25. Henry N. Guernsey, *Plain Talks on Avoided Subjects* (Philadelphia, 1899), p. 25.

26. The reality of masculine expectation was unavoidable: William Acton, for example, probably the most widely quoted English advocate of a chaste sex life, warned that only a careful moral indoctrination in secondary schools could avert the well-nigh universal social pressure on young men to experiment sexually. "Supported by such a public opinion [the young man] need not blush when tempted or jeered by the licentious. Innocence, or even ignorance of vice, will no longer be a dishonor or a jest." Cominos, "Late-Victorian Sexual Respectability," p. 40. Acton and like-thinking Americans frequently made this point.

27. Paul Paquin, *The Supreme Passions of Man; or, The Origin, Causes, and Tendencies of the Passions of the Flesh* (Battle Creek, Mich., 1891), p. 71. Cf. Elizabeth Blackwell, *The Human Element in Sex*, 3d ed. (London, 1884), p. 28.

28. S. R. Wells, *Wedlock; or, The Right Relations of the Sexes* (New York, 1869), p. 44.

29. Significantly, even in writers most explicitly evangelical in their orientation, purely religious arguments were employed infrequently and only in an ancillary capacity: the way in which arguments scientific in form, and dependent for their legitimacy upon the status of scientific knowledge, dominate debate even in this culturally sensitive area implies a great deal about the progress of secularization in nineteenth-century America.

30. "A Grave Social Problem," *British Medical Journal* 1 (January 14, 1882): 56.

31. A few radicals did assume an openly critical stance: all talk of absolutely interdicting adolescent sexuality and limiting it severely in marriage was, in the words of

one such author, mere "child's talk." For nature, he explained, "is a tyrant": the sexual impulse could never be suppressed completely. Misguided attempts to reach this end would result inevitably in mental and physical illness. J. Soule, *Science of Reproduction and Reproductive Control. The Necessity of Some Abstaining from Having Children—The Duty of All to Limit Their Families According to Their Circumstances Demonstrated* (n.p., ca. 1856), pp. 21, 32-34.

32. Sydney Elliot, *Aedology. A Treatise on Generative Life*, rev. ed. (New York, 1892), p. 181; C. A. Greene, *Build Well. The Basis of Individual, Home, and National Elevation* (Boston, ca. 1885), pp. 149-50; Caroline Latimer, *Girl and Woman. A Book for Mothers and Daughters* (New York, 1910), p. 141.

33. Such seductions could also have served to express hostility toward their employers. The biological mother might also have projected this hostility-shaded image as one mode of expressing rivalry and ambivalence toward the woman who actually cared for her children. It may also conceivably have mirrored the unwillingness of particular individuals to accept the role of *their* own parents in the inevitable sexual contacts between child and childrearer. This almost whimsically complex catalog demonstrates clearly the difficulties of interpretation in this area; there are simply no easy or one-dimensional explanations.

34. This discussion is not, of course, meant to imply that the sexual life of the "lower orders" in the mid-nineteenth century was necessarily less repressed than that of the would-be members of the middle class. Contemporary data would indicate that lower-class membership need not imply greater freedom of expression in matters sexual. Cf. Lee Rainwater, *And the Poor Get Children* (Chicago, 1960).

35. Alice Stockham, *Karezza. Ethics of Marriage* (Chicago, 1896), p. 77.

36. Male and female, they seemed to sense, were serving as ever more emotionally charged polarities, organizing about themselves an increasingly inclusive assortment of personality traits and behaviors. Every aspect of high culture, even Chrisianity itself, was shaped by this polarization. "Man," as one mid-century feminist put it, "must be regenerated by true and deep religious experiences, (Religion is feminine), or by the love and influence of Woman. . . ." Eliza Farnham, *Woman and Her Era* (New York, 1864), 11:44.

37. The first quotation is from John B. Newman, *The Philosophy of Generation* (New York, 1849), p. 63, the phrase concerning impotence from Drs. Jordan and Beck, *Happiness or Misery? Being Four Lectures on the Functions and Disorders of the Nervous System and Reproductive Organs* (New York, c. 1861), p. 18; the final quotation from R. J. Culverwell, *Self-Preservation, Manhood, Causes of its Premature Decline . . .* (New York, [1830]), p. 28. Emphasis on the "mortification" of the impotent groom on his wedding night was also standard. Cf. A. H. Hayes, *The Science of Life; or, Self-Preservation* (Boston, ca. 1868), pp. 180-81.

38. Jordan and Beck, *Happiness or Misery?* p. 39. A recent historian of psychiatry has suggested that the archetypical symptoms of nineteenth-century masturbatory insanity resemble those of the schizoid personality. Possibly true in particular cases, this interpretation would not be inconsistent with the argument we have tried to suggest. E. H. Hare, "Masturbatory Insanity: The History of an Idea," *Journal of Mental Science* 108 (1962): 9. A word of caution: despite our tendency to see this masturbation literature as characteristic of Anglo-Saxon Protestantism, the three most quoted authorities in the late 1830s and 1840s were French-speaking: S. A. Tissot, Leopold Deslandes, and C. F. Lallemand.

39. This sanction illustrates clearly a characteristic nineteenth-century emotional polarity—that between sexuality and maternity. It should also be noted that although virtually all nineteenth-century writers on masturbation noted that its devotees included females as well as males, this generally conceded observation never seemed to suggest the naturalness of sexuality in women.

40. Some clearly atypical medical authors were so dominated by such anxieties that their formulations starkly underline emotional themes normally presented in terms more indirect and ambivalent. A few, for example, warned that artificial phalli employed by female masturbators would create needs which no husband could ever satisfy. J. DuBois,

Marriage Physiologically Considered, 2d ed. (New York, 1839), pp. 26–27. (One Scottish physician even suggested the use of a kind of chastity belt to guard against this possibility. John Moodie, *A Medical Treatise; with Principles and Observations, to Preserve Chastity and Morality* [Edinburgh, 1848]). A related procedure was that of clitoridectomy as a radical cure for hysteria, nymphomania, and allied complaints. Cf. John Duffy, "Masturbation and Clitoridectomy. A Nineteenth-Century View," *Journal of the American Medical Association* 186 (October 19, 1963): 246–48; Guy Nichol, "The Clitoris Martyr," *World Medicine,* May 6, 1969, pp. 59–65; Isaac Baker Brown, *On the Curability of Certain Forms of Insanity, Epilepsy, Catalepsy, and Hysteria in Females* (London, 1866). This procedure was never widely practiced. Isaac Baker Brown, the London gynecologist who sought to popularize clitoridectomy, enjoyed little success and was, indeed, formally condemned by the Obstetrical Society of London as a result of his enthusiasm.

41. For representative example of the persistence of such anxieties, see C. S. Eldridge, *Self-Enervation: Its Consequences and Treatment* (Chicago, 1869), pp. 15–17, 25; J. E. Ralph, *Seminalia. . .* (New York, 1865), p. 81; E. Becklard, *Physiological Mysteries and Revelations in Love, Courtship, and Marriage* (New York, 1844), pp. 100–101; Joseph W. Howe, *Excessive Venery, Masturbation, and Continence* (New York, 1883), p. 41; Thomas L. Nichols, *Esoteric Anthropology* (London, n.d.), p. 84.

42. The English physician William Acton was probably the best known among such evangelically oriented authors. (Steven Marcus's *Other Victorians* contains a chapter analyzing Acton's writings; Marcus, however, presents Alcott's somewhat extreme views as typical of those accepted by his medical contemporaries.) In the United States such enthusiasts as John Cowan, Dio Lewis, and, to an extent, William Alcott exemplify the position of those similarly fearful of the perils implicit in the expression of sexuality.

43. W. Goodell, *Lessons in Gynecology* (Philadelphia 1879), p. 366.

44. Alcott, *Physiology of Marriage,* p. 153. The male child's oedipal anxieties and fear of female sexuality would appear to be thus neatly expressed in Alcott's intellectual ideogram—the mother dramatically betraying the child within her in succumbing to the father's sexuality.

45. Dio Lewis, *Chastity; or, Our Secret Sins* (New York, 1894, c. 1874), pp. 117, 113.

46. Henry C. Wright, *The Empire of the Mother over the Character and Destiny of the Race,* 2d ed. (Boston, 1866), p. 67.

47. One thinks of the Americans who consumed the oceans of whiskey and brandy distilled in nineteenth-century America despite the zealous admonitions of temperance advocates.

48. In what is probably the strongest passage in Steven Marcus' *Other Victorians,* the author underlines the tragedy inherent in the need of the urban poor to repress sexuality as a prerequisite to the achievement of a minimum human dignity (pp. 147–50).

49. Cominos, "Late-Victorian Sexual Respectability," p. 216.

50. We must, for example, define the appropriate demographic and economic realities, and this implies the evaluation of such factors as change in occupation and family size, age at first marriage, and patterns of internal migration. The precise definition of such parameters must precede any final evaluation of the relationship between these structural realities and the ideological formulations which help shape the formal and emotional perceptions of individuals in a particular generation.

Chapter 4

1. Cited by Morris Steggarda, "Charles Benedict Davenport (1866–1944): The Man and His Contributions to Physical Anthropology," *American Journal of Physical Anthropology* n.s. 2 (1944): 167. The best sketch of Davenport's life is that written by his long-time associate, E. Carleton MacDowell, "Charles Benedict Davenport, 1866–1944. A Study of Conflicting Influences," *Bios* 17 (1946): 3–50. Additional data on Davenport's work and especially on his place in the eugenics and immigration restriction movement

may be found in Mark H. Haller, *Eugenics: Hereditary Attitudes in American Thought* (New Brunswick, N.J., 1963). The memoir by Oscar Riddle, another of Davenport's long-time associates ("Biographical Memoir of Charles Benedict Davenport, 1866-1944," in *National Academy of Sciences, Biographical Memoirs* [Washington, D.C., 1948], 25: 75-110) is largely based on the previous study by MacDowell.

2. For the story of Davenport's efforts to have the Station established, see MacDowell, "Davenport," pp. 15-24.

3. "A History of the Quantitative Study of Variation," *Science* n.s. 12 (1900): 870. Davenport was prominent enough in biostatistics for Karl Pearson to have asked him to serve as American editor of *Biometrika* when the journal was founded in 1901. Davenport was also the author of the first American handbook on the subject, *Statistical Methods with Special Reference to Biological Variation* (New York, 1899).

4. "The Statistical Study of Evolution," *Popular Science Monthly*, September 1901, p. 459. In 1900 the ideas of Weissman were, as we have seen, still very much a matter of controversy. Davenport, for example, suggested that biometrics might be used in finally proving or disproving the existence of telegony, the idea that a woman's first mate might have an effect upon her children by a subsequent sire. Thus a woman having intercourse with a Negro might later have dark-pigmented children by a white father. "The Aims of the Quantitative Study of Variation," in *Biological Lectures from the Marine Biological Laboratory, 1899* (Boston, 1900), p. 272.

5. "Mendel's Law of Dichotomy in Hybirds," *Biological Bulletin* 2 (1901): 307-10. Davenport's diary, deposited with his papers at the American Philosophical Society Library, Philadelphia, notes his having written the article on November 27, 1900. MacDowell, "Davenport," p. 28.

6. For a number of references to articles in this controversy, cf. Beatrice Bateson, *William Bateson, F.R.S., Naturalist* (Cambridge, 1928), pp. 464-65, appendix, and William B. Provine, *The Origins of Theoretical Population Genetics* (Chicago, 1971).

7. "Euthenics and Eugenics," *Popular Science Monthly*, December 1910, p. 20; "Some Social Applications of Eugenics," *Medical Genetics and Eugenics* (Philadelphia, 1940), p. 40: cf., in this connection, "The Value of Zoology to Humanity," *Science* n.s. 16 (1915): 337; "Mendelism in Man," *Proceedings of the Sixth Annual Congress of Genetics* 1 (1932): 137, 140; Davenport to Henry H. Goddard, September 17, 1910; Davenport to Frederick Osborn, February 10, 1930.

8. "Some Social Applications of Modern Principles of Heredity," *Transactions of the Fifteenth International Congress on Hygiene and Demography* 4 (1912): 658.

9. C. B. Davenport and Gertrude C. Davenport, "Heredity of Skin Pigment in Man," *American Naturalist* 44 (1910): 642-72, 705-31. Cf. Curt Stern, *Principles of Human Genetics*, 2d ed. (San Francisco, 1960), p. 351. Over the years, however, Davenport rigidly applied the formula which had seemed to explain successfully the inheritance of skin color to other traits such as body build, otosclerosis, and susceptibility to goiter, though in the latter two conditions he assumed that one of the factors was on an autosome, the other on a sex chromosome. Davenport, *Body Build: Its Development and Inheritance* Eugenics Record Office, Bulletin no. 24, (Cold Spring Harbor, N.Y., 1924), p. 20; idem, *The Genetical Factor in Endemic Goiter*, Carnegie Institution of Washington, Publication no. 428 (Washington, D.C., 1932), p. 44; Davenport, Bess L. Miles, and Lillian B. Frink, "The Genetic Factor in Otosclerosis," *Archives of Otolaryngology* 17 (1933): 135-70, 340-83, 503-48.

10. Davenport to H. H. Laughlin, April 1, 1908.

11. Davenport, assisted by Mary Theresa Scudder, *Naval Officers. Their Heredity and Development*, Carnegie Institution of Washington, Publication no. 259 (Washington, D.C., 1919).

12. "Some Social Applications," pp. 3-4; "Inheritance of Some of the Elements of Hysteria," *Illinois Medical Journal* 24 (1913): 289-90.

13. *Naval Officers*, p. 9.

14. "The Nature of Hereditary Mental Defect," p. 5, reprinted from *Proceedings of the Fiftieth Annual Session of the American Association for the Study of the Feeble-minded* (1926). For similar statements, cf. Davenport and Morris Steggarda, *Race Crossing in Jamaica*, Carnegie Institution of Washington, Publication no. 395 (Wa-

shington, D.C., 1929), p. 469; Davenport, *The Feebly-Inhibited*, Carnegie Institution of Washington, Publication no. 236 (Washington, D.C., 1915), p. 119.

15. "Crime, Heredity, and Environment," *Journal of Heredity* 19 (1928): 312. For the development of the concept of cerebral localization, see Robert. M. Young, *Mind, Brain, and Adaptation in the Nineteenth Century. Cerebral Localization and Its Biological Context from Gall to Ferrier* (Oxford, 1970); William F. Bynum, "The Anatomical Method, Natural Theology, and the Functions of the Brain," *Isis* 64 (1973): 445-68.

16. "Mendel's Law of Dichotomy," p. 308. "Evidence of Man's Ancestral History in the Later Development of the Child," *Proceedings of the National Academy of Science* 19 (1933: 787; "Ontogeny and Phylogeny of Man's Appendages," *ibid.*, 20 (1934): 363.

17. Davenport to David Starr Jordan, February 6, 1912; "Heredity, Culpability, Praiseworthiness, Punishment, and Reward," *Popular Science Monthly*, July 1913, p. 35; "Light Thrown by the Experimental Study of Heredity upon the Factors and Methods of Evolution," *American Naturalist* 46 (1912): 129; "Crime, Heredity, and Environment," p. 307; "Heredity in Nervous Disease and its Social Bearings," *Journal of the American Medical Association* 59 (1912): 2141-42.

18. Cf. "Heredity of Constitutional Mental Disorders," *Psychological Bulletin* 17 (1920): 303; "Heredity in Nervous Disease," pp. 2141-42; Davenport to David Starr Jordan, February 9, 1922.

19. For the pioneering survey of this conflict, see Richard Hofstadter, *Social Darwinism in American Thought*, 1860-1915 (Philadelphia, 1944).

20. *Heredity in Relation to Eugenics* (New York, 1911), p. 80; "Heredity, Culpability, Praiseworthiness," p. 37; *Delineator*, April 1912, p. 272; Davenport to Frederick Osborn, December 23, 1932.

21. *Heredity in Relation to Eugenics*, p. 219; Davenport to Madison Grant, April 7, 1925. The story of Davenport's relationship to the eugenics and immigration restriction movements, as well as the fate of these movements in the 1930s, is excellently told by Haller, *Eugenics*; see also Kenneth M. Ludmerer, *Genetics and American Society. A Historical Appraisal* (Baltimore, 1972).

22. Castle to Irving Fisher, February 25, 1924, carbon in Davenport Papers; Pearl, *The Present Status of Eugenics*, p. 10. For earlier expressions of disquietude, see Castle to Davenport, November 10, 1910; William Bateson to Davenport, February 11, 1921; T. H. Morgan to H. F. Osborn, June 14, 1920, carbon in Davenport Papers; L. J. Cole to J. A. Detlefsen, January 19, 1914, Department of Genetics Papers, University of Wisconsin Archives. T. H. Morgan, the most important geneticist of Davenport's generation, was always careful to avoid the ingenuous reductionism which characterized Davenport's views of the determinants of behavior and "racial characteristics." Morgan et al., *The Mechanism of Mendelian Heredity* (New York, 1915), p. 210; Morgan, *Evolution and Genetics* (Princeton, 1925), pp. 206-7.

23. MacDowell, "Davenport," p. 34.

24. Though in the past decade a growing debate over the possibilities of "genetic engineering" recalls some of the moral and political themes which marked the eugenics movement.

25. Davenport emphasized as well the importance of constitutional factors at a time when most of his contemporaries found it easy to overlook them. The germ theory, he pointed out again and again, was only a partial explanation of disease processes. Everyone was exposed to the tubercule bacillus, but only some died of tuberculosis. Not all alcoholics exhibited delerium tremens, he argued, nor was goiter simply the result of iodine insufficiency.

Chapter 5

1. There is little published information on Beard's life, though he is referred to in almost every general history of psychiatry. An interesting short sketch was written by Charles L. Dana, "Dr. George M. Beard; A Sketch of His Life and Character, with Some Personal Reminiscences," *Archives of Neurology and Psychiatry* 10 (1923): 427-35.

Valuable as well are the recollections of A. D. Rockwell, a partner of Beard's in medical practice and coauthor of his early works on medical electricity, *Rambling Recollections: An Autobiography* (New York, 1920), esp. pp. 182–90. See also the contemporary obituaries by Rockwell, "The Late Dr. George M. Beard. A Sketch," *Medical Record* 24 (1883): 399–401, and W. J. Morton, "Obituary. George Miller Beard, A.M., M.D., New York," *Journal of Nervous and Mental Diseases* 10 (1883): 130–34. For an introduction to Beard's ideas and their relationships to later developments in medical psychology, see Henry Alden Bunker, Jr., "From Beard to Freud. A Brief History of the Concept of Neurasthenia," *Medical Review of Reviews* 36 (1930): 109–14. For more recent studies see Henri Ellenberger, *The Discovery of the Unconscious. The History and Evolution of Dynamic Psychiatry* (New York, 1970); Nathan G. Hale, Jr., *Freud and the Americans: The Beginnings of Psychoanalysis in the United States, 1876–1917* (New York, 1971).

2. To have specialized in such fields would, of course, have been impossible for a regularly educated young physician a generation or two earlier. Beard was, naturally enough, a vigorous and self-conscious defender of specialization. Beard and A. D. Rockwell, *The Medical Use of Electricity* (New York, 1867), p. 11. The growth of neurology as a specialty played an important role in the development of dynamic concepts of psychopathology, despite the prevalent somaticism of Beard's generation. Unlike the asylum physician, the neurologist in private practice had necessarily to spend much of his time with neurotic patients.

3. Beard, *The Psychology of the Salem Witchcraft Excitement of 1692 and Its Practical Application to Our Own Time* (New York, 1882), pp. 66–67.

4. "Physical Future of the American People," *Atlantic Monthly* 43 (1879): 727.

5. *Salem Witchcraft*, p. 84; Beard, "The Problems of Insanity. A Paper Read Before the N.Y. Medico-Legal Society, March 3d, 1880," reprinted from the *Physician & Bulletin of the Medico-Legal Society*, p. 3.

6. S. Weir Mitchell, for example, described hysteria as a "hated charge," and deplored the almost universal belief in the purely psychological character of its symptoms. *Lectures on Diseases of the Nervous System, Especially in Women*, (Philadelphia, 1881), pp. 21, 29; cf. W. S. Playfair, *The Systematic Treatment of Nerve Prostration and Hysteria*, (Philadelphia, 1883), pp. 23–23. For a recent interpretation of this syndrome, see Carroll Smith-Rosenberg, "The Hysterical Woman: Sex Roles and Role Conflict in Nineteenth-Century America," *Social Research* 39 (Winter 1972): 652–78.

7. *A Practical Treatise on Nervous Exhaustion (Neurasthenia), Its Symptoms, Nature, Sequences, Treatment* (New York, 1880), p. 3. Cf. ibid., p. 6; Beard, *Sexual Neurasthenia (Nervous Exhaustion). Its Hygiene, Causes, Symptoms, and Treatment, with a Chapter on Diet for the Nervous*, ed. A. D. Rockwell (New York, 1884), p. 86.

8. *American Nervousness* (New York, 1881), p. 8. Although Beard had discussed neurasthenia as early as 1869, his first book on it did not appear until 1880. This study, *A Practical Treatise on Nervous Exhaustion*, dealt only with the clinical aspects of neurasthenia. It was not until a year later, in 1881, that Beard outlined an etiology in his analysis of *American Nervousness*.

9. "Neurasthenia or Nervous Exhaustion," *Boston Medical and Surgical Journal* 80 (1869): 217. Although Beard differentiated neurasthenia from other nervous ailments by classing it as "functional," he did not imply in making this distinction that it was dependent upon psychological rather than somatic factors. His use of the term functional was an accepted one at the time: it described phenomena resulting from a physiological process, as opposed to those involving anatomical change. To Beard, however, the dichotomy between "structural" and "functional" was essentially artificial. "What the microscope can see, we call structural—what the microscope cannot see, we call functional." *Nervous Exhaustion*, p. 114.

10. *American Nervousness*, p. 17.

11. Ideas of neural pathology had been current in the medical world since the eighteenth century. (See, for example, Gernot Rath, "Neural Pathology: A Pathogenic Concept of the eighteenth and nineteenth Centuries," *Bulletin of the History of Medicine* 33 (1959): 526–41). It was the development of neurophysiology in the nineteenth century, however, rather than these earlier ideas, which seems to have inspired Beard.

12. *Sexual Neurasthenia*, p. 17. "The Case of Guiteau—A Psychological Study," *Journal of Nervous and Mental Diseases* 9 (1882): 104.

13. *American Nervousness*, p. 98. For similar analogies, see ibid., pp. 10, 12, 42. Beard was a fervent admirer of Thomas Edison and worked with him for a short time.

14. "The problems of insanity," p. 9.

15. *Sexual Neurasthenia*, p. 107.

16. "Are Inebriates Automatons?" *Quarterly Journal of Inebriety* 3 (1878): 9.

17. *Nervous Exhaustion*, p. 93.

18. *American Nervousness*, p. 78; cf. *Nervous Exhaustion*, p. 78.

19. Charles L. Dana, *Archives of Neurology and and Psychiatry* 10 (1923): 429-30.

20. The author of a modern essay on Beard, for example, introduces his subject with the reassuring observation that he "was taken seriously by Freud" and concludes that Beard was part of a revolt against the sterile mechanism of Helmholtz, Ludwig, and du Bois-Reymond. Philip P. Weiner, "G. M. Beard and Freud on 'American Nervousness,' " *Journal of the History of Ideas* 17 (1956): 269, 274. The writer of another study refers sweepingly to French psychiatry before Freud as largely "the 'fact-finding' which is commonly the pre-history of any science." Milton Gold, "The Early Psychiatrists on Degeneracy and Genius," *Psychoanalysis and the Psychoanalytic Reviews* 47 (1960-61): 37.

21. E. H. Van Deusen, superintendent of the Michigan Asylum for the Insane, and user of the term "neurasthenia" a year before Beard, noted that many of his neurasthenic patients were farm wives. He concluded that their affliction resulted from the social and intellectual deprivation of their isolated lives. Beard, practicing in New York, naturally associated cases exhibiting the same symptoms with the tensions of urban life. Van Deusen, "Observations on a Form of Nervous Prostration, (Neurasthenia)," *American Journal Insanity* 25 (1869): 447.

22. *American Nervousness*, p. 96; *Sexual Neurasthenia*, p. 238n.

23. For numerous references to this almost ritualistic belief, see Norman Dain, *Concepts of Insanity in the United States, 1789-1865* (New Brunswick, N.J., 1964). For other references to social stress as a cause of mental disease, see George Rosen, "Social stress and mental disease from the eighteenth century to the present: Some Origins of Social Psychiatry," *Milbank Memorial Fund Quarterly* 37 (1959): 5-32, and Mark D. Altschule, *Roots of Modern Psychiatry* (New York and London, 1957), pp. 119-39.

24. "The Case of Guiteau—A Psychological Study," p. 112.

25. When Beard used the word "sociology," he meant the sociology of Comte and not what the word has come to mean today. Beard read Comte, Taine, and Buckle and was obviously influenced by all three.

26. "The Cosmic Law of Intemperance. A Contribution to the Scientific Study of the Temperance Question," *Michigan University Medical Journal* 3 (1872): 396.

27. *American Nervousness*, p. 114.

28. Ibid., pp. 293, 338-39, 344-46; *Atlantic Monthly* 43 (1879): 724.

29. *The New Cyclopaedia of Family Medicine. Our Home Physician: A Popular Guide to the Art of Preserving Health and Treating Disease* (New York, 1881), pp. xviii-xxiii.

30. The comparison between Beard and Barnum was made in the *St. Louis Clinical Record*, 7 (1880): 93. The review of *American Nervousness* by Spitzka appeared in ibid., 8 (1881): 122. More representative of medical opinion of Beard are the tolerant and interested, but not uncritical, comments in the *Medical Record* 20 (1881): 296-97 and the *Chicago Medical Gazette* 1 (1880): 167. Even reviewers in lay publications, however, criticized Beard's obtrusive egotism and his substitution of assertion for research. Cf. New York *Tribune*, July 15, 1881, p. 6; *Independent*, July 14, 1881, p. 11.

31. Franz Carl Miller, ed., *Handbuch der Neurasthenie* 1893). The first fifty pages of this handbook—in agate type—consisted of the bibliography and history of this new disease.

32. The discussions of neurasthenia by Freud and Durkheim are of particular interest. Freud's effort to disentangle "die eigentlichen Neurosen" from the psychoneuroses is particularly illuminating, both in respect to the internal development of Freud's

thought and its relationship to the medical assumptions of his day. See, for example, "Uber die Berechtigung von der Neurasthenie einen bestimmten Symptomkomplex als 'Angst-Neurose' abzutrennen," *Gesammelte Werke* (London, 1952), 1: 315–42, and "Die 'Kulturelle' Sexualmoral und die Moderne Nervosität," ibid., 7: 143–67, esp. pp. 148-9. For Durkheim, see *Suicide: A Study in Sociology*, trans. John A. Spaulding and George Simpson (London, 1952), pp. 67–77.

Chapter 6

1. The now-classic discussion of the influence of pietism in American history is that by H. Richard Niebuhr, *The Kingdom of God in America* (New York, 1937). W. G. McLoughlin has provided a more recent synthetic discussion of "Pietism and the American Character," *American Quarterly* 17 (1965): 163–86.

2. *The Sanitary Condition of the Laboring Population of New York. With Suggestions for its Improvement. A Discourse (with Additions) Delivered on the 30th December, 1844, at the Repository of the American Institute* (New York, 1845). Cf. the discussion in this pamphlet with its evaluation by George Rosen, *A History of Public Health* (New York, ca. 1958), pp. 237–39. Rosen contends (p. 238) that "this study already contains in essence the principles and objectives that were to characterize the American sanitary reform movement for the next 30 years."

3. This generalization is based partially on a search for items of public health concern in half a dozen American medical journals between 1843 and 1847. The comparative lack of concern is unmistakable and is emphasized by the English origin of many of those items found directly relating to public health. With the 1850s, the interest of American physicians began to increase.

4. The most important source of information for Griscom's life is the memoir by his son, J. H. Griscom, *Memoir of John Griscom, LL.D., Late Professor of Chemistry and Natural Philosophy; with an Account of the New York High School; Society for the Prevention of Pauperism; the House of Refuge; and Other Institutions. Compiled from an Autobiography, and Other Sources* (New York, 1859). Cf. E. F. Smith, "John Griscom," *Dictionary of American Biography* 8 (New York, 1931–32): 7. The manuscript division of the New York Public Library contains a collection of Griscom's incoming correspondence. For the background of Quaker pietism and benevolence see S. V. James, *A People Among Peoples: Quaker Benevolence in Eighteenth-Century America* (Cambridge, Mass., 1963).

5. Formal theological positions were remarkably unimportant in comparison with the common dedication of such men to spiritual activism and social improvement. Griscom, a Quaker, could write of Thomas Chalmers, a Scottish Presbyterian, "It would be difficult to name any writer of the past or present century, entitled to a higher rank . . . as a defender and expounder of theological truth." *Memoir*, p. 379. Chalmers was, significantly, a pioneer in social welfare as well as a prominent theologian and popularizer of natural theology.

6. A student of science in Jeffersonian America has described Griscom's chemical lectures as atypically successful and long-lived. John C. Greene, "Science and the Public in the Age of Jefferson," *Isis* 39 (1958): 20.

7. From a letter of Griscom's, August 27, 1847. *Memoir*, p. 365. Cf. Joseph Murray, Jr., to Griscom, February 13, 1817, Griscom Correspondence, The New York Public Library.

8. On ventilation, see Henry Vethake to Griscom, November 27, 1819; Jacob Bigelow to Griscom, October 29, 1822, Griscom Correspondence. On Griscom's yellow fever interests, see James Hardie, *An Account of the Yellow Fever Which Occurred in the City of New York, in the Year 1822* (New York, 1822), pp. 51, 71; New York City, Board of Health, *A History of the Proceedings of the Board of Health, of the City of New York, in the Summer and Fall of 1822* (New York, 1823), pp. 230–42.

9. Unfortunately, almost no documents illustrating the younger Griscom's personal life seem to have survived. Perhaps most significant in illuminating Griscom's spiritual

life is his careful memoir of his father; its tone leaves little doubt of the son's pietistic orientation.

10. Philip Van Ingen, *The New York Academy of Medicine. Its First Hundred Years* (New York, 1949), p. 20. Van Ingen also notes that Griscom was among the first group of trustees elected when the Academy was chartered (p. 43). For other biographical material see S. W. Francis, *Biographical Sketches of Distinguished Living New York Physicians* (New York, 1867), pp. 45-59; [Philip Van Ingen], *A Brief Account of the First One Hundred Years of the New York Medical and Surgical Society* ([New York], 1946), p. 43; "New York Medical and Surgical Society. First 100 Years. Biographies. Vol. II," Rare Book Room, New York Academy of Medicine, pp. 475-84. This typed sketch is the most detailed account of Griscom's life available.

11. "Our Creator afflicts us with diseases," Griscom elaborated, "that we may know how frail and dependent we are. But he has also given us a knowledge of the laws which regulate our growth, and our lives, so that by attending to them, and living purely and uprightly, we may avoid those diseases, in a great degree." Griscom, *First Lessons in Human Physiology; to which are Added Brief Rules of Health. For the Use of Schools*, 6th ed. (New York, 1847), pp. 132-33. A principal motive in his writing of texts for the study of such comparatively novel subjects, Griscom explained to parents, "has been the desire to render the study of our frames subservient to moral improvement, by furnishing the young reader with incontestible evidence of a Great First Cause." *Animal Mechanism and Physiology; Being a Plain and Familiar Exposition of the Structure and Functions of the Human System* (New York, 1839), p. vii. All of Griscom's specific appeals for public health reform called at least in passing for efforts to raise the level of public knowledge; he urged, for example, at one point the establishment of a "Hygiological Society" to be composed of physicians and laymen and dedicated to the spread of hygienic truths. *Anniversary Discourse before the New York Academy of Medicine Delivered in Clinton Hall, November 22d, 1854* (New York, 1855), p. 52.

12. Griscom, *Improvements of the Public Health, and the Establishment of a Sanitary Police in the City of New York* (Albany, 1857), p. 3. Such seemingly primitivistic appeals to the contrast between the health of the rural, even savage, life and urban conditions are to be found in virtually all of Griscom's writings. Like natural theology itself, such ideas were little questioned in ante-bellum America. For a discussion of the emotional resonance in this period between the idea of sin and the unnatural, virtue and the natural, see Charles E. Rosenberg, *The Cholera Years: The United States, 1832, 1849, and 1866* (Chicago, 1962), p. 132 and passim.

13. In addition to his frequent reiteration of the standard warnings of his generation against tightly laced corsets and alcohol, Griscom wrote books on the problems of ventilation and—in amusingly apocalyptic tones—the evils of tobacco. *The Use of Tobacco, and the Evils, Physical, Moral, and Social, Resulting Therefrom* (New York, 1863); *The Uses and Abuses of Air: Showing Its Influence in Sustaining Life, and Producing Disease* (New York, 1850).

14. *Uses and Abuses of Air*, pp. 137n, 143.

15. Such allegations were made in editorials in D. M. Reese's *American Medical Gazette*, accusing Griscom of a twenty-year dedication to the hope of feeding from the "public crib." "That Consumption Hospital," ibid. 8 (1857): 112-13; "Medical politics," ibid., p. 113. Philip Van Ingen's history of the New York Academy of Medicine notes that Griscom had been involved in reprimanding Reese for allegedly unethical conduct. Van Ingen, *New York Academy of Medicine* (New York, 1949), pp. 90-91, 115-16.

16. New York City, *Annual Report of the Interments in the City and County of New-York, for the Year 1842, with Remarks Thereon, and a Brief View of the Sanitary Condition of the City* (New York, 1843). This report had been ordered printed in "four times the usual number." The source of Griscom's political influence in 1842 and thus the explanation of his appointment as city inspector is, in the absence of manuscript evidence, obscure.

17. *Sanitary Condition*, p. 8, n.2. Like many of his contemporaries, Griscom habitually emphasized the economic gains to be realized through public health reform; one feels, however, that such hard-headed appeals were in part rationalizations for a more basic humanitarian commitment.

18. There was no American equivalent of the hostility felt by certain prominent British sanitarians to physicians among lay advocates of public health. Griscom based all of his proposals upon the impossibility of any but physicians properly fulfilling the duties of a health officer; in keeping with this emphasis was Griscom's assumption that existing medical knowledge was adequate to the explanation and thus prevention of a good portion of the sickness which burdened the city. In 1842 Griscom outlined his essential organizational point of view in regard to New York's Board of Health. New York City, Board of Aldermen, *Communication from the City Inspector, Recommending a Reorganization of the Health Police*, April 24, 1843. Doc. No. 111, pp. 1314-20.

19. The first portion of this quotation is from *Sanitary Condition*, p. 1, n.2; the second from Griscom's *Annual Report for 1842* p. 173, n. 16.

20. Griscom was also consistently critical of both the exploitative behavior of many of the city's property holders and the culpable failure of many among the wealthy to ventilate their mansions and observe moderation in eating and drinking—all sins more deserving of condemnation than the almost involuntary misdeeds of the poor. See *Sanitary Condition*, p. 20, n. 2.

21. *Uses and Abuses of Air* p. 92, n. 13. The etiological position assumed by Griscom—quite common in the 1840s—was termed by contemporaries "contingent-contagionism," the conviction, that is, that many infectious diseases were contagious only in such confined quarters as hospital wards and slum apartments. This belief provided an excellent vehicle for the expression of social criticism as well as for an explanation of some of the logical dilemmas implicit in either contagionism or noncontagionism.

22. "The Where, the When, the Why, and the How, of the First Appearance and Greatest Prevalence of Cholera in Cities," *Bulletin of the New York Academy of Medicine* 3 (1866): 6–26, and his comments at pp. 49–50. His bias in favor of an etiology which justified sanitary reform is equally apparent in his discussion of yellow fever; he argued, for example, that it was of little practical significance whether the city's filthy docks and slips had given rise to yellow fever or simply provided "a richly manured soil in which the germs of that disease, introduced from abroad, would grow with redoubled vigor. . . . It is enough to know that such conditions are inimical to human life, and should never be permitted." *A History, Chronological and Circumstantial, of the Visitations of Yellow Fever in New York City* (New York, 1858), p. 21. Cf. Rosenberg, p. 196, n.12.

23. For the testimony of these city missionaries see *Sanitary Condition*, pp. 24–38, n. 2; New York, *Annual Report of Interments . . . 1842* pp. 167–71, n.16. More than a few prominent New York clergymen became active in medical and public health affairs— Henry Bellows, for example, and William Muhlenberg. (Bellows directed the Sanitary Commission during the Civil War, while Muhlenberg founded St. Luke's Hospital.) Perhaps most professional in his career as city missionary-*cum*-public health expert was S. B. Halliday, active for half a century in the saving of souls and the improvement of health conditions. It is clear that the original motivations for Halliday's concern with environmental reform, nurtured during decades of work for a succession of New York religious charities, lay in his conversion during the revivalistic enthusiasm of the early 1830s. Cf. S. B. Halliday, *Lost and Found: or Life Among the Poor* (New York, 1859). The relationship between the city mission movement and the growing demand for environmental reform is a complex one. For a more detailed account see Carroll S. Rosenberg, *Religion and the Rise of the American City: The New York City Mission Movement, 1812–1870* (Ithaca, 1971).

24. *New York Journal of Medicine* 4 (1845(: 30. In a city with a paucity of institutional structure and organizational models, it was natural that Griscom should have drawn upon the personnel and pattern of activities of the city missions, just as he depended upon the city's dispensaries. In almost all his proposals for board of health reorganization, Griscom suggested that the dispensary physicians, the only medical men who understood tenement conditions, be made district health officers. On the dispensaries see Charles E. Rosenberg, "Social Class and Medical Care in Nineteenth-Century America: The Rise and Fall of the Dispensary," *Journal of the History of Medicine* 29 (1974): 32–54.

25. John Ordronaux, *Prophylaxis, an Anniversary Oration Delivered before the New York Academy of Medicine, Wednesday, December 19th, 1866* (New York, 1867), pp. 16, 68.

26. Both in his purely evangelical work and in his temperance agitation, Hartley was a consistent advocate of the need for methodical house-to-house visitation; it was such visiting which, for the first time, brought numbers of middle-class New Yorkers into contact with slum conditions. The basic source for Hartley's life is a *Memorial of Robert Milham Hartley, Edited by His Son, Isaac Smithson Hartley, D. D.* ([Utica, N. Y.], 1882). The preceding paragraph is synthesized from his detailed biography. For evaluations of Hartley's place in the development of American social welfare, see R. H. Bremner, *From the Depths: The Discovery of Poverty in the United States* (New York, 1956), pp. 35-38; Roy Lubove, "The New York Association for Improving the Condition of the Poor: The Formative years," *New York historical Society Quarterly* 43 (1959): 307-27. The most important source for Hartley's ideas and activities are the annual reports of the A.I.C.P. for its first three decades; there are also some valuable surviving manuscript sources—including the minutes of the Association's board of managers—at the Community Service Society, 105 East 22d Street, New York. For the city mission background of Hartley's early work and the significance both practical and theological of house-to-house visiting, see Carroll S. Rosenberg, *Religion and the American City*, esp. Chap. 9.

27. Hartley, *Memorial*, pp. 229, 288, 297, respectively, for the quoted passages. These are typical of many similar entries.

28. The institutional history of the A.I.C.P., like Hartley's personal biography, demonstrates an evolution from pietistic beginnings to a more secular benevolence. Though ordinarily considered a pragmatic—if in some ways moralistic and status-oriented—response to urban conditions, the Association actually began as an outgrowth of the New York City Tract Society. This organization had, by the early 1840s, found itself so preoccupied with the economic needs of the poor that its managers feared their primary objective of converting all New Yorkers to evangelical Protestantism might be lost in the demands of day-to-day meliorism. Hence their establishment of a separate organization, the A.I.C.P., to deal with the material ills of the poor. (John H. Griscom was a member of the Association's first executive committee, as well as serving as a volunteer visitor and committee member for his district.) Though the A.I.C.P.'s object was not formally the salvation of souls, the moral and psychological views of poverty entertained by the spokesmen of this new organization were identical with those expressed for many years by New York's evangelical leaders. For a detailed treatment of these developments see Carroll S. Rosenberg, *Religion and the American City*.

29. *An Historical, Scientific, and Practical Essay on Milk as an Article of Human Sustenance; with a Consideration of the Effects Consequent upon the Unnatural Methods of Producing it for the Supply of Large Cities* (New York, 1842).

30. Hartley, *Memorial*, pp. 235, 331. Cf. pp. 29-30, 128, 144-45, 208, 212, 232.

31. New York City Board of Health, *Majority and Minority Reports of the Select Committee of the Board of Health, Appointed to Investigate the Character and Condition of the Sources from Which Cow's Milk is Derived, for Sale in the City of New York,* (New York, 1858), pp. 169-70.

32. For an important discussion of the background of such images of "infection" and the gradual and complex secularization of this concept, see Owsei Temkin, "An Historical Analysis of the Concept of Infection," in *Studies in Intellectual History* (Baltimore, 1953), pp. 139-44. See also the discussion of the interaction between scientific throught and religious values provided by L. G. Stevenson in two significant articles: "Science Down the Drain. On the hostility of Certain Sanitarians to Animal Experimentation, Bacteriology and Immunology," *Bulletin of the History of Medicine* 29 (1955): 1-26, esp. pp. 3,4n.; and "Religious Elements in the Background of the British Anti-Vivisection Movement," *Yale Journal of Biology and Medicine* 29 (1956): 125-27.

33. New York Association for Improving the Condition of the Poor, *Fourth Annual Report* (1847), p. 23; *Third Annual Report* (1846), p. 22.

34. R. H. Bremner has written an account of the A.I.C.P.'s one substantial experiment in this area; "The Big Flat: History of a New York Tenement House," *American Historical Review* 64 (1958): 54-62. Cf. A.I.C.P., *Fifth Annual Report*, (1848), pp. 18-19; *Tenth*

Annual Report, (1853), pp. 26–27; Board of Managers, Minutes, April 10, 1854, Community Service Society.

35. It was always assumed, of course, that such reforms would have an inevitable spiritual effect. At the eleventh annual meeting of the A.I.C.P., for example, the influential clergyman T. L. Cuyler made this point of view explicit in praising the Association's just-completed housing report. "The sanitary statements of the Report," he proposed, "show that where cleanliness and ventilation are neglected, disease and mortality are proportionately increased. And where the body is unclean, and the dwelling wretched, there is commonly a corresponding moral degradation. . . . Sanitary reform," Cuyler urged, "is intimately connected with the spread of true religion. The dwellings of the poor are to be looked after as well as their souls," N.Y.A.I.C.P., *Eleventh Annual Report* (1854), p.6.

36. N.Y.A.I.C.P., *First Report of a Committee on the Sanitary Condition of the Poor in the City of New York* (New York, 1853). Though less famous than the Shattuck Report of 1850, this document seems to have been quoted with equal frequency in the dozen years after its publication. Also revealing is the detailed discussion of this report the succeeding year in the Association's *Eleventh Annual Report* (1854), pp. 19–29. Hartley, who wrote all the Association's annual reports, significantly began his discussion with a quotation from Thomas Chalmers: "That all our sufferings and evils (so far as they exceed those inseparable from a finite and imperfect nature) may be traced to ignorance or neglect of those laws of nature which God has established for our good, and displayed for our instruction," ibid., p. 19.

37. Long-time A.I.C.P. supporters were, for example, influential in the New York Sanitary Association (founded 1859), though the Association itself was modeled after the British Health of Towns Associations, while similar ties existed between the A.I.C.P. and the Citizen's Association. For a discussion of the events leading to the passage of the Metropolitan Board of Health Bill and the place of these organizations, see G. H. Brieger, "Sanitary Reform in New York City: Stephen Smith and the passage of the Metropolitan Health Bill," *Bulletin of the History of Medicine* 40 (1966): 407–29.

38. N.Y.A.I.C.P., *A Plan for Better Distribution of Medical Attendance and Medicines for the Indigent Sick, by the Public Dispensaries in the City of New York* (New York, 1845). On dispensaries see A.I.C.P. *Eight Annual Report* (1851), pp. 20–22; *Ninth Annual Report* (1852), pp. 38–39. The two dispensaries were the DeMilt and the Northeastern.

39. Griscom retained his formal adherence to the Society of Friends, "whose tenets," he explained late in life, "are regarded by me as most in accordance with Scripture teachings, as the most liberal in sentiment, and most truly democratic in practice of all sects." Francis, *Biographical Sketches*, p. 54. We have been unable to determine whether Griscom was an orthodox or Hicksite Quaker, His humanitarian environmentalism is, indeed, Griscom's most significant—and endearing—characteristic. He even blamed poor ventilation for the sluggish behavior of school children who normally received the rod instead of the fresh air they actually needed. *Uses and Abuses of Air*, p. 51, n.13. Hartley is consistently harsher than Griscom in his social and individual judgments—a harshness intensified by his rigid Manchesterian views.

Chapter 7

1. December 13, 1921. *From Maine Street to Stockholm: Letters of Sinclair Lewis, 1919–1930*, ed. and intro. Harrison Smith (New York, 1952), p. 90. A portion of this letter is quoted by Mark Schorer in his *Sinclair Lewis, An American Life* (New York, 1961), p. 326. My impression of Lewis's life is based primarily upon this exhaustive study, upon Lewis's published letters, and upon the memoir written by his first wife, Grace Hegger Lewis, *With Love from Gracie: Sinclair Lewis, 1912–1925* (New York, 1955). There has, been comparatively little serious criticism of *Arrowsmith*. Lyon N. Richardson has, however, provided a useful study of differences between the texts of the serialized and the book versions. "*Arrowsmith*: Genesis, Development, Versions," *American Literature* 27 (1955–56): 225–44.

2. Perhaps it was inevitable that the most thoroughly corrupt and one-dimensional of Lewis's central figures should have been the minister of a gospel in which he placed no belief. Mark Schorer has sympathetically described Lewis's youthful attachment for evangelical religion while he was attending Oberlin Academy. *Lewis*, pp. 50–52.

3. The author's intention is unmistakable. The sentence in question reads: "The days of pioneering, of lassies in sunbonnets, and bears killed with axes in piney clearings, are deader now than Camelot; and a rebellious girl is the spirit of that bewildered empire called the American Middlewest." *Main Street* (New York, 1920), p. 1.

4. Paul de Kruif has published an account of these events in his memoir, *The Sweeping Wind* (New York, 1962), pp. 9–57.

5. De Kruif's recollection and Schorer's reconstruction of this boisterous meeting are essentially in agreement. Cf. Schorer, *Lewis* pp. 337–41 and De Kruif, *Sweeping Wind*, pp. 60–67.

6. On February 13, 1923, for example, Lewis wrote to his friends at Harcourt, Brace "It gives me joy to inform you that De Kruif is perfection. He has not only an astonishing grasp of scientific detail; he has a philosophy behind it . . . and in all of this there's a question as to whether he won't have contributed more than I shall have." This letter was written at sea. Lewis and De Kruif were in the midst of the ocean cruise during which *Arrowsmith* was planned and blocked out. *From Maine Street to Stockholm*, p. 125, and see also pp. 122, 126–27. De Kruif received a fourth of the royalties from *Arrowsmith*. Lewis's gracious prefatory acknowledgment of De Kruif's help—though not on the title page—was an undoubtedly sincere expression of his gratitude.

7. "Jacques Loeb, the Mechanist," *Harper's* 146 (January 1923): 182–90; "Our Medicine Men. By One of Them," *Century Magazine* 104 (1922): 416–26; 593–601; 781–89; 950–56; "Medicine," in *Civilization in the United States. An Inquiry by Thirty Americans*, ed. Harold Stearns (New York, 1922), pp. 443–56.

8. It has been a prolonged parturition; many of the criticisms voiced by Max Gottlieb and Arrowsmith are still heard in the basic science departments of our better medical schools.

9. *Century* 104 (1922): 788. De Kruif entertained a roseate view of the dedicated and "noncommercial" nineteenth-century practitioner.

10. Carl Ludwig, possibly the greatest teacher of physiology in the second half of the nineteenth century, was the mentor of many of the leaders in the first generation of American academic physiologists. George Rosen, "Carl Ludwig and his American Students," *Bulletin of the History of Medicine* 4 (1936): 609–50.

11. *Century* 104 (1922): 782. Martin Arrowsmith was born in 1883 and when he entered medical school in the first decade of this century, the vast majority of medical students were not college graduates. Many had no college or university training at all.

12. This sentence is a conflation of remarks made by De Kruif in Stearns, *Civilization*, p. 451, and in *Century* 104 (1922): 594.

13. *Arrowsmith*, p. 270.

14. It is clear that this is Lewis's explicit intention; no one had experienced more acutely than he the bitterness of American success. Martin is shown to be repulsed by the prospect of becoming a "Man of Measured Merriment," of succumbing to "the shrieking bawdy thing called Success." (*Arrowsmith*, p. 323). As the novel ends, Arrowsmith looks forward to years of research on quinine. And, he exclaims joyously, "probably we'll fail!" These are the final words of *Arrowsmith*. Paul de Kruif recalls protesting that the "probably" should be "possibly"; that no one begins a project with the conviction that he will fail. "That shows you've missed the whole meaning of Arrowsmith," Lewis sadly replied. *Sweeping Wind*, p. 116.

15. *Arrowsmith*, p. 124. Lewis, it must be noted, made use of this device for passing judgment on American values before he met De Kruif. In *Babbitt*, he phrases an explicit criticism of Zenith in the words of Dr. Kurt Yavitch, "the histologist (whose report on the destruction of epithelial cells under radium had made the name of Zenith known in Munich, Prague, and Rome) . . . " *Babbitt* (New York, 1950), p. 100.

16. De Kruif's list of those actual persons upon whom the characters in *Arrowsmith* were based is to be found in Schorer, *Lewis*, pp. 418–19. The letter which contains this

"key" is deposited in the Rare Book Room of the New York Academy of Medicine (Paul de Kruif to Archibald Malloch, April 16, 1931). De Kruif is careful to emphasize that Lewis attempted to capture the "spirit," not the physical characteristics of these men.

Though my interpretation emphasizes the ways in which Max Gottlieb is a reflection of Loeb, elements of Novy's life and work can easily be discerned in the fictional professor's character. Novy, like Gottlieb, was famous for having destroyed the premature theories of others and, again like Gottlieb, noted for the unfailing reliability of his experimental findings. Novy, moreover, placed constant emphasis upon the importance of controls in biological research—a methodological emphasis familiar to readers of *Arrowsmith*. See Ruth Good, "Dr. Frederick G. Novy: Biographic Sketch," *University of Michigan Medical Bulletin* 16 (1950): 257-65.

17. Grace Hegger Lewis comments in her memoir of Lewis upon the enthusiastic tone of De Kruif's marginal comments on the *Arrowsmith* manuscript in her possession. *With Love from Gracie*, p. 257. De Kruif's less enthusiastic retrospective evaluation of Max Gottlieb may be found in *Sweeping Wind*, p. 109.

There is little question, however, of the influence exerted upon the youthful De Kruif by the ideas and personality of Jacques Loeb. The most convincing evidence is to be found in the worshipful tone adopted toward Loeb in De Kruif's journalistic ventures. See, for example, "Loeb," *Harper's* 146 (January 1923): 189-90. In *Civilization in the United States* (p. 456), he unhesitatingly classes Loeb as the greatest of American biologists.

18. *Arrowsmith*, p. 39.

19. Loeb, *The Mechanistic Conception of Life* (Chicago, 1912), p. 35. A biography of Jacques Loeb is needed. Fortunately, however, a useful memorial sketch is available, written by his long-time associate W. J. V. Osterhout, "Jacques Loeb," *Journal of General Physiology* 8 (1928): ix-lix. Loeb was born in 1859 in Mayen, Germany, and died in 1924.

20. It has, for example, been suggested recently that the post-Romantic generation of German biologists were conspicuously unenthusiastic in their reception of Darwinism because the transmutation of species was "only too well remembered from the days of Naturphilosophie and speculative science." Owsei Temkin, "The Idea of Descent in Post-Romantic German Biology: 1848-1858," in *Forerunners of Darwin, 1745-1856*, ed. Bentley Glass, Owsei Temkin, and William Straus Jr. (Baltimore, 1959), p. 355.

21. See Paul F. Cranefield, "The Organic Physics of 1847 and the Biophysics of Today," *Journal of the History of Medicine* 12 (1957): 407-32; Cranefield, "The Nineteenth Century Prelude to Modern Biophysics," *Proceedings of the First National Biophysical Conference* (New Haven, 1959), pp. 19-26; Owsei Temkin, "Materialism in French and German Physiology of the Early Nineteenth Century," *Bulletin of the History of Medicine* 20 (1946): 322-27. In this thoughtful paper Professor Temkin differentiates clearly between the French and German varieties of "materialism." J. H. Northrop, Nobel Prize-winning chemist, contemporary of De Kruif's at the Rockefeller Institute, and one of the models for Terry Wickett, has clearly shown the place of his and his teacher Jacques Loeb's work in the continuing struggle between vitalism and mechanism. "Biochemists, Biologists, and William of Occam," *Annual Review of Biochemistry* 30 (1961): 1-10.

22. Loeb, *Mechanistic Conception of Life*, pp. 61, 123.

23. This and the two succeeding quotations from *Arrowsmith* are to be found on pages 278, 298, and 406, respectively.

24. A central episode in *Arrowsmith* is the West Indian plague epidemic, during which Martin is to test the effectiveness of his new bacteriophage. He is, however, torn between the physician's human desire to heal and the scientist's willingness to use human controls as conclusive evidence of the scientific worthlessness of most clinical findings. *Century* 104 (1922): 424. Lewis, presumably with De Kruif's guidance, had become convinced that the vast majority of medical knowledge consisted simply of post hoc conclusions. *Arrowsmith*, p. 124, and esp. p. 120. Or, compare De Kruif's explanation in *Microbe Hunters* (New York, 1926), pp. 235-36, for Theobald Smith's having deserted medicine for laboratory science.

25. *Century* 104 (1922): 785.

26. Ibid., p. 951. De Kruif did trace this spirit to what he considered its German origin.

27. *Arrowsmith*, p. 321.

28. *Century* 104 (1922): 950.

29. Osterhout. "Jacques Loeb," 7 *Journal of General Physiology*, p. lviii. Bernard De Voto has, in a well-known attack on American literature in the twenties, criticized Lewis harshly for his intellectual failure in allowing his hero to reject the community of American science. *The Literary Fallacy* (Boston, 1944).

30. The conclusion of Arrowsmith would, of course, seem particularly relevant to critics of a psychological persuasion. Arrowsmith's final decision is a rejection of maturity, of responsibility, of wife and child for an idyll with the virile Terry Wickett —an idyll sanctioned by the purity of Nature.

Chapter 8

1. In this brief compass I will avoid the structural problem of tracing the means through which such a small group of well-motivated and goal-directed men were able to effect a particular desired change in the larger society.

2. Fortunately, the personal papers of a good many of these agricultural chemists have been preserved in varying degrees of completeness—a fact which allows greater insight into individual motivation than is normally the good fortune of historians of science. Most extensive are the William Brewer Papers at the Yale University Manuscript Division, the S. W. Johnson Papers in the Biochemistry Department of the Connecticut Agricultural Experiment Station, New Haven, and the Evan Pugh Papers in the Penn State Collection, The Pennsylvania State University. Also important are the John P. Norton Papers and George Brush Papers at Yale, the Charles C. Chandler Papers in Special Collections, Columbia University, and the George C. Caldwell Papers in Cornell University's Collection of Archives and Regional History. Extensive extracts from the letters and journals of James F. Magee, another member of the Göttingen American colony, have been published: George Magee, ed., *An American Student Abroad* (Philadelphia, 1932). Selected extracts from the Pugh and Johnson Papers have also been reprinted: Elizabeth A. Osborne, *From the Letter Files of S. W. Johnson* (New Haven, 1913), and C. A. Browne, "European Laboratory Experiences of an Early American Agricultural Chemist—Dr. Evan Pugh (1828-1864)," *Journal of Chemical Education* 7 (1930): 499-517.

3. Most had pretensions to middle-class status even if not to possession of great wealth. A relatively large middle class—as minimally defined by freedom from immediate dependence upon day wages—meant a comparatively large pool of *potential* scientists, even if only a very small absolute number found anything congenial in so atypical a career. There is no full-length biography of Evan Pugh, but see Jacqueline Bloom, "Evan Pugh" (Master's thesis, Pennsylvania State University, 1960).

4. Benjamin Silliman, Jr., to W. H. Brewer, January 31, 1837, Brewer Papers; O. Wolcott Gibbs to George Gibbs, July 26, 1846, Gibbs Family Papers, State Historical Society of Wisconsin.

5. See Louis I. Kuslan, "The Founding of the Yale School of Applied Chemistry", *Journal of the History of Medicine* 24 (1969): 430-51. For details of the laboratory's operations one may consult the letterpress copybook kept to record its affairs and now deposited in the Manuscript Division, Yale University Library. The financial circumstances of the laboratory are described by J. P. Norton in a letter to Joseph Henry, December 5, 1848, Norton Papers.

6. The comparison between the degree of social acceptance granted students in Europe and America is taken from a revealing letter from C. M. Wetherill to J. F. Frazer, June 10, 1850, Frazer Papers, American Philosophical Society; George Brush to W. H.

Brewer, January 20, 1853, and William Craw to Brewer, December 19, 1852, Brewer Papers.

7. S. W. Johnson to Dear Sister, December 30, [1850], Johnson Papers, and S. W. Johnson to Dear Father, Mother, Brothers and Sisters, December 1, 1850, Johnson Papers. These letters were written during a period of spiritual crisis and are thus more overtly pietistic than SWJ's usual and later prose. J. C. Baston to SWJ, [1855], cited in Osborne, *Letter-Files*, p. 94.

8. Pugh kept a detailed journal during portions of his German and English student years. There is a typed transcript as well as the originals in the Pugh Papers. Many entries reflect his moral stance; see that for September 9, 1855, which explains his distaste for all "alkaloids"—including tea, coffee, and opium—because all were equally unnatural.

9. J. P. Norton, Diary, Entry for September 13, 1846, and August 3, 1851, Norton Papers.

10. Edward Hitchcock, "Private Notes," December 1842, Hitchcock Family Papers, Amherst College Library. The introspective Hitchcock had also to confess that "distinction among scientific men has been with me a most powerful motive of action." "Private Notes," December 1843. The emotional concordance between the life of science and that of the spirit found no awkward hindrances in the formal intellectual sphere. As is well known, arguments from design had become an unquestioned commonplace among American Christians of all denominations in this period.

11. Entry for November 21, 1853. Theodotus Burwell to W. H. Brewer, April 21, 1852. Brewer Papers: S. W. Johnson to [A. A. Johnson], [undated fragment, 1849-50]. Johnson Papers.

12. J. C. Arthur to E. F. Smith, May 13, 187 [8], Erwin Frink Smith Papers, American Philosophical Society.

13. *Address to the Cumberland County Agricultural Society at Their Fall Meeting, October, 1860* (Carlisle, Pa., 1860), p. 5.

14. A. A. Johnson to W. W. Johnson, December 10, 1858, cited in Osborne, *Letter-Files*, pp. 130-31.

15. W. O. Atwater to Carroll Wright, October 16, 1893, Reel 6, W. O. Atwater Papers, E. F. Smith Library, University of Pennsylvania; Thomas F. Hunt, quoted in San Francisco *Call*, November 21, 1912. "In our new conception of a successful life," Hunt elaborated, "we do not have prosperity without morality, but we do have prosperity because of morality."

16. Notice the following comments by Pugh, comparing American and German farmers: "But there is another consolation for the American scientific agriculturist—viz. we can safely say, that if our farmers should ever happen to be as ignorant as the German farmers we know they are not so *stupid* or so bigoted in following the old way." Pugh to Johnson, September 30, 1855. After forty years of work, however, S. W. Johnson had other thoughts. "An immense advantage enjoyed by the German investigator," he confessed in 1896, "consists in the fact that he has a clientele of landed proprietors who have themselves passed the strenuous discipline of the gymnasium and the university. . . ." "President's Address," *Proceedings*, Association of American Agricultural Colleges and Experiment Stations (1895-96), p. 45.

17. James F. Magee to Dear Brother and Sister, [1855], *An American Student Abroad*, p. 62; H. A. Rowland to J. C. Maxwell, March 1876, as cited in Samuel Rezneck, "An American Physicist in Europe: Henry A. Rowland, 1875-1876," *American Journal of Physics* 30 (1962): 885; Charles W. Dabney, Jr., to My dear Pa, October 6, 1879, C. W. Dabney Papers, Southern Historical Collection, University of North Carolina.

18. Pugh to SWJ, [1857], Pugh Papers; SWJ to A. A. Johnson, July 3, 1854, cited in Osborne, *Letter-Files*, p. 62.

19. Pugh to SWJ, October 31, 1854, November 14, 1855. See also Pugh to SWJ, March 15, 1855, in which Pugh discusses the possibilities of bringing a farm weekly "directly under our control." The symbiotic political alliance between agricultural scientists and administrators and "intelligent farmers" and farm spokesmen—that is, the more

prosperous and better educated in the agricultural community—despite its undoubted efficacy in stimulating agricultural productivity soon became a characteristic aspect of the experiment station heritage and in the twentieth century increasingly dysfunctional. The success of the stations in increasing productivity meant—if I may be excused the crudity—that among other things on the whole the rich got richer and the poor, poorer. Those with education and the values conducive to innovation, in addition to capital sufficient to allow a margin for innovation, benefited most prominently from technological advances in agriculture.

20. Pugh to SWJ, March 13, 1861, Pugh Papers. For the reference to the federal government, see Pugh to SWJ, April 19, 1862. As early as 1860, Pugh had suggested the possibility of arranging a congressional appropriation to support experimental work. Pugh to SWJ, August 16, 1860.

21. The mainspring analogy occurs in a long and important letter from Pugh to SWJ, December 1, 1854, Pugh Papers: Pugh, *Statement made by Dr. E. Pugh . . . of the Agricultural College in reference to the Proposition to Deprive the College of its Endowment* (Philadelphia, 1864), p. 5.

22. Pugh to SWJ, November 18, 1861.

23. Biographical material on Magee is to be found in Magee, *An American Student Abroad*. Lamborn left a large bequest and an extensive manuscript collection to the Philadelphia Academy of Natural Sciences. Unfortunately, there is nothing in this collection which sheds light on his German years.

24. Kimball to Pugh, January 19 and October 15, 1861, Pugh Papers; G. C. Caldwell, Diary, Entry for March 22, 1865, Caldwell Papers, Cornell University Collection of Archives and Regional History.

25. Chandler to Bishop Horatio Potter, January 25, 1862, Chandler Papers, Special Collections, Columbia University Library.

26. Samuel Halliday to Pugh, May 20, 1862, Pugh Papers; M. M. Rodgers, *Scientific Agriculture*, 2d ed. rev. (Rochester, N.Y., 1850), p. 17.

27. Pugh to SWJ, January 6, [1860], Pugh Papers. Cf. J. P. Norton to Solon Robinson, January 5, 1852, Letterpress book, Outgoing, Norton Papers. A fertilizer manufacturer, indeed, complained to Pugh that farmers sometimes assumed that a "guarantee" meant the guarantee of a crop. B. M. Rhodes to Pugh, April 11, 1862.

28. F. W. Cook to Pugh, August 14, 1861, Pugh Papers. Through the First World War experiment station administrators had to face the criticism of laymen who continued to assume that "an experimental farm" should be a source of profit.

29. G. Evans to J. P. Norton, March 19, 1849, Norton Papers; F. B. Hough to S. Haldeman, February 21, 1851, Samuel Haldeman Papers, Academy of Natural Sciences of Philadelphia.

30. Pugh to SWJ, March [16], 1855, Pugh Papers.

31. In 1875, for example, Orange Judd, the principal lobbyist in forcing the passage of Connecticut's pioneer experiment station, was a prosperous farm-newspaper publisher and intimate friend of W. O. Atwater, a European-trained and research-oriented chemist. Yet Judd felt that the immediate and most important goal of the stations was to stop "manure swindling"—that is, the sale of misrepresented chemical fertilizers. "We must," he explained to Atwater in discussing plans for the station, "have something going on that will furnish *frequent* items weekly perhaps though the press." Judd to Atwater, July 6 and July 23, 1875, Reel 1, Atwater Papers.

32. The best general history of agricultural research in the United States is still A. C. True, *A History of Agricultural Experimentation and Research in the United States, 1607-1925 USDA, Misc. Pub. 251 (Washington, D.C., 1937). More recent and useful, though concerned largely with the history of formal policy discussion, is H. C. Knoblauch, E. M. Law, and W. P. Meyer, State Agricultural Experiment Stations: A History of Research Policy and Procedure*, USDA, Misc. Pub. 904 (Washington, D.C., 1962).

33. E. A. Andrews to J. J. Abel, June 6, 1887, John J. Abel Papers, Welch Medical Library, The Johns Hopkins University.

34. Storer to SWJ, April 13, 1880, Johnson Papers; F. C. Stewart to L. H. Pammel, October 7, 1894, L. H. Pammel Papers, Iowa State University; Farlow to W. Trelease, January 5, 1885, Trelease Papers, Cornell University Collection of Regional History and University Archives.

35. J. B. Lindsey to E. W. Allen, September 9, 1906, Massachusetts File, Records of the Office of Experiment Station, Record Group 164, National Archives, Washington, D.C.

36. George Brush to W. H. Brewer, November 28, 1852, Brewer Papers.

37. Much of the western New York State region in which Johnson grew up was known in pre-bellum America as "the burned-over district," because of the frequency and intensity of the revivals which swept through these counties. For an excellent study of this area, see Whitney Cross, *The Burned-Over District: The Social and Intellectual History of Enthusiastic Religion in Western New York, 1800–1850* (Ithaca, N.Y., 1950).

38. To adequately document this point would demand another paper of the same length. For some examples of conflict between these aspects of the scientist's career, see the remarks concerning W. G. Farlow and F. H. Storer documented in n. 34 above.

Chapter 9

1. The best general history of agricultural research in the United States is still A. C. True, *A History of Agricultural Experimentation and Research in the United States, 1607–1925*, USDA, Misc. Pub. 251 (Washington, D.C., 1937). More recent and useful, though concerned largely with the history of formal policy discussion, is H. C. Knoblauch, E. M. Law, and W. P. Meyer, *State Agricultural Experiment Stations. A History of Research Policy and Procedure*, USDA, Misc. Pub. 904 (Washington, D.C., 1962).

2. Vol. 45, August 21, 1886, p. 548.

3. As one dean explained in 1897: "The entire area is covered with experimental crops. We deem it unnecessary to demonstrate that farming may be made to pay, or that under bad management it is a failure," E. Davenport to A. C. Bird, October 11, 1897, Dean's Letterbooks, Record Series 8/1/1, College of Agriculture, University of Illinois Archives. Cf. R. W. Thatcher to A. R. Dimond, March 13, 1910, Biochemistry Department Papers, Folder 58, University of Minnesota Archives.

4. J. B. Turner to Jonathan Blanchard (1848), Turner Papers, Illinois Historical Survey.

5. C. W. Dabney to Mrs. Dabney, March 16, [1881], Box 25, Dabney Papers, Southern Historical Collection, University of North Carolina, Chapel Hill; A. T. Neale to W. O. Atwater, March 13, 1882, March 17, 1884, Reel 1, Atwater Papers, Edgar Fahs Smith Collection, University of Pennsylvania, Originals at Wesleyan University, Middletown, Conn.

6. This attitude was not limited to fruits and vegetables. When, for example, the *Sacramento Record-Union* printed E. W. Hilgard's lectures without permission, the newspaper's manager argued that such lectures were not Hilgard's private property: "He is paid a salary by the university on behalf of the people of the state of California. . . . I believe a student has the right to take these lectures . . . and furnish the same for publication." W. H. Mills to Rev. J. H. Bonte, January 30, 1882, Box 7, Folder 167, Hilgard Papers, Bancroft Library, University of California.

7. S. M. Babcock, agricultural chemist at the Geneva Experiement Station, received, for example, an offer for such a position in 1884 from Lombard College in Galesburg, Illinois: "We want some one that can teach Chemistry, Physiology, Botany, Zoology, Geology, German, &c. The number of recitations will be about five per day." J. V. N. Standish to Babcock, July 22, 1884, Babcock Papers, State Historical Society of Wisconsin, Madison, Wis.

8. Erwin Frink Smith to W. A. Henry, May 10, 1886, E. F. Smith Papers, American Philosophical Society, Philadelphia, Pa.; S. H. Gage to the President of Trustees of the University of North Carolina, August 25, 1881, S. H. Gage Papers, Collection of

Regional History, Cornell University, Ithaca, N.Y.; Gage to W. Trelease, September 3 and September 12, 1881, William Trelease Papers, Collection of Regional History, Cornell University; Louis F. McInnis to William L. Broun, April 27, 1889, Broun Papers, Department of Archives, Auburn University, Auburn, Ala.; W. B. Stark to J. K. Patterson, May 6, 1889, Patterson Papers, University of Kentucky Educational Archives, Lexington, Ky.

9. George Atkinson to W. G. Farlow, April 15, 1896, Farlow Papers, Farlow Herbarium, Harvard University.

10. C. W. Dabney to Mrs. Dabney, Box 25, Dabney Papers.

11. One problem lay in the endemic status conflicts between scientists with station appointments—often in applied fields—and those in regular university departments. At Wisconsin, for example, the College of Letters and Sciences sought at one point to limit appointments in the College of Agriculture to men whose work lay exclusively in applied science. See W. D. Hoard to Charles Van Hise, October 12, 1908, and Van Hise to Hoard, October 14, 1908, Box 19, President's Papers, University Archives, University of Wisconsin. Half a year later Hoard complained again to President Van Hise of "the ill-concealed sneers of certain professors in the faculty of the College of Letters and Science toward the College of Agriculture." Van Hise replied weakly that jokes about a "cow university" were not meant seriously. Hoard to Van Hise, April 16, 1909, and Van Hise to Hoard, April 19, 1909, Box 19, President's Papers. Yet available evidence seems to indicate that proximity between state university and college of agriculture—as at Cornell, Illinois, Wisconsin, and Minnesota—was on the whole more intellectually satisfying and effective than separation of the institutions.

12. For an example of the use of Hatch funds to pay insurance premiums, see A. C. True to R. H. Miller, January 17, 1897, Maryland File, Records of the Office of Experiment Stations, NA, RG 164; for the expenditures for dissecting material, see True to H. R. Clark, April 5, 1895, Oregon File, OES.

13. *Agricultural Science* 4 (April 1890): 102.

14. April 14, 1890, Farlow Papers; cf. Thaxter to Farlow, March 4, 1889, December 31, 1889, March 13, 1890, and W. C. Sturgis to Farlow, March 29, 1898, and June 14, 1900.

15. Board of Regents, University of Wisconsin, *Annual Report for the Year Ending September 30, 1866*, p. 8. The general history of the University of Wisconsin College of Agriculture has been well documented: W. H. Glover, *Farm and College. The College of Agriculture of the University of Wisconsin. A History* (Madison, 1952); Vernon Carstensen, "The Genesis of an Agricultural Experiment Station," *Agricultural History*, 34 (1960): 13-20; Edward H. Beardsley, *Harry L. Russell and Agricultural Science in Wisconsin* (Madison, 1969).

16. "Report of the Professor in Charge of the Experimental Farm," Board of Regents, University of Wisconsin, *Annual Report for the Fiscal Year Ending September 30, 1882*, p. 44.

17. Remarks of W. A. Henry, Association of American Agricultural Colleges and Experiment Stations, *Proceedings of the Second Annual Convention . . . January 1, 2, and 3, 1889*, USDA, OES Misc. Bulletin 1 ([Washington, 1889]), p. 37.

18. The Wisconsin State Diaryman's Association had sought to encourage scientific study of their industry's problems as early as 1875. Glover, *Farm and College*, p. 81. Eric E. Lampard's excellent study of Wisconsin's dairy industry clearly documents the role of the experiment station in its growth: *The Rise of the Diary Industry in Wisconsin: A Study in Agricultural Change, 1820-1920* (Madison, 1963).

19. Henry to Babcock, August 31 and September 16, 1887, Babcock Papers.

20. In 1914/1915, the University of Wisconsin College of Agriculture and Experiment Station expended $127,180 for research. The Adams and Hatch appropriations totaled $30,000, the state contributed $75,456, and farm sales provided another $21,724. In addition, the state legislature provided $10,000 for the publication of experiment station bulletins and circulars (F. B. Morrison to J. H. Skinner, March 28, 1916, Box 12, College of Agriculture Papers, University of Wisconsin Archives).

21. Henry to Truman Fullenwider, March 3, 1908, Box 11, College of Agriculture Papers, University of Wisconsin Archives.

22. William Trelease, for example, though a fellow Cornellian, was restive under Henry's demands for practical performance (Trealease to W. G. Farlow, June 22, 1882, Farlow Papers). Agricultural chemist H. P. Armsby, not surprisingly, found himself "in hot water" on another occasion "for having talked sense" in regard to the margarine question. (Armsby to E. H. Jenkins, July 20, 1886, Incoming Correspondence, Director's Papers, Connecticut Agricultural Experiment Station, New Haven). Even S. M. Babcock, the "star" of Henry's staff, often found himself so distracted by visitors and shortcourse demands that he could not complete research projects. See Babcock to Mrs. Babcock, May 23, 1897, September 5, 1897, September 7, 1899, Babcock Papers.

23. For a contemporary description of the harsh conditions in which McCollum worked, see L. B. Mendel to T. B. Osborne, July 26, 1912, Biochemistry Dept. Records, Connecticut Agricultural Experiment Station. For analyses of the background of nutrition work at the Wisconsin and Connecticut experiment stations, see Stanley L. Becker, "The Emergence of a Trace Nutrient Concept through Animal Experimentation" (Ph.D. diss., University of Wisconsin, 1968).

24. This interpretation of Davenport's work is based on the records of the Illinois College of Agriculture during Davenport's tenure as Dean and Director of the Experiment Station. Most important are the College of Agriculture Letterbooks, 1888-1911 (Record Series 8/1/1), Experiment Station Letterbooks, 1901-1904 (Record Series 8/2/2), and Agronomy Letterbooks, 1899-1919 (Record Series 8/6/3).

25. [Davenport], *The Work and Needs of the Agricultural College and Experiment Station of the University of Illinois, February, 1903* (n.p., n.d.), p. 12; Davenport to W. J. Kennedy, February 1, 1906, Dean's Letterbooks (Record Series 8/1/1); Davenport to C. F. Mills, October 19, 1900, Dean's Letterbooks.

26. In 1911, for example, Davenport was forced by the state's dairy association to ask for the resignation of the head of his dairy husbandry department. Davenport to E. J. James, April 11, 1911, Dean's Letterbooks, Personal (Record Series 8/1/1).

27. As Davenport explained to a contemporary: "A man desiring to develop a department of economics or history, Greek or philosophy, is practically confined to internal conditions for the achievement of his ambition; fortunately it is not so with agriculture. The state of South Dakota, not the campus at Brooking, is your field. . . . If you can make your department indispensable to South Dakota, there is nothing you cannot have" (Davenport to A. N. Hume, October 9, 1913, File Drawer 6, Davenport Papers).

28. The following pages are based primarily on the papers of E. W. Hilgard at the Bancroft Library, University of California. For evaluations of Hilgard's principal work, see Hans Jenny, *E. W. Hilgard and the Birth of Modern Soil Science* (Pisa, Italy, 1961); Maynard A. Amerine, "Hilgard and California Viticulture," *Hilgardia* 33 (1962): 1-23. See also Mary L. Mayfield, "The University of California Agricultural Experiment Station, 1868-1924" (Master's thesis, University of California, Davis, 1966).

29. Years later Hilgard was happy to submit a claim for priority in establishing America's first experiment station (Hilgard to A. C. True, January 7, 1892, California File, OES).

30. Hilgard to F. A. P. Barnard, January 1, 1886, Hilgard Letterbooks, Hilgard Papers. For this bleak characterization of his correspondence, see Hilgard to A. L. Bancroft, March 25, 1886, Hilgard Letterbooks. Hilgard's avowal of empathy is taken from "Address to Agricultural and Horticultural Society," *Los Angeles Daily Republican*, October 7, 1877, clipping in folder 205, Box 9, Hilgard Papers.

31. Hilgard to Harvey Wiley, July 29, 1885, Hilgard Letterbooks.

32. Hilgard to G. W. Atherton, December 6, 1884, Hilgard Letterbooks.

33. Though the power to disallow claims was rarely invoked, the OES used the threat constantly, especially after it began the practice of making annual inspection trips to the several state stations. For a short account of the administrative history of the OES, see Milton Conover, *The Office of Experiment Stations, Its History, Activities and Organization*, Institute for Government Research, Service Monographs of the United States Government, no. 32 (Baltimore, 1924).

34. For a detailed discussion of the background and passage of this measure, see chapter 10.

35. N. E. Hansen, "Plant Breeding," Association of American Agricultural Colleges and Experiment Stations, *Proceedings of the Eighteenth Annual Convention . . . November 1-3, 1904*, USDA, OES Bulletin 153 ([Washington, D.C., 1905]), p. 119.

36. Raymond Pearl, *Modes of Research in Genetics* (New York, 1915), p. 169. Despite momentary embarrassments and gaucheries, this scientific entrepreneurship and the hopes upon which it fed helped create one of the institutional contexts in which academic genetics was to develop in this country. See chap. 12.

37. Within a few years, for example, of T. H. Morgan's first drosophila publications, Office of Experiment Station administrators were urging state directors to turn to the Morgan group at Columbia in their search for men to conduct breeding programs (E. W. Allen to H. W. Mumford, January 2, 1912, Illinois File, OES). Some even among the more alert and responsive members of the older generation of scientist-administrators felt real qualms in regard to hiring scientists with no specific farm training or orientation. See L. H. Bailey, "Training for Experimenters," *Agricultural Science* 5 (1891): 214-15; H. J. Waters to E. W. Allen, March 24, 1902, Missouri File, OES.

38. Probably the most articulate and dedicated of such spokesmen for the upgrading of station research was W. H. Jordan, director of New York's Geneva Station. See, for example, his "Function and Efficiency of the Agricultural College," *Science* 34 (1911): 780-81.

39. The comparatively rapid development of the scientific disciplines in the land-grant colleges and experiment stations surprised even contemporaries in the early years of this century. As Yale physiologist L. B. Mendel wrote after spending a week in Ithaca: "Incidentally my eyes were opened to the forces now enlisted in this country in the study of the branches of so-called agriculture. Many of us have certainly under-estimated the scientific possibilities of this movement" (Mendel to T. B. Osborne, Osborne Personal Boxes, no. 1, Biochemistry Department, Connecticut Agricultural Experiment Station).

40. William Bateson, for example, visiting the United States, in 1907, was shocked at the inelegant circumstances of the American professoriate. "To be a University Professor without private fortune," he explained, "is the meanest kind of lot. They are slaved to death; also no time for original research. Hours unendurably long" (Bateson to Beatrice Bateson, October 24, 1907, Reel A, Bateson Papers, American Philosophical Society). For examples of skepticism toward the USDA's scientific bureaus, see J. W. Coulter to E. F. Smith, July 14, 1888, Smith Papers, A.P.S.; W. J. Spillman to A. F. Blakeslee, November 1, 1911, Blakeslee Papers, A.P.S.; H. J. Conn to K. F. Kellerman, May 1, 1911, Conn Papers, Collection of Regional History, Cornell University.

41. The increasing success of the college of agriculture as an educational institution also played an important role in economic growth, helping create a consensus of values in farm leaders and thus conditions in which community receptivity toward innovation and respect for the role of science were maximized.

42. One might also discuss a number of tangible and permanently significant results of pre-World War I experiment station work—hybrid corn or the discovery of Vitamin A, for example. For a more detailed discussion of these innovations and their relation to both disciplinary and contexual realities, see chap. 11.

43. Henry to A. C. True, July 9, 1898, Wisconsin File, OES.

44. When, for example, small nurserymen in North Carolina complained of inspection fees, the Experiment Station council decided that "it seems better to insist on their still paying even if there are many forced out of business. There is more danger by far from the small nurseries than from the larger ones" (Minutes of Station Council, Entry for November 1, 1897, School of Agriculture, Research Division, University Archives, North Carolina State University, Raleigh). Even in the earliest years of agitation for the creation of experiment stations and fertilizer inspection, large manufacturers of chemical fertilizer were often in favor of such programs. See B. M. Rhodes to Evan Pugh, April 16 and June 23, 1862, Pugh Papers, Penn State Collection, Pennsylvania State University.

45. For general discussions of the Babcock test, see Lampard, *Rise of the Dairy Industry*, and Glover, *Farm and College*. For Henry's own version of the test's background, see W. A. Henry, "Notes on the Origin of the Babcock Milk Test, Dictated March 8, 1912," typed ms, Babcock File, Library of the University of Wisconsin College of Agriculture. It would take a separate monograph to detail the story of the Babcock test

and its implications for the dairying industry and the land-grant colleges. It might be noted, however, that by 1907, of some thirty-five programs in dairying at American agricultural colleges, Wisconsin had supplied instructors for Alabama, Colorado, Connecticut, Illinois, Indiana, Kansas, Maine, Maryland, Massachusetts, Michigan, Minnesota, Mississippi, New Hampshire, North Dakota, Ohio, Oregon, Pennsylvania, South Dakota, Vermont, and Washington (*Wisconsin Agriculturalist*, February 28, 1907, pp. 2–3).

46. Davenport to George H. Rankin, February 15, 1901, Dean's Letterbooks. The ultimately ambiguous quality of such dollars-and-cents arguments is apparent.

47. It must be recalled, moreover, that the existence of such technological innovations not only had a discrete effect on productivity but served as well to stimulate the industry by changing the image of dairying and attracting general farmers to this area of specialization—a special concern of station publicists.

Chapter 10

1. 24 *Stat.*, 440. President Cleveland had grave doubts as to the constitutionality of the Hatch Act, the first direct cash grant-in-aid to individual states. States in which independent experiment stations already existed could, if they chose, use the Hatch funds to endow these stations; otherwise they were to be departments within the individual state's land-grant college.

2. 34 *Stat.*, 63. The Hatch Act had also sanctioned the "verification" of experiments. The "original" in the corresponding phrase of the Adams Act implicitly forbade this. The most important sources for the history of the Adams Act are the papers of Dean W. A. Henry in the archives of the University of Wisconsin, in the Henry C. Adams Papers in the State Historical Society of Wisconsin, and in the Records of the Office of Experiment Stations (OES), Record Group 164, in the National Archives.

3. Much of True's success as an administrator was a result of his ability to assuage the suspicions of station leaders and to convince them that his ultimate loyalties lay not with the Department of Agriculture, but with the state stations. Cf. John Fields to A. C. True, February 8, 1901, OES, Oklahoma File; A. C. True to E. W. Hilgard, December 10, 1903, "Confidential and Personal," OES, California File. For a useful short account of its administrative history see Milton Conover, *The Office of Experiment Stations: Its History, Activities and Organization*, Institute for Government Research, Service Monographs of the United States Government, no. 32 (Baltimore, 1924).

4. E. W. Allen later characterized the policy of the Office of Experiment Stations as one of influence and not coercion, but the distinction is a fine one. Though the power to disallow claims was rarely invoked, True used the threat constantly, especially after the Office had begun the practice of making annual inspection trips to the several stations. But the Office had other, less formal means of exerting influence. One was the prestige which True came to have personally and his judicious use of it to help "deserving" scientists and administrators unable to cope with hostile factions. The Office and True, moreover, soon became a kind of central employment bureau for workers in the agricultural sciences. To ignore True's pointed advice was to cut oneself off from his patronage and indirectly from the possibility of advancement, for all the better institutions habitually turned to True for advice when they sought to fill a vacant position.

5. For an example of the use of Hatch funds to pay insurance premiums, see True to R. H. Miller, January 17, 1897, OES, Maryland File; for the expenditures for dissection material, see True to H. R. Clark, April 5, 1895, OES, Oregon File.

6. For attacks on station veterinarians performing routine preventive work, see True to A. J. Neale, April 1, 1896, OES, Delaware File, and True to W. D. Gibbs, March 6, 1902, New Hampshire File. For examples of the opposition of the Office to the use of Hatch funds for fertilizer testing, see True to H. J. Wheeler, January 26, 1898, Rhode Island File; True to C. E. Thorne, January 27, 1900, Ohio File; True to C. C. Thach, September 27, 1905, Alabama File.

7. True to Charles Curtiss, January 2, 1897, OES, Iowa File; True to T. L. Haecker, February 9, 1899, Minnesota File; True to M. A. Scovell, October 5, 1898, Kentucky File.

8. For Adams's acknowledgment that True had drafted the bill, see H. C. Adams to W. A. Henry, December 24, 1903, Dean's Papers, College of Agriculture, University of Wisconsin Archives.

9. Whitney, who assumed a dogmatic and controversial approach to problems of soil science, was particularly distrusted. The scientific aspects of his quarrel with station men, and in particular with E. W. Hilgard, is well summarized in Hans Jenny, *E. W. Hilgard and the Birth of Modern Soil Science* (Pisa, Italy, 1961), pp. 89–102.

10. For experiment station disillusion with Wilson, see Henry to Adams, January 27, 1905, Dean's Files, University of Wisconsin Archives; Hilgard to Henry, February 11, 1904, ibid., General Files. For expressions of resentment against the Department and hopes that the Adams Act might restore the balance of power, see Hilgard to True, December 3, 1903, OES, A. C. True Personal File; Hilgard to Franklin H. King, February 3, 1904, Franklin H. King Papers, State Historical Society of Wisconsin; Eugene Davenport to James G. Cannon, November 4, 1905, College of Agriculture Papers, University of Illinois; Henry to E. H. Jenkins, Director's Papers, Connecticut Agricultural Experiment Station, New Haven; P. H. Mell to Henry, February 23, 1906, Dean's Files, University of Wisconsin Archives.

Early in 1904, as if to underline the necessity of the increase in station funds, station leaders had narrowly defeated a provision in the agricultural appropriations bill which would have authorized the Secretary of Agriculture to "coordinate" the work of the stations. Cf. J. L. Hills to Redfield Proctor, February 14, 1904, and George Atherton to Boise Penrose, February 15, 1904, National Archives, Record Group 46, Records of the Senate, Petition File, 58A, J.1.

11. Eugene Davenport to W. J. Kennedy, February 1, 1906, College of Agriculture Papers, University of Illinois.

12. In Connecticut, for example, the experiment station worked closely with the state Pomological Society, with dairymen, and with tobacco growers. In Wisconsin, the station cooperated for many years with the State Horticultural Society and the State Dairymen's Association. In Louisiana, rice and cotton growers, sugar planters and processors all had ties with local stations. (Louisiana planters had, indeed, established a private experiment station before the federal subvention of 1887.) In New York, not only the raisers of fruit, poultry, and dairy animals, but even the peony and ginseng growers took an active interest in station research. Stations founded by individual states before the passage of the Hatch Act were always a product of the initiative and influence of organized farm groups. Cf. W. H. Glover, *Farm and College. The College of Agriculture of the University of Wisconsin, A History* (Madison, Wis., 1952); Vernon Carstensen, "The Genesis of an Agricultural Experiment Station," *Agricultural History* 34 (1960): 13–20; Carl Raymond Woodward and Ingrid N. Waller, *New Jersey's Agricultural Experiment Station, 1880–1930* (New Brunswick, N.J., 1932); Gould P. Colman, "A History of Agricultural Education at Cornell University" (Ph.D. diss., Cornell University, 1962), 1: 153, 273; 2: 412.

13. Jenkins, "The Corn Crop in Connecticut," *Proceedings, Connecticut Board of Agriculture*, 1904, pp. 196–97; "Communication from W. A. Henry read at Dinner in Honor of Dr. Babcock, held on February 9, 1916," mimeographed, Biographical File, Library of the University of Wisconsin College of Agriculture.

14. This was the case, for example, when True wished to assure favorable congressional action on appropriations for irrigation and nutrition research to be administered by his Office. W. R. Dodson to True, May 23, 1906, OES, Louisiana File: True to Eugene Davenport, December 5, 1900, Illinois File; True to M. A. Scovell, October 5, 1898, Kentucky File. Experiment station directors were even called upon for help when an antivivisection bill threatened to pass in Congress. Cf. H. H. Goodell to E. W. Allen, May 24, 1897, OES, Massachusetts File. Of course, college and station leaders could not influence every sort of legislation. Their effectiveness was limited to those measures which either immediately affected agricultural college or station interests or to those which could be cloaked in the benevolent neutrality of science.

15. Adams died in the summer of 1906, however, and he never concluded his campaign against the insurgent who opposed him for the nomination. Adams knew, however, that he could call upon the support of the dairymen's association and of what his friend E. W. Keyes called the "university influences." Keyes to H. C. Adams, February 16, 1906, Henry C. Adams Papers, State Historical Society of Wisconsin; Robert S. Maxwell, *La Follette and the Rise of the Progressives in Wisconsin* (Madison, Wis., 1956), p. 42.

16. Harvey Wiley to Franklin H. King, July 25, 1904, "Confidential," King Papers.

17. This is illustrated, for example, in the publication problems which plagued station scientists. A. C. True's files contain dozens of letters from workers asking permission to publish experimental results in technical journals before they were published in station bulletins. A paper, moreover, which would bring respect from fellow scientists might provoke only suspicion or even ridicule from the experiment station's rural constituents. Cf. H. J. Webber, *Science*, October 18, 1907, p. 510. On the scientist's indifference to more mundane standards of success, see editorial by C. S. Plumb in *Agricultural Science* 1 (July 1887):162-63, and remarks by W. O. Atwater in *Proceedings of the Third Annual Convention of American Agricultural Colleges and Experiment Stations*, USDA, OES Miscellaneous Bulletin no. 2 (Washington, D.C., 1890), p. 98. Consistent with this emphasis was the conviction of Atwater and other station leaders that the best station work would have to be done in connection with a university. Cf. W. O. Atwater to W. H. Brewer, May 29, 1889, William H. Brewer Papers, Yale University.

18. It is clear, however, that even in the 1870s and 1880s some scientists worked for the establishment of experiment stations because of the opportunity it might give them to do research. Cf. William McMurtie to G. H. Cook, September 13, 1884, George H. Cook Papers (Rutgers University, Rutgeriana Collection); W. O. Atwater to S. W. Johnson, January 7, 1873, S. W. Johnson Transcripts, Connecticut Agricultural Experiment Station, New Haven.

19. H. C. Knoblauch, E. M. Law, and W. P. Meyer, *State Agricultural Experiment Stations. A History of Research Policy and Procedure*, USDA Misc. Pub. no. 901 (Washington, D.C., 1962), pp. 55-109, contains an analysis of the policy statements made by agricultural college association leaders between the passage of the Hatch and Adams acts.

20. Eugene Davenport to H. C. White, April 9, 1906, College of Agriculture Papers, University of Illinois. It must be remembered that many of the Association's leaders not only shared a faith in science, but were men whose own stations' prosperity and personal reputations had benefited from their having sponsored successful research programs. The executive committee of the Association, it might be noted, had been the group which originally suggested to Congress the need for enactment of the 1894 provision which gave the power of audit to the Secretary of Agriculture. "Report of the Executive Committee," *Proceedings of the Eighth Annual Convention of the Association of American Agricultural Colleges and Experiment Stations*, USDA, OES Bulletin no. 24 (Washington, D.C. 1895), p. 17.

21. For Adams's tribute to Henry, see Adams to Henry, March 20, 1906, Adams Papers.

22. *Proceedings of the Sixteenth Annual Convention of the Association of American Agricultural Colleges and Experiment Stations*, USDA, OES Bulletin no. 123 (Washington, D.C., 1903), p. 55.

23. For Adams's interviews with Wilson and True, see Adams to W. A. Henry, December 4 and December 24, 1903, Dean's Files, University of Wisconsin Archives. For Henry's accounts of the background of the Adams Act, all of which are in essential agreement, see Henry, "The Work of Hon. H. C. Adams," *Breeder's Gazette* (Chicago), August 1, 1906, pp. 186-87; Henry, "Memorial to Henry Cullen Adams," *Proceedings of the Twentieth Annual Convention of the Association of American Agricultural Colleges and Experiment Stations*, USDA, OES Bulletin no. 184 (Washington, D.C., 1907), pp. 36-40; *Democrat*, (Madison, Wis.), February 17, 1906, p. 2.

24. A third hurdle which had to be overcome was created by an early split in college and station ranks. A number of college presidents and the National Association of State

Mining Schools hoped to have a bill subsidizing mining colleges pass Congress either in conjunction with the Adams Act or before it. Adams warned, however, that persistence in this scheme would end any possibility of passing either measure. Nevertheless, the matter remained in dispute until a coup by experiment station men removed Pennsylvania's George W. Atherton from the executive committee and replaced him with the reliable station man Liberty Hyde Bailey. Cf. Henry C. Adams to W. H. Hays, November 13, 1905, National Archives, Record Group 16, Records of the Office of the Secretary of Agriculture; Davenport to Adams, May 23, 1905, College of Agriculture Papers, University of Illinois; Adams to Henry, April 16, 1904; Henry to Adams, November 11, 1904, Dean's Files, University of Wisconsin Archives; Adams to L. H. Bailey, November 13, 1905; W. H. Jordan to L. H. Bailey, November 6, 1905, Liberty Hyde Bailey Papers, Cornell University Archives and Collection of Regional History.

25. Wiley's two fellow bureau chiefs threatened to remove all work related to soils, fertilizers, and plants from his Bureau of Chemistry.

26. Adams to Henry, January 13, February 11, 15, 1904, January 24, 1905, Dean's Files.

27. House Report No. 1883, "Increased Appropriations for Agricultural Experiment Stations, March 24, 1904," 58th Cong., 2d Sess. Adams wrote the report, but did not sign it. Adams to Henry, March 26, 1904, General Files, College of Agriculture, University of Wisconsin Archives. For the application of local pressure to committee members, see Henry to Adams, February 22, 1904, General Files; Adams to Henry, January 16, 1904, Dean's Files; Henry to Adams, February 12, 15, 1904, Dean's Files. It should be noted that the arguments advanced by Adams—as in this report or in his speeches on the House floor—emphasized not the importance of abstract research but the immediate financial benefits which the stations had already brought.

28. Adams to W. H. Hays, May 16, 1905, Records of the Office of the Secretary of Agriculture.

29. For Pennsylvania, see Adams to Henry, January 30, February 27, 1905, Dean's Files; Adams to Benjamin Casson, January 27, 1906, Adams Papers.

30. In desperation Adams had even drawn up a petition to have the bill brought to the House's attention and managed to collect two hundred and fifty signatures within a few days. Adams to Henry, February 27, 1905, Dean's Files.

31. Adams to L. H. Bailey, February 15, 1906, Telegram, Bailey Papers; Adams to James Wilson, February 19, 1906, Records of the Office of the Secretary of Agriculture. For actions of local station and college leaders, see H. J. Wheeler to H. C. Adams, February 20, 1906, Adams Papers; E. H. Jenkins to Morgan G. Bulkeley and to Frank P. Brandegee, February 19, 1906, Director's Papers, Connecticut Agricultural Experiment Station; Davenport to S. M. Cullom and A. J. Hopkins, February 6, 1906, College of Agriculture Papers, University of Illinois.

32. In each of these fields, it might be noted, experiment station scientists played a prominent part and in each Adams funds underwrote much early research.

33. James Wilson to the directors of the OES, March 20, 1906. This important policy statement in the form of a circular letter is conveniently reprinted in Knoblauch et al., *State Agricultural Experiment Stations*, pp. 236-37.

34. E. W. Allen to J. B. Lindsay, May 8, 1906, OES, Massachusetts File. For a clear statement of their aims after several years of experience, see E. W. Allen, "Scope, Purpose, and Plans of Adams Fund Investigations," *Proceedings of the Twenty-fourth Annual Convention of the Association of American Agricultural Colleges* (Montpelier, Vt., 1911), pp. 171-74.

35. For an account of Osborne's work, see Hubert B. Vickery, "Thomas Burr Osborne," *Journal of Nutrition* 59 (May 1956):3-26. For the objections of Connecticut farmers, see E. H. Jenkins to A. C. True, October 5, 1908, Director's Papers, Connecticut Agricultural Experiment Station.

36. A weakness in True's policy, at least to mid-twentieth-century eyes, was his narrow conception of the word "research." True uniformly disapproved proposals for the use of Adams funds to study economic or social questions. His interpretation was, of course, an inevitable consequence of the struggle which he had waged to raise standards in the stations. The social sciences were soft and thus suspect.

37. For a statement of the argument that the creation of the Adams Act simply underlined the need for the expansion of extension work, see W. A. Henry, *Proceedings of the Twentieth Annual Meeting of the Association of American Agricultural Colleges and Experiment Stations*, USDA, OES Bulletin no. 184, (Washington, D.C., 1907), p. 95. For True's use of the Adams Act to urge stations to increase pressure on the state legislatures for the support of extension work, cf. True to W. R. Dodson, October 12, November 4, 1908, OES, Louisiana File; L. L. Willoughby to True, February 16, 1907, Georgia File; True to H. L. Russell, October 12, 1907, Wisconsin File.

Chapter 11

1. E. V. McCollum's history of nutrition research is still indispensable. *A History of Nutrition: The Sequence of Ideas in Nutrition Investigations* (Boston, 1957). I have also benefited from an extended interview with Professor McCollum.

2. *Association of American Agricultural Colleges and Experiment Stations, Proceedings of the Fourth Annual Convention, 1890*, p. 91.

3. Medical historians, reflecting the priorities of their own discipline, emphasize, naturally enough, the medical discoverers in the conquest of the deficiency diseases. Historical accounts by biochemists, on the other hand, emphasize the background of protein chemistry against which the development of the deficiency-disease concept took place.

4. R. H. Chittenden, "Some New Viewpoints on Nutrition," *Popular Science Monthly* 73 (1908): 398. The availability of purified preparations of proteins created new opportunities not only in nutrition research; H. Gideon Wells, for example, used Osborne's proteins for experimental work with anaphylaxis.

5. For Hopkins's acknowledgment that the origin of his work lay in his interest in the metabolic effects of the several amino acids, see F. G. Hopkins to Thomas Osborne, August 4, 1912, Thomas B. Osborne Papers, Department of Biochemistry, Connecticut Agricultural Experiment Station. As late as March 14, 1913, Hopkins wrote to Osborne: "That such extraordinarily small amounts of the 'X factor' can act, rather diminishes the practical importance of the phenomenon; but not, I think, its theoretical interest" (Osborne Papers). Hopkins, unlike Mendel, Osborne, McCollum, and Casimir Funk, did have medical training and on several occasions in later life contended that a long-standing interest in the deficiency diseases had motivated his interest in nutrition research. Compare Hopkins's 1929 Nobel Prize address, "The Early History of Vitamin Research," in *Hopkins and Biochemistry*, ed. Joseph Needham and Ernest Baldwin (Cambridge, Mass., 1949), p. 196. Hopkins's recollections and his contemporary correspondence with Osborne are obviously inconsistent.

6. For Babcock's own account of these events, see S. M. Babcock to Paul de Kruif, October 10, 1927, carbon, Department of Biochemistry, University of Wisconsin. See also the reminiscences of E. V. McCollum, "My Early Experiences in the Study of Foods and Nutrition," *Annual Review of Biochemistry* 22 (1953): 1–16.

7. Ibid, p. 3. Babcock was a student of G. C. Caldwell at Cornell and S. W. Johnson had originally set Osborne, his son-in-law, to work on the plant proteins in the late 1880s. The "American colony" of mid-century students in Germany which we have already described at some length was still playing a key role in the development of American biochemistry. See Hubert B. Vickery, "The Influence of Samuel W. Johnson on the Chemistry of Proteins," *Yale Journal of Biology and Medicine* 13 (1941): 563–69.

8. E. V. McCollum to E. B. Hart, May 4, 1907, Biochemistry Files, University of Wisconsin.

9. McCollum, *History of Nutrition*, p. 223; McCollum, "My Early Experiences," p. 10. In the latter reminiscence, McCollum notes that in a year of Mendel's very thorough course in physiological chemistry he could not recall any mention of beriberi, scurvy, or rickets (p. 3).

10. Osborne to Mendel, July 29, 1911, Osborne Papers.

11. Funding, of course, tended always to be justified in applied terms. The director of the Connecticut Agricultural Experiment Station, for example, described Osborne's proposed research to the Department of Agriculture in the following terms: ". . . feeding experiments on the relative efficiency of different pure vegetable proteins in maintaining the nitrogen equilibrium. This goes to the root of the question of efficiency of protein from different sources in the feeding stuff." E. H. Jenkins to A. C. True, June 24, 1909, Director's Files, Connecticut Agricultural Experiment Station.

12. The preceding paragraphs have implied another relationship between science and American society. This is the connection between patterns of economic growth and trends in scientific research. An increasing need for rationalization of farm practice made funds available for the support of chemical laboratories. (In similar fashion, the support of nutrition work by the Carnegie Institution of Washington—indeed, the existence of the Institution itself—can be explained in terms of increasing economic complexity.) It is hardly a novelty to suggest that such relationships exist. They have, nevertheless, received comparatively little historical attention.

13. See, for example, A. R. Crabb, *The Hybrid-Corn Makers: Prophets of Plenty* (New Brunswick, N.J., 1947); G. H. Shull, "Beginnings of the Heterosis Concept," and H. K. Hayes, "Development of the Heterosis Concept," pp. 14-65 and 49-65, in John W. Gowen, ed., *Heterosis* (Ames, Iowa, ca. 1952). For a study of the development of hybrid corn as a case study in the relationship between pure and applied science, and one written from a somewhat different point of view than the present discussion see I. Bernard Cohen, *Science, Servant of Man. A Layman's Primer for the Age of Science* (Boston, 1948), pp. 176-95.

14. This generalization and the balance of the following pages is based largely on the records of the University of Illinois, College of Agriculture, especially the letterpress copybooks of Eugene Davenport, dean of the college and director of the experiment station, and the eight letterpress books of the Department of Agronomy covering the years 1899 to 1903. The records of the Connecticut Agricultural Experiment at New Haven, especially the director's correspondence, provided a second major source. See also chap. 10, preceding.

15. W. M. Hays to Senator Knute Nelson, February 6, 1896, Director's Letterbooks, Experiment Station Records, University of Minnesota Archives.

16. The importance of this study in encouraging maize breeding was, for example, particularly emphasized by Donald Jones, himself a pioneer in the field. Jones, "Biographical Memoir of Edward Murray East, 1879-1938." *National Academy of Sciences, Biographical Memoirs* 23 (1945): 217-42; Jones, "History of the Genetics Department of the Connecticut Agricultural Experiment Station," typed ms., CAES Library. Illinois corn-breeding experiments early in the 1890s had emphasized yield, but in the second half of the decade emphasis shifted to composition.

17. A. D. Shamel to Prairie Farmer Publishing Company, October 18, 1900, Agronomy Department Letterbooks.

18. Davenport to F. A. Warner, October 18, 1900; Davenport to George Williams, October 23, 1900, Director's Letterbooks. For work of the Agronomy Department with and for large seed corn growers see A. D. Shamel to F. A. Warner, December 16 and 23, 1901; January 2, 1902; and to J. Dwight Funk, October 31, 1901, Agronomy Department Letterbooks.

19. When experimenting, for example, with seed corn, college workers found that tenant farmers often falsified yields of improved seed corn, unwilling as they were to shift from accustomed varieties. A. D. Shamel to E. A. Gastman, January 7, 1902, Agronomy Letterbooks.

20. Shamel to C. F. Mills, November 12, 1901, Agronomy Letterbooks.

21. P. G. Holden to Charles Doty, February 16, 1900, Agronomy Letterbooks; cf. Shamel to W. H. Burke, April 2, 1900.

22. Davenport and C. G. Hopkins, agricultural chemist, the senior members of the college faculty, were both committed to the traditional "ear-to-row" selection methods. Many years later A. D. Shamel recalled their hostility to his use of selfing and cross-pollinating in continuing the corn-breeding work which the older men had begun with

P. G. Holden and which they had become somewhat discouraged with after 1900. Shamel to Holden, April 20, 1948, Copy in Historical File, Agronomy, College of Agriculture Papers.

23. The best account of Shull's work is to be found in his own—not uninterested —account cited in note 13 above and essentially corroborated by Donald Jones in his memoir of East (*National Academy of Sciences, Biographical Memoirs* 23 (1945): 217-42) Jones reprints a most illuminating exchange of letters between Shull and East (pp. 223-26) written during 1908 and 1909.

24. Jenkins to A. C. True, November 1, 1909, Connecticut File, Records of the Office of Experiment Stations, RG 164, National Archives. For a specific example of Jenkins's economic rationale in subsidizing corn research see Jenkins, "The Corn Crop in Connecticut," *Proceedings Connecticut Board of Agriculture*, 1904, pp. 196-97.

25. In the case of hybrid corn work at Illinois, for example, a good deal of misunderstanding was caused by chemist C. G. Hopkins's unilateral announcement to the press that the college had discovered a strain of corn which would have twice the protein content of standard varieties.

Chapter 12

1. Morgan was only senior author: T. H. Morgan, A. H. Sturtevant, H. J. Muller, and C. B. Bridges, *The Mechanism of Mendelian Heredity* (New York, 1915). The authors cited were checked in J. McKeen Cattell's *American Men of Science. A Biographical Directory* in the first three editions (New York, 1906, 1910, and Garrison, N.Y., 1921). There is, unfortunately, no monographic study of the introduction of Mendelianism to the United States. There are, however, many accounts and biographical sketches which relate to the beginnings of American genetics; a number will be cited below in relation to specific incidents. Useful material will be found as well in W. E. Castle, "The Beginnings of Mendalianism in America," in *Genetics in the Twentieth Century*, ed. L. C. Dunn, (New York, ca. 1951), pp. 59-76; Garland Allen, "Thomas Hunt Morgan: The Relation of Genetic and Evolution Theory, 1900-1925" (Ph.D. dissertation, Harvard University, 1966.

2. The term is drawn, of course, from *Drosophila Melanogaster*, the fruit fly central to the work of Morgan and his group. Bateson was English, though he had studied for a time with W. K. Brooks, at Johns Hopkins. Bateson, *Mendel's Principles of Heredity* (Cambridge, 1913).

3. As R. C. Punnett put it: "The ferment of new ideas was already working in the solution, and under the stimulus of Mendel's work they have rapidly crystallized out," *Mendelism*, 3d ed. (London, 1911), p. 131. For a discussion of the varied origins of the first generation of geneticists see A. H. Sturtevant, "The Early Mendelians," *Proceedings of the American Philosophical Society* 109 (1965): 199-204.

4. For an outline of these developments see A. C. True, *A History of Agricultural Experimentation and Research in the United States, 1607-1925*, USDA, Misc. Pub. 251, (Washington, D.C., 1937).

5. Manly Miles, *Stock-breeding: A Practical Treatise on the Applications of the Laws of Heredity to the Improvement and Breeding of Domestic Animals* (New York, 1879), p. iii.

6. J. S. Newman, "Answers to Inquiries," Alabama Department of Agriculture, *Bulletin Number Four* (Auburn, Ala., 1884), p. 54.

7. Morrow, University of Illinois, *Bulletin. The University Farms* (Champaign, Ill., 1885), p. 11. For representative discussion of the possible effects of dehorning bulls see Eugene Davenport to H. W. Collingwood, May 19, 1879, Director's Letterbooks, College of Agriculture Papers, University of Illinois.

8. True to J. McKeen Cattell, October 2, 1902, Personal File, Records of the Office of Experiment Stations, RG 164, National Archives. Cf. True to W. A. Henry, October 31,

1906, Wisconsin File; True to J. F. Duggar, October 17, 1906, Alabama File, RG 164, National Archives.

9. Nathan Allen, "The Intermarriage of Relations," *Quarterly Journal of Psychological Medicine* 3 (1869): 266.

10. A general aversion to the discussion of matters sexual may well have exacerbated the customary vagueness of such explanations. As one writer unwittingly expressed it: "My theory being based upon general physiological laws, I have been able to avoid all objectionable detail." George B. Starkweather, *The Law of Sex* (London, 1883), pp. vi–vii. These questions are treated in greater detail in chap. 1.

11. Insofar as I am aware, the Flexner Report of 1910 is still the best general description of the state of American medical schools in the early years of this century. Abraham Flexner, *Medical Education in the United States and Canada*, Carnegie Foundation for the Advancement of Teaching, Bulletin no. 4 (New York, 1910). Cf. R. P. Hudson, "Abraham Flexner in Perspective: American Medical Education, 1865–1910," *Bulletin of the History of Medicine* 46 (1972): 545–61.

12. See, among many other examples, Charles S. Minot, "On Heredity and Rejuvenation," *American Naturalist* 30 (1896): 100 and passim.

13. The full title of Wilson's book is not, of course, without significance. One could do no better than to read Wilson's study for an insight into the state of cytology at the turn of the century. E. B. Wilson, *The Cell in Development and Inheritance* (New York, 1902), esp. chap. 5, "Reduction of the Chromosomes, Oögenesis and Spermatogenesis," pp. 234–88. For an excellent, if brief, historical review of this theme in cytological work see Arthur Hughes, *A History of Cytology* (London and New York, ca. 1959), pp. 63–89.

14. "It soon became evident," in the words of H. J. Muller, "that the elements studied by the microscopist on the one hand and by the experimental breeder on the other hand were in fact to be identified with one another. Thus in a sense we may say that the east and west coasts of Mendelism had been discovered independently and that the explorers from both sides finally met. They later found, quite literally, that their 'maps' of the intervening terrain, made from their respective vantage points, agreed to a remarkable degree." Muller, "The Development of the Gene Theory," in Dunn, ed., *Genetics*, p. 79.

15. For a discussion of the social context in which the eugenics movement became involved with immigration restriction and racism see John Higham, *Strangers in the Land: Patterns of American Nativism, 1860–1925* (New Brunswick, N.J., 1955); Barbara Miller Solomon, *Ancestors and Immigrants. A Changing New England Tradition* (Cambridge, Mass., 1956). For examples of the specific use of hereditarian arguments in the immigration restriction movement see Carroll A. Smith, "Anglo-Saxon Science: The Scientific Rationale for Immigration Restriction" (Master's thesis, Columbia University, 1958).

16. For a study of the eugenics movement see Mark H. Haller, *Eugenics: Hereditarian Attitudes in American Thought* (New Brunswick, N.J., 1963).

17. Pearson, *Darwinism, Medical Progress and Eugenics. An Address to the Medical Profession*, Eugenics Laboratory Lecture Series, 9 (Cambridge, 1912), p. 7; Bateson, *Mendel's Principles*, 1913, pp. 303–5; W. E. Castle to Irving Fisher, February 25, 1924 (copy) C. B. Davenport Papers, American Philosophical Society. For the rejection of eugenics by prominent biologists in different situations, see T. H. Morgan to H. F. Osborn, June 14, 1920 (copy); William Bateson to C. B. Davenport, February 11, 1921, and in regard to the influence of Nazism, L. C. Dunn to J. C. Merriam, July 3, 1935 (copy), C. B. Davenport Papers.

18. The most conspicuous of these was Charles B. Davenport, who drifted farther and farther away from his zoological colleagues and, as the century advanced, became increasingly committed to the conservative ideology which became so much a part of the eugenics movement. See chap. 4, above.

19. L. C. Dunn, "Cross-currents in the History of Human Genetics," *American Journal of Human Genetics* 14 (1962): 1–13. Compare the contemporary remarks of Lewellys Barker, "Heredity in the Clinic," *American Journal of the Medical Sciences* 73 (1927): 597. The prominence of the holders of the doctor of philosophy degree in mid-twentieth-century medical school genetics departments is hardly surprising.

20. Practitioners, of course, have never given up the use of constitutional ideas; they are almost demanded by the variety and persistence of patterns of health and disease. In formal medical thought, however, emphasis on general contitutional factors did suffer relative decline in the first forty or so years of this century. This was, I believe, a consequence not so much of a formal and conscious rejection of such considerations, but of the difficulty of reducing constitutional factors to experimental situations or clinical research designs. As medical academicians became increasingly research-oriented and specialized, their publications naturally found little room for factors which could not be articulated in these terms.

21. For an example, see Haller, *Eugenics*, p. 87. The literature in this area, with interest intensified by the prohibition controversy, is also voluminous.

22. Although graduating with a doctorate from Harvard, Cole had originally attended Michigan Agricultural College. The following remarks are based on a reading of Cole's correspondence in the records of the Department of Genetics, University of Wisconsin Archives.

23. Cole to Morgan, November 20, 1911; February 12 and September 23, 1912; E. N. Wentworth to Cole, January 21, 1913; B. W. Kunkel to Cole, March 8, 1914; J. A. Detlefsen to Cole, January 16, 1914, Department of Genetics, University of Wisconsin Archives, 9/17/3. Even in Missouri, to cite another example, agricultural students in a general breeding course were taught Weismann and given Wilson's *Cell* and recent issues of *Biometrika*, founded but a short time before, as suggested reading. F. B. Mumford to H. R. Smith, February 5, 1904, University of Missouri, College of Agriculture Papers, Reel 35.

24. Farm belief, for example, in the influence of "previous impregnation" upon a mother's offspring by a later and different sire was—and in some circles still is—persistent. Cf. S. A. Beach to W. M. Hays, February 28, 1906, Records of the Office of the Secretary of Agriculture, RG 16, National Archives.

25. J. B. Dandeno to A. F. Blakeslee, February 27, 1907, A. F. Blakeslee Papers, American Philosophical Society. Blakeslee's search for a position is clearly if depressingly documented in his correspondence, especially in his letters to Roland Thaxter and W. G. Farlow. For the facts of Blakeslee's life see E. W. Sinnott, "Albert F. Blakeslee," National Academy of Sciences, *Biographical Memoirs* 33 (1959): 1-38.

26. W. D. Hoard to L. J. Cole, June 13, 1912; Cole to Hoard, June 14, 1912, Department of Genetics, University of Wisconsin. On Wilson, see Wilson to Addis Schermerhorn, November 18, 1898; Wilson to C. F. Curtiss, April 5, 1904, Private Letterbooks, James Wilson Papers, in the possession of Mrs. Janet Wilson Lehninger, Baltimore, Maryland.

27. Raymond Pearl, a long-time experiment station worker, shrewdly summarized the problem when he attacked the "perfervid oratory, loose thinking, and cheap advertising of men and institutions," which obscured the rather modest contributions which Mendelianism had made to practical breeding. The true, if modest, role of Mendelianism in breeding, he continued, "does lack the grandeur of the vision sometimes opened out by the extension lecturer in his zeal to inspire the farmers to do better things, and at the same time pave the way for increased appropriations for his institution." Pearl, *Modes of Research in Genetics* (New York, 1915) pp. 159, 169. Pearl worked at the Maine Agricultural Experiment Station at Orono before accepting a chair at the Johns Hopkins School of Hygiene.

28. L. H. Bailey to H. J. Webber, April 21, 1906, L. H. Bailey Papers, 21-2-84, Cornell University Collection of Archives and Regional History; E. W. Allen to H. W. Mumford, January 12, 1912, Illinois File, RG 164, National Archives.

29. Morgan, "Random Segregation versus Coupling in Mendelian Inheritance," *Science* N.S. 34 (1911): 384.

30. V. A. McKusick, "Walter S. Sutton and the Physical Basis of Mendelism," *Bulletin of the History of Medicine* 34 (1960): 487-97.

31. Some of the authors cited by Morgan et al. were still graduate students when the *Mechanism of Mendelian Heredity* was published in 1915; I have taken the the liberty of including these authors if they completed their degrees within the few years succeeding.

32. W. K. Brooks, whose influence as teacher of Morgan, Wilson, and Bateson cannot be overestimated, was, however, an American and his training was largely American. The role of Brooks does point up the influence which individuals and individual personality can play in the formation of intellectual trends. It illustrates as well the pivotal role of Johns Hopkins in the early years of American graduate education—the late 1870s and early 1880s. A. H. Sturtevant has recently emphasized the significance of Brooks in shaping the research interests of the men mentioned above: "Early Mendelians," p. 200. The best discussion of the teaching of biology at Hopkins in the early years and Brooks's place in it is in Hugh Hawkins, *Pioneer: A History of The Johns Hopkins University, 1874–1889* (Ithaca, 1960).

33. This is clear enough, but the mobility of academics, especially young ones, makes a tabulation rather difficult.

Bibliographical Note

In some ways it would be easier to compile a list of desiderata than a bibliography of science and nineteenth-century American social thought. Indeed, our very definition of the problem has changed in recent years. Historians have traditionally been concerned with formal thought—the role of science in the thought of men such as Jonathan Edwards and Thomas Jefferson, William James, and Lester Ward. We have, on the other hand, only recently come to accept the need for rather different kinds of studies, ones which concern themselves with the place of science in the system of belief and assumption through which Americans generally have ordered their world. The following brief pages do not seek to identify all those subjects which need investigation, nor even all those studies which might prove relevant or exemplary; rather, they attempt to provide some access to the available literature (and to supplement the more specific references within the individual chapters).

We do not have a general history which synthesizes this aspect of American history. Daniel Boorstin's, *The Americans* (in 3 vols., New York: Random House, 1958, 1965, 1973) represents our most ambitious attempt to locate the place of science and technology in a general synthesis of American social history. Nathan Reingold's *Science in Nineteenth-Century America: A Documentary History* (New York: Hill & Wang, Inc., 1964) provides a useful assortment of personal documents. Two collective volumes provide valuable if more limited studies of particular aspects of the interaction between science and American society: George H. Daniels, ed., *Nineteenth-Century American Science: A Reappraisal* (Evanston, Ill.: Northwestern University Press, 1972); David D. Van Tassel and Michael G. Hall, eds., *Science and Society in the United States* (Homewood, Ill.: Dorsey Press, 1966). There are useful studies of aspects of science in America devoted either to particular problems or periods; all provide at least some information on relationships between science and social thought: Brooke Hindle, *The Pursuit of Science in Revolutionary America, 1735–1789* (Chapel Hill: University of North Carolina Press, 1956); George H. Daniels, *American Science in the Age of Jackson* (New York:

Columbia University Press, 1968); Dirk J. Struik, *Yankee Science in the Making* (Boston: Little, Brown & Co., 1948); A. Hunter Dupree, *Science in the Federal Government: A History of Policies and Activities to 1940* (Cambridge, Mass.: Harvard University Press, 1957). Struik's quarter-century-old attempt to formulate an economic-determinist synthesis remains atypical; American historians of science and technology, as American historians generally, have been little interested in exploring Marxist points of view. Brief but useful are John C. Greene's articles on science in the new nation: "American Science Comes of Age," *Journal of American History* 55 (1968): 22–41; "Science and the Public in the Age of Jefferson," *Isis* 49 (1958); 13–25. For the period before 1820, the Institute of Early American History has sponsored valuable and still-useful bibliographical guides: Whitefield J. Bell, Jr., *Early American Science: Needs and Opportunities for Study* (Williamsburg: The Institute, 1955); Brooke Hindle, *Technology in Early America: Needs and Opportunities for Study. With a Directory of Artifact Collections by Lucius F. Ellsworth* (Chapel Hill: University of North Carolina Press, 1966). Bibliographical information can also be gleaned from the "Critical Bibliography of the History of Science and its Cultural Influences" which appears each year in *Isis*, the journal of the History of Science Society.

The shifting relationship between science and religion is one area in which historians have investigated the interactions between science and social thought. The problem has been traditionally seen in high-culture terms, but the pervasiveness of these influences implies a more general social relevance, especially in the more structured world order of the seventeenth and early-eighteenth centuries. The vogue of Michael Foucault, *Madness and Civilization: A History of Insanity in the Age of Reason* (New York: Random House, 1965), and Mary Douglas, especially *Natural Symbols: Explorations in Cosmology* (New York: Pantheon Books, 1970) and *Purity and Danger: An Analysis of Concepts of Pollution and Taboo* (London: Routledge & Kegan Paul, 1966), both illustrates and has encouraged the growing interest of historians in the shifting equilibrium between science and religion as a central element in the shaping of a modern world-view (*mentalité* in the similarly fashionable terminology of French social history). Keith Thomas's *Religion and the Decline of Magic* (New York: Charles Scribner's Sons, 1971) has illustrated the possibilities of this approach, as well as the possibility of dealing with levels of belief and strata of society thought normally inaccessible or inappropriate to historical analysis. Fortunately, a number of emotionally resonant issues in early America illustrate the significance of these issues and are well represented in the existing literature. The two most prominent are the debates over smallpox inoculation in Boston in 1721 and the Salem witchcraft controversy in the 1690s. Perry Miller's discussion of these incidents and their relation to the Puritan world-view and the status of the ministry is still of great significance: *The New England Mind: The Seventeenth Century* (Cambridge, Mass.: Harvard University Press, 1954); *The New England Mind: From Colony to Province* (Cambridge, Mass.: Harvard University Press, 1953), esp. chap. 13, "The Judgment of the Witches," and chap. 21, "The Judgment of the Smallpox." In relation to smallpox, see also Genevieve Miller, *The Adoption of Inoculation for Smallpox in England and France* (Philadelphia: University of Pennsylvania Press, 1957); John B. Blake, *Public Health in the Town of Boston, 1630–1822* (Cambridge, Mass.: Harvard University Press, 1959); Ola E. Winslow, *A Destroying Angel: The Conquest of Smallpox in Colonial Boston* (Boston: Houghton Mifflin Co., 1974). For other insights into the structure of attitudes toward science and faith in colonial America see also Cotton Mather, *The Angel of Bethesda*, ed. and intro. Gordon W. Jones (Barre, Mass.: American Antiquarian Society and Barre Publishers, 1972); Ernest Caulfield, *A True History of the Terrible Epidemic Vulgarly Called the Throat Distemper Which Occurred in His Majesty's New England Colonies between the Years 1735 and 1740* (New Haven: Beaumont Medical Club, 1939); I. Bernard Cohen, "Prejudice against the Introduction of Lightning Rods," *Journal of the Franklin Institute* 253 (1952): 393–440. For discussion of other incidents illuminating the shifting balance between secularism and a more traditional otherworldly orientation see Charles E. Rosenberg, *The Cholera Years: The United States in 1832, 1849, and 1866* (Chicago: University of Chicago Press, 1962); John Duffy, "Anglo-American Reaction to Obstetrical Anesthesia," *Bulletin of the History of Medicine* 38 (1964): 32–44; Lloyd G. Stevenson, "Science down the Drain," *Bulletin of the History of Medicine* 29 (1955): 1–26. On witchcraft see also Alan Macfarlane, *Witchcraft in Tudor and Stuart England: A Regional and Comparative Study*, (New York: Harper & Row, Publishers, 1970); Stanford J. Fox, *Science and Justice: The Massachusetts Witchcraft Trials* (Baltimore: The Johns Hopkins University Press, 1968); Paul Boyer and Stephen Nissenbaum, *Salem Possessed: The Social Origins of Witchcraft* (Cambridge, Mass.: Harvard University Press, 1974); and Thomas's *Religion and the Decline of Magic*, cited previously.

The debate over Darwinism has dominated historical discussion of science and religion in nineteenth-century America. Most of such analysis is devoted to more or less formal thought. For materials before 1961 see Nelson Burr, *A Critical Bibliography of Religion in America*, vol. 4 of *Religion in American Life* (Princeton: Princeton University Press, 1961). For useful or influential studies see also Richard Hofstadter, *Social Darwinism in American Thought*, rev. ed. (Boston: Beacon Press, 1955); Stow Persons, ed., *Evolutionary Thought in America* (New Haven: Yale University Press, 1950); Milton Berman, *John Fiske, The Evolution of a Popularizer* (Cambridge, Mass.: Harvard University Press, 1961); Frank Miller Turner, *Between Science and Religion: The Reaction to Scientific Naturalism in Late Victorian England* (New Haven: Yale University Press, 1974); Charles C. Gillispie, *Genesis and Geology: A Study in the Relations of Scientific Thought, Natural Theology, and Social Opinion in Great Britain, 1790–1850* (Cambridge, Mass.: Harvard University Press, 1951); Walter F. Cannon, "The Normative Role of Science in Early Victorian Thought," *Journal of the History of Ideas*, 25 (1964): 487–502. Still indispensable is Arthur O. Lovejoy, *The Great Chain of Being: A Study of the History of an Idea* (Cambridge, Mass.: Harvard University Press, 1936). See also William F. Bynum, "The Great Chain of Being after Forty Years: An Appraisal" *History of Science* 8 (1975): 1–28. In a more specialized area, recent studies of faith healing provide some guidance: Stephen Gottschalk, *The*

Emergence of Christian Science in American Religious Life (Berkeley and Los Angeles: University of California Press, 1973); Gail Thain Parker, *Mind Cure in New England: From the Civil War to World War I* (Hanover, N.H.: University Press of New England, 1973); Donald Meyer, *The Positive Thinkers* (Garden City, N.Y.: Doubleday & Co., 1965). For more general studies see Paul Carter, *Spiritual Crisis of the Gilded Age* (DeKalb, Ill.: Northern Illinois University Press, 1971), and Paul Boller, Jr., *American Thought in Transition: The Impact of Evolutionary Naturalism, 1865–1900* (Chicago: Rand-McNally & Company, 1969).

Science has played a prominent role in the debate surrounding a number of vexing social problems, and concern with such problems has led some historians to a growing interest in the social uses of scientific ideas. The woman's movement, for example, has recently focused attention on the ways in which scientific arguments have served to justify and articulate traditional female role prescriptions. (See the references in chap. 2.) Race has provided a similar focus of concern. Not surprisingly, since the seventeenth century scientific arguments have played some role in debates over race and an increasingly prominent one in the nineteenth century. See, for example, Winthrop D. Jordan, *White over Black: American Attitudes toward the Negro, 1550–1812* (Chapel Hill: University of North Carolina Press, 1968); William Stanton, *The Leopard's Spots: Scientific Attitudes toward Race in America, 1815–59* (Chicago: University of Chicago Press, 1960); Thomas F. Gossett, *Race: The History of an Idea in America* (Dallas, Texas: Southern Methodist University Press, 1963); William Sumner Jenkins, *Pro-Slavery Thought in the Old South* (Chapel Hill: University of North Carolina Press, 1935); Christine Bolt, *Victorian Attitudes to Race* (London: Routledge & Kegan Paul, 1971); John S. Haller, *Outcasts from Evolution: Scientific Attitudes of Racial Inferiority, 1859–1900* (Urbana, Ill.: University of Illinois Press, 1971); Samuel Stanhope Smith, *An Essay on the Causes of the Variety of Complexion and Figure in the Human Species*, ed. Winthrop D. Jordan (Cambridge, Mass.: Harvard University Press, 1965); George W. Stocking, Jr., *Race, Culture, and Evolution: Essays in the History of Anthropology* (New York: Free Press, 1968).

Historians and literary critics have also concerned themselves with the impact of nature in the shaping of a particularly American world-view and the place of attitudes toward science in the shaping of particular conceptions of nature. Probably the most influential studies of this question in our generation have been Henry Nash Smith's *Virgin Land: The American West as Symbol and Myth* (Cambridge, Mass.: Harvard University Press, 1950) and Leo Marx's *The Machine in the Garden: Technology and the Pastoral Ideal in America* (New York: Oxford University Press, 1967). Neither study, however, deals in a systematic way with the relationship between science and technology and the actual audiences for such organizing ideas. See also Hans Huth, *Nature and the American: Three Centuries of Changing Attitudes* (Berkeley and Los Angeles: University of California Press, 1957); William M. Smallwood, in collaboration with Mabel Smallwood, *Natural History and the American Mind* (New York: Columbia University Press, 1941); Roderick Nash, *Wilderness and the Ameri-*

can Mind (New Haven: Yale University Press, 1967). Nash provides a particularly concise and useful note on sources, pp. 237-46. Much of the study of this problem has, however, focused on literary sources and aesthetic concerns.

When we turn to the life of science and to the relationships between American culture and social attitudes and the encouragement of science, we find an abundance of institutional and biographical material, but little of it considered in terms parallel to those emphasized in Part Two of this book. There has been much recent attention to the "process of professionalization" and questions of definition and consequent quantification. See George H. Daniels, "The Process of Professionalization in American Science: The Emergent Period, 1820-1860," *Isis* 58 (1967): 151-66, and Joseph Ben-David, *The Scientist's Role in Society: A Comparative Study* (Englewood Cliffs, N.J.: Prentice-Hall, Inc., 1971), chap. 8, "The Professionalization of Research in the United States." Ben-David's work has the virtue of focusing on the scientific discipline and the institutional context in which that discipline is practiced, but concerns itself little with general cultural questions and the internal intellectual life of the particular disciplines. Probably the greatest single influence in our generation's view of science and the scientist has been the work of Robert K. Merton. For an overview of Merton's emphases see his recently collected essays, *The Sociology of Science: Theoretical and Empirical Investigations*, ed. Norman W. Storer (Chicago: University of Chicago Press 1973). For examples of monographic studies in this general framework see Diana Crane, *Invisible Colleges: Diffusion of Knowledge in Scientific Communities* (Chicago: University of Chicago Press 1972); Jonathon R. Cole and Stephen Cole, *Social Stratification in Science* (Chicago: University of Chicago Press, 1973). See also Warren O. Hagstrom, *The Scientific Community* (New York: Basic Books, 1965). These studies are important but emphasize "normative" standards within the sciences, the measurement and attribution of status, and distribution of information. Historians have yet to provide analyses of a truly contextual kind—that which describe the growth of the scientific disciplines as both an intellectual and social phenomenon within a particular social context. Surprisingly, there has been more interest in the social and ideological dimensions of engineering in America than in the shaping of the scientific disciplines. Perhaps this is a consequence of the engineers' somewhat ambiguous status and broader social influence of "engineering ideology" in the form of scientific management, efficiency, and even technocracy. See, for example, Daniel Hovey Calhoun, *The American Civil Engineer. Origins and Conflict* (Cambridge, Mass.: M.I.T. Press, 1960); Monte A. Calvert, *The Mechanical Engineer in America, 1830-1910: Professional Cultures in Conflict* (Baltimore: Johns Hopkins University Press, 1967); Raymond H. Merritt, *Engineering in American Society, 1850-1875* (Lexington, Ky.: The University Press of Kentucky, 1969); Edwin T. Layton, Jr., *The Revolt of the Engineers: Social Responsibility and the American Engineering Profession* (Cleveland: Case Western Reserve University Press, 1971); Samuel Haber, *Efficiency and Uplift: Scientific Management in the Progressive Era, 1890-1920* (Cambridge, Mass.: Harvard University Press, 1959); Raymond E. Callahan, *Education and the Cult of Efficiency* (Chicago: University of Chicago Press, 1962).

Index

Library of Congress Cataloging in Publication Data

Rosenberg, Charles E.
    No other gods.

    Bibliographical Note: p. 263
    Includes index.
    1. Science—History—United States.   2. Science—Social aspects—United States.
3. United States—Social conditions—1865–1918.   I. Title.
Q127.U6R618   301.24'3'0973   75–36942
ISBN 0–8018–1711–0 (hardcover)
ISBN 0–8018–2097–9 (paperback)